FOURTH EDITION

FITNESS MANAGEMENT

A Comprehensive Resource for Developing, Leading, Managing, and Operating a Successful Health/Fitness Business in the Era of the 4th Industrial Revolution

Stephen J. Tharrett, M.S.

©2017 Healthy Learning. Fourth edition. All rights reserved. Printed in the United States.

No part of this book may be reproduced, stored in a retrieval system, or transmitted, in any form or by any means, electronic, mechanical, photocopying, recording, or otherwise, without the prior permission of Healthy Learning. Throughout this book, the masculine shall be deemed to include the feminine and vice versa.

ISBN: 978-1-60679-391-6
Library of Congress Control Number: 2017942423
Book layout: Cheery Sugabo
Front cover design: Cheery Sugabo
Front cover photo: Syda Productions/Shutterstock.com

Healthy Learning
P.O. Box 1828
Monterey, CA 93942
www.healthylearning.com

Dedication

This book is dedicated to my family. To my wife, Denise, who has stood by me for 40 years, providing support, inspiration, patience, and love. To my children, Alyssa and Travis, for their love and support and for teaching me so much about what is required to be a leader. Finally to my father, John Tharrett, who passed away over two decades ago, an individual who was my hero growing up. While this project was a labor of love, I could not have done so without the unconditional love provided by my family.

S.T.

Acknowledgments

I want to begin by extending a special thanks to James A. Peterson, Ph.D., who, over the past 25 years has mentored and coached me as a writer. He has been my co-author on over 10 books, and until this 4th edition of *Fitness Management,* my co-author on the first three editions. Beyond being a mentor, Jim has been a close friend and an inspiration, something for which I'll always be grateful.

Secondly, I want to acknowledge all of the incredible people in this industry who have shared their passion and wisdom with me about the business of operating a successful health/fitness club.

Thirdly, I would like to thank the leaders and peers who served with me for 20 years at ClubCorp, including Robert Dedman Sr., Richard Poole, Bob Johnson, Doug Howe, Murray Siegel, and Steve Plakotoris, each of whom it was my honor to work with, and who gave me the opportunity to learn and grow by freely sharing their knowledge and love of the business.

Fourthly, I would like to acknowledge the incredible members of the ClubCorp athletic and tennis committees, over 40 strong dedicated and passionate leaders. Each of these special people (particularly the committee leaders, including Gordon Collins, Billy Freer, Tommy English, Nony Michulka, Rich Andrae, Jill Bauman, Vicki McGrath, Frank Martin, Mike Saldivar, Pam Koch, Jim Swieter, Teresa Thomason, and Bill Johnston, who just recently passed away) never hesitated to share their wisdom or heart. I also want to thank my wonderful assistant, Michelle Arnette, who (without knowing it) taught me many of the "ins and outs" of the business.

Fifthly, I would like to thank my colleagues and friends at the Russian Fitness Group, a group of dynamic and talented professionals, with whom I had the honor of working for nearly three years during my tenure as the company's CEO and managing director from 2008 to 2010. I want to extend a special thanks to my executive team at RFG, including Alla, Alexey, Dmitry K., Irina, Julia I., Julia K., and Roman. I also want to give a special thanks to Yana, who acted as my guardian angel during my three years in Russia, and Olesya, who served as my executive assistant, translator, teacher, and friend.

Lastly, I would like to acknowledge the industry leaders who have been so open and willing to share their knowledge and insights about the industry. Frankly, there are so many individuals to thank in this regard that I cannot begin to mention everyone who has impacted my professional life in a positive manner. On the other hand, I would like to personally thank those individuals who have served as role models for me during my extended tenure in the industry. With over 2,000 years of collective experience, these exceptional industry individuals are a true reflection of the nature of the industry. The list of those individuals to whom I am eternally grateful in this regard includes people such as Rick Caro of Management Vision, Norm Cates of the Club Insider, Frank Napolitano of 24 Hour Fitness, Spencer Garrett of Pierpont Racquet Club, Rob Goldman, Gary Klencheski, Mitch Wald, Carl Porter, Gale Landers of Fitness Formula, Steve Schwartz of Midtown Athletic Clubs, Tim Rhode, Bill McBride of Active Sports Clubs, Red Lerille of Red's, Rudy Riska, who spent more than four decades as the executive director of the Downtown Athletic Club in New York, Jim Gerber formerly of Western Athletic Clubs (now the Bay Clubs), Annbeth Eschbach of Exhale, and Robert Chaiken, as well as the countless other individuals with whom it was my honor and pleasure to serve during my involvement with the industry. In addition to the aforementioned industry leaders, I would also like to give very special thanks to John McCarthy, former executive director of IHRSA, who has been a mentor over the years and provided valuable insight into the writing of this book. Finally, thanks to the entire team at IHRSA, particularly Hans Muench, formerly the European Director of IHRSA, for their incredible efforts in advancing the industry over the past three decades.

I also would like to acknowledge the wonderful and talented people involved in other aspects of the industry who have shared a wealth of information with me over the years. In particular, I would like to thank Andy Richters of Matrix Fitness and formerly of Star Trac, Gary Klein of Keiser, Bob Taggert of T2 Fitness, Mike Zinda of Life Fitness, Stan Peterman formerly of Quinton and now with Technogym, Ken Germano, Dr. Cedric Bryant of ACE, Hervey Lavoie of Ohlson Lavoie, Richard Brunner formerly of Michigan State, and Brian Davidson, formerly of Life Fitness. Frankly, space does not permit me to list everyone who has been a trusted friend and business associate over the past 20 years. It goes without saying that their assistance has been invaluable.

A special thanks to Dr. Dee Edington, former dean of the School of Kinesiology at the University of Michigan and former director of the Wellness Research Center at the University, and Dr. Tom Sattler, former professor at the University of Illinois at Chicago, for their mentorship over the years.

Unfortunately, I am sure I have missed more names than I have mentioned. On the other hand, hopefully, all of the wonderful and talented people with whom I have been blessed to share this journey are aware of how grateful I am for the positive impact that they have had on my life. One key point is inescapable: we are all in an incredible business!

S.T.

Contents

Dedication 3
Acknowledgments 4
Preface 16

**PART 1: INTRODUCTION TO THE HEALTH/FITNESS
FACILITY INDUSTRY** 19

Chapter 1: The Health/Fitness Facility Industry: The Past, Present,
and Future 21
    Chapter Objectives
    An Industry Is Created: The Introductory Stage (Pre-1960s)
    The Industry Takes Off: The Growth Stage (1960s–2000)
    The Industry's Entry Into the Mature Stage of Its Life Cycle (2000–Beyond)
    What Does the Future Hold: A Glimpse at Several Future Health/
        Fitness Facility Industry Trends
    Reflections

Chapter 2: The Physical Activity Beliefs and Behaviors of Americans
and Their Implications for Health/Fitness Facilities 45
    Chapter Objectives
    Core Values of Americans Toward Physical Activity and Health
    What Physically Active Americans Say Are the Reasons That They
        Participate in Physical Activity and Exercise
    The Level of Fitness Consciousness Among Americans as a Predictor
        of Joining and Staying With Exercise
    What a Portrait of Those Individuals Who Exercise Can Mean to Health/
        Fitness Management
    Industry Driven Research on What Americans Are Actually Doing When
        It Comes to Physical Activity
    What the Centers for Disease Control and Prevention (CDC) Says
        About the Physical Activity Practices of Americans
    Reflections

**PART 2: MEMBERSHIP AND MARKETING IN THE HEALTH/FITNESS
FACILITY INDUSTRY** 55

Chapter 3: Why Consumers Join Health/Fitness Facilities 57
    Chapter Objectives
    Understanding the Differences Between a Health/Fitness Club and a
        Gym/Fitness Facility
    What Do Consumers Really Think About Health/Fitness Facilities
    Why Consumers Join a Health/Fitness Facility
    Reflections

Chapter 4: Subscription Models in the Health/Fitness Facility Industry 67
  Chapter Objectives
  Defining the Differences Between a Member and a Customer
  Traditional Subscription Offerings in the Health/Fitness Facility Industry
  New Subscription Models for Health/Fitness Facilities
  Traditional Membership Categories in the Health/Fitness Facility Industry
  Bundling Subscription Offerings
  Pricing Strategies for Membership and Other Subscription Models
  Reflections

Chapter 5: Marketing Essentials: Branding in the Health/Fitness Facility Industry 82
  Chapter Objectives
  The Essence of a Brand
  The Brand Value Equation
  Some Important Characteristics of Great Brands
  Guidelines for Building a Differentiated Brand for a Business
  Reflections

Chapter 6: Marketing Essentials: Understanding the Needs and Voice of Consumers 93
  Chapter Objectives
  The Value of Listening to the Voice of the Customer
  Tools for Capturing the Voice of the Customer
  Reflections

Chapter 7: Marketing Essentials: Communicating the Facility's Value Proposition and Generating Purchase Intent 100
  Chapter Objectives
  The Essence of Messaging the Club's Value Proposition
  General Marketing Approaches
  Traditional Strategies for Marketing and Promoting the Value Proposition of the Facility
  The New Normal: Digital Marketing
  Reflections

Chapter 8: Digital Marketplaces and Platforms for Promoting Health/Fitness Businesses 123
  Chapter Objectives
  Digital Coupon Sites
  What Is a Digital Middleman?
  Fitness Internet Middlemen
  A New Digital Marketplace for Generating Studio Clients
  Reflections

Chapter 9: Selling the Value Proposition of Your Facility........................... 131
    Chapter Objectives
    Understanding the Mathematics of Selling Facility Access
    Understanding the Sales Continuum
    Sales Stages Up Close and Personal
    Staging the Prospect Tour
    Corporate Sales
    Sales Management: Creating a Culture of Sales Success
    The New Normal: Online Prospecting and Sales
    Reflections

PART 3: ENGAGING AND RETAINING CLIENTS IN THE HEALTH/FITNESS FACILITY INDUSTRY 147

Chapter 10: Member and Client Retention and Tenure 149
    Chapter Objectives
    The Industry's Recent Experiences With Member/Client Retention
    Common Industry Definitions of Member/Client Retention
    Common Industry Definitions of Member/Client Attrition
    Calculating Membership Retention: Two Approaches
    Membership Tenure in the Health/Fitness Facility Industry
    The Value of Retention and Tenure
    Reasons Individuals Express About Remaining as Members
    Reasons Members Give for Terminating Their Engagement
    Proven Strategies for Improving Retention
    Reflections

Chapter 11: Customer Loyalty: The Art of Staging Memorable Customer Experiences........................... 167
    Chapter Objectives
    Understanding Customer Loyalty and Satisfaction
    Measuring Customer Satisfaction and Loyalty
    Customer Satisfaction and Loyalty as They Relate to Driving the Value of the Facility Experience
    How Customers Respond to Service Delivery and the Experience Provided by the Facility
    Defining a WOW Experience
    Creating Experiences That WOW Customers
    Reflections

Chapter 12: Creating a Service Culture That Drives Customer Loyalty 182
    Chapter Objectives
    The Service Profit Chain
    Defining a Service Culture

Creating a Service Culture in the Health/Fitness Facility Industry
Implementing Service Culture Values and Standards
Reflections

Chapter 13: Programming Essentials: A Primer for the
Health/Fitness Facility Industry 193
Chapter Objectives
The Value of Programming
The Keys to Great Programming
Program Offerings: Status Quo or Changing of the Guard
Reflections

**PART 4: THE BUSINESS OF DEVELOPING AND MANAGING A
HEALTH/FITNESS BUSINESS** 207

Chapter 14: Health/Fitness Facility Business Models 209
Chapter Objectives
Umbrella Business Models
The Different Facility Market Segments and Value Propositions in the Health/Fitness Facility Industry
The Different Price Point Models Used by Operators to Create Differentiation
Reflections

Chapter 15: Establishing a Health/Fitness Business 222
Chapter Objectives
What Are the Options a Club Has for Forming a Legal Entity?
Considerations to Account for When Filing for Legal Status for a Business
Obtaining a Federal Tax ID (Employer Identification Number) for Your Business
Deciding Whether to Buy or Build a Club
Getting the Business Started
Reflections

Chapter 16: The Health/Fitness Industry Financial Model 233
Chapter Objectives
Accrual vs. Cash Accounting
The Basic Financial Tools Used by the Health/Fitness Facility Industry
Reflections

Chapter 17: Budgeting, Forecasting, and Driving Profitability
in the Health/Fitness Facility Industry 252
Chapter Objectives
Budgeting in the Health/Fitness Facility Industry
Forecasting in the Health/Fitness Facility Industry

Industry Practices for Driving Revenues
Industry Practices for Controlling Expenses
Controlling the Leading Expense Categories
Reflections

Chapter 18: Buying, Leasing, Selling, and Raising
Capital for a Health/Fitness Business 269
Chapter Objectives
Traditional Approaches to Raising Capital for a Health/Fitness Business
Crowdfunding: A Non-Traditional Source of Capital
Buying and Selling a Health/Fitness Business
Leasing and Sale Leasebacks
Reflections

PART 5: STAFFING ISSUES IN THE HEALTH/FITNESS FACILITY INDUSTRY 285

Chapter 19: The People Factor: Employees in the
Health/Fitness Industry 287
Chapter Objectives
Employees vs. Independent Contractors
Exempt vs. Non-Exempt Employees in the U.S.
Full-Time and Part-Time Employees
Permanent and Temporary Employees in Europe
The Position Players in Health/Fitness Facilities
Offsite Position Employees in Multiple-Facility Operations
Compensation for Various Positions in the Health/Fitness Facility Industry
Benefits Provided in the Health/Fitness Facility Industry
Education and Skills Required of Health/Fitness Professionals
Education and Skills Required of Fitness Instructors, Group-Exercise Instructors, Personal Trainers, and Wellness Coaches
Organizational Alignment and Structure in Individual Health/Fitness Facilities
Organizational Alignment and Structure in a Multiple-Facility Operation
Reflections

Chapter 20: Building and Leading a Successful Team 308
Chapter Objectives
The Four Es of Building a Great Team
Recruiting and Selecting the Business's Team
Leadership
Developing Job Descriptions and Compensation Agreements for Employees
Reflections

PART 6: FACILITIES AND EQUIPMENT IN THE HEALTH/FITNESS FACILITY INDUSTRY 323

Chapter 21: Health/Fitness Facilities 325
   Chapter Objectives
   Types of Health/Fitness Facilities
   The Various Spaces Found Within a Health/Fitness Facility
   The Design and Construction Process
   Costs Associated With Design and Construction
   Examples of Health/Fitness Facility Designs
   Reflections

Chapter 22: Fitness Equipment for the Health/Fitness Facility Industry 356
   Chapter Objectives
   Cardiovascular Equipment
   Selectorized/Variable Resistance Equipment
   Free-Weight Equipment
   Cardiovascular Entertainment Equipment
   Other Frequently Required Equipment for Health/Fitness Facilities
   Purchase or Lease Equipment
   Reflections

PART 7: OTHER HEALTH/FITNESS FACILITY MODELS 373

Chapter 23: Sports-Performance Centers 375
   Chapter Objectives
   Introduction to the Sports Performance Training Market
   The Primary Forces Driving the Sports Performance Training Market
   Youth Sports Participation and What Lies Behind It
   Preventing Sports-Related Injuries in Youth
   The Role of Sports-Conditioning Programs for Youth
   Adult Sports Participation
   The Role of Sports-Conditioning Programs for Adults
   Overview of the Sports Conditioning Industry
   A Profile of the Market for Sports-Conditioning Programs in
      Health/Fitness Facilities
   Sports-Performance Center Metrics
   The Essential Components of a Sports-Performance Center
   Marketing Sports-Performance Centers
   An Overview of Several Leading Sports-Performance Operations
   Reflections

Chapter 24: Boutique Fitness Facilities 389
    Chapter Objectives
    Types of Boutique Fitness Offerings
    Boutique Studio Dynamics
    The Power of Boutiques
    Reflections

Chapter 25: Spas 399
    Chapter Objectives
    General Spa-Industry Data
    The Spa Landscape: Definition and Description
    Spa Consumer Profile
    A Profile of Why Consumers Use Spas
    Spa Visit Motivators
    Spa Facilities and Features
    Spa Space Requirements
    Spa Equipment
    Spa Service Offerings
    Spa Retail
    Spa Financial Parameters
    Marketing the Spa
    Spa Staff
    Reflections

PART 8: BUSINESS OPERATIONAL PRACTICES IN THE HEALTH/FITNESS FACILITY INDUSTRY 425

Chapter 26: Risk Management 427
    Chapter Objectives
    Risk Management Practices to Reduce Employee and Business Risk
    Essential Risk Management Practices to Reduce Member/User and Business Risk
    Automated External Defibrillators (AEDs)
    Reflections

Chapter 27: Front-of-the-House Operations: Physical Activity Departments 443
    Chapter Objectives
    Defining an Operating Practice
    Fitness Department (Fitness and Group Exercise)
    Aquatics Department
    Tennis Department
    Reflections

Chapter 28: Front-of-the-House Operations: Non-Physical
Activity Departments.. 459
    Chapter Objectives
    Defining an Operating Practice
    Front-Desk (Reception) Department
    Child-Care Department
    Reflections

Chapter 29: Administrative Department Operations 469
    Chapter Objectives
    Locker Rooms
    Laundry
    Housecleaning
    Accounting
    Reflections

**PART 9: OVERVIEW OF THE INTERNATIONAL
HEALTH/FITNESS CLUB MARKET**... 483

Chapter 30: Overview of the International Health/Fitness Club Market 485
    Chapter Objectives
    Historical Perspective
    Reflections

Chapter 31: The Asian Health/Fitness Club Market... 495
    Chapter Objectives
    Overview of the Asian Market
    Overview of the Health/Fitness Club Industry in Asia
    Membership Characteristics
    The Leading Players in the Asian Health/Fitness Club Market
    Opportunities and Challenges for the Asian Market
    Reflections

Chapter 32: The European Health/Fitness Club Market................................... 506
    Chapter Objectives
    Overview of the European Market
    Overview of the Health/Fitness Club Industry in Europe
    The Leading Players in the European Health/Fitness Club Market
    Opportunities and Challenges for the European Health/Fitness
      Club Industry
    Reflections

Chapter 33: The Latin American Health/Fitness Club Market..........................525
    Chapter Objectives
    Overview of the Latin American Market
    Overview of the Health/Fitness Club Industry in Latin America
    The Leading Players in the Latin American Health/Fitness Club Market
    Opportunities and Challenges for the Latin American Market
    Reflections

PART 10: THE FUTURE OF THE HEALTH/FITNESS FACILITY INDUSTRY..........................535

Chapter 34: The Future of the Health/Fitness Facility Industry..........................537
    Chapter Objectives
    Seven Important Demographic and Cultural Trends That Will Shape the Future of the Health/Fitness Facility Business
    Reflections

PART 11: CASE STUDIES AND OPERATOR INSIGHTS FROM THE HEALTH/FITNESS FACILITY INDUSTRY..........................547

Chapter 35: Customer and Member Chronicles..........................549
    Chapter Objectives
    Sun Wars
    Odor Eaters
    Naked Man on the Loose
    Peace and Harmony During the Holiday Season
    Beware of the Nose
    To the Rescue
    Cell-Phone Enforcer
    Reflections

Chapter 36: Employee Chronicles..........................562
    Chapter Objectives
    Health Hearsay
    A Lover's Quarrel
    Anyone Up for a Dip?
    A Little Affair
    Reflections

Chapter 37: Business Chronicles..........................571
    Chapter Objectives
    Closing a Club and Gaining Fans
    Drive-In Fitness Anyone?
    Now, Where Did You Say the Fitness Area Was?
    Reflections

Chapter 38: Retention and Programming Stories..579
   Chapter Objectives
   Engaging Members Into the Club Life
   Programming That Makes a Difference
   Reflections

Chapter 39: Words of Wisdom From Boutique Fitness Studio Operators......586
   Introduction
   The Story Tellers: Studio Operators Who Have Been Successful
   Reflections

APPENDICES..599
A. Leading Health/Fitness Industry Associations and Organizations............601
B. Leading Health/Fitness Industry Trade Publications....................................603
C. Profiles of Leading Global Health/Fitness Facility Companies..................605
D. Profiles of Leading U.S. Club and Boutique Fitness
   Facility Companies..608
E. Sample Marketing Materials From Leading Global
   Health/Fitness Operators..611
F. Profiles of Leading U.S. Health/Fitness Club
   Equipment Manufacturers..614
G. Sample Job Descriptions..618
H. Sample Structured Interview Questioning Format for a
   Fitness Director Applicant..633
I. Selected Operational Forms...639
J. Sample Design and Construction Checklist..646
K. Sample Member Satisfaction Survey...649
L. Sample Corporate Sales Checklist..653
M. Selected Risk Management Forms...656
N. Suggested References...674

About the Author..678

Preface

This book is designed to serve three distinct target populations. One group is the upper-level undergraduate and graduate students who are seeking to embark on a career in the health/fitness industry, be it a boutique fitness studio, commercial fitness facility, non-profit health/fitness facility, medical-based health/wellness facility, private club fitness facility, or any related business model that engages the public in pursuing a healthier and more active lifestyle. Another are young professionals who are already working in the industry and who are seeking information and insights that can help them expand their professional horizons and possibly move into management. Finally, the book is intended for seasoned industry professionals who want to know more about areas in which they may not have as much experience or knowledge as they would like to have.

As you read this book, keep in mind that the health and fitness industry is presently in the mature stage of its life cycle and is experiencing the segmentation and innovation that results from an industry's maturation. With maturity has come a demand by investors and owners for professionals with both strong business acumen and a passion and understanding of the dynamics of the industry. Sixty years ago, this industry was in its infancy, developed, operated, and pushed forward by entrepreneurs who had a passion for fitness and what they were doing. Circumstances forced these industry pioneers to focus on surviving first and creating an industry second.

Over the past several years, the industry has reached a level of maturity where many of the dynamics of the health/fitness facility business have changed. For example, over the past decade, financial markets have and will continue to invest in the industry. Concurrently, major industry figures are creating national and international health/fitness club companies and franchises. This maturation process has resulted in a shortage of leaders and managers who can take the industry to the next level, and help it continue to grow profitability on an ever-changing playing field. Much of this situation can be attributed to the fact that the industry had not established a formal educational process for bringing professionals into the industry. Only in the past year, through the efforts of the author and the American Council on Exercise, has a formal business management course and certification for fitness business management been introduced.

Over the years, one of the most pressing issues that other health/fitness business owners have brought to my attention is the critical need for a reliable mechanism for sharing the information that is needed to help better develop the future business leaders for the industry. This book is my attempt to help address that void. I have chosen to write it as a means of sharing with the readers the wealth of knowledge and passion that I have garnered from over 35 years of working with the most incredible people in the industry. In reality, this book presents the insights and wisdom of industry leaders who collectively have over 5,000 years of experience in the industry.

This book is separated into ten distinct sections, based on the skill sets needed to succeed as a leader and manager in this industry. Part 1 introduces the reader to the fitness, health, racquet, and sport club industry by touching on the history of the industry, the current practices and trends in the industry, and the attitudes and attributes of the consumer who chooses to be a member of a club. Part 2 focuses on health/fitness facility engagement and membership, starting with a review of why consumers join facilities, and progressing into the branding, marketing, and sales practices necessary to succeed in the business. Part 3 provides an overview of member and client retention and the process of utilizing great service and great programming to create memorable experiences for the businesses clients and members. Part 4 reviews the administrative business functions of the industry, beginning with the formation of a legal business entity, progressing to the financial standards and processes, and concluding with an examination of the key issues involved in buying, leasing, and selling a health/fitness business. Part 5 looks at the employee side of the health/fitness facility business, starting with a detailed overview of the people-related requirements, and concluding with a discussion of the essential aspects of leadership within the industry. Part 6 addresses the facility and equipment side of the business, covering topics ranging from facility design to equipment selection. Part 7 addresses three business models that, in the past decade, have changed the landscape of the health/fitness facility industry. Part 8 details the key operational and administrative issues within a health/fitness facility, beginning with an overview of the risk management practices in the industry and progressing through the most essential operating practices for both front-of-the-house and behind-the-house club operations. Part 9 addresses the emerging international market by providing an in depth overview of the health/fitness club markets in Asia, Europe and Latin America. Part 10 offers a picture of what the future may hold for our industry. Part 11 presents case studies of unusual management experiences, ranging from customer and member-related scenarios to employee and big business scenarios and club stories on member engagement and programming. Each case study provides an overview of an unusual or unexpected business event and the actions taken by the respective clubs and their leaders. The club stories provide insights into how some of the industry's best facility operators engage their clients, customers, and members and stage memorable experiences.

This book also features several appendices that contain examples of various operating policies and practices that can be implemented within a health/fitness facility from day one.

In conclusion, my primary goal in writing this book is to expand the horizons of its readers and provide them with a valuable resource that can help them in their professional development. If the publication of this book has a positive impact on the key issues attendant to the fitness, health, racquet, and sport club industry, then the effort involved in writing it will have been more than worthwhile.

S.T.

PART 1

INTRODUCTION TO THE HEALTH/FITNESS FACILITY INDUSTRY

Chapter 1
The Health/Fitness Facility Industry: The Past, Present, and Future

Chapter 2
The Physical Activity Beliefs and Behaviors of Americans and Their Implications for Health/Fitness Facilities

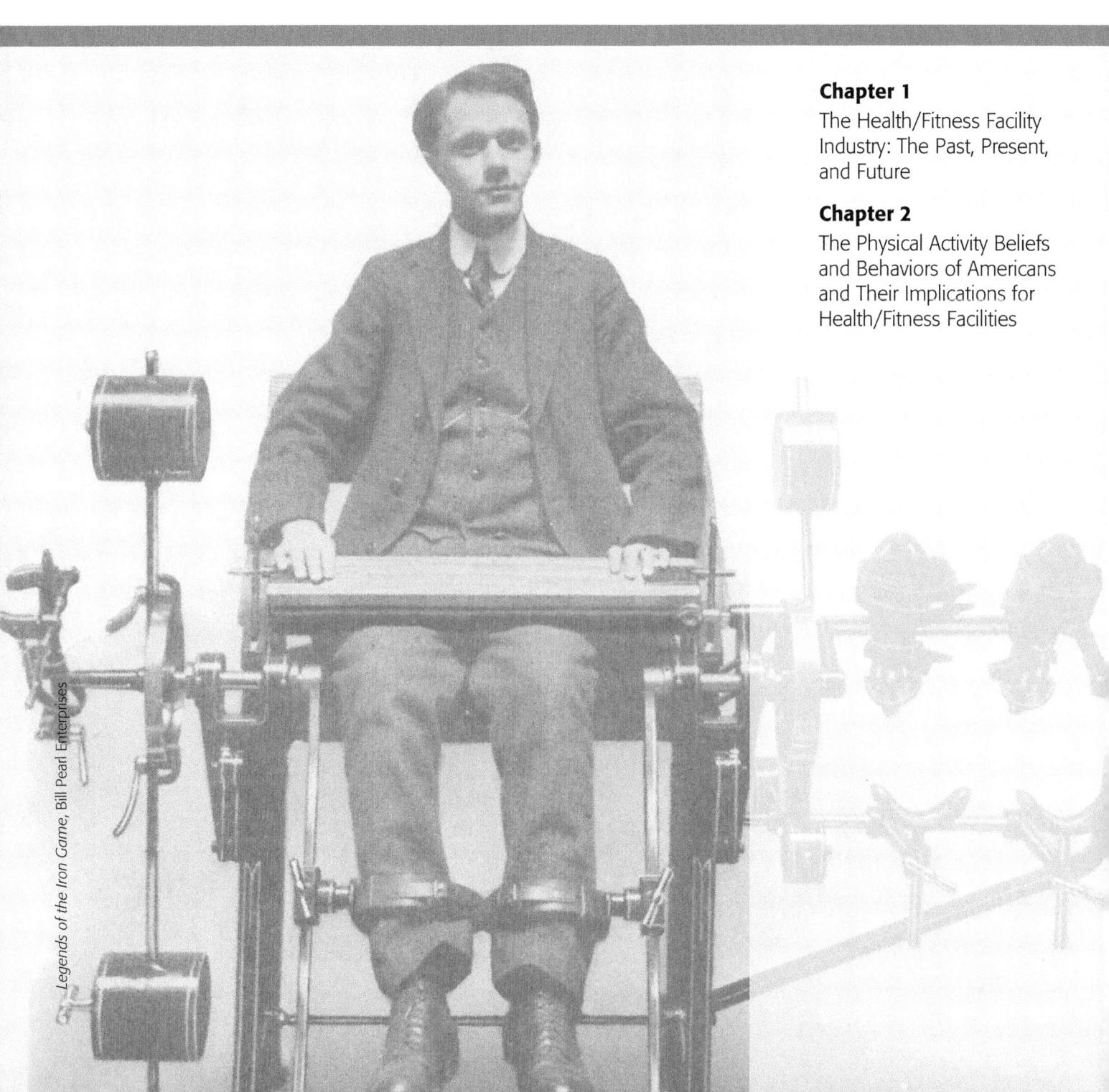

Legends of the Iron Game, Bill Pearl Enterprises

The Health/Fitness Facility Industry: The Past, Present, and Future

*"The true past departs not; no truth or
goodness realized by man ever dies; or can die;
but all is still here, through endless changes."*

—Thomas Carlyle 1795 - 1881

Chapter Objectives

The primary objective of this chapter is to share the heritage of the health/fitness facility industry. The chapter begins by reviewing the industry's history in order to provide insight into the cultural roots of the industry. This discussion is followed by a section that features a more in-depth look at the modern history of the industry (from 1970 forward), with particular emphasis on the state of the industry as of 2015. The chapter concludes by offering a review of existing trends that will impact the health/fitness facility industry over the next decade.

An Industry Is Created: The Introductory Stage (Pre-1960s)

The first officially documented fitness club, referred to at the time as a gymnastics club, was established in 1811 by Frederich Ludwig Jahn. Based in Germany, the club was originally called a Public Turn Platz. Shortly thereafter, it became known simply as Turnverein. Turnverein was developed to provide German men and boys with an organized social environment in which they could prepare themselves physically to protect their country against the French. Turnverein offered organized group classes, using body-weight movements, Indian clubs, dumbbells, ropes, and a variety of equipment that is common to many gymnastic and fitness clubs today. By the 1850s, approximately 150 Turnverein had been developed around the world, with the first American Turnverein opening in 1848 in Cincinnati, Ohio.

In 1847, the famous French strongman, Hippolyte Triat, opened a club in Paris, which he called "Gymnase Triat." Gymnase Traiat featured an open floor for conducting classes, as well as working out on exercise equipment such as suspended rings, parallel bars, dumbbells, barbells, Indian clubs, free weights, and other accessories. Gymnase Traiat was the first club to sell shares to the public as a means to raise the necessary funds to develop and operate the club. Gymnase Triat was also one of the first club facilities to conduct group-exercise classes to music, in this instance, music performed live by actual musicians. Hippolyte Traiat was the first operator to immerse prospects in the

> The first officially documented fitness club, referred to at the time as a gymnastics club, was established in 1811 by Frederich Ludwig Jahn.

club experience by allowing guests to observe classes from a specially designed deck overlooking the club's gymnasium floor. Triatt is also recognized as the inventor of portable parallel bars.

Hippolyte Triat's gymnasium club (circa 1840s)

In 1848, the first U.S. health club, a Turnverein club, was established in Cincinnati, Ohio. Shortly thereafter, the Boston YMCA opened its doors (1850). A decade later, the initial private athletic clubs in the U.S. began their operations. The first of these was the Olympic Club in San Francisco, which started in 1860. Subsequently, a mere eight years later, the New York Athletic Club opened its doors to members. These pioneering clubs had their roots in an industry culture that emanated from male-oriented social and sport clubs and institutes of physical culture. Interestingly enough, while women were not part of this male-dominated club culture, they were actively engaged in promoting exercise, as evidenced by Catherine Beecher's book entitled, *Housekeeper and Healthkeeper*, which was published in 1870. In 1898, the first woman's only athletic club opened in the U.S., appropriately named the Woman's Athletic Club.

These early athletic clubs (Olympic Club, San Francisco; New York Athletic Club, New York; Los Angeles Athletic Club, Los Angeles; Lille Athletic Club, France; Athletic and Cycling Club of Saint Petersburg, Russia; the Athletic Club of Florence, Italy, etc.) were developed to foster both social and business relationships and to promote a culture of physical activity. Each featured facilities that provided an environment for actively pursuing social networking and engaging in sport activities.

In 1894, Louis Durlacher, more commonly known as Professor Attila, opened one of the first commercial health/fitness clubs in New York City, Attila's Athletic Studio and School of *Physical Culture*. Professor Attila had opened his first club in London, approximately a decade earlier, which targeted providing training to Europe's kings, queens, and dignitaries. Attila's N.Y. studio went on to become one of the most famous of its type in the U.S., and upon his death in 1926, the club was turned over to his protégé, Sig Klein. Klein built on the reputation of Attila's studio when he opened his own gym in 1927, which he called Sig Klein's Studio of Physical Culture. Klein's studio subsequently operated for over five decades in mid-town Manhattan, finally closing its doors in the mid-1970s.

Professor Louis Attila's Athletic Studio and School of Physical Culture

In the mid-to-late 1800s, two significant milestones occurred in the fitness industry that would change the way people exercised in gyms and athletic clubs. The first breakthrough was the development of therapeutic exercise machines by Gustav Zander of Sweden. Dr. Zander believed that machines could provide a more efficient and effective means of rehabilitating individuals who were injured, training athletes, and enabling ordinary citizens to exercise.

In the 1850s, Zander started developing exercise machines that employed levers, springs, pulleys, and weights. One of the unique aspects of these machines was that the user could adjust the resistance by moving the weights either closer or farther away from the axis, thereby creating a form of variable resistance. By the 1870s, he had created a total of 27 distinct pieces of exercise equipment, which he later featured in the first studio he opened in the U.S., in New York City, in the 1880s.

The second significant event was the development of variable-resistance pulley equipment by Dudley Allan Sargent. In the 1880s, Sargent, director of the Hemenway Gymnasium and an assistant professor of physical education at Harvard, developed the first pulley-driven variable resistance machines.

Dr. Sargent felt that progressive resistance was required to provide balanced development of the body. Furthermore, he believed that in order to properly develop certain muscles, those muscles you had to be isolated during the course of the exercise movement. Eventually, he invented over 30 pieces of equipment, including the aptly named the abdominal pulley system and the chest pulley system. At one time, over 50 pieces of his equipment were located in the Hemenway Gymnasium at Harvard.

The Sargent pulley system in the early 1900s in New York City

By the early part of the 20th century, the type of athletic club operated by Professor Attila in the 1890s became even more prevalent, with noteworthy growth in a number of the larger urban markets, including New York, Boston, Chicago, Los Angeles, and Philadelphia. During the early 1900s, the primary concern of many men who might otherwise be interested in joining a health/fitness club was the pursuit of feats of strength and physique. During this particular time period, several pioneers in the exercise domain, such as Eugen Sandow, Bernarr Macfadden, Alan Calvert George Hackenschmidt, and Professor Attila, became the leaders and spokespeople for the growing field of physical culture. Bernarr Macfadden conducted traveling road shows with his family during the late 1890s and earlier part of the 20th century to promote physical activity.

In 1899, Macfadden published a journal, called *Physical Culture* (a magazine that subsequently was published for 50 years), which provided a public venue for promoting the benefits of physical activity, physical culture, and proper nutrition. A few years after starting Physical Culture, Macfadden inaugurated a second publication that addressed physical culture, *Beauty and Health for Women*. During that same general time period, Eugen Sandow also developed a chain of schools of physical culture, which were designed to instruct others on the art of physical-culture training.

In response to the publicity generated by Macfadden, Sandow, and others, gyms began to arise that provided an environment for individuals to pursue activities (e.g., weightlifting, gymnastics, and acrobatic arts) that focused on physical development. In 1902, the Milo Barbell Company was formed by Alan Calvert. Calvert's company provided the emerging "gym" industry with a new form of mass-produced, weight training equipment, which further helped to advance the relatively new cultural phenomena of exercising in a club. These physical culture gyms appealed to a relatively small audience of men whose fitness and sports goals differed considerably from the individuals who joined the socially oriented athletic clubs. Among the earliest efforts in this regard was a facility developed by John Fritze, who opened a gym in the 1930s in Philadelphia, PA, called Germantown, which was then followed on the West Coast by one built by Vic Tanny, which opened in 1939.

By the 1940s, the development of these "bodybuilding and weightlifting" gyms had come into vogue. One of the most renowned was Leo Stern's in 1946, followed shortly thereafter by Eastman's in 1947, and Harold Zinkin's in 1948. Relatively small, these original gyms offered memberships for around $60 annually.

In 1947, Vic Tanny permanently changed the landscape of the fitness club industry when he opened the first club dedicated to serving middle class Americans. Tanny's gyms provided an alternative to the "bodybuilding gyms" that heretofore had dominated the club landscape. By offering middle-class men and women an attractive and affordable workout environment, Tanny's gyms introduced American consumers to a different club environment, one that included mirrors, carpet, chrome equipment, saunas, and pools. Over the next two decades, Vic Tanny's gyms went on to become the largest chain of clubs in the world, with annual revenue of $24 million ($184 million in 2015 dollars).

By the early 1950s, additional gyms had sprouted up across the west, including Bill Pearl's in 1953. During the early 1950s, a legend in the club business, Ray Wilson, established his first health club chain, American Health Studios. Over the next two decades, Wilson opened eight distinct health club chains, including American Health Studios, Silhouette Figure Salons, Club International, Trim and Swim Health Clubs, and European Health Spas. Wilson is credited with being the first person to introduce alternate-day club access for men and women, wherein men worked out on Tuesdays, Thursdays, and Saturdays, and women used the club on Mondays, Wednesdays, and Fridays. Understandably so, Vic Tanny and Ray Wilson are considered the founders of the modern fitness club industry.

Two equipment innovations of special consequence (for the health/fitness club industry) occurred during the 1950s. One was the invention of the first prototype of the Universal Gym (i.e., a multi-station, weight training machine) by Harold Zinkin, a former Mr. California and a regular at Muscle Beach. Zinkin created the first Universal Gym in the late 1950s in a back room of his Palm Avenue gym in Fresno, California. During this same time period, the second equipment innovation to change the course of the industry was the introduction of the Quinton treadmill, a state-of-the-art aerobic exercise machine that was embraced as a useful tool by the medical community, as well as the fitness community.

> By the 1940s, the development of "bodybuilding and weightlifting" gyms had come into vogue.

In the 1950s, the basic passion and enthusiasm for fitness that existed in such club facilities as Klein's, Stern's, and Pearl's, as well as in large chains, such as Vic Tanny's and Ray Wilson's, were introduced into almost every household in America. This movement from gym to home was driven by renowned fitness industry legend Jack LaLanne. Using the new (at the time) medium of television to reach out to millions of Americans everywhere with his gospel message of "get up, work out, and feel better," LaLanne brought the benefits of physical conditioning into the American consciousness. The Jack LaLanne Show, which started in the early 1950s and continued until the 1980s, brought physical activity to televisions nationwide. In the process, LaLanne created a demand for knowledge about the pursuit of physical activity.

Subsequently, Jack LaLanne's name was licensed by Ray Wilson, a process that created Jack LaLanne European Health Spas, which evolved into the largest chain in America during the late 1960s. In the late 1970s, Jack LaLanne European Health Spas were sold to Health and Tennis Corporation, which over the next few decades, in turn, became Bally Total Fitness.

During the 50s and 60s, the equipment found in most fitness centers consisted primarily of free weights (York), free weight benches (York or homemade), stationary bicycles, self-propelled walking machines (treadmills), vibrating belts, and pulley machines. During the 1960s, the health/fitness industry received a huge boost from the roll-out of the Universal Gym. The original Universal Gym was a multi-station machine, whose system of weight stacks and pulleys brought resistance training to the masses by offering a relatively safe, easy, and fast approach to training.

> The original Universal Gym was a multi-station machine, whose system of weight stacks and pulleys brought resistance training to the masses by offering a relatively safe, easy, and fast approach to training.

The next decade witnessed the dawn of the modern health/fitness club industry, sparked by both scientific efforts to investigate the need for and the benefits of exercise and marketing research that opened up a new segment of consumers for the industry. During the late 1960s and early 1970s, a new type of health/fitness facility originated—the racquet club. Some of the earliest examples of this genre included Kings Court, Minneapolis, Minnesota; Mel Gorham's Court Club in Pacific Beach, California; the Midtown Tennis Club in Chicago, Illinois; and the Racquetball and Sports Clubs of Atlanta.

While the athletic clubs and the gyms that were previously popular continued to grow, it was the introduction of the racquet club that brought an entirely new audience to the industry. These racquet clubs consisted mainly of individually owned businesses that were operated by people who had a passion for the pursuit of racquet sports and physical activity. These facilities primarily consisted of indoor tennis courts, racquetball and handball courts, swimming pools, and small fitness centers. During this period, two industry-related associations formed—one representing indoor tennis clubs (National Indoor Tennis Association) and one representing racquetball clubs (National Court Club Association). Nearly a decade later, in 1981, these two associations were combined to form the International Racquet Sports Association (IRSA). Concurrent with the growth of racquet clubs was the continued expansion and evolution of gyms and club chains, such as Jack LaLanne's European Health Spas, Holiday Health Spas, Scandinavian Health Spas, Ray Wilson's Family

Fitness Centers, and the predecessor of Bally's, Health and Tennis Corporation, which was formed in 1962.

The Industry Takes Off: The Growth Stage (1960s–2000)

❑ *The 1960s and 1970s*

During the late 1960s and the decade of the 70s, five landmark events occurred that would forever change the landscape of the health/fitness facility industry and push it into its modern period beginning in the 1980s. The first notable occurrence was the development of Nautilus machines in the early 1970s by Arthur Jones, an unconventional eccentric who was at the forefront of an effort that questioned many of the standard prescription guidelines for training.

Based on the principle of variable resistance (first introduced by Gustav Zander in the 1850s), these resistance machines took the young industry by storm. For the first time ever, average Americans had equipment that they could use to muscularly condition themselves in a relatively short period of time. In the process, Nautilus became the standard piece of equipment for health/fitness facilities and began appearing in almost every gym, YMCA, athletic club, and racquet club in the United States. The popularity of this equipment led many racquet clubs and athletic clubs to convert one or more of their racquet courts into a "Nautilus Center," for which they charged additional fees to access the equipment.

The second milestone event was the introduction of the Lifecycle. Initially developed by Dr. Keene Dimmick in 1968, Ray Wilson subsequently purchased the rights for the Lifecyle from Dimmick, and shortly thereafter retained his first salesperson, industry legend Augie Nieto. Under the entrepreneurial leadership and spirit of Wilson and Nieto, the Lifecycle become the first commercial, electronically operated stationary bicycle. The Lifecycle, by providing a user-friendly, enjoyable way to perform cardiovascular exercise, helped advance the relatively young industry by motivating people to engage in stationary cycling.

The third significant event was the work of Kenneth Cooper, MD, who conducted groundbreaking research on the benefits of aerobic exercise. In his bestselling book, Aerobics, Dr. Cooper introduced the world to an easy-to-complete way to quantify the aerobic impact of physical activity and to the medical and health benefits of aerobic activity. Dr. Cooper's research and his resulting book produced a surge of interest in both exercise and health/fitness clubs that would springboard the industry into the mainstream of public life.

The fourth significant event of this period was the introduction of "aerobic dancing" by Jackie Sorenson and Jazzercise by Judi Sheppard Misset. These two women introduced the concept of group exercise, based on music and choreography, to the general public. These two programs became a driving force in the evolution of the fitness industry and the beginning of the industry's acceptance of women as an important audience for fitness.

The fifth and final noteworthy development involved the efforts of the American College of Sports Medicine (ACSM). ACSM, a renowned professional

> The Lifecycle, by providing a user-friendly, enjoyable way to perform cardiovascular exercise, helped advance the relatively young industry by motivating people to engage in stationary cycling.

association of sports medicine, medical, and exercise science specialists, led the way in developing and disseminating the first set of nationally recognized guidelines for exercise testing and prescription. First printed in 1975, these guidelines would subsequently serve as a benchmark for all health/fitness professionals for prescribing exercise and assessing fitness.

In addition to the aforementioned trailblazing factors, two other individuals also had a substantial impact on the industry in the 1970s—Arnold Schwarzenegger and Richard Simmons. A seven-time Mr. Olympia, Schwarzenegger became the face of Gold's Gym (and later World Gym). Subsequently, through his appearance in movies, such as Pumping Iron, he introduced an entirely new generation of people to the benefits of weight training. Concurrently, Simmons, with the introduction of his market-savvy videos, such as *Sweatin to the Oldies and Dance Your Pants Off*, became a fitness icon to millions of stay-at-home women. All told, over 20 million copies of Simmons' energizing and entertaining exercise videos have been sold to date.

As a result of the collective confluence of the previously noted developments, events, and individuals, the advent of the modern health/fitness and sport club industry occurred. During this significant period, the racquet-club industry grew quickly. At the same time, several new types of health/fitness clubs were introduced to the marketplace, including the Sports Training Institute of New York (facilities that offered a blend of physical therapy, personal training, and membership); Cardio Fitness Centers in New York City (corporate fitness centers that were staffed by exercise physiologists who had at least a master's degree); and Lucille Roberts women's only clubs.

❑ *The 1980s*

In 1981, the International Racquet Sports Association (IRSA) was formed by the merging of the National Court Club Association and the National Indoor Tennis Association. The formation of IRSA represented the first landmark event of the modern era. The early founders of IRSA, Rick Caro, Norm Cates, Curt Buesman, and others, had no idea at the time that the association they created in 1981 would go on, under the leadership of its founding director, John McCarthy, to become the leading voice for the health/fitness industry and would serve as a compelling factor in the emerging recognition of this industry as an essential part of the American culture.

According to early research conducted by IRSA, there were a total of approximately 6,200 clubs in 1982. By the end of the decade, eight years later, that number would rise to 13,854 clubs, servicing approximately 21 million Americans or 7.4 percent of the total population. This figure represented an increase of over 100 percent in the number of health, fitness, and sport clubs (Figure 1-1) over the eight-year period from 1982 to 1990. The 100 percent plus growth in the number of health/fitness clubs during the 1980s and the corresponding growth in the number of health/fitness club users (up to approximately 21 million) were fueled by several landmark activities, as well as the continued popularity of health/fitness facilities that was sparked by the landmark events of the 1970s.

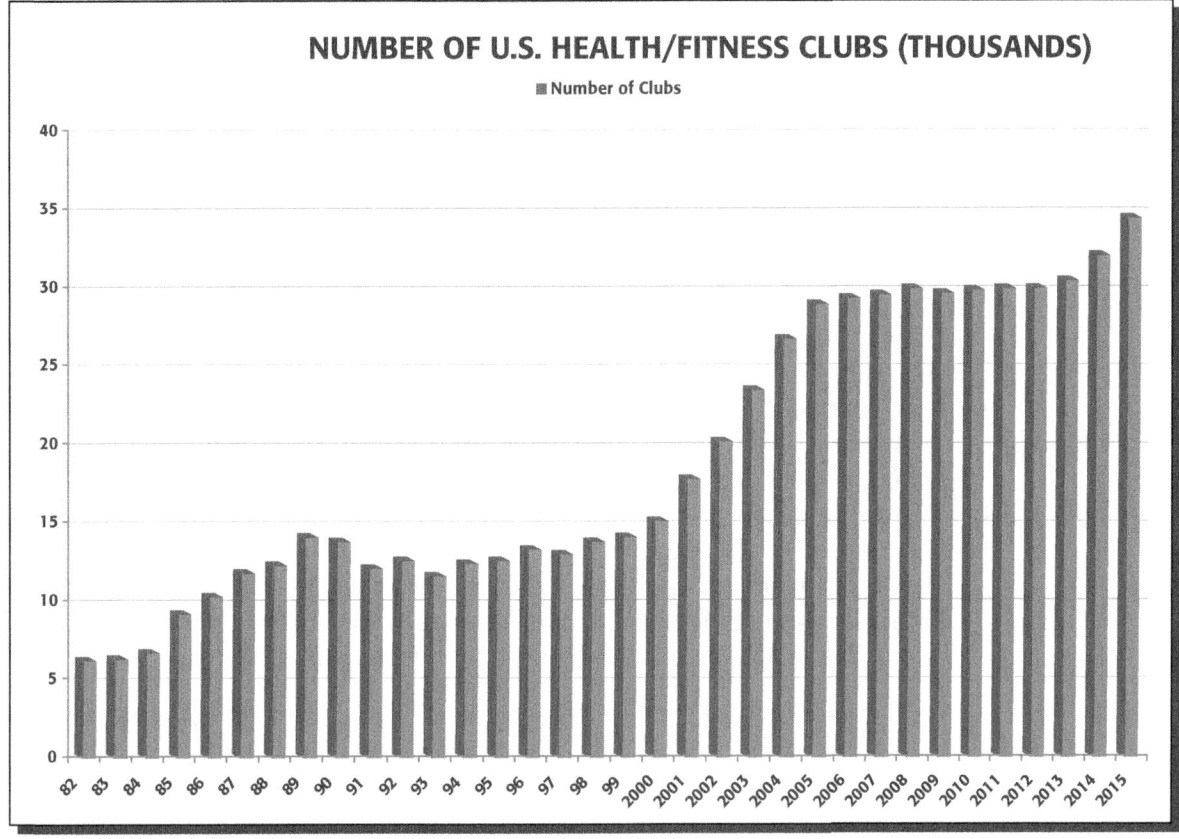

Figure 1-1. Number of U.S. health/fitness clubs

Comparatively speaking, the 6,200 clubs that existed when the decade of the 1980s began and the 13,854 clubs that brought the decade to a close represented a real mix. For one thing, the racquet and tennis clubs began to diversify, creating fitness centers out of existing racquet courts (the beginning of the multipurpose club), as more consumers expressed an interest in engaging in cardiovascular and resistance training. Individually owned and operated health/fitness clubs, commonly called "mom & pop" clubs, sprouted rapidly. Many of these clubs incorporated the term "Nautilus" in their commercial name as a means of attracting a wider audience. During this time period, Bally's became the industry leader, through its consolidation of many of the smaller chains (e.g., Holiday Health, Scandinavian, etc.).

In the process, Bally's became the face of the industry, much to the dismay of IRSA, which focused on representing health/fitness clubs that were committed to operating in a prudent, ethical manner. The emergence of Bally's was seen as both a positive and negative for the industry. On one hand, Bally's brought consumers to the industry; on the other hand, Bally's generated a considerable degree of negative publicity, on occasion, because of its aggressive business practices.

In addition to commercial health/fitness clubs, the 1980s saw the emergence of the corporate fitness center industry. Because research showed that employee-based fitness programs brought a return for the company, many corporations began to actively integrate on-site heath/fitness facilities into their employee offerings. One of the first was the Pepsi Center in Purchase, New York, under the leadership of Dr. Dennis Colacino. Eventually, corporations such as Exxon, Monsanto, and Johnson and Johnson became the benchmarks for this new segment of the industry during this period.

Cardio Fitness of New York, which initially arose in the late 1970s as a result of the enterprising endeavors of Dr. Jerry Zuckerman, was the first club chain in the 1980s to focus its efforts on offering its clients the opportunity to achieve scientific and medically based cardiovascular fitness, targeting corporate executives. Another institutional entry during the 1980s was the Fitness Company of New York, which was developed on both a scientific and corporate health model of fitness. The Sports Training Institute (STI) of New York, founded in 1975 by Dr. Michael O'Shea, was the first club group to bring a personal training model to the market. While STI eventually closed, its organizational structure and approach would become a model for the entire industry and one of the landmark events of the 1980s. Subsequently, club chains, such as Ray Wilson's Family Fitness Centers in California and 24 Hour Nautilus in Northern California, became major players in the low-dues dollar business segment of the industry. In later years, they joined together to become one of the largest organizational players in the industry—24 Hour Fitness.

Tennis Corporation of America (TCA), originally founded by Allan Schwartz as a tennis club, became a leading operator of both tennis clubs and sports clubs. The Midtown Tennis Club, TCA's first club, which was opened in 1969, was the largest indoor tennis club at the time. Several other highly regarded industry-based companies, including Fitcorp of Boston, a corporate fitness-based company, and Club Sports International of Denver (now known as Wellbridge), an operator of high-end sports clubs, were also established during this period. About this time, women's-only clubs began to flourish, with chains such as Lucille Robert's and Living Well Lady. As the 1980s came to a close and the number of clubs had reached in excess of 13,000 facilities, the diversity of club offerings had expanded to include such facilities as pure racquet/tennis clubs, multipurpose sports clubs, fitness only clubs, YMCAs, and corporate fitness centers.

As the number of clubs grew in the 1980s, so did the number of members who used the clubs and the manner in which they used them. While no accurate estimate of club patronage was available in 1980, by 1987 the industry was able to estimate that it served 17 million members, who on average used the club 72 times a year (about 1.4x a week) (Figures 1-2 and 1-3). The research also indicated that out of the 17 million members, approximately 30.6 percent (5.3 million) could be considered core members (i.e., individuals who use a particular club at least 100x a year) (Figure 1-4). This figure indicated that about one-third of all members actually were participating at their club at least twice a week.

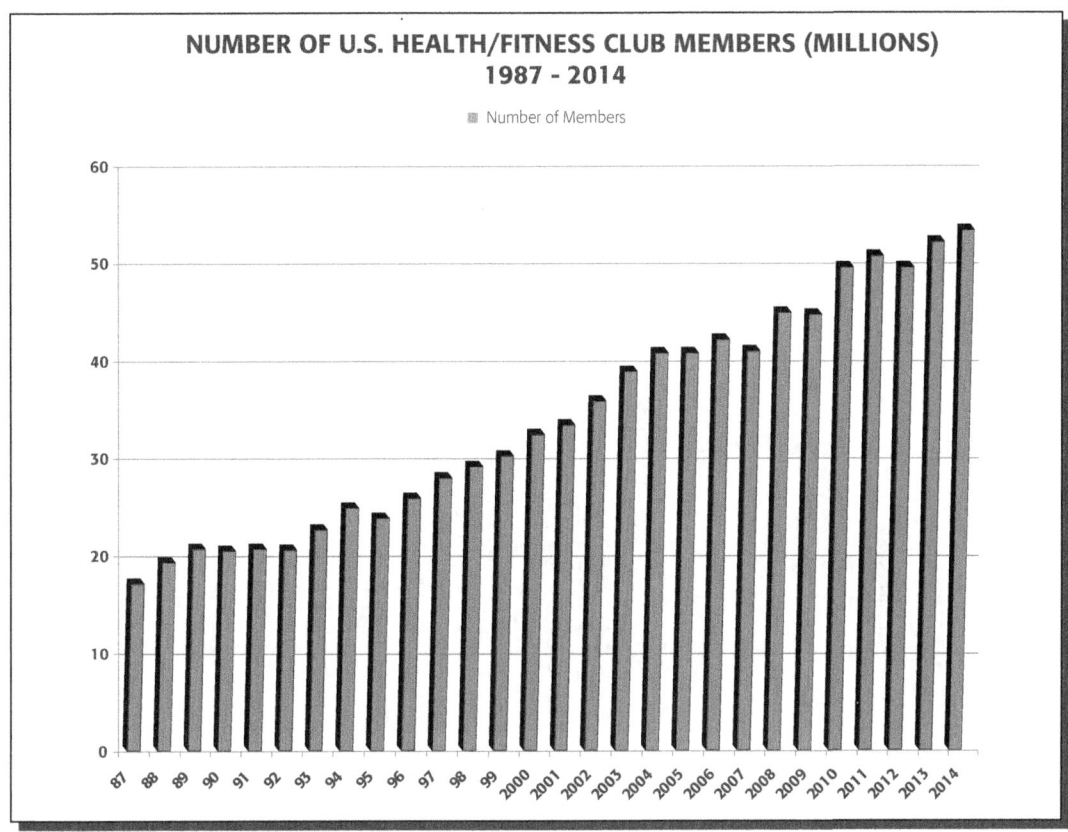
Figure 1-2. U.S. health club memberships

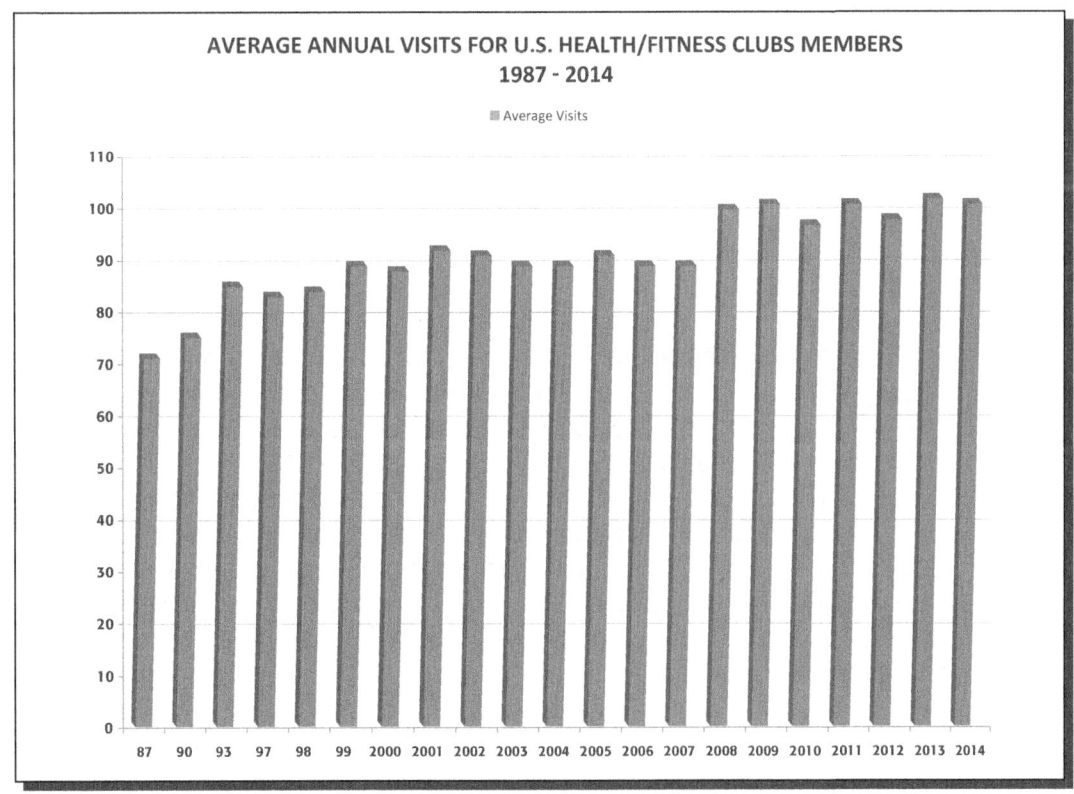
Figure 1-3. Average member visits annually

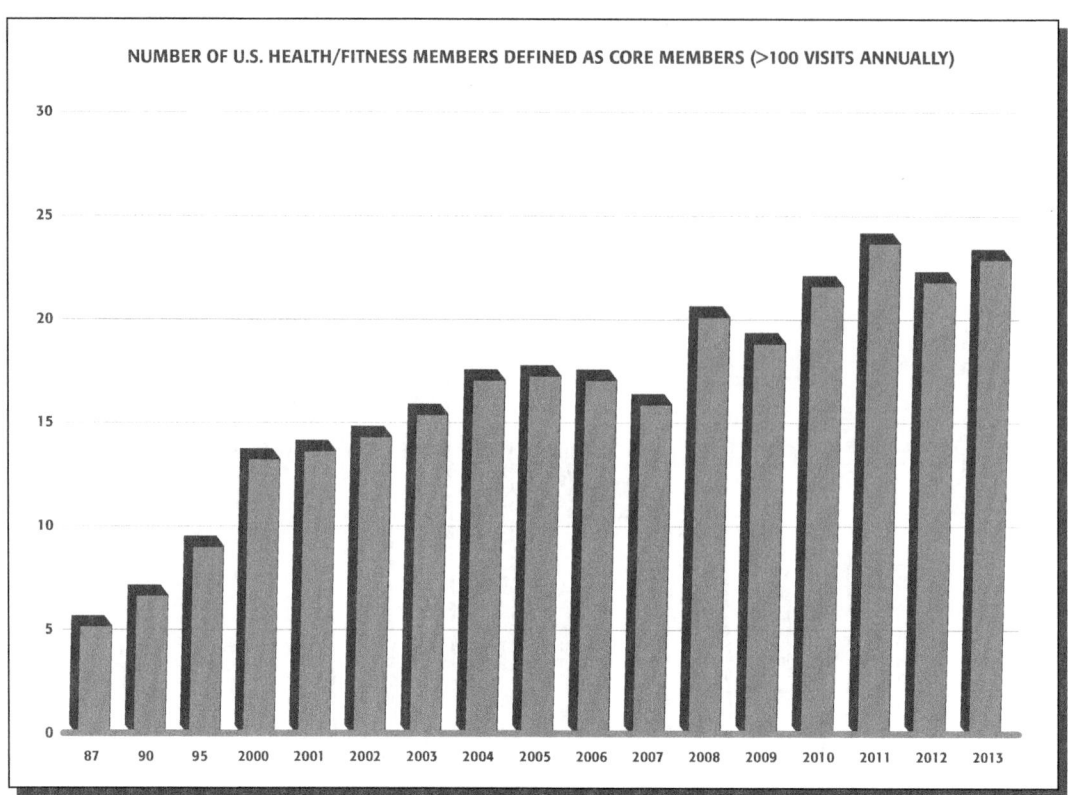

Figure 1-4. Number of core health club members

The rapid growth in the number of clubs and members during the 1980s was fueled by both documented data that supported both the need for and the value of engaging in physical activity on a regular basis and the impact that targeted programming had on popular culture. An outpouring of new research continued to show the "exercise is medicine" connection. Study after study linked regular exercise with a reduction in cardiovascular disease, as well as almost every other health-related disorder, including diabetes, high blood pressure, cancer, and obesity. While such data definitely played a role in helping bring more people to the clubs, a more likely factor in that regard was the introduction of programming that emphasized the trends of the popular culture.

Programming innovations were a main factor in club growth in the 1980s. The biggest program trend to influence the industry and a landmark event by itself was the explosion of aerobic group-exercise classes (commonly referred to as "aerobics"). The rapid growth of aerobics introduced an entirely new market to health/fitness clubs—women. The primary appeal of aerobics to women was its dance orientation and, arguably more importantly, its socialization of exercise. Jacki Sorensen and her aerobic dancing program, along with Judy Misset and her Jazzercise offering, took the country by storm, both introduced around 1969. These popular exercise modalities were soon followed by high-impact aerobics and then low-impact aerobics, which were popularized in the mid-1980s by Jane Fonda in her best-selling book, *Jane Fonda's Workout*, as well as shortly thereafter in a series of books and videos that collectively sold over 20 million copies. The movie "Perfect," with Jamie Lee Curtis, also helped to popularize the "aerobic dance" craze during this period. By the end of the 1980s, aerobic dance classes were bringing more people to clubs than any other activity.

In the mid-1980s, personal training became a program trend in the industry, particularly on the east and west coast. Concurrently, racquet sports also played a significant role in the growing movement by facilities to become more programming driven. The 1980s also saw the industry make a strong push toward raising the professional credibility of its instructors. In that regard, the American College of Sports Medicine undertook the preeminent role in the effort to certify health/fitness professionals. Joining ACSM in the effort were organizations such as the American Fitness and Aerobics Association (AFAA), the American Council on Exercise (ACE), the International Dance Exercise Association (IDEA), and the National Strength and Conditioning Association (NSCA). In response, each of these organizations offered educational and/or certification programs to support the growing demand by the industry for qualified health/fitness professionals.

Another significant occurrence in the 1980s was the rapid growth of a new factor in the health/fitness industry—fitness equipment manufacturers. While Nautilus continued to flourish as a manufacturer and distributor of resistance training equipment, new competitors arose to serve the emerging market. For example, during this period, Eagle, later to become Cybex, became a significant player in the resistance equipment business. Joining Cybex were companies, such as Body Masters, Paramount, and Universal.

On the cardiovascular side of the equipment equation, Life Fitness, founded by Augie Nieto of Lifecycle fame, led the way. Through the introduction of the Lifecycle, the Liferower, as well as subsequently the Lifestep, and the Lifetreadmill, Life Fitness took the lead in the manufacture and sales of cardiovascular equipment.

StairMaster was another successful equipment manufacturing company that originated in the 1980s, under the visionary leadership of Randy Peterson and Nicholas Orlando. StairMaster evolved from the landmark creation, manufacturing, and marketing of the StairMaster—the first mechanical stairclimbing machine. It could safely be argued that the StairMaster was the industry's signature product during the 1980s and might have been the most popular form of cardiovascular training equipment in the United States during this period.

The success of Life Fitness and StairMaster led other companies, such as Trotter, Unisen, and Precor, to enter the fitness equipment industry. During this decade, the motorized treadmill was even further popularized by companies such as Quinton and Trotter and later blossomed under the efforts of companies such as Precor, Unisen, and Life Fitness.

❑ *The 1990s*

At the beginning of the decade, a total of 13,854 clubs were operating in the United States. By the end of the decade, that total had grown to approximately 16,000 clubs, an overall increase of 15 percent (Figure 1-1). Concurrently, the number of club members increased by 36 percent from 21 million members at the beginning of the decade to 33 million by the end of the decade (Figure 1-2). During this period, the number of core members in health/fitness clubs increased by 100 percent, from just less than seven million to nearly 14 million.

> In the mid-1980s, personal training became a program trend in the industry, particularly on the east and west coast.

It is interesting to note that the average club member at the end of the decade used the club on average 89 times a year, up from an average of 72 times a year 10 years earlier (Figure 1-3). In a similar vein, the percentage of Americans who were members of clubs grew from just over 7 percent of the total population of the United States at the beginning of the decade to 13 percent of the population at the end of the decade.

All of the aforementioned data indicates that the industry grew more in terms of both the number of members using clubs and how frequently these members used the clubs, rather than being simply a by-product of the proliferation in the number of clubs. In other words, demand was growing faster than supply, a positive indicator for the continued growth of the industry.

A significant change in the market demographics of the average club member also occurred in the 1990s. During the growth period of the 70s and 80s, the typical member of a health/fitness club was a male between the ages of 18 and 34, with an annual income under $50,000. As the industry progressed during the decade, however, the demographics of club members changed.

The primary market for membership became individuals who were older (35 to 54), as well as more affluent ($50,000 to $75,000). By the end of the decade, the average age and household income of prospects continued to climb. At that point, a member was most likely to be between the ages of 35 and 54, equally likely to be male or female, and likely to be someone making in excess of $75,000 annually.

The aforementioned demographic swing, along with the new focus on family, would cause significant changes in the industry during the decade. It should be noted that during the 1990s, the total amount of retail spending in the industry had grown from around $6.5 billion in the early 1990s to $11.6 billion by the end of the decade, an increase of over 50 percent in consumer spending on health/fitness memberships (Figure 1-5).

As a result of both the under supply of health/fitness clubs and the growing financial performance of these commercial entities, the investment world began to look at the health/fitness club industry as a viable investment option. The movement of substantial equity into the industry from non-industry sources, such as equity groups, merchant banks, etc., represents one of the landmark occurrences in the 1990s for the industry. In fact, this influx of investment was a precursor of many of the changes that would take place in the 21st century.

From a club and facility perspective, the 1990s brought several significant changes, including:

- Consolidation and the formation of larger multi-club operators on a local, regional, and national scale (e.g., Bally, 24 Hour Fitness, Town Sports International, Wellbridge, Sport & Health, Lifetime Fitness, Club One, etc.)
- The establishment of fitness-only clubs (i.e., fitness- and exercise-only centers with no sports component)
- The development of large suburban multipurpose clubs that focused primarily on the family (e.g., Lifetime Fitness, Bay Clubs, Leisure Sports, etc.)
- The creation of multiple-modality studios (e.g., aerobics, spinning, Yoga, etc.)

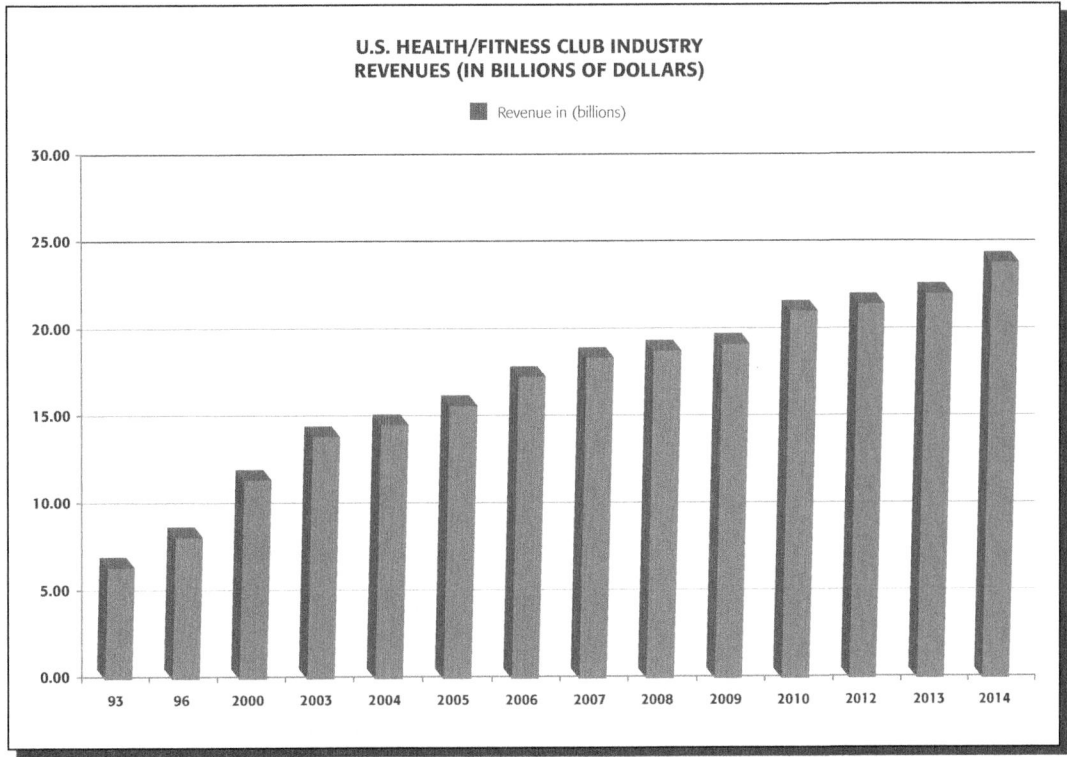

Figure 1-5. U.S. health club revenues

- The dawn of the club-based spa
- The creation of distinct club brands (e.g., Bally, Crunch, Equinox, 24 Hour Fitness, Lifetime Fitness, LA Fitness, etc.)
- The entry of hospital-based facilities into the industry, in large part driven by the aging population and the realization of the medical community that "prevention" should be an integral part of the medical business model
- The entry of expensive large-scale, community-owned and operated recreation centers, which would compete in the industry on a not-for-profit basis
- The expansion of the number of YMCAs and JCCs into a more competitive position in an attempt to serve the fitness market
- The development of apartment- and hotel-based fitness centers

The aforementioned changes in the types of health/fitness facilities and operations were driven by the evolving demographics, alterations in popular culture, additional research on the benefits of exercise, and the maturing of the industry from a purely business perspective. The 1990s also served as host to some of the most significant program and service trends to hit the industry since its earliest years. Among the more influential trends and program practices to arise during this period were the following:

- Spinning. Introduced by Johnny G in 1987, spinning became the rage during the early to mid-90s and has continued to be one of the industry's most sought-after group-exercise programs. Spinning served as the seed for a host of group-cycling programs that emerged on the market during this period (e.g., Schwinn, Keiser, Reebok, etc.); spinning involves group-based cycling that is done to music.

From a club and facility perspective, the 1990s brought several significant changes, including the creation of distinct club brands such as Equinox.

- Yoga and Pilates. As the average age of the club members continued to increase in the 1990s, classes in yoga and Pilates became mainstays of the industry. The trend was toward softer activity that emphasized stretching and movement, rather than aerobics. Yoga is an Eastern form of moving meditation that combines specific postures (asanas) and stretches with controlled breathing. Pilates is a form of exercise that is based on principles that were developed by Joseph Pilates in the 1920s.
- Weight training. Research showing the beneficial effects of resistance training on bone health, weight control, and overall health led to an enormous increase in the popularity of weight training, particularly among women.
- Personal training. The public's perception of personal training changed dramatically in the 1990s. Once considered a fringe program that appealed to a very small audience of affluent members, personal training became the primary program thrust of the industry during this period, as even more individuals recognized the value of receiving personalized attention and instruction. By the end of decade, clubs operated by Equinox and Sports Club/LA (which was purchased by Equinox in August of 2014) were often generating personal training revenue in excess of $2 million annually.
- Packaged group exercise. In the 1990s, the focus on "aerobics" had generally been replaced in the industry with "group exercise," and with it, an emphasis on having more diversity in group-exercise programming. In the process, programs, such as STEP, Body Pump, Spinning, Precision Cycling, Body Rage, and Kickbox Fitness, among others, became household names in the industry. By the late 1990s, Les Mills' packaged group-fitness programs (e.g., Body Pump, Body Rage, etc.) had become a dominant force

in the health/fitness club industry. Another major player in the packaged group-exercise domain that rose to prominence during the 1990s was Body Training Systems, which is now called Mossa.

- Kids' programming. By the end of the decade, most suburban clubs had come to realize that their ability to successfully attract a sufficient number of members would, in large part, be driven by their ability to offer a variety of youth-oriented programs.
- Seniors' programming. In the 1990s, the ever-increasing age level of the average club member, in part driven by the aging of the baby boomers, created a need for an entirely new focus of programming that was geared toward providing exercise alternatives for those individuals over the age of 50. For example, the development of Wellbridge was in response to this particular program trend.
- Day spas. By the end of the decade, the day-spa concept had taken hold in the industry, as many members perceived spa treatments to be an integral part of their overall approach to improving their level of well-being.

In 1996, possibly the most important landmark for the health and fitness industry ever to occur happened when the U.S. government released the *U.S. Surgeon General's Report on Physical Activity and Health.* In this report, the U.S. Surgeon General provided the American public with a clear, yet critical, message: Americans would benefit immensely from a regular program of physical activity. In essence, the message detailed the fact that engaging in physical activity on a regular basis contributes significantly to reductions in many health-related disorders. Furthermore, if specific activity guidelines were followed, individuals could improve their health and prolong the quality of their life. The full impact of this report has yet to be completely realized, since most Americans have not fully embraced the significance of the report. Nonetheless, the impact of this particular report on the industry was very significant.

The 1990s also served as a springboard for some of the most significant equipment innovations in the industry since the development of StairMaster, Lifecycle, and Nautilus machines. Among the critically acclaimed equipment concepts that occurred during this period were the following:

- The elliptical trainer. Precor introduced the concept of elliptical training in 1995. Named the EFX, the Precor elliptical trainer had a major impact on equipment-based training. The elliptical trainer was designed to provide a low-impact, comfortable approach to training that would slowly lead to a significant decrease in the popularity of such activities as indoor cycling and mechanical stairclimbing. As of 2015, according to IHRSA's 2015 Health Club Consumer Report, elliptical training is now the second most popular form of equipment training in health/fitness clubs.
- The spinning bike. The introduction of the spinning bike was a new twist on the bicycle ergometers of the 70s and 80s (for example, those that were manufactured by Body Guard and Monarch). The spinning bike allowed members to train in social groups, while simultaneously controlling the intensity level of their training.
- Plate-loaded resistance equipment. First introduced by Hammer in the late 1980s, but subsequently popularized in the 1990s, plate-loaded

equipment combined the safety features of selectorized machines with the impact of free-weight training.
- Treadmills. While treadmills had been around for over 40 years, companies, such as Star Trac, Life Fitness, Quinton, and Precor brought new dynamics to this particular type of equipment in the 1990s. In the process, treadmills became one of the most popular pieces of equipment in the industry, as manufacturers included programming options, as well as audio and visual entertainment, as a basic feature on their products—all at a reasonable cost.
- Pilates-based equipment. While Pilates equipment has been around since the 1920s, it was essentially introduced to the club industry during the 1990s. By the end of the decade, Pilates equipment, continuing to grow in popularity, became one of the fastest growing trends, according to data released by IHRSA at the end of the decade.
- Personal entertainment systems. The introduction of Cardio Theater in 1991 by Tony Deleede (and later Broadcast Vision) was a landmark occurrence in the industry. For many consumers, the introduction of Cardio Theater changed the way that they perceived their club experience.

The final noteworthy event that occurred in the 1990s was the change in direction taken by the International Health, Racquet & Sportsclub Association (IHRSA). From its inception and through the first half of the 1990s, IHRSA (formerly IRSA) had focused its efforts on being an association of quality clubs. This focus allowed it to develop resources to upgrade the professionalism of its membership. During the later half of the 1990s, however, IHRSA undertook a conscious shift in its strategy. In the process, IHRSA became an industry trade association, one that focused on public advocacy for the industry and one that expanded its role in the growing international market. This change in direction allowed IHRSA to partner with other organizations in an attempt to establish a more significant voice for the industry in public policy and industry promotion.

The Industry's Entry Into the Mature Stage of Its Life Cycle (2000–Beyond)

From 2000 to 2015, the number of health/fitness facilities increased by over 100 percent, while the number of club members grew by slightly over 60 percent.

At the beginning of the new century, the United States had almost 16,000 health/fitness facilities that served approximately 33 million members. By 2015, the number of U.S. clubs had grown to 34,500, with approximately 54 million members (Figures 1-1 and 1-2). During this period, the percentage of Americans who were members of clubs increased from approximately 13 percent of the population in 2000 to 18.5 percent of the population by 2015. In other words, in a period of approximately fifteen years, the number of health/fitness facilities had increased by over 100 percent, while the number of club members had grown by slightly over 60 percent. Since 2012, the compound annual growth rate of membership has been 1.7 percent, compared to a compound annual growth rate of 5.2 percent for facilities during the same time period.

The aforementioned trend (the number of clubs growing faster than the member population) is the polar opposite of what occurred during the 1990s, when the growth in membership outpaced the growth in clubs, and demand exceeded supply. A review of industry data going as far back as 1987 shows that the average number of members per facility has dropped over the past 27 years from over 2,000 per club to approximately 1,570 per club. By 2015, the health/fitness facility industry was entrenched in the mature phase of its life cycle, a period in which an industry experiences declining growth, downward pressure on pricing, and further differentiation.

The apparent reason for the aforementioned situation is an overdevelopment in the number of clubs, which, in turn, has outpaced the growth in overall membership. In other words, the industry has been carving the pie into smaller pieces, rather than effectively growing the size of the pie. Club growth had created saturation in several significant markets, such as New York, Los Angeles, and Chicago, as well as in other major metropolitan markets. In these areas, the number of clubs far surpassed the growth in market demand. Most of this shift in supply and demand has been fueled by the influx of investment capital and the growth strategies of various regional and national club chains, including 24 Hour Fitness, LA Fitness, Equinox, Town Sports International, Planet Fitness, and Life Time Fitness, among others.

The supply-and-demand equation has been further tilted by the fact that a significant portion of the club growth has occurred in what is commonly referred to as "fitness boxes"—club models that look and feel the same and that lack any real unique brand differentiation. Another contributor to this excess supply of clubs and the resulting pressure on membership growth at the club level has been the rapid growth of small box franchise operations since 2005 (e.g., Anytime Fitness, with close to 3,000 facilities worldwide, and Snap Fitness, with over 1,400 facilities), the rapid emergence of high-volume, low-priced clubs (e.g., Planet Fitness, Blink, Crunch, etc.) since 2008, and finally, the explosion of boutique fitness studios that begin around 2010. On the other hand, all of the blame for this oversupply cannot be attributed entirely to the growth in the number of commercial clubs and boutique studios, given that a significant growth in not-for-profit facilities (e.g., community-based facilities, university-based facilities, and medical-based models has also occurred). (See Figure 1-6.)

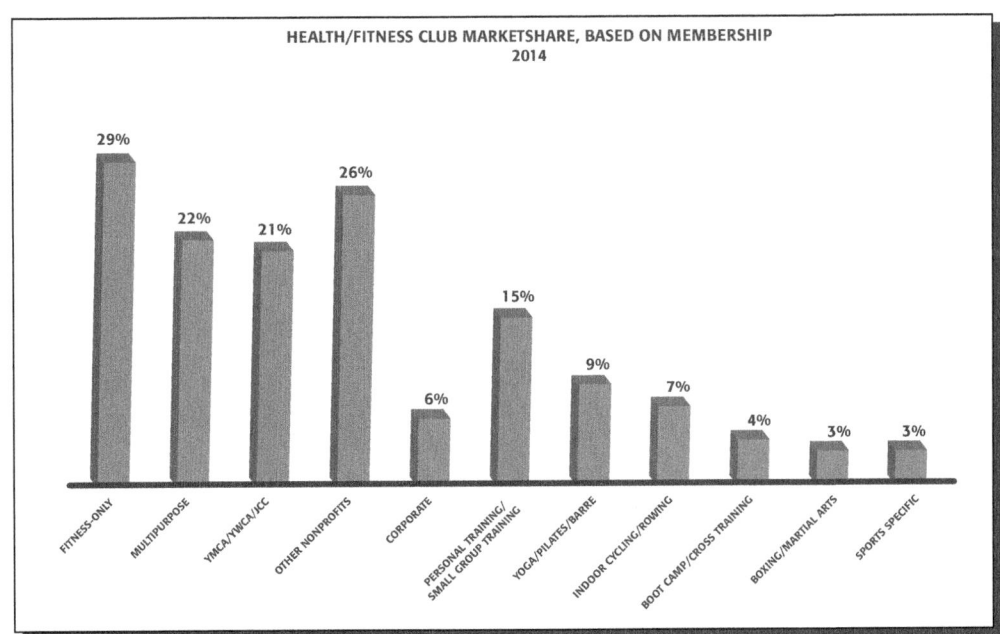

Figure 1-6. Industry mix of various types of health/fitness facilities

During the first 15 years of the new century, the industry has had more success generating usage from its existing members, rather than attracting new members to the market.

Looking closer at industry research, as detailed in *IHRSA's 2015 Global Report*, it is apparent that during the first 15 years of the new century, the industry has had more success generating usage from its existing members, rather than attracting new members to the market. In 1990, average club members used their club 79 times a year, while by 2015, that usage figure had increased to approximately 102 visits a year. Furthermore, the number of core members (i.e., those individuals who utilized their club more than 100 times a year) had increased to over 23 million, or approximately 44 percent of the total membership base.

In fact, the most active club members were those individuals who were over the age of 55. The available statistics indicate that by 2015, the industry had managed to elicit greater usage from its existing membership, to a greater degree than it had been able to drive additional non-members into the clubs. As a result of these trends, the industry currently faces four key challenges: an oversupply of clubs in certain markets; an insufficient influx of new members; downward pressure on pricing, and a lack of product differentiation.

In 2015, industry statistics indicate that the demographic profile of a U.S. club member was shifting. By 2015, the U.S. health/fitness club member profile was as follows (refer to Figures 1-7, 1-8, and 1-9):

- Fifty percent of members were women and 50 percent were men, statistics that represent a shift from five years earlier, when men composed 53 percent of members and women 47 percent of members. In essence, since 2010, membership has swung from being heavily weighted toward men to now being relatively well-balanced.
- The 25 to 34 and 35-to-44 age groups encompass the two largest segments of club membership at 20 percent and 18 percent respectfully, having grown by over 140 percent over the last 20 years.
- Those individuals who are 18 to 24 years of age, once the cornerstone of the industry in the 1980s, now account for 11 percent of the industry's membership.
- Nearly 42 percent of all health/fitness club members belong to boutique fitness facilities.
- Forty-two percent of all members have household incomes over $100,000 annually, with 14 percent of members having household incomes over $150,000 annually. Arguably, the industry has emerged as the playground for only the most affluent in our society.
- Approximately 52 percent of health/fitness club members have a four-year degree or higher, while less than 19 percent have only earned a high school education.

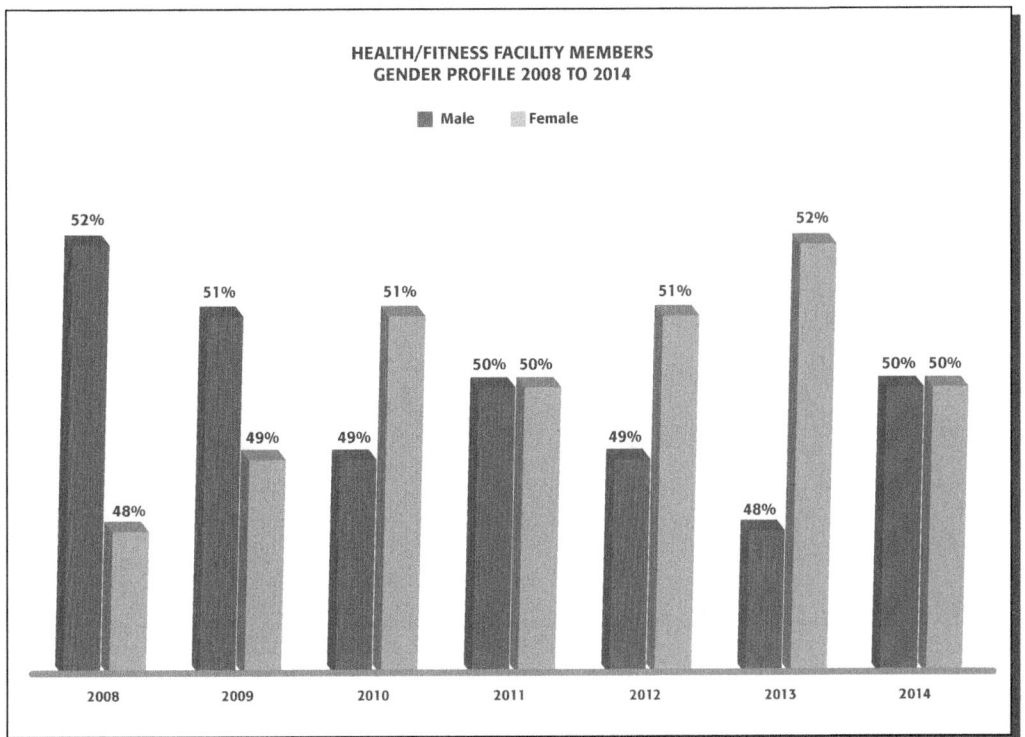

Figure 1-7. U.S. health club membership gender mix

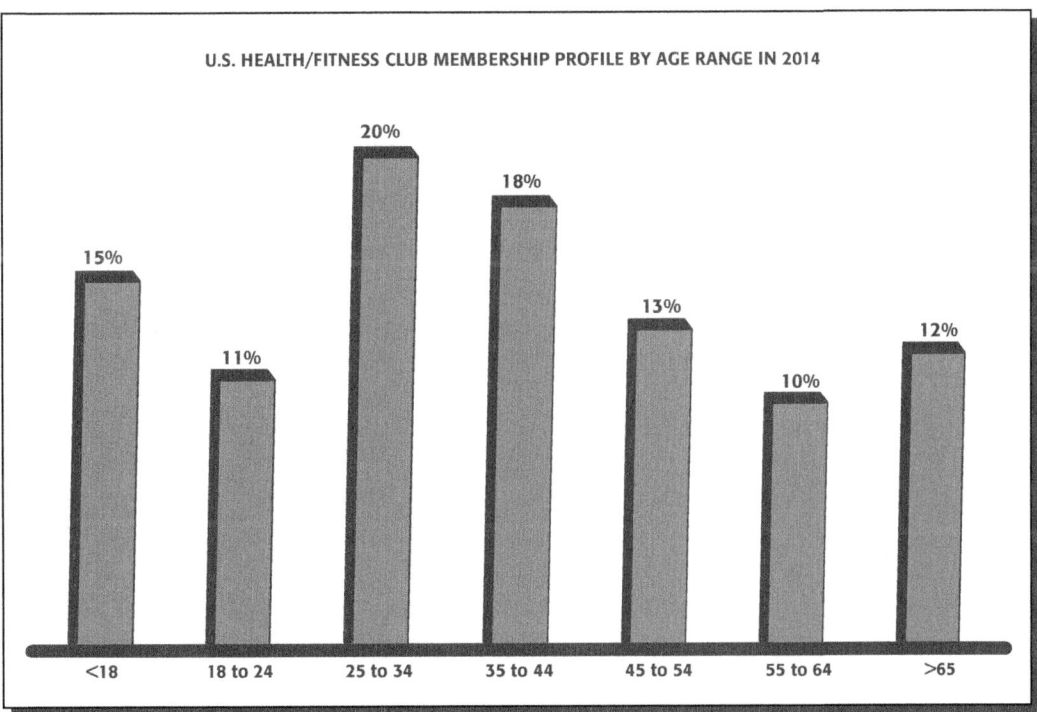

Figure 1-8. U.S. health club membership by age

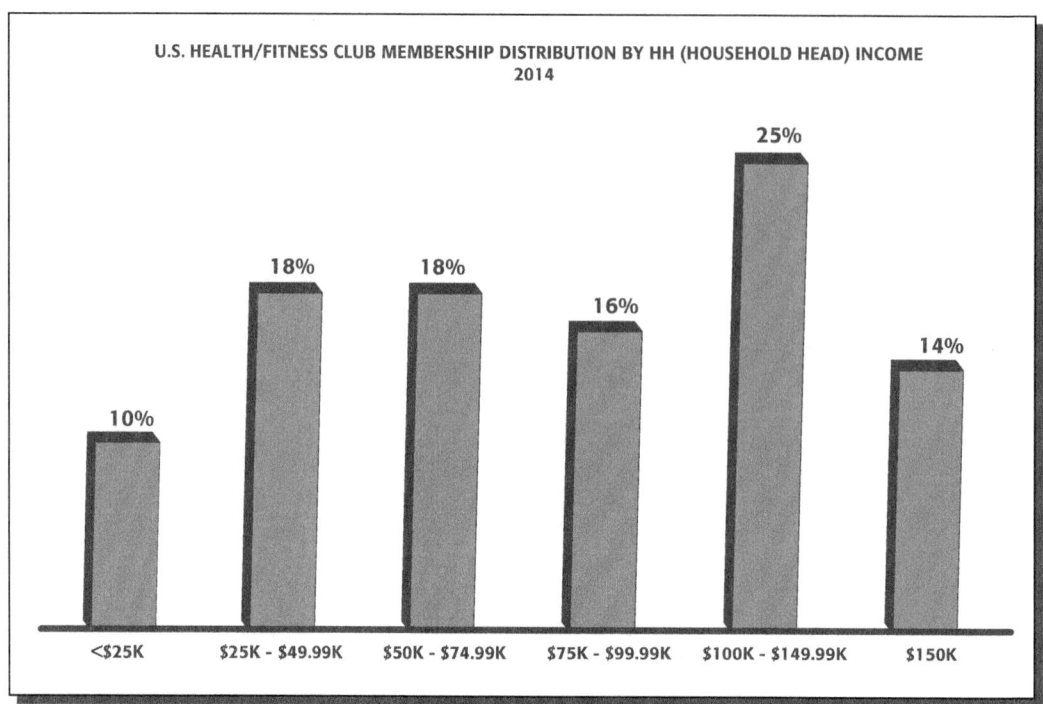

Figure 1-9. U.S. health club membership segmentation by household income

What Does the Future Hold: A Glimpse at Several Future Health/Fitness Facility Industry Trends

By 2015, a number of health/fitness club industry trends had shifted, as the facilities, equipment, and programs employed in the industry reflected the new demographics and psychographics of the American population. These trends represent the true state of the health/fitness club industry, as of 2015, and are precursors for what the industry can expect over the next one to two decades. Among the most significant trends that have evolved over the past few years are the following:

❑ Facilities

- High-volume, low-priced clubs (HVLP). These are clubs that offer limited amenities, 24-hour access in most cases, an abundance of equipment, and relatively limited staffing, all for under $20 a month (in most cases, for less than $10 a month). Examples of HVLP facilities include Planet Fitness, Crunch, Blink, Retro Fitness, and Youfit.
- Boutique fitness studios that are designed to appeal to niche markets (e.g., cycling studios, such as SoulCycle; Pilates studios; yoga studios, such as Core Power Yoga; personal training studios; cross training studios; high intensity interval training studios, such as Orange Theory and Barry's Bootcamp; and barre studios, such as Pure Barre and The Bar Method).
- Small franchise operations—facilities that provide convenience and affordability (e.g., Anytime, Snap, etc.).

❑ Equipment

- Cardiovascular equipment with personal media centers, that include a variety of features, such as LED touch screens, smart phone attachments, Internet connectivity, as well as cloud software applications, which provide the ability to monitor and store personal performance data
- Functional fitness accessories, such as TRX, Bosu balls, kettlebells, Indian clubs, etc.

❑ Programs and services

- Boot camps, high intensity interval training classes, and "extreme" training camps. These programs typically encompass leverage functional movements and push exercisers to relatively extreme levels of conditioning, such as mixed martial arts, and elite athlete training.
- Fusion fitness involving activities that blend diverse modalities, such as yoga and cycling, Pilates and weight training, yoga and Pilates, etc. This approach is designed to cater to consumers who want/need variety in their workouts for motivational purposes.
- Core fitness classes that concentrate on engaging the core musculature in the exercise workout
- Packaged group-exercise programs, such as Les Mills, Mossa, Zumba, and Tabata, which offer predictable, entertaining, and effective exercise routines. These programs provide great efficiency for clubs, as well as compelling and constantly changing exercise routines for participants.
- Youth sports performance conditioning. The growing epidemic of childhood obesity and America's fascination with organized youth sports help fuel this trend.
- Group training. As a result of the recession of 2008/2009, as well as an evolving consumer attitude toward materialism, group training offers members modified individualized attention in a small social setting at a lower cost.
- Internet-based training. As technology has evolved and consumers have become more technology-savvy and time-pressured, clubs have begun to offer a variety of Internet-based services, including personal training on the Internet.

At the present time, the U.S. industry continues to face challenges brought on by an increasing demand from the public and government for professional accountability. As a consequence of IHRSA's and the industry's efforts to have the industry accepted as a mainstream entity and the maturation of the U.S. health/fitness club industry into a $30 billion undertaking, both the public and the government have begun to place ever greater demands on the level of accountability of both the industry and the professionals involved in the delivery of fitness services. Among the examples of some of the public and government expectations that have either occurred or are in the process of transpiring (as of the publication of this book) are the following:

- State-level legislation that mandates the placement of automated external defibrillators in every health club (as of 2015, 11 states have passed legislation requiring health clubs to have AEDs)
- State-level legislation seeking to mandate the registration or licensure of personal trainers

- State-level legislation governing the operation of spa services
- Introduction of the Affordable Care Act and the impact of its regulations on companies that encourage its employees to engage in preventative health programs, including exercising at health/fitness clubs
- Higher expectations by the public for business practices grounded in integrity from all health/fitness club operators
- Expectations from the financial world for greater accountability and standardization of accounting practices in health/fitness clubs
- Expectations from investors for quarterly earnings performances that are consistent with Wall Street expectations
- Expectations by the public that the franchising of health/fitness clubs will continue. In that regard, beginning in 2003 and continuing through 2015, the industry has witnessed a substantial growth in the level of franchising groups, such as Anytime Fitness, Gold's, Snap, and Crunch, among others.

Reflections

While the health/fitness industry may seem to be a relatively young industry, its roots go back over two centuries. In fact, the innovative actions and practice of the industry pioneers in the 19th and 20th centuries offer a wealth of insights that today's health/fitness club operators would be wise to learn and leverage. By understanding and, more importantly, appreciating the efforts of the trailblazers and the forefathers of the industry, the future leaders can be better prepared to more effectively shape the course of the industry for decades to come.

The Physical Activity Beliefs and Behaviors of Americans and Their Implications for Health/Fitness Facilities

2

"Approximately 25 percent of Americans are inactive, while more than 60 percent of American adults do not engage in the recommended level of physical activity."

—Physical Activity and Health – A Report of the U.S. Surgeon General

Chapter Objectives

In order to gain a greater understanding of the physical activity practices of Americans and ultimately their potential suitability as health/fitness club members, it is important to understand the values and attitudes that Americans have toward physical activity. In that regard, research has shown that the values and attitudes held by individuals are the major determinants of their behavior. In other words, the core determinant of a person's actions is that individual's core values, which are at the heart of the attitudes and beliefs they have. In fact, the success of the U.S. health/fitness club business is extremely dependent upon the physical activity beliefs and behaviors of Americans.

This chapter provides an overview of the available research pertaining to both the attitudes of Americans toward physical activity and their actual physical activity behavior. The information in the chapter is designated to help club owners and club management better position their clubs for success by enabling them to more fully understand and act on the beliefs and behaviors of those individuals that they potentially serve.

> The success of the U.S. health/fitness club business is extremely dependent upon the physical activity beliefs and behaviors of Americans.

Core Values of Americans Toward Physical Activity and Health

When Americans are asked to rank their core values and how those values align with their overall satisfaction with life, health and fitness are an integral part of their response. According to research conducted by Roper Starch for IHRSA in 2001, which was later updated in a report released in 2007 entitled Fitness American Style, Americans rank health as the third most important value behind family and spouse. Concurrently, they rank fitness seventh among their top eight values (family, spouse, health, friends, career, diet, fitness, and money). It is interesting to note that both health and fitness are rated as more important than money (refer to Figure 2-1).

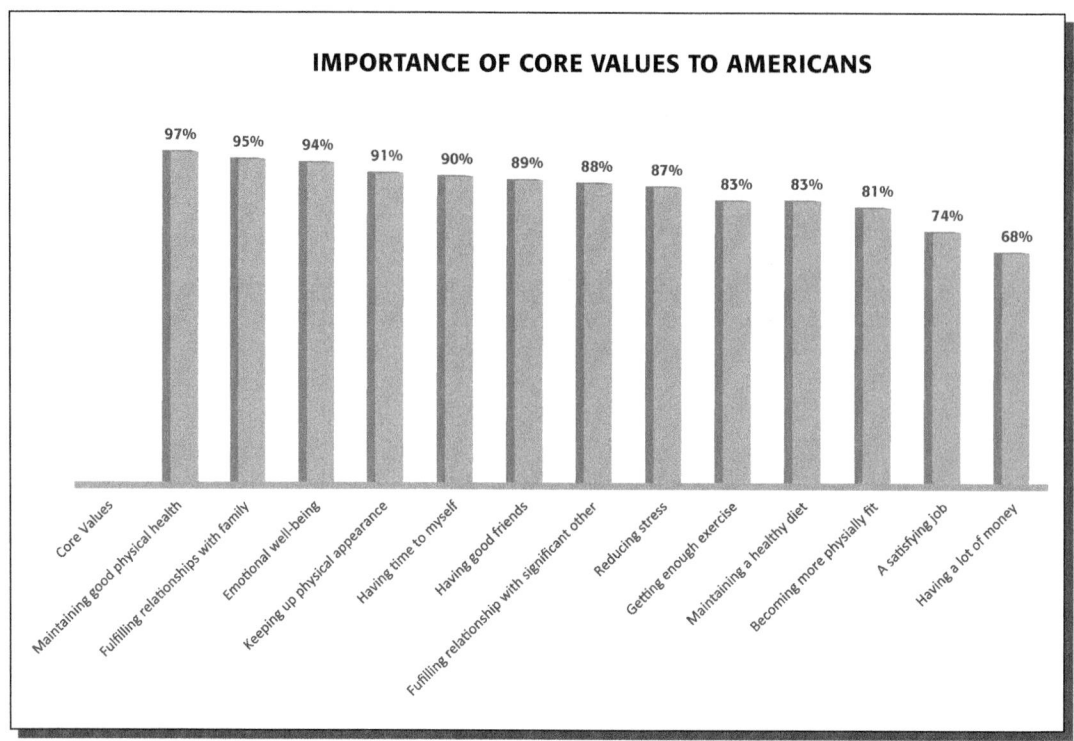

Figure 2-1. Importance of core values to Americans

On the other hand, when indicating the importance of each value to their overall level of satisfaction with life, health and fitness seem far less relevant to Americans than values, such as family, spouse, and money. Taken at face value, it is evident that when Americans prioritize their values, that health and fitness are important, but when measured as a contributor to their overall level of satisfaction with life, health and fitness are not as important as other values, such as family, friends, and career.

When Americans are questioned in greater depth about their attitude toward the importance of health and fitness, they share the following viewpoints:
- 97 percent of Americans state that it is essential and/or important to maintain good health.
- 91 percent of Americans believe that it is essential and/or important to keep up their physical appearance.
- 83 percent of Americans say that it is essential and/or important to get enough exercise.
- 81 percent of Americans feel that it is essential to become more physically fit.
- Women are far more likely than men to believe that fitness is essential to good health (nearly 60 percent of women versus 50 percent for men). Women are also more likely (40 percent to 31 percent) than men to feel that fitness is important to appearance.

- 74 percent of Americans are satisfied with their physical health, while a similar number (73 percent) are satisfied with their physical appearance. Only 49 percent are satisfied with the amount of physical activity they get.
- Younger men seem more satisfied than younger women with their health and appearance. As both groups age, however, men become less satisfied, while women become more satisfied.

When this data and the supporting research are examined, the following conclusions can be drawn:

- While Americans understand the importance of being healthy and fit, they don't see as much value in actually exercising to obtain the health and fitness that they claim that they value so much.
- Women, more than men, understand the importance of fitness to health and well-being.
- Americans, as a rule, and men, more than women, are generally satisfied with their health, appearance, and fitness. As a result, they already see themselves as having met the value equation with regard to their health and fitness. As a consequence they are less likely to see themselves as having a need to actually engage in an activity, such as exercise (refer to Figure 2-2).

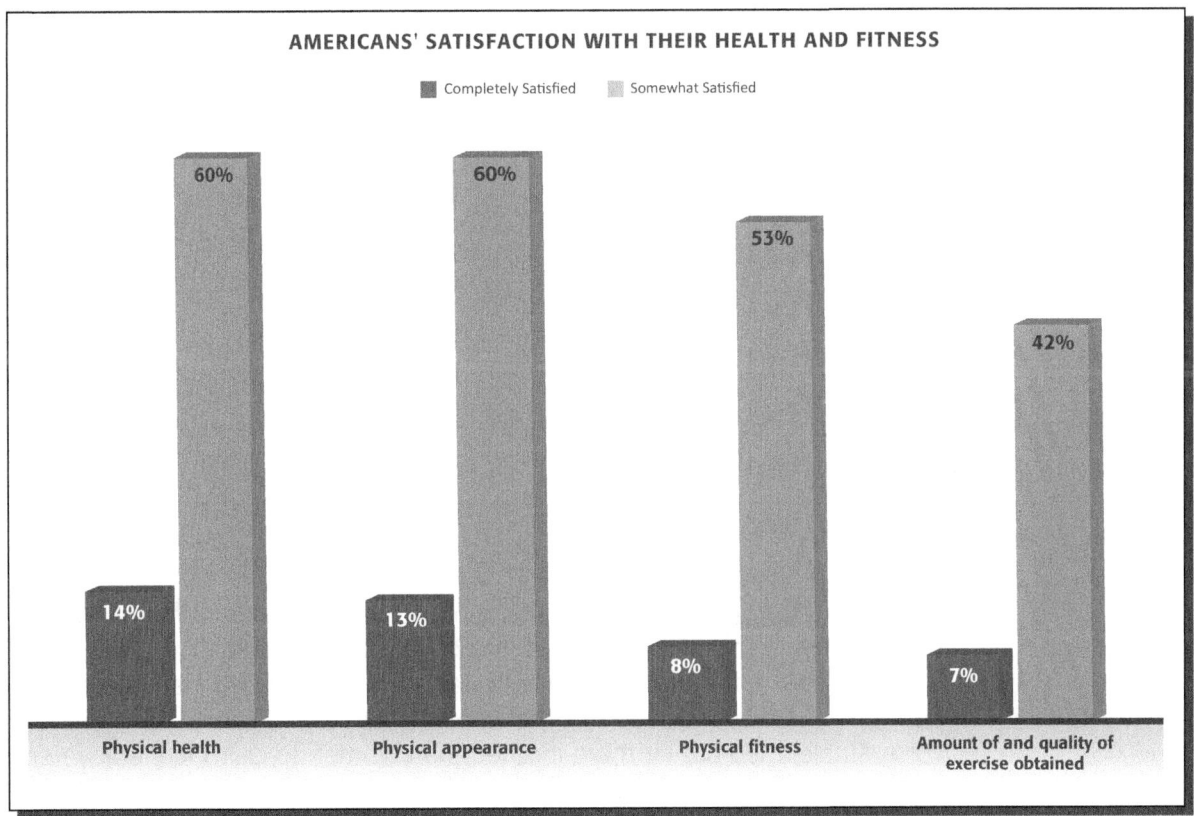

Figure 2-2. Americans' satisfaction with their health and fitness

What Physically Active Americans Say Are the Reasons That They Participate in Physical Activity and Exercise

When men and women are asked for the reasons why they engage in physical activity (exercise and sports), their responses indicate that multiple variables influence their actual behavior. Figure 2-3, based on research conducted by Roper Starch on behalf of the International Health, Racquet & Sportsclub Association (IHRSA) in 2001, provides a concise overview of the multiplicity of reasons Americans give for exercising.

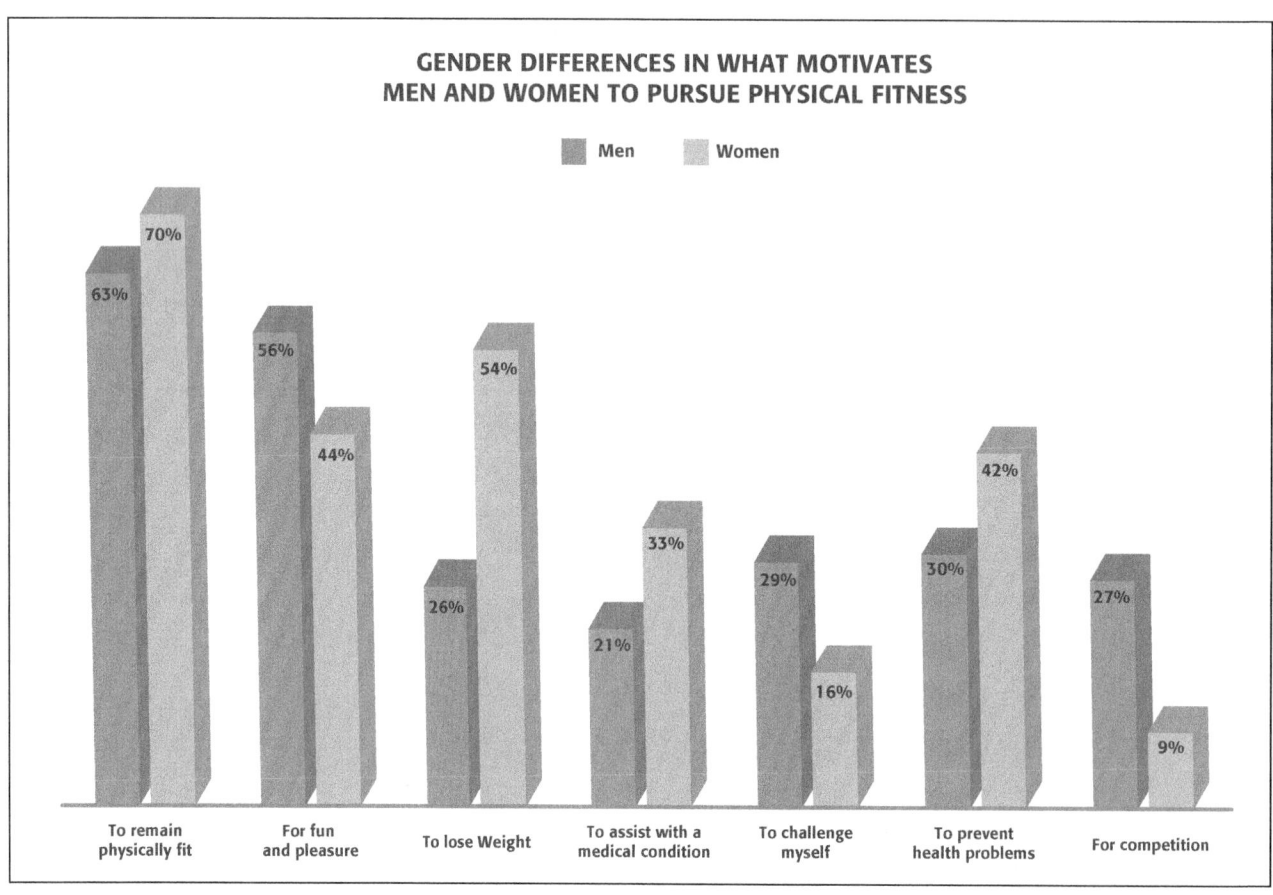

Figure 2-3. Men's and women's motivations for exercise

It is clear from Figure 2-3 that men and women have different reasons for exercising. This information is important because understanding these gender-related differences can assist health/fitness club owners/managers in developing club-based programs that can help attract and retain club members. For example, men are far more inclined than women to claim fun, enjoyment, personal challenge, and competition as driving forces for their exercise habits. Women, in turn, are far more inclined to see losing weight, staying fit, and helping prevent or assist with health-related conditions as their primary reason for exercising.

The Level of Fitness Consciousness Among Americans as a Predictor of Joining and Staying With Exercise

According to the research conducted by American Sports Data in 2003 and supported by the work of Dr. Rod Dishman, Americans can be classified in one of four categories of fitness consciousness: non-believers, indifferent, uninitiated believers, and hard-core participants. Understanding these categories and the accompanying traits and characteristics can assist clubs both in attracting new members and retaining existing ones. Figure 2-4 offers an overview of the traits associated with each basic category.

Non-Believers (2% of the population)	Indifferent (16% of the population)	Uninitiated Believers (63% of the population)	Hard-Core Participants (17% of the population)
Do not embrace the fitness lifestyle	No real interest in fitness	Believe fitness has value	Embrace fitness
Don't believe exercise is important	Negative attitude toward fitness	25% are sedentary and 26% are very active	Doers and believers; apostles of exercise
Sedentary lifestyle	Likely to claim they are not healthy	70% claim to be overweight	Regard their health as excellent
Male dominated	Equally likely to be male or female	More likely to be a woman and younger	57% male
Least educated	Low income and education	37% are college educated	49% are college educated and 38% are making in excess of $75K

Figure 2-4. Traits attributed to each of the basic categories of fitness consciousness

It is evident that those who are non-believers or indifferent are not qualified candidates for membership in a health/fitness club because the values and beliefs that they hold toward exercise would be very difficult to change when attempting to entice them to join a club. Even if they were sold a membership through effective "closing techniques," they would be unlikely to ever use their membership. The individuals who have hard-core, favorable attitudes toward fitness represent approximately 16 percent of the population, a total which closely parallels the percentage of Americans who are currently health club members (18 percent).

ClubIntel, a firm co-founded by the author, has undertaken several market-feasibility and club-concept studies, which scrutinized a number of suburban, high-income markets. In some investigations, 35 to 40 percent of consumers were found to belong to health/fitness clubs. These statistics suggest that the industry, as a whole, is close to extracting all of the low hanging fruit and needs to develop strategies that will attract the uninitiated segment (64 percent) of the population if it is to continue to grow the membership market.

What a Portrait of Those Individuals Who Exercise Can Mean to Health/Fitness Management

In the work that Roper Starch conducted for IHRSA in 2001, exercisers and non-exercisers were identified by a set of personality or psychographic characteristics. Grasping the nuances of these classifications can help club operators better understand the dynamics of how to develop and deliver a personalized club experience that can help attract and retain members. According to Roper's research, there are a total of six classifications: balanced holistics, conscientious preventers, social competitors, abracadabras, woulda-shouldas, and sit-com skeptics. An overview of the key attributes that characterize each of these six different and important groups involves the following:

- *Balanced holistics (13 percent).* These individuals view exercise as important to both their emotional and physical health. They exercise regularly and focus on reaching a state of internal harmony. They are twice as likely to be club members in comparison to the average American. They define themselves as socially confident, goal-oriented, energetic, and intelligent. They are more likely to be female (58 percent), college educated (32 percent), have a higher household income (average of $42K), be married (69 percent), and younger (40) than the average American. Finally, this group is two-and-a-half times more likely to exercise "religiously" than the general public.

- *Conscientious preventers (8 percent).* This group takes a balanced approach to physical activity and sees exercise as an avenue for the prevention of health-related problems and as a means to manage existing conditions. Individuals in this group are twice as likely to be club members and describe themselves as health-conscious, family-oriented, religious, and perfectionists. They are more likely to be older women (60 percent female, average age of 55); college-educated (32 percent); and have a higher income (average of $46K) than the average American.

- *Social competitors (20 percent).* These individuals prefer to spend their time in an environment that is social, engaging, and competitive. They are no more likely than other Americans to be club members. They describe themselves as professional, ambitious, risk-taking, and outgoing. They are also more likely to be male (62 percent) and single than the average American. They tend to fall within the average range with regard to their level of college education and income, but are younger than the average American. These individuals would represent many of those who visit boutique fitness studios such as HIIT and CrossFit-style studios.

- *Abracadabras (14 percent).* These individuals tend to be deconditioned and have little desire to pursue exercise. They describe themselves as less socially skillful, health conscious and energetic than the general population. This group is skewed toward married women with kids at home.

> Social competitors represent many of those who visit boutique fitness studios such as HIIT and CrossFit-style studios.

- *Woulda-shouldas (12 percent).* These are people who exercise, though not on a regular basis, and who tend to feel self-conscious about themselves. They describe themselves as out of shape, emotional, shy, and undisciplined. They are most likely to be women (73 percent) and married (60 percent), who have average earnings and slightly less college education than the general public.
- *Sit-com skeptics (12 percent).* Members of this group see exercise as nothing more than a craze that is pursued by self-absorbed individuals. They feel that a reasonable diet and clean living are the answer to good health. Generally speaking, they tend to be older married males (70 percent married and 56 percent male), with less education and less household income.

At first glance, a question might arise concerning what value exists in being aware of the aforementioned information. In essence, the answer is fairly straightforward. If club owners/managers were to create a profile questionnaire for their member prospects and existing members and then categorize these individuals into one of the six groups categorized by Roper, they would then have an enhanced capability of creating programs and services that would allow them to better tailor the club experience to each group's needs and interests.

Industry-Driven Research on What Americans Are Actually Doing When It Comes to Physical Activity

Up to this point, much of this chapter has addressed the beliefs and values that Americans have about exercise and sports. As was previously stated, understanding those values and beliefs will help club operators and/or fitness professionals better understand how they can exert greater influence on changing the exercise and sports behavior of the public and, as a consequence, grow their membership base. This section of the chapter presents an overview of the actual reported physical-activity behavior of Americans. The information is designed to provide further insight into the relationship between values, beliefs, and behavior when it comes to exercise.

In the 2002 American Sports Data (ASD) report on Trends in U.S. Physical Fitness Behavior, physical fitness activity was divided into three distinct categories: fitness, recreation, and outdoor activity. The fitness category included such activities as aerobics, aquatics, free weights, Pilates, yoga, etc. Recreation involved participating in such undertakings as basketball, football, ice-skating, tennis, racquet sports, volleyball, etc. Outdoor activity consisted of engaging in activities such as hiking, rock climbing, mountain biking, skiing, etc. According to Figure 2-5 (based on data compiled in the aforementioned 2002 American Sports Data Report), American involvement in physical-fitness activities on an active basis had increased from 42 million in 1987 to nearly 51 million in 2002 (it should be noted that "active" is defined as participating 100 times in at least one activity annually).

> American involvement in physical-fitness activities on an active basis increased from 42 million in 1987 to nearly 51 million in 2002.

	1987	1990	1993	1997	2000	2002
Millions	42.3	51.5	50	52.6	51.7	50.9
Percent of Total U.S. Population	19.7	23.2	21.8	21.8	20.8	19.8

Figure 2-5. Annual American involvement in physical fitness pursuits on an active basis

A review of Figures 2-5 and 2-6 indicates that the percentage of Americans who report being actively involved in physical fitness activity (fitness, sports, outdoor) has continued to drop since 1990, falling to a level of below 20 percent of the population in 2002. It is interesting to note that participation in fitness-only activities has increased from just over 27 billion participation days in 1987 to 30 billion participation days in 2002, although the number of individuals participating in sports activity and outdoor activity has remained relatively flat at 8.3 billion participation days and just under 1.4 billion participation days, respectively (refer to Figure 2-7). This data, along with other statistics provided by the ASD's research conducted earlier in the century, indicate the following macro trends in physical-fitness behavior:

- The number of core or active participants in physical-fitness activity has continued to grow over the past 15 years, but as a percentage of the population, it has remained flat.
- Women are more likely than men to be core or active participants.
- Individuals who are 55+ are the largest segment of active participants.
- Thirty-four percent of those individuals with college degrees are active, while just 13 percent of those individuals who do not have a college education are active.
- Men are far more likely than women to be involved in an outdoor activity.
- Over the past 10 years, participation in club-based activities, such as high-impact aerobics (40 percent), step aerobics (30 percent), mechanical stairclimbing (10 percent), and stationary cycling (30 percent), have all declined.
- During the past 10 years, the following activities have shown continuous growth in participation: spinning (10 percent), elliptical training (100 percent), free weight training (50 percent), yoga (100 percent), and Pilates (150 percent).

What the Centers for Disease Control and Prevention (CDC) Says About the Physical Activity Practices of Americans

The CDC conducts annual research to measure the physical activity practices of Americans and to assess how these physical activity practices impact the health of the nation. In their 2012 report, the CDC indicated that less than half of all Americans (48 percent) meet the 2008 Physical Activity Guidelines advocated by the CDC of engaging in at least 150 minutes a week of moderate-intensity aerobic activity/75 minutes of vigorous-intensity aerobic activity, as well as at least two days of muscle-strengthening activities.

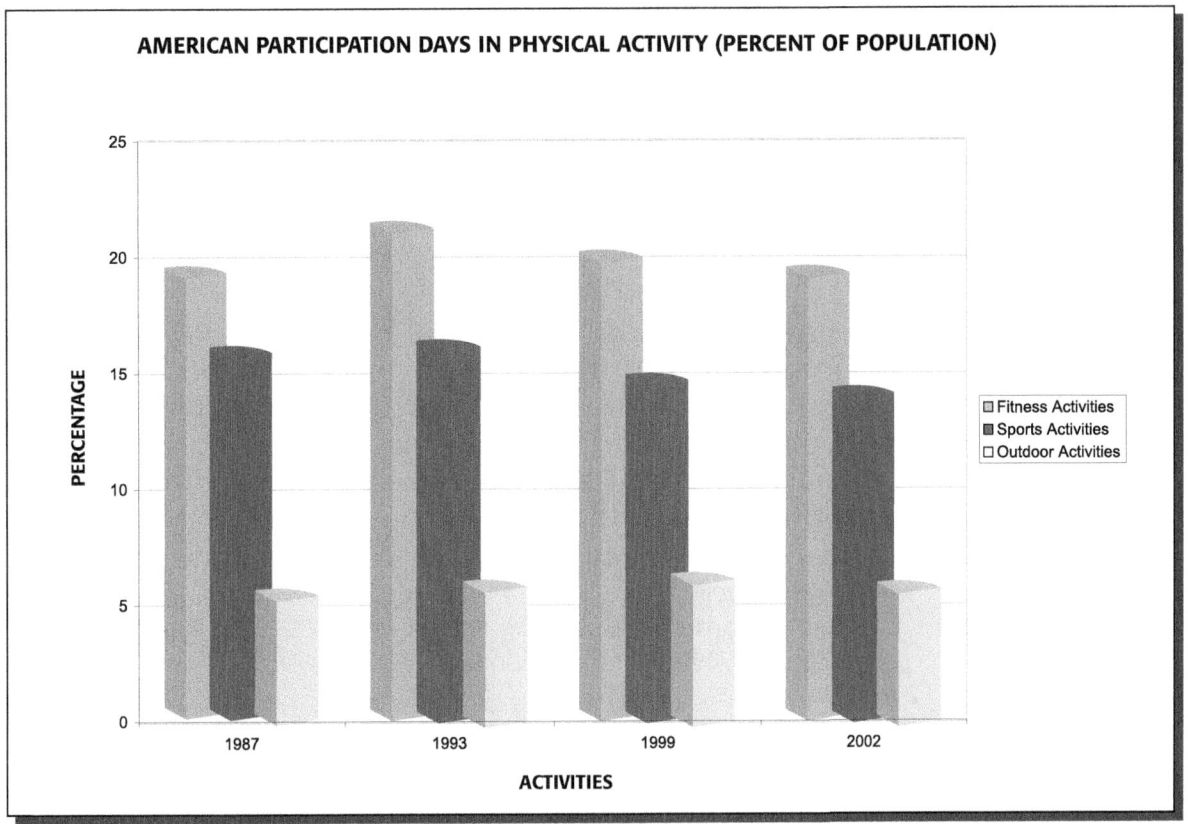

Figure 2-6. Percent of the American population that engages in selected physical activities

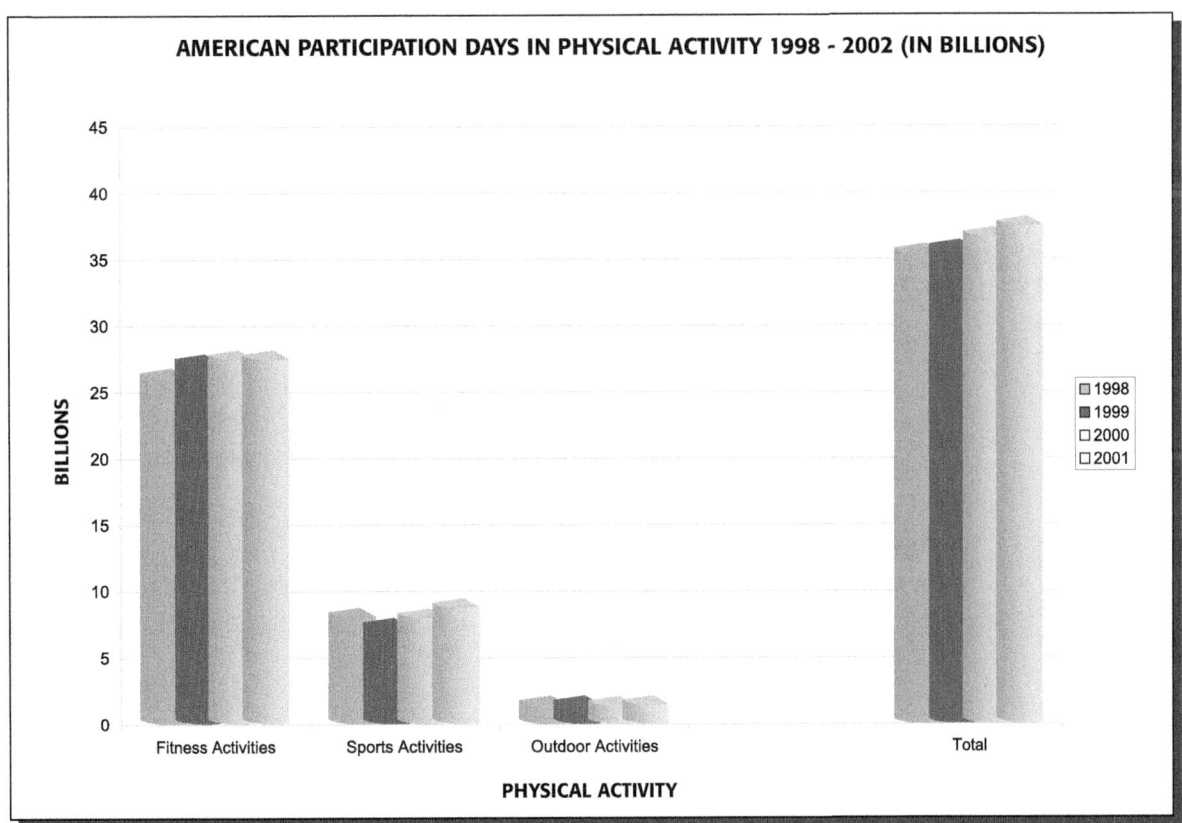

Figure 2-7. Total number of days in which Americans engage in physical activity

The report also shows that men (52 percent) are more likely than women (48 percent) to meet the recommended guidelines. The CDC study points to household income and educational attainment as being powerful determinants (the more income an individual earns and the higher that person's educational attainment, the more likely that individual will meet the physical activity guidelines) of whether Americans meet the government's physical activity guidelines.

Reflections

- Americans, in general, understand and acknowledge the fact that exercise and fitness are important to their health. Furthermore, they tend to view both factors as important values in their overall value hierarchy.
- While 80 percent of Americans claim that exercise is important, only 19 percent have adopted the appropriate behavior, in some fashion, that is consistent with this belief.
- Despite all the information about the benefits of physical activity, in particular its ability to improve an individual's health and reduce the risk of contracting numerous health-related diseases, less than half of all Americans achieve the recommended level of physical activity.
- While the fitness consciousness of Americans is higher than ever before (according to research and the media), actual fitness behavior is at one of its lowest points in 20 years. Obviously, a real disconnect exists between what the brain knows and the body does.
- Physical fitness behavior has become the domain of a more educated and more affluent segment of the American population. As such, exercise behavior appears to be tracking alongside other macro-demographic and economic trends in the U.S.
- Health and leading a balanced life seem to be overtaking appearance as a prime factor in whether an individual engages in physical activity on a regular basis, although among younger adults, appearance is still the primary motivator.
- One key to attracting people to exercise and fitness is to better understand the personality dynamics of individuals and have the club tailor its messaging and programming to address those dynamics. For example, if someone is an uninitiated social competitor, then the club's message and offering must be different for that person than it would be for an uninitiated, balanced holistic individual. Likewise, if the club's members are core users who could be classified as conscientious preventers, they should not be expected to be attracted to the same message and offering as the previously mentioned group.

It is important to be aware of the differences in what factors motivate women and men and how an individual's age, education, ethnicity, and related demographic profile can affect that person's behavior. This understanding can help club and studio operators to adapt their efforts to attract and retain members accordingly.

Part 2
Membership and Marketing in the Health/Fitness Facility Industry

Chapter 3
Why Consumers Join Health/Fitness Facilities

Chapter 4
Subscription Models in the Health/Fitness Facility Industry

Chapter 5
Marketing Essentials: Branding in the Health/Fitness Facility Industry

Chapter 6
Marketing Essentials: Understanding the Needs and Voice of Consumers

Chapter 7
Marketing Essentials: Communicating the Facility's Value Proposition and Generating Purchase Intent

Chapter 8
Digital Marketplaces and Platforms for Promoting Health/Fitness Businesses

Chapter 9
Selling the Value Proposition of Your Facility

Why Consumers Join Health/Fitness Facilities

3

"Physical fitness is not only one of the most important keys to a healthy body, it is the basis of dynamic and creative intellectual activity."

—John F. Kennedy

Chapter Objectives

This chapter explores the attitudes, beliefs, and reasons that consumers indicate influence their decision to join a health/fitness facility. As part of the discussion surrounding consumer attitudes about clubs, in particular joining a health/fitness facility, the commercial differences between a health/fitness club and a gym/fitness center are detailed.

Understanding the Differences Between a Health/Fitness Club and a Gym/Fitness Facility

To the general consumer, the perception of a fitness club, fitness center, and gym is essentially the same. Once individuals become a member though, they begin to see the difference between the various entities. As a result, the reasons that they had for joining begin to separate themselves from the reasons that they remain a member.

A fitness center, or a gym as it is commonly referred to by many consumers, is a facility that provides them with the tools to pursue their fitness and/or exercise objectives. The tools of the trade for fitness centers and gyms encompass several items, including the equipment with which people need to exercise (e.g., treadmills, elliptical trainers, resistance machines, free weights, etc.); the programs that provide the appropriate environment for personal exercise adherence (e.g., group exercise, personal training, small group training, etc.); and the staff who provide the requisite guidance and instruction (instructors, trainers, counselors, etc.) with regard to effectively and safely engaging in the chosen exercise routine. Among the global examples of fitness centers/gyms are 24 Hour Fitness, U.S.; Fitness First, U.K.; McFit, Germany; LA Fitness, U.S.; Planet Fitness, U.S.; and Fizkult, Russia.

> Among the global examples of fitness centers/gyms are 24 Hour Fitness, U.S.; Fitness First, U.K.; McFit, Germany; LA Fitness, U.S.; Planet Fitness, U.S.; and Fizkult, Russia.

A club is a different animal all together. The original definition of a club states that a club is an environment in which people of similar interests and social standing gather together to network, socialize, and pursue their personal goals. As such, a club implies that the participants have similar interests and backgrounds, have some desire to network and socialize, and have the opportunity to pursue their respective goals.

Accordingly, a health/fitness club offers an environment that provides the tools for individuals to pursue their fitness goals. It is also an entity that allows its members to interact, network, socialize, and engage with other members whose backgrounds are somewhat similar. Examples of global health/fitness clubs include David Lloyd Leisure, U.K.; Eastbank Club, U.S.; Houstonian, U.S.; Hillside City Club, Istanbul, Turkey; Oase Health & Sport, Germany; and the New York Athletic Club, U.S.

It should also be noted that a number of boutique fitness facilities that currently operate should also be classified as clubs, since their clients clearly represent individuals with a common passion and pursuit. In fact, much of what keeps the members of these boutique entities engaged is the social camaraderie that exists in these facilities. These facilities not only provide an environment for the pursuit of a person's fitness goals, they also accommodate the client's desire for a sense of community.

In the modern marketplace, the health/fitness club industry has done relatively little to help consumers differentiate between these two offerings (clubs versus gym/fitness centers). Clubs tend to have higher retention rates than gym/fitness centers, because the experience that members have depends not only on the outcome of their exercise achievements, but also on the development of interpersonal relationships. The reasons why people join a health/fitness club vs. a gym/fitness center tend to closely parallel each other, but the reasons members remain at each type of facility differ drastically.

> The reasons why people join a health/fitness club vs. a gym/fitness center tend to closely parallel each other, but the reasons members remain at each type of facility differ drastically.

What Do Consumers Really Think About Health/Fitness Facilities?

Before the reasons why people join a club can be discussed, it is necessary to understand the perceptions that the general public has about clubs. In that regard, in Fitness American Style, a study conducted in 2001 by Roper Starch on behalf of IHRSA, the public was asked to share their perceptions of clubs. Among the most interesting insights that were derived from the results of this research undertaking were the following:

- Americans, in general, hold a positive view of health/fitness clubs.
- Approximately 66 percent of those individuals polled believe that a club membership is usually worth the money, if a person makes good use of the membership. In other words, consumers perceive the value of a club membership is closely correlated to how the member uses the club.
- Six in 10 consumers indicated that a club offers the member more knowledge and expertise on exercise and fitness than they could otherwise obtain on their own. It would be interesting to know if this belief was as strong currently as it was ten years ago, since information on exercise and fitness is relatively rampant on the Internet.
- Approximately 56 percent of the individuals polled indicated that they thought health/fitness clubs were fun. On the other hand, when the differences between former members and non-club members are examined, the fun element is not as prevalent a perception among non-members.

- Nearly half (48 percent) of the individuals polled indicated that they thought health/fitness clubs were only for people who are fit—the basic perception being that if you are not fit and want to get fit, don't go to a fitness club.
- Forty-five percent of the individuals polled believe that clubs are for young people. At the present time, that perception might be somewhat different since a large segment of individuals over the age of 45 currently are members of clubs, at least in the U.S.
- Thirty-one percent believe that clubs are a place that a person goes to pick up someone (a perception originally espoused in the movie *Perfect*, in the late 1980s).
- The biggest negative perception was that clubs are overcrowded (an opinion held by 62 percent of non-members and 73 percent of members). The fact that such a significant majority of respondents perceive clubs as being crowded, especially former members, is problematic (given that overcrowding is a common reason that people give for dropping their membership).

In 2007, another report commissioned by IHRSA, *Fitness American Style III*, was released. In this report, consumers were asked to compare health/fitness clubs to other businesses in the community (Figure 3-1). Among the most interesting insights from this study were the following:

- The club industry is perceived favorably to other retail operators, including Starbucks, when it comes to the industry's commitment to providing its customers with good service.
- The club industry is seen more favorably than other businesses when it comes to being seen as engaged in their local community and being environmentally conscious.
- The products and services that clubs offer are perceived as having better value than those offered by other businesses, with the exception of the services offered by Federal Express and Johnson & Johnson (not displayed in the graph).
- Clubs are seen as being less innovative in their product and service offerings than other industries (not a real surprise).

While members of the public, in general, express positive perceptions about health/fitness clubs, both from a general perspective and when compared to other businesses, consumers also have some lingering negative perceptions about clubs. It is interesting to note that these negative perceptions closely align with the reasons that members give for resigning their membership. Another important insight is that while positive perceptions are important influencers of consumer behavior, negative perceptions, even if less prevalent than the positive perceptions, tend to have a stronger influence on behavior.

Why Consumers Join a Health/Fitness Facility

Consumers join health/fitness clubs for a variety of reasons. According to *Fitness American Style III*, prepared for IHRSA in 2007, the top three reasons that new members gave for joining their club were as follows:
- Get in shape (64 percent of respondents)
- Convenience of a place to work out (54 percent of respondents)
- Stay in shape (49 percent of respondents)

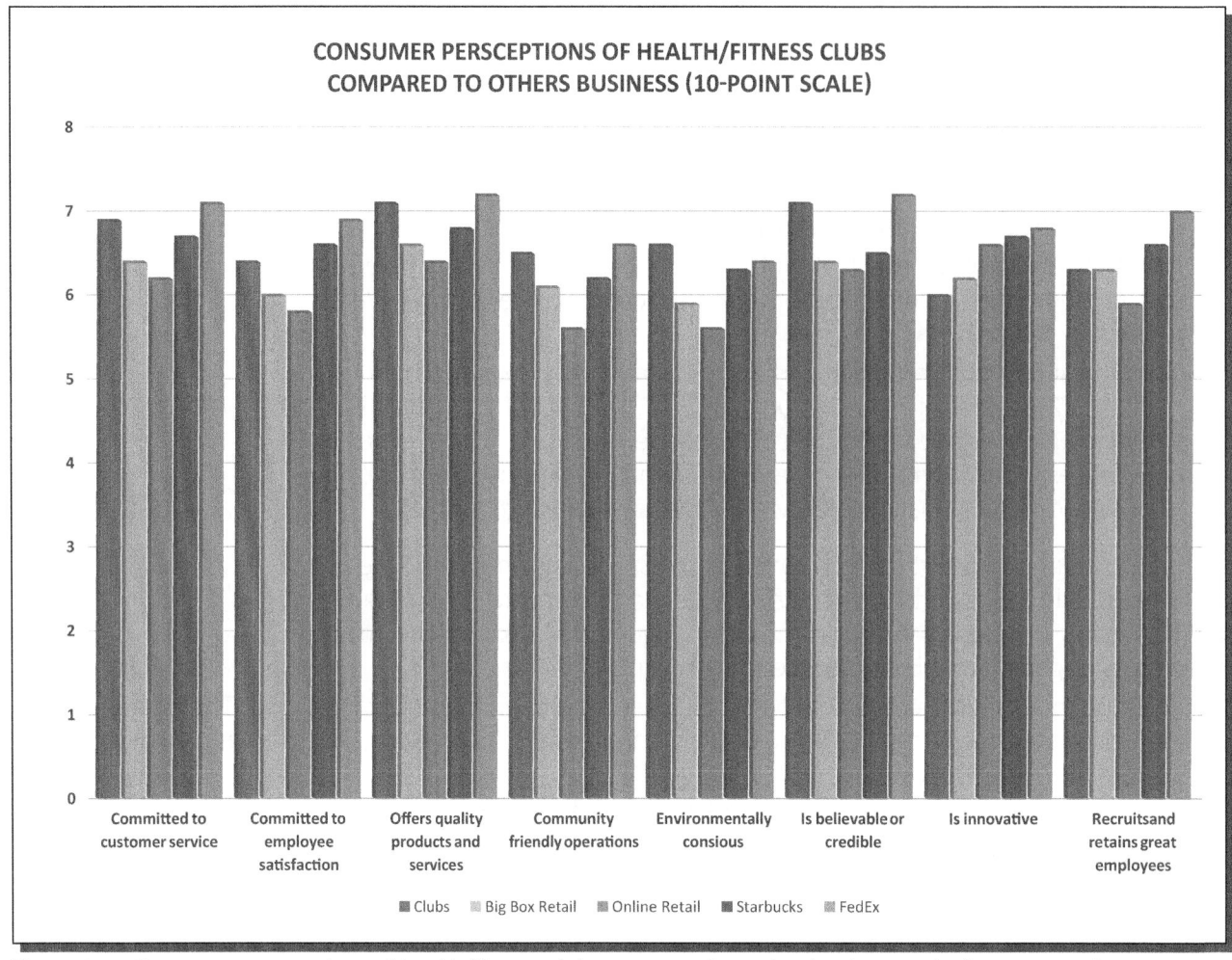

Figure 3-1. Consumer perceptions of health/fitness clubs compared to other businesses in the community

Subsequent studies conducted by IHRSA in 2008, 2011, and 2012, as well as in 2013, as reflected in *IHRSA's 2013 Trend Report*, show that while consumers still place the aforementioned three reasons among their top 10, understandably, other reasons arise that have a significant impact on their desire to join a health/fitness club.

Figure 3-2 graphically illustrates the trends from 2001, 2004, 2007, 2008, 2011, and 2012, as they relate to the reasons consumers give for joining a health/fitness club. Among the insights that can be derived from these trends are the following:

- Getting in shape, staying in shape, and staying healthy have consistently been at the top of the list for prospective members with regard to their reasons for becoming a health/fitness club member. In 2012, 58 percent of members surveyed indicated that these were the primary reasons they joined a health/fitness club.
- According to *Fitness American Style III*, needing a place to exercise was the third most frequently given reason for joining a club in 2007 (49 percent), a significantly lower response rate than in either 2004 or 2001, when nearly 60 percent of respondents indicated that this factor was their

primary rationale for joining a club. In IHRSA's most recent research on the issue, released in 2013, the club's location, particularly the convenience of the location, was the third leading reason behind a consumer's decision to join a health/fitness club, with 45 percent of those individuals surveyed indicating that this factor influenced their decision to join.

- According to *Fitness American Style III*, in 2001 and 2004, close to 60% of respondents indicated that they joined a club to provide them with the motivation to exercise. In 2007, however, only 20 percent of respondents indicated this factor was their primary reason for joining. The data in *IHRSA's 2013 Trend Report* did not directly address the issue of motivation. It did, however ask questions on topics that relate to motivation. One of those new questions showed that among the top four reasons for joining a club was a desire to make progress toward achieving personal goals.
- According to date from the 2013 IHRSA Trend Report, approximately one-third of consumers join a health/fitness club to have fun.
- Surprisingly, only 12 percent of consumers who participated in IHRSA's study indicated that having access to fitness professionals was an important reason for their decision to join a health/fitness club.

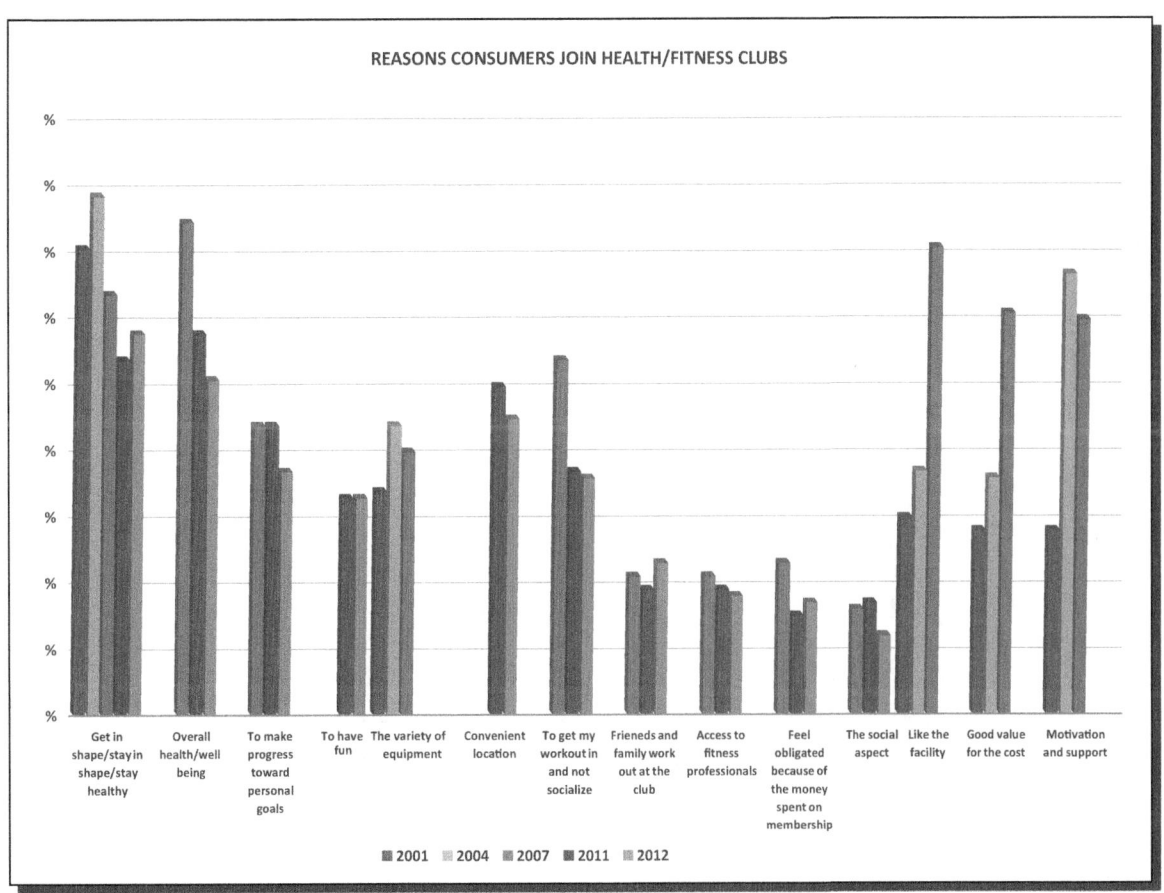

Figure 3-2. Trends in the reasons that consumers give for joining health/fitness clubs

It appears that as the 21st century has progressed, consumers moved from an "extrinsic goods" perspective (i.e., assigning their basic reason for joining a club in terms of either the look or the cost of a facility or the amount of equipment in the facility) to more of an intrinsic reasoning (i.e., placing greater emphasis on achieving their personal goals and enhancing their overall level of well-being).

In the 2013 IHRSA Trend Report, the researchers also looked at the differences between why men and women join a health/fitness club. The differences, which are considerable, are reflected in Figure 3-3. The most salient points derived from this comparison of the reasons why different genders join a health/fitness club were as follows:

- Men, more so then women, are more likely to indicate that having fun, socializing, and feeling obligated because of their recent expenditure to become a member of the facility as their primary reasons for joining a club.
- Women, more so than men, are more likely to indicate that convenience, getting in shape/staying in shape, enhancing overall health, access to group exercise and being a place to work out rather than to socialize as reasons for joining a club.

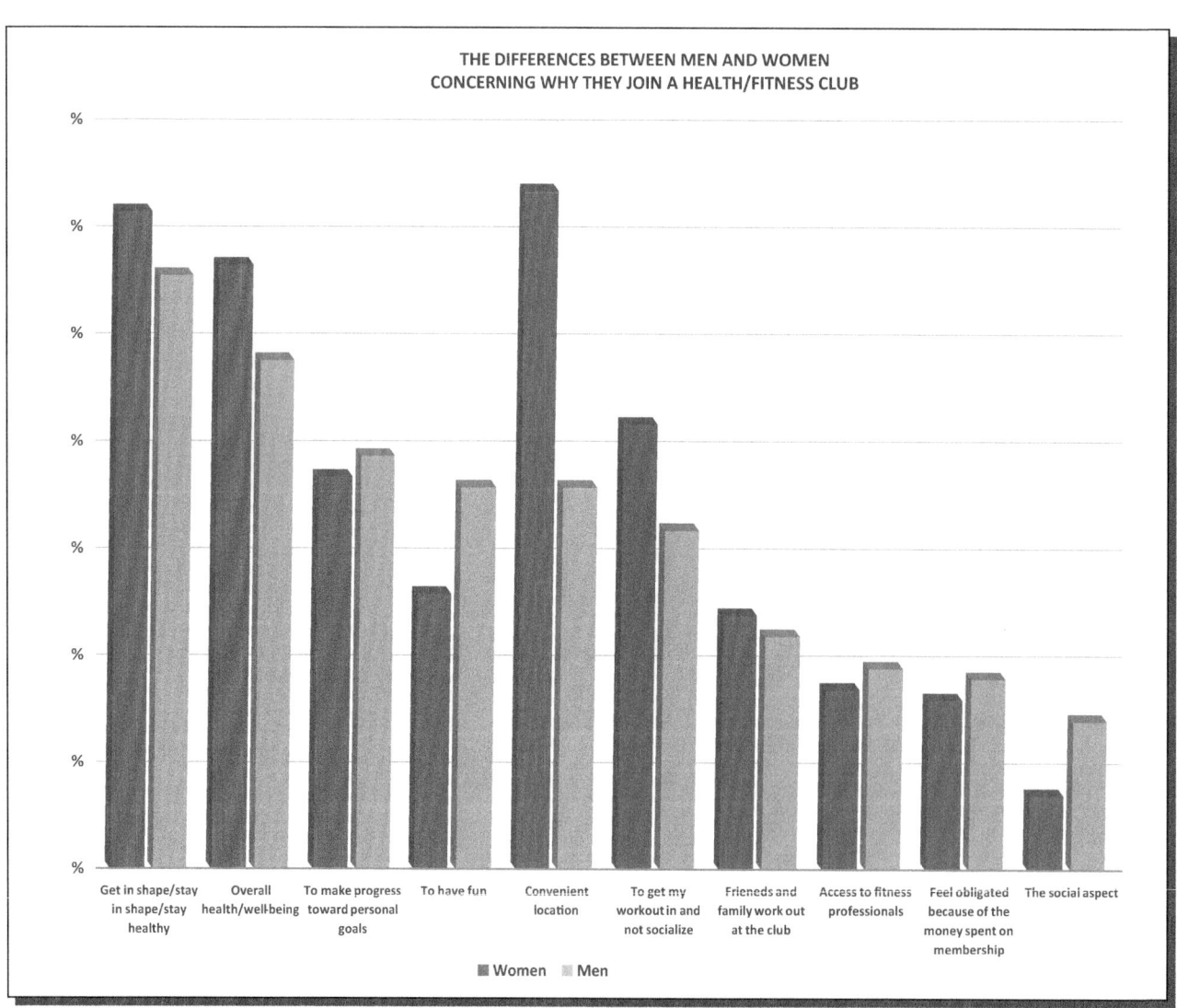

Figure 3-3. The differences between men and women concerning why they join a health/fitness club

In *IHRSA's 2013 Trend Report*, the researchers also explored the differences between generations with regard to their reasons for joining a health/fitness club. These differences, which are noteworthy, are reflected in Figure 3-4. The most compelling differences brought forth by this comparison between generations regarding their rationale for joining a health/fitness club were as follows:

- The Eisenhower generation, which represents adults born prior to 1946, is significantly more likely than other generations examined in the study to indicate that their reasons for joining a club are getting in shape/staying in shape, improving their overall level of health, having access to a variety of exercise equipment, and being in a convenient location.
- Baby boomers, those adults born between 1946 and 1964, place strong emphasis on achieving overall health, the convenient location of the club, getting in shape/staying in shape, and getting their workout in, rather than socializing, as their leading reasons for why they joined a club.
- Members of generation Y, otherwise known as the millennial generation (i.e., individuals born between 1981 and 2000), are more likely to mention having friends/family as members, having fun, and getting/staying in shape as their important reasons for joining a club.

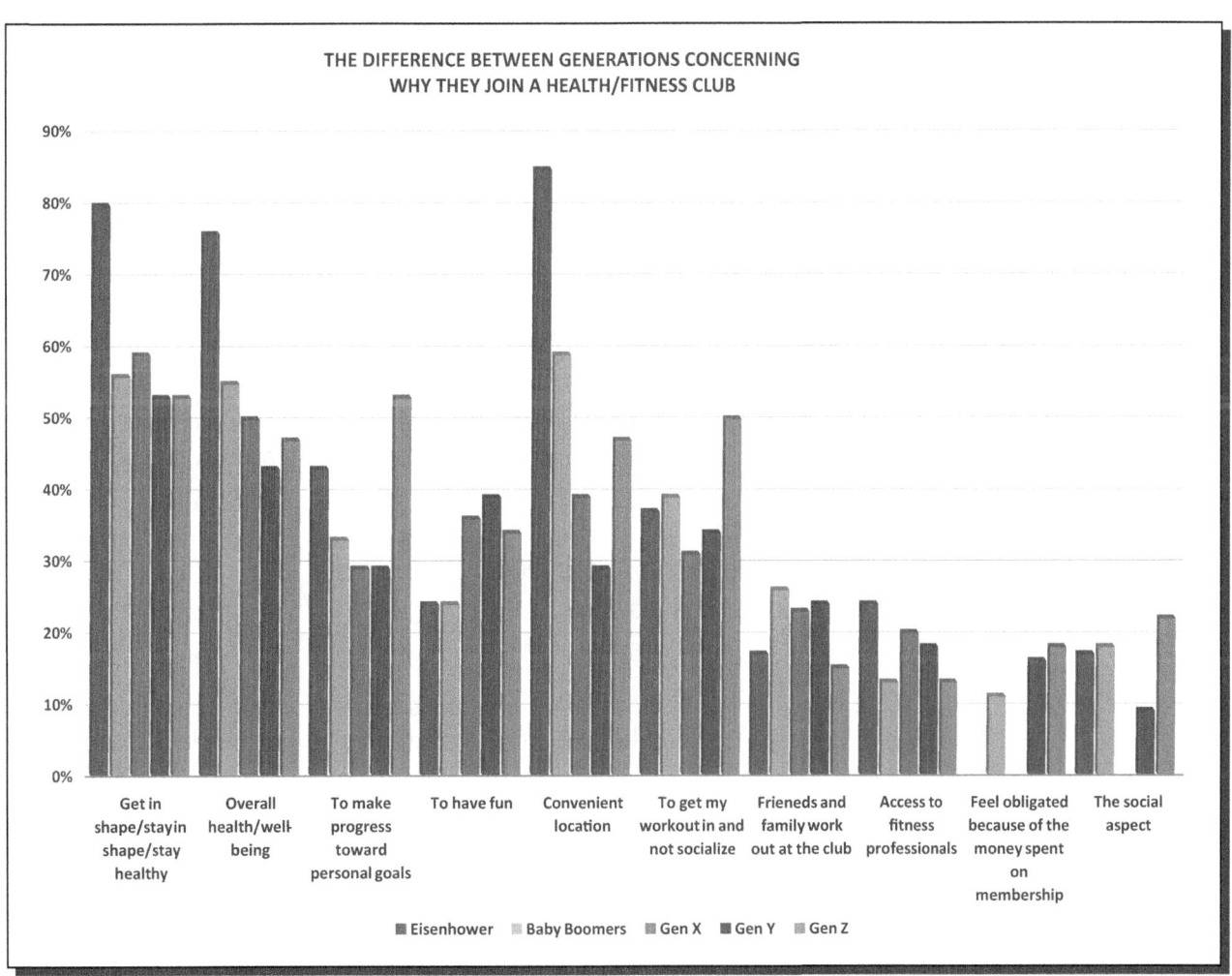

Figure 3-4. The differences between generations on why the join a health/fitness club

Another interesting question the researchers asked as part of *IHRSA's 2013 Trend Report* involved ascertaining what consumers perceived to be the barriers to joining a club. Being aware of perceived barriers for becoming a member of a facility is important to better understanding joining behavior. Arguably, perceived barriers can often overwhelm good intentions. As a result, they can impact the influence of rational reasons for joining and even remaining a member of a club. Figure 3-5 provides a graphic representation of these barriers. As such, the leading perceived barriers according to the research were as follows:

- "The club is too expensive" (e.g., "I cannot afford it") was the top barrier expressed by consumers, with 51 percent of consumers indicating this factor as an obstacle in 2012, down from 61 percent in 2008.
- "I exercise elsewhere" was the second most mentioned barrier to joining a club, with 28 percent of consumers indicating this factor as their primary obstacle, down from 34 percent a few years earlier.
- "No time" was the third most often mentioned barrier to joining a club, with 18 percent indicating this factor as their primary obstacle, up from 19 percent in the survey conducted the previous year.
- "I feel out of place" rounded out the list of the top five barriers, with regard to joining a club, with 15 percent of consumers expressing this rationale.
- Among the various generations, the barrier of cost (i.e., the club is too expensive) is strongest among baby boomers and lowest among generation Z.
- Members of generation Y are the most likely to indicate a lack of availability of someone to assist them as a barrier to joining a club.
- Women, more so than men, are likely to indicate that the cost of joining the facility, feeling out of place, and feeling out of shape as their primary barriers to joining a club.
- Men, more so than women, are more likely to indicate "no time," "I don't exercise," and "the location of the club" as their main barriers to joining a club.

Research presented in a report entitled, *Why People Don't Join*, prepared by IHRSA in 2006, listed the following top reasons as being given for not joining a club:

- A lack of time
- The membership costs too much.
- The club was intimidating.
- A lack of a social support network

It is interesting to note that the reasons for not joining a club in 2006 are not too dissimilar from the barriers that consumers expressed in 2012.

Reflections

As was indicated previously in this chapter, understanding why people join or don't join a club is important to creating a club environment that is conducive to attracting and retaining members. As a result, several essential insights can be gleaned from the information presented in this chapter, including the following:

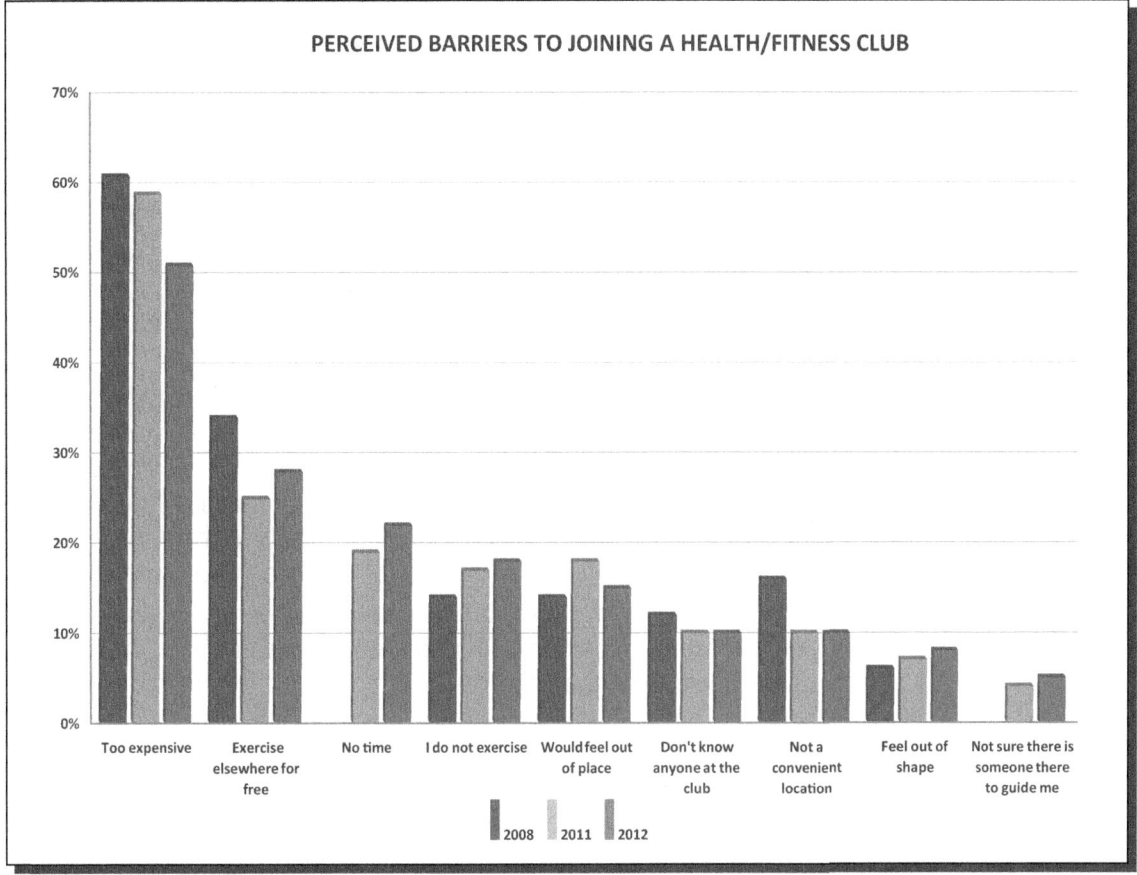

Figure 3-5. Perceived barriers to joining a club

- The general public has a relatively favorable impression of the health/fitness facility industry. The public's perception of the value of the industry's product offering, its focus on customer service, and its involvement in the community, as well as the basic environmental consciousness of the industry, is better than most big-box retailers and other service organizations.
- Consumers definitely perceive value in the investment of joining a facility, but that investment is highly correlated with usage. The perceived value of a health/fitness membership drops precipitously if the member does not take advantage of the product and service offerings of the club.
- Consumers also believe that health/fitness facilities offer a "fun" environment, a perception that is different than the opinions expressed about exercise itself.
- Consumers still retain some negative perceptions about health/fitness clubs. In particular, consumers view clubs as being overcrowded (a strong influencer of member retention), a place for young and fit people, and a pick-up place. What is most interesting to note is that some of these perceptions have been around for decades, and yet the industry has not been able to shake them off. The perception of overcrowding may be the most damaging, especially since club members and former club members have a stronger awareness of this factor than non-members. This perception may be one reason boutique fitness studios have grown in popularity, since they offer a more intimate physical environment.

- Regardless of an individual's gender, the primary reasons for joining a facility are related to getting in shape, staying in shape, improving health, and enhancing self-image. Granted, women look more closely at feeling better and looking better, while men are more inclined to focus on the availability of the facility and the possibility of gaining muscle. Each of these variables impacting the decision to join a club also plays a role in why individuals remain a member, a topic that will be addressed in the next chapter.
- Women place much greater emphasis on the quality of the club's staff, and whether friends or family are members of the facility. While not detailed as a leading reason, women believe that the cleanliness of a facility is also very important.
- Men who want to join a club tend to evaluate the facility more than the anticipated experience. In that regard, among the factors that men perceive as important are the availability of a variety of exercise equipment, the convenience of the club, and the existence of a competitive environment. Men also seem to be more inclined to look at a club for health reasons, a factor that is counter to what they express when asked about exercise.
- Members of generation Y seem to be far more concerned with the club's ability to assist them in looking better and feeling better about themselves, which is much different than the reasons expressed by the other primary generation—the baby boomers. For baby boomers, it's about losing weight and looking better.

Facility operators should consider the aforementioned insights, not just with regard to why individuals choose to join a health/fitness facility, but also as a window into the minds and emotions of members once they have joined. It should be kept in mind that if people join a club for a specific reason, that reason becomes the foundation for their expectations. As such, if they are unable to achieve those expectations (for any reason), they are more than likely to terminate their membership.

> If people join a club for a specific reason, that reason becomes the foundation for their expectations.

Subscription Models in the Health/Fitness Facility Industry

4

"Membership has its privileges."

—American Express Ad Campaign from the 1990s

Chapter Objectives

To a substantial degree, the financial success of the health/fitness facility industry is dependent upon its ability to offer an experience that attracts and retains clients. According to the report, *2015 IHRSA Profiles of Success*, approximately 69 percent of industry revenues are derived from membership (mean data reflected in the IHRSA report of all health/fitness club revenues coming from membership dues), making sustained membership growth the top priority of facility operators. Among health/fitness facilities that don't offer memberships, such as boutique fitness facilities, it is the number of clients who regularly purchase either fitness packages or unlimited access (subscription model) to their facilities that have a substantial impact on their profitability. This chapter reviews the types of subscription (e.g., membership) offerings currently offered by operators in the health/fitness facility industry, and then discusses pricing and structures. Finally, the chapter examines what these membership policies and procedures mean to the facility operator.

Defining the Differences Between a Member and a Customer

The health/fitness facility industry is unique in that to a great degree, its success depends equally on selling and retaining memberships and/or clients, whereas in most other hospitality industries, success depends more heavily upon generating a continuous stream of customers. With regard to the impact of membership on the level of success that a health/fitness facility achieves, it is important to note that some very important differences exist between customers and members. In order for a health/fitness facility to perform well financially, it must clearly understand these differences and create an experience that drives membership, not customer traffic. While the differences between a member and a customer are often subtle, they are nonetheless, very important.

A customer can be defined as an individual who pays a fee to purchase a product or to access a service, such as a health/fitness facility visit. A customer asks for no other privilege other than the right to use the service that they have paid for and understands that the fee is based upon the level of service provided

> The health/fitness facility industry is unique in that to a great degree, its success depends equally on selling and retaining memberships and/or clients, whereas in most other hospitality industries, success depends more heavily upon generating a continuous stream of customers.

or used. Customers are people who gain access based on a fee and have no commitment to the business that they are accessing. In essence, a customer is involved in a transactional experience, in which success is measured by the direct outcome of the actual transaction.

A member, on the other hand, is someone who pays for the privilege and right to use a health/fitness club, as well as the privilege to associate with other individuals of similar interests and backgrounds. Members establish an agreement with the business that they intend to honor. Members take a sense of ownership in the organization they join, connecting not to a service or facility, but to other people (members and staff) within the same organization. A member expects certain privileges, which, in most cases, extend far beyond just access to a service. Members pay not just for access, but for the unfettered privilege (schedule-wise) to access, with no restrictions placed on them when they access the service. Membership involves an emotional engagement between the club and the member. As a consequence, members have expectations about their membership experience that reach far beyond the mere transaction of gaining access to a facility.

Traditional Subscription Offerings in the Health/Fitness Facility Industry

During the modern era of the health/fitness facility industry, the subscription offerings of facilities have varied, ranging from a customer-driven model of daily access for a fee to a subscription model that is based on the payment of annual dues for the privilege of open-ended access year-round. At the present time, the industry has three relatively traditional approaches to how they bundle access (e.g., membership) offerings:

- *Annual contract with annual renewal.* The membership contract was first introduced back in the 1940s by Vic Tanny, and based on *IHRSA's 2013 Profiles of Success*, represents approximately 17 percent of the industry's membership accounts. Annual membership contracts are an agreement between the club operator and the member, which commits the member to a membership obligation of at least one year, and in many cases, two to three years. In essence, the member is agreeing to pay the club operator a set fee (usually discounted) for the privilege attendant to a long-term membership, whether they actually use the club or not.

    In the past, many clubs offered lifetime contracts, but in recent years, the length of a contract is determined by laws that exist in most states. At the present time, most states limit a club membership contract to three years, and in many states, that limitation is set at one year in duration. These annual membership contracts can also include certain discretionary provisions, for example, requiring the member to pay for their annual membership in advance or having an automatic renewal for another contract period.

    According to data from 2015, approximately 11 percent of these membership contracts are paid up-front, while another 41 percent of clubs allow members to make regular installment payments (e.g., bi-monthly or monthly), usually through electronic funds transfer (i.e., automatic withdraw from a bank account or credit card). Among those clubs that offer annual membership contracts, 27 percent automatically renew them for the contract period when the initial contract ends, while 47 percent offer members the opportunity to choose whether they want to renew.

A member perceives a value in the annual contract based on the opportunity to gain privileges for a reduced fee (a price-driven decision). The facility operator, on the other hand, sees value in the agreement arising out of the fact the club has received an agreed-upon amount of dues (resulting in a higher retention level of dues) and a predictable revenue stream, that might otherwise not be available if a member chooses to leave before the membership year is out.

Many consumers who are looking to join a health/fitness facility view membership contracts as legal agreements that require them to commit to a set length of membership and a specific financial outlay, even though they are not sure that they will either want or need to use the club for the time commitment set forth in the contract. As detailed in Chapter 3, many members indicate that this contractual obligation is a motivational factor for using the club. Membership contracts tend to be used most frequently by clubs that offer high-volume membership sales at lower price points, while also experiencing a high volume of member turnover (attrition).

- *Month-by-month (short-term) privileges.* This type of membership offering has been around the industry for years. Month-by-month memberships or subscription offerings, often referred to as short-term memberships, provide a member with club privileges for a period of time, typically one month. In turn, the member commits to paying one month's dues in advance. This type of membership package, based on data from 2015, is offered by 35 percent of all clubs, making it the most popular offering in the industry. Many members and prospective members believe that the month-by-month membership is their more attractive option, because it does not require them to make a commitment beyond a month's period of time. At the same time, owners tend to find this type of membership offering desirable, because it presents less of an up-front, price-based barrier to joining their club.

  On the other hand, this short-term membership offering also has some downsides for both the member and club owner. For the member, a month-by-month membership is easier to terminate and requires less of a commitment to using the club. For the club, a month-by-month membership tends to be associated with higher turnover than with a membership contract, and as a result, also offers slightly less financial security to the owner and operator of a club.

  Month-by-month memberships tend to be used frequently by facilities that are focused on providing a higher degree of member service and serving a more affluent population of members. These clubs tend to focus less on the volume of membership and more on the quality of the membership. It should be noted that many clubs that offer a month-by-month membership still require members to sign a one-year agreement that commits the individual to one year, but affords them the right to cancel their membership agreement with a month's notice.

- *Annual contract, with a month-to-month renewal option after the first year.* This type of membership (e.g., subscription) agreement is the most recently initiated contractual offering of the industry. Years ago, the industry discovered that by offering a blended membership package, they were able to provide an offering that appealed to prospective members more than the standard contract with an automatic renewal. A blended package also gives a club more financial protection than a month-by-month membership.

A driving force behind the development of this type of membership offering was research showing that if a member was engaged for a full year, they would be far more likely to stay active in the club going forward. As such, owners believe that a blended-membership package presents a viable strategy to reduce the first-year attrition of a month-by-month membership, yet offers the member the ability to stay or leave as they choose, commencing with their first-year anniversary. This type of membership package is offered by approximately 35 percent of the industry and is the second most popular membership option among club operators. This membership package is equally popular among the high-volume low-price health/fitness clubs as it is among higher-priced clubs that serve an affluent member base.

New Subscription Models for Health/Fitness Facilities

In the past few years, coinciding with the emergence of boutique fitness studios (e.g., personal training studios, cross training/HIIT studios, barre studios, and yoga studios), a new subscription model has emerged that is a hybrid of the aforementioned membership plans and the old pay-as-you-go approach. This hybrid model, which can be described as a hybrid subscription model, allows prospective clients to select a "package" that allows them a specified number of visits over a period of time for a set fee. This new approach has allowed boutique fitness studios to generate higher fees than if they used the "typical" membership dues model described in the previous section. Examples of these hybrid subscription models include the following:

- *Fixed number of sessions.* This type of subscription package typically defines the number of classes and/or visits a client or member can use over a given period of time. The most common of fixed session packages are five, 10, 20, and, in some instances, 50 sessions. In each case, these packages carry an expiration date after which the client cannot access the services that they originally purchased. For example, a facility that sells a package comprised of ten classes may require the client to use those 10 sessions over a period of 90 days.
- *Fixed number of sessions a week.* This type of subscription package allows a client the ability to purchase a specified number of visits or classes each week for a specific period of time that may range from a month to one year. This approach provides a client or member with more structure by putting them in a position in which they have to use the facility a set number of times each week. For example, they might purchase a 10-week package that offers two sessions a week. A more radical version of this model is one that offers guaranteed space for the number of weekly visits chosen. In this instance, not only are the number of visits each week set, but the client is also limited to a specific class during each of those visits. For individuals who have a very structured life these guaranteed classes are highly valued.

- *Unlimited access.* This type of subscription model gives the client the opportunity to take as many classes as they wish during the course of a month, as long as space is available. This type of subscription model is extremely appealing to those clients who are core users and who seek the flexibility to use the facility whenever they desire.

Traditional Membership Categories in the Health/Fitness Facility Industry

As was previously detailed in this chapter, most health/fitness facilities have developed three core membership offerings. To help personalize these offerings, the industry has gone one step further and created special membership categories that allow prospects and members the opportunity to further customize their membership experience. In this regard, the categories most frequently offered by clubs include the following:

- *Individual membership.* This type of membership bestows the privileges of membership on one designated individual for a specified dues rate. The most frequently selected type of membership, this particular membership category is most popular among clubs that are located in urban settings.
- *Couples membership.* This type of membership bestows membership privileges to two individuals for a specified membership dues rate. In some cases, clubs refer to couples as two people from the same family (e.g., a married couple, a parent and child, etc.), while in other markets, a couple might be defined as two individuals who live or work together. This basic category is most often employed in large metropolitan markets. Recently, however, it has gained considerable popularity in suburban markets.
- *Family membership.* This type of membership provides membership privileges to an entire family, usually defined as two adults and their offspring who are under the age of 21, for a specified membership dues rate. This particular category is popular in the suburban market. The greatest challenge with this category of membership ensues when a club has a large family using the membership, which can result in a club losing potential dues revenue that might otherwise be derived from selling separate memberships to several members of the same family. To address this challenge, many clubs have pursued two approaches. The first is to limit the number of children that can be included in the family membership. If a family exceeds that number, the facility charges an additional fee for each child added over the preset limit. The second approach, one that is currently the most frequently used, involves offering either an individual or couples membership, and then providing the flexibility of being able to add on to the core membership as few or as many individuals (children) as desired for a specific fee per add-on.

> Most health/fitness facilities have developed three core membership offerings: individual, couples, and family.

While the three previously mentioned categories dominate the industry, facilities employ some less frequently offered membership categories to target specific niche markets. The following categories provide a sampling of the growing trend in the industry to branch out to less typical membership offerings:

- *Singles membership.* This category does not involve an individual membership, which could be purchased by a single or married person, rather it is a membership offered only to someone who is single. This category is popular in urban markets that have a large population of young, single professionals.
- *Junior membership.* First offered in the country-club industry, junior memberships provide membership privileges to younger individuals who might not yet have the earning potential and expendable income to purchase a standard full-privilege membership. This type of membership usually has an upper age limit for eligibility, such as being over the age of 21 and under 30. The Cambridge Group of Clubs in Canada, for example, offers two membership categories that could be classified as junior-style memberships—intermediate executive (ages 31 to 34) and young executive (under age 30), each of which enables an individual to join the facility at a price reduction. The Houstonian, a luxury club located in Houston, Texas, also offers a junior associate membership category that allows a young adult, between the ages of 23 and 29 to transition from their family membership to an individual membership at a reduced monthly fee.
- *Seniors membership.* This category of membership is offered in markets that have a high concentration of seniors (usually defined in the industry as individuals who are over the age of 55). This category allows senior adults to have full club privileges at a reduced cost.
- *Corporate membership.* This category is very popular among clubs that are located in settings surrounded by a high concentration of businesses. A corporate membership usually allows groups of individuals from a specific company to join a club at a reduced rate. Many club operators define a corporate membership as a group of five or more individuals from one firm.
- *Off-peak membership.* In many markets, club operators offer customized off-peak or non-prime time memberships that restrict the hours that a member can access the club in return for a lower dues payment. For example, a club might create an off-peak membership that limits an individual's access to the facility to between the hours of 9 a.m. and 5 p.m. on weekdays, and after 11 a.m. on weekends at a dues price-point that is 10 percent to 20 percent less. The rationale for establishing this category of membership is three-fold. For one, they target consumers who might not otherwise be drawn to the club. Second, they provide an attractive price-point for consumers who have flexible time schedules. Finally, they generate memberships and the accompanying revenue during periods when the club has lower usage. Off-peak memberships are similar to what airlines and hotels define as dynamic pricing, a technique in which the price of a seat or bed is determined by supply and demand.
- *Executive membership.* Sometimes referred to as a VIP membership, this category of membership is relatively new to the industry and is based on packaging special benefits with the membership, such that a member will pay additional dues for the perceived extra benefits included in the category. Among the examples of special benefits often that are packaged into this type of membership are complimentary locker rental, access to a special locker room with custom features, discounts on club services, a specified number of complimentary services each month, etc.

Executive memberships are typically offered by high-end clubs that target a more affluent consumer base. The former Reebok club, currently owned and operated by Equinox and based in mid-town Manhattan, offers an executive membership category that has a premium of at least $100 a month over its standard membership, which provides access to a special locker room and other privileges. The Bay Clubs, based in California, and the Houstonian, based in Houston, Texas, also offer an executive category of membership.

- *Multiple-club membership.* With the expansion of club chains, many club operators have found value in offering a membership option that gives members access to more than one club in a chain. Most of the regional club chains (e.g., Fitness Formula in Chicago; Healthworks Fitness Centers for Women in Boston; New York Sports Clubs, in New York; Equinox in multiple demographic markets; and Bay Clubs in California; etc.) currently offer multiple-site memberships.

In fact, a number of national chains provide both regionally based and nationally based multiple-club memberships as well (e.g., Equinox, Planet Fitness, and 24 Hour Fitness). This type of membership offering has gained popularity with members because of the convenience factor, especially for those members who commute within a specific market or for those individuals who travel around the country or world. For the club operator, this category affords an outstanding monetization strategy, since it provides an avenue for up-selling and adding incremental dues dollars at minimal cost. ClubCorp, a publically held club company, based in Dallas, Texas, offers both regional and global membership packages that generate upwards of $40 million annually to the company's bottom line.

Bundling Subscription Offerings

Up to this point, this chapter has reviewed how facilities package their memberships or subscription offerings from the perspective of a particular category and type of contract. In most cases, the industry sees differentiation of access privileges (e.g., membership) as being based on the length of the contract, the type of alternative subscription model, the category of membership, and the associated pricing. In essence, the industry, as a whole, has created multiple membership and subscription offerings, using a commodity and goods approach, in which the difference in the offerings is based mostly on how the product is priced and wrapped.

In recent years, several of the leading health/fitness facility operators have created differentiation in their subscription offerings, not just on the basis of category and price, but also on what additional benefits they ultimately roll into the offering. This approach to differentiation follows a service or experience model, which allows clubs to create greater separation from their competitors, as well as to generate improved margins on their membership offerings. Examples of how clubs bundle their various membership offerings (categories and contracts) include the following:

- Package a specified number of complimentary personal training sessions with the subscription.

- Incorporate certain discounts to various club services, such as childcare, dining, massage, spa services, etc.
- Include special privileges to certain areas of the facility, such as the executive locker rooms, the Pilates room, the private training area, the boot camp area, etc.
- Include affiliated services with other service providers, such as restaurants, dry cleaning, car washes, etc.
- Incorporate charging privileges at the facility.

Over the past few years, several innovative facility operators have been exploring offering outcome-driven memberships (e.g., weight loss, anti-aging, sports achievement, healthy back, etc.), which, instead of providing specific privileges for a monthly fee, promise a specific outcome, bundled with specific services. This approach is less about providing access and more about tailoring the membership to the specific needs of the prospective customer base.

Pricing Strategies for Membership and Other Subscription Models

The health/fitness facility industry, in general, has developed a replicable model for the pricing of its membership packages and categories. This pricing model is based on a fee associated with entry or access to the membership privileges and then another fee associated with the actual usage of that privilege. In that regard, the two core types of club charges are initiation fees and dues:

❑ Initiation Fee

The initiation fee is the up-front fee a prospective member pays to a facility for the privilege of becoming a member and associating with the individuals who belong to that club. The initiation fee is often used as a differentiating factor for clubs, with those clubs that charge a higher upfront fee often being seen as more exclusive and less crowded. Research conducted both by IHRSA in the United States and by the Fitness Industry Association (FIA) in England shows that members who pay a higher initiation fee tend to remain members for a longer period of time, especially those individuals who are on a month-by-month membership. As a result of this research, the initiation fee is also seen as a pricing strategy related to gaining a greater level of commitment from members, which, in turn, enhances membership retention level of the facility.

> Initiation fees range from a low of $0 to as high as $24,000 in the commercial health/fitness club industry.

Initiation fees range from a low of $0 to as high as $24,000 in the commercial health/fitness club industry. According to IHRSA's *2015 Profiles of Success; the Annual Industry Data Survey of the Health and Fitness Industry*, the average initiation fee for all clubs in 2014 was $49, with a middle range of $1 to $115 (Figure 4-1). At the commencement of the 21st century, the average initiation fee, according to IHRSA data, was $150.

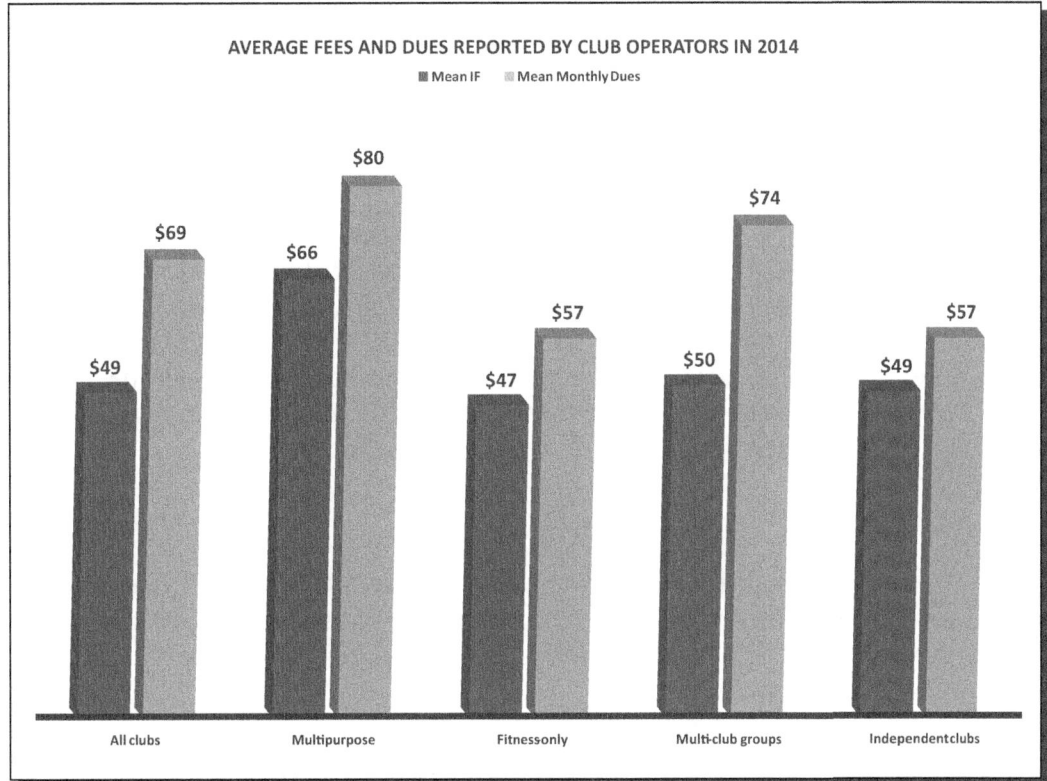

Figure 4-1. Dues and initiation fee ranges for the health/fitness club industry as reported by club operators

The initiation fee often is classified under other names, such as enrollment fee, administrative fee, processing fee, induction fee, etc. The tendency in the industry is for high-volume low-priced clubs to refer to their initiation fees as administrative or processing fees, which allows them to generate additional income, despite the fact that they proclaim that they have no initiation fees. Initiation fees are more common in clubs that sell month-by-month memberships. Clubs that sell membership contracts rarely charge initiation fees, instead offering low up-front processing fees.

In most cases, initiation fees are collected by the club at the time the new member enrolls for membership. Initiation fees are normally collected via a check, credit card or debit card. Since 2000, a new approach has arisen with regard to the pricing and collection of initiation fees. Taking the lead from the car industry, many clubs are now offering installment initiation fees, which allow a member to put down a percentage of the initiation fee upfront, and then over a period of time, pay off the balance of the initiation fee. In most cases, the initiation fee balance is included with the monthly billing of dues. In some cases, clubs are promoting initiation fees similar to car leases, in which they show the initiation fee as a monthly payment to be made over a designated time period. This strategy allows clubs to charge a higher initiation fee, but also enables the member to have more flexibility to complete the payment.

Another recent innovation practiced by a number of facilities involves moving away from straight enrollment fees and migrating toward charging two fees—a processing fee (described as the actual administrative costs of setting up a membership) and a one-time enrollment fee. This approach enables those facilities to reduce their initiation fee to zero to attract customers and to still collect an administrative fee.

One of the more innovative pricing practices in the industry involves charging a resignation fee rather than an initiation fee. In this scenario, the member does not have to pay an upfront fee to join, but rather they must pay a fee at the time they resign. The caveat with this approach is that the longer the individual remains a member of the facility, the lower the resignation fee, with the resignation fee being entirely eliminated after the member has been active for a given period of time, typically one or two years.

❏ Dues

Dues are the subscription fees charged to members for the ongoing privilege of being a member. Dues allow the member the freedom to access the various privileges of the club, per the terms of the membership they have purchased. Dues, as previously discussed in this chapter, are typically billed on either a monthly basis or an annual basis.

Since the advent of the great recession in 2008, many clubs have introduced a payment schedule that involves billing the member every two weeks, rather than once a month. This approach actually enables clubs to generate greater revenues than if they charged and billed on a monthly basis.

Clubs bill dues using various methods, including monthly statements from the club, billing through a designated charge card, pulling from a debit card, or an electronic funds transfer, also known as EFT. The most popular form of billing dues is through EFT, with the second most popular being credit card billing. A few clubs exist, however, that have members pay their dues monthly, using a coupon that they forward in with their check. EFT is the predominant method used in the industry, because it allows members to be automatically charged for their dues. Furthermore, EFT enables the club to receive its dues income, with limited liability for uncollected dues income (typically under 10 percent uncollected in any month).

Dues for health/fitness club memberships range from a low of around $10 a month (e.g., low-price high-volume clubs or budget gyms) for an individual to as high as $400 a month for some individual memberships. The average monthly dues for all clubs, according to the 2015 edition of the *IHRSA Profiles of Success*, were $69 a month, with the mean monthly rate based on the type of club, ranging from $48 to $107 a month (Figure 4-2). In fact, from 2000 to 2013, the average monthly dues collected by clubs has remained relatively flat, a situation that actually involves a decline in relative revenues, when accounting for the net present value of the dollar.

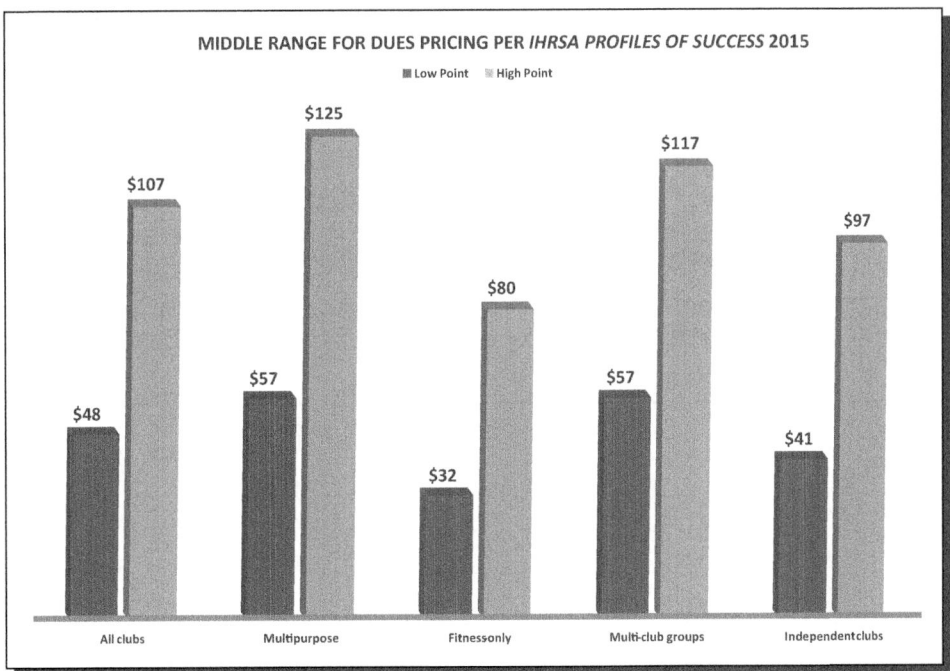

Figure 4-2. Middle range for dues pricing per *IHRSA Profiles of Success*

In the most recent edition of *IHRSA's Health Club Consumer Report*, which was published in 2015, consumers were asked what they pay for membership on a monthly basis. The average price consumers reported that they paid was $52 a month, nearly 25 percent less than reflected in the pricing that operators indicated that they charged (this difference in pricing is likely due to differences in sample size and survey methodology). Figure 4-3 provides an overview of the average fees paid by consumers from 2008 through 2014.

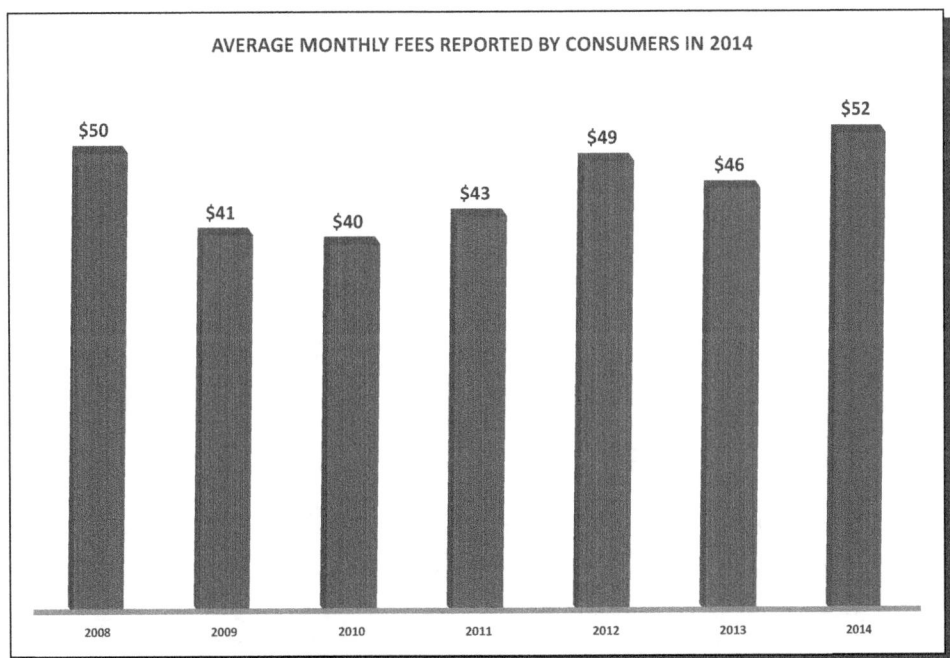

Figure 4-3. Average monthly fees reported by consumers in 2014

According to the same *Health Club Consumer Report*, 70 percent of consumers indicated that they pay under $50 a month for membership, while 41 percent of members paid less than $25 a month. On the other end of the spectrum, 11 percent of consumers indicated that they pay over $100 a month for dues, while 6 percent indicated that they pay over $150 a month (Figure 4-4). Another interesting pricing insight from the *2015 IHRSA Health Club Consumer Report* involves the differences in the average amount that individuals pay for their club membership, based on general facility type, with members of boutique clubs paying anywhere from 1.5x to 2.5x the amount that the average health/fitness club member pays for dues (Figure 4-5).

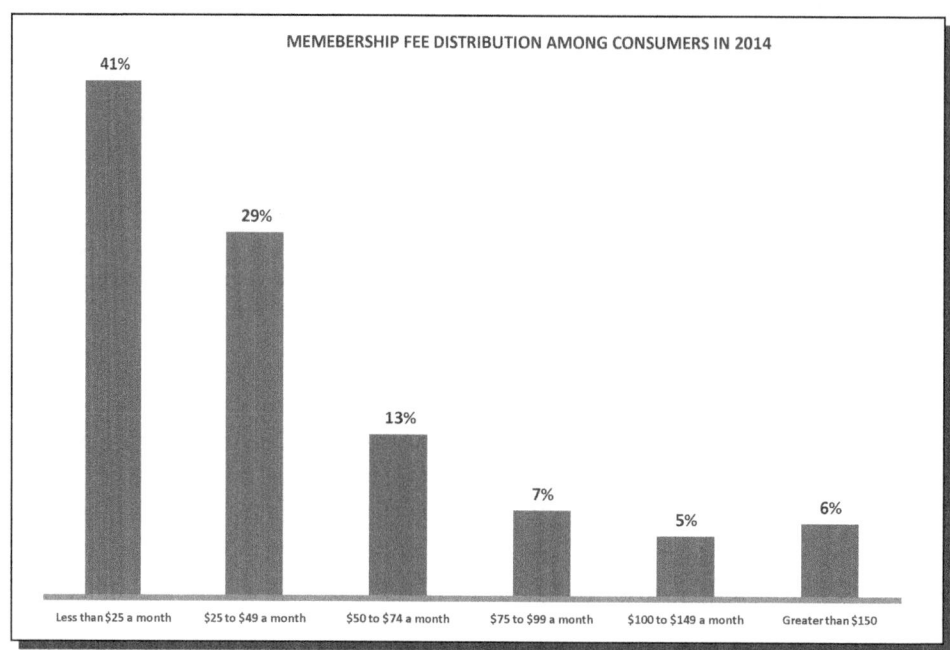

Figure 4-4. Membership fee distribution among consumers in 2014

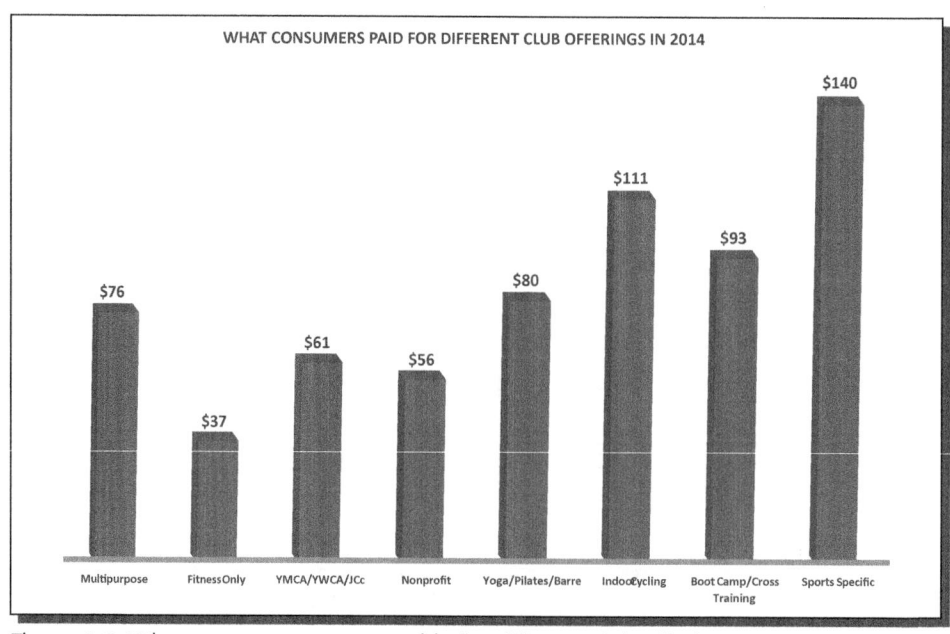

Figure 4-5. What consumers pay monthly for different club offerings

While the data in Figures 4-2 and 4-3 reflect industry averages, with regard to dues pricing, the industry has increasingly moved toward a dues-pricing strategy as a point of brand differentiation (e.g., a commodity- or goods-differentiation model). Furthermore, since 2008 this commodity-based pricing strategy has created considerable downward pressure on club prices across the industry. Among the various dues-pricing strategies that are employed in the industry are the following:

- *Under $20 a month.* Clubs that offer memberships that are priced at this level are referred to as "high volume-low priced" facilities in the U.S. and as budget clubs in Europe. This strategy has grown in popularity over the past five years and is exemplified by several U.S. club operators, such as Planet Fitness (monthly dues range from $9.95 to $19.95 a month), Blink in New York (monthly dues range from $15 to $20 a month), Crunch franchise clubs ($9.95 to $19.95 a month), and Cardinal Fitness (now Charter Fitness) in the Midwest, YouFit in the Southeast, as well as a number of European club companies, such as McFit in Germany (under 18 euros a month), Basic-Fit in the Netherlands (under 18 euros a month), and the Gym Group in the United Kingdom (under 20 pounds a month).

> **Members of boutique clubs pay anywhere from 1.5x to 2.5x the amount that the average health/fitness club member pays for dues.**

Clubs that take this approach to pricing tend to focus on delivering a "fitness box" that provides a workout facility that has abundant equipment, offers limited to no amenities (e.g., no towels, no locker room facilities or very limited changing facilities, etc.), provides no programming or limited programming (some budget operators have recently introduced virtual group-exercise programming), and has limited staff, other than salespeople. In recent years, in an effort to enhance the efficiency and profitability of these low-priced clubs their operators have moved to an online method of membership sales and sign-up, thereby eliminating the need for sales staff.

As part of their business model, these clubs target high-volume membership sales in order to generate the revenue that they need to be profitable. On average, most of these facilities need to have a membership base of over 7,000 members per club. In fact, many of them boast member counts of 15,000 or more.

- *$20 to $49 a month.* Based on a premise that is often referred to as affordable fitness, this pricing strategy seems to be the most popular approach to membership pricing in the market, especially among the major fitness-only domestic multiple-club operators that have a national presence, such as LA Fitness, 24 Hour Fitness, and Gold's Gym, as well as several regional players, such as X-Sport Fitness, based in Chicago and The Rush (recently purchased by Gold's Gym), based out of Tennessee. Several international clubs, such as Fitness First in the UK and Germany, also subscribe to this model.

Clubs that adopt this approach focus on providing a medium-to-large "fitness-only box"—one that is very well-equipped and offers the basic amenities. For example, 24 Hour Fitness and LA Fitness currently design their clubs at 40,000 to 45,000 square feet.

This type of club provides basic programming opportunities for members, especially in the area of group exercise. Due to their low pricing, these facilities focus more on their equipment offering and convenience, than on service. In most instances, these clubs have limited staffing and programming.

Similar to the facilities that subscribe to "budget pricing," these clubs also target high-volume membership sales in order to generate the revenue that they need to be profitable. As a rule, the average club in this membership-pricing category has between 4,000 and 10,000 members per facility.

- *$50 to $79 a month.* This pricing strategy has grown in popularity over the past 10 years. It is the strategy most often taken by independent clubs in smaller markets and local/regionally based multiple-club operators (e.g., Wisconsin Athletic Clubs, Wisconsin; and Atlantic Coast Athletic Clubs, Virginia, Maryland, and Pennsylvania). Clubs that leverage this pricing approach are focused on delivering a service-driven experience for their members. As such, they provide a balance of more-than-adequate facilities, plentiful equipment, amenities, program options, and reasonable levels of staffing.

  These are the clubs that have shifted their focus from mostly on sales to achieving a balance of membership sales and membership retention. These clubs, depending upon their size, will normally have membership levels ranging from 2,000 to 5,000 members, with the exception of the clubs in smaller geographic markets.

- *$79 to $99 a month.* This pricing strategy reflects what is frequently defined as the premium market segment, i.e., the high-service and quality-experience area of the club industry. This strategy is popular among many regional club operators (e.g., Sport and Health Clubs in the Washington, DC area; Fitness Formula Clubs in Chicago; and Active Sports Clubs in California), as well as in larger independent club operators in small- and medium-sized markets.

  Clubs that take this approach primarily focus on the goal of delivering high levels of member service. Facilities in this category normally commit to having a greater level of finish-out for their facilities (i.e., the level of interior finish, such as type of tile, lighting, etc.), as well as providing a relatively wide variety of equipment. These clubs offer considerable programming options, especially in the area of group exercise. These clubs are also focused on providing a reasonably high staff-to-members ratio. Depending upon their size, these facilities will normally have between 1,500 and 4,000 memberships.

- *$100 a month or more.* This pricing strategy is often referred to as the upper-premium and luxury segment of the industry, depending on whether the price point falls above or below $150 a month. This pricing differentiation strategy is employed by operators who are targeting the affluent segment of the market (i.e., households earning over $150,000 annually). Facilities in this strategic pricing category focus on delivering a high-end service experience that offers resort-type hospitality.

  This approach has been undertaken by several well-known independent club operators, including the Houstonian, Houston, and the East Bank Club, Chicago, as well as some regional and national club operators, such as the Bay Clubs located in California and Equinox, with clubs in eight major U.S. markets and two international markets. International operators such as David Lloyd Leisure in the U.K. and Companhia Athletica in Brazil also adhere to this model. These clubs provide luxurious physical environments that are supported by well-trained staff, as well as innovative and extensive programming. In addition to these upper-premium and luxury club models, many boutique fitness facilities have membership or alternative subscription offerings that are priced over $100 a month, and, in many instances, at over $200 a month.

Since 2008, the industry has been immersed in the mature stage of its life cycle and consequently, the average initiation fee charged by U.S. facilities has declined, as have the average dues. In fact, in terms of real dollars (current revenues adjusted for inflation compared to a decade earlier) club dues have actually declined.

Reflections

Without question, decisions concerning membership pricing, procedures, and policies are some of the most important issues with which club operators will ever have to deal. In that regard, this chapter has addressed the following key points:

- Membership is the heart of the health/fitness facility industry, contributing over 65 percent of a club's overall revenue, in most cases.
- Membership is about privileges and benefits, not just about access. Membership is about connecting with the club's people.
- Clubs have many options for packaging their membership offering. As such, they can institute membership categories that are grouped by such factors as age, size of group, family status, level of privileges, access to multiple sites, etc.
- Clubs can offer their membership packages on a month-by-month basis or through contracts of specified periods of time.
- When pricing memberships, clubs can consider both initiation fees and dues as a means to separate themselves from their competitors. Research shows that higher fees usually lead to greater membership retention. In reality, average membership pricing (fees and dues) has declined since 2008, a situation that is a reflection of the industry's mature life stage and its inability to differentiate itself, other than on pricing. All factors considered, over the long run, predatory pricing practices can cause immeasurable damage to the industry.
- Clubs should not fall prey to pricing as the main differentiation of their club membership offering from their competitors. Rather, they should consider the benefits and privileges, as well as the level of service they provide as a means to create a differentiated competitive advantage.

> **Decisions concerning membership pricing, procedures, and policies are some of the most important issues with which club operators will ever have to deal.**

5 Marketing Essentials: Branding in the Health/Fitness Facility Industry

"Branding is about everything."

—Tom Peters

Chapter Objectives

Over the past decade, branding has become a prominent focus of successful health/fitness club businesses. Unfortunately, for the majority of health/fitness club operators, branding extends no further than the logo, and possibly the colors, that represent their brand. This chapter explores the branding universe, beginning with a discussion of a brand's essence and the brand value equation. The chapter then discusses the characteristics of a great brand and finishes with an overview on how a health/fitness club can build a differentiated brand.

The Essence of a Brand

A club's or studio's brand is its reputation; it's the promise of value that a facility offers the market and the immediate thought that a consumer, prospect, client, and/or member has when the club's name is mentioned. People don't have relationships with products or facilities. Rather, they have trust in and are loyal to brands. Facilities and products are one-dimensional. In contrast, brands are multi-dimensional, with many layers, tenets, and beliefs that can generate a passionate following of people, each of whom may find a brand's promise compelling and relevant.

Brands have a purpose, often called a mission, that people can embrace. Brands are personally relevant and speak to each client, customer, guest, or member with a distinctly differentiated attitude and voice. Brands can inspire people to join a community. In the case of a health/fitness club, they can inspire people to make a change in their life. Brands can rally people for or against something. Brands can activate a passionate group of people to do something as powerful as reframing the world (think Google or Apple). Finally, brands are as much a reflection of what a facility's clients, customers, guests, and members experience as it is the message the club communicates through marketing.

> Over the past decade, branding has become a prominent focus of successful health/fitness club businesses.

The Brand Value Equation

The value of a club's brand is impacted by the relationship between three core elements (Figure 5-1). The first element, which is the numerator, is the facility's brand promise. The second and third elements are the denominators in the brand value equation. The first of these two numerators reflects the club's ability to fulfill the intangible and tangible expectations of its clients and/or members as expressed in its brand promise. The third element and second denominator is the by-product of the facility's ability to consistently deliver on the brand promise.

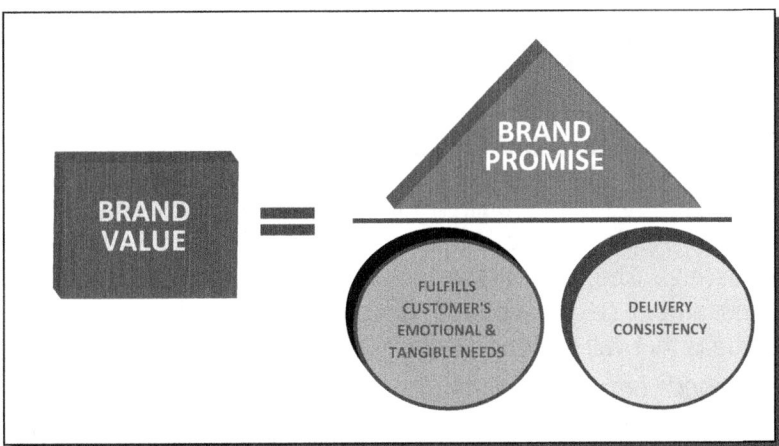

Figure 5-1. The three core elements of a club's value equation

❏ *Numerator*

- *Brand promise.* As expressed in the first section of this chapter, a facility's brand promise represents the promise of value the club offers the market. The promise communicates to members and prospects what they can expect to receive by engaging themselves with the facility's brand, or the value they will receive from engaging with the brand. The brand promise sets the table for the club's members and prospects by letting them know the value they will receive from the facility, both tangibly and intangibly. For example, at Haven on the Lake, a mind-body retreat located in Columbia, Maryland, its brand promise is "to provide an environment that embraces the body and spirit to promote personal vitality."

❏ *Denominator*

- *Fulfills clients'/customers' tangible and emotional expectations.* Brand value is highly dependent upon the facility's ability to fulfill the tangible and intangible, or emotional, expectations that members have established as a result of the promise the brand has made. The ability to fulfill these expectations is critical to the power of a club's brand. Using the aforementioned brand promise of Haven on the Lake, members expect to escape and reconnect, to align their mind with their body, and to enhance their personal vitality. If a member at Haven on the Lake achieves each of the core elements of the promise, then the power of the brand is enhanced. On the other hand, if a member enhances their physical health but is unable to connect with their spirit to improve their vitality, then the power of Haven on the Lake's brand is diminished. As such, it is better to underpromise and overdeliver, than it is to overpromise and not be able to deliver.

- *Delivers consistently.* Possibly the greatest challenge in creating and sustaining the power of a brand is the ability of the club to consistently, day in and day out, deliver on its brand promise. If a facility fulfills the value expectations of each member 95 percent of the time, or meets the expectations of 95 percent of its members, it is creating a "brand gap" that reflects the difference between what it is promising and what it is delivering. The consequence of inconsistency is a weakening of the club's brand.

Some Important Characteristics of Great Brands

Great brands are frequently built around a compelling and powerful promise (e.g., Amazon, Apple, Harley Davidson, and Lego), a uniquely differentiated experience (e.g., Ikea, Starbucks, and Walt Disney), and, in some cases, a cultural movement (e.g., Facebook, Google, and LinkedIn). Among the most common traits that will be found in great brands are the following:

- *Great brands are unique and relevant, respected, and trusted.* Great brands are more than a name, they emotionally engage people. In the health/fitness club industry, Exhale, founded in 2002 and which currently operates over 20 barre, yoga, and spa boutique studios throughout the U.S., is extremely unique,

Exhale has established an extremely unique and relevant brand promise that appeals to a highly passionate audience.

relevant, and respected by its clients and members. Exhale's brand speaks to the joining of mind and body through exercise, meditation, and holistic spa treatments. Since its inception over a decade ago, Exhale has established an extremely unique and relevant brand promise that appeals to a highly passionate audience.

- *Great brands define and fulfill the aspirations of the customer or, in the case of a club, the aspirations of its members.* One of the leading reasons people pursue the offerings of a health/fitness club is to fulfill their physical aspirations, as well as, in some instances, their emotional aspirations. According to IHRSA's 2013 Trend Report, one of those aspirations that the majority of members who join a club have is to get in shape/stay in shape and get healthy. The key for a facility is to understand what those aspirations are and then make sure its brand delivers on them. Two brands from the health/fitness club industry that clients and members indicate fulfill the aspirations are CrossFit and Exhale.

- *Great brands differentiate the experience, which is manifested through all touch points of a client's, customer's, and/or member's experience with the brand.* Differentiation requires a holistic effort that encompasses the totality of a member's experience with a facility's brand. It requires the integration of every touch point between the brand and its members. These touch points may include the club's web page, social media outlets, member interactions with staff, the facility and equipment, and even the interactions that occur between members. Ensuring your club's experience is manifested through each of these touch points requires a commitment to the details and the discipline to execute consistently. A great example from outside the health/fitness club industry of this differentiated experience manifested through every touch point of the customer experience is Disney.

- *Great brands create and own a unique "brand character," one defined by their attitude, their beliefs, their heritage, and their voice.* Great brands have a lot in common with individuals, as they develop, evolve, and own a distinct personality. For brands, this distinct personality is manifested through its attitude, beliefs, and voice. A brand's attitude is its inner persona. A brand can have a caring attitude, a trusting attitude, a defiant attitude, an arrogant attitude, an energetic attitude, and the list goes on.

What is important to a facility is that its brand embraces an attitude that clients, customers, and prospects can sense when they come into contact with the brand. A brand's beliefs are its values, what it holds dear, and the foundation behind the decisions the club makes. Members should be able to feel those values through the interactions it has with the brand.

Finally, every great brand has a distinct voice, which is the way it expresses itself to its clients and customers. A voice is how the brand communicates with its audience. A brand's voice is composed of the words, colors, images, sounds, and even aromas it uses when it communicates. Great brands speak with one voice, not multiple voices. A great example of two brands in the health/fitness club industry that consistently speak with a distinct voice are Equinox and Planet Fitness. Both of these brands have a unique character that consumers and members can sense when they interact with the brand, in-person or online.

> A great example of two brands in the health/fitness club industry that consistently speak with a distinct voice are Equinox and Planet Fitness.

Equinox is an example of a brand that has a unique character that consumers and members can sense when they interact with the brand.

- *Great brands consistently deliver on their promise. As detailed earlier in this chapter, the ability to deliver consistently, day in and day out, is a hallmark of all great brands.* Firms such as Apple, Disney, and Southwest Airlines are passionate about consistently delivering on their promise. To deliver on their respective promises consistently, each of these firms has developed standards, employee training programs, protocols, and monitoring systems that help ensure that their clients and customers experience the power of the company's promise.

Guidelines for Building a Differentiated Brand for a Business

❑ *Understand the value proposition of the business from the perspective of the prospects, consumers, and members of the club.*

- *What is it about the facility's brand that attracts them, engages them, and enamors them?* What is it about the club's brand that turns them off or serves to detract prospective clients and customers? Is its value proposition unique to the marketplace? If not, can the facility make it so? If the club is in the process of being developed, then certain points need to be addressed in establishing the facility's brand, including the following:

- *Who is the target audience (e.g., income demographics, interests, and lifestyle practices)?*
- *What attributes of the brand will garner the greatest appeal, buzz, and purchase intent (e.g., amenities, facilities, programs, or the community of members)?*
- *What personality attributes and voice speak to the heart of the targeted audience (e.g., do they prefer an edgy attitude and defiant voice or do they prefer an attitude that is comforting and a voice that is soothing)?*
- *What can the club offer the market that is unique and different than what the competitors offer?* For instance, at Planet Fitness, the fact is heavily promoted that the club makes "no judgments," an attribute they believe is unique to the marketplace. At O2 Max, a Los Angeles, California-based fitness studio, the studio's founder recognized an opportunity to provide a multidimensional fitness experience for young people (e.g., middle school age, high school age, college students, and young professionals) that bridges the online and offline worlds to provide a very personal experience that is flexible in meeting the changing needs, goals, and schedules of its clients and/or members.
- *What are the touch points of the club's brand that will clearly communicate its value proposition?* Touch points are the moments of interaction between a club brand and the member. Touch points include, but are not limited to, each interaction with the facility's staff (sales, reception, trainers, and instructors), the club's website, its Facebook page, direct mail pieces, community interactions, and so forth. For example, at Equinox, one of their most effective tools for engaging members and disseminating valuable health and fitness information is through their blog entitled Furthermore, which can be accessed on their website. Core Power Yoga, a national chain of yoga studios, also creates engaging touch points with its followers through its blog entitled At the Core. At Red's, a privately owned multipurpose club located in Lafayette, Louisiana, staff focus on each physical interaction with the member, while the individual is in the club. At Red's, interactions are fostered that help ensure members "feel" the brand's promise. To that point, the owner, Red Lerille, does not have a desk. Instead, he chooses to circulate throughout the club, making sure that he and his staff interact with each member of his facility.
- *What are the offerings that currently exist in the marketplace, and what offerings appear to be in demand and are not currently served?* In reality, nearly every market has a "big box" club. As such, the issue arises concerning what can a non-big box club offer that a big box facility doesn't? At EZIA Performance Labs, a fitness studio based in California, it was determined that taking a holistic approach to personal performance coaching that incorporated skilled professionals from the fitness, coaching, and healthcare fields and that was supported by a proprietary software platform would provide them with a unique and differentiated value proposition.

The best way for a facility to discover what its value proposition is, and how it's perceived in the marketplace, is to conduct some basic market research. Club operators might want to consider some or all of the following actions to clarify their facility's value proposition and its relevance in the marketplace:

The best way for a facility to discover what its value proposition is, and how it's perceived in the marketplace, is to conduct some basic market research.

- *Benchmark the facility and competitors through clue scanning.* Clue scanning is a market research approach that involves putting the club, in this instance, in the shoes of the member. The objective of clue scanning is to pick-up on the obvious cues that each brand communicates to its members (e.g., marketing messages, pricing, membership categories, programs, and staff interaction with the members), as well as the subtle cues that are often ignored by operators, but of which members and consumers are acutely aware (e.g., atmosphere, lighting, aroma, colors, sounds, and member-to-member and member-to-staff interactions) because they are engaging with the club on a daily basis.

  Clue scanning goes beyond physically visiting each club and engaging with it as if the visitor is actually a member. It also necessitates interacting with whatever touch- points that a member is likely to experience, such as a club's website and social media outlets. The end result of effective clue scanning is gaining a deeper appreciation for how members experience the club, and how consumers and members experience the competitors of the facility.

- *Conduct focus groups with member and non-member groups.* Focus groups are a qualitative research technique that allows the club to explore the experiences, perceptions, and feelings of its audience. By conducting focus groups with members, facility operators can obtain insights into the emotional aspects of the member experience, and what experiences drive value from the member's perspective. Conducting focus groups with resigned members, prospects, and/or individuals from the community can offer insights in how the market perceives the club's brand and what its competitive advantages or disadvantages might be.

  When conducting focus groups with its members, clubs should organize sessions with at least two to three groups. Furthermore, if it is facilitating sessions with non-member groups, then it will also want to have at least two to three groups in order to collect sufficient qualitative data to uncover what each audience perceives about the facility's brand and the experience it offers. Each group should have between 8 and 12 participants.

  If a group doesn't have a club and, instead, is developing a facility, then it should consider conducting focus groups within the community to better understand what the market needs or is seeking. The same principles apply to conducting focus group sessions within the community, as it does with a club's clients and/or members.

- *Perform a demographic and psychographic study of the target market.* Your target market will typically live or work within a 12- to 15-minute radius of the location that is selected for the club (approximately a three-mile radius). For fitness studios, that radius will be even smaller. Understanding the demographics (e.g., age ranges, gender ratio, household income levels, education levels, family status) and psychographics (e.g., spending patterns, hobbies, interests, type of car the prospective members drive, discretionary spending patterns) of the community can assist in shaping a value proposition that will appeal to specific audiences that might otherwise be underserved in the community.

- *Conduct an attitude, awareness, and usage study (AA&U).* An AA&U study, sometimes called a brand health study, is a market research approach used extensively in other industries to ascertain a brand's image, personality traits, level of awareness, overall appeal, and its uniqueness within the marketplace in comparison to its competitors. AA&U studies bring forth insights that can help shape what a club's value proposition needs to be, define how a club can more effectively deliver on its existing brand promise, determine whether the brand's message is coming through or not, and, finally, ascertain whether a club's value proposition has staked out a unique competitive advantage in the marketplace. Figure 5-2 is an example of an AA&U matrix that brings forth the personality traits of several brands and clarifies which traits each of those bands owns in the marketplace.

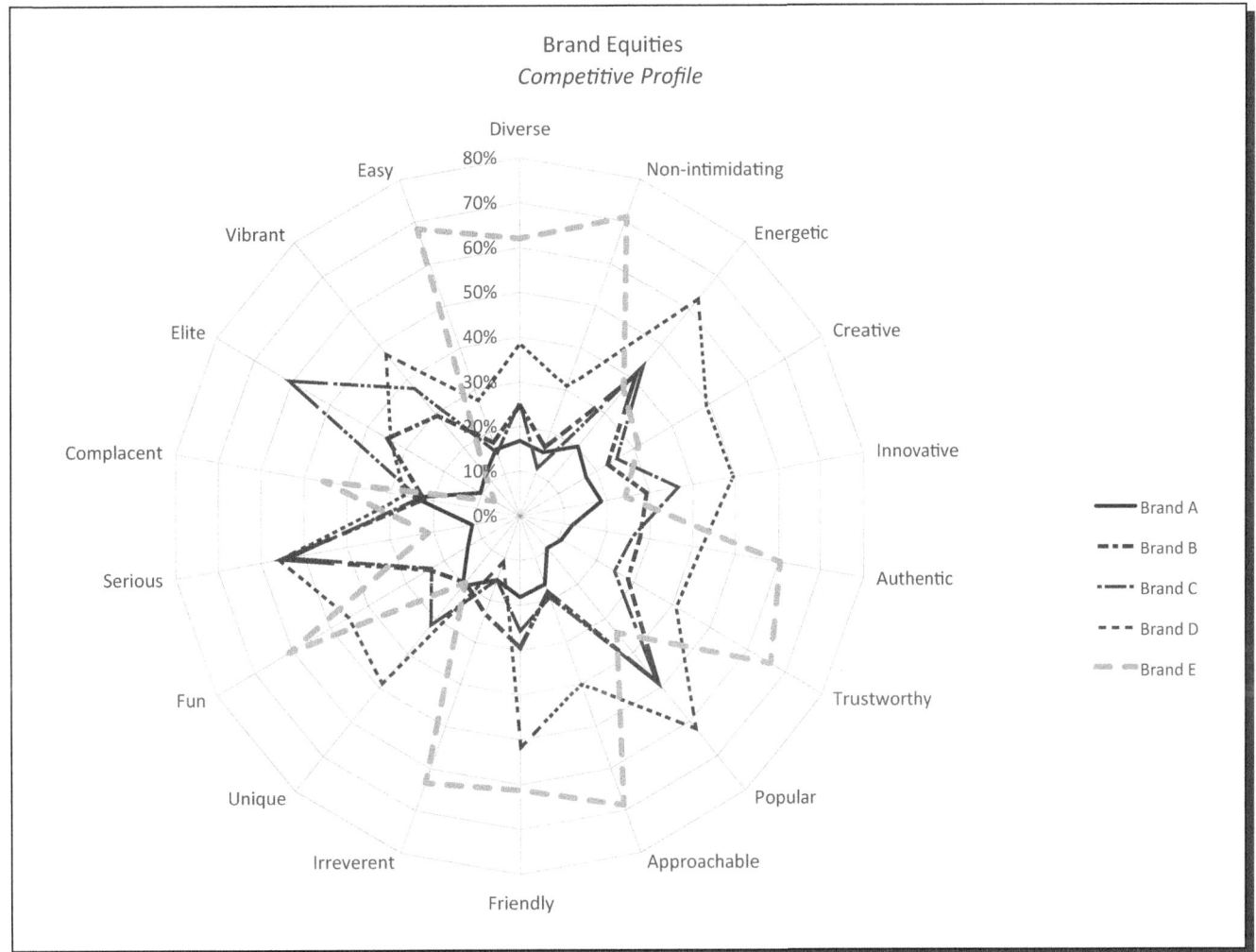

Figure 5-2. Brand equities competitive profile

❏ *Establish a brand promise based on the club's value proposition.*

Make sure that the club's brand promise is authentic, member- and/or customer-centric, compelling, well-differentiated, narrowly focused, and emotionally engaging. A brand promise must be customer-centric, not product-centric. It must also be emotionally engaging, so that the customer or member establishes an emotional memory of the experience. For example, in the health/fitness club industry, the Eastbank Club in Chicago and the Houstonian

A brand promise must be customer-centric, not product-centric. It must also be emotionally engaging, so that the customer or member establishes an emotional memory of the experience.

in Houston have established themselves as "being" brands. Both of the aforementioned clubs are recognized by their respective communities and members as prestigious and exclusive health and fitness clubs.

A great example of a well-thought out, compelling, and emotionally engaging brand promise (one that evolved from conducting the types of market research set forth in the previous section) is Lego's, which states, "The joy of building, the pride of creation." This brand promise is what drives Lego. Anyone who has ever played with Legos, or observed a child interacting with Legos, understands and feels the power of its promise.

❑ *Build a brand platform.*

Once a brand promise has been established by a club, then it needs to create the platform for launching it. A brand platform is typically composed of two core elements—the brand style guide and the brand-operating standards.

- *Brand style guide.* The brand style guide sets forth the standards for how the club's brand will communicate its value proposition and identity. The brand style guide includes the brand promise, the brand's name, and the brand's tagline if the facility chooses one, the brand attitude, the brand voice, the logo or mark, the color palette, the typography, and other key graphic requirements for how the club will communicate to the world at large who and what it is. A brand style guide can also set forth expectations for the aroma and sounds that will be associated with a facility's brand. Some companies even establish a brand dictionary or thesaurus that establishes the actual language of the brand. Most organizations pursue professional assistance in the creation of their style guide.

- *Brand operating standards.* The operating standards are the "absolutes" that pertain to how the club will deliver on its brand promise. These standards should address the operating expectations (e.g., client-service expectations, cleaning expectations, coaching expectations, and equipment expectations) that the facility expects to meet each and every day. All factors considered, the simpler they are the better. On the other hand, the club should make sure that these standards are detailed enough to ensure that no matter who is working, the expectations are clear.

❑ *Consistently deliver on the brand promise.*

The club should make sure everyone on the team understands the promise, and, just as importantly, is well-trained in being able to deliver on the brand's promise, operating standards, and style guide. The facility should assess what its members expect and how well the club is meeting those expectations.

In reality, the devil is in the details. Too often, clubs think that if they communicate their brand promise, that's all they have to do. To successfully establish and sustain a brand, clubs must ensure that everything they do is in proper alignment with their promise (e.g., purpose, values, voice, colors, and brand standards). In other words, the color palette used in the club, the sounds and smells throughout the club, the manner in which phones are answered, the appearance and tone of the facility's website and social media pages, the behaviors of the employees and/or contractors, the type of programming offered, etc. must all consistently support the brand promise of a club.

> To successfully establish and sustain a brand, clubs must ensure that everything they do is in proper alignment with their promise.

❑ *Share the facility's story.*

The club should establish an attitude and voice for its brand, one that can be consistently communicated internally and externally. As such, it should identify and acknowledge storytellers, those individuals who are passionate about telling the facility's story. Great brands make sure to tell their story. Telling the story involves spreading the organization's brand message through authentic and credible means.

A club's best approach to sharing stories is having members share their experiences about the club with other individuals. People see friends and associates as the most trusted source of information about a brand.

Another credible and invaluable storytelling mechanism, though less so than friends and associates, is through the leaders of the facility. At ClubCorp, founder and chairman Robert Dedman, Sr., was the consummate storyteller. He believed that stories were the most effective means for spreading the gospel of the ClubCorp brand.

David Patchell-Evans, the founder and CEO of Goodlife Fitness, a Canadian firm that owns and operates approximately 300 clubs in Canada, is also an outstanding storyteller. Patch, as he is known in the health/fitness club industry, has his own website, where he spreads the gospel about his brand and its philosophy. In addition, he makes regular appearances before public audiences, sharing his passion for the Goodlife Fitness brand. In the book, Karaoke Capitalism, the authors are quoted as saying, "Stories translate information into emotion," and great brands are all about emotional engagement.

❑ *Be authentic.*

Authenticity means being real, being trusted, and delivering an experience that the community and, more importantly, the members believe is credible. A great brand will be authentic when members put their trust in the brand promise and, consequently, the experience they receive. Authentic brands are not copycats; they don't copy what others do. For example, consumers look at Apple as authentic, because its products are unique, innovative, and, most importantly, inspire trust from its customers. Examples of some authentic brands in the health/fitness club industry include Eastbank Club, Chicago, Illinois; Red's, Lafayette, Louisiana; Houstonian, Houston, Texas; Gainesville Health and Fitness Center, Gainesville, Florida; Exhale, U.S.; and CrossFit.

Reflections

Branding is a critical business function, one that is essential to the process of establishing and sustaining a successful and profitable business. Branding does not occur overnight, or even in one year. Rather, it is an ongoing process that requires commitment, diligence, and perseverance. The following checklist is intended first as a topline summary of this chapter's discussion of branding and second as a simple guide for clubs to take the right steps to create and deliver its brand:

- *Identify the club's brand value proposition.* Make sure it's crystal clear, especially those tangible and intangible factors that help reinforce the value proposition.
- *Craft a brand promise around the drivers of the facility's value proposition.* Using the drivers of the value proposition, create a brand promise that is authentic, unique, differentiated, and compelling.
- *Build a platform for delivering the club's brand promise.* Establish the brand's purpose, values, attitude, and voice. Create a brand style guide and brand operational standards.
- *Be consistent in fulfilling the facility's brand promise.* Make sure that everyone involved with the operation and delivery of the brand embraces its promise, is committed to its tenants, is disciplined in executing on the brand platform, and, finally, makes no compromises in the messaging and delivery of the brand's value proposition.
- *Become an effective storyteller.* Be an advocate of the club's brand, become its spokesperson in the community, as well as among the facility's clients and/or members. Finally, find other individuals who are passionate about the club's brand value proposition and leverage their voice to get the story out.

> Branding is an ongoing process that requires commitment, diligence, and perseverance.

Marketing Essentials: Understanding the Needs and Voice of Consumers

6

"The aim of marketing is to know and understand the customer so well the product or service fits him and sells itself."

—Peter Drucker

Chapter Objectives

As Peter Drucker's quote states, the primary aim of marketing is to know and understand the customer, or, in the case of the health/fitness facility industry, to know and understand its prospective members and members. Knowing and understanding the customer requires a commitment to listening and learning from the voice of the customer. As such, the first goal of this chapter is to provide a rationale for why it is so important for health/fitness facility operators to listen to the voice of the customer or member. The second goal is to highlight some of the tools, both traditional and digital, that an operator can employ to listen to the members of a club, and, consequently, to develop a deeper understanding and appreciation for what its members and clients are saying.

The Value of Listening to the Voice of the Customer

Most health/fitness facility operators fail to understand the value of listening to the voice of the customer. Listening to the voice of the customer provides clubs with an understanding of their clients' attitudes, beliefs, and behaviors. As a consequence, facility operators gain insights that can help shape how they interact with, communicate with, appeal to, and serve their clients and members.

Listening involves a host of market research approaches (e.g., tools), each aimed at learning about the interests, needs, and wants of the audience of the club (consumers, clients, and members). It also enables clubs to better understand the experience of those respective audiences with their brand. Market research provides insights that allow facilities to better tailor their offerings (e.g., products, services, and value proposition), to align with the desires, interests, and needs of a specific audience. In that regard, it helps clubs to craft their message to attract and captivate members.

> Listening to the voice of the customer provides clubs with an understanding of their clients' attitudes, beliefs, and behaviors.

Tools for Capturing the Voice of the Customer

> Capturing the voice of the member is essential if a club wants to understand the attitudes, feelings, and experiences of its clients and members.

Capturing the voice of the member is essential if a club wants to understand the attitudes, feelings, and experiences of its clients and members. Facility operators should never assume that they know what their members are experiencing, feeling, or thinking. All too frequently, operators assume that because they regularly walk the floor of their facility, engaging with members who openly express their feelings, that they understand the dynamics driving the behavior of their clients and members.

Capturing the voice of the member requires a disciplined approach to using a variety of invaluable tools, each of which provides a unique and different perspective that will enable a club to create an accurate profile of its members and, equally important, what they are experiencing. The result of this enriched database of information about the facility's members is a level of insight that will allow the club to initiate and execute strategies that can have a material impact on improving its business. Among the tools that facilities can use to obtain such information are the following:

❑ In-Depth Interviews (IDIs)

In-depth interviews (IDIs as they are known as in the world of consumer insight research) offer an up close and personal approach to understanding the emotional aspects of a member's experience with the facility. As such, this tool can enable the club to gain the perspective of members on a particular topic of relevance to its business. IDIs are considered a qualitative research approach, which refers to the fact that they offer up insights that are not statistically quantifiable, but rather are deep in perspective.

The objective of an IDI is to explore an individual's emotional sentiment toward a product, program, service offering, or experience. This tool offers a voice that is not biased or influenced by others that might speak louder or more frequently. By obtaining a deep understanding of the emotional context around an individual's experience or sentiments, it provides management with valuable insights it might otherwise never know. Since an IDI only captures one person's perspective, most researchers will conduct sessions with multiple individuals. As a result, the individual perspectives can be viewed collectively, which, in turn, can produce deep insight into the psyche of a club's members.

IDIs are conducted using open-ended questions to bring out views that are not typically detected with more structured approaches, such as surveys. The IDI process is designed to be flexible and free-flowing, which enables the interviewer to explore an individual's beliefs in greater detail. IDIs should be facilitated by professionals who are experienced in this particular form of customer discovery.

❑ Focus Groups

Focus groups are another effective tool that management can employ to learn more about member attitudes, beliefs, and behaviors. Focus groups are a potent discovery tool to use when trying to determine the potential appeal of a specific program or service the facility is considering offering, or when the club is trying to capture the feelings that members may have concerning a particular program or service that it may have recently introduced. As such, focus groups can serve an excellent means for unearthing what drives value in an individual's overall member experience. They can also provide a framework for designing a member survey, which, in turn, can yield quantitative insights into the member experience.

Focus groups, like the previously described IDIs, are a qualitative research approach that offers a non-quantifiable, but highly insightful, perspective on the customer's feelings around a particular topic. While IDIs are highly individual in nature, focus groups leverage both individual opinions and groupthink (groupthink is the dynamic that occurs when individual opinions are expressed among a group of individuals with different perspectives and opinions).

Most consumer insight professionals prefer to enlist between 8 and 12 individuals in a focus-group session. To obtain a reasonable level of confidence in the feedback provided around a given topic, researchers will conduct several focus-group sessions, each comprised of a different group of randomly selected individuals. The collective feedback obtained from multiple focus groups will help bring forward themes that can help shape a specific or general business strategy.

Ideally, focus groups should be led by an independent facilitator. Such an approach would provide a less-intimidating and controlled environment for members to express their beliefs. While management should not be involved in facilitating the focus-group sessions, most professional facilitators will allow management to observe the sessions from a distance.

❑ Surveys

Surveys are a practical method for assessing how members feel about their club experience or uncovering their sentiments pertaining to a particular service the club offers. Surveys are frequently used to measure overall member loyalty and the accompanying key drivers of member loyalty. On the other hand, surveys can also be used to explore member feelings toward specific programs or initiatives.

Surveys are frequently used to measure overall member loyalty and the accompanying key drivers of member loyalty.

Surveys are a quantitative research approach that provides statistically reliable and valid data, produced by the discovery process. Consumer insight professionals and researchers will often refer to a survey's value by referencing the level of confidence offered by the data, such as a level of confidence of +/- 3 percent. As a consequence, the responses to a survey, if it is organized and administered properly, can provide data that is statistically reliable and quantifiable, and, therefore, of great value when developing business strategy.

Surveys are typically conducted using one of three approaches—over the phone, in-person, or online. Each approach has its strengths and weaknesses, a discussion which is beyond the scope of this chapter. In the health/fitness facility industry, the most frequently used approach involves administering an online survey, using one of the many available Internet-based survey tools. Among the most prominent online survey tools are the following:

- Survey Monkey (www.surveymonkey.com). Survey Monkey offers both a free version and a subscription-based version. The free version is great for small informal surveys. On the other hand, if conducting more complex surveys with larger groups or specific analytic needs are desired, then the company offers a few levels of fee-based versions of its survey.
- Survey Gizmo (www.surveygizmo.com). While Survey Gizmo does not offer a free version, it does have a low-cost tool that provides some advanced features. It also has more expensive versions, with more advanced features.
- Zoomerang (www.zoomerang.com). Zoomerang is similar to Survey Monkey, offering both a free program, with limited features, and more advanced versions, which are designed to enhance the utility of the survey tool.

Online surveys enable faculty operators to invite members to participate in the process, using a variety of Internet-enabled devices, such as their computer, tablet, or smart phone. A professionally conducted online survey will typically generate a response rate of between 15 and 30 percent. In other words, 15 to 30 percent of the individuals who were invited to participate in the survey completed it. A response rate of this magnitude will usually offer a high level of confidence in the response data and, as a consequence, provide club operators with an abundance of valuable insights.

In order to avoid survey fatigue (a situation in which consumers no longer desire to share their opinions), operators should limit the number of surveys that they conduct on an annual basis. As a rule, when surveying members to ascertain the overall member experience, doing so once or twice annually is typically sufficient. By the same token, when utilizing a survey to address a specific topic, clubs should restrict how often they employ this particular tool as well, preferably to once or twice a year.

❑ Real-Time Customer Experience Tracking Systems

One of the newest trends in the health/fitness facility industry involves real-time voice of the customer (VOC) tracking platforms that measure the customer and/or member experience on a daily basis across all touch points of the club experience. These real-time tracking systems provide club management with instant feedback concerning how well they are delivering on their customer promise. In that regard, these systems yield quantitative metrics on service performance, along with commentary on issues impacting the members' daily experience.

These real-time experience tracking systems can monitor both the transactional elements of the member experience (e.g., cleanliness, program offerings, staff availability, and equipment function) and the emotional components of the experience (e.g., sense of being cared for, value of the experience, and love for the club). Typically, these VOC systems send out a daily survey invite to a randomly selected group of members who visited the facility that day (some systems invite members who have been in the facility sometime during the last 90 days and consequently are not real-time).

Members can then respond to the survey invite on their smart phone, tablet, or computer. As members complete the survey, their responses are immediately uploaded into the system, hence the term "real-time feedback." While there are numerous firms that offer these VOC platforms, four firms that have the greatest visibility in this regard in the health/fitness facility industry are:

- Inmoment (www.inmoment.com)
- Medallia (www.medallia.com)
- The Retention People (www.theretentionpeople.com)
- Listen 360 (www.listen360.com)

❏ Comment Feedback System

Comment feedback systems are one of the oldest tools used by health/fitness facility operators to ascertain information regarding any positive or negative experience that a member may have had in the club. This type of feedback system is commonly referred to as a comment card approach. In this system, the members, having experienced either a favorable or unfavorable experience, can share their feelings (e.g., praise, rage, discontent, and frustration) by completing a comment card and depositing it in the club's approved repository. Such an effort could range from having boxes with comment cards located throughout the club, to web-based feedback systems that are hosted either on a club's website or in kiosks that are located in the club.

❏ Open Door/Open Floor

This approach to listening involves senior management (e.g., club manager and department heads) designating a specific time that members and clients can drop in and talk. It also mandates management should spend a portion of each day out in the club talking with members. The combination of getting out and talking with members and also leaving time on the schedule for members to walk in and meet with club staff enables management to foster an environment of trust. As such, trust fosters open and honest dialogue that allows management to better understand the needs, wants, and experiences of the club's members.

❏ Social Media Listening

Social media listening, also referred to as social media monitoring, is the process of the club listening to what its members are saying about it on the various social media platforms. Social media listening entails more than listening. It also involves vigilant monitoring of what is being communicated on the various social media platforms and assessing how those messages are impacting the club's brand message and reputation.

Social media listening is the 21st century approach to listening to the gossip that members have to say about their experience when they believe that no one is listening.

Why should management monitor what's being said about the club on the Internet? The voice-of-the-member tools that have been previously highlighted in this chapter require management to be proactive in approaching its members to solicit feedback, whether it is conducting focus groups, sending out a survey invitation, or providing a flexible feedback system on the club's website. Social media listening, on the other hand, while proactive in a sense, does not involve management soliciting member feedback. Rather, it entails listening to what members say about their experience when they are not solicited for feedback. It's the 21st century approach to listening to the gossip that members have to say about their experience when they believe that no one is listening.

At the present time, consumers, including club members, especially those individuals under the age of 35, tend to share their experiences and feelings, most often their complaints, via one of the many social platforms that exist, such as Facebook, Google Plus, Instagram, Twitter, Yelp, and YouTube. In fact, a survey conducted by a prominent market research firm showed that 42 percent of today's consumers will share a complaint through social media. To a degree, social media has become the key forum that individuals employ to express their issues with an experience they have had. More often than not, it's a negative experience, rather than a positive one. As a consequence, if a club is not attuned to what is being said on these social platforms, it is undoubtedly missing out on what its members are saying about it when it isn't proactively soliciting feedback.

> Social media has become the key forum that individuals employ to express their issues with an experience they have had.

As small business owners, most health/fitness facility operators can't afford to purchase expensive software to monitor the leading social media platforms. Fortunately, there are several free tools that operators can avail themselves if they want to listen in to what their members are saying in the social universe. Among the free social listening devices are the following:

- Hootsuite/Tweet Deck. These two social media platforms offer search columns that scan Twitter in real time, thereby providing the club with an ear to what members might be saying on Twitter.
- Icerocket. Icerocket focuses on blogs, but has a "big buzz" feature that scans activity on Facebook, Twitter, and images on Flickr.
- Social Mention. This platform scans and aggregates activity on Facebook, Twitter, and YouTube. As part of its toolkit, it offers basic analytics to help a facility identify positive and negative sentiment.

If a club wishes to dig deeper into the member feedback nuggets that are often deposited on the various social media platforms, it can purchase one of the many software systems designed for social media listening. The software it purchases will depend on the scope of its needs and expectations. For example, does the club want to monitor the basic social media platforms, such as Facebook and Twitter, or does it want to explore other platforms, such as Yelp and industry-specific consumer blogs? With regard to software systems that are designed for social media listening, a number of quality programs exist, such as Brandwatch and Digimind Social, as well as several niche providers, such as Meltwater Buzz and NetBase. A few of the firms that offer real-time voice of the customer platforms also have social listening tools, such as Inmoment, that enable a club to integrate social listening with the proactive voice of the customer tracking.

Reflections

If one of the primary objectives of the club is to understand its customers (e.g., members), and use that information to enhance its business value proposition to attract and retain more members, then learning how to leverage the various voices of the member tools is essential. In reality, becoming a great listener does not require the club to use every tool in its toolkit. It does, however, require that it understands which tools will provide it with the greatest insight into the needs, wants, and experiences of its members. As a consequence, the information afforded by these tools can facilitate the efforts of the club to create a value proposition that engenders member loyalty and advocacy.

7 Marketing Essentials: Communicating the Facility's Value Proposition and Generating Purchase Intent

"Clarity trumps persuasion."

—Dr. Flint McGlaughlin

Chapter Objectives

Seth Godin said, "Marketing is no longer about the stuff you make, but about the stories you tell." Communicating your facility's or studio's value proposition is storytelling, a story that says to your audience: "Come experience me because I am exactly what you need." In this chapter, our first goal is to frame what lay at the heart of all great marketing. Our second objective is to provide an overview of various marketing approaches, from traditional marketing strategies such as print advertising and direct mail, to the newest digital strategies being used by today's savvy marketers.

The Essence of Messaging the Club's Value Proposition

> Marketing, when dissected to its most basic elements, is nothing more than storytelling.

Marketing, when dissected to its most basic elements, is nothing more than storytelling. When telling a story, the storyteller is sharing information that the person believes will be entertaining, important, interesting, or relevant to those individuals at whom the story is targeted. Good storytellers know their audience. As a result, they are able to craft stories to capture the attention of the listeners.

If someone were to carefully listen to storytellers, that person would find that they adapt their story to fit their audience, understanding the subtleties of the people whom they are targeting. When the storyteller does their job well, the audience is captivated, embraced within the grasp of the storyteller's every word.

The same basic principle applies to marketing. When marketers do their job effectively, they are sharing a message that can be entertaining, interesting, helpful, or relevant to their audience. More importantly, persuasive marketing captures the attention of its intended audience and provides these individuals with a compelling rationale for considering whether to become a member of the club or client of the studio. As Ann Handley, chief content officer for Marketing Props states, "Make the customer the hero of your story."

It is important to note that marketing is a process, not an event. It begins, as detailed in Chapter 6, with the goal of understanding the needs, interests, and wants of the consumer. It then progresses through a series of initiatives and actions intended to capture the consumer's attention. Subsequently, in the process, it drives purchase intent.

Marketing may have a starting point and even a middle point, but it never has an ending point. Marketing is not a stagnant process. Rather, it is an undertaking that must evolve over time and adapt to ever-changing tastes of the consumers, as well as to the value proposition of the facility's brand.

One of the key issues that arises is what should the club expect of its marketing efforts? In other words, what objectives should the facility establish for its marketing efforts? In that regard, clubs should base their marketing endeavors on the following premises:

- Marketing should effectively communicate the facility's brand promise and value proposition, such that prospective clients and/or members, as well as existing clients and/or members, understand the benefits and value of the club's offering.
- Marketing should establish the facility's brand's identity in the marketplace, differentiating it from the competition.
- Marketing should provide a compelling rationale for consumers to purchase the club's offering. In other words, it should drive purchase intent.

Marketing should establish the facility's brand's identity in the marketplace, differentiating it from the competition.

- Marketing should capture the attention of the desired audience and then compel them to learn more about the facility's value proposition.
- Marketing should not be viewed as selling. Instead, it should be seen (in this instance) as a club letting consumers know what the facility has to offer them, so that they want to buy it.

Messaging the value proposition of a club's brand can take many forms. In that regard, the most commonly recognized approaches include advertising, buzz marketing, direct mail, Internet marketing, and public relations. In each instance, no matter what messaging or promotion technique is incorporated, the ultimate goal is threefold: build, enrich, share, or promote the club's brand's image and reputation; bring awareness of or attention to the benefits that the brand offers; and influence or drive purchase intent among the targeted audience.

It is important to understand that not all messaging and promotional strategies are created equal. As such, a facility's approach to promoting and messaging its brand will be heavily influenced by a number of variables, such as the life stage of its audience (e.g., age and generation), lifestyle (professional and personal interests and practices), place of residence or employment, gender, and level of income. The next two sections highlight the messaging and promotional (marketing) strategies that are likely to be the most cost-effective and successful at generating both purchase intent and purchase activity for a health/fitness club.

General Marketing Approaches

As shared in the previous section, marketing serves several purposes, each critically important to the overall success of the business. In general, there are three core approaches that marketers use to frame their storytelling.

Brand or Identity Marketing

This form of marketing focuses on building the image or identity of your club's brand in the marketplace. You might say that brand marketing is akin to an x-ray of your brand, as it exposes the soul of your brand. It involves communicating what your brand promise is and the attributes that comprise it. This marketing approach leverages your brand's slogans, taglines, colors, and images. Its goal is to communicate to the marketplace who you are and why you are different than everyone else in the market. No brand can be successful without integrating brand marketing into its promotional mix. Most brand marketing involves the use of images and short messages that speak to the attitude of your brand.

Content Marketing

Over the past decade, content marketing has become extremely important. Content marketing involves providing informative content that educates and informs the consumer. It demonstrates to consumers your expertise on a topic, but it also educates the consumer, with the desired outcome being that a well-informed consumer is more likely to select your brand when they are shopping. Examples of content marketing platforms include newsletters (print or digital),

The goal of brand or identity marketing is to communicate to the marketplace who you are and why you are different than everyone else in the market.

blogs, website-based articles, video channel on YouTube, column in a local newspaper, or even sponsored segments on radio.

Call-to-Action Marketing

Call-to-action marketing, as its name implies, involves promotions that are designed to drive customer traffic into your facility. Call-to-action promotions do not inform or educate, nor do they promote the brand's image; instead, they are designed to create a compelling reason for the consumer to act immediately. Call-to-action promotions are built on the following principles:

- *Create a sense of urgency.* If you want consumers to act promptly, research indicates you have to establish a sense of urgency in their mind, what some might refer to as a fear of missing out. This typically involves establishing a deadline for responding.
- *Create an offer they can't refuse.* Consumers respond best when they know a deal exists. As a result, call-to-action promotions need to extend an offer, whether it's a free class, free two-week membership, special gift, or discount. Research in the health/fitness club industry shows that consumers respond best to complimentary trial offerings.
- *Make the promotion eye-catching.* Whatever media you leverage for call-to-action marketing, the visuals need to pop out. Bland doesn't work when it comes to call-to-action marketing; innovative, creative, and disruptive imagery is more likely to catch consumer's attention.

Call-to-action marketing, as its name implies, involves promotions that are designed to drive customer traffic into your facility.

Traditional Strategies for Marketing and Promoting the Value Proposition of the Facility

❏ Advertising

Advertising represents a very broad-stroke approach to marketing in the health/fitness facility industry. As a rule, advertising is not a targeted approach to marketing. Rather, it is a method for earmarking a larger, less-targeted audience. Advertising can take many forms, including the following:

- *Print media.* Print media advertising includes placing advertisements in such venues as newspapers, magazines, company newsletters, etc. Print media varies in its effectiveness. If a club is located in a small market that has a relatively small local paper, then print advertising can be an effective approach for generating traffic. On the other hand, if a club is located in a large market, such as New York, the success of print advertising is highly dependent on the audience to which it is speaking, the demographic radius from which it will be pulling, and the scalability of its business. For example, New York Sports Clubs, with over 90 facilities in the New York metropolitan region, has had considerable success with print advertising.

The cost of producing a quality print ad can run thousands of dollars, while the cost to place it can range from a few thousand dollars to over $25,000.

At the least, print advertising can be very expensive. Not only must a club pay for the expenses involved in the production of the advertisement, it is also responsible for the cost of its placement as well. The cost of producing a quality print ad can run thousands of dollars, while the cost to place it can range from a few thousand dollars to over $25,000, depending on the size and relative location of the ad (quarter-page, half-page, full-page, back cover, etc.), whether it's black and white or color, the circulation of the specific print medium in which the ad appears (number of subscribers), and, finally, the geographic location of the market of the print medium.

Clubs that choose to use print media may want to consider using other forms of print media, such as local community circulars or flyers, which are less expensive and can be more easily targeted to a specific audience. Two club companies, in particular, that have set themselves apart with their print advertising are Companhia Athletica, with corporate offices in Sao Paulo, Brazil, and Equinox Fitness, with its corporate offices based in New York, New York.

At Companhia Athletica, three of their most successful print marketing campaigns (each subsequently won awards) were the "Body Fat Imprisonment" campaign in 2007, the "Flowers" campaign in 2009, and the "Switch Your Routine" campaign in 2010. Equinox, which many professionals in the marketing community consider the leader in print marketing, received acclaim for its 2008 "Happily Ever" campaign, which generated considerable positive press and social media commentary, its 2010 "My Body. My Biography" campaign, its 2014 campaign entitled, "Equinox Made Me Do It," and finally, its 2017 "Commit to Something" campaign.

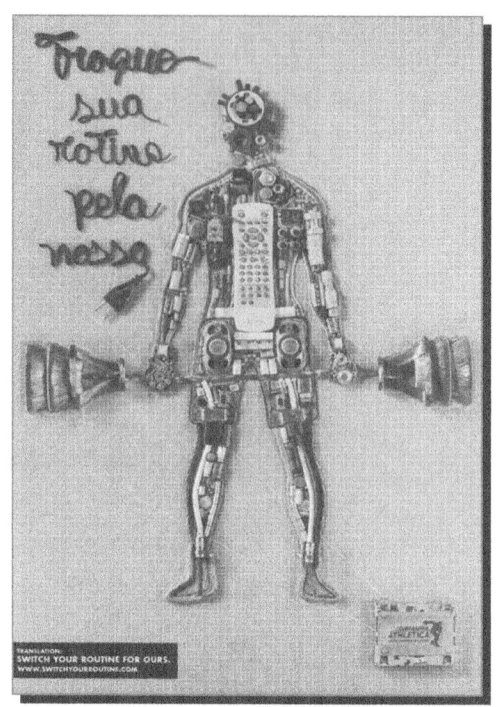

At Companhia Athletica, two of their most successful print marketing campaigns were the "Body Fat Imprisonment" campaign in 2007 (above left) and the "Switch Your Routine" campaign in 2010 (above right).

- *Radio.* Advertisements placed on radio stations and Internet radio (e.g., Pandora, Soma.fm, Slacker, Spotify, TuneIn, etc.) should align with a demographic audience that is similar to the demographics that the club wishes to target. In fact, every station/platform has detailed information on the demographics of its audience, which can help a club determine with which station/platform it should place its advertising dollars. In reality, radio advertising is not inexpensive. On the other hand, if a club or studio is relatively selective in how and where it advertises, such an approach can be effective. In markets with a high commuter population radio advertising can be especially productive. Some traditional radio stations, at no extra cost, may also agree to broadcast live from a club, a scenario that can provide a level of added visibility to the facility's marketing efforts.
- *Local and regional cable television.* Using cable television to communicate the facility's desired message can be a very effective approach to advertising, especially if a club does it on a regional or local level. Broadcast television advertising is particularly effective at reaching Baby Boomers. On the other hand, it is important for a club to keep the cost of production and placement of an ad on cable television in mind, when deciding whether this approach is an appropriate way for it to advertise.

  In recent years, a number of marketers have been taking the advertisements that have been produced for television and posting them on their YouTube pages. One club group that subscribes to this approach is Brick Bodies, based in Maryland. They do an excellent job of leveraging YouTube to post their television advertisements. In essence, they are leveraging their production investment many times over.

As with any form of advertising, it's important for the facility to understand its audience. For example, many young adults from the millennial generation don't watch television. Instead, they stream shows from Netflix and Hulu, platforms that often don't show advertisements. Accordingly, if a club is trying to appeal to the millennial generation, advertising on the local television stations may not be the best use of its advertising dollars. Instead, to reach this audience, it would be more effective to post its video content on YouTube. Another example of knowing who the audience is and whether television advertising is right for the club revolves around the advent of DVRs. These devices allow consumers to record their favorite shows and then play them back, while skipping over advertisements.

In recent years, a number of marketers have been taking the advertisements that have been produced for television and posting them on their YouTube pages.

- *Billboards and banners.* Billboard advertising can be an excellent option for advertising, especially in large, urban markets, such as Dallas, Houston, and Los Angeles, where people spend considerable time commuting in their cars. Billboards and banners, if placed along the appropriate thoroughfare, can bring considerable attention to the club. For example, in Moscow, Russia, the number-one source of leads for the top club operators is generated by banners that are hung over the streets (drivers in Moscow typically spend several hours each day in traffic). Like most advertising efforts, billboard advertising involves both production and placement costs. With billboard advertising, similar to other media, the club can pay for the space it chooses to use for a given period of time.

❑ Club Marketing Literature

Clubs need to develop marketing literature that will articulate the "story" of their club. These marketing materials can be used as handouts, when they're utilized outside the club, as well as when prospects are visiting at the club. Examples of some of the most effective marketing literature and media used by clubs include the following:

- *Print brochures.* Every club should consider having a print brochure. The brochure should represent the image of the club and tell the story of the club. An effective brochure, in this instance, should feature a number of items, including pictures, testimonies by members, bullet points on the attributes and benefits of the club, a map with the location of the club, and information on how to contact the club (including email and website addresses). Sample brochures are included in the appendices of this book.

    Cost-wise, a wide variety of print options are typically available. It is money well-spent, however. A quality color brochure might run as high as one to two dollars a brochure, when the club prints 500 or more at a time.

- *CD/DVD/flash brochure.* One of the most recently developed tools that a club can leverage to market and promote itself is an actual CD, DVD, or flash drive brochure. At a minimum, these high-tech brochures should contain a virtual tour of the club, clips of member testimonies, information about the club in story format, and a direct link to the club's website. CDs and DVDs are a relatively inexpensive item to produce, generally ranging from 50 cents to one dollar to replicate, while flash drives typically run a few dollars for a one or two gigabyte drive.

No brand can be successful without integrating brand marketing into its promotional mix. Most brand marketing involves the use of images and short messages that speak to the attitude of your brand.

❏ Coupons in Local Circulars

For many local, independently owned clubs and fitness studios, one of the most cost-effective ways to reach consumers in the community is to distribute coupons in a local community circular. Most small communities have a local circular that is distributed to residents on either a weekly or monthly basis. Research into consumer purchasing behavior has demonstrated that coupons are highly valued by shoppers of all generations. Print coupons are most effective when used to promote an offer to Baby Boomers. Typically, circular coupons are call-to-action promotions that provide a time-sensitive and discounted offer to consumers.

❏ Direct Mail

Direct mail marketing is, and has been, one of the most effective lead-generation tools for fitness clubs and studios for decades. Direct mail allows the facility to send a compelling and engaging message to the audience it is targeting. Not too dissimilar to a drone, direct mail can hone into the exact audience the club would like to target, even down to the exact street address. While the typical direct mail campaign will generate a response rate that varies from 0.5 percent to 3 percent, if the facility establishes the right audiences it would like to reach, it can achieve response rates as high as 5 percent. The more targeted a club's initial audience, the higher its percentage of responses will be.

No matter the type of direct mail effort a facility chooses to adopt, it should carefully consider several factors, including the following:
- *Keep it clean and simple.* Because consumers want the direct mail effort to get directly to the point, clubs should make their message pop immediately. People don't want to read too much. Instead, all factors considered, they would rather the message slap them across the face.

- *Make it pop.* The mailboxes of consumers, both the physical ones and the virtual ones, are constantly getting inundated with promotion materials. Accordingly, if a direct mail piece does not grab their attention immediately, then chances are, it will be clicked to the trash folder or thrown into an old circular file.
- *Make it personal.* Nothing says a message cares more than making it personal. If club operators are using direct mail, they should hand-address the mailers and possibly sign their name.
- *Extend an offer.* Direct mail is most effective when the message includes a time-constrained offer. In other words, when a club is making an offer, it should put a deadline on it. For example, if the facility is extending a complimentary 20-minute training session as its offer, the direct mail piece should indicate when the offer is good until. There is nothing like a deadline to get people to respond, often on the last day of the offer.
- *Acquire quality mailing lists.* Obviously, the best source for names to contact would be provided by the members themselves. On the other hand, if individuals are just launching their business, they should seek out the assistance of a firm that specializes in providing direct mail lists (both physical addresses, as well as email and phone numbers). Before purchasing a mailing list, however, it is essential that every effort be undertaken to make sure that it comes from a reputable organization.

Lead Boxes

Lead boxes were among the first marketing tools employed by operators of health/fitness facilities. Lead boxes involve placing a box or container, accompanied by a promotional offer, at synergistic locations within an entity's primary market. The most frequently used approach is for a club to place its lead boxes in retail locations, where the demographics of the retail customers align with the facility's targeted client base. A common practice, especially among big box, low-priced clubs, involves providing a promotional piece that extends to the public a chance to win something when they complete the form and drop it in the lead box. In order for lead boxes to be successful, they need to be checked on a regular basis. Just as importantly, if a prize is offered, it needs to be actually awarded.

Member Referral Programs

Member referral programs have been around the fitness industry for over a century. Most referral programs provide incentives to existing members to either bring in friends or refer them to the membership sales team. In some instances, clubs even offer incentives to the individual who was referred. Some facilities have a permanent referral program, while others prefer to run referral programs a few designated times each year.

One of the downsides of referral programs is what is referred to as "referral fatigue." This condition arises when members stop referring people to the club. This situation occurs because instead of generating "word of mouth" buzz through the loyalty of members, clubs are eliciting positive referral behavior (i.e., bribing) through incentives.

❑ Community Engagement

Community engagement refers to the process of establishing relationships with key groups within your respective community, an undertaking that is often referred to as public relations. Community engagement entails developing and managing the brand image and reputation through relationships in the community. A few examples of how a studio can get involved within its community and therefore embellish the image and reputation of its brand include the following:

- *Sponsor community activities.* A club can get involved with community activities by serving as a host or sponsor for a local community event. The Atlantic Club, with two clubs in New Jersey, supports as many community events as it can, having made this policy a central part of their marketing efforts. The Goodlife Fitness Centers in Canada, with sites around the country, get involved in sponsoring both national and local events as a means of supporting the communities in which the facilities are located.
- *Support charitable events in the community.* Today's consumers, especially Millennials, are socially conscious and want to give back to their community. One way clubs or studios can build on this dynamic to drive awareness of its brand, and drive new member growth is to get involved in supporting local charities. One example of this is Exhale, a New York–based group of barre, yoga, and spa studios that sponsors local charity events within each of the communities it does business.

One way clubs or studios can drive awareness of their brand and drive new member growth is to get involved in supporting local charities.

- *Become a health and fitness resource for the community.* A facility could contact the local press and see if a staff member of the club could write a question-and-answer column for the paper, or a blog for its online publication. In the letter instance, instead of going to the local media, the club could also create its own blog and develop it as a resource for the community.
- *Establish strategic partnerships.* Another effective community engagement approach, especially for an independent facility, involves pursuing strategic partnerships or cross-promotional relationships. These partnerships and relationships involve establishing a synergistic relationship between the club and another business, such that each entity benefits. For example, a club that provides nutritional coaching support might create a strategic partnership with a local health food store, or, if the club provides integrative health programs, establish a relationship with a local physician's group or hospital. Examples of strategic partnerships include the following:
  - ✓ *Alliance with local restaurants.* Clubs can approach restaurants whose clientele have the same demographics and establish a relationship in which both organizations are marketing the others to its clients. This approach can be as simple as employing table-top advertising, or could involve special coupons that members and customers receive when they use the club or restaurant.
  - ✓ *Alliance with local healthcare organizations.* By establishing an informal relationship with other healthcare organizations, a club could gain valuable leads.
  - ✓ *Alliance with local homeowner associations.* A club could establish a relationship in which new homeowners obtain, as part of their homeowner membership, a coupon that enables them to join the club at a discounted price or possibly to receive a one-month, complimentary membership.
  - ✓ *Alliance with local realtors.* Clubs can work with local realtors to create special welcome gifts. These gifts could be included with all new home purchases or could be positioned as a special-benefit package, if individuals satisfy some set of predetermined criteria that would be set by the local realtor. In an urban market, a club might want to work with local apartment/condominium landlords to create the same type of package.

The New Normal: Digital Marketing

The world of marketing has changed dramatically over the past decade. Today's consumers are more likely to learn about a product or, for that matter, purchase a product online. Market research shows that no matter the generation (e.g., Millennial, Generation X, or Baby Boomer), if retailers want to reach consumers where they shop, then they need to have a digital marketing strategy. Furthermore, that digital strategy has to address consumers' propensity for shopping and buying products on their mobile devices. The balance of this section will highlight the various digital strategies that clubs can use to reach consumers.

Market research shows that no matter the generation (e.g., Millennial, Generation X, or Baby Boomer), if retailers want to reach consumers where they shop, then they need to have a digital marketing strategy.

❑ Internet Advertisements

Over the last few years, Internet advertising has become extremely popular. The most common forms of Internet advertising include banner advertisements, pop-up advertisements, video advertisements, and mobile advertisements. The vast majority of Internet advertisements are defined as pay-per-click, or PPC advertisements, meaning the advertiser only pays for their promotion when someone clicks on their ad. The caveat to these PPC advertisements is that what you pay is based on a bidding process around specific keywords. For example, Google Adwords, the most popular and largest digital advertising platform, allows businesses to establish their own budget framework (i.e., timeframe for their promotion, total funds they want to spent, etc.). When using Google Adwords, you first bid for keywords. Once you've purchased these keywords, then your promotion will pop-up on the consumers screen whenever they type in one of the keywords in their search engine. If the consumer then clicks on your promotion, you pay a specified amount for that view, hence the term pay-per-click.

So what are some of the best platforms for club operators to use for Internet advertising? According to digital marketing experts, the leading Internet advertising sites are:

- *Google Adwords.* This is the largest PPC platform. Google Adwords targets user behavior (people searching for specific information) using key words. When a consumer types in specific words or phrases that align with those keywords, an advertisers promotion will appear.
- *Bing Ads.* Bing Ads is smaller than Google Adwords, but is still a highly effective. It uses a similar approach as Google Adwords around keywords, but does so at a lower cost.
- *Facebook Advertising.* Facebook advertising is considered the most cost-effective of the big three, as they allow advertisers alternatives to pay-per click promotions using keyword searches. Something Facebook allows

advertisers to do that Google Adwords or Bing Ads doesn't is the ability to target a specific niche of consumer demographics and interests rather than just framing it around keywords. Additionally, Facebook allows advertisers to use video content and images so even if consumers don't click on the club's advertisement, they still see it.

Persuasive marketing captures the attention of its intended audience.

Club operators should be aware that Internet advertising is not the marketing panacea that some would make it out to be. With the advent of software such as Ad Blocker, which block Internet advertisements from appearing on keyword searches, a club's Internet advertisements may never be seen by segments of the intended audience.

❑ Buzz Marketing

Buzz marketing is commonly referenced as word-of-mouth (WOM) promotions that take place in the social media universe. If and when these promotional efforts "catch" fire, the process is referred to as viral marketing. Buzz marketing relies solely on the passion and loyalty of existing members and the relationships these members have with other individuals in the community. These buzz creators include connectors, mavens, and experts; all members whose connections, relationships, and acknowledged expertise engender trust and speak to authenticity.

Nothing is more powerful than the authenticity of a recommendation from a trusted friend or associate. When a facility's members are spreading the gospel about the club's brand, the buzz subsequently garners unadulterated mindshare (communicated with minimal external interference) with the targeted audience. When buzz is generated organically (i.e., member-driven) by the club's members, rather than being driven through non-authentic means (i.e., paid-for referrals) then your business is more likely to experience the phenomena called "going viral." When buzz goes viral, it refers to the fact that the "word" has spread quickly and broadly, which is the pinnacle of any marketing effort.

Buzz is not something that a club can buy. Rather, it is something that the business has to earn. When a facility successfully fulfills its promise to its members, when it exceeds what the members expect, and when it establishes an emotional connection with its members, it generates loyalty and advocacy. It is this loyalty and advocacy that lead to buzz and, ultimately, to the brand promise of the club going viral. Examples of prominent buzz marketing platforms that can be leveraged by marketers include the following:

- *Social media.* Facebook, LinkedIn, Tumblr, Twitter, YouTube, and Instagram, as well as various other social media platforms, have become the primary vehicle for buzz at the present time. Nothing spreads further faster than buzz circulated by friends on Facebook or Twitter. Equinox, a U.S.-based operator of premium and luxury clubs, has over 125,000 likes on its Facebook page and 48,000 plus subscribers to its YouTube site. Both sets of numbers are a testament to the ability of Equinox to leverage the voice of its members through social media. Another example of an organization that has embraced the use of social media is McFit, a German budget club operator. McFit has over 132,000 likes on Facebook and over 6,500 subscribers on YouTube, which is indicative of its approach to using social media as a tool for generating buzz. Possibly the best example of how effective social media can be at creating buzz is CrossFit, whose Facebook page has generated over 2.8 million likes, along with a fanatical following.

  Social media marketing is all about sharing relevant and timely content (information that the club wants people to read and, in turn, the individuals want to read) across the platforms that the facility's members and prospective members visit. In most instances, this undertaking will require a club operator to post content across a variety of social media platforms, a process that will be discussed in the section on social media that appears later in this chapter.

  Finally, not all social media is created equal. While Facebook is the grandaddy of them all, and a platform every club should be on, deciding what other platforms to have a presence on depends upon knowing where your members spend their time. For instance, Instagram has become popular among Millennials and Generation X. Snapchat, one of the newest social media platforms, is extremely popular among younger Millennials.

- *Blogs.* Blogs (which are a website or a web page that is regularly updated and managed by one individual or a small group of people) are part of a social media activity. On the other hand, they differ from sites such as Facebook, Twitter, and YouTube in that they rely more heavily on experts and celebrities to drive buzz. There are blogs whose authors are celebrities that have enormous fan bases. Getting one of these celebrity bloggers to share the club's story can generate an incredible amount of buzz about its brand. If an individual's goal is to be perceived as an expert source, that person can create their own blog, such as done by Equinox, which has its blog entitled Furthermore that can be accessed through its website. Chris

Brogan, founder of New Marketing Labs, is quoted as saying, "No matter what, the very first piece of social media real estate I'd start with is a blog."

In the current marketplace, the majority of consumers, a group that includes a club's prospective members, explore their opportunities by searching the Internet.

As Seth Godin, an acclaimed author and speaker on marketing, states, "The future belongs to marketers who establish a foundation and process, where interested people can market to each other. Ignite consumer networks, and then get out of the way, and let them talk." This premise is the essence of buzz.

❏ Website and Landing Page

Every club needs to have a branded website that is a virtual replication of the facility's experience. In the current marketplace, the majority of consumers, a group that includes a club's prospective members, explore their opportunities by searching the Internet. Accordingly, if the prospective members of a facility are testing the waters, trying to identify what health/fitness facility can best fulfill their needs, the club needs to have a website that will capture their attention, draw them in, and tell the story of the facility.

A well-designed website can enhance your brand's reputation, strengthen its image, and heavily influence purchase intent. On the other hand, a poorly designed website can drive prospective members away. As such, a website that draws people in and drives purchasing behavior must adhere to the following principles:

- *Align it with the brand of the facility.* In other words, the design of the club's website must adhere to the club's brand style guide, as well as communicate the attitude and voice of the brand of the business. The appearance and tone of the site must be a perfect reflection of the experience that clients would have if they visited the facility.

- *Leverage key word searches.* When consumers are seeking information on a subject on a website, in this instance, health/fitness clubs, they will usually type in selected key words or phrases. As such, it is extremely important that the website of a facility is linked with certain essential words and phrases so that when consumers type them into Google, the club's name appears at or near the top of the list. Google and other search engines, such as Yahoo or Bing, have developed key word advertising, which allows entities (individuals or organizations) to purchase keywords. In the health/fitness facility industry, when these words are entered into the search engine, that club's site will appear prominently on the page.

Without effective marketing, a club, as well as its brand, will become lost among the numerous offerings of which consumers can avail themselves.

If a facility prefers not to spend money on keyword advertising, something some club operators may be hesitant to do, such a club must ensure that its website is professionally designed, so that during organic searches, the facility's name appears near the top. This practice, commonly referred to as search engine optimization (SEO), is critical to having a web address that pops out when consumers enter certain words and phrases into their search engine.

In order for a club's site to appear near the top during organic searches, the facility needs to make sure that the content is relevant, topical, fresh, and, most importantly, linked to the keywords that consumers use when they search for health/fitness clubs online. The key point, in this regard, is that when consumers search online, a facility wants to be the first club that appears.

- *Create a landing page other than a home page.* Landing pages are referred to by Internet marketers as "squeeze pages." As such, their primary purpose is to funnel those individuals who visit the page to where the club wants them. Whereas websites require visitors to search the site for what they want, or possibly for what the facility wants them to see, landing pages take consumers right to the source. Research shows that landing pages can be up to 75 percent more effective than a home page in converting search traffic into leads and, eventually, into business.

Ideally, a club wants to have a landing page for every campaign it undertakes in order to help ensure that visitors only receive what is relevant to them. Among the tips for creating effective landing pages are the following:

- ✓ Offer a simple focused message that makes it evident to the searcher that the club has what they want.
- ✓ Make the landing page compelling and include an offer, such as a guest pass, a reduced fee on a training session, or a complimentary service. Keep it simple and limit the offers or calls to action.
- ✓ Make sure to collect basic information about the searcher, such as the individual's name, email address, and basic interests.
- ✓ Have a confirmation, to the individual, when a person engages on the page.

All factors considered, creating landing pages for the various campaigns and promotions of a facility is not an easy task. In that regard, one option that is open to club operators to leverage one of the numerous online software platforms available in the marketplace that allow businesses to create effective landing pages and the accompanying tools to manage the conversion process (i.e., turning visitors into clients). Two of the most popular of these platforms are Lead Pages and Click Funnel. These two platforms provide marketers not only with tools to create effective landing pages, they also include features that clubs can employ to collect information on visitors and then convert them to clients.

- *Make the website easy to navigate.* Once a consumer enters a facility's website, the club should make it relatively easy for them to navigate the site. Ideally, most visitors to a site will enter through a dedicated landing page. On the other hand, regardless of whether the landing page or home page is their first point of entry, the facility wants to make it intuitive for them to find what they want. Because fancy graphics and extensive wording are more likely to distract and turn consumers away, the website should be kept clean and simple. The Equinox website is an excellent example of a website that is intuitive and compelling.
- *Make sure to provide a trial pass or offer on the home page and landing pages.* When consumers visit a facility's home page, or are directed to its landing page, one of the first things that they should see is an offer to register for a complimentary trial. Offering a complimentary trial (e.g., guest pass, complimentary training session, or complimentary class) enables the prospect to experience the club's brand. As part of the trial registration, the facility should obtain enough information about the person so the sales team of the club can follow up with them directly. For example, Equinox's home page has a button for scheduling a visit. On 24 Hour Fitness's website, once an individual enters the non-member landing page, a button exists that the visitor you can click to download a free pass. The Lifetime Fitness home page also has a button that an individual can click on to try one of its facilities for free.

> Research shows that landing pages can be up to 75 percent more effective than a home page in converting search traffic into leads and, eventually, into business.

❏ Social Media

Social media has become one of the hottest platforms for marketing and messaging. It is one, if not the most important, way to share relevant content with a specific audience. The "experts" would lead everyone to believe that social media is a "slam dunk," with regard to generating fans, followers, and, of course, prospect traffic. In reality, social media can be an outstanding marketing tool, which, in combination with other marketing strategies, can be effective in generating consumer interest and purchase intent.

In the current marketplace, success requires that a club have a compelling online presence.

Because social media is not an exact science, and if it's not managed properly, it can be a drain on a facility's time and resources, as well as be ineffective in driving client and/or member traffic. The key to leveraging social media as a marketing tool for a business is for the club to focus its efforts on a select few social media outlets, those that the facility believes that prospects and clients are most likely to be connecting with on the Internet. Equinox Fitness, based in New York City, does an outstanding job with its social media efforts, making it an essential ingredient in the value proposition for its brand.

Among the tips that can help a club leverage its social media efforts and, in the process, contribute to its overall success in generating customer interest and purchase intent are the following:

- *Limit the number of social sites the facility engages.* Contrary to the pervading mantra, the most effective approach for a club is to focus its social media efforts on two or three of the most respected and useful sites. In identifying the social media platforms that it will utilize, a facility should try to identify to what its prospective members and members are most likely to gravitate. Facebook, obviously, has an incredible reach and can generate a large fan base if used properly. For example, McFit, a budget club operator, based in Germany, has over 132,000 likes on its Facebook page, making it one of the most followed Facebook pages in the health/

fitness facility industry. CrossFit, which has over 12,000 locations, has garnered over 2.8 million likes on its Facebook page. Facebook allows entities to carry on a two-way dialogue with fans by sharing stories, photos, and even video content.

Google+ is newer, but it is also an excellent platform for clubs to carry on dialogue with its existing and future clients. Being on Google+ will drive a facility's relative rankings on Google, giving the club a greater profile outside of its website. If one of a facility's primary points of differentiation is its level of expertise attendant to a given topic area, or a club wants to provide regular insights into its brand, Twitter or possibly even LinkedIn can bring value, as can Instagram and Tumbler. For example, Todd Durkin, owner of Fitness Quest 10 in San Diego, has over 22,000 followers on Twitter.

- *Consider using a social media management tool.* Most club operators and marketing directors don't have the time either to create content or to effectively leverage social media. Consequently, social media management systems, such as Hootsuite and Buffer, are invaluable tools in the current social media-driven marketing environment. Both of these social media management platforms allow users to craft content, schedule posts across multiple platforms, stagger the release of posts across platforms, analyze performance, and stay on top of the buzz. Another excellent tool for managing social media is the mobile social media platform Everypost.
- *Keep it simple, but authentic.* A facility should remember that the authenticity of its social media efforts are important, given that savvy consumers will know when its releases are automated. As a result, clubs should balance their use of automated tools, such as Hootsuite or Buffer with more personalized releases. As John Jantsch, author of Duct Tape Marketing, states, "Bring the best of your authentic self to every opportunity." His primary point is that being authentic is critical, especially when it comes to social media messaging.
- *Be professional.* A club should be aware that anything it releases on social media is a reflection of its brand, and its brand is everything. Because the releases will likely be seen around the world, the facility must do whatever it can to ensure that everyone is seeing and feeling the essence of its brand. Accordingly, club operators should not delegate the management of its social media efforts to just anyone. They need to make sure that whoever is handling its social media efforts is professional and clearly understands the tenants of the facility's brand's value proposition and style guide.
- *Size does not matter, quality does.* The pervading thought among individuals and businesses is that the more fans and followers that an entity has, the more successful it is. The real key to leveraging social media is to attract the right audience and convert them to true advocates of the entity's brand. Having 500 fans who are passionate about what the facility is and what it has to offer is significantly better than having 5,000 followers who have little to no real interest in the club, other than to say that they are a fan.

The key, in this regard, is for a facility to use its social media to carry on authentic and trusted dialogue with its audience, not just send out a constant stream of information. Having a lot of likes on Facebook means nothing, unless people are actually conversing on the club's site.

Having a lot of likes on Facebook means nothing, unless people are actually conversing on the club's site.

- *Build a trusting relationship with the audience.* Too many businesses, including health/fitness facilities, use social media to talk to their audience, rather than carrying on a conversation with them. Those entities that are most successful with social media have a conversation with their audience; they listen, discuss, respect, and follow through. If all a facility does is to send out sales pitches or one-sided news, then it is disrespecting its followers.
- *Social media should be a conversation with friends.* Tim O'Reilly and Sarah Milstein, co-authors of The Twitter Book, reaffirmed the importance of using social media to carry on a trusted dialogue, when they stated, "The biggest mistake we see companies make when they first hit Twitter is to think about it as a channel to push out information."

❑ E-Mail Promotions

Email promotions, often referred to as email blasts, are today's version of yesterday's direct mail campaigns. Email promotions allow an operator to cover a larger and often more targeted audience in real time. Furthermore, the response rate for an email blast is typically higher than it is with standard direct mail. Well-designed email campaigns can generate an open rate (the rate at which the receivers of the promotion open the email) in excess of 30 percent and click-through rates from 3 percent to 5 percent, and sometimes as high as 10 percent (the rate that people open any attachment or link that accompanies the email).

The first requirement for a successful email campaign involves having a qualified database of consumer emails. The larger and more qualified that database, the more likely the club's email promotion will generate the required number of inquiries and sales. Therefore, if facility operators wish to be successful with their email promotions, they first must become proficient in collecting valid email addresses from clients and prospects. One of the most productive approaches to collecting valid email addresses from consumers and prospects is to require consumers to provide their email address whenever they access an offer on your website, social media site, or through an Internet advertisement.

Given that managing an email campaign can be time consuming for club operators, a number of exceptional online platforms exist that can ease the burden associated with managing email promotions. Among the leading platforms for managing a concerted email campaign are ActiveCampaign, CakeMail, MailChimp, and Sendinblue.

❑ SMS Promotions

> Text messaging is reported to have a response rate of 45 percent compared to 6 percent on average for email messages.

Texting is the most widely and frequently used app on a smartphone. According to research conducted by Pew Internet, 80 percent of Americans text, 97 percent of whom do it on a daily basis. According to Mobile Marketing Watch, text messages have an open rate of 98 percent compared to 20 percent for email. Additionally, text messaging is reported to have a response rate of 45 percent compared to 6 percent on average for email messages. In a study facilitated by the Direct Marketing Association, 44 percent of consumers indicated they would rather receive product details and marketing messages through text over other messaging channels. Finally, according to a report from Exact Target, 25 percent of marketers are presently using SMS messaging to generate sales. What all this means is that consumers are more likely to be reading and responding to text messages than any other form of digital messaging.

When using SMS, a business needs to send a simple and succinct message to the consumer that can be read in five seconds (research shows text messages on average are read in five seconds or less). To engage consumers, the text should contain a link back to a landing page or similar digital destination. If the SMS message is compelling, personal and relevant, the consumer will click on the link and immediately be taken to a landing page where they can act on the SMS offer. The challenge of SMS marketing, not unlike email promotions, is acquiring phone numbers, and as a result is often more effective as a marketing tool once you've established a relationship with a prospect.

One of the most critical areas for facility owners to focus on is marketing.

❑ Mobile Platform

Approximately 80 percent of all consumers use their smartphone to search the Internet, with a nearly equivalent percentage using their smartphones to shop. Global Web Index reported that, in 2015, 46 percent of shoppers used their smartphone to make a purchase. When you consider that approximately two-thirds of Americans own a smart phone, 80 percent of them use it to shop, and close to 50 percent make a purchase on their smartphone, it makes mobile the new frontier for promoting what your business has to offer. According to Google, nearly 90 percent of mobile searches lead to action, and more than 50 percent to sales. The point behind sharing this data is to bring forward how important it is for every fitness business to design their marketing with mobile top of mind by:
- Having a website that is optimized for mobile. Google has made it essential that businesses have a mobile-friendly website if they want to enhance their SEO.
- Leveraging SMS marketing messages as highlighted in the previous section.

- Making sure consumers can purchase your offerings via their mobile device, whether that involves purchasing a guest pass, membership or ancillary service.

Reflections

Without effective marketing, a club, as well as its brand, will become lost among the numerous offerings of which consumers can avail themselves. More often than not, the best value propositions mean nothing, unless they are messaged effectively. As a result, one of the most critical areas for facility owners to focus on is marketing. As such, they need to get their story told in the marketplace so that consumers flock to their business. The following checklist is intended both as a topline summary of this chapter's discussion of how a club can most effectively message its value proposition and as a simple guide for what steps a facility should take to market its brand.

- *Know which customers the club wants to serve, and know what these individuals desire.* Before embarking on a marketing campaign, a facility should take the time and allocate the financial resources to do research and understand, as intimately as possible, whom the target audience is and what will appeal to them.
- *Create a marketing plan.* Before a club starts the journey of becoming a viable business, it should create a plan that sets forth its core marketing objectives, identifies its marketing assets, highlights a timeline for its promotional efforts, and establishes a budget to achieving its plan.
- *Focus on using marketing assets that align with what the club is and who its audience is.* A facility should not get caught up trying lots of things. Instead, it should focus on what actions will have the greatest impact on it being able to reach its targeted audience. This approach often is referred to in marketing agencies as building an entity's media mix.
- *Establish a multidisciplinary, or omnichannel Internet presence.* In the current marketplace, success requires that a club have a compelling online presence, one that includes a strong mobile presence. Accordingly, the facility should make sure that it allocates the resources to develop and sustain an online presence that will touch its targeted audience where they search and shop.
- *Remember it's a process.* Marketing, like branding, does not have a starting point and an ending point. Marketing is an ongoing process in which the facility seeks to understand its audience and then focuses on creating and sending a message that will pierce the hearts of those individuals.

> A facility should focus on what actions will have the greatest impact on it being able to reach its targeted audience.

Digital Marketplaces and Platforms for Promoting Health/Fitness Businesses

8

"It is a whole sale conversion to a better, faster, cheaper, more flexible way of doing business."

—Jeffrey Rayport, assistant professor,
Harvard Business School

Chapter Objectives

In the past decade, businesses have seen the way they promote their businesses, and the manner in which consumers purchase their wares, change dramatically. Shopping has moved from the brick-and-mortar world to the virtual world, even when the product being sold has traditionally been sold in a brick-and-mortar setting. Two of the biggest disrupters in this shift to digital marketplaces shopping have been digital coupon sites and digital middlemen platforms. These two digital business models have had a significant impact on how consumers, including fitness consumers, shop for and purchase products and experiences. Correspondingly, they have changed the way most retail businesses, including health/fitness facilities, market and sell their wares.

This chapter will explore the digital marketplace phenomena. The exploration of digital marketplaces will begin with digital coupon sites. Next digital middlemen will be discussed, concluding by briefly addressing the newest digital disruptor, a blend of mobile application and cloud-based B2B platform.

Digital Coupon Sites

Digital coupon sites are digital marketplaces that allow businesses to offer coupons and special promotions to consumers in an effort to generate purchasing behavior. According to market research data on consumer use of coupons, 82 percent of consumers indicate digital coupons are a more convenient option compared to printed coupons. Digital coupon sites are not dissimilar from the traditional print circulars and coupon booklets that local consumers browse to find coupons and special offers. The biggest difference between the traditional coupon distribution platforms and digital coupon sites is the extent to which a business can promote its business proposition to a large audience of interested consumers in their local market. The largest, and possibly the most recognized, platforms are Groupon and Living Social. There are also less well-known sites such as Coupons and Retail Me Not that offer small businesses an opportunity to introduce their products to the marketplace.

> In the past decade, businesses have seen the way they promote their businesses, and the manner in which consumers purchase their wares, change dramatically.

How Do Digital Coupon Sites Typically Work?

- First, the sites only promote your offer to the local market, thus ensuring that you are reaching prospects that are most likely to engage with your facility.
- Second, digital coupon sites typically restrict when and how long the offer will be made available to consumers. This builds on the principle of scarcity, which is a powerful influence on people's purchasing behavior.
- Third, the sites require you to have a special offer—for example, a one-month membership plus a personal training session for $45, a $35 class for $10, or a $100 personal training for $40. In most instances, digital coupon sites want your offer to represent a 50 percent or greater discount on the retail price. Again, consumer research shows that consumers love discounts and they love coupons.
- Fourth, the sites typically take 50 percent of the revenue generated by a promotion; paying the seller the remaining 50 percent once the revenues are collected. Some digital coupon sites allow you to place your promotion for free, then take a specified dollar amount for each coupon downloaded or redeemed.

What Are the Benefits and Risks of Incorporating Digital Coupon Sites Into Your Marketing Strategy?

Like any marketing strategy used to promote your health/fitness facility, you must weigh the return on investment (ROI) that can be expected. As a small business, health/fitness facilities have limited capital resources, and as a result, they need to assess the ROI of their marketing spend. In an article that appeared in Inc.com earlier this decade, the authors indicated that according to a study conducted by Rice University, 32 percent of merchants indicated their promotion on Groupon was not profitable, and 40 percent indicated they would not do it again. What this research indicates is there are benefits to obtain, but also risks to consider. What follows are some of the benefits and risks of integrating digital coupon sites into your facility's marketing strategy.

❑ Benefits

- *They attract a lot of customers.* A well-designed coupon on a site such as Groupon can attract a considerable number of consumers. Operators need to be careful that the offer does not cannibalize sales to existing customers, and also have a way to further monetize customers who engage with the facility as a result of using a digital coupon.
- *It promotes your business.* Digital coupon sites expose your business and its value proposition to a wide audience within your market, and very often at a much lower cost than more traditional marketing approaches.
- *It can help build relationships with customers.* They key is to create offers that are built around driving multiple visits rather than a single visit.
- *It can generate incremental revenue.* If the offer is priced correctly, it can generate incremental revenue your facility might not otherwise have generated.

❑ Risks

- *The offer can attract deal-seekers who may not fit your membership profile.* Since digital coupon sites are known for attracting deal-seekers, the customers you attract may not be individuals who align with your desired membership profile.
- *They can negatively impact your brand's reputation.* Anytime you offer large discounts or provide giveaways, it detracts from your brand. Discounting does not generate brand loyalty, nor does it elevate a brand's reputation. If you operate a budget club, then discounting is not as likely to damage your reputation compared to if you operated a premium club.
- *It may not be profitable and may even lose money.* If you don't package your promotion correctly, it increases the likelihood the business will lose money on each coupon redeemed. Not every promotion has to generate a profit, but you don't want it to cost the business too much either.
- *Facebook or other digital site may afford you a better ROI.* While digital coupon sites offer brands great exposure and generate god customer traffic, there are other digital platforms that could do the same for less.

Tips for Generating a Favorable ROI Using Digital Coupon Sites

- *Decide ahead of time what it is you want to achieve from the promotion.* Is your goal to make a profit on the redemption of each coupon? Is it to drive high traffic through the door and monetize a portion of the traffic? Similar to any other marketing strategy, it's important to clearly define the desired goal. By establishing clear goals, it will be easier to frame your offer.
- *Don't give it away free, and don't offer a percentage discount.* Freebies will literally kill your business and brand unless you place a strict limit on the number of offers that can be redeemed. Furthermore, don't say 50 percent off or 70 percent off; instead, establish a clear price point for your promotion that will catch people's attention. For example if you are a premium club whose monthly membership runs $100 a month, you might consider offering a month's membership for $45.
- *Keep your costs in mind.* You always want to know what it will cost you to fulfill your commitment. For example if you pay your personal trainers $50 for a session, and you offer a coupon for a $55 training session, understand that after the digital site takes their cut you'll end up with $30 or less. In essence, each person who comes in will cost you $20. If you get 100 visitors that will cost you $2,000. This may or may not be a good investment compared to spending $2,000 on direct mail. The point is: understand what your costs will be and if those costs are justifiable.
- *Don't make it a habit.* In the world of marketing, you have to have a blend of content marketing, image marketing, and call-to-action marketing. Doing too much of one and not enough of another can be disastrous. What we are saying is that offers on a digital coupon site are an excellent tool for generating consumer traffic, what one would a great digital call-to-action promotion. Like any call-to-action promotion, you want to use them sparingly. In the big scheme of things, doing a digital coupon promotion a few times a year should be the limit. Use them judiciously to get the best ROI.

> In the world of marketing, you have to have a blend of content marketing, image marketing, and call-to-action marketing.

What Is a Digital Middleman?

A digital middleman is a business that leverages the Internet to offer consumers attractive alternatives to traditional shopping experiences. A good Internet middleman provides added value the traditional producer can't provide and offers a service the consumer desires. For example, Airbnb offers homeowners a virtual platform to market and rent their property, while offering a convenient and cost-effective means for reserving convenient and affordable lodging that consumers crave.

With the emergence and evolution of digital middlemen—such as Airbnb, Amazon, Just Eat, Nimbl, Open Table, Soothe, and Uber—comes the billion-dollar question: When is the business relationship between seller, middleman, and buyer a symbiotic one that lifts all parties and when does that relationship become parasitic or even cannibalistic and potentially wipe out a business or even industry? Let's take a look at these three relationship constructs.

- *Symbiotic relationships.* In this relationship, the Internet middleman brings added value to the seller's value proposition (e.g., offers greater convenience) while also helping the seller tap a new source of revenues. The buyer receives something they want, such as greater convenience or a lower price. The middleman benefits by growing their business and generating a profit. A great example of this would be Instacart, which has Whole Foods as a client. Consumers benefit by being able to purchase Whole Foods groceries online and get same-day delivery without leaving their home. Whole Foods benefits by reaching a new audience and driving incremental revenue at little to no extra cost. Instacart earns revenue by marking up the food price to consumers and by charging consumers a nominal fee. Everyone wins!
- *Parasitic relationships.* In this relationship, the consumer and middleman tend to receive benefit while the seller may or may not benefit. For example, Just Eat, GrubHub, and Seamless (note that GrubHub and Seamless are two distinct brands but owned by one entity) benefit the consumer by allowing them to order home-delivery food from a variety of restaurants, hence greater selection and convenience for the consumer. Each of the aforementioned Internet middlemen benefit by receiving a commission that ranges from 12 percent to 14 percent of the sale. The seller benefits from gaining new incremental sales, but may not generate incremental profit because of the commission paid to the middleman. If the restaurant fails to account for the commission in their marginal costs, then it could result in their losing money on the sale. If the restaurant's profit margin exceeds the cost of the commission paid the Internet middlemen, then it's a symbiotic relationship, but if the commission exceeds their profit margin, then it becomes a parasitic relationship.
- *Cannibalistic relationships.* This relationship is an example of Schumpeter's "creative destruction," where new and innovative business models make it impossible for some businesses to survive. In this relationship, one party loses while the others gain benefit. Take Uber, for example. The consumer wins through lower prices and greater convenience. Uber wins by generating revenues and profit. Existing car transportation businesses lose because

> A good Internet middleman provides added value the traditional producer can't provide and offers a service the consumer desires.

they are at a competitive disadvantage (higher operating costs, government taxes, and less convenience). This, of course, is capitalism at its finest, but for those whose industry is imperiled, it may not seem that way.

Fitness Internet Middlemen

The health/fitness industry now finds itself entrenched in a digital middleman economy, a march led by ClassPass (classpass.com), Dibs (ondibs.com), and Fitreserve (fitreserve.com) in the U.S. and PayAsUGym (payasugym.com) in the United Kingdom.

According to the *2016 International Fitness Industry Trend Report—What's All the Rage* released in the late fall of 2016 by ClubIntel, approximately 13 percent of fitness businesses indicated they participate in an Internet middleman–driven program, up from 3 percent in 2013. While 13 percent may not appear to be a large percentage, in some markets such as New York, Chicago, and Los Angeles, the percentage of health/fitness facilities that participate in one of the Internet middleman platforms exceeds 25 percent.

The U.S. market leader and the first to really introduce the health/fitness industry to the digital middleman phenomena is ClassPass, originally branded as Classtivity. ClassPass extends fitness consumers a subscription (membership) giving them the opportunity to engage in unlimited fitness classes or gym visits each week at over 8,000 studios around the globe for between $105 and $200 USD a month (price varies by market). In addition to offering consumers the ability to access unlimited classes for a set monthly fee, consumers can also purchase limited monthly access, such as access to three, five, or 10 classes of a reduced rate (e.g., five classes for $55 a month in Dallas, $60 in Chicago, and $75 in New York). As of year-end 2016, ClassPass had enrolled over 3,000 studios and clubs in over 35 markets, including the U.S., Canada, and the UK. According to recent releases, ClassPass books over 1.5 million reservations a month.

> The U.S. market leader and the first to really introduce the health/fitness industry to the digital middleman phenomena is ClassPass.

According to its founder, ClassPass is a monthly membership subscription that extends consumers a unique opportunity to work out at multiple clubs and studios, and for operators, brings them enhanced market awareness, new client traffic, the possibility of obtaining new members, and of course, incremental revenue growth. By purchasing a membership subscription ranging from $105 to $200 a month, a consumer can go online and reserve a spot in a class from among various clubs/studios (e.g., barre, cycling, dance, HIIT, Pilates, and yoga) in their market. The only caveat for the consumer is that they are limited to three visits at any one studio or club over the course of a month. For consumers who purchase limited access packages, for example five classes a month, the number of visits they can make to a specific facility are limited to two visits.

Since ClassPass first entered the market, more start-up Internet middlemen have entered the fray, both in the U.S. and the UK. One of the more successful competitors is a company called FitReserve based out of New York, which launched in the fall of 2014. FitReserve (like ClassPass) offers consumers a monthly subscription that allows them to register for over 13,000 classes at approximately 300 studios throughout New York City and Boston. FitReserve

> In 2016, approximately 13 percent of fitness businesses indicated they participate in an Internet middleman–driven program, up from 3 percent in 2013.

allows consumers to visit each of their partner studios up to four times per month, more frequently than members of ClassPass. FitReserve also does not "black out" classes, meaning FitReserve members have access to a studio's entire schedule. ClassPass, at least at this moment, does not provide their members with total access to classes at their partner properties. Finally, FitReserve has created three limited access offers that serve the needs of fitness consumers from novice to enthusiast. The three options are: access to five classes a month at $79 (just under $16 per class); access to 10 classes a month at $149 a month (approximately $15 a class), and 20 classes for $249 a month (approximately $14 a class). These rates are designed to be more in line with the pricing offered by clubs and studios, therefore, supporting each business's value proposition. Recently, FitReserve created prepaid packages that allow consumers to prepay for 10 classes a month for a three-month period ($425), six-month period ($799), or one-year period ($1,499). Like ClassPass, FitReserve offers fitness consumers a discount ranging from 25 percent to 60 percent on the cost of an individual class/session/visit if it were purchased directly from a facility.

The third major entrant to the U.S. fitness Internet middleman market is a company called Dibs. Dibs' value proposition is more closely modeled after platforms such as Open Table for restaurants and, to some degree, many of the hotel booking platforms. The founder of Dibs describes the platform as a B2B (business to business) platform with a consumer-facing value proposition that leverages real-time dynamic pricing—a principle used by airlines and hotels. The platform allows studios or clubs to establish their minimum and maximum price points and then uses sophisticated algorithms to offer consumers real-time prices based on the studio's/club's supply-and-demand dynamics: if the demand is high and supply is low, the price received goes up; if the demand is low and supply is high, the price drops. Dibs generates its revenue by taking a percentage of the fee that the studio obtains from each registration, similar to what GrubHub and Just Eat do in the restaurant segment. From the consumers' perspective, Dibs will allow them to book a class at any partner studio with the understanding they will pay a price based on the studio's price parameters and supply-and-demand dynamics. To gain access to the most popular classes, consumers will pay more, and for less popular classes, they will pay a lower fee (think: airlines' capacity and load models).

In the United Kingdom, PayAsUGym.com is the UK market leader in offering the health/fitness club industry a viable Internet middleman platform. PayAsUGym, as of the fall of 2015, has 2,300 gyms and studios and 430 pools in its network. Like most of the other fitness Internet middlemen, PayAsUGym offers consumers a subscription model that allows them to acquire access to the over 2,300 gyms and studios and 430 pools in their network. The platform allows consumers to select from a single one-day pass, a five-visit pass, a 10-visit pass, or a monthly pass. For example, if you reside in London, a monthly unlimited pass can range from under 50 pounds to just over 100 pounds, while a single-visit pass might run from as little as 5 pounds to over 12 pounds. Similar to its compatriots in the marketplace, PayAsUGym has rules regarding how its members or clients use its network of gyms, studios, and pools, specifically:

- Members are limited to three visits at any one facility and one visit to what they have designated as premium gyms, studios, and pools.
- Members can freeze their membership for 10 pounds a month, during which time they can make one visit to a network affiliated property.
- Members must reserve space in classes. Classes can be restricted by the participating gym or studio. Once a reservation is made, if the member fails to cancel at least 12 hours in advance, they are charged a cancellation fee.

Five Tips to Successfully Partnering With Fitness Internet Middleman

1. *Don't devalue your brand by discounting so deeply (e.g., accepting a 50 percent to 60 percent discount).* Negotiate for a price that reflects the value of your studio/club to the consumer. Remember, these Internet middlemen need your studio or club to enhance their value proposition, so stand hard and negotiate for more. Even a few dollars more per class can make a significant difference. The more studios or clubs under your umbrella, the more negotiating power you have. By way of example, in video gaming, the digital platforms get 30 percent, and the developer/publisher gets 70 percent. Massage Internet middleman Soothe takes 30 percent of revenues and gives the remaining 70 percent to the massage therapist. While neither is ideal, it's sure better than what is being offered by the middlemen players in today's fitness market. In the restaurant business, the Internet middlemen take a percentage of revenues, in some cases as much as 14 percent, but even in these instances, the restaurants control the pricing. As the seller, you are incurring all the risk and all the cost, so make it worth your while.

2. *Protect your existing client base.* Your clients are paying fair market price to engage with your studio or club. They shouldn't be shoved out to accommodate a lower-paying guest who has no intent of becoming a member or regular client. This means that if you have classes that presently have high member occupancy levels (greater than 80 percent), don't open them up to low-paying guests. Take, for example, the yoga studio that was getting 75 percent of its visits from ClassPass. In essence, the guests were pushing out the regular clients. Furthermore, make sure you provide more for your members and regular clients than you do for the Internet middleman guests, such as making sure the members get the top instructors, the most convenient times, the signature classes, the best music, and the most care. If you do this, you are likely to lessen switching behavior and not sacrifice high-margin business for low-margin business.

3. *Limit your offerings.* If you look at these Internet middlemen services from a yield management perspective (what airlines and hotels do with seats and rooms), then you can lessen the parasitic elements of the relationship and garner greater benefit. First, limit these guests to those classes with low occupancy percentages (below 50 percent occupancy). If offering gym time, place a limit on the hours they can access the gym. One studio told us that when they limited the classes that ClassPass guests could use, the guests tended to leave negative online reviews (another reason these transient guests are not good for business). If all your classes have occupancy levels under 50 percent, then you have an entirely different set of issues to address, and ClassPass or another Internet middleman might be what you need.

> Make sure you provide more for your members and regular clients than you do for Internet middleman guests.

Second, make sure that any classes you are opening up to Internet-driven guests are at times that are unappealing to your existing client base. You might even consider creating a few classes you know members will never visit and use these as your offering for Internet-driven guests. Third, manage the process. Monitor usage and occupancy on a daily basis so you know when the guest traffic may be interfering with your client's experience. This management process is referred to as yield management.

4. *Create a conversion incentive.* If you want more visitors to convert to your studio or club, then find an incentive that says to them it's a better value to be a regular client than a temporary visitor. This involves demonstrating the benefits of being part of your community (e.g., access to best instructors, best classes, etc.) rather than a transient visitor. Remember that these Internet-driven guests will pass through your door no more than three times in a month, so you need to capture their heart and feet at the onset. Like the famous line from the Tom Cruise movie *Jerry Maguire*, you have to get them at hello.

5. *Monitor switching behavior.* One of the dangers that come with any Internet middleman service is the possibility of existing clients, even the loyal ones, abandoning you for the middleman. If they can get what they perceive to be an equivalent offering for half the price, they will. Those who are at the highest risk of switching are infrequent users (less than twice per week), the quiet ones, and those you don't have as much personal contact with. It is critical that you monitor usage and identify the high-risk clients and reach out to them. Don't give them a reason to abandon you.

A New Digital Marketplace for Generating Studio Clients

In 2016, MyFitnessPal, a fitness app owned by Under Armour, partnered with the largest cloud-based scheduling software platform for the health/fitness industry. The partnership allows individuals who use the MyFitnessPal app to find, book, and schedule class at nearby fitness facilities within the Mindbody network. Mindbody presently serves over 50,000 fitness clubs and studios, and the MyFitnessPal application has over 100,000 users. This new marketing platform is neither Internet middleman nor coupon site, but rather a hybrid model that leverages a popular mobile fitness app and a popular B2B cloud-based scheduling platform to introduce fitness enthusiasts to classes and programs at different facilities. In early 2017, Mindbody partnered with Google Reserve, an online platform that allows consumers to use Google's search capabilities to find fitness studios near them and consequently book classes at those studios.

Reflections

Digital marketplaces, whether they be Internet middlemen or digital coupon sites, offer operators an opportunity to drive new customer traffic, often at levels unachievable using other more traditional marketing approaches or even digital marketing approaches. Concurrent with the opportunity they present to grow business, they also present risks that can negatively impact a health/fitness facilities brand and result in unprofitable business. If managed correctly, both Internet middlemen and digital coupon sites can provide operators with a means to extend their reach and grow their business.

Selling the Value Proposition of Your Facility

9

"Selling is a noble profession."

—Robert Dedman, Sr., founder of ClubCorp

Chapter Objectives

The health/fitness facility industry has been about membership sales since the inception of the modern era in 1947, when Vic Tanny launched his first commercial health club. Since then, the health/fitness club industry's business mantra, so to speak, has been about sales. Whether it was Bally's in the 1960s and 1970s, 24 Hour Fitness in the 1980s and 1990s, or Lifetime Fitness and Planet Fitness during the early part of the 21st century, industry leaders have emphasized sales, be it membership sales or product sales. This chapter undertakes an in-depth look at sales, beginning with a discussion of the mathematics of sales. The chapter then reviews the sales process (e.g., membership or facility privileges), starting with lead generation and ending with sales closure. The chapter concludes with a discussion of corporate sales, online membership sales, and sales management.

Understanding the Mathematics of Selling Facility Access

As was discussed previously, a thriving customer base (e.g., membership) is at the heart of every successful health/fitness facility. The challenge of sales is to make sure that the facility's membership level continues to grow, thus ensuring the overall profitability and vitality of the club. According to the published report, *IHRSA's 2015 Profiles of Success, The Annual Industry Data Survey of the Health and Fitness Industry*, clubs that were members of IHRSA had an average net membership growth of 4 percent in 2014, which was nearly identical to the growth seen in 2013. The reported growth among the IHRSA clubs that were sampled for *Profiles of Success* contrasts with to data reflected in IHRSA's 2015 and 2014 *Health Club Consumer Report*, in which overall membership for the industry from 2012 to 2013 grew by 1.7 percent in 2014. From 2012 to 2015, as reflected in IHRSA *2016 Health Club Consumer Report*, the compound annual growth rate for members was 1.7 percent. As reflected in the data, the sample of clubs reported in *IHRSA's Profiles of Success* experienced membership growth more than double this number. Based on data from 2015, as reflected in Figure 8-1, the average IHRSA member club sold approximately 738 memberships in

> A thriving customer base is at the heart of every successful health/fitness facility.

2014, with the numbers ranging from 175 to as many as 1,254 memberships over the course of the year, based on the facility's business model. In fact, some of the larger club big-box operators that have membership levels of over 10,000 have to sell as many as 5,000 new memberships annually to maintain a stable membership base.

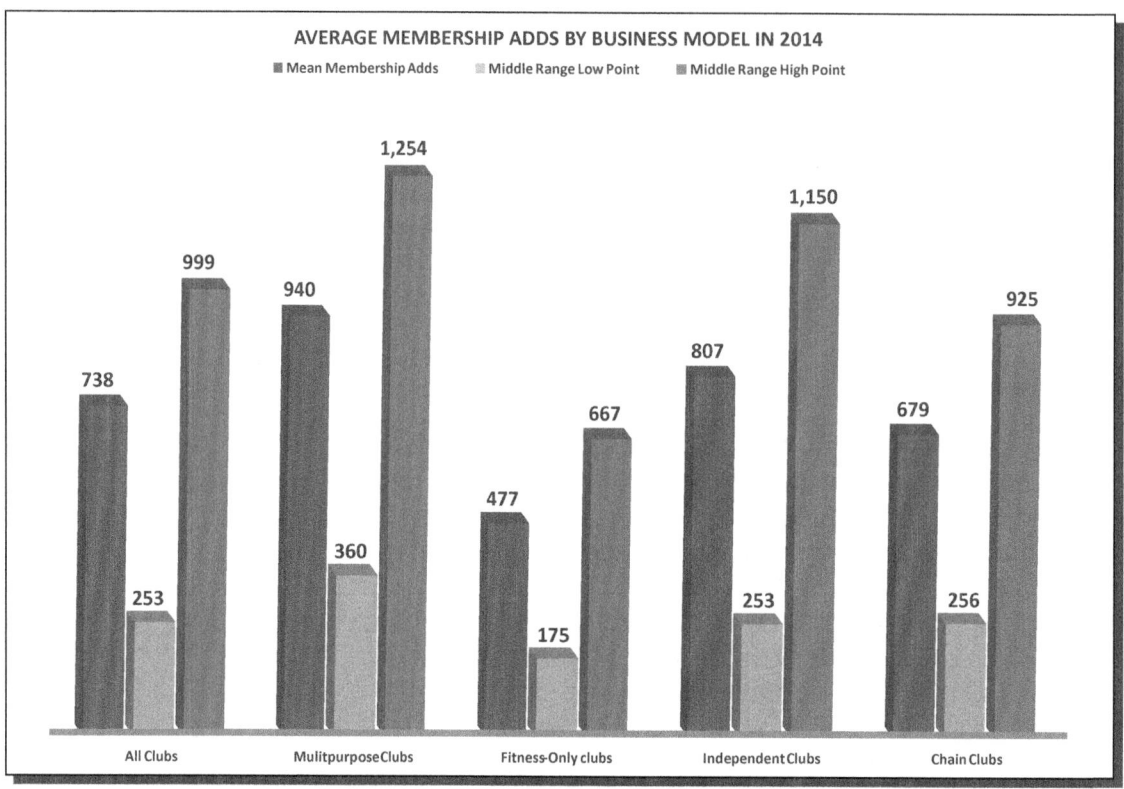

Figure 9-1. Average membership adds by club business model in 2014

What is most evident from the aforementioned figure is the fact that most clubs, whether small or large, fitness-only or multipurpose, independent or part of a multi-chain company, are generating new sales on an annual basis at a rate ranging from 20 percent to 50 percent of their base membership. The point to note is that when it comes to membership sales, health/fitness clubs have established a historical pattern requiring a relatively high rate of membership sales. In 2014, the median number of total sales for clubs over 60,000 s.f. was 1,241 memberships, if that number is converted to a weekly sales rate, the average club over 60,000 s.f. ends up having to sell 24 memberships a week. If the 2014 annual sales ranges indicated in Figure 8-1 are examined, the average sales required on a weekly basis for the majority of clubs would range from a low of three sales a week to a high of 24 sales a week.

It is interesting to note that some of the clubs operated by big box players, such as Lifetime Fitness, LA Fitness, 24 Hour Fitness, and Planet Fitness, often have to sell between 50 and 100 memberships a week. As such, depending on the club business model (budget, low-priced, midlevel, premium, or luxury), a high performing salesperson will sell between three (luxury club) and 30 (low-priced) memberships a week. In other words, most clubs will need to have at least two full-time membership salespeople. In fact, high sales-volume clubs, such as Lifetime Fitness or LA Fitness, will often need to have as many as 8 to 15 membership salespeople.

Understanding the Sales Continuum

Membership sales involve three distinct stages: identifying leads, qualifying prospects, and closing the sale. Each of the sales stages is like a filtering screen, with the number of people at each stage being screened until it becomes a smaller population with better qualifications for membership. As Figure 8-2 indicates, the sales process can begin with 100 leads that then develop into 30 prospects, and finally result in 15 sales.

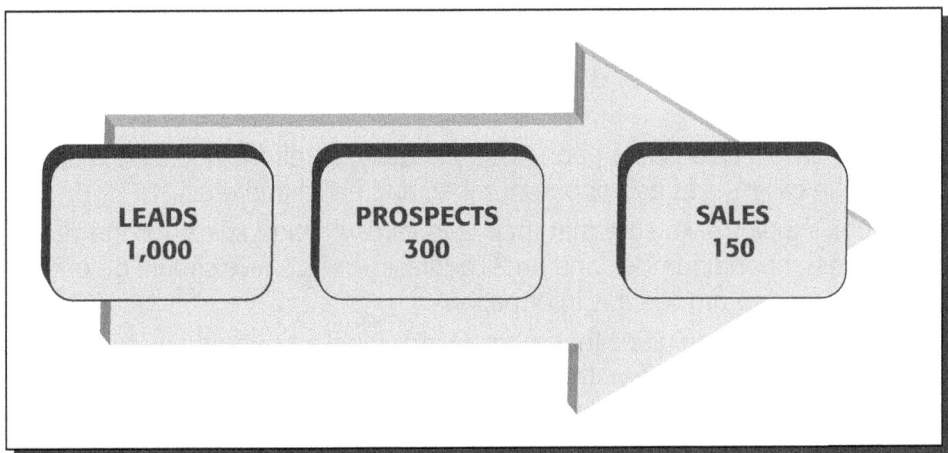

Figure 9-2. Membership sales continuum

Using the aforementioned example as a reference, a facility that requires 20 new memberships a week and has a closing ratio of 50 percent (means the club is able to convert half of its prospects to members), would need to generate a total of 40 prospects a week. To generate 40 prospects, the facility knows that it will need at least 200 leads each week, meaning that only 20 percent of leads will express sufficient interest in what the club has to offer to be classified as a prospect for membership. When examined in this perspective, the sales process requires a business to create a large reservoir of leads in order to produce the required level of membership sales. While the percentages tend to vary from market to market and club to club, the average club can expect to convert 20 percent to 50 percent of its leads to prospects and 20 percent to 80 percent of its prospects to actual members.

Sales Stages Up Close and Personal

❑ Identify Leads

A lead is defined as an individual whose demographics (personal characteristics and behaviors) align with the demographics of a club's audience and who has given an indication that they might be interested in a club's or studios offering. Examples of leads include individuals who complete a lead card, individuals who respond (i.e., call, complete an information form online, or possibly walk in) to a promotion, and individuals who respond to an email blast, text message, or social media promotion. Leads are just that, individuals who, when exposed to the features and benefits of the club, may become more interested and eventually decide to join the club.

The process of generating leads should be considered the top priority of the sales team and the marketing department. By generating a sufficient reservoir of leads, a club can be assured of generating a sufficient number of sales. The lead generation process involves two distinct phases. The first phase is marketing, which is designed to generate consumer interest and awareness of the club, while the second phase is lead tracking or database mining, which enables a club to place a name and general contact information with a lead. Because marketing was reviewed in the previous three chapters, this chapter does not reexamine this aspect of lead generation. Instead, this section details some of the key aspects of database mining (personal information gathering), including the following:

- Every time a club gets a phone call or inquiry, an effort should be made to get the caller's address, phone number, and email address.
- Clubs should make sure that their lead cards provide space for the name, address, phone number, and email address. An incentive should be offered to the lead to provide this information.
- For any marketing piece that gives an individual an opportunity to respond to the marketing offer, the response form should require the lead to provide the appropriate contact information (e.g., at the minimum name and email address).
- If a club is engaged in a health fair or community event, contact information should be collected on every individual with whom the club comes into contact.
- A club should make it a habit for its sales staff to collect the required contact information on every individual with whom they come in contact.
- If a club utilizes guest passes as a marketing strategy, the guest pass should include space for the contact information.
- If the club extends complimentary guest passes or trial visits using its website or Facebook page, then as part of the process of obtaining the guest pass, the inquiring individual should have to provide that person's contact information. An example of this online approach is used by Lifetime Fitness. On Lifetime's website, shoppers are offered an opportunity to try out one of their clubs for free. After clicking on the button that says "Try Us for Free," shoppers are taken to a page where they are asked to provide their name, email address, phone number, and region of the country in which they reside, along with identifying their primary interest, after which they hit the submit button. By completing this short form, the shopper receives a guest pass, and Lifetime Fitness has obtained the information they need to pursue that person as a lead.

> The process of generating leads should be considered the top priority of the sales team and the marketing department.

As the aforementioned points indicate, generating leads is a full-scale effort that ties marketing to information collection.

❑ Qualifying Prospects

A prospect is a lead who has expressed a need for or an interest in what the facility has to offer. A prospect differs from a lead in that that person has been identified as having a desire, need, or want that can be filled by the services offered by the club. Accordingly, a prospect is more likely to become a member or client than someone who is a lead.

A prospect is more likely to become a member or client than someone who is a lead.

Turning leads into prospects and qualifying people as prospects occur in many ways. The most critical factor in qualifying prospects is to talk with the lead/individual and identify that person's desires, needs, and wants and then get that individual to express it to the salesperson. Several core marketing strategies exist that are relatively likely to be successful at generating prospects, including names received from member referrals, guest visits from distributed guest passes and trial memberships, and referrals from corporate accounts. In the end, to turn a lead into a prospect requires that a conversation take place between the salesperson and the individual who is a prospective club member, during which the salesperson picks up an indication that qualifies the lead as a prospect. Among the more common indications that a lead is now a prospect are the following:
- An individual indicates verbally or non-verbally that the club offers them an opportunity to fulfill a specific need.
- The individual has been a member of another health/fitness facility in the past.
- The individual has a history of being physically active and is looking to resume exercising.
- The individual is looking for a way to achieve a personal fitness or weight-loss goal.
- The individual contacted the club, based on the recommendation of a current club member.
- The individual has taken a tour of the club or has utilized a guest pass they received and has actually used the club.

When a salesperson determines that a lead has become a prospect, it is that person's responsibility to move forward with the final process of closing the sale.

❑ Closing the Sale

The steps involved in closing a sale refers to the process of moving a prospect to the point where that person decides to make a purchase. As such, the procedure of moving a prospect to membership usually takes place in one of two ways. The first way is what is referred to as relationship selling, in which prospects choose to make a purchase (e.g., become members), because the facility has demonstrated to them that the club can fulfill an expressed need. The second method is often referred to as "high-pressure sales," a practice in which the sales representative, using specific "closing" techniques, applies pressure on the prospect to join.

Relationship selling is likely to generate the highest closing percentage (i.e., the percentage of prospects who actually make a purchase, such as acquiring a membership) and the highest quality member. "High-pressure" closing techniques (i.e., high-volume sales), on the other hand, usually produce lower closing percentages and low-quality or often unqualified buyers (e.g., members).

The primary differences between the two basic methods of closing are as follows:

- *Relationship selling.* This approach to selling is preferred by those clubs that are interested in bringing in members who will remain members. A technique that is most frequently practiced in premium clubs and boutique facilities, this approach to turning a prospect into a buyer (e.g., member) involves an in-depth process of uncovering a prospect's needs and then connecting the club's services to the expressed needs of the prospect. The process involves creating a series of benefit statements that enable the prospect to see how the club can fulfill their expressed needs (e.g., benefit them). This process does not intimidate the prospect, and it does not employ discounting or other rehearsed processes to move the prospect to membership. The relationship sale involves the following simple steps:
  ✓ Asking questions of the prospect so that that an individual's needs can be determined. Normally, at least two expressed needs must be identified. The questions usually start as open-ended probes (no definitive answer) and then move into closed probes (yes- or no-type questions).
  ✓ When a need is uncovered, the salesperson will reiterate what has been said and then create a benefit statement that connects a particular service to the expressed need of the prospect.
  ✓ When a prospect confirms (verbally or non-verbally) that the benefit exists, then the membership salesperson will confirm the benefit.
  ✓ After confirming the benefit agreed to by the prospect, the membership salesperson will repeat the process to inject yet a second confirmed benefit into the process.
  ✓ Once the prospect has confirmed that the club benefits them in at least two ways, the membership salesperson will ask for the sale in a non-intimidating way.

  Relationship selling is far more effective in generating quality sales, whether it be membership sales or another type of sale, than high-pressure selling. Typically, such a technique will lead to a very high closing ratio. The primary challenge with relationship selling is the time it can take to close the sale. While "high-pressure" sales tactics are geared to close a prospect immediately, it is not uncommon for a prospect exposed to relationship selling to take a day, or even longer, to make the final purchase commitment.

- *High-pressure closing.* Clubs and salespeople who use this process start by asking questions that uncover a prospect's needs and vulnerabilities.

> Relationship selling is far more effective in generating quality sales, whether it be membership sales or another type of sale, than high-pressure selling.

While uncovering the prospect's needs is an important facet of this process, what is more important is identifying the prospect's vulnerabilities, such as time, cost, support of a significant other, self-confidence, etc. When the salesperson identifies the vulnerability, the next step involves having the salesperson use a rehearsed script that has a proven record of intimidating and pressuring the prospect, based on that individual's specific vulnerability, to sign up for membership or purchase a personal training session.

Vic Tanny clubs, which initially opened in 1947, were the first facilities in the health/fitness club industry to leverage this approach to sales. The Vic Tanny organization later introduced the high-pressure methodology to a host of other clubs and club companies, including Health and Tennis Corporation (rebranded later as Bally Total Fitness). In an article that appeared in Time magazine in 1961, the leadership of Vic Tanny was quoted as saying, "If you fail to get an appointment, then take a gun out of your desk and shoot yourself." This quote exemplifies the intensity and ethics that underlie clubs that rely on "high-pressure" selling.

The following example can help illustrate this process. For example, a salesperson has uncovered the fact that the prospect has low self-esteem and does not perceive that he has sufficient funds to join the club. A possible high-pressure closing technique that this salesperson might use is to say, "You don't want to continue feeling so bad about yourself, so why don't you join now and get started with changing your image? I know you don't think you have the necessary funds for joining, so the club is prepared to offer you a $0 initiation fee and reduced membership dues of $19 a month if you sign up for a two-year contract."

Sales representatives who use this approach in an attempt to turn a prospect into a member tend to discount the price of the memberships that they are selling and present multiple closing lines, before allowing the prospect to leave. In many cases, the sales representative will tag team with another representative to further intimidate the prospect. While this approach to closing is considered inappropriate by much of the industry, consumers are likely to face such strategies from clubs who depend on high-volume sales.

Staging the Prospect Tour

Previously in this chapter, the various strategies for moving a lead to a prospect and then turning that prospect into a member were discussed. Among the many approaches employed in the health/fitness facility industry in this regard, the club tour is the strategy that has been shown to produce the highest percentage of prospects from leads and also to generate the highest percentage of memberships from prospects. A salesperson who has mastered the art of the club tour can be assured of generating quality prospects and membership sales. As a rule, staging the winning club tour involves the following steps:

❑ Begin the Tour With a Relaxed Q-and-A Session

When salespeople first meet prospects, they should sit down in an open, non-intimidating setting. The salesperson should offer the prospect a beverage or water and then proceed to uncover the following key pieces of information:

> The club tour is the strategy that has been shown to produce the highest percentage of prospects from leads and also to generate the highest percentage of memberships from prospects.

- Are they currently a member of a health/fitness club, and if so, what activities do they currently pursue?
- If they are currently a health/fitness club member, why are they considering another club?
- Do they currently exercise? If yes, what kind of exercise do they currently perform? If not, what factors do they feel will help them be more likely to engage in a regular exercise program?
- What is it that they would like to accomplish as the result of joining the club? Do they have any specific goals that they have established?
- Are there any activities that are of particular interest to them, such as group exercise, yoga, running, weights, etc.?
- Do they have a friend or associate who currently uses the club?
- Do they prefer a competitive or social atmosphere or are they more inclined to prefer a relaxed, private atmosphere?
- How much time do they have available at the moment to learn about the club and the benefits it can offer?

The aforementioned inquiries are the most critical questions that should be asked. Obtaining answers to these questions will not only increase the chances of the membership sale being closed, but the information can also prove invaluable in arranging the prospect's first visit to the club. In addition, this information can be used by a club's fitness department to help identify those members who may be at a heightened risk for attrition. Furthermore, the information obtained by this process can help the entire club to focus on improving membership growth and retention.

❏ Start the Tour at the Prospect's Hot Spot

It is critical that the club tour begins in the area that the prospect indicates as having the highest importance to them. It is important to keep in mind that because the "club shoppers" of today are very knowledgeable about clubs, giving them a "canned" tour is one of the worst things that a facility can do. As such, it can turn them off and detract from the club staff's level of professionalism.

Club operators should remember that most "club shoppers" have already checked the club out online, including taking a virtual tour of the club, if the facility's website offers one. Accordingly, the tour should be personalized for each prospect, based upon the aspects that the prospects indicated were their priorities in the Q-and-A session. A salesperson should not waste time taking the prospect through the entire club, unless the salesperson asks the prospect first about such a tour, or the prospect indicates they want to see the entire club during the initial Q-and-A session.

❏ Introduce the Prospect to the Experts

It is critical during the tour that the salesperson introduces the prospect to the club's experts in the prospect's indicated areas of interest. If the tour has been scheduled in advance, arrangements should be made for the experts to be present during the tour. For example, if the prospect is interested in group exercise, then the group-exercise coordinator or an instructor should be made available. If the prospect is interested in free weights, then the fitness director or a personal trainer should be present to answer the prospect's questions. If the tour is unscheduled and an expert is not available, an effort should be made to get the fitness director or an available fitness professional to show the prospect around the fitness area.

A salesperson should never lead off a tour of the fitness area by saying, "This is our cardiovascular room," or "We have Life Fitness equipment." These statements are obvious. Furthermore, to the club shopper, who has probably been a member of other clubs, or visited other clubs, either in person or online, these statements indicate a lack of professionalism and understanding of the prospect's specific needs by the individual leading the tour.

Instead, the salesperson should focus on what sets the facility apart (e.g., unique points of differentiation) from all the other clubs. The salesperson should address what the key differences mean to the prospect and why the individual should join the club. At this time, the salesperson should focus on the benefits provided by a club membership that are unique to the prospect.

❑ Extend an Invitation to Try the Club That Day

The salesperson should make sure that the prospect is given the opportunity to use the club that day, if the prospect desires. Better yet, the prospect should be connected with another member or a staff person who can provide any needed assistance.

❑ Introduce the Prospect to a Member

From a sales perspective, nothing is stronger than the testimony of a member in showing a prospect the value of a club. The introduction between a prospect and a member should be short and brief. The club should always keep in mind that a satisfied member can be their best salesperson.

❑ Provide a Brochure/Club Information Package

Every prospect should be provided with the club's brochure, which will enable certain parts of the information presented in the brochure to be referenced during the tour.

❑ Use the Club's Program/Events Calendar

The tour should include a brief review of the club's program and/or events calendar. It is important that the prospect gets a feel for the various activities that the club sponsors, along with a sense of the traditions of the club. This situation also represents a great opportunity to allow prospects to ask any questions that they may have and it gives the salesperson an excellent chance to elaborate on the level of activity in the club.

❑ Ask for the Sale

After the tour is completed, the salesperson should sit down with the prospect in a non-intimidating setting and ask if the prospect has any further questions. After answering the prospect's questions, the salesperson should ask for the sale. If the tour went as planned, the sale will be made. If the sale doesn't occur, the salesperson should make sure that the prospect is given a guest pass and then follow-up with the prospect at a later date to see how the individual's visit to the club went.

Corporate Sales

Corporate membership sales involve a unique process and situation in the health/fitness club industry. In urban markets and suburban markets with a high concentration of businesses, corporate membership sales present an unparalleled opportunity for facilities to develop large reservoirs of leads and prospects, which often result in high closing rates. For many health/fitness clubs, the corporate market represents a majority of their membership growth opportunity. According to *IHRSA's 2007 Profiles of Success*, clubs at that time, on average, generated 15.6 percent of all membership sales from corporate memberships, a quantitative measure that is no longer available in IHRSA's more current research reports. It should be noted that for some clubs and club companies, whose primary markets are in high-density business settings, corporate membership sales can easily account for 50 percent or more of overall sales. Since the process of generating corporate leads and prospects, along with the process of closing those leads, is different than the typical sales process, this section of the chapter reviews the most effective approaches for selling memberships to the corporate market.

> For some clubs and club companies, corporate membership sales can easily account for 50 percent or more of overall sales.

❑ Learn and Understand the Corporate Mindset Toward Club Memberships

The club's first step should be to learn about the corporate fitness arena and what corporations are seeking when they purchase corporate memberships. In this regard, the University of Michigan's Health Management Research Center produces an annual report detailing the current research on the benefits and costs associated with worksite wellness. This report offers a useful overview of the cost benefit data that corporations typically consider when they evaluate the need for a corporate membership program. Another excellent resource is the 1998 IHRSA publication, *The Corporate Market: How to Capture and Keep Corporate Memberships*.

In general, most corporations purchase corporate memberships for one of the following reasons:
- Use it as a tool for recruiting high-caliber talent. Many corporations indicate that fitness memberships are a benefit frequently sought by new employees.
- See it as a means to help improve employee morale and productivity.
- See it as a means to reduce healthcare-related costs for the company (current research validates the fact that low-risk employees cost companies considerably less than moderate and high-risk employees).

- See it as means of improving the image of the company.
- See it as a means to reduce worker's compensation costs, absenteeism, and work-related disability.

While most companies pursue a fitness membership program for their employees based on one or more of the aforementioned factors, they also evaluate a corporate fitness membership program based on a club being able to provide one or more of the following services:

- Corporations look for health/fitness programs that address fitness, nutrition, health education, health screening, and behavioral change.
- Corporations look for membership packages that offer more than just memberships, e.g., provide access to specific programs, such as back care, weight loss, stress management, health fairs, health-risk screening, etc.
- Corporations look for clubs to provide them with reports on employee usage of both the club in general and specific programs in particular. These reports should provide the corporation with detailed insight into how much use their employees are getting out of the membership.
- Corporations prefer a situation where clubs offer a variety of options for billing, including the options of dues sharing with employees, payroll deduction, discounted fees, etc.

❑ Identify the Club's Corporate Market

Once a club gains an understanding of the corporate market, its next step should be to develop a list of the most appropriate corporations to pursue. Among the most effective means for accomplishing this task are the following:

- *Identify which corporations are represented by the club's current membership.* This step can be done by doing a search of the club's membership roster and identifying the corporations listed on the membership applications. If the club has a good relationship with its members, it might also consider having discussions with those members of the club who are known to be affiliated with local companies. Clubs should always keep in mind that its members are the best source of information in this arena.
- *Compile a list of companies that fall within the club's market area.* While not as effective as utilizing the club's membership roster, this strategy is a good alternative. Clubs should focus primarily on those companies that are located within a few miles of the club.
- *Find out who the decision-makers are at the corporations.* In most cases, either the human resources department or the medical department is involved in the process of deciding whether to purchase health/fitness club memberships for their company's employees. In smaller companies, it might be the manager or president of the company. Of course, if a club has a good relationship with its members, it may be able to find out from them who the key decision-makers are at the companies at which they work.
- *Learn about the company's values and needs.* As part of the process, clubs should make an effort to learn as much about a company as it can. The club can start the effort by searching the company's website. The best approach in this regard, however, is for a club to talk to its members who

Corporations look for health/fitness programs that address fitness, nutrition, health education, health screening, and behavioral change.

are employed by the company. The club should learn as much as it can from these discussions with its employees.

❑ Develop a Corporate-Presentation Package

> A club needs to prepare a professional presentation about the club and the value of corporate memberships.

Most companies, both small and large, expect the sales process to feature professionally presented materials. As a result, a club needs to prepare a professional presentation about the club and the value of corporate memberships. Among the key elements that such a presentation package might include are the following:

- *Develop a PowerPoint or digital presentation.* A PowerPoint or other digital presentation should be put together that not only tells the story of the facility, but also integrates information on the benefits of fitness and wellness for the corporation.
- *Make the presentation company relevant.* The materials should be customized to the respective company with which the club is dealing.
- *Have a printed presentation package or digital presentation on a flash drive.* The facility should leave a professionally done package with the company after its presentation is completed. In this regard, the most recent trend is for a club to provide a flash drive with the digital presentation that includes an embedded link to the facility's website.
- *Get away from a standard corporate discount package.* The club should avoid making its presentation a discount presentation. The facility's primary goal during a presentation should be to increase the perceived value of what it has to offer the company.

❑ Get an Audience at the Corporation

This step is often the most challenging aspect of corporate sales. Similar to the typical membership sale, converting a lead into a prospect can be a demanding task. Furthermore, getting an opportunity to meet with the corporation can be a long tedious process. Clubs experienced in corporate sales have found the following approaches to be effective in getting the club's foot in the door:

- *Arrange for a member referral.* The best approach for getting an audience at a corporation is for a facility to have one of its existing members introduce a designated person from the club to the company decision-maker by setting up an appointment for them. If members cannot set up an appointment for that person, then the member should be asked to at least provide an introduction for the salesperson.
- *Build relationships in the community.* If possible, appropriate staff members from the facility should join the local chamber or business-networking group. They should establish relationships that they can later use to help get them an audience at the targeted company.
- *Forward a personalized invitation.* If the company contact is known, the club should forward an invitation inviting them to the club for a special presentation. The invitation should be compelling and eye-catching. The

more professional and out-of-the-ordinary it is, the more likely it is to get the company's attention.

- *Always confirm an appointment with a follow-up call.* Whether the facility's appointment is obtained by an invitation or a personal introduction, the club should be sure to follow-up by phone and/or email to confirm the appointment.

❏ Make the First Appointment a Learning Experience

In corporate sales, the first appointment is not designed to close the sale, but rather as a means to learn about the company's needs and wants (sound familiar?) and to present general information on the benefits the club can offer. At this meeting, typically more time is spent learning about the company than presenting information on the facility. The basic goal of this first meeting should be to have the company agree to have the club forward a proposal specific to the company.

❏ Forward a Customized Presentation

Upon completion of the initial meeting, the facility should prepare a customized proposal on membership for the company. The proposal should be relevant to what the club has learned about the company. The proposal might include an invitation for the contact to use the facility or possibly an invitation that allows the company to send its employees to the club for a week's complimentary usage. Some facilities have developed special activities at the club, such as featured evenings for the targeted companies. In any event, the facility should make sure to follow-up its proposal with a call to confirm that its proposal has been received. The call should include an inquiry about when a good time to follow-up might be.

In corporate sales, the first appointment is not designed to close the sale, but rather as a means to learn about the company's needs and wants and to present general information on the benefits the club can offer.

❏ Maintain Contact

Once its proposal has been forwarded to the company, the club should be vigilant with following up. The facility will often find that it may take a few months between the time it forwarded its initial proposal and the next meeting it has with the company.

❏ Be Prepared for Additional Meetings and Counterproposals

When pursuing corporate sales, the club needs to be prepared for the fact that it will typically have to deal with additional meetings and revised proposals. It is a rare event that a club's first proposal becomes the one the company accepts.

❏ When Closing the Sale, Throw a Party for the Company

Once the company agrees to the club's proposal, then a special function should be held at the club in honor of the company, welcoming the company to the facility.

❑ Make Sure to Assign a Corporate Representative

Over the years, clubs have found that it is essential for them to assign a staff person to represent the account and maintain ongoing contact with the company representative once the contract has been signed. More often than not, corporations need and want hand-holding. Accordingly, facilities should make sure that they have a staff person meet with the designated corporate representative on a regular basis. These meetings should include updates about the level of usage by company employees and other relevant data to the company representative. Maintaining regular contact with the company can help assure ongoing support from the corporation.

It is important to understand that corporate membership sales are a high-reward and high-risk approach to membership sales. While corporate sales can lead to a relatively large number of sales, they can also often lead to high level of member turnover.

Sales Management: Creating a Culture of Sales Success

The clubs that constantly achieve membership sales success, not to mention achieve their sales goals related to other services, such as personal training, are fully aware of the fact that sales must become part of the facility's culture. The most critical part of creating a sales culture is to establish disciplined sales-management practices. In the health/fitness facility industry, a disciplined sales management approach would encompass several activities, including the following:

- *Identify and appoint a sales manager.* It is extremely important that a staff person be accountable for the club's overall sales performance. The sales manager should be the individual who helps establish sales goals, leads sales meetings, offers coaching and instruction for the sales staff, and otherwise supports the efforts of the sales staff.
- *Establish sales goals for the team and individuals.* The sales manager, working with ownership and/or management, needs to establish annual, monthly, weekly, and even daily sales goals for the sales team and individual sales staff (e.g., membership and personal training). Many facilities set goals, based on the number of membership units sold or personal training packages sold. The wise sales manager, however, focuses on sales goals founded in dollar volume. The individual and team sales goals that are established should be somewhat of a stretch, so that if they're achieved, the club exceeds its baseline sales parameters for being successful.
- *Monitor and track sales performance.* The sales manager should implement a system that allows the club's sales performance to be tracked on a daily, weekly, monthly, and annual basis. The system should enable the sales manager and sales staff to identify positive and negative sales trends.
- *Conduct weekly team and individual sales meetings.* The sales manager needs to have weekly sales meetings with the team that focus on results, challenges, and solutions. Concurrently, the sales manager needs to meet individually with their sales team members to provide support, coaching, and education.

Sales must become part of the facility's culture.

- *Create special incentives.* Sales are filled with highs and lows. Sales managers need to create incentives that reward exceptional performance and also help drive performance during down times. While these incentives can be ongoing, in many cases, they should be designed to be employed during specific time periods.
- *Recognize success.* Sales managers need to realize how important recognition is to salespeople. Accordingly, a means to recognize individuals who perform well should be designed and implemented. Such an undertaking can produce very positive results.
- *Compensate the sales staff, based on performance.* Salespeople need to be compensated, based on how well they achieve their individual and team sales goals.
- *Integrate the sales team with the operations team.* Club managers and sales managers both need to realize that the greatest level of membership sales success comes when the sales team and the operations team work together. Unfortunately, some facilities forget this precept and create organizational silos (individual pockets of focus), in which membership sales are not connected to the other areas of the club. An effective sales manager will realize that the entire club staff can have a positive impact on the success of the sales department and will do whatever is feasible to integrate the two.
- *Hold the sales team collectively accountable.* The club manager needs to hold the sales manager accountable for the facility's level of sales performance against the predetermined sales plan. By the same token, the sales manager should hold the sales staff accountable for their individual and team performance.

The New Normal: Online Prospecting and Sales

Over the past several years the health/fitness club industry has seen rapid development in the use of online prospecting and sales systems. This trend not only has reduced the number of salespeople employed by a club, but, in many instances, has eliminated them entirely from the process. Beginning with the advent of "budget clubs" in Europe and "high-volume, low-price clubs" in the United States, membership sales have moved out of the hands of a trained sales staff into the realm of the "cloud." With the advent of the boutique fitness facility market, sales of training packages and classes have also moved online. This new approach to sales relies on the following three critical factors:

❑ Attracting Prospects With a Very Low Price

Industry practice over the last few years has shown that if a club is able to effectively market itself through an attractive pricing offer (typically under 20 Euro or $20 a month), then it does not need to have sales staff involved in such tasks as generating leads, providing tours, and conducting sales sessions. All factors considered, it appears that when the price is low enough, a club can generate a plentiful quantity of leads and prospects, without the involvement of a sales team.

❑ Demonstrating the Club Value Proposition Over the Internet

With the advent of 3D technology and interactive modeling, facilities are able to provide prospects with virtual tours of the club online. In addition, websites can go beyond just providing virtual 3D tours. They can also provide member testimonials, class schedules, staff qualifications, etc. In essence, with the proper technology, everything that was once done in person in the club can now be done online.

❑ Allowing a Prospective Member to Apply and Pay Online

With the advancements in technology and online payment systems, clubs are able to have their entire membership application and dues-collection process conducted and completed over the Internet. This approach involves having the member actually complete an online application for membership, including providing the necessary payment information. After the membership application is completed and the payment method is approved, members receive their initial new-member information online. Shortly thereafter, they also receive their membership card and related materials in the mail. Examples of clubs that successfully leverage this approach to membership sales include the Gym Group, a leading budget club operator in the UK; McFit, a leading budget club operator in Germany; and Blink, a high-volume, low-price club chain owned and operated by Equinox Fitness. In all three of these examples, these chains:

- Offer memberships at low cost (less than $20 a month and less than 20 euros a month).
- Perform extensive Internet and social media-based marketing, an effort that promotes their price and the great value proposition.
- Have elaborate websites that allow a prospect to tour their clubs, view their offerings, and obtain any information that might otherwise be critical to the decision to purchase a membership. Prospects can see the club, view member testimonials, and even observe parts of the club life.
- Have an online membership application and payment process.

None of these clubs have a dedicated sales staff. Each of these companies generates, on average, between 5,000 and 10,000 members per club, and, in many instances, even more.

Reflections

As elucidated by the information presented in this chapter, sales are a continuation of a club's membership and marketing efforts. More importantly, sales are a by-product of disciplined business practices that require a detailed system of checks and balances.

PART 3
Engaging and Retaining Clients in the Health/Fitness Facility Industry

Chapter 10
Member and Client Retention and Tenure

Chapter 11
Customer Loyalty: The Art of Staging Memorable Customer Experiences

Chapter 12
Creating a Service Culture That Drives Customer Loyalty

Chapter 13
Programming Essentials: A Primer for the Health/Fitness Facility Industry

Courtesy of Exhale, New York, NY

Member and Client Retention and Tenure

10

"Every company's greatest assets are its customers, because without customers there is no company."

—Michael LeBoeuf, author of
How to Win Customers and Keep Them for Life

Chapter Objectives

Members are the heart of every club. Without them, health/fitness clubs would cease to exist. It is a widely held belief in the industry that membership is all about sales. In reality, however, building and sustaining a profitable membership, or client base if operating a fitness studio, requires a balanced approach between the process of selling and retaining memberships.

Membership retention is about engaging members in the club experience so that they continue to stay a member. The more members stay, the fewer the number of memberships a club has to sell. In other words, membership retention involves the process of engaging members in the club experience and consequently, retaining them long after the sale.

This chapter provides an overview of membership-retention data in the health/fitness facility industry. The chapter also discusses what retention and attrition are and how they are measured. In addition, the chapter looks at membership tenure and the value of a member. Furthermore, the chapter details several of the variables known to influence a facility's membership retention level and some of the steps that clubs can take to affect those retention variables.

> Membership retention is about engaging members in the club experience so that they continue to stay a member.

The Industry's Recent Experiences With Member/Client Retention

According to a report published by IHRSA, *One Million Strong—An In-Depth Study of Health Club Member Retention in North America*, the average one-year retention rate for North American clubs for the period 2012 to 2015 was 67.2 percent. After individuals had been members of a health/fitness facility for two years, the retention rate was only 44.4 percent, nearly the same percentage as reported for U.S. clubs over the past decade. What this data indicates is that despite efforts by the industry since the onset of the 21st century to focus on membership retention, the numbers have changed very little (Figure 10-1).

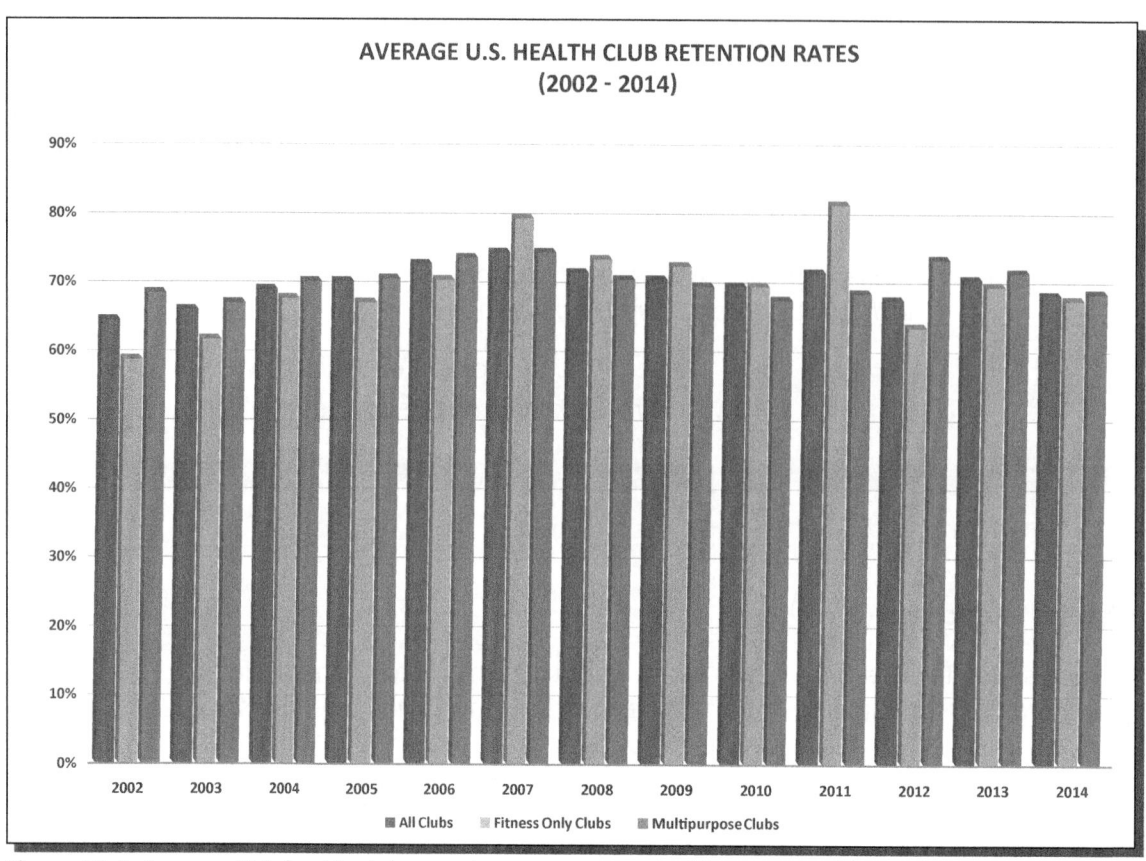

Figure 10-1. Average U.S. health club retention rates as reported in annual editions of *IHRSA's Profiles of Success* (2002–2014)

Over the first five years of the 21st century, the industry made considerable improvement in its average membership retention rate, going from 65 percent in 2000 to 71 percent in 2005. Starting in 2005, and continuing over the next decade, retention percentages for the industry have remained relatively steady. By 2014, the industry's retention percentage was 69 percent. It should be noted, that while the industry's overall average level of retention was 69 percent, some business models, such as independent clubs and clubs over 60,000 square feet, had average retention levels of approximately 79 percent.

The key takeaway from these statistics is that once the industry decided to focus on retention at the beginning of the century, it was able to improve its performance, but after the initial spurt of improvement during the first five years, it was unable to sustain that achievement. It is interesting to note that some of the largest and most prominent players in the industry have been unable to duplicate these industry-wide retention levels. According to Lifetime Fitness's public filings before it returned to the private domain, its retention rates floated between 62 percent and 65 percent over the most recent five years. Equinox, one of the premier operators of quality clubs in the industry, has indicated, off the record, that its retention rates tend to fluctuate around 65 and 70 percent.

It should be noted that a number of club operators have achieved membership retention levels that far exceed the industry averages reported in the IHRSA data. Among the examples of these high performing clubs are the Eastbank Club in Chicago, a large multipurpose club that has historically achieved retention levels exceeding 80 percent; Stonecreek Club and Spa, based in Covington, Louisiana, whose retention levels in 2013 hovered around 84 percent; and the Houstonian in Houston Texas, which has experienced retention levels of around 97 percent over the years.

IHRSA's 2016 Health Club Consumer Report, which is based on a large-scale survey of health club consumers, calculates membership churn, based on the industry's overall membership growth and changes in the membership status of respondents. In 2015, the rate of overall membership churn was 20 percent. As such, the rate of membership churn over the past few years has fluctuated between 19 percent and 23 percent, which would represent an industry retention rate of approximately 77 percent to 83 percent (refer to Figure 10-2). The reason the consumer levels vary from the retention levels reported by operators is because the consumer data only reflects whether a respondent no longer has a club membership and does not look at specific club patterns. Consequently, the consumer data reflects a higher retention percentage.

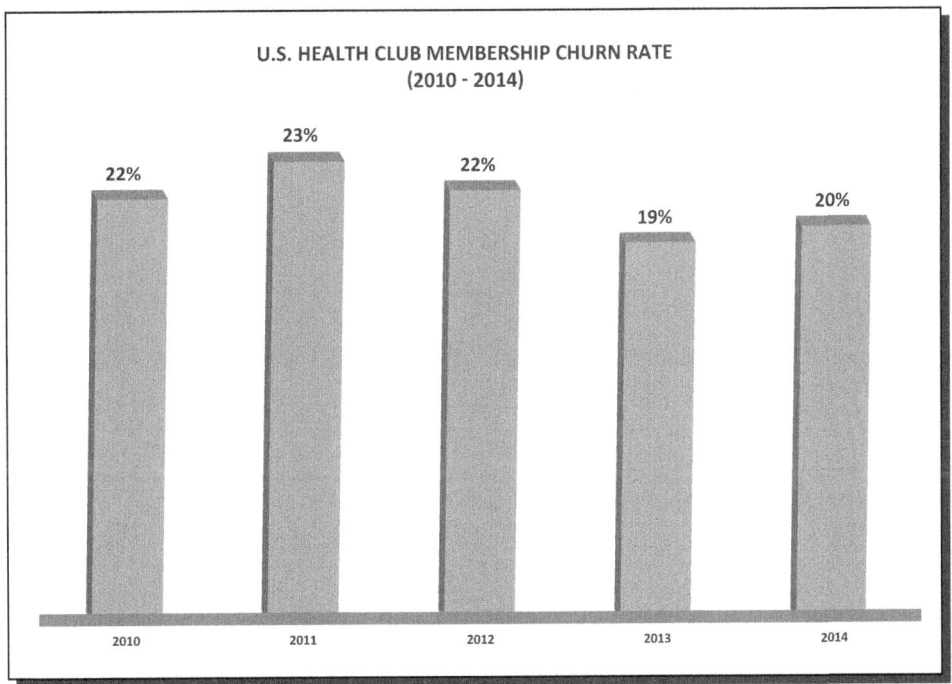

Figure 10-2. U.S. health club membership churn rate (2010–2014)

According to IHRSA's survey data, the average number of membership terminations a facility experiences has declined steadily over the past decade, going from an average of 1,300 in 2000 to an average of 750 in 2009 and an average of 737 at the end of 2014. On an absolute basis, this situation is a significant improvement in the average club's ability to retain members.

According to the aforementioned data concerning the average number of new memberships sold and the average number of memberships cancelled, the average club in 2013 experienced fewer membership terminations than sales, a repeat of what occurred in 2011 and 2012 and a reversal of fortune from the trends experienced in 2009 and 2010.

Figure 10-3 provides a visual representation of net membership growth trends for the industry over the past several years. Unfortunately, as facilities continue to experience slowing new membership sales, due to increasing competitive pressures, retention efforts will need to intensify, if indeed, the industry wants to continue growing over the next decade.

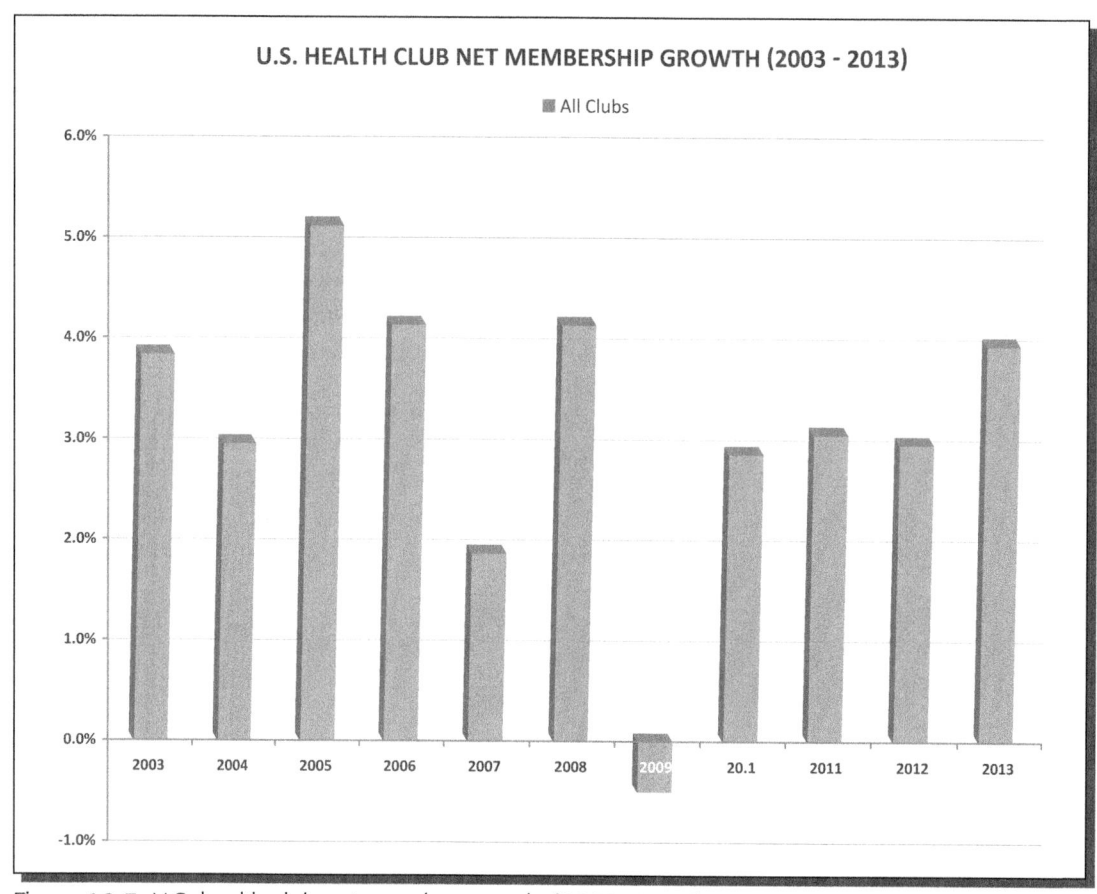

Figure 10-3. U.S. health club net member growth (2003–2013)

The retention data presented in Figures 10-1 and 10-2 are a reflection of U.S. clubs that were surveyed by IHRSA. In a three-part study of the UK health club industry, conducted by Dr. Paul Bedford of the UK and published in *The White Report: A UK National Retention Report*, it was found that the average attrition rate of UK members in 2012 at the end of their first year of membership was 44 percent, which is equivalent to a retention rate of 56 percent.

In 2015, Dr. Bedford conducted a similar retention study of U.S. clubs, using the same methodologies. The results of Dr. Bedford's North American study were published by IHRSA in a report entitled, *One Million Strong: An In-Depth Study of Health Club Member Retention in North America*. The average retention rate after one year for North American clubs was 67.2 percent, approximately 11 percentage points higher than it was for the UK clubs. At the two-year mark, the average retention rate for the North American clubs was 44.4 percent. Figure 10-4 shows the average retention rates in the UK for the period of 2009 to 2012.

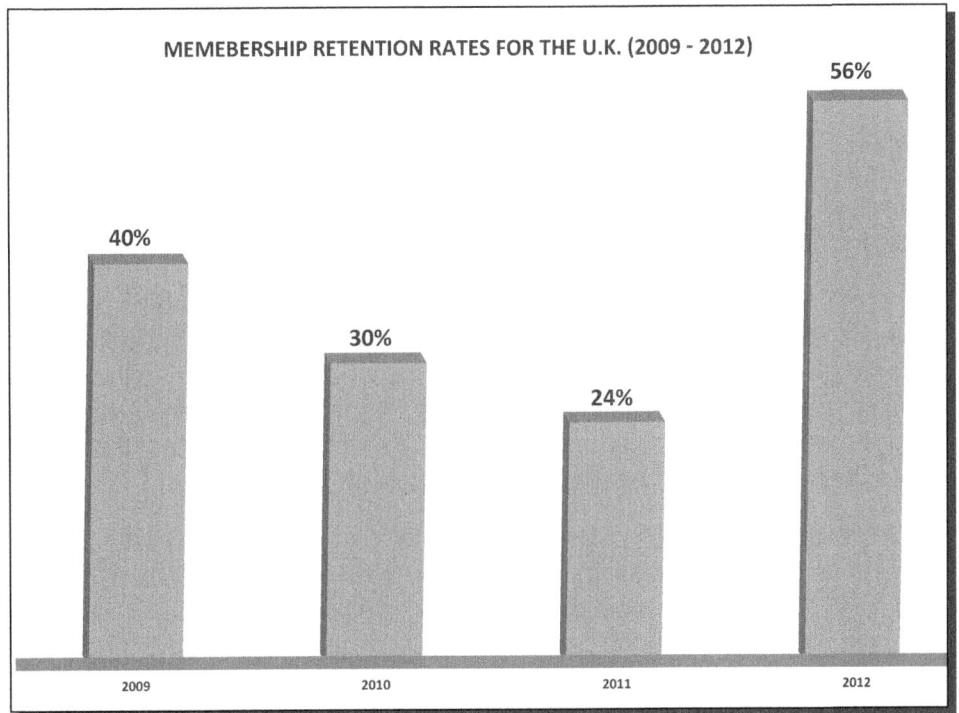

Figure 10-4. Membership retention for UK clubs, as reported in the *2013 White Paper*

Common Industry Definitions of Member/Client Retention

General Definition

Membership retention encompasses the business outcome of a club holding on to (keeping) its members after the initial membership sale, as well as the subsequent enrollment of the new members. As in any successful business, the objective is to retain the highest possible number of clients for the longest possible period of time (e.g., tenure). In the health/fitness facility business, retaining members is as important, or even more so, than retaining clients can be for other businesses, given that members represent the "lifeblood" of clubs.

The health/fitness club business is an example of a form of "closed economic model," one in which clubs are dependent on their ability to monetize their business from a restricted or limited market of clients (e.g., members). As a result, retention becomes a key driver of long-term profitability. As such, the majority of health/fitness facilities measure retention on an annual basis.

A Slightly Different Perspective on Member Retention

In their groundbreaking research on membership retention in the United Kingdom, Paul Bedford, Ph.D., and Melvyn Hillsdon, Ph.D., defined retention as the proportion of members who remain a member for a predetermined period of time (e.g., three months, six months, 12 months, 18 months, etc.). This definition takes into account the variable of a member's tenure. The rationale for tying membership tenure into the retention equation lies in the understanding that the longer a member remains with a facility, the more likely it is that person will spend money in the club.

Common Industry Definitions of Member/Client Attrition

General Definition

Membership attrition, which is the opposite of retention, represents the departure of members from a club. Attrition of customers, like death and taxes, is inevitable for any business. Similar to the other two factors, most clubs would prefer to minimize and delay it as long as possible.

In the case of the health/fitness club industry, delaying and, if possible, preventing the attrition of members can have a very positive impact on a club's financial performance. Each time a member leaves a club, that facility loses a valuable source of income. Furthermore, the expenses involved in replacing that member costs far more than it does to provide an environment that might otherwise help that member decide to remain with the club.

While the majority of clubs measure attrition on an annual basis, some health/fitness clubs monitor this important metric on a monthly basis. These operators believe that monitoring monthly attrition provides an additional perspective with regard to the seasonality of the health/fitness club business. For example, publicly held U.S. companies, such as Town Sports International, often report their monthly attrition figures as part of their monthly calls with investors.

An Alternate Perspective on Member Attrition

In their aforementioned groundbreaking research on attrition and retention in the United Kingdom, Dr. Paul Bedford and Dr. Melvyn Hillsdon defined member attrition (as opposed to their description of member retention) as the rate of member churn or turnover per 1,000 members. Arguably, attrition is best measured not as a percentage of the total membership, but instead as a turnover rate, based on an objective and comparable metric. Such a methodology enables a club to objectively measure its attrition at any point in time. The data reflected in Figure 10-6 is based on this approach to calculating attrition.

Calculating Membership Retention: Two Approaches

❑ The IHRSA Methodology for Calculating Attrition and Retention:

- Begin by calculating the number of members at the beginning of each month. Next, add the number of new members and deduct the number of dropped members, which provides the number of members at the end of the month. This calculation then becomes the number of members at the beginning of the next month.
- Take the number of members at the beginning of each month, and then add them together and divide by 12 (i.e., the number of months in the year). This calculation gives a facility its average member count for the year.
- Calculate the total number of members who resigned during the year.

- Divide the average member count by the total number of members who terminated their membership during the year, which will yield a club's annual attrition rate.
- Subtract the annual attrition percentage from the integer "one," which will provide the club's annual retention rate.

Figure 10-5 illustrates an example of employing IHRSA's recommended approach to calculate a club's annual attrition and retention levels.

	# Members	Resigned Members	Attrition %
January	3,200	60	1.9%
February	3,250	80	2.5%
March	3,300	90	2.7%
April	3,350	85	2.5%
May	3,350	90	2.7%
June	3,325	100	3.0%
July	3,275	105	3.2%
August	3,250	120	3.7%
September	3,275	95	2.9%
October	3,350	85	2.5%
November	3,350	90	2.7%
December	3,300	100	3.0%
YE	3,298	1,100	33.3%

Figure 10-5. The IHRSA methodology for calculating membership attrition and retention levels

❑ The Approach Used by Dr. Paul Bedford, of the UK, for Calculating Attrition and Retention

As part of their research efforts, Dr. Paul Bedford and Dr. Melvyn Hillsdon proposed using a form of "survival analysis" for accurately measuring a club's retention level and attrition rate. Their approach takes into account the time between events, as well as the proportion of members who remain at specific points in time. It is postulated that this approach provides a more accurate reflection of member retention than the methodology recommended by IHRSA, since it takes into account both the proportion of involvement and the tenure of the relationship.

As shown in Figure 10-6, the three clubs (A, B, and C) have identical retention rates after 14 months. It should be noted, however, that with the exception of a few months, club A has been able to sustain a much higher level of retention at key periods of time. As a result, club A has a greater level of cash flow and profitability.

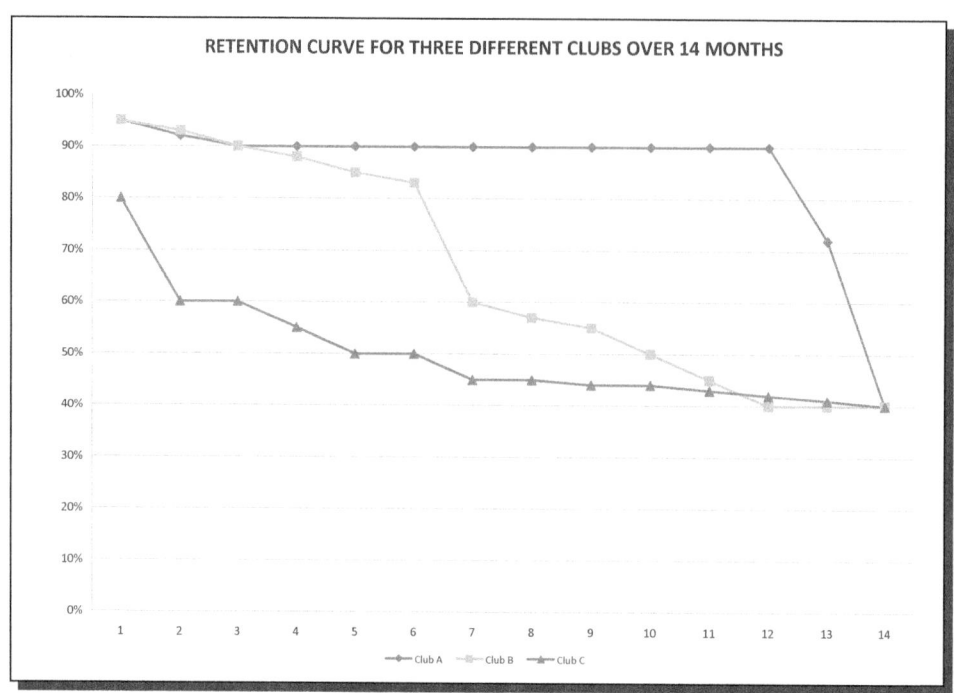

Figure 10-6. Retention curve by club

Membership Tenure in the Health/Fitness Facility Industry

Membership tenure refers to the time that an individual remains a member of a given facility. According to data published in *IHRSA's 2016 Health Club Consumer Report*, the average tenure of a health/fitness club member was 4.9 years in 2015, down from 5.3 years in 2013. Since 2010, membership tenure has consistently hovered around 4.5 years (Figure 10-7).

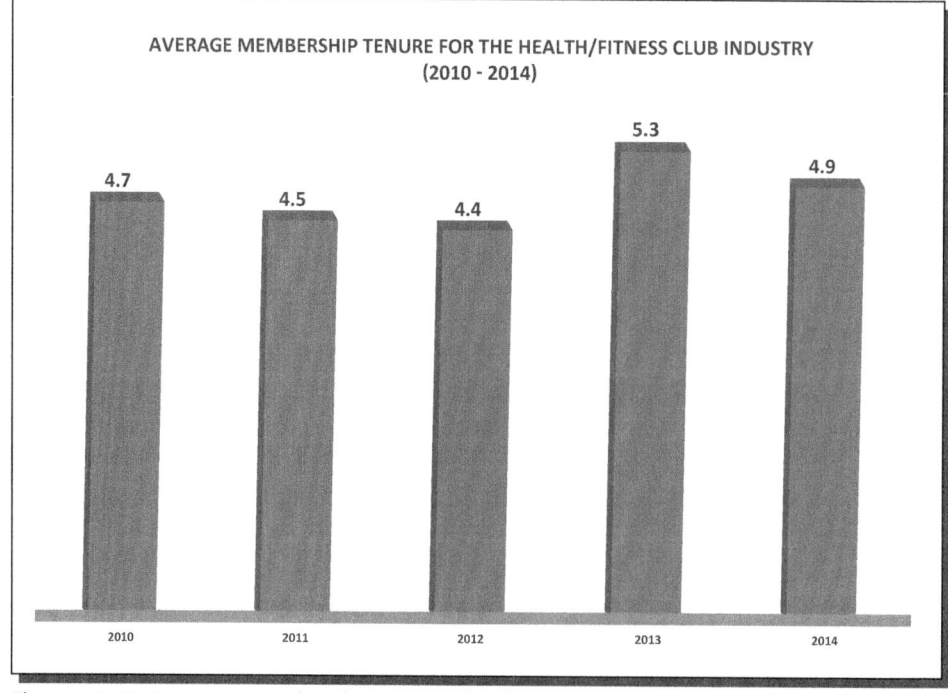

Figure 10-7. Average membership tenure for the health/fitness club industry

Membership tenure is directly influenced by a member's delight with their experience, and consequently, with the level of loyalty that they have established with their facility. As such, data from *IHRSA's 2016 Health Club Consumer Report* points to some relatively interesting relationships between the tenure of an individual's membership and certain behavioral and demographic attributes, including the following:

- *Gender impacts membership tenure.* For the past five years, men have demonstrated greater longevity as members of health/fitness facilities than women, in most cases at least six months to 18 months longer (Figure 10-8).
- *Age impacts membership tenure.* Membership tenure appears to take a dramatic leap once an individual turns 45. By the time an individual reaches the age of 55, membership tenure is double the overall industry average, more than twice what it is for adults 25 to 34 (Figure 10-9).
- *Household income impacts membership tenure.* How much a person earns has a direct relationship to membership tenure, with those individuals with a higher household income remaining a member longer (Figure 10-10).
- *Frequency of usage may impact membership tenure.* Membership tenure appears to be linked to member usage, with those individuals who use the club more frequently having the longest tenure (Figure 10-11).

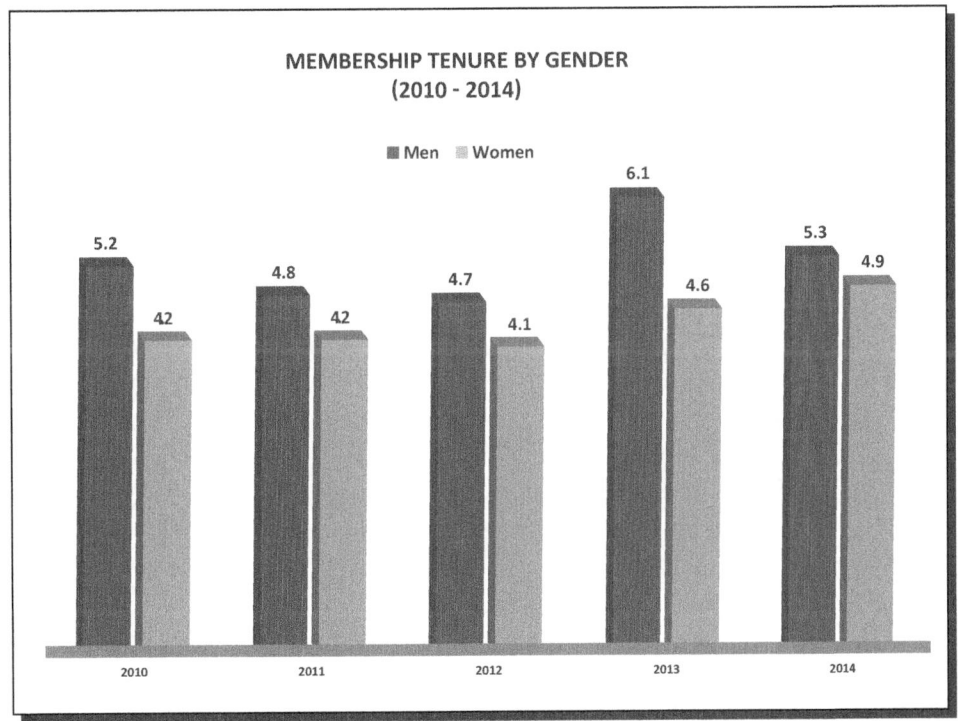

Figure 10-8. Membership tenure by gender

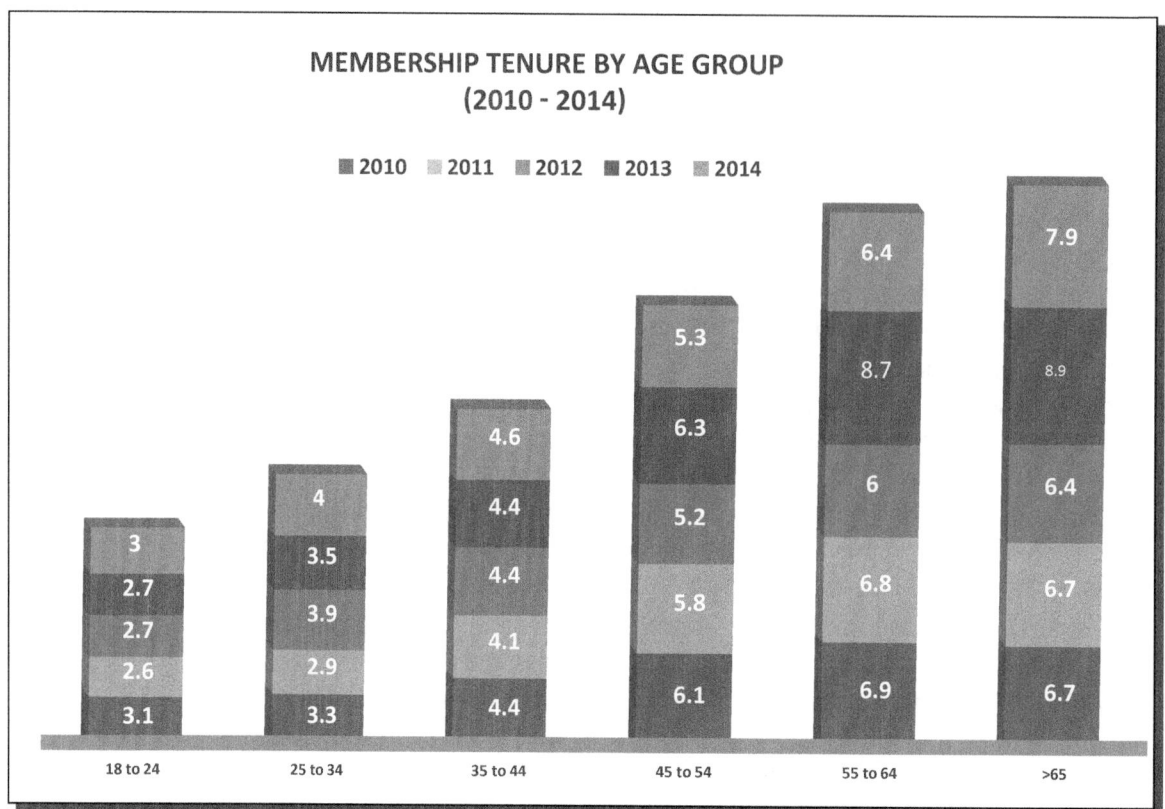

Figure 10-9. Membership tenure by age group

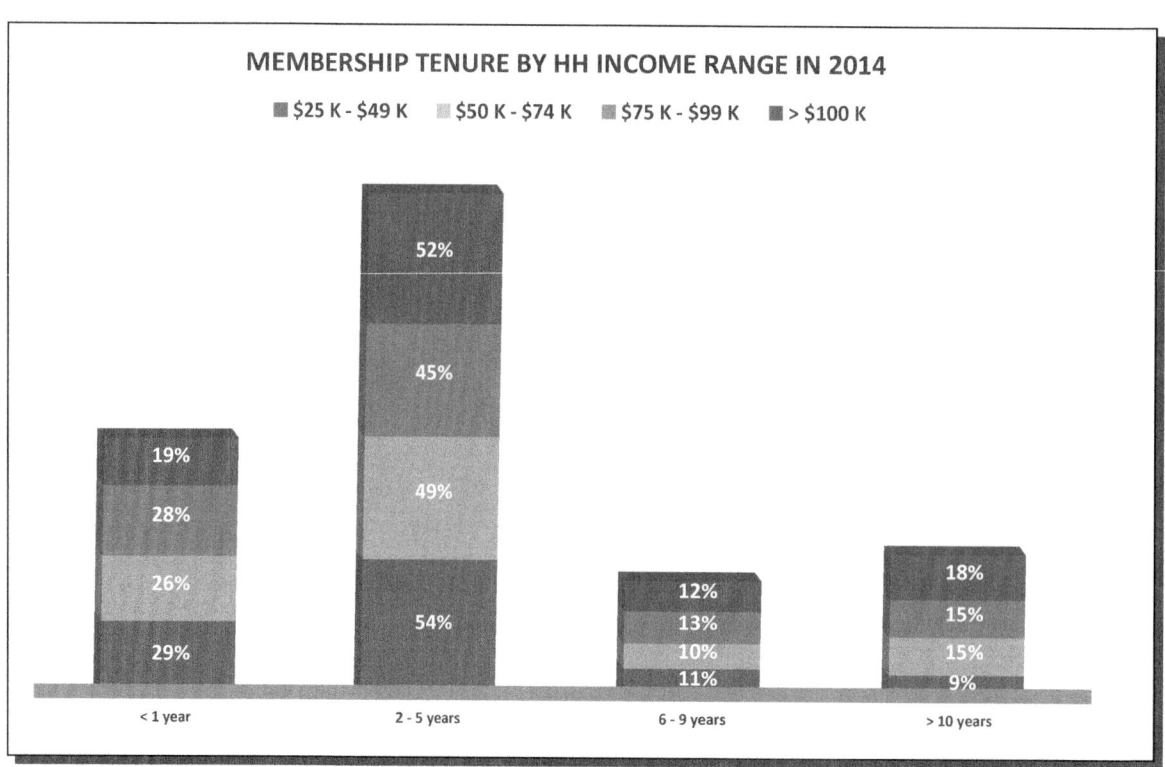

Figure 10-10. Membership tenure by HH income range

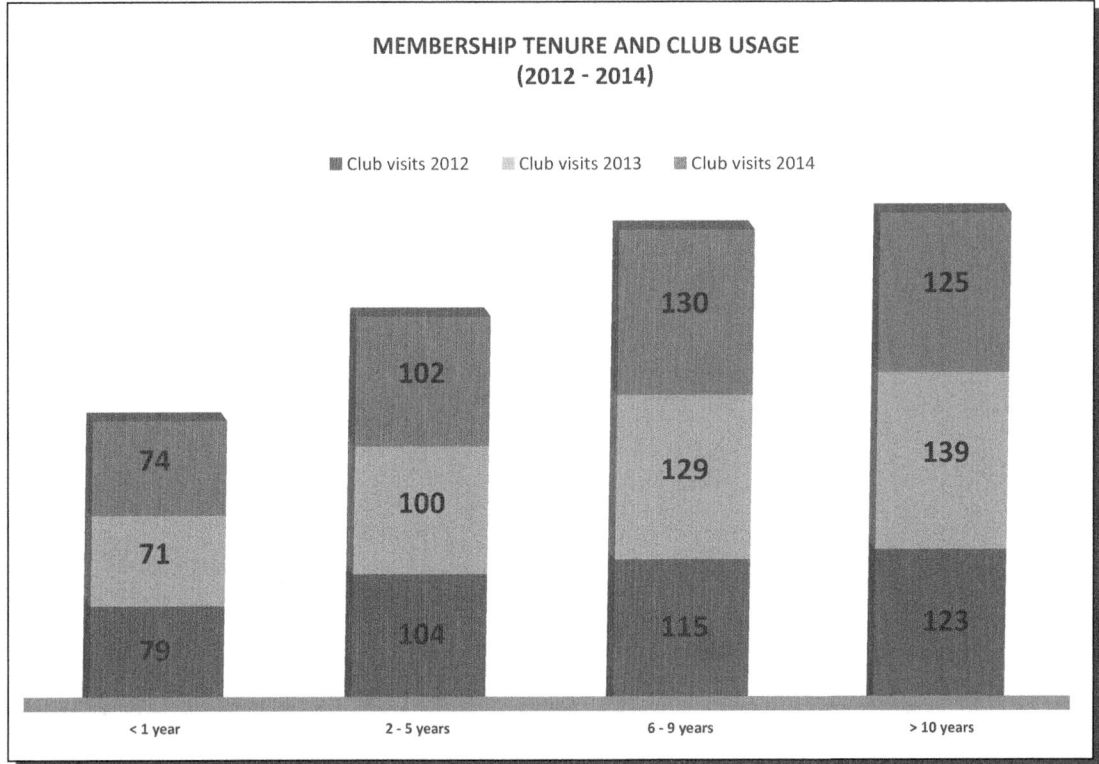

Figure 10-11. Membership tenure and club usage

Membership tenure is intimately linked to membership retention. Obviously, unless a member retains their membership, they will be unable to increase their tenure. To club operators, tenure speaks to the lifetime value of a member, a topic that is addressed in the next section.

The Value of Retention and Tenure

With regard to member retention and tenure, two key questions arise: what is the real value of driving retention to both a club and the industry, and why is it so important? An answer to both inquiries is provided by Dun & Bradstreet, a renowned financial research firm that states that the primary reason most businesses fail is that they either lack sales and/or fail to retain their existing customers.

In the health/fitness facility industry, the value of retaining a customer (i.e., member) is even more significant than in many other businesses, because of the fact that a limitless supply of new customers for their business offerings does not exist. A better idea of the "real dollar" value of a typical club member can be obtained by looking at statistics on average membership pricing and average membership tenure, using data that appears in *IHRSA's 2014 Health Club Consumer Report*. Figure 10-12 illustrates the difference in value between an average club member, a member of a typical fitness-only facility, and a member of a multipurpose facility.

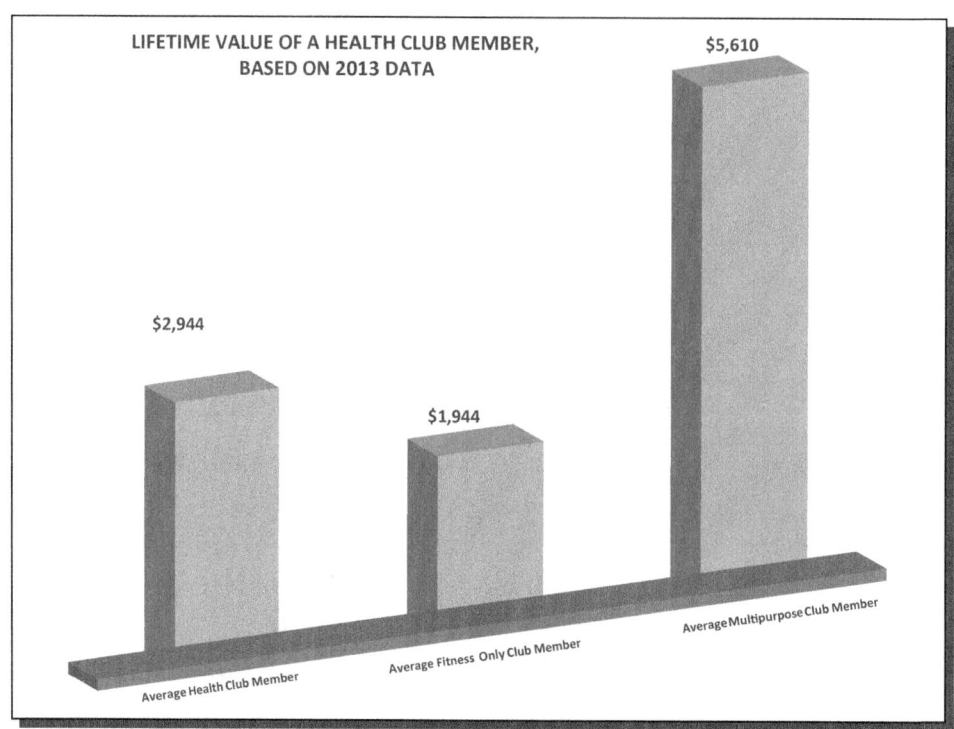

Figure 10-12. The value of a member

In the case of the "average health/fitness club member," according to the statistics detailed in Figure 10-12, the average facility, in 2013, had a value equivalent to $2,944 based on the average tenure of members and the average price the individuals paid for membership dues. It is interesting to note that when the value equivalent of an individual who is a member of a multipurpose club is compared with a member of a fitness-only club, the impact of tenure and pricing can be seen. As such, the member of a multipurpose club is worth nearly three times as much as a member of a fitness-only facility, before factoring in incremental spending on ancillary services.

Given the recent IHRSA statistics (2013 data) that indicate that the average health/fitness club lost 776 members and that the worth of each member, as reflected in Figure 10-12 is $2,944, it would mean that the average club allowed $2.3 million in revenues to walk out the door in the past year. As such, if the average club could decrease its attrition level by just 5 percent, thereby retaining an additional 39 members, that facility would save approximately $115,000 in dues annually.

It should be noted the aforementioned example does not factor in the potential impact of member referrals or consider the value those referrals might bring to the bottom line. It also does not account for the fact that the longer an individual remains a member, the more incremental spending takes place. As such, it is obvious that when a member leaves a club, especially the earlier a member leaves a facility, the club's profitability will be negatively impacted.

All factors considered, the value of retaining a club member becomes even more important during periods of economic volatility, such as during recessionary periods or times when the economy is experiencing financial bubbles. Not surprisingly, when people are less secure about their financial position, they are less likely to spend money on a new purchase (e.g., a club membership). On the other hand, they are also more likely to stay with existing investments.

Given the experiences that occurred during the economic turmoil that occurred between 2008 and 2010, existing members who had already invested in a club membership tended to use their club more frequently. As a consequence, they were less likely to surrender their membership. On the flip side, during the most recent recessionary period, new sales in clubs experienced a significant downturn. As a result, when the economic environment is less than ideal, retention becomes an even more critical factor to the profitability of a club.

Reasons Individuals Express About Remaining as Members

The reasons members give to researchers regarding why they are health/fitness club members do not vary significantly from the rationale that they provide for joining a club. In other words, the expressed intentions of people immediately after joining a club do not shift much from the reasons that drove them to become a member in the first place.

In *IHRSA's 2013 Health Club Trend Report*, consumers indicated a host of reasons for utilizing their membership. The leading reason, shared by approximately 60 percent of members, was the need to stay healthy, followed closely by the desire to feel better about themselves, as well as the need to stay in shape.

A study of 24,000 members of UK health/fitness clubs in the earlier part of the 21st century that was conducted by Paul Bedford, Ph.D., explored the importance of customer interaction to a member's decision whether to remain a member. His research, which involved over 24,000 individual interviews, identified several of the key elements that impact an individual's decision to remain a member, all of which go beyond the reasons detailed in IHRSA's studies. His research uncovered several interesting factors, including the following:

- *Members want to be recognized.* Members indicated that they wanted to be approached by members of the club's staff. Members indicated it was important to be welcomed to the facility with a hello and smile, and, just as importantly, to be recognized for making an effort to get to the club.
- *Members want to know that staff is available to assist them if needed.* The individuals in these interviews made it clear that they valued receiving coaching and guidance, especially when the staff was proactive in approaching them. The members also indicated that staff should not interrupt them when they are actively exercising, and that staff should be sensitive to reading a member's cues about when they wanted to be approached.
- *Members want to be confident in how they use the club.* Individuals interviewed in this study indicated that it is important that they have confidence in how to navigate the club. Members do not want to be seen by other members as being a "rookie" or someone who looks out-of-place in the club setting. Fitting-in is a critical determinant of a member's experience. If members sense that they look out of place, they will be far more likely to resign their membership. One example given in the

interviews conducted by Bedford involved the use of an exercise card. Members reported that they felt embarrassed to have only one exercise card, when other members had either several stapled together or even had a diary for recording their exercise practices.

- *Members want to have a level of competence in how they use the club.* Those individuals interviewed indicated that it was important for them to understand the relevance of exercise to their specific needs. These individuals believe that it is important for them to see the connection between what their goals are and the exercises and programs in which they are engaged.

Reasons Members Give for Terminating Their Engagement

In IHRSA's 2013 Trend Report, the reasons people gave for terminating their membership were explored. While 16 formal reasons were explored, the following five variables rose to the top (Figure 10-13): it was too expensive/I could not afford it; I was not using my membership; I could exercise somewhere else; it was too crowded; and I felt out of place.

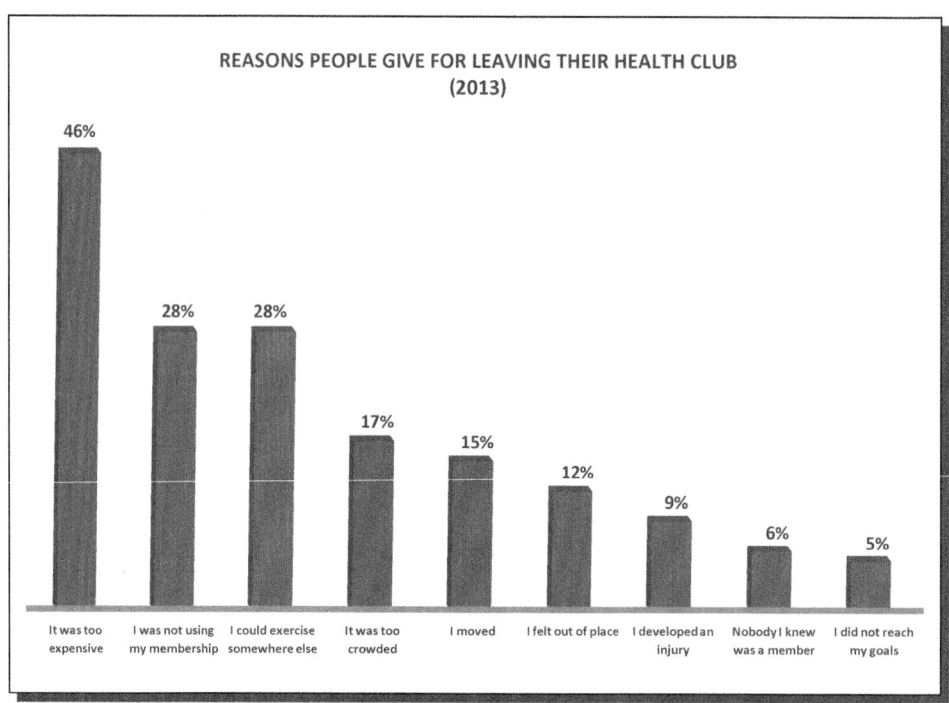

Figure 10-13. Reasons people give for leaving their health club

If the aforementioned reasons that members express for leaving a club are compared to the rationale provided for joining a facility (along with the drivers of member satisfaction, as well as with responses related to consumer perceptions of the club experience), a few responses stand out. The first is overcrowding, which existing members indicated is a barrier to overall satisfaction with the club experience. This factor was also listed as a leading negative perception by consumers. It would appear that the perceptions of consumers are valid. Even worse, it seems that the industry has been unable to overcome an important negative influencer of member satisfaction and membership retention.

The second factor is not achieving their goals, which is among the leading reasons why people join a health club in the first place. Looking at the data, it would appear that while an individual's aspirations to achieve their health and fitness goals is a strong driver of joining a facility, when they don't achieve those aspirations, that failure leads to them deciding not to remain a member.

The most often cited reason for leaving has to do with cost, which also plays an influential role in why they join. When this rationale is considered, along with some of the other reasons given by members for giving up their membership, it can be seen that the cost issue has more to do with what the member gets for what they pay. It is not the actual cost, but whether they use the club often enough. Do they achieve their goals, and do they feel comfortable? When usage is low, results are not achieved. Subsequently, if and when members don't feel comfortable, then they perceive the club as being too expensive.

The aforementioned reasons also indicate that clubs, arguably, may have a responsibility to help members achieve their goals, feel comfortable with their environment, and engage with the club so they are visiting frequently enough to receive a benefit. This premise is supported by data cited in the IHRSA publication entitled, Why People Quit. In this investigation, researchers explored the reasons that people expressed for choosing to resign. This study focused on the elements of the club experience that were influenced by management's approach to the business. The most dominant of these factors was overcrowding, which is something easily within the control of management. A possibly more interesting set of reasons for leaving a facility than overcrowding is an array of three factors that are even more directly linked to management:

- *Dissatisfied with staff.* This factor suggests that the members are either dissatisfied with the qualifications of staff, the level of staffing, or the manner in which staff treats members. In studies conducted by the author's company, ClubIntel, the predominant factors influencing member loyalty relate directly to the level of satisfaction or dissatisfaction with the staff and the approach that staff takes in acknowledging and caring for members.
- *Lack of attention from staff.* This factor is a simple measure to interpret. Members feel that the club staff does not focus their efforts on providing them with assistance and guidance. This issue tends to be exasperated by the industry's current love affair with paid personal training, which has resulted in many clubs forgoing any type of service to members who are unwilling to pay additional fees for guidance.

In research conducted in the United Kingdom by Dr. Paul Bedford, in which he interviewed over 24,000 club members, the issue of attention from club staff also arose. It seems that in many cases, members had not been approached by staff, since they joined their club, which, in numerous instances, had been over one year. Similarly, one of the findings of research on member loyalty that the author's company has conducted with clients, is that one of the most powerful influences on member loyalty relates to the level of attention that members receive from staff. All factors considered, the more acknowledgement and care that members receive from staff, the higher their loyalty scores and, consequently, the higher their retention levels.

> While an individual's aspirations to achieve their health and fitness goals is a strong driver of joining a facility, when they don't achieve those aspirations, that failure leads to them deciding not to remain a member.

- *Unresponsive management.* This factor refers to the inability of management to resolve member issues in a timely and satisfactory manner. It is related to the communication and transparency between management and the members. Similar to the previous factor, this same issue has arisen in research conducted on retention by the author, when assessing the drivers of member loyalty.

In another study commissioned by IHRSA in the early part of the 21st century, members were asked why they resigned, and how these factors would impact their decision to rejoin. They indicated reasons that were very similar to the aforementioned issues, including the following:

- ✓ No exercise partner
- ✓ Lost interest
- ✓ Did not fit in
- ✓ Favorite staff left

These responses, like the others detailed in this chapter, indicate that individuals expect clubs to provide attentive, caring, supportive, and professional staff, programs that help them achieve their goals, and a social environment that motivates them to continue their membership.

Proven Strategies for Improving Retention

The process of retaining members ultimately revolves around the club's ability to deliver experiences that are personally relevant and are delivered with an attentive and caring attitude. Among the proven approaches for driving member retention are the following:

- *Don't sell the club short.* Retention begins at the time of joining. Research shows that members who pay an enrollment fee stay longer than those who don't. Furthermore, the higher the initial fee, the higher the retention level. The key point is that the club operator should assign a real value to the membership experience. If membership is given away, all factors being equal, members will feel their membership is not worth very much. One exception seems to exist to this rule, involving budget clubs, where the dues payment is under 20 euro or $20 a month. It appears that at this low-price point, membership retention may actually increase slightly.
- *Identify the members' fitness needs and focus on getting them to the goal.* The data is clear that with regard to membership retention, it is crucial that members achieve their fitness goals. This process not only involves identifying what those goals are, but also developing a program that provides a realistic avenue for them to be achieved. Finally, all clubs should provide monitoring, support, and encouragement to their members so their members' goals can be achieved.
- *Connect the new member to other members.* Most members express a strong desire to have a partner or to feel a sense of belonging. Satisfying this desire requires getting the members to meet other members and establish friendships. Clubs can accomplish this goal by having the staff introduce new members to other members. They can also achieve this objective by organizing and implementing such undertakings as welcoming

parties, new member/existing member activities, member chat spaces, niche interest groups on Facebook, partner programs, etc. It is interesting to note that among boutique studios this sense of connection or community is one of the key value drivers.

- *Staff and members need to connect.* Clubs need to establish a service culture that is passionate about caring for the members. The staff should be encouraged to meet with members, learn about them, and respond to their needs and feedback. Responsive, friendly, and supportive are three key attributes of an attentive and caring staff.

- *Get the members active.* The research is very clear about the "use-it-or-lose-it" aspect of membership. Members who are more active, especially in the initial stages of their membership, are far more likely to remain members (IHRSA and FIA data both reflect this phenomena). This observation is reinforced by data from IHRSA's Health Club Consumer Report, which shows that members who use the club more frequently have longer tenure. As such, clubs need to establish systems that introduce new members to club-based activities in a non-intimidating way and then track their activity-involvement levels so they can monitor, support and acknowledge each member's efforts to be physically active. Facilities might even consider offering incentive programs tied to activity during an individual's first three months of membership.

- *Be attentive to the members' comments and interests.* Club management needs to establish a system for maintaining an open dialogue with its members. This process should involve the use of such factors as a feedback system, service recovery system, focus groups, voice of the member (VOM) surveys, social media listening and even member committees. The members need to perceive management as being interested in and responsive to their experiences.

- *Keep the facility clean and well-maintained.* While not a primary reason given by members for quitting, research shows that whether the club was kept clean and whether the club kept its equipment and facilities updated had an impact on the desire of individuals to maintain their club membership. Members want to feel that the dues they are paying are going back into the club. Facilities need to keep this factor in mind and let members know when the club is doing something to upgrade its facilities or equipment.

- *Make retention a part of everyone's job description.* All employees, from the membership sales staff to the manager to the housecleaning staff, must view the process of helping retain members as an integral part of their job. Salespeople help retention by not selling the club short and by helping connect members at the time of joining. The fitness staff drives retention by helping members achieve their fitness goals and helping connect the members to other members. The front desk staff can have a positive impact on retention by making members feel welcome and responding to member comments. The house maintenance staff affects retention in a positive manner by keeping the club clean and by looking for ways to respond to member needs.

> All employees, from the membership sales staff to the manager to the housecleaning staff, must view the process of helping retain members as an integral part of their job.

> Retention begins with a culture within the club that focuses on connecting people, creates memorable experiences, and always puts the member first.

Reflections

As facility operators attempt to identify strategies that can help them retain members, they should remember that retention begins with a culture within the club that focuses on connecting people, creates memorable experiences, and always puts the member first.

Customer Loyalty: The Art of Staging Memorable Customer Experiences

11

*"Customer satisfaction is worthless.
Customer loyalty is priceless."*

—Jeffrey Gitomer, American
author and business trainer

Chapter Objectives

In the previous chapter, the value of a membership and the importance of retaining members in driving the profitability and vibrancy of a club were addressed. As research indicates, members either stay in or leave a facility based on whether their experience at the club meets or does not meet their expectations and needs. Research also shows that in the majority of instances, the situations in which member expectations were not met revolved around the connection of members to members, members to the staff, and members achieving their goals.

This chapter explores the importance of the fact that clubs need to establish a culture that fosters intense member loyalty, which, in turn, requires a passionate commitment to stage memorable experiences that meet and exceed the expectations of their members. The chapter examines how individuals who belong to clubs respond to experiences that they encounter as members of a club and the impact that these experiences have on their level of emotional engagement and loyalty. The chapter then reviews the importance of creating memorable experiences. Finally, the chapter details the process of creating the experiences that drive member retention.

> Members either stay in or leave a facility based on whether their experience at the club meets or does not meet their expectations and needs.

Understanding Customer Loyalty and Satisfaction

❏ Defining Customer Satisfaction and Customer Loyalty

Member satisfaction is defined as the collective feeling or sense of fulfillment that members have about their experience with a facility. When members are satisfied with their experience, it reflects the fact that the club has objectively met their needs and allowed the members to achieve the initial expectations that they had when they joined the facility.

Satisfaction is a non-emotional response. It does not create an undying or fanatical desire to continue to use a product or service, or, in the case of a club, to remain a member. What it does refer to is the fact that the club has temporarily met each member's expectations and that unless a better service or experience arises in the market, each member will continue to utilize their current facility.

The potential downside of this factor, from a business perspective, is threefold. First, once a member is satisfied, their expectations change, resulting in a higher level of performance having to be delivered by the club to drive the satisfaction of that individual going forward. Second, member satisfaction only allows a facility to retain the member until such time as either a perceived better experience is offered by the club or another facility in the market brings forth an experience that a particular member may perceive to be better. Finally, it should be kept in mind that member satisfaction does not generate member loyalty. Because it does not fully engage the emotions and passions of the member, it does not create the bond that can either retain members for life or can drive them to spend more at the club.

Member loyalty occurs when a business captures the heart and soul of the customer. The following quote from Lord Burleigh (English statesman, 1521 – 1598) does an excellent job of putting member loyalty in proper perspective, "Capture their hearts, and you have their hands and purses." What Lord Burleigh was saying is that loyal members are those individuals whose heart and soul are one with the club. When members become the apostles and disciples of a facility, or as Ken Blanchard coined in his book, *Raving Fans*. "Raving members" are individuals who have the highest level of retention and who spend the most money in their club.

❑ The Value Equation Underlying Customer Satisfaction and Loyalty

Oscar Wilde once said, "Nowadays, people know the price of everything and the value of nothing." Well, it's the understanding and appreciation of value that drives member loyalty. How does a club first achieve member satisfaction, and then move beyond it to establish member loyalty? It begins with understanding the underlying elements of how a customer, or in the case of the club business, a member, perceives value and how that value creates either satisfaction or emotional passion and loyalty. As such, a member's perception of value can be calculated using the formula reflected in Figure 11-1.

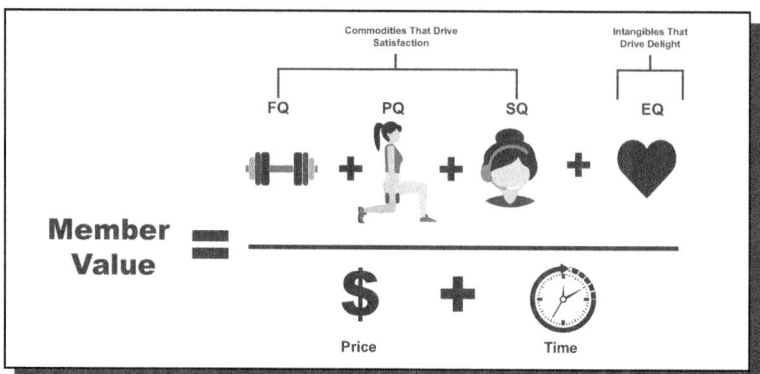

Figure 11-1. Member value equation

Numerator:

- FQ or facility quality is defined by the overall quality of a facility and includes several elements, such as cleanliness, amount of equipment, variety of equipment, accessibility of equipment, design of the facility, condition of the facility, etc.
- PQ or product quality is defined as the overall quality of a club's offerings, based on the expectations that the members have. It includes an array of elements, such as quality of group exercise classes, availability of group exercise classes, variety of programs, quality of personal training program, availability of wellness programs, etc.
- SQ or service quality is defined as the level of service a club provides, based on the expectations of the members, and includes a number of elements, such as smiles, greeting members by name, fast and courteous attention, service recovery, management's appreciation of the members, etc.
- EQ or emotional quality is defined as the level of emotional attachment that is created for the member by the club experience and depends on a variety of elements, such as relationships with staff, relationships with other members, a sense of pride in the club, existence of member tribes, etc.

Denominator:

- Price reflects the actual cash price that individuals pay to use the facility and is comprised of enrollment fees, dues, and, on occasion, fees for extra services. It may also involve whether the payment is made monthly or annually.
- Time reflects the time that an individual must allocate to gain benefit from being a member of the club, which involves elements, such as visits per week, time spent each visit, and any time allocations involved in getting to and from the facility. Time can also be reflected in the availability of programs and whether a member has to adapt their schedule to participate in those programs.

Member satisfaction occurs when the numerator is higher than the denominator. On the other hand, loyalty can only occur when the emotional quality in the numerator is incredibly high. For example, Apple has created an incredibly high level of customer loyalty, because all of the elements in the numerator in its perception-of-value equation are powerful, particularly the emotional quality. An article that appeared in the January 2011 edition of *Advertising Age*, written by Doug Levy and Bob Garfield, indicated that if someone Googles "I love Apple," that individual will get 3.27 million hits, more than any other firm, including Starbucks, which received 2.7 million, Zappos with slightly more than 1.1 million hits, and AT&T wireless with only 21,000 hits.

Everyone is aware of the fact that Apple products are not inexpensive (typically, they're more expensive than comparable products). The key point to keep in mind is that the numerator contributors, when combined together, are far more valuable and powerful than the costs reflected in the denominator. The basic takeaway is that for facilities to establish a high value, they must deliver the facility, product, and service, along with emotional engagement, at a level far greater than the actual cost and time required for a member to use the club.

> For facilities to establish a high value, they must deliver the facility, product, and service, along with emotional engagement, at a level far greater than the actual cost and time required for a member to use the club.

Measuring Customer Satisfaction and Loyalty

The standard approach for measuring satisfaction is to survey the membership on a regular basis, asking a series of questions or proposing specific statements to which members can then respond, using a simple five-point Likert scale, for example, a basic scale commonly employed in surveys. The Likert scale (a simple Likert scale is five points, while more advanced scales can be seven, nine, or 11 points) is a standardized psychometric tool that allows researchers to easily assess respondent answers. By employing this scale, researchers are able to accurately measure the degree of delight, satisfaction, or dissatisfaction that exists around a specific situation, series of situations, or an entire experience. The basic five-point scale is as follows:

> 5 = strongly agree
>
> 4 = agree or somewhat agree
>
> 3 = not sure, or neither agree or disagree
>
> 2 = disagree
>
> 1 = strongly disagree

The most frequently used and quoted metric or indicator of member loyalty is called the "*Net Promoter Score*," a measure that was introduced in 2003 by a Harvard University professor, Fred Reichheld. The term *Net Promoter Score (NPS)* is actually a trademarked title of Reichheld, Bain & Company. The fundamental purpose of the *Net Promoter Score* is to clearly identify those customers and/or members who are actual promoters of a particular business (loyal members, raving fans, etc.).

While Net Promoters are typically determined by using an 11-point scale, the metric can also be applied, using the aforementioned simple five-point Likert scale. A Net Promoter, or a loyal member (raving fan), is a member or customer who rates the club as either a 9 or 10 on an 11-point scale or a five on a five-point scale (Figure 11-2).

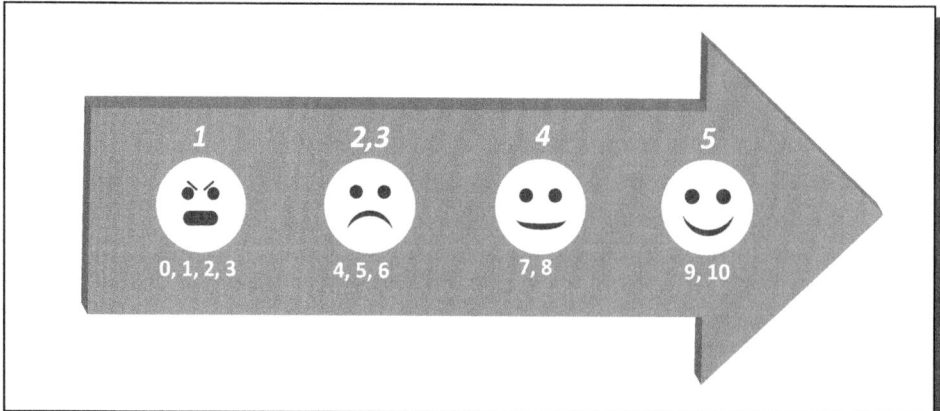

Figure 11-2. The 11-point and five-point scales for determining the *Net Promoter Score* of member loyalty

The *Net Promoter Score* is determined by taking the percentage of members who rate a facility as a Net Promoter (nine or 10 on an 11-point scale and five on a five-point scale) and then subtracting that number from the percentage of members who rate the club as a detractor (0 through six on an 11-point scale and one to three on a five-point scale). The resulting number is the facility's *Net Promoter Score* (Figure 11-3). A score of zero or better is considered adequate, a score of approximately +25 is deemed as good and a score greater than +50 is thought to be excellent.

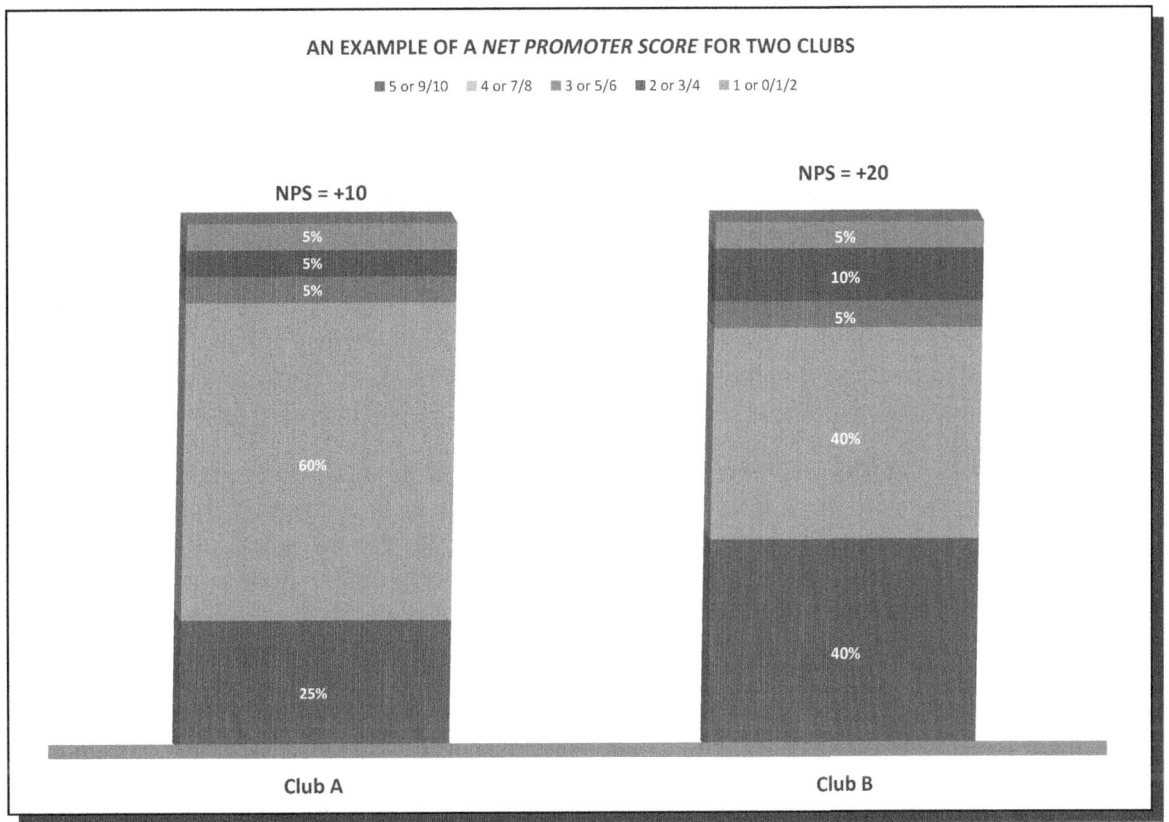

Figure 11-3. An example of the *Net Promoter Score* for two different clubs

Figure 11-3 depicts two clubs—one, Club A, with a *Net Promoter Score* of +10, and the other, Club B, with a NPS score of +20. The club with the positive 20 score is definitely doing a better job at creating an environment that promotes member loyalty. In reality, a number of club operators, with a score similar to that of Club A (25 percent of members gave the club a five, while another 60 percent gave the club a four on the survey), would tend to think, "Hey, we have 60 percent of the members who are either satisfied or delighted with their experience, so we must be doing a good job." The underlying error in this type of logic is that they don't understand that a merely satisfied member has no emotional buy-in, and that with more detractors than promoters, the club is in real danger of losing members.

A number of businesses focus on one simple question to determine their overall *Net Promoter Score*—"How likely are you to refer a friend or colleague?" Truth be known, many researchers believe that this single question and the resultant *Net Promoter Score* are not a true indication of customer loyalty. Rather, it is a score that indicates how likely a member is to refer another member. The pervading rationale of these researchers is based on the premise that a club or studio needs to develop its *Net Promoter Score*, using the responses to a series of questions. As such, in the health/fitness facility industry, one leading market researcher has built the "Member Loyalty Score" (MLS) off of members' responses to the following four questions:

- How likely are you to remain a member over the next 12 months?
- How likely are you to refer someone for membership over the next 12 months?
- How would you rate your overall experience with the club?
- Do you love the club?

In reality, taking the responses to these four questions and calculating the percentage of responses that fall into each of the three response categories (promoter, passive, detractor), totaling them up, and then subtracting detractors from promoters provides a far more accurate portrayal of a club's member loyalty than the single *Net Promoter Score*. Figure 11-4 shows the results of a facility that used a survey that measured each of the four aforementioned questions in order to determine its level of member loyalty. In this example, the club scored from +15 to +37, a tally that ranges from just okay to very good.

With a *Net Promoter Score* in hand, a facility can more easily identify the general level of loyalty that exists within its membership. Even with a *Net Promoter Score* in hand, businesses should also be aware of how important it is for them to get a reading on other important issues, as well as most importantly, to understand the specific variables that contribute to driving its *Net Promoter Score* upward.

To obtain an accurate read of a club's NPS, or preferably its MLS score, the facility should regularly conduct surveys (preferably once a quarter). Some club operators have implemented real-time voice of the member (VOM) tracking systems that provide a daily real-time means for measuring, monitoring, and managing the experience of its members. These VOM systems can provide an excellent means for clubs to keep its pulse on the member experience, as long as they measure more than one metric. Examples of the leading VOM systems that are presently utilized by clubs and studios in the health/fitness facility industry are hosted by Medallia, The Retention People, and Listen 360.

Customer Satisfaction and Loyalty as They Relate to Driving the Value of the Facility Experience

While it is important to be aware of the reasons that members have for using a facility, work from other industries show that understanding a customer's level of loyalty or satisfaction is equally important in determining how a business can perform better at retaining its customers. An FIA report from 2001 entitled *Winning the Retention Battle*, studied member satisfaction and the drivers

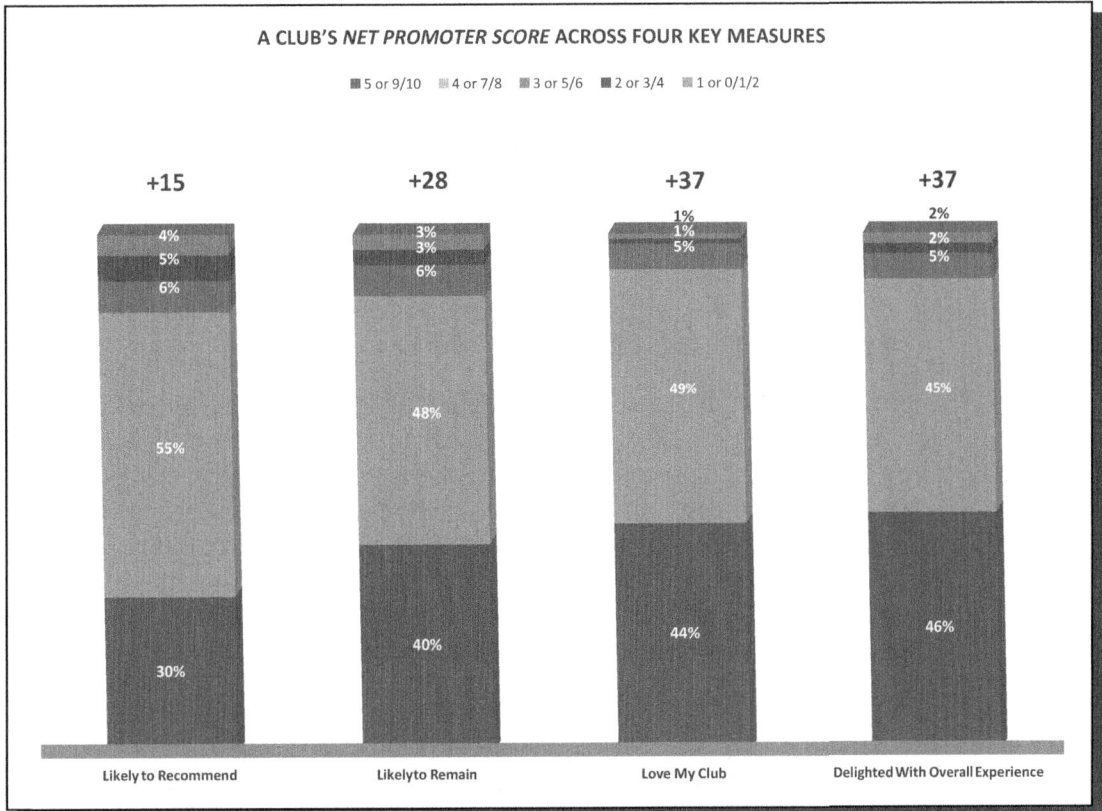

Figure 11-4. A club's *Net Promoter Score* and scoring distribution

behind it. When members were asked what the most crucial factors were driving their level of satisfaction with the club experience (scores over one), the following factors were indicated:

- Overall quality of the staff (rating of 1.16). This response not only reflected the knowledge and expertise of the staff of the facility, it also measured the club's level of attentiveness in serving the members.
- Club management (1.15). This measure refers to the management practices of the facility with regard to servicing the members, as well as management's responsiveness to issues raised by members.
- Level or member compaction (1.08). This score is an indication that one driver of satisfaction relates to whether members feel the existence of personal space or if they feel "caged-in."
- Feel like they fit in (1.02). This result is based on the premise that members believe that their level of satisfaction is drawn, at least in part, from feeling a sense of being perceived to fit in, or not standing out as being different.
- Social ambiance (1.02). This reply reflects the fact that a facility that affords members a chance to socialize with other members and, in essence, connect with other member is important to their overall club experience. This measure is also an indication that the club needs to provide a socially engaging environment.

Similar to the aforementioned findings, the researchers also identified the following categories as receiving the highest percentage of agreement, with regard to being rated as excellent or very good (9 or 10 on a 11-point scale) in their contribution to member satisfaction:

- Overall value for the money spent (54 percent) and general club atmosphere (52 percent) received the two highest totals, with regard to having a role in the satisfaction levels of members.
- Fitting in (46 percent), social ambiance (36 percent), and not too crowded (36 percent) were close runner-ups, with regard to the factors that are important to the level of member satisfaction.

In a 2007 study conducted on behalf of IHRSA, *Fitness American Style III*, the researchers looked at member satisfaction with the club experience. They found that 91 percent of current members were either very satisfied or somewhat satisfied with their facility. It should be noted that because research on customer loyalty that has been conducted since the publication of the aforementioned study also considers multiple other attributes that can drive customer loyalty, the responses reflected in this earlier IHRSA-commissioned study may not be the best barometer of member loyalty.

If this IHRSA study is examined more closely, only 42 percent of respondents indicated that they were very satisfied. In this report, 93 percent of members indicated that they would be very likely or somewhat likely to refer a friend as a member to the facility. What is not known, however, is the true percentage of promoters and passives that comprise this number, and whether an overall positive *Net Promoter Score* existed. It is interesting to note that members who indicate that they had an excellent relationship with the staff scored significantly higher on overall satisfaction with their club than those individuals who did not have an excellent relationship with the staff of the facility.

In fact, research undertaken by the FIA in 2001 and research reported in *Fitness American Style III* from 2007 both indicate that members who are very satisfied with their club experience are more frequent users of the facility. In addition, according to data included in these studies, those members who responded that they were very satisfied with their club experience were significantly more likely to refer someone for membership.

Such indications have been further reinforced by research, involving member surveys that have been administered by the author. These efforts have shown that members who score their level of delight or satisfaction with the club experience a five on a five-point scale are five to six times more likely to indicate they will remain a member or refer a friend or associate for membership (Figure 11-5).

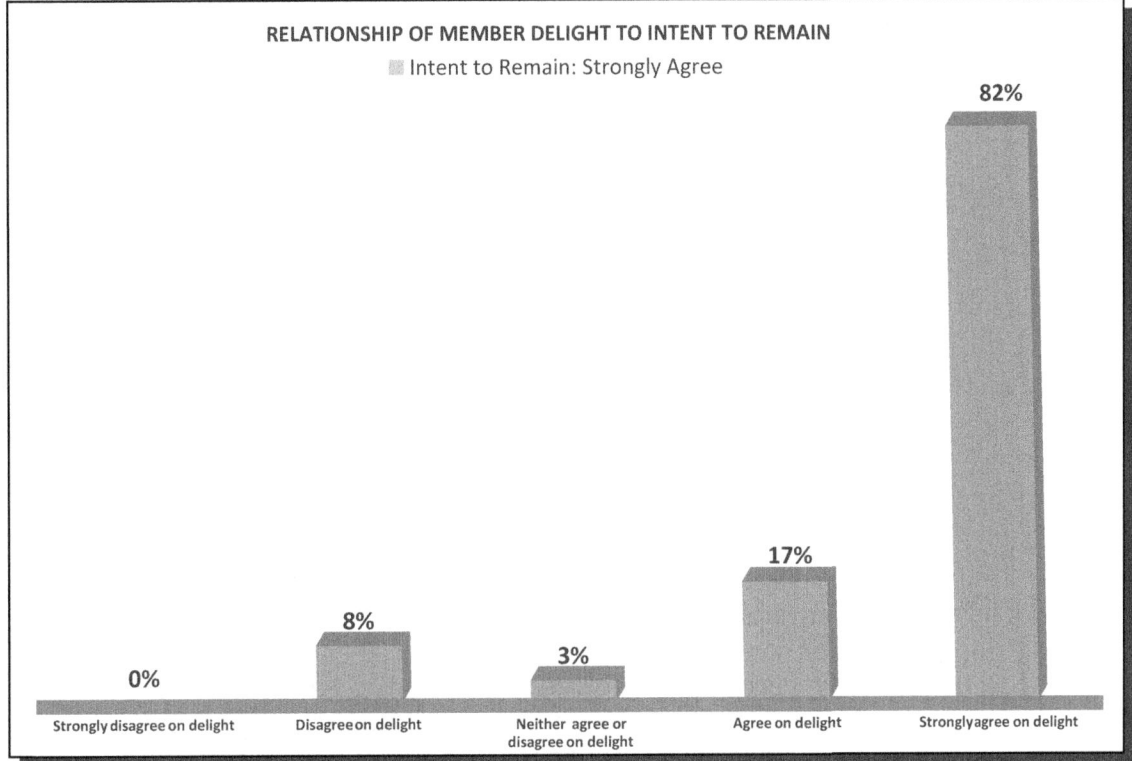

Figure 11-5. Relationship of member delight to intent to remain

How Customers Respond to Service Delivery and the Experience Provided by the Facility

When individuals decide to become members of a facility, they join with certain preconceptions and expectations. For some, those factors may involve achieving a certain fitness goal, while the objective of other individuals may be to meet other people within the club setting. Regardless of whether one or more of these factors is the primary reason driving their joining a facility, each of these variables affects whether they remain a member. In this regard, these factors may include such diverse matters as personal attention from staff, recognition from the club, facility cleanliness, program variety, program convenience, meeting other members, and a host of other reasons. In reality, because club operators cannot always identify these expectations (a well-conducted member survey can actually identify the key expectations that a club's members have), they must be prepared to create and deliver experiences that can meet or exceed expectations of which they may not even be aware.

A facility's first indication of how members have accepted or perceived the delivery of the club's experience is by the response they make (both verbally and non-verbally) to inquire about the facility. Collectively, the members' responses then become an important factor in whether, as well as how, club operators and their staff adjust the services and experiences they provide.

Research conducted on how individuals respond to their experiences indicates that four basic responses exist—one of which is good, one of which is outstanding, and all of which can be used to drive a club's ability to retain its members:

❑ Outrage

Outrage is an emotional response that members have when their experience has fallen well short of their expectations. Members who exhibit outrage feel great emotional displeasure and a sense of betrayal. When clubs do not deal immediately with member outrage, they are contributing to the formation of what can be called, "business terrorists," people who go out of their way to harm the business. Many of the individuals in the health/fitness facility industry are familiar with this response. Most clubs tend to ignore members who respond with outrage, not realizing that they are creating terrorists.

Over the past decade with the evolution of the Internet, outraged customers have used social media to voice their unhappiness. Some outraged consumers search for vengeance by posting complaints on company Facebook pages or other social platforms, such as Yelp, while others take a more aggressive stance and create "complaint sites" or "gripe sites." As such, several of America's leading companies, including one former leading health/fitness club operator in the United States, have been the target of dedicated gripe sites. Because these sites can damage reputations and profitability, finding ways to avoid creating customer outrage should be a priority for every business. When a club or business is able to actually overcome the outrage (not an easy thing to do), it is building a strong bridge to retaining that customer and/or member.

❑ Dissatisfaction

> In one large global fitness club company's semi-annual survey of its members, it was determined that over 50 percent of the members who experienced an inconvenience never filed a complaint.

Dissatisfaction is an unemotional response that members have when they do not receive the service or experience they expect. This response often occurs when a club makes its members "sacrifice" something of importance, the absence of which then becomes an inconvenience. Dissatisfied members normally don't tell the club about their sense of dissatisfaction. In one large global fitness club company's semi-annual survey of its members, it was determined that over 50 percent of the members who experienced an inconvenience never filed a complaint. This statistic is a great example of what happens with members who are dissatisfied with the club experience; they may have a problem, but they don't voice it. Rather, they might grumble to other members of the club or show up less often at the club. An example of a circumstance that could result in a degree of member dissatisfaction could be something as simple and basic as a trainer arriving five minutes late for an appointment with the member or the sauna not working. Eventually, dissatisfied members will leave the club if they are not identified. On the other hand, they are easily taken care of if the source of their dissatisfaction is addressed by the club.

❏ Satisfaction

To many individuals in the health/fitness club business, member satisfaction is considered the end point, the response of choice. A satisfied individual means that the club has been able to meet the member's expectations. A satisfied member is not necessarily a happy member, rather an individual who, for now, will continue as a member. Satisfied members are often the first to leave when a new club opens elsewhere, because although they are satisfied, they have not developed a sufficient sense of loyalty to the club. Far too often, satisfied members are relatively unknown to the club, because they haven't expressed their true feelings to the club.

> A satisfied member is not necessarily a happy member, rather an individual who, for now, will continue as a member.

❏ Delight

Delight occurs when the club exceeds a member's expectations. In other words, the club has provided an experience that was both memorable and beyond the member's perceptions or expectations. Delight is an indication of an emotional buy-in or personal ownership. Delighted members are often referred to as "business apostles"—individuals who "tell and sell" the club's story to others. Typically, club operators know who these individuals are, because they are often the most active, outgoing, and loyal members of the facility.

In the late 1990s and early 2000s, ClubCorp sponsored research that was designed to identify how the various aforementioned member responses impacted retention and profitability. In particular, ClubCorp wanted to better understand how these responses affected the members' desire to remain a member and their willingness to refer others for membership. This research found that delighted members were twice as likely to remain a member over the next 12 months as a satisfied member and one tenth as likely to leave. Furthermore, a delighted member was nearly 10 times as likely as a satisfied member to refer someone for membership. The conclusion, which paralleled research results in other customer-service environments, was that a delighted member is the most valuable member a club has. These findings support the contention that a club should create a service and experience culture that is focused on driving member delight.

In her book, *Understanding Customers*, the author, Ruby Newell states, "It takes 12 positive experiences to make up for one unresolved negative experience." As a consequence, when someone looks at the outcomes of delight versus outrage, it becomes evident that individuals understand and respond to these emotional responses immediately. When the membership retention and membership sales implications of these figures are considered, it is very clear that clubs can benefit by creating a culture that is focused on delivering the service necessary to create experiences that drive a member's sense of delight, which collectively enhances their level of member loyalty.

Defining a WOW Experience

> If a club wants to have a positive impact on member retention, it needs to have a service culture that is focused on creating and sustaining experiences that exceed the expectations of members.

As the previous sections pointed out, if a club wants to have a positive impact on member retention, it needs to have a service culture that is focused on creating and sustaining experiences that exceed the expectations of members. In that regard, two critical issues arise: what is meant by the term "an experience" and what role does a club's service culture have in driving these experiences. In order to address those issues, the first step is to understand the relationship between service and experience. Both factors are defined as follows:

❏ Service

Service is the process by which a club's people and systems are able to deliver the club's facilities, programs, and other amenities to the member across every touch point. Service is the process that the club employs to deliver its product. Service requires people and systems that can repeatedly deliver the club's product, with minimal sacrifice or hassle on the member's part.

The following example can help illustrate the differences between service and experience. A club offers yoga classes for novices, beginners, and advanced members. The classes are the club's product. The manner in which the club's instructors teach those classes and interact with the members is the service the club provides. If the service provided by the club enables members to participate freely, with minimal inconvenience, and enjoy the class, then the club is servicing the members with minimal sacrifice by the members.

If instead, the yoga class instructors require members to say a pledge, ask beginners to perform advanced work, and never smile, the club's service in this instance would be requiring the members to make some degree of sacrifice to participate. In other words, in the context of service, the club should think of it as the delivery mechanism for all of the experiences it provides to members. Great service occurs when members sacrifice the least and benefit the most, while poor service exists when the club makes its members exert a considerable sacrifice.

❏ Experience

An experience involves the interplay of a club's product, the service process, the expectations and needs of the member, and finally, the ability of the facility to create the desired circumstances around a theme. In essence, an experience is what members receive or perceive they receive based on how the club themes the service it provides and how it impacts the members' expectations. It should be noted that experiences can be good or bad. Accordingly, the goal of the facility should be to create experiences that require minimal sacrifice on the part of the member and enhance the member's sense of member delight.

One positive example of creating a desired experience is a class offered by the various Crunch clubs in New York City. These Crunch clubs have developed a group exercise class called cardio striptease. The theme of the class is, of course, striptease. The club's product is a group exercise class. The service is the manner in which the instructor delivers the class, hopefully with passion, dressed in full striptease attire which is later removed, of course, and encouraging the members to do the same. While the foregoing is an extreme example, other programming efforts, such as fireman's aerobics, hell week, antigravity yoga, etc., also illustrate how clubs can create an experience at the micro-level.

Creating Experiences That WOW Customers

Clubs can achieve noteworthy success with their members by creating a service culture that is focused on delivering unique experiences that not only exceed member expectations, but also help facilitate member delight and loyalty. Among the relatively simple steps that a facility can take to become more experience-oriented are the following:

❏ Establish a Theme

The first step in creating a unique and differentiating membership experience is to identify a unifying theme. By establishing a theme for the experience that the club intends to provide, it can focus each aspect of its business toward the fulfillment of that particular theme. For example, the Telos Fitness Center, based in Dallas, Texas, operates around providing an Athenian theme. Each aspect of its design, product mix, and service culture is focused on reinforcing this Athenian theme, from the Greek columns in the lobby, to the God and Goddess awards for members, and finally to the Spartan training, based on the ancient Greek approach to fitness as medicine.

Another example of theme building is Crunch Fitness, based in New York City, which has developed a theme that is designed to deliver out-of-the-box, non-judgmental experiences. When an individual enters a Crunch facility, that person can easily see that the design of the club, the attire of the staff, the names of the classes and programs, and the service approach of their staff all align with the facility's basic theme.

Another example of a health/fitness operation that is built around a theme are the fitness studios owned and managed by Exhale, whose offices are located in New York City. Exhale's theme is focused on mind and body, attempting, in essence, to make each facility an out-of-body retreat. Exhale's facilities, programs, and service culture all center on creating experiences based on that particular theme. At a more micro-level, numerous clubs and studios have developed classes and programs around a highly recognizable theme, such as boot camp, fireman's aerobics, SWAT classes, etc.

❏ Add the "ING"

According to B. Joseph Pine and James H. Gilmore in their insightful book, *The Experience Economy*, when a club takes a particular product and service and thinks of that item in the context of adding an "ING," then the club is more likely to generate the desired experiences. An excellent example of this concept in practice occurred when Johnny G. created Spinning. What was once just riding a stationary bike (e.g., taking a spin) became a hot experience. By creating Spinning, he made the class more appealing as an experience. The key point for clubs to consider in this regard is for the facility to think about the action-oriented aspects of its products and services.

❑ Build the Proper Stage

> **Creating experiences is like putting on a play.**

Creating experiences is like putting on a play. In the first act, the club needs to construct the proper stage or set design. Facilities that want to create positive experiences have to first develop an appropriate theme and then make sure the stage for acting out that experience has been established. For example, at the Rochester Athletic Club (RAC) in Rochester, Minnesota, an area of the club, called the Neighborhood, was established. To make the theme come alive, the operators of the facility took what were formerly indoor tennis courts and constructed a replica of an old Midwestern town, complete with ice cream shop, storefronts, pedestrian walkways, and a miniature golf course. As a result, The RAC's facilities are designed to look and feel like an old-time neighborhood.

Another industry group that focuses on building the proper setting is Crunch clubs, which feature a theme that is non-judgmental and out-of-the-box. When individuals enter the Crunch club in West Hollywood, for example, they will notice that as they walk to the locker rooms, they can see the profiles of people in the showers or that when members are on the exercise floor, that all the mirrors are round and on stands. Crunch also places signs throughout their club with off-the-wall expressions that support their theme. As intended, the members of Crunch clubs definitely get the sense they are immersed in an unusual experience.

❑ Have the Right Props

Just as a stage is normally needed to put on a play, clubs also need the right props. From a club perspective, the props are the equipment, the signage, the physical amenities, the classes and programs, and even the staff attire. It is critical that the club's props align with the designated theme of the facility. At Crunch clubs, for example, several outrageous signs are posted throughout the club. Most members stop and read the signs and have a laugh—a process that is part of the intended experience. The Crunch staff can be found wearing cut-offs, earrings, and other unusual items, all of which reinforce the predetermined theme of Crunch clubs. Each Crunch club also offers classes such as cardio striptease and cardio funk, both of which align with their theme. In a similar vein, at Exhale, a New York-based operator of mind-body studios, its theme of a mind/body retreat is reinforced by props such as curtains, chairs, candles, and other items that make the members and guests feel as if they are escaping from the world.

❑ Have the Club's Staff See Their Job as Acting

Actors are adept at stepping into a character and creating the atmosphere desired by the director. For a club's staff, they too need to know the theme of the facility and then be able to "act" in a manner that reinforces that theme. For example, at Oase Health and Sport in Germany, its theme is built around being a "home away from home." Accordingly, the employees at Oase try to act not as staff, but as members of the family, encouraging interactions between individuals that create a sense of family. As such, the art of acting by the club staff is an essential aspect of what could be considered the club's "service culture."

❑ Ensure That the Staff Is Focused on Creating Transformations

Not only must a club's staff members be focused on acting, they should also be prepared to deal with each individual member in a manner that allows them to personalize the experience for that member. Transformations occur when an experience takes on a high degree of personal relevance. In essence, a club's staff needs to find ways to help members experience a change that is consistent with the members' personal expectations and needs. As such, these transformations require a strong "service culture." A great example of a fitness business that has prospered by fostering member transformations is CrossFit, in large part because of the social support network that its members offer each other.

Reflections

A high level of member loyalty should be the destination for every club operator. It is essential that every operator is aware of the fact that with high levels of loyalty come increased levels for member advocacy, higher levels of membership retention and tenure, and finally, an increased level of member spend. In order to pursue this admirable and worthy goal of "best-in-class" member loyalty, club operators need to keep the following factors in mind:

- *Make the customer value equation the framework for delivering the customer experience.* Every element of the value equation plays a role in building value. Finally, club operators need to remember that emotional quality is the turbo booster for delivering memorable experiences that foster member loyalty.
- *Understand that loyalty is not just one number*—it's a total package. Club operators should never get caught looking at just one measure of loyalty. They need to understand what goes into driving loyalty and then set their goals.
- *Measure what they expect.* Clubs can't achieve industry-leading levels of member loyalty unless they know their starting point, their goals, and then monitor their progress toward achieving their goals. Furthermore, club operators need to measure what drives loyalty, otherwise they will be challenged to create an environment that is conducive to driving the achievement of their facility's member-loyalty targets.

> A high level of member loyalty should be the destination for every club operator.

12 Creating a Service Culture That Drives Customer Loyalty

"The member is king."

—Robert Dedman, Sr.

Chapter Objectives

The previous chapters in this section looked at member and client retention and how this critical business factor is affected by a facility's ability to create memorable experiences for its customers. In turn, it was pointed out that a club's success in creating memorable experiences relies heavily on having a service culture. This chapter details the role of service in creating memorable experiences for the club's members and what steps are needed to establish and sustain a service culture.

The Service Profit Chain

According to Leonard Schlesinger of Harvard University in his article, "How Does Service Drive the Service Company," the "service profit chain" lies at the heart of growing a business's profitability. Like a "chain," the process has several interrelated links. Profitability is driven by customer loyalty, which is influenced by customer delight. Customer delight is affected by outstanding external service to the customer, which, in turn, is driven by delighted employees who are the recipients of great internal service (refer to Figure 12-1). Simply stated, in club terms, profitability is driven by loyal members, who have a sense of delight that is derived by their having engaged in memorable experiences at the facility. These member experiences are delivered by a staff with a strong internal and external service culture. It is the aforementioned "service profit chain" that lies at the center of membership retention and the ability of a club to create memorable member experiences.

> Profitability is driven by loyal members, who have a sense of delight that is derived by their having engaged in memorable experiences at the facility.

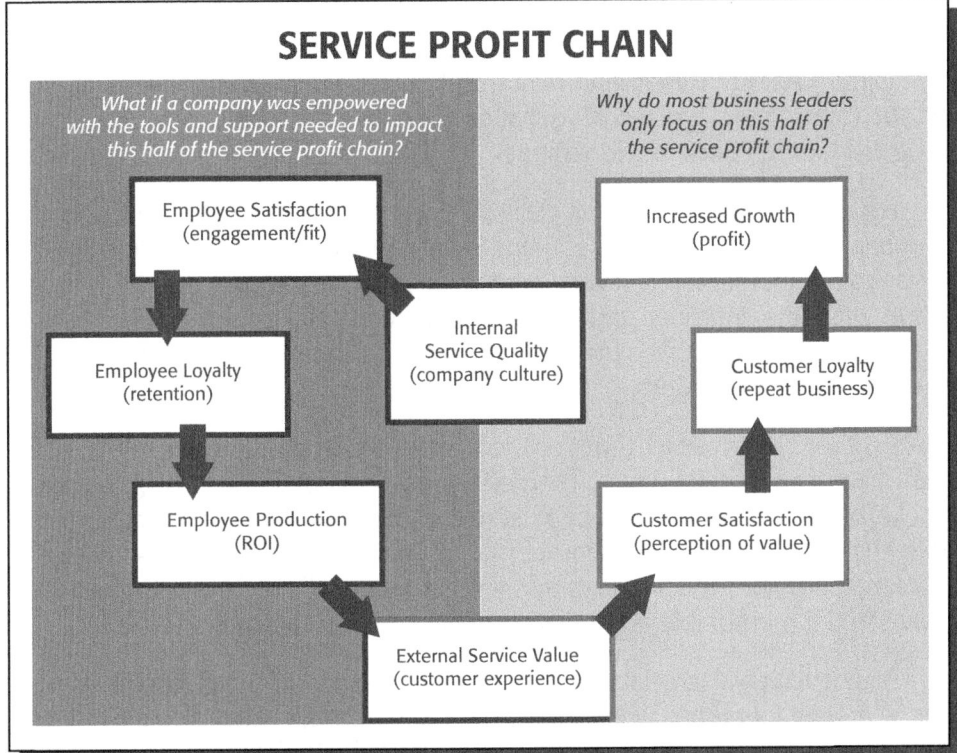

Figure 12-1. The service profit chain

Defining a Service Culture

The key to the club staff providing great service that is focused on delivering memorable member experiences starts with the establishment of a service culture. A service culture is a system of customs, habits, and conventions, the values, words, and works attendant to this culture help create and sustain a long-term environment in which the staff are passionate about and are empowered to act with a "servant's heart," delivering whatever is required to provide the club's members with a personally relevant and memorable experience. Establishing a service culture therefore becomes one of the most essential elements in any health/fitness facility's operating model, as well as a vital competency for management.

Creating a Service Culture in the Health/Fitness Facility Industry

Establishing an appropriate service culture in the club industry can involve a number of steps, including the following:

❑ Create a Set of Core Business Values Around Service

The core foundation of all cultures is a set of values. Whether it is a societal culture, such as the ones that exist in England, China, or Germany, or a business culture, such as witnessed at Ben & Jerry's, Starbuck's, Nordstrom's, or BMW, the heart of every culture is based on a set of values that lie behind every decision that is made. If a facility wants to establish a service culture, its values must be consistent with the service expectations of its membership. As the authors of the book, Karaoke Capitalism, Jonas Ridderstrale and Kjell A. Nordstrom, stated in their landmark text, "Values are magnets, values attract." As such, having the right values will attract people who have a "servant's heart," a central theme in any service culture.

For example, at ClubCorp, a Dallas, Texas-based private club company, the company's founder, Robert Dedman, Sr., established a service culture for the organization that featured several core values that focused on service. The first value was, "the member and guest is king." With this one precept, Dedman established a framework for how he expected each employee to interact with the members of ClubCorp.

Another fundamental ClubCorp value that Dedman constantly referred to was, "warm welcomes, magic moments, and fond farewells." When Dedman spoke of this underlying company sense of purpose, he was referring to the role that each employee plays in making sure that all members receive a personalized welcome when they arrive, a personalized farewell when they leave, and a memorable and magic experience while they are in the club.

Another core value established by Dedman was to call each member by their name at least four times when they were in the club. This practice was intended to reinforce the culture of personalizing each member's club experience.

A final value that Dedman preached was "to deliver a Cadillac for a Chevrolet price." As such, his underlying desire was to overdeliver on the company promise or to deliver a far greater value than for which the member actually paid. Over the years, the company values and attitudes instilled by Dedman have served ClubCorp very well.

In a similar approach, Red Lerelle, of Red's in Lafayette, Louisiana, has established some very basic business values for his company that speak to service. At Red's, every employee understands that they are to smile and say hello and goodbye to every member. At Red's, everyone knows that it is their job to do whatever it requires to take care of the members. These values, established by Red when he founded his club over five decades ago, continue to set the framework for the club's service culture.

❑ Create a Tradition of Service Values by Starting at the Top

In every culture, the values and traditions that are attendant to that culture are sustained by leaders who embody those values and traditions. These leaders act in a manner that supports the core values of the culture.

In the club business, one of the steps that can help create a tradition of great service is to reinforce the values in word and deed at all times. At Red's, for example, Red can be found training new employees on the importance of saying hello and goodbye to members of his club, most often by being seen throughout the club saying hello or goodbye. By the same token, at ClubCorp, when Robert Dedman, Sr. visited a club, he could often be found talking with members and asking what he could do to help them. In both Red's and Dedman's world, the service values started with them. In other words, they did whatever it took to demonstrate the service values that they wanted to inculcate within their organization's culture.

❑ Establish Courses of Action that Reinforce the Values and Service Culture

In any culture, it takes more than one individual to spread the service culture. According to anthropologists, a culture is sustained by artifacts, tradition, myths, legends, and heroes. In other words, once an entity has the values of a culture established, it must have the people and stories to keep it alive and vibrant with the individuals who are part of that endeavor. As previously discussed, not only does it take leaders who will share relevant stories attendant to the service culture and believe in a manner consistent with the core values of the culture, it can require much more.

In the club business, for example, leaders must identify key staff members who embrace the service culture of the facility and will "walk it and talk it." These employees become the club's storytellers and heroes. Accordingly, facilities should undertake an effort to collect employee recollections of the company's service culture so that they can be shared with the other employees.

> Leaders must identify key staff members who embrace the service culture of the facility and will "walk it and talk it."

At ClubCorp in the 1980s and 1990s, the company encouraged employees to make note of stories that exemplified the service culture, and then to share those stories with their fellow employees by means of the company's website and through daily staff lineups at each respective ClubCorp facility. Sharing their own stories of a service experience during such a lineup can result in a "magic moment" for those staff members who are conveying their remembrances.

In the process, these individuals become one of the service culture's storytellers. In 2008, when I first took the reins as CEO for the Russian Fitness Group, one of the first endeavors that I embarked on was to instill the company's culture at all levels of the organization. To accomplish this objective, a "culture leadership team," composed of 30 team members from the corporate office and clubs, was established. This group of 30 employees was assigned the responsibility of spreading the company culture.

The team members were deeply involved in immersing the organization's employees in the culture of the company. One particularly potentially helpful step that team members took was to visit the various clubs in the group and to share personally relevant stories that spoke to what the company culture was all about. Among the other steps that can help reinforce the service culture within a club are the following:

- Create a system to recognize outstanding service. Employees are far more likely to embrace a service culture when they are recognized for actions that align with the club's service culture. At ClubCorp, for example, this recognition program was called STAR Recognition. Other clubs have different names for their recognition programs. The key, however, is to recognize employees who live the service culture, regardless of the term utilized to acknowledge the effort.

- Develop a cultural immersion program. Facilities need to initiate an ongoing education program for all of their employees. At the heart of that training program should be a module dedicated to both the club's service culture and how employees can become the apostles for that service culture. At ClubCorp, the first educational effort an employee is exposed to is a video that explains the service culture at ClubCorp. At the Russian Fitness Group, a course entitled, "Culture; the Ultimate Competitive Advantage," was conducted annually. All company and club leaders were expected to attend. Furthermore, it's essential that the facility's educational program on its service culture is an ongoing one, not just a one-time delivery.
- Loosen the knot. One of the most common complaints from customers is that when they need something done, that employees have to ask their supervisors for instructions or permission to act. In reality, however, if a facility wants to have a genuine service culture, it should empower its employees to act according to the culture. It should trust its employees to make the right decisions. At Nordstrom's, for example, employees are given the freedom to deal with customers, based solely on the company's service values. Fortunately, many clubs give its employees the freedom to make the right decision, based on an environment of trust. The key point that should be noted is that the process should be grounded in the clubs' service culture and how the clubs educate and support that culture.
- All decisions need to be founded in the club's service values. Many businesses establish service values, but then act outside them. For example, ClubCorp, at least up until the early part of the 21st century, had a core philosophy that was based on the precept that the "member is king." If a situation subsequently occurred where the employee had to make a choice with regard to a particular action, that person's choice had to be consistent with the value that the "member is king." If the employee's decision ran counter to that value, then the first link in ClubCorp's service culture chain had been broken.
- Document the core values and practices of the facility's service culture. It is critical that the values and practices of the club's service culture be documented and shared with each of its employees. ClubCorp, for example, gave each of its employees the "basics card," which was a small, wallet-sized card on which are noted the values and philosophies that are at the heart of the company's service culture.

    The card that each employee of Red's receives lists eight specific values that are at the heart of Red's service culture. The card utilized at Red's serves as a statement of the service-culture standards at Red's. Not only does it help all Red's employees to know the service culture expectations at Red's, it also furnishes them with a constant reminder of those expectations. The following eight values are listed on the Red's card:
    - The members are number one.
    - Make eye contact, smile, and say "Hello" and "Goodbye."
    - Show up on time and ready to work.
    - If a member has a problem, solve it. Keep them happy.
    - If you've got time to lean, you got time to clean.
    - I don't know the answer; I'll find out, so check back with me.

- Have a positive attitude; be enthusiastic about your job.
- Stay in shape.

At the Russian Fitness Group, organizational values were documented through various media. For example, a screen saver was developed for all of the company's computers that displayed the company's values. Another step that was undertaken was to give coffee/tea mugs to each employee, on which were listed the company's core values. The point to keep in mind is that like ClubCorp and Red's, a way was found to put the core values in front of each employee on a daily basis.

❏ Provide a Means for Members and Clients to Communicate With Management About Their Experiences at the Club

A service culture requires a high degree of openness by management. As such, management must be open to listening to the members and fostering an environment of trust between the members and the staff. Members must feel like they can share both their praise and their concerns openly and know that management and employees will respond to the members' efforts to communicate with them in a manner that helps ensure a better member experience. Among the approaches that clubs can utilize to elicit and enhance feedback from their members are the following:

- Open door/open floor. This approach to listening involves management leaving time for members to drop in and talk. It also mandates management should spend a portion of each day out in the club talking with members. The combination of getting out and talking with members and also leaving time on the schedule for members to walk in and meet with club staff allows the club to foster an environment of trust. Red Lerille of Red's is an exceptional example of this approach. Red spends most of his day engaging with members, walking around the club, and attending to the needs of members.
- Member committees. At ClubCorp, the facilities have committees made up of members. These committees serve dual roles. Not only do they provide valuable feedback on the experiences of the members, they also allow the members to become involved in identifying experience solutions. The number of committees varies from club to club. Some facilities only have a few committees, while others have more than a dozen, such as a social committee, racquet sport committee, membership committee, group-exercise committee, etc.
- Focus groups. Focus groups are an effective way for facilities to learn more about what their members feel. Focus groups allow a club to bring together groups of members in a non-intimidating environment and identify what they feel and believe about their experiences in the facility. Ideally, focus groups should be led by an independent facilitator, who can provide a less intimidating environment for members to express their emotions about their club experience.
- Voice of the member (VOM) surveys. Surveys are a practical method for assessing how members feel about the club experience. In this regard, surveys should be conducted at least once annually. Within the industry, numerous facilities, such as Fitness Formula Clubs in Chicago,

> Management must be open to listening to the members and fostering an environment of trust between the members and the staff.

Illinois; Atlantic Coast Athletic Clubs, Charlottesville, Virginia; Houstonian, Houston, Texas; and World Health, Edmonton, Canada, conduct member surveys to measure how well they are delivering the member experience and ascertain how their members feel about key touch points involving their experiences at the facility. One of the newest trends in the industry involves real-time voice of the member tracking (VOM), which measures the member experience on a daily basis. These real-time tracking systems provide club management with instant feedback on how well they are delivering on their service culture. They also provide quantitative metrics on service performance and offer commentary on issues impacting members.

- Feedback system. Every club should offer members some form of a feedback system, or as it is more commonly known, a comment-box system, that their members can use to share their concerns and praises. This undertaking can range from having boxes with comment cards left available throughout the club, to web-based feedback systems. Clubs, such as ACAC in Charlottesville, Virginia; Bay Clubs in California; Eastbank Club in Chicago; Virgin Active in England; and Intenso in Germany, all offer some type of a feedback system that their members can use to share their thoughts, concerns, and praises.
- Social media listening. Currently, as a rule, clients want to provide feedback to club staff in real-time. All too frequently, however, especially among those individuals who are members of Generation Y, that feedback is shared on one of the many social media platforms, such as Facebook, Twitter, Yelp, and YouTube. Accordingly, club operators need to stay abreast of the chatter that arises in the social media, and when that chatter is negative, respond to it in real time.

As Danak Boyd, social media researcher for Microsoft, states, "The way you can understand all of social media is as the creation of a new kind of public space." In other words, club operators need to understand that social media is a public space where consumers often share their delight or outrage with a service experience. As such, it is important that these operators take the time to understand the chatter that is occurring in these new public spaces about their business.

❑ Eliminate the Sacrifices That a Member Has to Make

James Gilmore and Joseph Pine, in their book entitled, *The Experience Economy*, are quoted as saying, "Companies need to focus on understanding customer sacrifice, which equals the gap between exactly what the customer wants and what they ultimately settle for." Eliminating sacrifices, or as Adrian J. Slywotzky and Karl Weber, the authors of the book *Demand: Creating What People Love Before They Know They Want It*, refer to them, hassles, is a critical aspect of any service culture.

The process of creating and sustaining a service culture requires that a club look at its operations and identify the sacrifices or hassles that members must make in order to use the facility. In that regard, a member can sacrifice in a number of ways, including a loss of convenience, self-esteem, achievement of fitness goals, friendships, etc. When a club identifies sacrifices that its members must make, it should remove them. For example, many facilities require members to hand over their keys and ID just to get a towel. All factors considered, these clubs are asking members to make some degree of sacrifice just to use a towel. On the other hand, if members can obtain a towel without all of that inconvenience, it could easily be argued that they would feel much better.

Another example of a member sacrifice that is commonly experienced by members currently in the health/fitness facility industry is being unable to obtain general fitness advice and guidance from trainers without opening their wallet (again). A primary reason many individuals join clubs is to gain help in achieving their desired health/fitness goals. If and when they are unable to receive such assistance as expected, the situation becomes an enormous sacrifice. In reality, too many club operators construct inadvertent barriers, thinking that they will save money. Instead, however, they create member sacrifices that eventually help drive members away.

❑ Create a Service Recovery Approach That Can Patch the Gaps

Even in the best service culture, mistakes occur. According to the data shared by Dr. Leonard Schlesinger in his article, "The Service-driven Service Company," customers who have a bad experience can be turned around with the proper service-recovery process. The data on customer service indicates that up to 95 percent of customers will make a repeat purchase if the problem they experience is addressed promptly and correctly. This type of insight makes it imperative that a club's service culture include a service-recovery process. In developing a service-recovery process, either manual or digital, clubs should make sure to address each of the following steps:

- Listen. The first element of a service-recovery process is to listen to the members. This endeavor begins with having a system, featuring elements such as those discussed previously, that allows a club's members to voice their issues. It is imperative that the members be allowed to express their concerns either anonymously or not. Employees should be willing to listen attentively when members bring up an issue of concern to them. If the issue is brought up through a survey or other medium, then management needs to contact the individual and hear what that person has to say. Over the past few years, many clubs have found that their website or social media sites, such as Facebook or even company-sponsored social platforms, can provide an outstanding forum for listening to members and conducting a two-way dialogue with them.
- Empathize. Whenever a member shares an issue with the club's employees, they need to empathize and show that they understand the member's perspective on the issue. This attitude needs to be communicated clearly to the individual.
- Apologize. It is imperative that the member with a relevant issue over their experience in the club receives an apology from the individual employee with whom they shared their concern or from management, if the comment is communicated online through a digital feedback platform, such as a VOC platform. The apology from the employee should be imparted on

behalf of the club, indicating that the staff of the facility regrets the situation. The apology should be made promptly. If the concern is expressed to an employee in person, then the apology should occur at that time. If the issue comes to light at a later time (e.g., by a letter, submission on the club's website or Facebook page, or via another communication medium), then the apology needs to be delivered verbally and in person, if possible, as soon as the issue has come to the attention of management.

- Respond. Once the club has become aware of the issue and has apologized, it should take action to address the matter. As indicated on the aforementioned values card that is utilized at Red's, "solve it and keep them happy." If the issue has been brought to the attention of a line employee, the employee should be empowered to solve the issue. If the issue is beyond that person's scope of responsibility, then it should be immediately brought to the attention of an employee or supervisor who can solve the issue. If the issue cannot be resolved immediately, the club should make sure that someone gets back to them as soon as possible. The employees at Red's are instructed to respond to such a situation by stating, "I don't know the answer; I'll find out, so check back with me." If an issue is raised anonymously, management still needs to act promptly to address the situation.

  The key in service recovery is to empower the employee team to respond to issues promptly with solutions and when the employee does not have a solution to a particular problem, the club should make sure that the employee knows where to go for the solution. Whenever and however the club is responding, the club should inform the member that it is taking action to address the situation. Finally, in the multi-tasking, real-time environment that exists at the present time, people expect to hear from the facility in real-time. Accordingly, clubs need to establish a precedent for responding to all issues as quickly as possible and solving the issue as soon as possible thereafter.

- Communicate the response. When an issue occurs that needs to be addressed, management should begin the process of solving the matter by letting the member know that it is aware of the situation and will take prompt action in a diligent manner, something that should be done at the time it learns of the issue. When the issue is raised anonymously, a note can be either placed on a communication board in the club or on the club's website or Facebook page, or relayed through a Twitter feed, informing the membership in general of an issue that has come to management's attention and of the action the club plans to take concerning the situation. If the issue is raised in person, members should immediately be informed of the action the club is taking. Members need to have prompt feedback that the club understands their issues and how it plans to deal with them.

- Follow up. The final critical aspect of the service-recovery process is for a club to make sure that once it has taken action on a member issue, it clearly and promptly communicates to the member what the outcome of the action is. If the issue was raised anonymously, then the club should post the resulting action on a comment board or a digital screen at the club or on the club's website or chosen social media page.

It should be noted that the service-recovery process applies just as much to employee-related issues, as it does to member issues. Clubs that can properly and effectively address an employee-related issue are far more likely to have employees who are able to act in an appropriate manner when member-related problems occur.

Implementing Service Culture Values and Standards

Creating and sustaining a service culture is not an easy process. Examples of possible service values and standards that club operators might consider as they create their own service values and culture include the following:

❑ Greeting members:

- Always smile and make eye contact.
- Call the member by name.
- Personalize the greeting by saying more than just "hello."
- Always greet members by standing and extending a hand.

❑ Professionalism and education:

- Make sure that the staff has the appropriate certifications and education and share this information with members by posting it within the club, as well as making it available on the website of the facility.
- Always have the staff share information of value with members, when the opportunity arises.
- Always have a solution or know how to find the solution.
- Instill in all employees the understanding that their number one job is to be there for the members, no matter what.

❑ Social engagement and member interaction:

- Never have staff walk by a member without saying hello and introducing themselves.
- Make it a practice to introduce members to other members.
- Ask members in a genuine and caring fashion if they need assistance.
- Foster a relationship with the members and learn something unique about them.
- Focus on listening and empathizing with the members before responding.

❑ Programming of the facility:

- Offer a variety of programs for a variety of needs.
- Be flexible in the club's program offerings, both in terms of interests served and when the programs are offered.
- Find ways to determine the program interests of the members.

❑ Justice and safety for members and employees:

- Don't play favorites; treat every member and employee as an equal.
- Become aware of the personal interests of both the members and employees and have the staff act appropriately.
- Talk about "we" and avoid using "me."
- Create an environment that is not intimidating for the members or employees.

❑ Self-esteem of members and employees:

- Focus on knowing everyone's goals and make an effort to provide what it takes for them to be achieved, including providing guidance, support, and recognition.
- Never let a member or an employee feel like their needs are a burden; instead, let them know they are valued.
- Provide an environment that speaks to greater perception of body and mind awareness and comfort.

❑ The facility:

- Keep it clean and make it everyone's job to keep it clean.
- Keep all equipment in working order unless an alternative is provided.
- Make the facility convenient to use.
- Make the facility seem like a second home or office.

Reflections

Creating and sustaining a service culture is an absolutely essential aspect of a successful health/fitness club. As such, this factor should be the first and foremost issue that facility operators address if they want to create memorable member experiences and enhance their club's level of membership retention.

Programming Essentials: A Primer for the Health/Fitness Facility Industry

13

"A club without programming is like a smartphone that can't access the Internet; it may look cool and sound cool, but it can't get you connected."

—Stephen Tharrett,
from *101 Programming Strategies for Engaging Members in Health/Fitness Clubs*

Chapter Objectives

According to consumer research on why people either join or leave a health/fitness club, programming plays an important role in both decisions. Since prospective members, current members, and former members all tend to view programming as a critical part of the health/fitness club value equation, it is essential that facility operators understand the dynamics involved in programming the activities that their club offers. Initially, this chapter explores the role that programming plays in membership. It then provides an overview of the variety of program opportunities that exist for facilities. Finally, the chapter concludes by detailing the key steps involved in successful programming.

The Value of Programming

Programming engages members in the facility experience, creating opportunities for members to become actively involved in the club. Market research indicates that individuals join clubs for a variety of reasons, including social engagement (women of all ages and seniors of both genders), group activities (women), challenge and competition (men), and achieving fitness goals (both genders). By the same token, research has also been able to identify some of the primary reasons members give up their facility membership, including not achieving their goals, not feeling as being in place, not being able to make social connections with other members, not feeling engaged by the club, not being able to sustain motivation and interest, not having a training partner, and not using the facility frequently enough. When these factors affecting a member's decision to either join or leave a facility are examined closely, it becomes evident that the club's programming has the ability to influence each in a positive fashion. As a result, a facility that is interested in enhancing its membership sales and membership retention levels needs to become adept at programming.

> According to consumer research on why people either join or leave a health/fitness club, programming plays an important role in both decisions.

All factors considered clubs should look at programming as the "play" or "theatre" that they put on to foster the memorable experiences that members desire. Hypothetically, creating these memorable experiences is like putting on a play, with the facility being the stage for the play, the equipment serving as the play's props, and the staff as the actors in the play. In this scenario, programming becomes a series of one-act plays that the facility's staff put on to entertain and engage the members. Programming has the ability to create connections between members, help motivate individuals to achieve their personal goals, help members establish training partnerships, offer competitive challenges for members, and entertain members. Programming is one of the most viable strategies that a facility has for meeting and exceeding the expectations that most individuals have as a member of a club. Furthermore, effective programming is one of the best tools a facility has for differentiating itself from its competitors.

> Effective programming is one of the best tools a facility has for differentiating itself from its competitors.

The Keys to Great Programming

A number of critical steps are involved in the efforts by health/fitness facilities to develop and execute an effective program strategy that enhances membership retention and sales. Among the essential steps that can help provide club operators with a simple process for achieving successful programming are the following:

❑ Understand the Market Served

The first step in programming, like the first step in developing almost any new business, involves obtaining an understanding of the market for that entity's products and services, in this instance, the club's members. The discovery process for a facility to understand its members should begin with the club opening the lines of communication with its members and determining their interests, needs, and wants. As such, conducting focus groups and surveys on a regular basis can help provide a facility with the basic information it might need.

At a minimum, every club should ask a series of questions of all of its new members that enables it to determine what the program and activity interests of these individuals are. Another excellent step, in this regard, is to keep track of what activities members participate in when they are in the facility. As this information is collected, the club should create a file on the interests and participation level of each member, as well as a record of the programs in which each individual is engaged. Subsequently, this information may help to facilitate efforts by facilities to provide member-centered programming.

❑ Have a Purpose and Vision

The club's second step in developing its programming approach should be to establish a purpose and vision for its programming. This purpose and vision need to align with the facility's overall mission and address the needs and desires of the membership. The purpose and vision should be based on its answers to the following questions:
- Is the club's programming designed to drive member involvement and participation?

- Is the club's programming designed to enhance the sale of memberships?
- Is the club's programming an integral part of the club's brand differentiation process?
- Is the primary purpose of the club's programming seen more as providing incremental revenue?
- Is the club's programming part of its experience theme?

At best, every club needs to establish a purpose and vision for its programming that can be stated in one paragraph and serve as the framework for its programming efforts. At ClubCorp facilities, for example, the purpose of programming was to drive member involvement in each club and create memorable experiences that can help enrich the lives of the members and build relationships.

❏ Get the Members Involved

One of the best-kept secrets about programming is that the more a club's members take ownership in its programming efforts, the better it will be for the club. This statement is particularly true among Millennials, who expect to collaborate with the brands they purchase from. When members take a sense of ownership in a club's programming, and collaborate in the creation of those programs, those individuals will be more likely to help the club design its programming efforts to meet their personal interests and needs and assist the club in getting other members to participate in the club's activities. Among the steps that clubs can employ to successfully get their members involved in their programming are the following:

- Establish member committees that act as liaisons with the membership and serve as ideation centers for programming.
- Identify member loyalists and get them involved in the programming at a volunteer level.
- Provide recognition and rewards for the members who become involved in the club's programming efforts.
- Establish a platform on social media that allows members to offer suggestions for programming.

❏ Get the Employees Involved

The ability of a facility to get its employees involved in its programming efforts is an essential factor with regard to whether it will be able to deliver exceptional programs. All factors considered, employees who participate in the planning and execution of the club's programming are more likely to assume an enhanced sense of ownership and responsibility for the success of the club's programming. Since the majority of employees in the fitness facility industry are Millennials, instituting a collaborative approach to programming will leverage one of this group's core values. Each facility should initiate its programming efforts by having the staff assigned to the task brainstorm about program ideas. Subsequently, the club should appoint employee teams to flush out the various possible programs in more detail. Finally, the facility should assign particular programs or program initiatives to specific employees and hold them accountable for their efforts. Most importantly, clubs should never make programming a one-person show.

Clubs should never make programming a one-person show.

A club's annual program plan should feature a mix of ongoing programs and special-event programs such as fitness games.

❏ Create an Annual Program Business Plan for the Club

Once the facility understands and executes the aforementioned steps, it then needs to develop an annual program plan for itself. An annual program plan allows the club to establish goals, timelines, schedules, and a system of accountability for its program offerings. The annual program plan serves as the facility's roadmap for programming success. The essential components of such an annual program plan include the following:

- Address specific "S.M.A.R.T. objectives." As such, the club should begin the process of developing an annual plan for its programming efforts by identifying specific objectives that should be achieved yearly that are simple, measurable, attainable, realistic, and trackable. These objectives should be consistent with the club's overall objectives and values. Examples of S.M.A.R.T. objectives include the following:
    ✓ Achieve an average of 3,000 participants each week in group exercise.
    ✓ Increase member retention from 65 percent to 70 percent by the end of the year.
    ✓ Generate an additional $30,000 each month over the prior year in program revenue.
- Establish a blended mix of programs. The facility should ensure that the success of its programming efforts is not dependent on just one type of programming, such as group exercise. Rather, its programming efforts should incorporate a variety of program options, including fitness programs, group-exercise programs, health-promotion programs, social programming, etc. Furthermore, the club's annual program plan should feature a mix of ongoing programs (i.e., programs that are offered on a daily or weekly basis, such as personal training, group-exercise classes, etc.) and special-event programs (i.e., programs that are conducted once a month or at certain designated times, such as fitness games, adventure outings, etc.).

- Create a program booklet and calendar. Most highly successful facilities develop both an annual program calendar and a quarterly program calendar. Program calendars serve to provide a club's members with a timetable of the facility's programs so the members can arrange their personal and business calendars to participate in the programs that are of interest to them. Producing a program booklet that can be given to its members is another productive step that facilities can take. These booklets feature a description of the offerings on the club's program calendar, thereby making it easier for the members to select the programs in which they are interested. These program calendars and booklets can be made available to the members through a variety of possible platforms, for example, posting on the club's website, posting on the club's Facebook or Instagram page, publishing in its newsletters, and the various distribution channels that the club uses to interact with its membership..
- Establish core marketing and promotional strategies for each program. As part of its annual program plan, the club should identify how it plans to market its programs to its members. The top three to five strategies should be detailed in the plan and then implemented to the degree possible. For example, some clubs employ posters and flyers to promote their programs, while others utilize their club's newsletters, website, and social media platforms. A number of facilities use displays and interactive media to promote their programs. Because most clubs will not be able to use every possible marketing tool, they should make a concerted effort to identify the strategies that it plans to use and then do the best it can to execute them.
- Assign each program to an employee and include a timeline for its implementation. As part of its annual program plan, the facility should assign an employee to be held accountable for the delivery of the program. As such, many larger clubs have program directors who have overall responsibility for the club's entire programming efforts. Unfortunately, however, many smaller facilities cannot afford a program director. In these instances, the club should appoint someone who is held accountable for each program.
- Build a basic financial plan for programs as part of the program plan. Another aspect of a club's program plan that should be included is itemized revenue and expense goals for the overall program and for each of the programs offered. While the financial portion of the program plan does not need to be detailed, it should, at a minimum, provide a framework for which employees can be held accountable.

❏ Constantly Market, Promote, and Sell

Some facilities develop a plan for programming, get their members and employees involved, and have all the materials that they need to offer the various programs, and yet their members still don't participate in the programs. A question arises concerning how such a scenario could occur. In this regard, one of the biggest pitfalls for club programming is the failure of many clubs to let their members know what programs are being conducted and when they are offered. Too often, facilities feel that if they simply put a poster up, or post information on the Facebook page, that their members will sign-up for the activity. In reality, nothing could be further from the truth. Because members are constantly exposed to a variety of marketing messages and materials, clubs need to be creative and disciplined in their approach to marketing and selling their programs. Among the steps that facilities can take to successfully market and sell its programs are the following:

- Touch all of the senses with its marketing efforts. Most members of a facility will respond to the club's marketing efforts if the facility blends the media it uses to promote its programs and these efforts touch the various senses of its individual members. For example, the club can stir a person's visual senses by using video content that runs on screens throughout the club and on the club's Facebook and YouTube pages. It can affect an individual's sense of hearing by using audio marketing through the facility's audiovisual mediums. It can also market a particular program by addressing a person's sense of smell, through the use of such contrivances as lighted incense or scented candles. Still other clubs might appeal to the member's sense of touch by using an interactive display to promote their programs.
- Think about targeting marketing efforts toward specific member audiences. Instead of using generic posters, videos, or displays, facilities should develop direct-mail pieces, invitations, targeted text messages, email blasts, and social media page postings to enhance member awareness. By using its records of member interests and activity patterns, clubs can create special invitations that are targeted to provide information on specific programs to specific member groups.

Every facility has the opportunity to script and stage programs that are tailored to the needs and interests of its members.

- Establish sales goals for each program. The facility should ensure that each program has a measurable target and then should share that information with its employees. Creating measurable targets (metrics) for each program will make it easier to hold employees accountable for each program's success.

- Teach employees the importance of leveraging their relationships to sell the club's programs. For whatever reason, most employees are uncomfortable with "selling" and shy away from it. As a result, many facilities find that even the best-planned sales goals and marketing efforts often fall short. In reality, clubs need to educate their employees to understand the fact that the relationships that they have with the facility's members is often the best avenue for program sales. Accordingly, clubs should establish incentive and reward programs that support the sales efforts of their employees. Such programs can have a meaningful impact on a facility's efforts to market and sell its programs.

❑ Feedback Is the Breakfast of Champions

Even after the facility has undertaken each of the aforementioned programming steps and the club's members have responded by participating in the activities offered in numbers never anticipated, the club has one more critical step to complete—obtain feedback from its members about its programming efforts. The most effective programmers in the health/fitness facility industry make a concerted effort to get feedback from the members and employees at the conclusion of every program. By soliciting feedback from all parties involved, the club will help lay a framework for continuous growth in its programming efforts, as well as continued success in those endeavors. Feedback provides information concerning what everyone really thinks about the club's programming. It also offers an objective look at the successes, opportunities, and possible limiting factors that may exist within a facility's programs.

Program Offerings: Status Quo or Changing of the Guard

Research shows that the commercial health/fitness facility industry offers a wide variety of programming options for members. According to data presented in *IHRSA's 2014 Profiles of Success,* the number of core programs offered by clubs has increased over the past four years to 69. Figure 13-1, based on data from *IHRSA's 2014 Annual Profiles of Success,* details the top facility program offerings from 2003 through 2013.

Several key observations can be made as a result of reviewing this data. First, the program offerings highlighted in these reports, which cover a span of 10 years, reflect a tendency for commercial facilities to offer the same programs (e.g., lack of innovation). Second, while global macro-trends indicate an emerging need for programs that serve seniors, youth, and those individuals with lifestyle-related health problems (e.g., obesity, diabetes, arthritis, etc.), commercial clubs seem to have decreased the number of programs they offer to serve these distinct populations over the past decade. Third, social programming continues to represent a minor portion of most clubs' program offerings, despite the growing emergence of social networking.

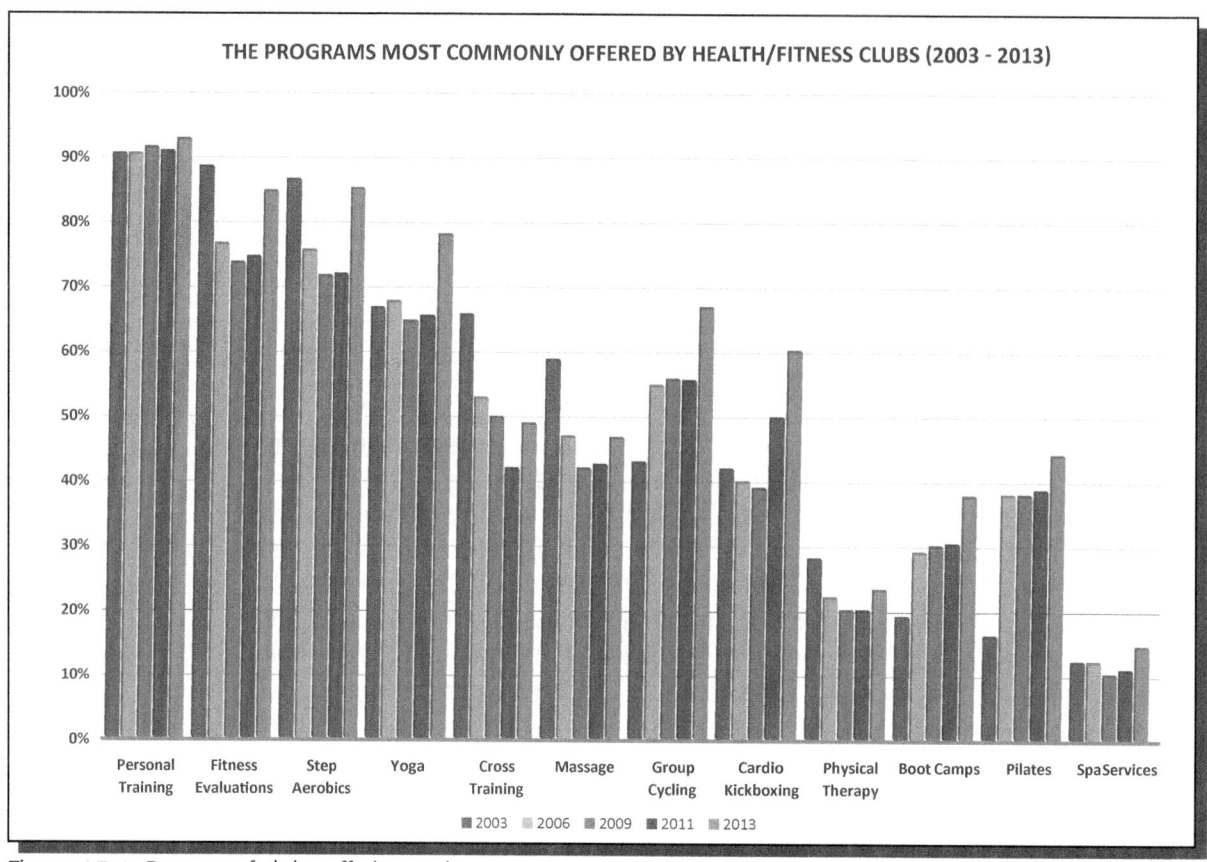

Figure 13-1. Percent of clubs offering various programs 2003–2013

As such, based on the information reflected both in Figure 13-1 and within the pages of the 2014 Profiles of Success report, commercial health/fitness facilities have not fully grasped the value of creating and delivering programs for niche audiences. A similar programming shortcoming exists for the newest generation of members whose interests lie in social connectivity.

In 2016, ClubIntel conducted a trend study of the global health/fitness facility industry that looked at programming trends, among others. As such, when the programming trends reported by this 2016 study are compared with the program interests expressed by club members in IHRSA's 2015 Health Club Consumer, several intriguing insights are observed.

First, among seven highly popular program formats offered by clubs in 2014 (e.g., personal training, boot camp classes, yoga, group cycling classes, aquatic classes, barre, and Pilates), in every instance, the percentage of facilities and professionals offering the programs far exceed the actual level of consumer participation. Second, the popularity of certain programs in which members indicate they participate differs considerably from what is reflected as the most popular among the club offerings (Figure 13-2).

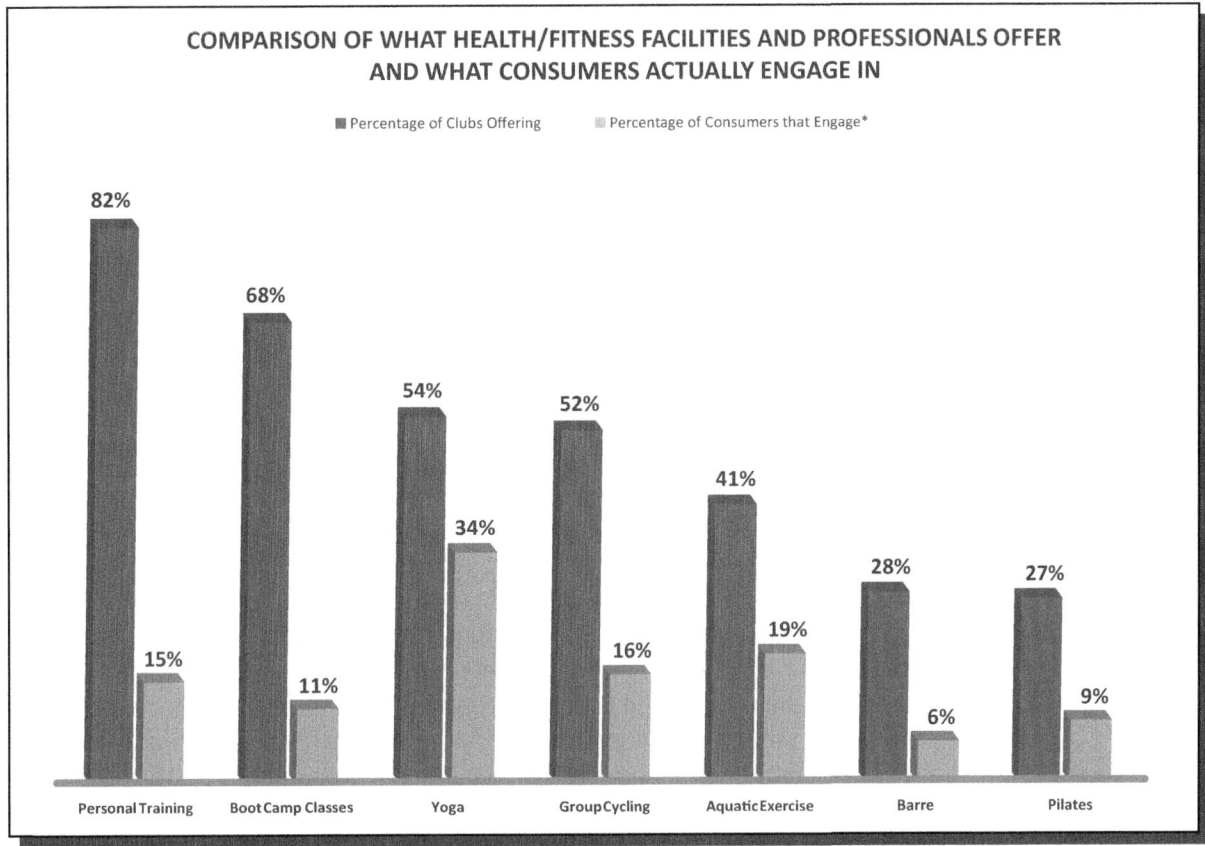

Figure 13-2. A comparison of what clubs offer and what members say they do

These insights would imply that club operators may not be as attuned to general consumer needs and wants as they should be. Instead, they are responding to niche audiences and to "hype" emanating from the health/fitness facility industry, rather than to the general voice of the member.

Each year, the American Council of Exercise conducts a survey of personal trainers to identify up-and-coming trends for the next year. Figure 13-3 provides an overview of the top seven fitness-related trends identified by this survey for the years 2004, 2009, and 2012. It is interesting to note that the trends indicated by the trainers don't seem to align with the programming trends reflected in the two aforementioned reports.

2004	2009	2012
Balance Training	Boot Camp Workouts	Obesity Awareness
Fusion Classes	Budget Workouts	Whole Life Fitness
Shorter Duration Workouts	Specialty Classes	Behavior Modicication
Wellness Coaching	Circuit Training	Technology Based Training
Flexible Workouts	Kettlebells	Community Fitness
Corproate Fitness	Senior Fitness	Senior and Youth Fitness
Functional Fitness	Technology Based Training	Corproate Fitness

Figure 13-3. ACE's annual fitness trends to watch

While most clubs and facilities remain fixated on sticking with the tried-and-true programming elements of past years, many independent facilities and multi-club operations, as well as boutique fitness studios, have begun pushing the envelope by introducing programs that appeal to smaller niche audiences, as well as to the socially engaged Millennials. Among the examples of programming trends that have attracted what some people refer to as "program groupies" are the following:

- Fusion fitness: These are classes that combine multiple activities, often incorporating activities as diverse as Pilates and kickboxing; rowing and weight training; and yoga and eating chocolate. According to the 2016 International Fitness Industry Trend Report, 45 percent of health/fitness facility settings offer fusion-style classes.
- Small-group training (traditional and HIIT): Facilities have begun to transform their personal training programs from one-on-one to small/mid-size group sessions that involve one instructor coaching four to six members. As group sessions have evolved, clubs and trainers have constructed the group sessions around a number of themes, such as SWAT boot camp or dance boot camp. According to the aforementioned International Fitness Trend study, 57 percent of health/fitness facility settings offer small-group, fee-based training. One of the fastest growing programs in health/fitness facilities over the past three years according to the aforementioned study is HIIT small-group training, which experienced 59 percent growth from 2013 to 2016.

Cross training is one of the programs most commonly offered by health/fitness clubs.

- Pre-packaged group exercise: Les Mills, began the trend of leveraging pre-packaged group programs in the 1990s, when it instituted BODYPUMP, as well as such subsequent classes as BODYCOMBAT, RPM, and BODYBALANCE, among others. Another company whose packaged programs are offered in over 1,000 clubs worldwide is Mossa, formerly Body Training Systems. Furthermore, over the last few years, Zumba, has taken pre-packaged programming to a new level, as has Flirty Girl Fitness. As such, the 2016 trend study previously quoted shows that 43 percent of health/fitness facility settings offer pre-choreographed (packaged) classes.

- Boot camp: Boot camp classes, which first arose on the scene at the turn of the century, have evolved into a programming stable of most health/fitness clubs. Currently, these classes are offered both indoors and outdoors and are conducted featuring a host of themes. In fact, boot camp classes are an offshoot of the small-group training phenomena that has occurred in the health/fitness facility over the past decade. According to the previously quoted trend study, 63 percent of health/fitness facility settings offer boot camp-style classes.

HIIT classes have emerged as one of the top trends in personal and small-group training since 2010.

- High intensity interval training classes (HIIT). HIIT has become all the rage in recent years. HIIT programs, which are also referred to as metabolic training, combine intervals of extremely intense cardio or resistance training with less-intense resistance movements, such as bodyweight-oriented movements. These classes have emerged as one of the top trends in personal and small-group training since 2010. One indicator of the popularity of these programs was the release of the Les Mills Grit series of classes, which are based on the underlying principles of HIIT. A class such as Beach Body Fitness's Insanity is also an example of HIIT training. As such, HIIT group classes (more than six individuals) are offered by 58 percent of health/fitness facility settings, according to the 2016 trend study. According to the same survey, HIIT classes grew by 87 percent from 2013 to 2016.
- Fitness tours and adventures: While programming outside the four walls of the facility has existed for decades, only in the past five years have clubs, particularly, public recreation facilities, begun to embrace the social significance of offering a wide array of program opportunities that bring together members of like interests who enjoy participating and socializing in exotic and far-flung fitness adventures.
- Clans with fans: One of the newest trends, although it is still in the growth stage, is offering programs targeted at small passionate audiences of members. Classes such as pole-dancing fitness, lap-dancing fitness, sport dancing, and

Fitness tours and adventures are an example of programming trends that have attracted what some people refer to as "program groupies."

yoga and wine, among others, show that if a facility appeals to small passionate audiences of members, it can have a significant impact on the overall engagement of a club's membership base. In reality, these programs for clans have spurred the development of the boutique fitness club industry.

- Virtual group fitness: The explosion of budget clubs and 24/7 clubs, along with the flexibility afforded by smart phones, tablets, and computers has spawned an entirely new way of delivering fitness, both at the club level and offsite. The most popular virtual group-exercise class programs are offered by Fitness on Demand, Wexar Virtual, Les Mills, and WellBeats, formerly Fitness on Request. These virtual classes allow members to take a virtual instructor-led class whenever they desire. According to the 2016 trend study referenced previously in this section, club-held virtual group fitness classes grew by 390 percent between 2013 and 2016, with just over 10 percent of all clubs indicating they offer these virtual experiences in their clubs. Another trend in virtual fitness classes involves group exercises that members can download or stream from a club-sponsored digital platform (e.g., YouTube) through a subscription. According to the previously mentioned 2016 trend study, 10 percent of clubs indicate they offer this service to their members. As such, Crunch Fitness currently offers virtual classes to which members and consumers at large can purchase a subscription and either download or stream to their Internet-connected device of choice from the company's website.

- Use of fitness wearable devices to support client training. From 2013 to 2016, the health/fitness industry has seen the use of fitness wearables as a tool to support client training increase dramatically, increasing from 11 percent of facilities in 2013 to 29 percent of facilities in 2016. Fitness wearables, especially devices and systems such as those sold by MyZone and Polar, have become mainstays in many cycling and HIIT programs. These devices and their accompanying systems allow users to track their own performance while exercising, but also allow them to upload performance data to the cloud to review at a later date. Additionally, systems such as MyZone and Polar provide digital scoreboards, which post the heart rates and power output for each student in class, thereby offering both a social support structure and competitive element to inspire class participants.

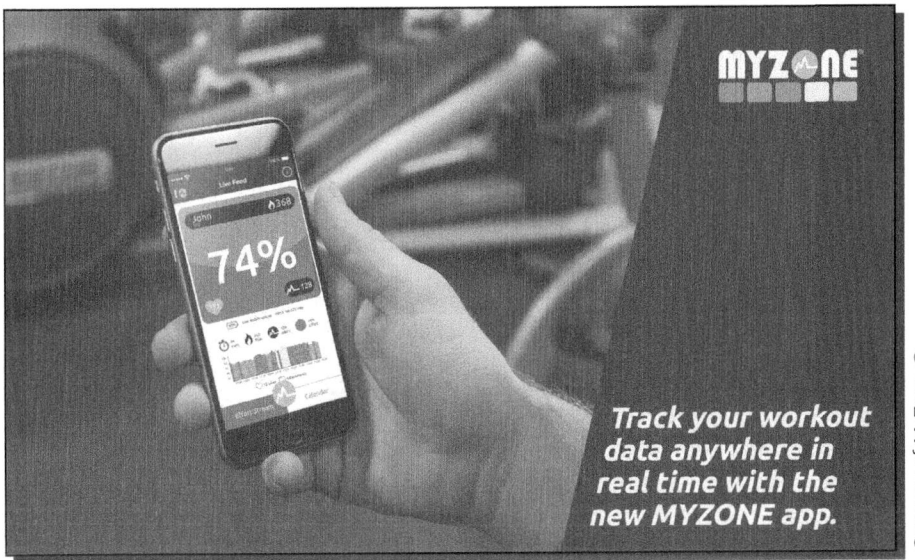

The health/fitness industry has seen the use of fitness wearables as a tool to support client training increase dramatically.

The question arises that begs asking, "Will operators continue to lean heavily on the programming basics, such as personal training, group cycling, and massage, or will they embrace the newest trends such as virtual fitness classes, HIIT small group training, barre, aerial yoga, adventure races, and fusion-style classes. Furthermore, will clubs and studios explore other ways to introduce innovative activities to their members?" Truth be known, no immutable answer exists to such an inquiry. Without question, however, change must occur if the industry is to evolve and properly serve its newest member constituencies.

Reflections

Programming is a tool that club operators can use to engage, connect, entertain, motivate, and recognize members. Every facility has the opportunity to script and stage programs that are tailored to the needs and interests of its members.

In reality, the ability of clubs to leverage that opportunity will provide the fuel to drive member engagement and participation, as well as, ultimately, member loyalty and retention.

PART 4
The Business of Developing and Managing a Health/Fitness Business

Chapter 14
Health/Fitness Facility Business Models

Chapter 15
Establishing a Health/Fitness Business

Chapter 16
The Health/Fitness Industry Financial Model

Chapter 17
Budgeting, Forecasting, and Driving Profitability in the Health/Fitness Facility Industry

Chapter 18
Buying, Leasing, Selling, and Raising Capital for a Health/Fitness Business

Health/Fitness Facility Business Models

14

"If you don't have a competitive advantage, don't compete."

—Jack Welch

Chapter Objectives

The health/fitness facility industry, like many other industries that have reached the mature phase of their life stage, has seen the business models that comprise its universe evolve and differentiate. This chapter will begin by discussing the umbrella business models in the health/fitness facility industry, and then dig down and briefly explore the various value propositions (operating concepts/models) that entrepreneurs and experienced veterans have introduced within each of these.

Umbrella Business Models

In the health/fitness facility industry, there are three basic models from which to choose: an independent club/studio operator, a part of a multiple-unit operation (regional or national), or a franchise (single, district, or regional). A review of each of the three types of models can help reveal the benefits and risks associated with each option:

❑ *Independent Facility.* An independent club model involves a business that operates independently of any other club, studio or business association. As such, the development and operation of the business is solely dependent upon the facility's ability to build the systems and hire the people to operate profitably. It should be noted that individually owned and operated boutique fitness studios would also fall into this category. Over 50 percent of the health/fitness clubs operating in the U.S. are independently owned and operated, including industry leaders such as Red's in Lafayette, Louisiana; Franco's in Mandeville, Louisiana; the Gainesville Health and Fitness Center in Gainesville, Florida; the Rochester Athletic Club in Rochester, Minnesota; the East Bank Club in Chicago, Illinois; and Fitness Quest 10 in San Diego, California. Among the benefits of establishing the business as an independent club are the following:
- The facility can be designed and operated as part of the local community, thereby creating a product unique to the demographics of the market in which it is located.

> Over 50 percent of the health/fitness clubs operating in the U.S. are independently owned and operated.

- The ownership group of the business has control of the business's destiny and can create the systems and structures it deems necessary.
- The club or studio can establish a brand for itself in the local community that is built on the values and goals of the ownership group.
- The club or studio will not be burdened with some of the overhead costs normally associated with being part of a franchise or multiple-club operation.
- Concurrent with the aforementioned benefits, the owner and operator of an independent club or boutique fitness studio also face several challenges that the other operating models do not have, including:
  - ✓ Independent operators will not have access to the capital, operating, and marketing resources that the other operating models can offer.
  - ✓ Independent operators may find themselves at a disadvantage with the other business models when it comes to purchasing power, marketing clout, and talent recruitment.

The health/fitness club industry was founded by independent operators whose talent and passion helped forge the $30 billion-plus U.S. industry that presently exists. It is these same types of entrepreneurial spirits that are driving the growth of the boutique fitness studio market. At present, other than boutique fitness facility operators, the current landscape portrays an environment that is less friendly to those individuals who operate independently.

❑ *Multiple-Unit Operation.* The multiple-unit business model exists today because it affords owners and operators several distinct advantages when it comes to accessing capital, recruiting talent, and controlling a particular market. Multiple-club firms currently occupy a significant portion of the entire health/fitness club market. A multiple-unit operation can be national, such as 24 Hour Fitness, LA Fitness, Lifetime Fitness, Equinox, or boutique studio operator Core Power Yoga; regional, such as Town Sports International (Northeast corridor), Bay Clubs (California), or Sport and Health (Washington, Maryland, and Virginia); or local, such as Wisconsin Athletic Clubs (Milwaukee), Fitness Formula (Chicago), Healthworks Fitness Centers for Women (Boston), or Village Sports Clubs (Phoenix). In the current global economy, multiple-club operations can also position themselves as multi-national or global club companies, such as Virgin Active (United Kingdom, Italy, South Africa, Spain) or Basic Fit (Belgium, France, Luxembourg, Netherlands, and Spain).

Being part of a multiple-club or multi-studio operation offers several business advantages when compared to being an independent club operator, including:
- Access to capital for growth
- Business systems and programs that can assist in operating a club or studio more efficiently and profitably
- Talent sources and intellectual capital that can enhance the opportunities in a given market and help grow local talent
- Cost efficiencies driven by volume purchases
- Branding and marketing as provided by the parent company

Concurrent with the aforementioned advantages, being part of a multiple-club or multi-studio operation also has several potential downsides about which a business operator should be aware, including:

- The local business operator will normally have less control of their destiny and less freedom to operate their business as they desire, because they will need to fit their efforts into the systems, policies, and procedures of the parent company.
- The business operator may find that the facility is less unique to its market than it would prefer or expect since it must function according to the branding and operational model established by the parent company.
- The business will most likely have to assume the name of the parent company and thereby forfeit any direct identity with its local market (e.g., 24 Hour Fitness, LA Fitness, Virgin Active, Fitness First, Core Power Yoga, etc.). Some multiple-club operations, such as Wellbridge (e.g., Bel Air Athletic Club, Colorado Athletic Clubs, and Sport and Wellness Clubs), allow their clubs to have individual identities.

❑ *Franchised Business Operation.* The franchise model has become one of the most popular approaches for entrepreneurs to enter the industry. Some of the largest and most well-known brands in the industry (companies such as Anytime Fitness, Gold's Gym, Planet Fitness, and Snap Fitness) are all built on a franchise framework, as well as some of emerging boutique fitness studios such as Barry's Boot Camp, Pure Barre, and Orange Theory. Owning and operating a franchised club or fitness studio provides some of the advantages of both an independent operation and a multiple-club operation. The franchising model is based on the principle that local business owners will have greater success connecting their club or studio to the local community and making it successful if they have an ownership stake in the business, while at the same time benefiting from being associated with a recognized brand that provides operational and marketing assistance. Since 2000, specialty franchises, such as Curves, Anytime Fitness, Snap Fitness, and more recently Barry's Boot Camp, Pure Barre, Orange Theory Fitness, and Retro Fitness, have established themselves as leading franchise operations and, consequently, have helped to reshape the industry by establishing greater value to the franchise model.

A franchise can be purchased for one club, for a district or an entire region. Franchisers, such as Anytime Fitness or Gold's, require potential investors to meet certain financial expectations before they can assume a franchise. These expectations include the requirement that the franchisee must demonstrate the level of financial backing that would be needed to build and operate the franchise. Most franchisers charge the franchisee an up-front franchise fee that can range from as low as $5,000 to as high as $35,000 and an annual fee that can run between 3 percent and 6 percent of the franchisee's annual revenues. In addition, there are other costs associated with having a franchise, including the cost of purchasing the operational and retail products needed for the club through the franchiser's business system.

> **The franchise model has become one of the most popular approaches for entrepreneurs to enter the industry.**

The advantages to a health/fitness club operator who chooses to become a franchised operation include:

- Obtaining the rights to a nationally recognized brand that will immediately position the new business in the marketplace
- Access to the business systems created by the franchiser, such as design plans, equipment discounts, operations manuals, marketing templates, insurance, etc.
- Access to national marketing programs and the ability to share costs on marketing and advertising programs
- Access to educational programs and conventions operated by the franchiser
- Ability, as a local owner, to control the destiny of their business as long as they meet the criteria established by the franchiser

Concurrent with the aforementioned advantages are some disadvantages, including:

- Upfront capital for the franchise fee, something the club or fitness studio would not have if it operated independently or was part of a multiple-club operation
- The annual cost of maintaining the franchise
- An association with a specific brand, especially if that brand proves to be the wrong one for the club's particular community. A club should be aware of the fact that the consumer will associate it with a specific brand, even if it operates differently than most of the others who use that franchise brand.
- Limitations in the club's or studio's flexibility to operate the business as it desires, because of the requirements of the franchise agreement

The Different Facility Market Segments and Value Propositions in the Health/Fitness Facility Industry

The health/fitness club industry has evolved into a diverse array of operating models or concepts, each offering consumers a different value proposition based on the type and scope of facility, type and quantity of equipment made available, programs offered, services rendered, and pricing approach. The reason for having such a diverse array of value propositions or club concepts is the result of operators' efforts to differentiate themselves in the marketplace, to capture a position or audience that is uniquely their own. Unfortunately, too many operators and entrepreneurs fall prey to the most common denominator in any industry where staking out a space a business can own occurs, and that is to revert to price as the leading point of differentiation. Pricing models will be discussed in the section that follows this one. All said, this section will bring forward the leading health/fitness operating concepts or value propositions that exist in the marketplace (Figures 14-1 and 14-2).

CHAPTER FOURTEEN

Health/Fitness Facility Business Models

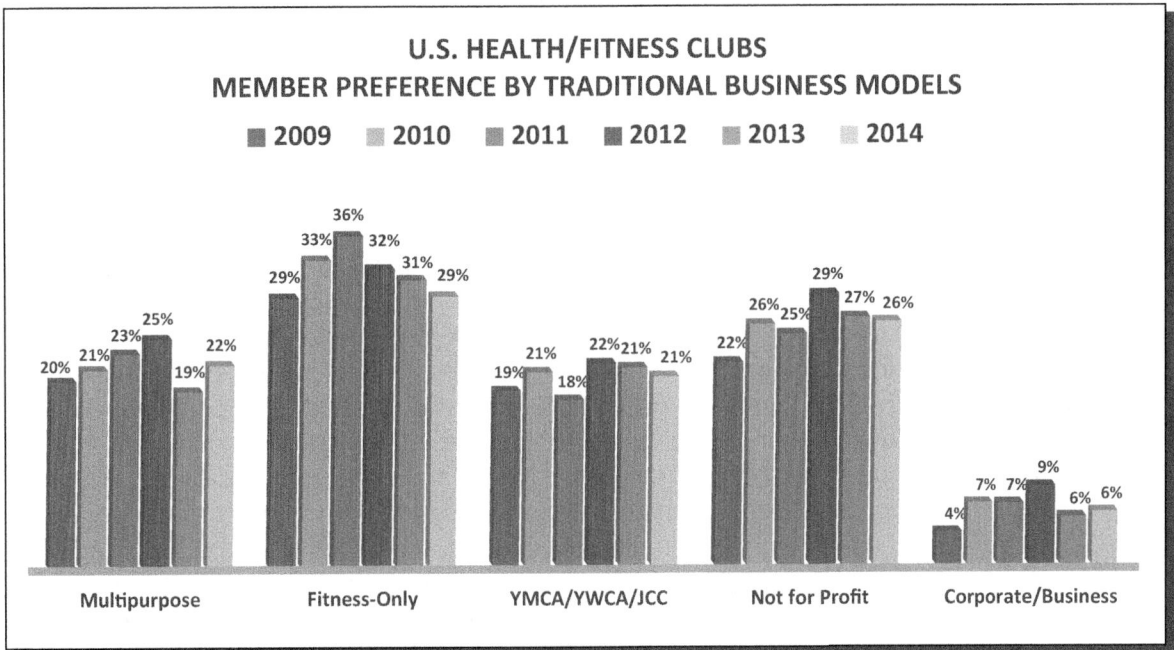

Figure 14-1. U.S. health/fitness clubs member preference by traditional business models 2009 to 2014

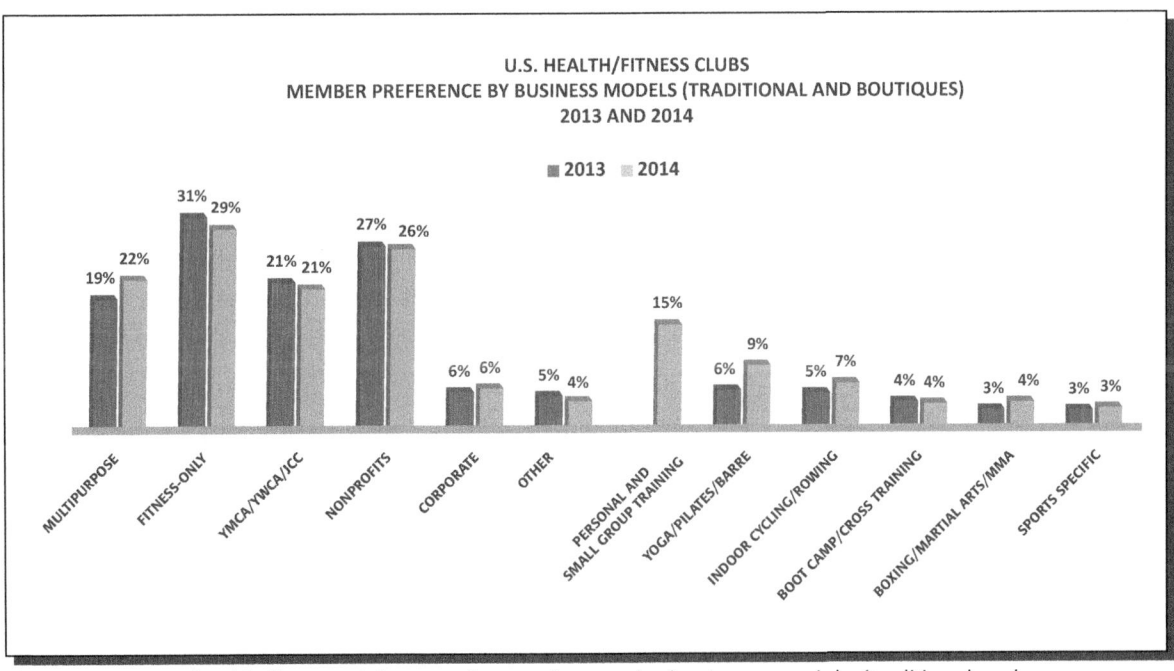

Figure 14-2. U.S. health/fitness clubs member preference by business models (traditional and boutique) 2013 and 2014

> *Fitness-only clubs.* Fitness-only clubs are clubs whose product offering is composed primarily of a variety of fitness equipment, fitness instruction and coaching, possibly personal training, and in many instances group exercise studios and the classes that are attendant to having these studios. Among the leading U.S. operators of fitness-only clubs are Anytime Fitness, Crunch Fitness, Gold's Gym, 24 Hour Fitness, Planet Fitness, and Equinox. Within this particular segment, most operators have differentiated themselves on price, access, or the inclusion or exclusion of a specific element such as group exercise classes, personal training, etc. For example, fitness-only clubs such as Planet Fitness, Retro Fitness, Blink, and Crunch franchises have staked their position to what the health/fitness club industry defines as the high-volume low-price model (e.g., budget club or value club) where monthly dues are under $20 a month. Equinox, on the other hand, has staked their position on elegant facilities, dynamic and engaging group fitness programs, leading-edge personal training, and state-of-the art technology. Consequently, Equinox's price point exceeds $150 in most markets. According to IHRSA's *2016 Health Club Consumer Report*, the average monthly fee paid by a member of a fitness-only club is $41, while approximately 33 percent of consumers frequent this particular club concept. Since 2013, the percentage of consumers frequenting these types of facilities has declined.

> *Multipurpose clubs.* Multipurpose clubs represent a diverse range of clubs whose facilities and associated offerings extend beyond just fitness. From a facility perspective, multipurpose clubs will provide spaces for other activities, spaces such as group exercise studios, pools, racquet courts, sport courts (e.g., basketball, volleyball), spa zones, child-care centers, and even cafes. In essence, multipurpose clubs could be considered lifestyle malls, providing a little, or in some cases, a lot of everything that an individual may want to use in pursuing their health and fitness goals. Among the leading independent multipurpose club operators in the U.S. are clubs such as the Eastbank Club in Chicago; the Houstonian in Houston, Texas; and Red's in Lafayette, Louisiana. Some of the leading regional and national companies who operate multipurpose clubs include the Bay Clubs based out of San Francisco, California; Fitness Formula in Chicago, Illinois; LA Fitness based in Los Angeles, California; Lifetime Fitness with offices in Minneapolis, Minnesota; and 24 Hour Fitness located in San Ramon, California. In this segment, differentiation tends to leverage more than one element, often relying on a combination of facilities and services offered, and the price point that is associated with that offering. For example, Lifetime Fitness has established a value proposition that is built on providing a well-designed facility of over 110,000 square feet offering nearly every imaginable kind of activity for families at an affordable price (ranges from $40 to $160 for an individual membership and for a family $75 to $340 a month, depending on the market and level of access). On the other end of the spectrum are the Bay Clubs located in California, which position themselves as sports resorts, whose facilities are similar in scope to Lifetime Fitness, but whose programming, staffing levels, and level of service are reminiscent of a resort. As a result, their price points are considerably higher than those of Lifetime Fitness, with individual memberships going for close to $200 a month and family memberships in some instances approaching $400 a month.

According to data from IHRSA's *2016 Health Club Consumer Report*, the average fee paid by a member of a multipurpose club is $76 a month (approximately double than the average price paid for a fitness-only club), while approximately 22 percent of consumers frequent them.

❏ *Boutique fitness studios.* Boutiques are the new players on the block, having established a powerful presence in the past few years. According to IHRSA's *2016 Health Club Consumer Report*, 35 percent of consumers frequent a boutique fitness studio. Boutique studio operators have been able to accomplish what their larger siblings—the big-box players, regional firms, and franchise companies—have been unable to do: fulfill the needs of niche and highly passionate interest groups. These studios have evolved into exercise destinations that serve specific fitness clans, groups of people who are passionate about pursuing a specific type of exercise regime. A sampling of the types of niche studios that have evolved over the last decade include:

> Boutiques are the new players on the block, having established a powerful presence in the past few years.

- *Personal/small group training studios (15 percent of consumers frequent).* Personal training studios vary considerably, often being based on the training principles espoused by its founder. The types of personal training studios vary considerably, a sampling of which include: those that utilize standard fitness equipment (e.g., cardio equipment, variable resistance machines and free weights) and those that use more functionally based apparatus such as TRX, ropes, tires and kettlebells. According to a study conducted by the Association of Fitness Studios (AFS) in 2015, 42 percent of studio operators indicated their focus was personal training. According to data brought forward by IHRSA's *2016 Health Club Consumer Report*, the average member of a personal training/small group training studio pays $92 a month.

- *Cross-training/boot camp/HIIT studios (4 percent of consumers frequent).* These studios focus on offering a dynamic setting for conducting group training centered on a multi-movement framework that leverages the use of more functional equipment and accessories, along with structured workout regimes using bodyweight movements as well as equipment. Within this segment of the studio market are clubs dedicated to offering a high-intensity interval-style workout, such as franchise operators Barry's Boot Camp (17 locations and growing) and Orange Theory (over 500 locations opened). Four established brands operating in this sphere are CrossFit, Barry's Boot Camp, Iron Tribe Fitness, and Orange Theory. According to data from the aforementioned IHRSA report, approximately 4 percent of consumers frequent these studios paying an average of approximately $106 a month.

- *Yoga studios.* Yoga studios might possibly be the most popular type of fitness studio. Not all yoga studios are alike. There are some that focus on a particular style of yoga (e.g., Hatha, Vinyasa, Ashtanga, power yoga, Ienger, Kundalini, Bikram, hot yoga, and even aerial yoga), while others may offer a variety of yoga styles in an effort to broaden their appeal (e.g., Pure Yoga, Yoga Works). According to AFS's 2016 study of studio operators, approximately 2 percent indicated they operate yoga studios. Two of the most prominent operators of yoga studios are Core Power Yoga and Yoga Works. IHRSA's *2016 Health Club Consumer Report* does not track data exclusively for yoga studios and instead lumps it in with the other leading mind-body studio offerings such as barre and Pilates. According to their data, 9 percent of consumers frequent one of these three mind-body studio offerings, paying on average approximately $87 a month.

- *Pilates studios.* Pilates studios are a key player in the mind-body studio segment (also includes yoga and barre studios) and represent an important consumer niche. Pilates studios focus primarily on providing equipment-based instruction and training, both on an individual level and in group sessions. According to AFS's 2016 study of boutique studios, approximately 4 percent reported being Pilates studios. There are also studios that also offer mat-based class instruction. Pilates studios often focus on delivering a specific style of Pilates methodology based on the background of the lead instructor or founder (e.g., Balanced Body, Fletcher, Stott, Power, and Winsor). Finally, some Pilates studios may differentiate themselves by offering Gyrotonics. IHRSA's *2016 Health Club Consumer Report* does not track data exclusively for Pilates studios and instead lumps it in with the other leading mind-body studio offerings such as barre and yoga. According to their data, 9 percent of consumers frequent one of these three mind-body studio offerings, paying on average approximately $87 a month.

Barre studios have blossomed over the past several years.

- *Barre studios.* Barre studios have blossomed over the past several years. Barre is based on the movement principles originally espoused by Lotte Berk, incorporating movement principles from ballet, Pilates, and Yoga. In New York, Physique 57, a Barre-based studio, which opened its first studio in 2006, has since grown to occupy multiple studio locations. Barre Code, a Chicago-based Barre studio, opened its first studio in 2009 and has since expanded to 24 locations in 10 states. Two of the largest Barre Studio operators are Pure Barre with approximately 300 locations in North America and the Bar Method with approximately 72 locations in the U.S. Interestingly, in the UK, there are still official Lotte Berk studios in operation. IHRSA's *2016 Health Club Consumer Report* does not track data exclusively for Barre studios and instead lumps it in with the other leading mind-body studio offerings such as Pilates and yoga. According to their data, 9 percent of consumers frequent one of these three mind-body studio offerings, paying on average approximately $87 a month. At Physique 57, a premium barre studio operation with studios in multiple markets, a monthly unlimited membership to its New York–based studios runs approximately $340.

- *Sports performance studios.* One segment of the studio industry that gained popularity during the first decade of the 21st century, but whose growth has since flattened, is the sports training segment. This segment focuses on providing coaching and training intended to enhance athletic performance. These studios may follow the principles of a specific discipline, with national franchises such as Athletic Republic, Parisi Speed School, and Velocity Sports Performance leading the way, and independent operator D1 Sports. IHRSA's *2016 Health Club Consumer Report* reported that approximately 2 percent of members use these studios, paying on average $131 a month.

- *Multi-disciplinary performance studios.* These are unique studios that have chosen to integrate several disciplines to help individuals enhance their fitness, health, and overall level of physical performance. According to AFS's 2016 study of boutique studios, approximately 25 percent reported being multi-disciplinary. Many of these studios combine a variety of health- and fitness-oriented disciplines, among the most common modalities incorporated include: personal training, sport-specific training, small-group training, chiropractic, massage, nutritional counseling, and even acupuncture. There are also numerous multi-disciplined studios that combine disciplines such as HIIT and cycling, or cycling and yoga. Two examples would be Ezia Performance Labs in San Diego, California, and FNS Training Center in Santa Clara, California.

- *Group cycling studios.* Group cycling exploded onto the health and fitness club scene in the early 1990s. Since its introduction to the health/fitness club market, group cycling has evolved into one of the industry's most popular classes. In the middle of the last decade (2000 to 2010), entrepreneurs saw an opportunity to establish an even more unique group cycling experience by creating studios dedicated to group cycling, attracting the most extreme devotees of group cycling. According to AFS's 2016 study of boutique studios, approximately 4 percent reported operating group cycling studios. The most often cited example of success in this genre of the studio segment has been SoulCycle based in New York, which in just the past several years has opened over 80 studios and is now a sub-brand of Equinox. FlyWheel and CycleBar are franchise operators with studios in numerous U.S. markets. According to data published in IHRSA's most recent Health Club Consumer Report, approximately 7 percent of consumers frequent cycling studios, paying on average $112 a month.

> One segment of the studio industry that gained popularity during the first decade of the 21st century, but whose growth has since flattened, is the sports training segment.

Studios dedicated to group cycling attract the most extreme devotees of group cycling.

The Different Price Point Models Used by Operators to Create Differentiation

The previous two sections highlighted the high-level umbrella business models that define the health/fitness club industry, as well as the specific operating models and value proposition offerings that define the current state of the industry. As brought forth earlier in this book, a club's value equation is dependent on six elements (facility quality, product quality, service quality, emotional quality, price, and time), of which price is only one component. As a result, price should never be the sole determinant of a business's value proposition. Unfortunately, in many mature industries, including the health/fitness club industry, operators often define themselves by this one element, often eschewing the other elements. Therefore, it is important to understand how the industry has modeled its offerings based on price. What follows are the pricing models which have come to define for many in the industry the market segment in which they operate.

❑ *Budget clubs (under $20 a month)*. Budget clubs, or as many in the industry would prefer to call them, high-value or high-volume low-price clubs, are those club businesses whose offering is priced at $20 or less on a monthly basis, the majority of whom offer memberships at under $15 a month and several who offer memberships for only $10 a month (e.g., Planet Fitness, Crunch, Fitness Connection, Fitness Evolution, Gold's Gym Express, and Youfit). According to IHRSA's *2016 Health Club Consumer Report*, approximately 41 percent of consumers belong to clubs whose price point falls within this range. These clubs tend to be fitness-only facilities focused on offering a good level of facility quality that is highlighted by an expansive array of fitness equipment, minimalistic changing rooms, and in some instances, small group exercise rooms. The majority of budget clubs have a footprint that encompasses less than 20,000 square feet. These clubs tend to have limited staff (usually one or two on duty at any moment in time), no programming to speak of (some offer a limited group class schedule or virtual group exercise classes), and no amenities (i.e., locker room supplies, towels, etc.). In the U.S., some of the leading national and regional budget club operators include Planet Fitness, Crunch, Blink, Retro Fitness, Youfit, Chuze Fitness, and Fitness Connection. This segment of the club industry grew by nearly 70 percent from 2014 to 2016, and during this time period was the second fastest growing segment of the club industry behind boutique fitness studios.

❑ *Economy clubs ($20 to $49 a month).* Economy clubs represent a step up from the budget club segment. The majority of clubs in this segment are priced between $29 a month and $49 a month, depending on the market they do business in. According to the aforementioned IHRSA trend report, approximately 28 percent of consumers belong to clubs whose price point falls within this range. For example, an LA Fitness membership in Dallas, Texas, can be obtained for $29 a month, while in California or the Northeast it may go for $49. These clubs tend to be fitness-only, but many, such as LA Fitness clubs, are multipurpose facilities. Clubs who operate in this price range tend to leverage their facility quality (variety of spaces, reasonable level of finish out, and abundance of equipment) and product quality (group exercise classes, child care, etc.), while often shunning any serious attention to service quality and emotional quality. These clubs may range in size from 5,000 square feet (e.g., Anytime Fitness) to 50,000 square feet (e.g., LA Fitness). In the U.S., some of the leading national and regional club operators in this segment include Anytime Fitness, LA Fitness, X-Sport Fitness, 24 Hour Fitness, and Gold's Gym.

❑ *Mid-market clubs ($50 to $74 a month).* Clubs that operate in this segment represent a blend of fitness-only and multipurpose facilities. Like those clubs operating in the economy sphere, the price point is influenced by location, and consequently a membership in one market could be $59 and in another $79 a month. According to data from the previously mentioned IHRSA trend report, 13 percent of consumers indicate they are members of clubs whose price point falls within this range. Clubs operating in this segment tend to add an additional element to their value equation, adding the service quality element to the facility quality and product quality elements that are the domain of the economy clubs. By bringing forward a more refined service experience built around better staffing (level of staffing and competency of staffing) and additional programming, these clubs offer their members a more enriching and rewarding membership experience, which in turn enables them to set a higher price point. In the U.S., some of the leading national and regional club operators in this segment include 24 Hour Fitness, Gold's Gym, Wisconsin Athletic Clubs, and a few of the Fitness Formula clubs in Chicago. This segment of the club industry, along with the economy segment discussed in the previous paragraph, grew by

> The budget club segment of the club industry grew by nearly 70 percent from 2014 to 2016.

Multipurpose clubs could be considered lifestyle malls, providing a little, or in some cases a lot, of everything that an individual may want to use in pursuing their health and fitness goals.

only 2 percent from 2014 to 2016 and represents an industry segment that is facing challenges in a club environment where budget clubs and premium clubs appear to be prospering.

- ❑ *Premium clubs ($75 to $99 a month).* Premium clubs tend to leverage all or most elements of the value equation, taking the facility quality, product quality, and service quality that define the mid-market clubs and introducing a higher level of service quality and offering certain aspects of the emotional quality. In most instances, these clubs are multipurpose, though there are a few that are fitness-only. These clubs also offer a higher level of finish to their facilities, along with a greater commitment to having qualified staff available to serve the members. Premium clubs also offer an extensive variety of programming. According to the 2016 IHRSA Consumer Trend Report, approximately 7 percent of consumers belong to clubs whose price point falls within this range. In the U.S., some of the leading national and regional club operators in this segment include Lifetime Fitness; Sport and Health, Washington, D.C.; Fitness Formula in Chicago, Illinois; and Merritt Clubs, Maryland. This segment of the industry grew by 21 percent from 2014 to 2016, second only to budget clubs among traditional health/fitness club settings.

- ❑ *Premium-plus clubs ($100 to $149 a month).* Premium-plus clubs represent a step up from the premium segment and approach what might be defined as a near-luxury experience. These clubs are almost always multipurpose clubs, with Equinox being one of the few in this segment that operates nearly exclusively as fitness only. This segment separates itself from the premium segment through the level of service and hospitality that is provided, as well as the variety and quality of programs offered. Many of these clubs have spas, which add an element of elegance and exclusivity. In addition, clubs in this segment also have higher end finishes. Clubs operating in this segment could be compared to a Hilton or J.W. Marriott hotel in terms of the experience. According to the 2016 IHRSA Consumer Trend Report approximately 5 percent of consumers belong to clubs whose price point falls within this range. In the U.S., several of the leading national and regional club operators in this segment include Lifetime Fitness (certain clubs in targeted markets); some clubs operated by Equinox Fitness, and Village Health Clubs and Spas, Phoenix, Arizona.

❏ *Luxury clubs and boutique clubs (over $150 a month).* Luxury clubs represent a very small segment of the industry, and according to IHRSA data serve approximately 6 percent of all health club consumers. Luxury clubs set themselves apart on several levels, but most notably on their level of hospitality and service and ability to foster the emotional aspect of the club experience. In these clubs, it's all about creating a highly personal experience for each member. These clubs, like their compatriots in the hotel business, are focused on building an enriching and long-lasting relationship with the member such that it is their second home so to speak. Among the most prominent U.S. clubs in this segment are the Houstonian, Houston, Texas; Eastbank Club, Chicago, Illinois; New York Athletic Club, New York; most Equinox Fitness clubs; and to a slightly lesser degree the Bay Clubs in California.

As indicated in the header, many boutique clubs and studios price their experience similar to the luxury clubs. While the majority of boutiques do not offer a luxury experience, what they do provide that allows them to command this price point is a very personally relevant experience for the member. These boutiques studios build their value proposition around the following: delivering a highly personal experience, fostering a community of equally like-minded and passionate enthusiasts, and finally, providing an inspiring environment that makes it easier for members to gets results.

> Many boutique clubs and studios price their experience similar to the luxury clubs.

Reflections

The health/fitness club business has evolved into one that is built around a variety of value propositions. An owner/operator can choose to be a part of a group of clubs (corporate or franchised) or operate on their own, they can select to operate a niche boutique studio or pursue their dreams by running a large multipurpose club, and finally, they can select to operate a budget club at a low price point where sales volume is the key to profitability or entertain operating a luxury club where success hinges on creating an elegant environment, outstanding hospitality and providing enriching and rewarding experiences that foster lasting memories.

15 Establishing a Health/Fitness Business

"Whenever you see a successful business, someone once made a courageous decision."

— Peter F. Drucker

Chapter Objectives

The process of establishing a health/fitness business can be relatively complicated.

The process of establishing a health/fitness business can be relatively complicated. This chapter begins with a review of the basic legal requirements. Next, the chapter covers the all-important question of whether to purchase a club or build a club, followed by an overview of the various approaches for financing the development and growth of the business. Finally, the chapter details the key steps that are necessary to help turn a business venture into a great business organization.

What Are the Options a Club Has for Forming a Legal Entity?

In general, there are five options to select from when establishing the legal structure for a club. These five options all have their benefits and risks. What follows is a brief overview of each option.

- *Sole Proprietorship (SP).* A sole proprietorship is the most basic business structure. A sole proprietorship has no formal legal requirements and always has a single owner, the individual who is creating the business. As a sole proprietor, you can reference the business under your own name or indicate you are "doing business as" (d.b.a.) under a specified name. If you decide to go into business as a sole proprietorship and operate under a d.b.a., then you will be required to file for a certificate "for doing business as" with the state government. Operating as a sole proprietorship has few if any advantages for a club owner, and lots of disadvantages; the most significant of those disadvantages being:
  - The business has no insulation from liability, and all liability and debt become the personal responsibility of the owner. If legal action is brought against your business, then your personal assets are at risk.
  - The business will terminate upon the death or incapacity of the individual who is the owner.

- If your intent is to operate a fitness club and lease space, then a sole proprietorship becomes even more of a risk, since you would be personally responsible for the lease.

❑ *Partnerships.* Partnerships are designed to be a simple business structure for companies that have more than one owner. There are two general types of partnerships: general partnerships and limited partnerships.

  - *General partnership (GP).* General partnerships require relatively little legal assistance to be formed, and the taxes from the business enterprise are pass through, meaning they are only taxed once. A general partnership can be written, oral, or implied. A general partnership typically consists of two or more individual's doing business as co-owners. In a general partnership, each partner is an agent of the partnership and can legally bind the other partner to any agreement entered into by the other partner on behalf of the business. In essence, each partner has joint and severable liability, meaning that one individual or all of the individuals can be held accountable for the debt and legal liability of the business. Finally, either partner has the ability to dissolve the partnership at any time.

  - *Limited partnership (LP).* Limited partnerships require a legal agreement between the involved parties and a certificate of limited partnership. Limited partnerships have a general partner who typically manages the business, and in many instances also has the largest financial investment in the business. This legal structure allows there to be limited partners, individuals who have a financial stake in the business, but who are not involved in managing it. In a limited partnership, the partners can be individuals or corporations. Limited partnerships are similar to general partnerships in that the partners have joint and severable liability. A limited partnership exists as long as the general partner is involved, or until all partners agree to terminate the arrangement. A limited partnership is one option a club owner might consider if the intent is to have multiple stakeholders in the business and the entrepreneur intends to have the largest stake in the business. If the entrepreneur will not be the majority owner, then a limited partnership may not be the best solution.

  - *Corporations (C-Corp).* Corporations, also known as C-Corps, are legal entities that provide significant and substantial liability protection for the owners, also known as shareholders. It should be noted that individual owners are not shielded from liability in instances where they provide a personal guarantee for a bank loan. C-corporations tend to be the legal structure of choice for larger companies, primarily due to issues revolving around liability and taxation. The disadvantage of a C-corporation and the primary reason why an independent club with one or more owners would not want to operate under this structure is the issue of double taxation. A C-corporation is taxed twice; first the profits of the company itself are taxed, and second, any income generated by the shareholders (for example, salaries and/or profit distributions) is taxed at the individual level. When a corporation is formed, it must file articles of incorporation with the state where it intends to have an office. The articles of incorporation must include a listing of the owners, directors, and officers. A corporation is required to have both bylaws and annual meetings of its directors and officers, with

There are two general types of partnerships: general partnerships and limited partnerships.

the directors and officers representing the owners. Corporations may issue stock, both common and preferred. Stock enables individuals and organizations to have an ownership stake in the business. A corporation may exist for perpetuity.

- *S Corporations (S-Corp).* An S corporation is a hybrid corporation that combines the features of various business structures. An S-Corp provides owners or shareholders with limited liability for corporate activities, including legal issues and debt. Another upside of an S-Corp is the benefit of pass through taxation, which means income is taxed once when it is passed through to each of the respective owners (e.g., payroll and/or ownership distribution). For a club owner, whether as the sole owner or as one of several owners, an S-Corp is an attractive option. You should consult with a legal professional, as well as an accountant, before pursuing this structure.
- *Limited Liability Corporation (LLC).* An LLC combines elements of a corporation, a sole proprietorship, and partnership structure to create a dynamic and flexible legal entity that is well-suited for individual owners as well as multiple owners. An LLC insulates the owner(s), referred to as members, from the legal liabilities of the business, with the exception of when an owner provides a personal guarantee for a loan. LLCs also provide the business itself with limited liability. LLCs provide the same tax benefit for owners as does an S-Corp, meaning that taxes are passed through to the individual owner(s). The owners of an LLC can choose to be taxed as partners or as an S-Corp, or as a sole proprietor if owned by a single individual. LLCs do not have to hold meetings of the shareholders or maintain minutes of meetings (a requirement of a C-Corp). For a club owner, whether as the sole owner or as one of several owners, an LLC is an attractive option. You should consult with a legal professional, as well as an accountant, before pursuing this structure. While it has numerous advantages, your local accountant and attorney may feel your business would be better served under another legal structure.

Considerations to Account for When Filing for Legal Status for a Business

Selecting the legal structure for a new business is just the first step in the process. Once it has been determined what legal structure is best for the business, then the owner needs to address some other key decisions. While these issues may differ slightly from state to state, the major ones are similar no matter where a business is formed. Following is a list of issues owners should carefully consider when forming a new legal entity:

- *Identify the legal name for the business.* It is advisable to conduct an online search to make sure that the name that has been selected is available.
- *Identify a registered agent and registered office for the business.* A registered agent is someone that is designated to officially receive and send legal papers on behalf of the business entity. If forming an LLC or C-Corp, then this step is a requirement. While owners can identify themselves or a business partner to be the registered agent, it is advisable to select your attorney or accountant to be the registered agent with the state.

CHAPTER FIFTEEN — *Establishing a Health/Fitness Business*

- *Identify the owner(s) of the legal entity.* If the plan is to have one owner, it's easy, but if there will be partners or shareholders (members in an LLC), then owners must address this in the formation of your legal entity.
- *Create a company agreement.* This is a legal document that provides specific details about the company, including how decisions will be made, how owners will interact, and in the event an owner wants to get out, how that will be addressed.

Once you complete the filing, the state will forward you a Certificate of Filing and later a Certificate of Formation.

Obtaining a Federal Tax ID (Employer Identification Number) for Your Business

Once the legal business structure has been established, the next step is to file for a federal tax identification number (EIN). The EIN is the business's "social security number," a form of the business's fingerprint and is the means by which the government keeps tabs on the business. Once the business has received a Certificate of Formation as a legal entity, then it can file for its EIN, either online through the government (www.irs-tax-id.com) or through an attorney or accountant. The process only takes minutes when done online and once the business is registered, the government will provide confirmation of the business's Federal EIN. The Federal EIN is used in a variety of ways, including when doing the following:

- Opening a bank account for the business
- Paying taxes for employees of the business
- Filing local, state, and federal tax returns for the business
- Completing various government forms such as a W-9
- Setting up accounts with suppliers

Deciding Whether to Buy or Build a Club

Once individuals have successfully navigated the decision-making path of what legal structure to assume and what type of club model under which they want to operate, the next major business hurdle they face is to decide whether they want to build a club or purchase a club. It should be noted that if you decide to acquire a franchise the decision of whether to build or purchase remains a decision that needs to be taken. All factors considered, this decision is as important as any owners will make and more than any other will impact their initial capital requirements and their ability to achieve profitability. It is essential that the individuals who are making this critical decision (whether to build or buy) fully understand the various factors that affect each choice. Such an understanding can help them decide which option is the best course of action for them.

> The decision whether to buy or build a club is as important as any owners will make and more than any other will impact their initial capital requirements and their ability to achieve profitability.

❏ *Building a Club.* If the decision is made to build a club, two standard courses of action can be taken. One is to purchase land, and then proceed to build a free-standing club structure (Greenfield). This approach to building requires not only that the land be purchased, but also that the club operators have the capital to build a free-standing building. This course of action is normally the most capital intensive, because it requires the funds both to purchase the property (ranging from $2 to $20 a square foot), and also to build a free-standing structure (ranging from $75 to $400 a square foot). By the time the process is completed, anywhere from $2 million to $20 million could be spent on the club. (It should be noted that some U.S. operators have spent as much as $40 million for clubs that exceed 100,000 square feet in size.) Besides the large outlay of cash, when a club is built from scratch, the membership also has to be built from scratch. As a result, the cash flow from the club's operations at its opening will normally not support the facility's operating expenses. It is common in the industry for free-standing clubs to not reach profitability until the end of their second or third year of operation and not begin to provide any return on their assets until at least their third year. Of course, exceptions to this rule exist.

Another option that operators have for building a club is to lease space in a strip mall, office park, or office building. In this instance, the operator will still have to build out the facility, but the costs will be less. In this scenario, the landlord usually provides the shell structure, along with an allowance for tenant build out (usually ranging from $15 to $50 a square foot). A typical tenant finish-out may range from $50 to $250 a square foot, depending on the club concept and market it will be located in (note that some boutique facilities can be constructed for as little as $20 a square foot), which is considerably less than building from the ground up. This contribution of the shell and core by the landlord reduces the amount of up-front capital that is needed by the club's owner. Similar to a free-standing club, the time needed to generate enough membership to reach profitability will often take approximately 18 months to three years. In this scenario, the owner's initial level of debt will not be as great. However, some additional built-in overhead (e.g., rent) will exist if this option is chosen.

> An attractive alternative to building a club is to purchase an existing club or franchise.

❏ *Buying a Club.* An attractive alternative to building a club is to purchase an existing club or franchise. When individuals purchase a club, they have two options—one is to purchase the entire business and the other is to purchase only the assets of an existing club's business. Most attorneys will advise individuals to purchase only the business assets, an option that will allow them to avoid assuming the liabilities of the existing business. The primary advantage of purchasing an existing club begins with the cost of purchase. As a general rule of thumb, most clubs will have an enterprise value (the value of the business before accounting for debts and related liabilities) equal to three times to six times their EBITDA (earnings before interest, taxes, depreciation, and amortization). As a result, the majority of clubs normally sell for far less than they would cost to build. Another benefit of purchasing an existing club involves the fact that purchasers are also getting an existing membership and an existing cash flow. In other words, the time it will take a club to reach profitability and gain a return on assets or equity will typically be far shorter than if they built the club from the ground up. On occasion, an existing club can reach profitability immediately and provide returns on the purchased assets as early as the first year. (It should be noted that the process of purchasing is far more complicated than the aforementioned discussion indicated and will be covered more thoroughly in later chapters.)

Chapter Fifteen — Establishing a Health/Fitness Business

Getting the Business Started

To this point, the chapter has addressed the primary challenges facing a prospective club or studio owner, which revolve around the legal framework for the business, deciding whether to purchase or build and finally, the different approaches that can be taken to finance the development, expansion, or growth of a club or club company. The final critical step in starting a health/fitness club or studio involves establishing a business framework that will enable the club to be successful. In that regard, several key steps can be undertaken by owners that can help them establish an appropriate framework for their business, including:

❑ *Establish a Clear Vision for the Business.* The vision of any business revolves around three distinct narratives: the mission statement, the brand promise, and the theme. The mission statement, often referred to as the purpose, is a succinct statement that clearly communicates to both a club's customers and its employees who and what the business is. At ClubCorp, their mission statement articulated the fact they would be the "world class leader in delivering the private club experience." This simple statement makes it clear what the intentions of the business are and whom they intend to serve. Lifetime Fitness, a national operator of premium and luxury clubs, has as their mission statement: "To provide an educational, entertaining, friendly and inviting, functional and innovative experience of uncompromising quality that meets the health and fitness needs of the entire family." This statement of purpose by Life Fitness makes it clear that they are in the business of offering an extraordinary experience for each of its members. For any business, it is imperative that they provide a mission statement that allows their team and customers to understand the overall focus of the business.

> The vision of any business revolves around three distinct narratives: the mission statement, the brand promise, and the theme.

The second essential narrative is the club's customer or brand promise. The promise is the commitment that the club makes to each and every customer of its business, a commitment that must be consistently delivered on. At ClubCorp, the promise was to "build relationships and enrich lives." At Haven on the Lake, a mind-body retreat based in Columbia, Maryland, their brand promise is: "To provide an environment that embraces the body and spirit to promote personal vitality." The brand promise not only lets a club's customers know what to expect, more importantly, it enables the club's staff to be aware of what experience they are expected to deliver to the club's members.

The final piece of the vision puzzle is the theme. The theme is the driving force behind the experience the club intends to provide its members. Many businesses forget to establish a theme. As a result, their business tends to lose focus on the experience it is trying to create. An example of where a club is using a predetermined theme in an appropriate manner is at Crunch. Their theme speaks to "making no judgments." When individuals visit one of their clubs, they definitely can pick up on the fact that the Crunch employees are making an effort, with the help of their facilities and programs, to act out that theme.

❑ *Create an Organizational Culture and Strive to Maintain It.* Culture is often defined as the traditions and practices that make a country, business, or people unique. With regard to a business setting, its culture is what makes

> **The first step that a business must take in order to create a culture is to identify its core values.**

a business unique from any other. Culture for a business is like culture for a country; it speaks to what is unique and special about the business and in what each and every employee can take pride. Culture begins with the establishment of core values and traditions, which are then sustained through stories told by the "leaders and heroes" of the business. Over time, these stories become the myths of the business, and the heroes become the legends.

The first step that a business must take in order to create a culture is to identify its core values. The core values serve as the foundation behind every decision a business makes. They are the roots of the business that nourish it and sustain it. At ClubCorp, their core values included a philosophy where the member/guest is king, a mandate for every employee to plan their work and work their plan, an unwavering commitment to integrity, and a firm belief in the necessity to exhibit character at all times. At Red's in Lafayette, Louisiana, their core values reflected such precepts as "greeting each member with a smile," "saying hello and goodbye," and "if you have time to lean, you have time to clean." Although simple, the aforementioned values are powerful influencers of positive business behavior.

The second step in creating a business culture is to establish specific philosophies and practices that, when replicated over time, will become traditions. At the Ritz Carlton, for example, they speak of "ladies and gentlemen serving ladies and gentlemen." Similarly, at ClubCorp, the discourse of "creating a refuge for the member, a home away from home" is commonly expressed. The philosophies of both companies serve as a framework for the actual practices in which their employees engage. Over time, as employees repeat these mantras and engage in these practices, they become traditions. Even more importantly, over time, employees will tell stories about how certain employees carried out these practices in a special way. When this occurs, myths and storytellers have been created, which are critical to sustaining the culture the business has developed.

❏ *Perform a SFSWOT (Success, Failures, Strengths, Weaknesses, Opportunities, and Threats).* The SFSWOT allows you to put historical performance in perspective by providing a framework for prioritizing the objectives and strategies that will comprise your business plan. The SFSWOT process should not be done in isolation; rather, it should involve key members of your team, such as your group exercise coordinator, spa coordinator, aquatics coordinator, etc. Furthermore, to facilitate the SFSWOT, you will need to gather historical data on your club's or studio's performance, as well as any other data relevant to the businesses performance. The elements of the SFSWOT are as follows:

- *Successes.* These represent the performance outcomes that you and your team believe are indicative of success. For example, you might consider prior year revenue growth of 10 percent a success or the introduction of a highly popular spa service as a success. The key is to identify those performance achievements that ownership and club management would consider a success.

- *Failures.* These represent performance outcomes that by all measures would be considered failures. While we are taught not to dwell on our failures, understanding what performance outcomes were not successful can shed light on how you need to proceed with your efforts for the upcoming planning period. For example, you may have introduced a HIIT class the past year in which attendance was minimal and consequently the program cost you more than it earned.
- *Strengths.* Strengths represent those attributes of the club, along with past and present performance achievements, that you feel set you apart. For example, you might consider the personal trainers to be one of the club's strengths because of their education level and relationships skills, or you might feel that your group exercise program is a strength because of attendance levels and favorable comments received from members.
- *Weaknesses.* Weaknesses represent attributes of your department along with past and present performance achievements which you feel hinder your ability to be more successful. For example, you might consider not having sufficient group exercise studios or not enough functional training accessories as a weakness. Another possible weakness may be your payroll margin as a percentage of revenues.
- *Opportunities.* Opportunities represent areas of your business where your team can leverage its strengths to create a stronger value proposition, greater operating efficiency, enhanced member loyalty, or increased revenue. For example, after studying your successes, failures, strengths, and weaknesses, you might spot an opportunity that will allow you to garner greater member participation and increase revenues.
- *Threats.* Threats can represent competitors, people, practices, and related attributes of your business that, if unchecked, will have a negative impact on the performance of your department. For example, the fact that you don't have enough space to offer spa services might inhibit your ability to grow revenues.

❑ *Establish Long-Term and Short-Term Business Objectives.* Before the business ever opens its doors to serve its future members, it needs to establish both long-term objectives (e.g., 10 to 20 years out) and short-term objectives (e.g., one-year, three-year, and five-year). Together, these objectives can help establish a road map for the club's business journey and help inform the club's investors and employees where it is planning to go and how it plans to get there.

The long-term business goals are often referred to as BHAG's (big hairy audacious goals). These goals represent what the club ultimately wants to achieve. While these goals should be clear and succinct, at the same time, they should not be as specific as those the club establishes for the short term. An example of a BHAG for a health/fitness club might be "to be recognized as the premier health/fitness club in the market, as reflected by capturing 15 percent of the market." If this goal were part of a club's plan, then it should be relatively clear to everyone what the club planned to accomplish in the future. Just as importantly, it could also serve as a marker for the club's progress over the years.

> Long-term business goals are often referred to as BHAG's (big hairy audacious goals).

The club's short-term business goals need to be S.M.A.R.T. (simple, measurable, attainable, realistic, and trackable).

The club's short-term business goals need to be S.M.A.R.T. (simple, measurable, attainable, realistic, and trackable). All factors considered short-term goals serve as the benchmarks for the beginning of a club's business journey. Examples of short-term business goals might include:

- Enroll 100 personal training clients by the end of year one.
- Achieve 2,000 members at the end of year one.
- Achieve revenues of 3 million dollars at the end of the first year and seven million dollars by the end of the fifth year.
- Achieve an annualized return on assets of 12 percent for each of the first five years.
- Open up a second club by the end of the third year of business.

❑ *Establish Replicable Operating Standards and Systems.* When a business is young, the club owner can often oversee every step that is taken. As time passes, however, the business' success will not depend on the ability of a single person. Rather the club's staff must be able to replicate the practices that drive the club's success. In that regard, the club must have clearly defined standards and systems.

Standards set the expectations for how a specific practice should be carried out. Standards need to be simple and clear. In essence, standards convey a description of the outcome that the club expects from an operational practice. Standards do not tell employees the "how," but rather the "what" and "when" a particular practice/action needs to be achieved. An example of a standard might be, "Every member will receive an orientation to the fitness floor that includes an exercise prescription." As such, this standard communicates the expectation, but not the path to be taken.

Systems are the processes and resources that the club provides to its employees that enable them to achieve the standards. More importantly, systems create consistency in the club's service delivery across space and time. Systems can include such factors as employee education programs, procedural documents for the handling of membership sales, procedural documents for accounting practices, etc. If the club does not establish business systems, even simple ones, it may find that its employees will tend to take the steps that are best for them and not necessarily the best for the business.

❑ *Establish an Accountable Organizational Structure.* Every business, especially a health/fitness club business, needs to have an organizational structure that brings decision-making relatively close to the member or customer. This scenario involves creating a flat organization where as few layers as possible exist between the customer or member and the employee who is making the decision concerning what should be done. This process of creating an accountable organizational structure requires the following key steps:

- Create a clear structure showing the relationships of each position to the members and to the other employees. Make sure to have as few layers between the customer and the owner as possible.
- Create a job description for each position that is based on accountability and not on tasks.

- Establish a model for open communication up and down the organizational structure. Eliminate communication holes and traps by doing away with positions of power.

By addressing these issues up front, the club can create an organizational structure where every employee takes a sense of ownership in the success of the business. Samples of organizational charts and job models are included in the appendices.

❑ *Hire the Best and Then Provide a Continuous Learning Environment.* The truest indicator of how successful a particular club business will become lies in the talent of the people it employs. As a consequence, club owners and operators need to hire the best people. According to Jim Collins, author of Good to Great, the best employees are those individuals who embrace the company's values and culture and have disciplined focus, disciplined thought, and disciplined action. As such, it is imperative that business leaders take the time to select and hire the best individuals. Furthermore, to keep the best, the club needs to provide an environment that promotes continuous learning and growth. In addition, the club needs to establish a culture that encourages employees to learn new skills and provide the support, both financially and time-wise, for employees to take advantage of learning opportunities. In addition, clubs should budget for educational efforts and programs, bring in outside speakers, establish regular in-house education, expose employees to other job roles, and promote those individuals who demonstrate that they are leaders and achievers.

> The truest indicator of how successful a particular club business will become lies in the talent of the people it employs.

❑ *Remember That Service Delivery Stays Close to the Member.* Many businesses create hurdles and barriers that force their customers to sacrifice something as part of their experience. When individuals create a business, they should establish a framework that eliminates member sacrifice. More importantly, the framework should enable its frontline employees (i.e., those employees who directly interact on a daily basis with the members) to do the delivery and, if necessary, the recovery of the services. For example, if a member comes to a fitness instructor and has a concern about an issue, the member should not be made to wait while the instructor chases down a supervisor. Instead, the club should have a policy of empowering instructors to act on their own to solve issues.

❑ *Create a Standard Financial Model and Budgets.* A final key to achieving success in a business is to create a financial model that everyone can understand and work with. The financial model should be based on establishing budgets that the respective club staff can work from and by which they can monitor the club's financial performance. As a matter of practice, club owners/operators should make the budget available to the appropriate staff members so that they know what has to be achieved and how they have performed over the course of the budgetary period, financial-wise. The club's financial model should also include simple reporting tools that enable the club to monitor the key financial indicators on a daily, weekly, monthly, quarterly, and annual basis.

Reflections

Establishing a health/fitness business can be daunting and requires that the owner take a disciplined approach to the process.

Establishing a health/fitness business can be daunting and requires that the owner take a disciplined approach to the process. This process involves several key steps, including establishing the legal structure for the to-be-operated club, identifying the appropriate business model, identifying the financial needs required to pursue development of the new business, raising the capital to launch the business, and finally, putting in place the proper systems and structures so that your team can deliver on the vision for the business.

The Health/Fitness Industry Financial Model

16

"Losing money is inherently evil."

—Robert Dedman, founder of ClubCorp

Chapter Objectives

Initially, this chapter reviews basic accounting methodologies, followed by a review of the basic financial tools that are used to measure financial performance in the health/fitness facility industry. The chapter concludes by presenting an overview of benchmark financial data from the industry.

Accrual vs. Cash Accounting

In general, the business world employs two methods for accounting for the financial performance of a business: cash accounting and accrual accounting.

- *Cash Accounting.* Under cash accounting, a business accounts for all revenues and expenses as they are incurred by the business. This method is sometimes referred to as "checkbook" accounting. When using the cash accounting method, a club must record every revenue collected and every expenditure incurred on the day on which it occurred. This approach to accounting is typically used by smaller organizations, such as boutique fitness studios, that need to closely manage their cash flow. All factors considered this "checkbook" approach provides them with the control that they need.
- *Accrual Accounting.* Accrual accounting is the method employed by most businesses. In accrual accounting, a business accounts for its revenues not as they are generated, but how they are earned. With regard to expenses, a business using accrual accounting accounts for these outlays not as they may actually be expended and paid for, but as they are represented by the operating practice. For example, a club receives a quarterly rent statement from its landlord for $300,000. In accrual accounting, the business would account for this payment as $100,000 in each of the months covered by the agreement, while in cash accounting, the $300,000 would be accounted for when the bill was paid. Another example might involve a situation in which a club sold $360,000 in annual membership contracts in January. In accrual accounting, the club would only allocate 1/12 of that amount ($30,000) to January's revenues, along with any carryover accruals from

> Accrual accounting is the method employed by most businesses.

the previous 11 months. In contrast, in cash accounting, the entire sum of $360,000 would be accounted for at the time it was received. Accrual accounting practices are governed by specific rules. The International Financial Reporting Standards (IFRS) are used around the globe, while Generally Accepted Accounting Principles (GAAP) are employed in the United States. Interestingly, if a company operates business around the world, then it may be required to maintain two sets of books. These two standardized systems spell out exactly how a business should account for its expenses and revenues when it's using accrual methodology.

The Basic Financial Tools Used by the Health/Fitness Facility Industry

As the health/fitness club industry has matured, the tools for measuring financial performance have also become more sophisticated. The three most important financial tools and the information each provides are as follows:

> As the health/fitness club industry has matured, the tools for measuring financial performance have also become more sophisticated.

❑ *The Balance Sheet* (refer to Figure 16-1). The balance sheet provides a quick snapshot of the financial health of the club on a day-to-day, week-to-week, and period-to-period basis. The balance sheet tells the business exactly how healthy its finances are at any point in time. The balance sheet lets the club know what its assets are, what its liabilities are, and what its equity in the business is.

- *Assets.* The assets of a business are the cash value of its business holdings—property, equipment, land, etc. In turn, its holdings are defined as either short-term (current) assets or long-term (non-current) assets. A club's short-term assets are those assets or holdings of the business that can be turned into cash (e.g., become liquid) over the next 12-month period of time. Examples of short-term assets include:
  - ✓ Cash in the bank and cash equivalents (short-term CDs, etc.)
  - ✓ Short-term physical assets that could be sold over the next year, such as small equipment
  - ✓ Accounts receivables that are due and not collected (i.e., the money members owe the club, but have not paid yet, such as dues and personal training fees)
  - ✓ Prepaid expenses (i.e., expenses the club has paid ahead of time to save money, such as utilities or phone expenses)
  - ✓ Inventory items (e.g., merchandise with a shelf life of less than one year)
  - ✓ Deferred taxes

  In most successful health/fitness club businesses, current assets, based on business model, would typically represent between 20 percent and 40 percent of its total assets. According to the published report, the *IHRSA 2015 Profiles of Success*, in 2014, the average club had current assets equal to 30 percent of its total assets, with a range of 14 percent to 39 percent. Just as importantly, the majority of its current assets should be either cash or cash equivalents. If the club's current assets are more heavily weighted toward inventory, it may end up having to write that off the inventory as an expense and potentially have to pay taxes on that inventory. By the same token, if the club has a large accounts receivable,

CHAPTER SIXTEEN

The Health/Fitness Industry Financial Model

Sample Balance Sheet			
Assets		**Current YTD**	**Prior YTD**
Current Assets			
	Cash	$500,000	$450,000
	Cash equivalents	$50,000	$25,000
	Accounts receivable	$100,000	$150,000
	Inventory	$50,000	$60,000
	Pre-paid expenses	$25,000	$20,000
Total Current Assets		$725,000	$705,000
Non-Current Assets			
	Equipment	$500,000	$525,000
	Building	$3,000,000	$3,000,000
	Property	$500,000	$400,000
	Less accumulated amortization and depreciation	$300,000	$225,000
	Net of property and equipment	$3,700,000	$3,700,000
	Investments	$250,000	$200,000
Total Non-Current Assets		$3,950,000	$3,900,000
Total Assets		$4,675,000	$4,605,000
Liabilities			
Current Liabilities	Accounts payable	$125,000	$120,000
	Accrued expenses	$75,000	$100,000
	Current maturities on debt	$200,000	$190,000
	Deferred taxes	$50,000	$25,000
Total Current Liabilities		$450,000	$435,000
Non-Current Liabilities	Long-term debt	$1,500,000	$1,800,000
	Capital lease obligations	$300,000	$400,000
	Other long-term liabilities	$100,000	$100,000
Total Non-Current Liabilities		$1,900,000	$2,300,000
Total Liabilities		$2,350,000	$2,735,000
Owner's Equity			
	Common stock	$1,985,000	$1,670,000
	Preferred stock	$0	$0
	Retained earnings	$240,000	$100,000
	Paid in capital	$100,000	$100,000
Total Owner's Equity		$2,325,000	$1,870,000
Total Liabilities and Owner's Equity		$4,675,000	$4,605,000

Figure 16-1. The balance sheet

then it is in a position of losing a portion of that to bad-debt expense and having to write that portion off. Not having sufficient short-term assets (less than 10 percent of total assets) can result in a club experiencing cash-flow problems, as well as an inability to cover important expenses during seasonal changes in financial performance.

The club's long-term assets are those holdings and financial instruments of the business that are not expected to be collected over the next 12 months. Examples of long-term assets include:

✓ Property (land and buildings)
✓ Leasehold improvements (e.g., the capital the club has placed into a leased space to make it operational, such as new carpeting, new showers, tenant finishes, etc.)
✓ Equipment (e.g., treadmills, resistance training equipment, etc.)
✓ Security deposits and lease deposits
✓ Loan fees
✓ Depreciation (deducted)

The non-current assets of a financially healthy health/fitness club should range between 60 percent and 85 percent of its total asset value. According to the published report, the *IHRSA 2015 Profiles of Success*, the average club had non-current assets equal to 71 percent of its total asset value, with a range of 61 percent to 86 percent. Just as importantly, the club's long-term assets should lean toward property, equipment, and deposits because these assets are more easily sold. If the club has substantial dollars tied up in leasehold improvements, it is less likely to recoup them, and consequently they hold less value for potential suitors.

- *Liabilities.* The club's business liabilities are the financial obligations it has—in essence, the money it owes to others as part of operating its business. Liabilities are defined as either short-term (current) liabilities or long-term (non-current) liabilities. In the best of cases, the club would prefer that its total liabilities not exceed more than 70 percent to 75 percent of the value of its total assets, with less being better. According to the published report, the *IHRSA 2015 Profiles of Success*, the average club had liabilities equal to 60 percent of its total assets, an increase of approximately several percentage points when compared to five years earlier. According to the IHRSA data, clubs had total liabilities that ranged from 45 percent to 70 percent of total assets. Given those statistics, it is important to note that financial experts on occasion talk about "leverage," which is a reference to the liabilities that a business has. When those liabilities exceed 80 percent of the business's assets, the business is considered to be highly leveraged.

The current liabilities of the club are those obligations that will be due and payable within the next 12 months. Examples of current liabilities include:

✓ Accounts payable (these are invoices that the club has not paid for, but for which the club has already used the service)
✓ Notes payable (e.g., any loans that come due during the current year)
✓ Income taxes that are due
✓ Deferred revenue (this is revenue from contracts or agreements that have been collected, but not earned. For example, if the club

sells one-year membership contracts, it must reflect all revenue not attributed to the current operating period as deferred revenue and therefore a current liability.)
- ✓ Deferred rent (any rent the landlord agrees can be paid at a later date)
- ✓ Deferred taxes

A rule of thumb with regard to current liabilities is that they should never exceed the value of the club's current assets (current ratio) and, ideally, should be equal to 50 percent of the value of the club's current assets (referred to as a club's current ratio).

The long-term liabilities (debt) are those obligations and expenses, while not due during the next 12 months, will be due sometime thereafter. In the health/fitness club industry, it is recommended that the club's long-term debt not exceed a value of 40 percent to 50 percent (e.g., in 2014, the average club had long-term debt equal to 45 percent) of its total assets, a decrease of several percentage points from several years earlier. In the publication, the *IHRSA 2015 Profiles of Success*, the average long-term debt for clubs ranged from 20 percent to 60 percent of total assets. It should be noted, on the other hand, that some club companies, which are underwritten by private equity and/or venture capital, look favorably on carrying a high debt load (i.e., a situation that is commonly referred to as being highly leveraged), since it is one way to generate business growth. In fact, a number of private equity firms assume debt levels equivalent to 80 percent to 90 percent of assets in an effort to stimulate business growth. The downside of this approach is the liability of such debt and the strain it can place on a club's operating cash flow. During challenging economic times, such as the economic slowdown from 2008 and 2011, many of the operators who were highly leveraged experienced loan defaults and bankruptcies because of their inability to cover their debt payments. Examples of long-term debt include:
- ✓ Future interest and principal payments on loans from financial institutions
- ✓ Deferred revenue from long-term contracts (an example might be a five-year corporate membership contract)
- ✓ Deferred rent (oftentimes, a landlord will agree to provide a tenant with a window of no rent with the stipulation that the rent must be paid at a later date when the club is more profitable)
- ✓ Deferred taxes

- *Owner's equity.* Owner's equity represents the owner's actual investment in the club, which can include any initial dollars invested, as well as any dollars earned over the life of the business. Owner's equity can vary, depending on whether the club was established as a corporation, a limited liability corporation, a partnership, or a sole proprietorship. Owner's equity is determined by subtracting the total liabilities of the business from the total assets of the business. In the case of a financially sound club, the owner's equity will usually be in the neighborhood of 20 percent to 40 percent of the total asset value. In the case of more mature clubs, however, it may be closer to 50 percent of the total assets. In 2014, according to IHRSA data, the average club reported owner's equity of 40 percent, slightly less than it was before the onset of the most recent recession in 2008. Situations also exist, especially in highly leveraged clubs and club companies (i.e., clubs carrying a high level of long-term debt), where the owner's equity might be as low as 10 percent. Examples of owner's equity are as follows:

- ✓ *Corporations.* In corporations, the owner's equity can exist in a number of forms, including capital stock (common or preferred), paid in capital (actual cash put into the business), and retained earnings not distributed to the stockholders (money the business makes and then puts back into the business).
- ✓ *Partnerships, limited liability corporations (LLC), and sole proprietorships.* In these business structures, the owner's equity can exist as contributions in cash or kind (sole proprietor or partnership) and cash generated by the withdrawal of assets (partnerships). Investors and lending institutions will look at a club's balance sheet as one way of evaluating its current financial health and its ability to be profitable over the long run.

> Investors and lending institutions will look at a club's balance sheet as one way of evaluating its current financial health and its ability to be profitable over the long run.

- *Balance sheet indicators.* A few critical financial ratios or key indicators, based on the information furnished on a club's balance sheet, can be used to provide a quick glimpse of a club's overall financial health. The most frequently used balance sheet–based indicators are current ratio, acid-test ratio, debt-equity ratio, interest-coverage ratio, return on equity, return on invested capital, and return on fixed assets.
    - ✓ *Current ratio.* The current ratio is an indicator of a club's financial liquidity (cash in hand) within the next 12-month period. The current ratio is determined by dividing the value of the club's current assets by the value of its current liabilities. For example, if a club had a total of $1,000,000 in current assets and $500,000 in current liabilities, then its current ratio would be two. A current ratio above two is considered excellent; a ratio between one and two is deemed to be good; a ratio between .6 and one is regarded as fair; and a ratio that is less than .6 is considered poor. In 2014, the median current ratio for clubs surveyed by IHRSA was 1.4. It should be noted that if a club generates a significant portion of its revenue from the sale of annual memberships, then the current ratio may fall below one, because deferred revenue represents a current liability. For example, in my former company in Russia, nearly all memberships were annual memberships. As a result, the company had a significant amount of deferred revenue reflected on its balance sheet, which resulted in its current ratio being around .5 to .6. If not for the deferred revenue, the current ratio would have been closer to 1.5.
    - ✓ *Acid-test ratio.* The acid-test ratio is a measure of a club's "quick" liquidity or its ability to generate cash immediately. The acid-test ratio is determined by taking the club's current assets and subtracting out that portion attributable to inventory and prepaid expenses, and then dividing by its current liabilities. A financially sound club operation should have an acid-test ratio of one or higher. For example, if the club has $1,000,000 in current assets, of which $300,000 is in inventory and $200,000 is in prepaid expenses, and has $500,000 in current liabilities, then its acid-test ratio would be one.

- *Debt-to-equity ratio.* The debt-to-equity ratio is a good measure of a club's leverage (in other words, the value of the owner's equity in comparison to the total liabilities that the club carries). The debt-to-equity ratio is measured by taking the total liabilities of the business and dividing them by the total owner's equity. For example, if a club has $4,000,000 in total liabilities and the owner's equity was $1,000,000, then the debt-to-equity ratio would be four. In 2014 the average debt-to-equity ratio in the club industry according to IHRSA's data was approximately 1.5, lower than it was in 2009 when it was 1.8. The higher the ratio, the greater the debt is in comparison to the owner's equity, and the more likely the club is highly leveraged. A review of the last several years' worth of industry data shows that 2012's leverage-oriented ratios (debt-to-equity, interest-coverage, etc.) were lower than in previous years, indicating that in 2012, clubs were less likely than in previous years to experience debt-related problems.

- *Interest-coverage ratio.* The interest-coverage ratio is frequently used by investors as a measure of the balance between a company's ability to grow and pay down its existing debt. It represents the amount of available cash to cover interest payments on existing debt. For example, a club that generates $500,000 in cash annually and has interest payments of $250,000 would have an interest coverage ratio of 2. Ideally, clubs need to have an interest-coverage ratio of at least 2, if they want to be assured of being able to cover their interest payments, and have capital available for growth, as well as for emergencies. According to the publication, the *IHRSA 2014 Profiles of Success*, the average club in 2014 had an interest-coverage ratio of 5.2, with a range of 1.9 to 13.2. All factors considered, if a club has an interest-coverage ratio that is too low (i.e., below 1.5), it is likely to have potential problems with cash flow, while if its ratio is relatively high (i.e., over 4), it may not have sufficient debt to successfully grow its business.

- *Return on equity.* Return on equity is a measure that is used by investors to assess the value of their investment. Return on equity is determined by taking the net income (earnings before taxes) and dividing it by the cash or equity invested. In an investor's mind, this ratio tells them how well their investment is working for them in generating cash flow. On average, most venture-capital groups look for returns in excess of 40 percent, while other investors are likely to be satisfied with returns of 20 percent to 30 percent. According to the publication, the *IHRSA 2015 Profiles of Success*, the average return on equity in 2014 for the industry was 19 percent, up over 5 percentage points from earlier in the decade. For owners who reinvest in their own club, such as when undertaking an expansion of an existing facility, they may be satisfied with a return of 15 percent to 20 percent. For example, if a club owner were to invest $250,000 for a fitness-center expansion and, as a result, generated an additional $50,000 in cash flow as a by-product of having more members who are spending more money, their return on equity would be $50,000/$250,000 or 20 percent. Another way of looking at return on equity is what is called return-on-invested capital. This measure

> Return on equity is a measure that is used by investors to assess the value of their investment.

represents the return an investor generates on the capital that individual invests in a project. If an investor puts in $100,000 for a club expansion and over the next five years, generates, on an annual basis, an additional $25,000 in cash, then that person's annual return-on-invested capital (AROIC) is 25 percent.

✓ *Return on fixed assets.* Return on fixed assets is another measure used to assess the value of an investment. Return on fixed assets represents the profitability of a business measured against the amount the business holds in its fixed (non-current) assets. To some investors, this measure is considered a more valuable indicator of how well their money is working for them than is the return-on-equity ratio. For example, if a club had $2,000,000 in fixed assets and, as a result, produced an additional $200,000 in cash flow for the club, then the return on fixed assets would be $200,000/$2,000,000 or 10 percent. While many club investors look for returns on fixed assets of 20 percent to 25 percent, ranges of 10 percent to 15 percent are considered acceptable. In 2012, the average return on fixed assets for the industry was 9.7 percent, nearly the same as it was four years earlier in 2009 during the height of the recession. The basic reason investors and owners see this measure as a more realistic assessment of their return is because they have their money tied up in the assets of the business. In turn, the cash they generate is a result of how well that equity is doing for them.

As can be seen, understanding the nuances of a club's balance sheet is essential to understanding the value and financial health of that business.

❑ *The Profit-and-Loss Statement or Statement of Income* (see Figure 16-2). The profit-and-loss statement is a financial tool that is used to reflect a club's operating performance over a given period of time. The standard practice in the health/fitness club industry is to produce both monthly and year-end profit-and-loss statements. Several club chains divide the year into 13 operating periods of four weeks each and compile a profit-and-loss statement for each of the four-week periods, as well as an annual statement. Finally, a few clubs actually provide a weekly profit-and-loss statement that reflects their operating performance on a weekly basis. Some businesses refer to the profit-and-loss statement as a statement of income or a statement of operations.

The profit-and-loss statement is designed to show the club operator how well the club is performing financially over the designated time period by providing information on actual performance, planned performance, and the variance-to-plan performance. With each profit-and-loss statement, the club operator can get an accurate update on how the club is performing, both actually and against budget, for the given period, as well as year-to-date. This type of information allows the operator to make decisions regarding such factors as membership sales, revenue strategies, and expense control in a timely and effective manner. It is important to remember that the profit-and-loss statement is typically based on an accrual system. In other words, it measures financial performance based not only on both the cash generated and spent, but also on allocations for cash yet to be received or yet to be

Profit and Loss Statement				
		YTD Actual	YTD Plan	YTD Variance
Revenues				
	Membership	$2,450,000	$2,300,000	$150,000
	Fitness	$600,000	$550,000	$50,000
	Spa	$265,000	$250,000	$15,000
	Food & Beverage	$125,000	$100,000	$25,000
Total Revenues		$3,440,000	$3,200,000	$240,000
Expenses				
	Fitness	$600,000	$563,000	$37,000
	Spa	$175,000	$162,000	$13,000
	Food & Beverage	$90,000	$88,000	$2,000
	Tennis	$250,000	$245,000	$5,000
	Membership	$300,000	$292,000	$8,000
	Marketing & Sales	$100,000	$96,000	$4,000
	G & A	$250,000	$255,000	-$5,000
	Other Operating Expenses	$150,000	$138,000	$12,000
	Rent	$200,000	$200,000	$0
	Utilities	$230,000	$215,000	$15,000
	Property Taxes	$120,000	$120,000	$0
Total Operating Expenses		$2,465,000	$2,374,000	$91,000
EBITDA		$975,000	$826,000	$149,000
EBITDA Margin		28%	26%	
	Depreciation	$130,000	$130,000	$0
	Interest	$350,000	$350,000	$0
Net Income		$755,000	$606,000	$149,000
	Principal	$75,000	$75,000	$0
	Capital Replacement	$100,000	$95,000	$5,000
Profit Before Taxes		$710,000	$566,000	$144,000

Figure 16-2. The profit-and-loss statement or statement of income

spent during a given period of time. As such, the profit-and-loss statement provides a reflection of both planned performance and actual performance. One of the most useful tools in the health/fitness club industry, for understanding the profit-and-loss statement is the book—Uniform System of Accounts for the Health, Racquet, and Sportsclub Industry—which was developed under the leadership of IHRSA. This document establishes specific categories within the profit-and-loss statement for budgeting and monitoring financial performance in the industry. The key profit-and-loss categories (revenues, department expenses, undistributed expenses, fixed expenses, EBITDA, and EBIT) that the industry employs to monitor and evaluate a club's financial performance include the following:

- *Revenue categories.* The revenue portion of the profit-and-loss statement is intended to provide the club operator with a means of budgeting and tracking the revenue-producing aspects of the business. The primary revenue areas or revenue departments on a profit-and-loss statement include:

  ✓ *Membership.* The membership revenues are those revenues that are generated through the membership dues paid by members on a monthly basis and the initiation fees that members pay upon joining a club. For boutique facilities, this might be the money earned from the sale of unlimited class passes. A club must record all revenues from these two areas on the profit-and-loss statement under the category assigned to the membership revenue department. In the instances where a club uses membership contracts, the club can only reflect on its profit-and-loss statement the amount of revenue from the contract that has been earned during the period of time reflected on the profit-and-loss statement. For instance, if a club receives $1,200 from a member upon joining for one-year's dues, then on the monthly profit-and-loss statement, only $100 of those dues can be reflected on the statement. In the health/fitness club industry, according to the publication, the *IHRSA 2015 Profiles of Success*, approximately 60 percent to 90 percent of all club revenues come from the membership department. As such, a number of companies in the health/fitness club industry are trying to reduce their dependence on membership revenue by introducing monetization strategies that can generate additional revenues. In that regard, some clubs who have implemented these monetization strategies, particularly large multi-purpose clubs, report that they generate closer to 50 percent of their overall revenue from their membership department. An interesting divergence from this trend of decreasing dependency on membership revenues is seen in those clubs that have positioned themselves in the high-volume, low-priced segment of the industry (e.g., Planet Fitness, U.S.; Gym Group, England; and Mcfit, Germany), in which dues can actually represent in excess of 90 percent of the revenue of the business.

  ✓ *Fitness.* The fitness department generates the second largest amount of revenue in the club industry. Revenues earned from personal training, small group training, group-exercise classes, Pilates classes, and locker rental are examples of income that could all be attributed to this particular department. According to industry data from 2014, the average fitness department contributes in the neighborhood of 10 percent of a club's total revenues, nearly identical to the percentage contributed four years earlier. At the Russian Fitness Group based in Moscow, its clubs, on average, generated 16 percent of all revenues from fitness. In reality, in a number of clubs (e.g., Equinox Fitness), the fitness department generates upwards of 20 percent of the total revenues.

  ✓ *Spa.* The spa department contributes revenues by providing such services as massages, facials, pedicures, manicures, and related activities that are delivered in a spa environment. In the last few years, the spa department has developed into a significant revenue source for many health/fitness clubs. In fact, spas can generate as much as $10,000 per treatment room per month. According to the publication, the *IHRSA*

> Approximately 60 percent to 90 percent of all club revenues come from the membership department.

2014 Profiles of Success, the average club generated 2.5 percent (with a range of 1.7 percent to 8.4 percent) of its revenues from its spa. At the Russian Fitness Group based in Moscow, the average club generated 10 percent of club revenues from its spa operations.

✓ *Tennis.* The tennis department generates revenues through court fees, instructional lessons, and programming. In multipurpose clubs, tennis might be the second largest contributor of revenues. Industry data shows a tennis department can easily generate between $25,000 and $50,000 in revenue per outdoor court and $50,000 to $100,000 per indoor court on an annual basis.

✓ *Pro shop.* Financially, the pro shop is the source of the net revenues that are generated by merchandise sales. In most clubs, this contribution is relatively small when compared to total club revenues. According to the published report, the *IHRSA 2015 Profiles of Success*, the average club generated 1.1 percent of all revenue from retail sales (with a range of 0.5 percent to 2.5 percent). In some clubs, the pro shop may generate as much as $500,000 to one million annually, though, on average, most generate less than $100,000 in annual revenues.

✓ *Food and beverage.* The food-and-beverage department generates revenues through the sale of food and beverages and by conducting special functions, such as parties. In most health/fitness clubs, the food-and-beverage operation is not a comparatively large contributor to the club's revenues because their operations usually don't consist of much more than a snack bar or smoothie bar. According to IHRSA data from 2015, the average club generated 3 percent of its revenues from food and beverage (with a range of 1 percent to 6 percent). Some clubs, such as the East Bank Club in Chicago, generate millions of dollars in food-and-beverage revenue through multiple outlets, including private parties. On the other hand, most food-and-beverage departments are fortunate if they achieve a 10 percent margin.

✓ *Youth services.* The youth department is a relatively recent undertaking for most of the clubs in the industry, but one that shows promise as a meaningful source of revenue. The youth department generates revenues by holding parties, providing youth programming, and offering childcare services. In 2015, according to IHRSA statistics, youth programs generated between 0.9 percent and 4.5 percent of club revenues.

✓ *Other revenue.* A number of clubs generate revenue from services that do not fall into the standard accounting categories on the profit-and-loss statement. In these instances, these revenues are often reflected under the category of "other revenues." The most significant sources of other revenue in the health/fitness club industry are revenues from space rental, physical therapy, and other medically related services. Some club chains, such as the Bay Clubs in California, lease space to physical therapy businesses. The revenues from these leases are normally reflected as other revenue on the club's profit-and-loss statement or are established as an entirely new revenue category.

• *Departmental expenses.* Departmental expenses are that part of the profit-and-loss statement where the expenses incurred by each of the

> The most significant sources of other revenue in the health/fitness club industry are revenues from space rental, physical therapy, and other medically related services.

operating revenue departments in the delivery of their respective services and the generation of their respective revenues are listed. In other words, the departments of membership, fitness, spa, tennis, pro shop, food and beverage, and youth all have expenses that are directly associated with the services they provide and the revenues they generate. On the profit-and-loss statement, the expenses generated by each department are placed in an account that best reflects its activity or function, either within a department or as part of the overall profit and loss statement. Examples of the accounts that are reflected either in each department or as part of the overall profit and loss statement include:

✓ *Payroll.* This category of expenses represents the cost of employee wages and commissions. Payroll includes such items as salaries, hourly wages, commissions for employees, incentive pay for employees, etc. For example, the commission that the club pays a personal trainer would be considered wages, just as would the wages paid to a group-exercise instructor by the club, or the commission given to one of the club's sales representatives. Payroll (benefits and payroll taxes included) alone can represent approximately 15 percent (e.g., budget club) to 50 percent (e.g., luxury club) of a club's total operating expenses, depending on the business model, and as much as 75 percent to 80 percent of any given department's operating expense.

✓ *Benefits.* This expense category represents the cost of providing basic benefits to the club's employees. These costs will vary, depending upon the benefits a club offers to its employees. The standard benefit package normally includes health benefits (hospitalization, dental, vision) and federally and state-mandated payments, such as FICA, FUTA, and SUTA (the payments made for Social Security, Medicare, etc.). Additional employee benefits that many clubs offer include such items as club contributions to a company-sponsored savings plan [401(k)], life insurance, long-term disability insurance, etc. Normally, the cost of employee benefits can range from as little as 15 percent of a club's total payroll expense to as high as 30 percent of its total payroll expense.

✓ *Education and training.* This expense category involves the expenses associated with the ongoing education of the club's employees. This category can include the cost of sending employees to conventions and conferences, funding continuing education credits, providing in-house training, and providing scholarships for pursuing coursework at local colleges. As a whole, the industry does not apply any standard allocation to this area. It would be in the club's best interest, however, for club operators to consider allocating funds equal to one to three percent of payroll for this expense category.

✓ *Total payroll.* Total payroll represents the combined cost of wages, salaries, benefits, education, and taxes (payroll plus benefits). According to the report, the *IHRSA 2015 Profiles of Success*, the average club spent 41.9 percent of all of its revenues on total payroll, with a range of 37 percent to 46 percent. Clubs that have a brand that depends on delivering a highly personalized, customer service-oriented experience will tend to have a higher total payroll cost (with a range of 40 percent to 50 percent), while some of the high-volume, low-price operators that provide minimal staffing tend to have a total payroll that does not exceed 12 to 15 percent of its total revenue.

- ✓ *Supplies.* This category of expenses varies from club to club. As a whole, this category includes expenses associated with cleaning supplies, general maintenance supplies, paper supplies, locker room amenities, etc. The industry average for this category is approximately two percent of the total revenues generated by a club.

- ✓ *Advertising/promotions/marketing.* This expense category represents the costs associated with marketing, promoting, and selling a club, and for a specific department doing the same for its products and services. For a particular department, such as fitness, this expense would include such items as the cost of flyers, posters, pamphlets, post cards, and other marketing pieces used to promote the department's services. Expenses emanating from efforts to promote activities in the membership department would involve internal departmental promotions, rather than external club promotions. Normally, the cost of external marketing is allocated to an undistributed expense category for marketing.

- ✓ *Printing.* This expense category is used to allocate expenses associated with printing efforts by the club, including club brochures, letterhead, envelopes, newsletters, and other hard-copy documents.

- ✓ *Dues and subscriptions.* This expense category is used by clubs to expense items, such as club subscriptions for newspapers, magazine subscriptions for the club, subscriptions to special-interest publications, etc. The largest part of this expense category would arise from the costs involved with providing professional membership dues for employees (e.g., ACSM, NSCA, etc.), association dues for the club (e.g., IHRSA, ISPA, IDEA, etc.), and dues for local and community associations and groups (e.g., Chamber of Commerce, Rotary, etc.).

- ✓ *Contract labor.* This expense category is used to allocate the costs associated with retaining the services of outside professionals. For example, contract labor could include such items as attorney fees, accounting firm fees, outside speaker fees, special instructors, etc. In fact, many club operators pay their personal trainers and group-exercise instructors out of a contract-labor account, based on their mistaken belief that these providers are not employees, but rather independent contractors. As a result, they attempt to save on the cost of providing benefits to these individuals. Unfortunately, most club operators are misinformed about what constitutes an independent contractor. As such, they are running a risk in expensing these costs to this particular account. (Note: The issue of independent contractors is addressed in later in this book.)

- ✓ *Maintenance and repair.* This category of expenses is associated with the general costs of maintaining the club's facilities and providing minor repairs to the facility. For example, if the club hires an exterminator to service the club, this expense would fall under this category. Another example of an expense assigned to this category would be if the club had to purchase some parts to repair a treadmill.

Contract labor could include such items as attorney fees, accounting firm fees, outside speaker fees, special instructors, etc.

✓ *Cost of goods sold.* This category of expenses only applies to departments that sell retail items. The cost of goods sold represents the cost of an inventory item that is removed as it is sold from the inventory. For example, if the club purchases 500 shirts for $10 each, it would have a total of $5,000 in inventory. Later, if it sold all 500 shirts for $10,000, then its inventory cost for the shirts would be $5,000 (50 percent of the total revenue received from the sales). In most clubs, the cost of sales usually runs between 60 percent and 80 percent for their retail operations (e.g., the pro shop), though the inventory cost at many clubs runs much higher. As a rule, the cost of sales can be relatively high when a club holds too much inventory of an item and is later forced to write it off or it experiences shrinkage of inventory.

While the aforementioned expense categories are the primary departmental expense categories that exist on the profit-and-loss statement of most health/fitness clubs, they are not the only ones that occur. Furthermore, some clubs prefer not to include these categories as departmental expenses, and instead incorporate them as overall club expense categories. Clubs that want to monitor their costs in detail should create even more definitive expense categories. Establishing such categories can help them maintain an even firmer grasp on their expenses.

- *Undistributed expenses.* Undistributed expenses are associated with the overall operations of the club, rather than for running any specific department. In most club operations, these are expenses that emanate from the successful operation of the club that have no direct association with a specific department. In these situations, clubs allocate such expenses to the undistributed-expenses category. The most significant categories for undistributed expenses typically include the following:

    ✓ *Sales and marketing.* The cost of sales and marketing is an expense that is generated by efforts to market the club, such as advertisements in the media, websites, direct-mail pieces, and related sales materials. On average, most health/fitness clubs spend approximately two to five percent of their revenues on sales and marketing (e.g., averaging 2.6 percent in 2014). In fact, major multiple-club operators, such as 24 Hour Fitness, LA Fitness, and Equinox Fitness, frequently devote more of their resources to this undertaking, often reaching as high as 5 percent of their revenues.

    ✓ *Utilities.* Utility expenses include the costs of such items as electric, gas, water, and telephones. Most clubs lump these items as an undistributed expense, while some club operators might distribute them as departmental expenses. The industry average for clubs is to spend between four and seven percent of operating revenues on utilities (e.g., averaging 5.8 percent in 2014). For clubs in the Northeast and West, especially California, utility expenses can often run as high as 10 percent of their revenues.

    ✓ *Member services.* The cost of member services is an undistributed expense that is associated with the delivery of special member services and member relations. Expenses that fall into this category might include the cost involved in conducting focus groups, surveys, member-reward programs, and member-appreciation functions.

> On average, most health/fitness clubs spend approximately two to five percent of their revenues on sales and marketing.

- ✓ *G and A (general administration and accounting).* G and A is an undistributed expense that entails the costs involved in running the accounting department and in providing general management (e.g., manager, assistant manager, office assistant, etc.). It should be noted that in many clubs, the management and accounting areas are actually set up as departments, with their own expenses, and are treated as a separate department. Besides payroll, costs, such as postage, credit-card charges, bad-debt expense, and EFT (electronic funds transfer) charges are normally debited to this accounting category. According to IHRSA's *2015 Profiles of Success*, the average club spent 7.8 percent of revenues on G and A, with some clubs spending as much as 8 percent of revenues.
- ✓ *Capital replacement and repair.* This undistributed expense involves the costs associated with funding the ongoing upkeep and repair of the club's facilities. In most instances, capital costs involve items that either cost more than $500 or have a depreciation period of at least three years. Examples of capital replacement costs include such expenses as the funds allocated for buying new exercise equipment, buying computers for the staff, replacing carpet, expanding an area within the club, or replacing or repairing a piece of equipment (e.g., an air conditioner). On average, in the club industry, a facility spends approximately 2 to 5 percent of its total revenues (in 2014 according to IHRSA the average facility spent 5.7 percent of revenues) on capital replacement and repair depending on the age of the property and the competitive environment. As a rule, some clubs may find that they need to allocate up to 15 percent of their revenues every five to seven years to handle their larger capital needs, such as a club expansion. In reality, many successful club operators handle this situation by accruing expenses over a few years to make sure that the funds are available for these larger capital requirements.

- *Fixed expenses.* Fixed expenses are considered those expenses that are not directly impacted by a club's operation, but rather the expenses that are recurring and relatively consistent year in and year out. The standard fixed-expense categories for the profit-and-loss statement include:
  - ✓ *Insurance.* This particular category includes the costs associated with providing property, general liability, key-man, and professional liability insurance. In the health/fitness club industry, these costs average between 1 percent and 2 percent of the club's total operating revenues. In 2014, the average club expended 1.1 percent of its revenues toward insurance payments. In fact, a few club operators feel insurance is not a fixed expense, but rather an expense that can be controlled through risk-management practices. As a consequence, in their operations, insurance is categorized as an undistributed expense.
  - ✓ *Rent.* Rent is probably the largest single expense for most clubs, other than payroll. The industry average for rent in 2014 was 10.6 percent, with a middle range between 12 percent and 20 percent of the club's total operating revenues. In some markets, such as Los Angeles, London, New York, Moscow, etc., the high cost of real estate can drive rent costs as high as 25 percent to 35 percent of revenues. Among

> An indicator of a club's profitability and earnings, EBITDA is used by investors and owners as a benchmark for valuing a company and benchmarking its operating efficiency.

boutique fitness studios rent can consume as much as 25 percent of total revenues. In order for a club to be profitable, it should make every effort to keep its rent payments below 15 percent of its total revenue. In most instances, rent is derived from the lease a club operator enters into, many of which run at least five years and more often for 10 years. A number of landlords also include what are called CAM costs into the rent. CAM costs are the landlord's costs for common area maintenance. In fact, class A office spaces (i.e., office space located in highly desirable locations and newer buildings) in many large, urban markets can have CAM costs that run as high as $10 to $15 a square foot. As such, it is essential that club operators get clarification of the CAM costs for a particular space and not make an operating or lease decision purely on the quoted rent cost.

✓ *Real estate/property taxes.* Real estate/property taxes contribute the fee that the club pays local government for occupying its property. If the club owns its land and building, then its property taxes are based on the assessed value of the property and building. On the other hand, if the club leases its space, its property tax will be based on an assessment of the leasehold improvements on the facility.

✓ *Management fees.* Management fees are expenses that usually only occur in clubs that are part of a multiple-club operation. In a multiple-club operation, the ownership group or the management parent normally charges a management fee for the expertise, services, and guidance that it provides to each particular club. In addition, in some independent clubs, ownership creates a separate management company for the business that then charges a fee to the club for the services of the owner. The majority of multiple-club operators charge a base management fee, which typically ranges from three to six percent of a club's total operating revenue.

✓ *Depreciation.* Depreciation is the actual cost that a business incurs as a result of the loss in value of its fixed assets. Most clubs utilize a standard depreciation table to determine the depreciation schedule for its fixed assets. For example, property and buildings are depreciated over 20 years and equipment over 5 to 10 years. According to IHRSA's data from 2014, the average club annually expended close to 6 percent of its revenues toward depreciation and amortization.

✓ *Principal and interest.* Principal and interest represent the costs associated with paying down debt and include the interest on any loan balance, as well as the amortized amount of principal on those loans. The interest portion of this expense line averaged 2.5 percent of revenue in 2014 according to the published report, the *IHRSA 2015 Profiles of Success*.

- *EBITDA (earnings before interest, taxes, depreciation, and amortization).* EBITDA is determined by taking the total revenues of the club and deducting the departmental expenses, undistributed expenses, and fixed expenses. The only expenses not counted in this expense category are the costs of depreciation and amortization, interest, taxes, capital replacement, and capital repair. EBITDA is not a GAAP accounting metric; rather, it's a management performance metric. An indicator of a club's profitability and earnings, this

> An indicator of a club's profitability and earnings, EBITDA is used by investors and owners as a benchmark for valuing a company and benchmarking its operating efficiency.

number is used by investors and owners as a benchmark for valuing a company and benchmarking its operating efficiency. For example, if a club that generates four million dollars in revenue has two million in department expenses, $500,000 in undistributed expenses, and $500,000 in fixed expenses, its EBITDA would be $1,000,000 or 25 percent of revenues.

As a rule, the club industry utilizes broad EBITDA benchmarks to indicate the operating effectiveness of a club. In 2014, according to IHRSA's research, the average club had an EBITDA margin that was equal to 17 percent, with a range of 12 percent to 19 percent, depending on the type of club. Figure 16-3 shows industry EBITDA margins from 2012 and 2013. Lifetime Fitness, an operator of high-end multi-purpose clubs, reported EBITDA margins in its public documents (before It went private) of 28.8 percent and 28.6 percent for the year's ending 2012 and 2013. Equinox, which is privately held, has reported EBITDA margins of approximately 25 percent. At McFit in Germany, reports have circulated of EBITDA margins approaching 35 percent. Under most circumstances, a club that is leasing space will find it a challenge to ever exceed an EBITDA margin of 30 percent, due to the impact that rent has on its overhead.

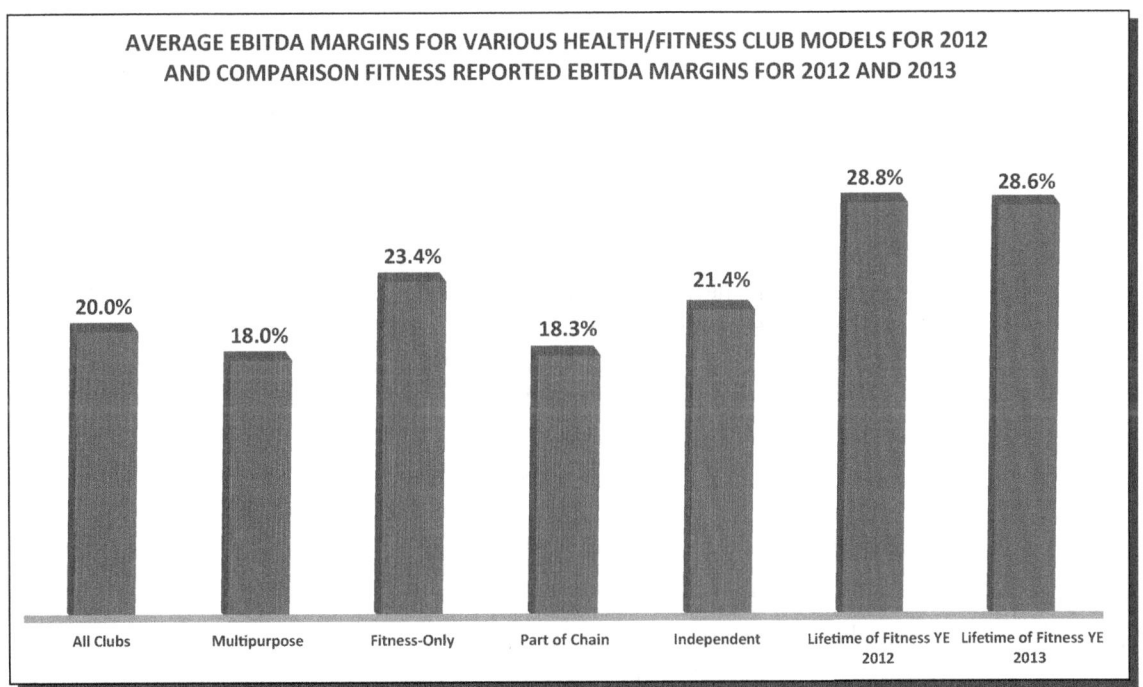

Figure 16-3. EBITDA benchmarks in the health/fitness industry

- *EBIT.* EBIT stands for earnings before interest and taxes and represents the net cash flow before interest and taxes that the club owner is able to earn. EBIT is derived by taking the calculated EBITDA and then deducting the expenses associated with capital replacement, depreciation, interest on loans, and amortization of a loan (the principal that is paid). On average, a club operator can expect this factor to range between 2 and 10 percent of the total revenues, with a range of 6 to 8 percent the most likely scenario.

❑ *The Departmental Income Statement.* The departmental income statement is a detailed profit-and-loss document for a specific department. While the profit-and-loss statement provides a look at the financial performance of a club for a specified period of time, a departmental income statement provides each operating department within a club a comprehensive summary of the revenues, expenses, and net cost of operating that particular department. For the club operator, the departmental income statement can be a useful tool for helping evaluate the performance of a specific department and holding the respective department head (supervisor) accountable for the financial performance of that department. Many of the top club operators in the industry expect their department heads and supervisors not only to develop a departmental income budget, but also to then use the departmental income statement as a tool for monitoring the success of their department.

The IHRSA book, Uniform System of Accounts for the Health, Racquet and Sportsclub Industry, provides a detailed description of the various departmental income statements that are employed in the industry. A list of the most common departments within the health/fitness club industry includes membership, aquatics, fitness, spa, pro shop, racquet sports, food and beverage, and children's programs. For each of these departments, a complete accounting of the revenues, expenses, and net cost of the department can be determined and then compiled in a departmental income statement. Having such detailed accounting for each department can help a club operator hold each department head accountable for the financial success of that individual's respective department.

In IHRSA's *2015 Profiles of Success*, they reported the profit margins for the various revenue departments in a club. These profit margins represent the margin between revenues generated and expenses incurred per a departmental income statement. Unfortunately, IHRSA does not indicate whether the clubs surveyed allocated the same expenses to their departmental calculations for the profit margin, and consequently these margins may not be based on the same income and expense parameters. Figure 16-4 provides a graphic representation of these profit margins for the various departments represented in an earlier IHRSA report from 2014.

Reflections

Understanding the basic principles of accounting is an essential first step in being able to understand and manage the financial performance of a club. Furthermore, being familiar with the key accounting and financial metrics used to measure performance, and what those benchmark metrics are for the health/fitness club industry, will allow professionals to lead and manage their businesses to greater financial performance.

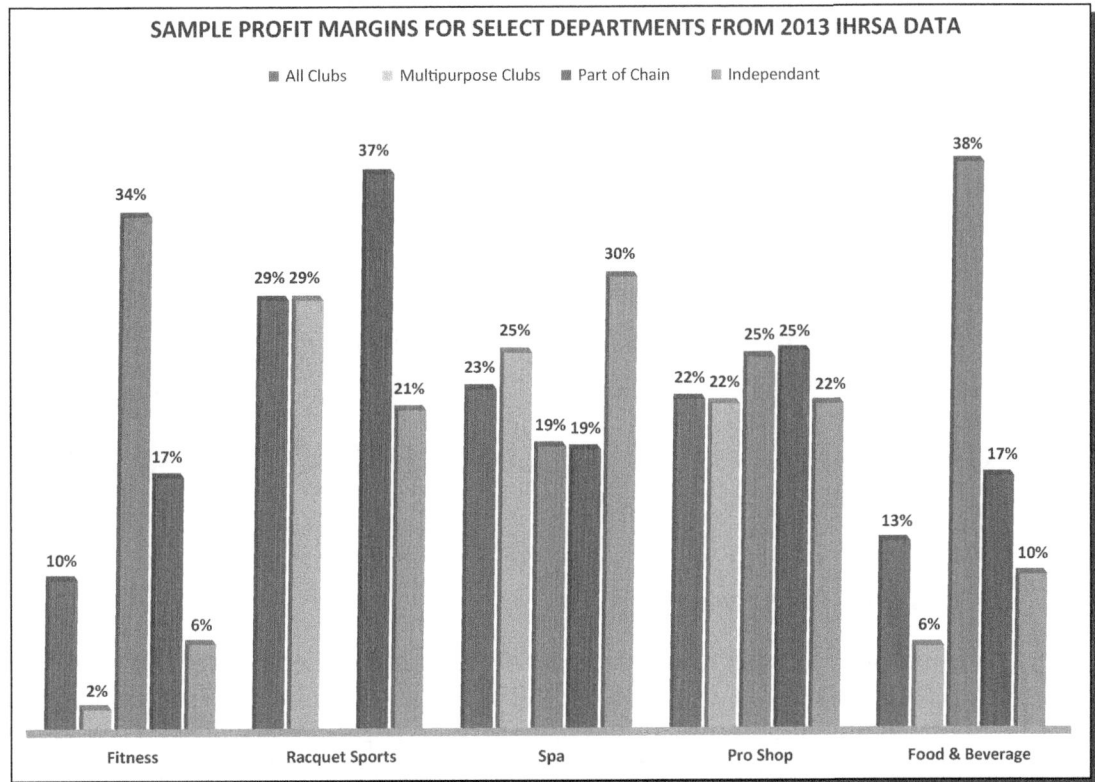

Figure 16-4. Sample profit margins for select departments from IHRSA's 2013 Data Success

17 Budgeting, Forecasting, and Driving Profitability in the Health/Fitness Facility Industry

"The company without a strategy is willing to try anything."

—Michael Porter

Chapter Objectives

The previous chapter reviewed how the industry keeps score of its financial performance, but not how it establishes its financial targets or drives the achievement of those financial targets. This chapter initially offers an overview of the budgeting and forecasting process, and then concludes with an examination of the most effective industry practices for driving profitability and achieving budget targets.

Budgeting in the Health/Fitness Facility Industry

The practice and process of budgeting exists in every business. Creating a budget is the first step in driving a successful financial plan and achieving profitability. Budgeting is simply the process of creating financial targets for the business, based on an understanding of the underlying forces that shape the operations of the business. In the club industry, budgets are done on an annual basis, usually beginning three to four months prior to the start of the next fiscal year. A club budget is a best estimate of its future financial performance, based on a thorough knowledge of the current year's financial performance, current market conditions, and the operational forces that will impact its financial performance going forward. At all times, a budget is a living, breathing document that serves as a roadmap for a club's financial targets.

> Creating a budget is the first step in driving a successful financial plan and achieving profitability.

Most clubs initially create a five-year budget prior to opening for business and then once they're open and operating, develop an annual operating budget. Two primary approaches to budgeting exist in the industry: zero-based budgeting and trend-line budgeting.

- *Zero-Based Budgeting.* Zero-based budgeting involves the process of building a budget from scratch, using such factors as information on pricing, market forces, expected usage levels, projected staffing levels, etc. When a club develops a zero-based budget, it uses its knowledge of the market and market conditions to build a template of what it expects to occur and what these circumstances will mean from a financial perspective. Zero-based budgeting is used most often when developing a new club or making a significant change in the operation of an existing club. When a club uses the zero-based approach to budgeting, it must take into consideration a host of assumptions, examples of which are shown in Figure 17-1.

Revenues	Expenses
1. What will be the expected number of members or memberships at the beginning of the year and the end of the year?	1. What will be the club's total hours of operation?
2. What will be the net gain in membership each accounting period?	2. What will be the total number of FTE (full-time equivalents) that will be required for each area of club operations (fitness, spa, front desk, classes, etc.)?
3. What will be the average monthly and annual dues for each membership?	3. What will be the average hourly rate for each FTE by area?
4. What will be the average enrollment fee collected with each membership?	4. What percentage of revenues, based on industry averages, will be allocated to payroll?
5. What percentage of memberships will participate in personal training services?	5. What will be the cost of benefits as a percentage of total wages?
6. What will be the average fee collected for personal training services?	6. What will utilities be, based on square footage and an average cost per square foot?
7. What percentage of membership will participate in services such as massage, athletic leagues, court reservations, group classes, special events, etc.?	7. What are the expected unit costs for various expenses, such as supplies, uniforms, printing, etc., as a percentage of revenue?
8. What will be the average price for each service at the club (e.g., massage, classes, leagues, court fees, event fees, etc.)?	8. What are the expected unit costs for insurance, property tax, capital repairs, etc., per square foot for the club?
9. How many guests will use the club and what will be the average guest fee?	9. What is the total club square footage?
10. What percentage of the revenues does the club want to derive from dues, personal training, etc.?	10. How many members will the club have?
11. What revenues does the club expect per member or per square foot of the facility?	11. What is the club's target for EBITDA and EBIT as a percentage of revenue?

Figure 17-1. Examples of basic assumptions and questions used in the zero-based budget process

The questions included in Figure 17-1 are the types of queries that club operators must ask and be able to answer if they want to pursue a zero-based budget process. Figure 17-2 presents an example of a zero-based budget for a fitness department.

Assumption	Volume	Unit Cost	Weekly Budget #	Annual Budget #
Level of membership	2,000	NA		
% of members taking personal training each week	5% (100)	$50	$5,000	$260,000
Average fee for personal training	$50	NA		
% of members taking paid exercise classes each week	5% (100)	$10	$1,000	$52,000
Average fee for classes	$10	NA		
% of members taking other fee-based services each week	10% (200)	$5	$1,000	$52,000
Average fee collected for other services	$5	NA		
Total Revenue			**$7,000**	**$364,000**
# FTE for department	10 (400 hours)	$10	$4,000	$208,000
Average hourly rate for FTE	$10	NA	NA	
% of commission on personal training	50%	50%	$2,500	$130,000
Benefits as a % of payroll wages	15%	15%	$600	$31,200
Other expenses as a % of department revenues	25%	25%	$1,000	$52,000
Total Expenses			**$8,100**	**$421,200**
Department Net				**-$57,200**

Figure 17-2. An example of a zero-based budget for a fitness department

As can be seen in Figure 17-2, a zero-based budget requires that the club operator make accurate assumptions with regard to several factors, including membership levels, pricing, volume of traffic for services, and selected other categories. Many club operators believe that using zero-based budgeting forces them to stay attuned to the factors that are impacting their market and business. As a consequence, they are more likely to achieve their budgetary predictions or estimates.

- *Trend-Line Budgeting.* Trend-line budgeting is the most commonly used budgeting practice for multiple-club operations and independent-club operations. The trend-line budget process is based on the principle of clubs building their next year's budget off the past financial trends of their business and then extrapolating forward, based on those trends. This method of budgeting is assumed to be more accurate and predictable, because it relies on a known history of financial-performance trends and then applies certain assumptions to those trends. A downside of this approach is its overreliance on past performance trends and its shortsighted view of current and future market forces. In any event, trend-line budgeting is an effective approach to budgeting, one that is much easier to apply when working with multiple-club entities and mature properties. Figure 17-3 illustrates the revenue, payroll, other operating expenses and EBITDA trends, in millions for a club over a three-year period.

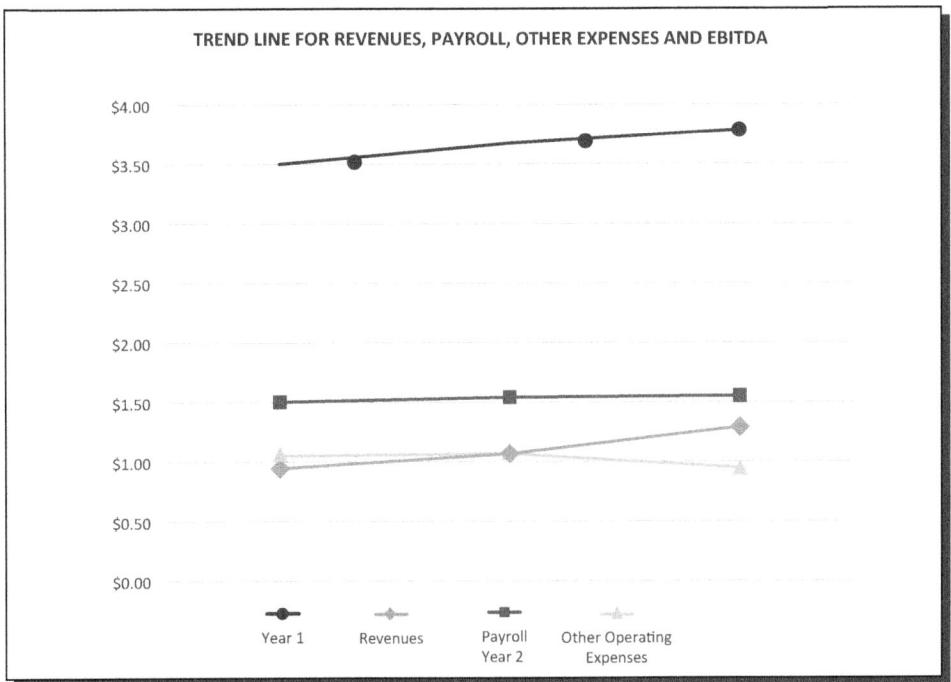

Figure 17-3. Trend line budgeting; revenue, payroll, other operating expenses and EBITDA trends for a health/fitness club

As can be seen in Figure 17-3, the club's revenues have grown consistently over the past three years. At the same time, payroll has decreased slightly, and as a consequence EBITDA has increased slightly each year. For the next calendar year, using the trend-line budgeting process and assuming that its revenues and expenses will increase in proportion with the results of prior years, the club could assume that its EBITDA will increase as a result of the trends in revenues and expenses. When using the trend-line budgeting process, club operators need to consider a number of assumptions and questions (for ease of understanding, the data in Figure 17-3 serves as a reference for the assumptions and questions). Figure 17-4 lists several of these assumptions and questions.

As Figure 17-4 illustrates, the trend-line budgeting process requires both an understanding of a club's prior year's financial-performance trends and the ability to foresee both the expected and unexpected with regard to external and internal business forces. For example, when the 2008 financial crisis hit the global marketplace, club operators preparing for their 2009 budget had to reconsider their past financial performance and apply new thinking to those trends in order to establish a realistic budget for the upcoming year. If club operators tried to extrapolate their financial performance from 2007 and 2008 (trend-line budgeting) to 2009, they most likely would have had unrealistic forecasts. Instead, operators had to adapt their approach to using trends and reconsider some of their most basic assumptions. For example, at the Russian

Revenues	Expenses
1. What is the average percentage rise in revenues for each of the last five years?	1. What has been the average percentage increase in expenses each of the last five years?
2. What is the expected or assumed percentage increase for revenues in the upcoming year due to CPI?	2. What is the expected or assumed percentage increase in payroll and other expenses due to CPI?
3. What is the expected or assumed percentage increase in revenues due to either pricing or usage increases?	3. What is the expected or assumed percentage increase in payroll due to merit increases or the addition of new staff?
4. Is the club adding a new service that will bring new revenues?	4. What are the expected or assumed percentage increases in other expenses, such as utilities, benefits, hospitalization, etc., due to unexpected or rumored market conditions?
5. Is a new competitor moving into town that might pull members from the club?	5. Does the club have any outstanding liabilities that are expected to come due?
6. Is there an indication of a new business or residential development coming in that would cause a higher-than-expected bump in membership levels?	6. Does the club have any delayed capital repair that it must address in the coming year?

Figure 17-4. Examples of basic assumptions and questions used in the trend-line budgeting process

Fitness Group, the company had experienced over 10 percent growth in cash revenues in 2006, 2007, and during the first six months of 2008. When preparing the 2009 budget, the company could have assumed the same basic revenue trends would continue, and therefore it could have budgeted for at least a 10 percent revenue increase in 2009. Instead, the company took into consideration the impact of the economic downturn and budgeted for flat revenue growth (and concurrently for lower expenses), the result of which was an EBITDA plan for 2009 that was only slightly higher than forecasted for 2008.

Forecasting in the Health/Fitness Facility Industry

Forecasting is an extension of the budgeting process. It is normally undertaken to more accurately predict financial performance over a shorter period of time than an annual budget, such as on a quarterly or monthly basis. The process of forecasting is a mainstay of both the public market and those club operators desiring to enter the public market. In recent years, many, if not most, multiple-club operators have moved toward quarterly forecasting as a means to create more accurate financial predictions than they normally would obtain from their annual budgets. The main difference between budgeting (an annual process) and forecasting (normally a quarterly process) is that with forecasting, the club is looking at its budget, then taking the most recent external and internal business events, and finally using those factors to create a more accurate estimate of its financial performance for the upcoming period (usually a quarter). By forecasting, the club can better predict its future financial performance and cash position. Forecasting is also an excellent tool for developing club leaders who are able to take greater accountability for the club's financial performance. Figure 17-5 illustrates a club budget, examples of recent business events, and their application to a quarterly forecast.

Category	Annual Budget	Next Quarter's Budget	Recent Events	Quarterly Forecast
Membership dues	$2,000,000	$500,000	In the last quarter, the club lost 50 members at annual dues of $50,000.	$487,500
Gross operating revenues	$3,000,000	$750,000	Price increase occurred in all services of 10%.	$762,500
Payroll	$1,200,000	$350,000	Wage increases go into effect at 5%.	$367,500
Other expenses	$1,000,000	$250,000	As predicted	$250,000
Total expenses	$2,200,000	$600,000	See above	$617,500
EBITDA	$800,000	$150,000		$145,000
Loan payment	$300,000	$75,000	No payment for quarter	$0
EBIT	$500,000	$75,000		$145,000

Figure 17-5. An example of forecasting, using an existing annual budget

As Figure 17-5 indicates, the forecast for the next quarter has been adjusted from the original budget, because the operator has taken into account several recent external and internal business changes. As a result of the forecast, the operator is better prepared to manage the club's cash flow for the upcoming quarter and to make adjustments in the club's operations, if they're needed, to compensate.

Industry Practices for Driving Revenues

❑ *The Sources of Revenue.* Research conducted by IHRSA indicates that the largest source of revenue for clubs comes from membership dues. In the publication, the *IHRSA 2015 Profiles of Success*, it was reported that between 60 percent and 90 percent of the average club's total revenue is derived from membership dues. As a result, it can be seen that membership sales and retention play a critical role in driving a club's overall revenue. The other 20 percent to 40 percent of a club's revenue, and in some instances 50 percent of its revenues, must be generated from other monetization sources, including:

- *Personal training.* Personal training is the second largest source of revenue in the industry (e.g., based on data reported by IHRSA in 2014, personal training inclusive of small group training accounts for approximately 5 to 15 percent of a club's revenues), with the possible exception of tennis revenue in those clubs that offer tennis. In IHRSA's *2015 Profiles of Success*, personal training contributes approximately 7.2 percent of the average clubs revenue while small group training generates on average another 1 percent of revenues. According to the above report, the typical club reports having 200 personal training clients, which represents approximately 9 percent of the member base for the average club participating in the survey. In a separate research conducted by IHRSA and reported in its *2016 Health Club Consumer Report*, 12 percent of consumers report participating in personal training at least once during the prior year. In fact, with regard to personal training, a few club companies (e.g., Equinox Fitness, U.S. and World Class, Russia) indicate that they are able to attract close to 20 percent of their members for personal training. In other words, if the club has 1,000 members, it can expect to see 50 to 100 sessions involving personal training a week, and if the club has 5,000 members, it can expect to see 250 to 500 personal-training sessions a week. According to data from IHRSA's *2015 Profiles of Success*, the average hourly rate charged by clubs for an individual personal training session is $60, compared to an average of $55 reported by members in the *2016 Health Club Consumer Report*. Figures 17-6 and 17-7 compare reported personal training participation rates and fees for training as reflected in data from the aforementioned IHRSA reports. As a rule, personal training fees tend to range from $40 to $125 an hour, with the highest U.S. rates found in New York, Los Angeles, and San Francisco. With these types of numbers, it is not unreasonable for a club of 1,000 members to generate as much as $7,500 a week in personal-training revenues or $360,000 annually, while a club of 5,000 members can derive as much as $37,500 a week or $1,950,000 annually from personal training. The Eastbank Club, based in Chicago, generates over $3 million in personal training annually. Equinox Fitness, which operates approximately 90 clubs throughout the U.S., and World Class, which operates approximately 60 clubs in Russia, both indicate having clubs that generate over $2 million in annual revenues from personal training. Over the past few years, duet and small group training have emerged as significant contributors to the personal training revenue stream of clubs. In the most recent IHRSA data, over 30 percent of members prefer to participate in duet and small group training. While the fees for group training run less than they do for individual sessions (according to IHRSA data an individual will spend from 25 percent to 50 percent less, depending on whether it's a duet or small group), the volume of training that can be conducted can more than make up for the reduced fee.

> Over the past few years, duet and small group training have emerged as significant contributors to the personal training revenue stream of clubs.

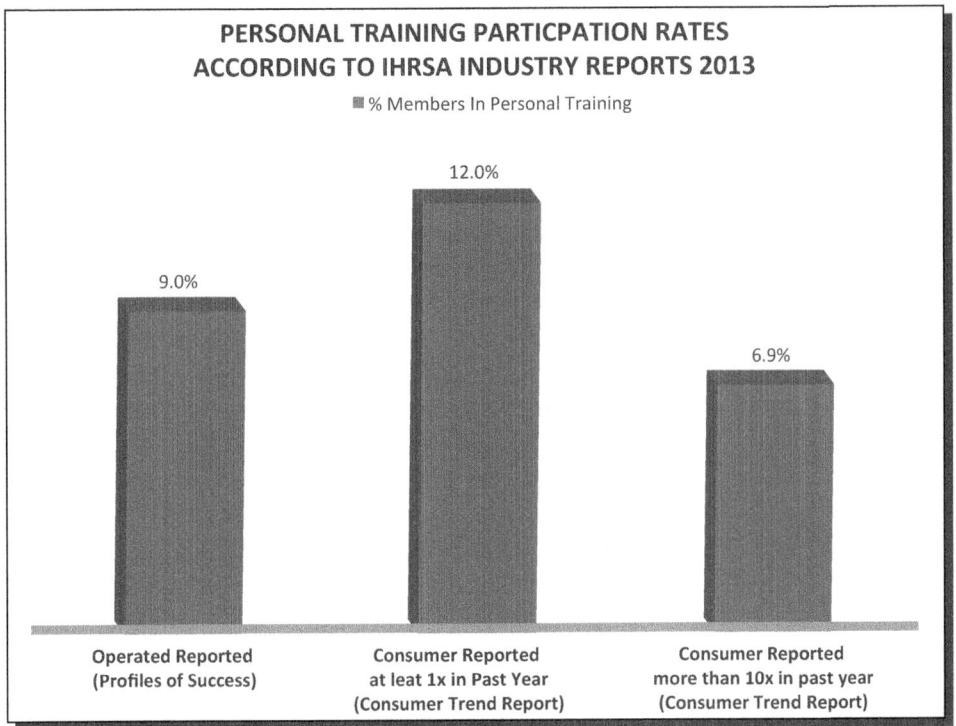

Figure 17-6. Comparison of personal training participation rates from IHRSA research

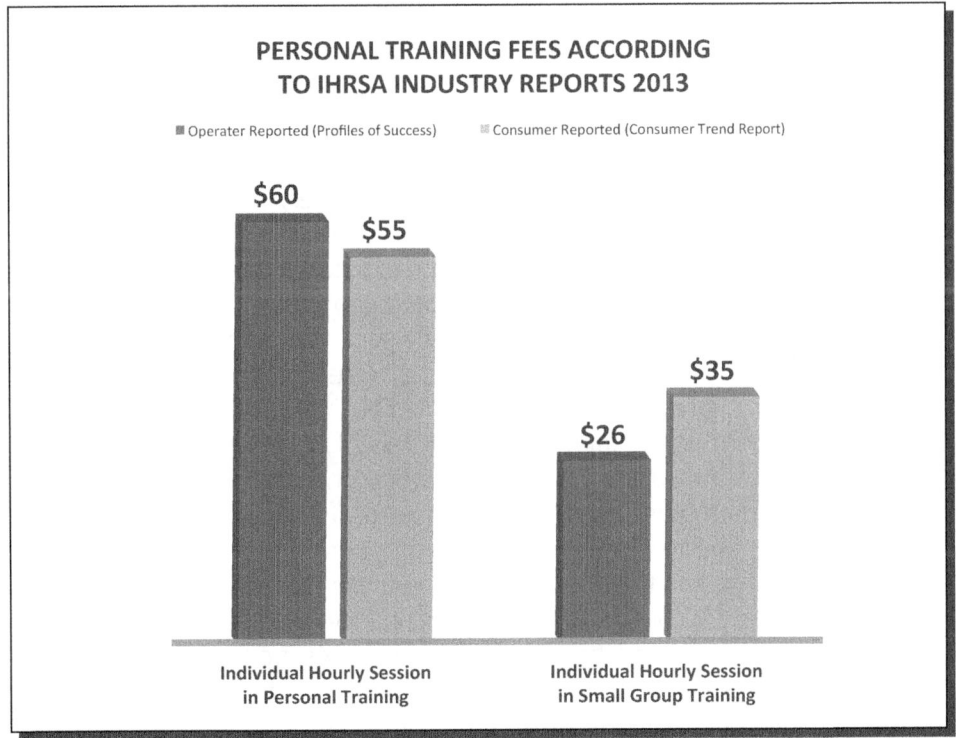

Figure 17-7. Comparison of personal training fees from IHRSA research

- *Tennis services.* In clubs that have tennis courts and tennis services, tennis is often the largest source of revenue after membership. In clubs with tennis, the largest single generator of revenue is providing tennis lessons (individual and group). Lesson revenue can account for as much as 80 percent of all tennis revenues. Other sources of revenue for tennis include court fees (indoor courts), youth programs, leagues, tournaments, and pro-shop sales. A club with outdoor courts can annually expect to generate between $25,000 and $50,000 in revenue per court, with the best clubs approaching $75,000 per court, while a club with indoor courts can expect to derive $35,000 to $100,000 per court. Club operators usually generate an average of $40,000 for an outdoor court and $75,000 for an indoor court. The reason indoor courts generate significantly more revenue is due to court fees. As previously indicated, lesson revenue is the top source of tennis revenue, with the average fee charged for a one-hour private lesson ranging from $40 to $60. Court fees range from a low of $10 per court hour to as high as $100 per court hour, depending upon the market in which the club is located. It should be noted that 10 percent to 40 percent of a club's members may be actively involved in tennis lessons on either an individual or group basis.

> Spa services have grown into a prime source of revenue for the health/fitness club industry.

- *Spa services.* Spa services have grown into a prime source of revenue for the health/fitness club industry. According to the publication, the *IHRSA 2015 Profiles of Success*, in 2015, the average club generated approximately 42.5 percent of its revenues from spa services. In some clubs, this source of revenue might only involve the delivery of massage, while in other clubs, it might involve a number of activities, including massage, facials, body treatments, pedicures, manicures, and even hair service. According to research conducted by ISPA (the International Spa Association), massage is the leading revenue source in the spa-service category, followed (in order) by facials, pedicures, manicures, and body treatments. In most instances, massage will account for at least 50 percent of the spa-service treatments. Research conducted by the spa industry shows that a typical treatment room could generate as much as $10,000 a month, while a pedicure station usually generates approximately $3,000 a month. In the club industry, anecdotal research indicates that a club can expect to generate about $3,000 to $10,000 a month from a single treatment room, assuming occupancy levels of 60 percent to 70 percent. The same research also shows that between one percent and five percent of a club's members will be active users of its spa services. In a 2016 study of the private club fitness and spa industry, the researchers found that the average spa treatment room in a private club–based spa generated approximately $50,000 with average occupancy levels of 44 percent. With regard to pricing, a one-hour massage can range from as low as $40 in some mid-western clubs to as high as $130 in some of the high-end clubs in the more affluent markets. In fact, some club-based spas, such as those operated by Village Health Clubs and Spas headquartered in Phoenix generate over $2 million annually.

- *Youth programs and services.* In the last several years, the children's program and activity areas have become a significant source of revenue for many health/fitness clubs. In 2014, according to the publication, the *IHRSA*

2015 Profiles of Success, youth programming generated approximately 2 percent of a club's total revenues. Activities conducted in these areas, such as birthday parties, sports camps, dance classes, martial arts, tumbling, after-school camps, holiday camps, swim lessons, and swim teams can provide significant revenues. In fact, youth programs in suburban clubs, such as the Bay Club in Redwood City, California, Franco's in Mandeville, Louisiana, and ACAC Fitness & Wellness in West Chester, Pennsylvania, all contribute significantly to each club's overall revenue numbers.

- *Pilates.* One of the newest sources of revenue for the industry has evolved from offering Pilates to club members. By combining both private instruction and group instruction, many clubs have seen Pilates become their second largest source of revenue. For example, Health Works Fitness Centers for Women, a woman's-only chain of clubs located in Boston, has one Pilates center that grosses close to a half a million dollars a year. In some of Equinox Fitness's clubs, where the Pilates studio occupies 600 to 800 square feet, sources indicate they generate between $20,000 and $50,000 a month in revenue. For boutique Pilates studios, this is their number-one source of revenue.

- *Group exercise classes.* Over the past few years, many clubs have begun to establish signature group exercise classes that carry an additional fee. These signature classes might be high-level versions of existing classes (e.g., special group cycling classes with heart rate monitoring), specialty classes (e.g., aerial yoga and hot yoga) or boot camps. According to data from the *2015 Profiles of Success* published by IHRSA, clubs on average charge an additional $10 for these classes. Among many of the boutique fitness facilities, the fee for a single session ranges on average from $15 to $25, with some of the premium boutiques setting individual class fees as high as $35. The emerging trend among boutiques is to charge a fee for unlimited and restricted access to all their classes, in which case the fees range from $130 to $350 a month, depending on the type of classes offered.

- *Other revenue-generating programs.* In addition to the aforementioned four sources, clubs have developed a variety of services that can contribute to revenue growth. For example, ClubCorp's Rivers Club in Pittsburgh, Pennsylvania generates over $200,000 annually in locker-rental income. The East Bank Club in Chicago derives over seven million annually in food and beverage revenue. Many clubs (e.g., Bay Clubs, etc.) have found that leasing space to a physical therapy operator can bring in as much as $100,000 annually from fixed leases and revenue sharing. Still other clubs have leveraged activities, such as special events, leagues, adventure programs, and social events into significant sources of new revenue.

❏ *Increasing the Revenue Stream From Each Revenue Source.* As a rule, clubs have four primary strategies that they can employ to increase their revenue output from the aforementioned revenue sources: increasing the pricing, increasing the usage rate of the services that they offer, leveraging a subscription model, and adding new products and services.

- *Price increases.* Many club operators assume that the best approach to driving revenues is to increase the price of a service. While price increases can generate significant bumps in revenue, especially if applied to membership dues or personal training, such increases can also have a negative impact if club operators do not take into consideration their club's market position and the value of the club's personal training offering. Many clubs make it a practice to increase their dues or personal training fees two to three percent every year, irrespective of market conditions, while others carefully consider the dynamics of the marketplace and their club's niche before passing on any price increases. In reality, if the club is delivering a great product and its members are delighted with their overall experience, then an annual price increase equal to the consumer price index (CPI) or slightly higher can usually be accommodated.

Operators need to understand that pricing is generally influenced by two primary forces. The first factor is the influence of competitive market conditions. For example, if a club's competitors in a particular market are continually decreasing their pricing, it will make it challenging for that club to increase its prices, even if it offers a fantastic experience. The second major influence on pricing is related to supply and demand. For example, if a club has more people requesting a service than it can serve, then the facility is in a position to raise its prices. On the other hand, if far more of a supply of a service existed than what the market was demanding it is likely that the club would be unable to increase its prices.

- *Increasing volume.* Another effective approach for driving revenues is to increase member and guest participation in fee-based services. While the health/fitness club industry, as a whole, tends to shy away from this approach, all factors considered, it is the most effective strategy for generating relatively large increases in revenue. For example, multiple-club operators, such as Equinox Fitness and 24 Hour Fitness, focus much of their non-dues revenue efforts on internal selling. To effectively increase member usage of fee-based services, clubs should consider the following approaches:
  - ✓ *Sales management.* The best clubs closely manage the sales of their primary revenue sources, such as personal training, massage, and other services, just as they do membership. The top revenue-producing clubs establish sales targets for their teams and each individual employee, and then closely monitor each entity's sales performance. Not only do these clubs establish challenging sales goals for both the sales teams and individuals, they then hold the teams and employees accountable for their performance against these goals. All factors considered, Equinox Fitness, based in New York, may do this better than anyone else in the industry.
  - ✓ *Sales training.* Fitness staff (e.g., trainers, instructors, and therapists) tends to be relationship people who often shy away from sales. As a rule, many individuals view sales in a negative light. Accordingly, many top club operators make a concerted effort to provide continuous sales training for their employees that can help make them more comfortable about selling themselves and the services of their clubs. During my tenure as the CEO of the Russian Fitness Group, targeted sales training was provided for our trainers and therapists.
  - ✓ *Selling upfront.* The top revenue-producing clubs have learned that the best time to sell a service, such as personal training or massage, is when the member first joins the club. Many club groups, such as

Equinox Fitness, 24 Hour Fitness, and Bay Clubs, bundle special-service packages that the membership sales team makes new members aware of when they join the club. This process is often referred to as up-selling the club's services. Club operators should keep in mind that, all factors considered, new members represent the best audience for sales.

✓ *Internal marketing.* All too often, some clubs believe that by putting a poster on the wall, their members will automatically sign-up for the offering. In reality, to effectively make members aware of the services it offers, the club should utilize a variety of marketing tools, such as interactive displays, direct-mail invitations to members, SMS messages to members, postings on Facebook, newsflashes on their website, newsletter messages, and audio-visual messages, utilizing the club's internal audio-visual entertainment equipment.

✓ *Relationships and making the call.* Members who respect and trust the employees of the club are much more likely to purchase a service from those employees. The same can be said about members who know and respect other members. The top revenue-producing clubs make an effort to utilize their employees and members as salespeople. Having employees make sales contacts or extend invitations to the members that they know can contribute significantly to revenue generation. Members who are provided an incentive will often serve as apostles for the services offered by the club and invite their friends to join them to participate in a fee-based service.

- *Moving to a subscription model for monetized services.* One of the newest approaches being used by club operators to increase the revenues generated from existing sources revolves around a subscription model of revenue generation. A subscription model, which is the primary approach used for membership, offers members a specified volume of services each week or month for an agreed-upon fee. For example, rather than sell a package of 10 personal training sessions, a club might instead charge a set monthly fee for personal training based on the member having two sessions each week. To further leverage this subscription approach, some clubs have gone to putting the subscription on automatic electronic funds transfer. This approach ensures the club receives its money each month while requiring the member to make a concerted effort to use the subscribed number of sessions each week. The subscription model is also popular among many boutique fitness studio operators, where they provide clients with the opportunity to subscribe to unlimited access, or in some instances guaranteed access to certain classes for a set monthly fee.

- *Adding new products and services.* The third strategy for effectively driving revenues is to introduce new products and services to the club's members. For example, if the club does not offer spa services, adding these services can generate new revenue streams. By the same token, if the club does not offer Pilates, including a Pilates center in the facility can help drive revenues for the club. In reality, the opportunities for adding new products and services are virtually endless. One proven strategy for identifying new sources of revenue is to create a club-based revenue team, consisting of employees from different areas of the club. This revenue team should then

The opportunities for adding new products and services are virtually endless.

be empowered to meet on a regular basis and brainstorm new ideas for generating revenue. When the revenue team identifies a revenue idea that has consensus, then management can work with them to develop an execution strategy.

Industry Practices for Controlling Expenses

While driving revenue is critical to growing a club's profitability, controlling expenses also plays a vital role. The process of controlling expenses involves having systems and practices in place that can help prevent the club from needlessly wasting money. At the same time, the process can help the club invest its money more wisely in its people and assets.

> The top expense categories for clubs are wages and salaries, benefits, utilities, and lease costs.

❑ *The Leading Expense Categories.* According to the publication, the *IHRSA 2015 Profiles of Success*, the top expense categories for clubs are wages and salaries, benefits, utilities, and lease costs.

- *Wages and salaries.* According to the most recent industry studies, wages and salaries comprise approximately 37 percent to 47 percent (a figure that includes employee benefits and taxes) of every dollar in revenue that the club generates. If the related benefit costs are subtracted, then payroll is probably closer to 30 percent to 35 percent of gross revenues. This figure approximates the total of all other departmental undistributed expenses combined. Wages and salaries include the salaries of supervisors, the hourly wages of the non-exempt employees, commissions paid to personal trainers and other instructors, wages paid to group-exercise instructors, and bonuses provided to any employee of the club. For most clubs, the wages paid to group-exercise instructors and the commissions paid to personal trainers and others constitute the largest single payroll expense.

- *Benefits.* Benefit costs can range from 15 percent to 25 percent of the actual wages and salaries. These costs include club contributions to social security taxes, hospitalization benefits, disability insurance, retirement type accounts, and education. The single largest contributor in recent years has been hospitalization costs, which have grown at rates over 12 percent annually the last several years.

- *Utilities.* Utility costs normally range between 4 percent and 10 percent of a club's operating revenue, depending upon its geographic location. The largest contributors to utility costs are heating, and air conditioning, and expenses attributed to the operation of the pools and whirlpools.

- *Leases.* For clubs that rent space, the cost of rent can be a club's second largest expense after wages. According to the IHRSA's Uniform System of Accounts and the IHRSA's *2015 Profiles of Success*, lease rates can run as high as 20 percent of a club's revenue (it should be noted that in some global urban markets, such as New York, London, and Moscow, rent can consume as much as 30 percent to 35 percent of a club's revenues). Successful club operators look to keep their lease rate under 15 percent of revenues. According to the publication, the IHRSA's *2015 Profiles of Success*, in 2014, the average lease for a health/fitness club was approximately 11 percent of revenues. Many clubs get lulled into a state of complacency by assuming that they have a fixed based rent and they fail to consider the common area maintenance (CAM)—costs that landlords pass through, which represent the club's share of the building operating costs assumed by the landlord. In most markets, landlords like to offer triple-net leases, which means the club pays the landlord a base rent, CAM costs, utilities, and property taxes. In most urban markets, the lease rates for class "A" space run approximately $30 to $70 a square foot per year, while the lease rates for class "B" space tend to be in the neighborhood of $20 to $30 a square foot per year. CAM costs can run another $6 to $15 a square foot, depending upon the market in which a club is located. In smaller markets rent rates for space in strip malls run in the neighborhood of $15 to $20 a square foot.

Controlling the Leading Expense Categories

Achieving profitability requires that the club operator put systems in place for controlling the large and small expenses that can often erode the revenue gains that a club makes. Among the most effective strategies that the industry employs to help monitor and control operating expenses, thereby facilitating growth in profitability, are the following:

❑ *Managing Wages and Benefits Expense.* Since wages and benefits contribute, on average, close to 42 percent of all operating expenses, it makes sense that by effectively managing its payroll, the club can also better manage its expenses. Examples of the most effective strategies for managing payroll include:

- *Scheduling for less than 40 hours.* Smart operators avoid scheduling their full-time non-exempt employees for 40 hours and instead schedule them for 32 to 35 hours a week. This approach has two advantages. First, it provides leeway if an employee is asked to serve a few more hours, and second, it allows the clubs to avoid both overtime and overlapping schedules.
- *Not scheduling employees during low-usage periods.* Many clubs save wages by limiting their level of scheduling during low-usage times. While it is important to be fully staffed during peak-usage periods, during times when members are not using the facility, management can limit their scheduling of employees to only provide the necessary level of employee coverage. If additional staffing is required when special functions are held, these situations can be handled with exempt employees (e.g. supervisors).
- *Monitoring and avoiding overtime.* Since overtime costs a club 50 percent more than regular time, wise club operators make it a practice to carefully monitor employee hours to avoid overtime. In this regard, software programs are available that will provide the club with reports that indicate when its employees are approaching overtime. In which case, the club can make whatever adjustments are necessary in its employee schedules to avoid overtime situations. An overtime situation that often arises due to scheduling issues is personal trainers, typically your highest-paid non-exempt employees. Many personal trainers, due to client load, often work 50-plus hours a week. Since many clubs allow trainers to schedule their clients, they often get overlooked when it comes to overtime. Consequently, management needs to pay close attention to the hours its personal trainers work.

> Achieving profitability requires that the club operator put systems in place for controlling the large and small expenses that can often erode the revenue gains that a club makes.

- *Going to flat rates versus percentage commission.* Personal trainers and massage therapists are often paid a commission on the revenue they generate. The industry norm for commissions tends to vary from 40 percent to 60 percent, with some clubs paying as much as 80 percent commission. Instead of paying a commission, many clubs pay a flat rate for personal training and/or massage. This approach enables the club to avoid providing wage increases every time the fees for services offered by the club are raised.
- *Group-exercise classes.* For many club operators, the cost of offering group-exercise classes can be very substantial. The average wage for a class instructor can vary from an average as low as $18 a class in some midwestern markets to $100 per class in the large urban markets, such as New York and San Francisco. When the fact that some clubs offer as many as 100 to 150 classes a week is considered, the enormity of the potential costs involved becomes apparent. At the Russian Fitness Group, the group-exercise payroll often ran has high as 10 percent of the clubs membership revenue. The top club operators make it a habit to establish specific attendance requirements for a class to continue and when attendance falls below those specified levels, the class is eliminated. The primary goal of most clubs is to offer only the classes that appeal to members and thereby only pay the wages for those classes that bring value to each club's program offerings.

❑ *Managing Operating Supply Costs.* In most clubs, the costs associated with operating supplies, printing, and other miscellaneous supplies can run as high as 5 percent of revenue and, if uncontrolled, much higher. The most effective approaches to managing these expenses include:
- *Using a purchase-order system.* A purchase-order system requires that before employees can purchase an item for the club, they need to obtain a price quote and submit it to management for approval. If subsequently approved by management, the purchase order becomes the basis for an order. This approach allows management to monitor expenses against budget to insure that funds are not expended for unnecessary items.
- *Par stock and inventory.* A par stock is a term that connotes a process that involves purchasing sufficient quantities of supplies and creating an inventory of those items for the club to pull from in times of need. In reality, many clubs unfortunately wait until they run out of an item before attempting to restock the item by purchasing it. With a par-stock process, the club purchases items based on its usage experience, keeping an inventory sufficient to cover a particular period of time. Under the par-stock process, when the club's inventory drops to a certain level, it purchases the standard reorder quantity. This approach is similar to an open-to-buy system in retail. The par-stock method allows the club to buy in bulk, which saves money, but it also allows it to closely monitor the usage of products and control its shrinkage (e.g., inventory loss due to theft).
- *Preferred vendor arrangements.* Clubs can negotiate with vendors to obtain preferred status and thus gain discounts. If a club is willing to purchase its supplies from one or two vendors, it can often negotiate a discounted

> If a club is willing to purchase its supplies from one or two vendors, it can often negotiate a discounted price schedule.

price schedule. In large multiple-club operations, this approach can involve a significant savings opportunity. In this regard, independent-club operators should consider using industry-association programs, such as the programs offered by IHRSA.

❑ *Utility Costs.* As previously discussed, utility costs typically represent 4 to 7 percent of revenues, and in some instances as much as 10 percent of a club's operating revenue in certain markets. Most clubs can save on their utility costs by incorporating one or more of the following strategies:
- *Converting electric heating appliances to gas.* Gas is usually less expensive than electric, especially when it comes to heating pools, water heaters, whirlpools, and washers.
- *Using light-saver switches.* Many clubs use automatically controlled lighting systems that turn off lights in rooms when they are not in use. Far too many clubs waste money by keeping lights on in particular areas, even though those rooms are not in use. These clubs rely on their employees to turn off the lights as appropriate, an approach that is not always as effective as automated systems.
- *Installing water restrictors in the showers.* Water restrictors are devices that can be added to showers that reduce the total volume of water that is dispensed. Over time, these implements can save considerable costs in water bills.
- *Insulating the club.* Most utility companies will provide the club with incentives if it upgrades the level of insulation in the club. In many cases, utility companies will even cover most of the cost for such improvements. The upside for the club comes with the reduced cost of heating and cooling.
- *Negotiating with the utility company for a flat rate.* Club operators can often negotiate with the utility company to establish a flat utility rate that is reviewed on a semi-annual basis. Not only can this practice save money, more importantly, it can also enable the club to more accurately forecast its utility costs.
- *Installing low-energy lighting.* Many utility purchasing groups offer incentives to businesses that install low-energy lighting systems. Such incentives allow a business to spend less in the conversion process, with savings subsequently being realized on their monthly utility bill.

❑ *Leases.* In most cases, leases are non-negotiable once they're in place. At least, this situation is what most operators assume. As a result, many club owners pay higher-than-needed rent and CAM costs. The first step for the club in managing its lease expense is to know its lease terms inside and out. By knowing the terms of its lease, the club can identify when unnecessary costs are passed through, such as high CAM costs and rent increases, when none exist in the lease. Even more important than knowing its lease, the club should be fully aware of a situation when the opportunity exists to renegotiate its lease. Landlords are open to renegotiating leases under several possible circumstances, including: when a new building owner becomes the landlord, when the landlord is looking to extend leases, and when lease rates for other spaces are going at a lower rate than what the club currently pays. For example, during the economic downturn that extended from 2008 to 2010, a number of landlords provided temporary lease relief to their tenants. At the Russian Fitness Group, for example, the company was able to negotiate rent reductions on several of its properties, saving the company hundreds of thousands of dollars in the process. All factors considered if the club has established itself as a worthy and reliable tenant and has built a good relationship with the landlord, then the club is in a better position to renegotiate more favorable lease terms.

❏ *Capital Repair.* In the IHRSA's publication, the *2015 Profiles of Success*, it is noted that in 2014, clubs, on average, spent $154,627 on reinvestment (approximately $47,000 of it on fitness equipment), a statistic that represents on average 3 percent of revenues. As indicated previously, this outlay represents a significant allocation of cash for most club operators. Some operators feel that by limiting their allocation for capital reserve that they can bring more of their existing revenue to the bottom line. At first glance, this attitude might make sense, since it decreases the out-of-pocket cash that a club has to spend, thereby increasing the EBIT and profit before tax (PFT) of the club. Unfortunately, this reasoning ends up costing clubs money, both in the short-term and even more so in the long-term. By allocating 3 to 6 percent of its revenues to capital repair and replacement and then using it, the club is investing in its physical assets, an approach which, in turn, helps to drive revenues and prevent costly operational maintenance costs. By investing the full capital replacement on an annual basis, the club can also help prevent having to spend much larger sums in future years, when a particular physical asset reaches a point where it requires major renovation and repair. IHRSA data from a study conducted in 2016 showed that the clubs that reinvested the most in their facilities experienced the highest levels of revenue growth during that same time period.

Reflections

By incorporating annual budgeting and quarterly forecasting, a facility operator can develop realistic and achievable financial targets for its revenues, expenses, and earnings. These financial targets can then be used to foster individual and team accountability for the business's financial performance. Once in place, these targets can assist the facility operator in determining which revenue-enhancement and cost-control strategies are needed to achieve particular financial targets.

Buying, Leasing, Selling, and Raising Capital for a Health/Fitness Business

18

"Our business is really simple. When you look at a deal and its structure looks like an octopus or spider, just don't do it."

—Timothy Sloan, CFO Wells Fargo

Chapter Objectives

As the industry continues to evolve and become more financially sophisticated, club and studio owners and operators need to acquaint themselves with as many of the overriding issues surrounding the purchasing, financing, and sale of health/fitness facilities as possible. In that regard, this chapter will review the information and processes that a club or studio operator should know concerning how to raise capital for a facility, how to buy a business, how to sell a business, or simply how to properly evaluate a lease for the space that a club or studio might occupy. Initially, the chapter discusses the key issues attendant to raising capital, including the newest form of capital acquisition crowdfunding, and then concludes by examining several of the most relevant factors involving buying, leasing, and selling clubs.

Traditional Approaches to Raising Capital for a Health/Fitness Business

Whether you're an entrepreneur start-up seeking seed capital, a mature business seeking funds to expand the business to leverage market trends, or a club company desirous of acquiring a competitor to expand market share, understanding the dynamics of raising capital is an essential business competency. This section will address the various routes a club owner can pursue to raise the capital they need for the business. So, where can business owners find the money to capitalize their vision?

> Understanding the dynamics of raising capital is an essential business competency.

❑ *Personal Equity.* Personal equity is the cash an owner personally contributes to the venture. In most instances, entrepreneurs have minimal equity to put into a deal, while more established business veterans may have a larger well of funds to pull from. Typically, new business owners (entrepreneurs), in this case future club or studio owners, may have a small stash of cash that they have saved over the years that can be applied to the venture. It is important for owners to contribute equity to their venture, even if it's not very much. Investors always want to know owners have "skin in the game," meaning they have capital at risk if the venture does not succeed. If pursuing a small business loan, the lender will require an equity contribution.

> Raising capital from family and friends brings with it certain risks, particularly if the venture does not succeed.

- ❑ *Friends and Family.* The term *friends and family* refers to family members, friends, business associates, existing clients, and acquaintances. Friends and family are those most likely to place trust in a new owner's vision and have an intimate knowledge of their expertise. Depending on the amount of capital being sought (usually smaller capital requirements), friends and family can often provide the balance of funding an entrepreneur requires. Raising capital from family and friends brings with it certain risks, particularly if the venture does not succeed. When raising capital from family and friends, it is best to have an attorney first draw up a term sheet and later an operating agreement that spells out what the investor will get in return for their contribution of capital. In most instances, friends and family will want to get their investment back within a given time frame along with some form of return on their investment. Others may want a percentage stake in the business along with participation in any profits the business generates.

- ❑ *Angel Investors.* The term *angel investor* (also called *angel*) defines investors who are not typically part of your inner circle and are successful business people who provide financial backing (start-up or growth capital) for entrepreneurs and start-ups. The Securities and Exchange Commission defines an accredited individual angel investor as a natural person who has a net worth in excess of one million dollars at the time of their investment or has annual income for the past two years in excess of $200,000 ($300,000 for a household) and expects similar earnings over the next few years. Typically, angels seek to invest their money in ventures they believe hold significant potential to be successful while generating high returns on their investment. As such, angels place a lot of faith in the person behind the venture. Most angels are not millionaires; instead, they are successful business people (lawyers, physicians, entrepreneurs, successful small business professionals) seeking to earn better returns on their money than they would in other investments such as bonds, the stock market, certificates of deposit, etc. Typically, they will invest smaller amounts of capital (most often under $50,000), but in turn will not seek control of the business, and will have lesser financial expectations than venture capital groups and private equity organizations. Over the past decade there has been significant growth in angel networks. Angel networks are angel investors who come together as a collective group to invest in viable start-up businesses. These angel networks pool the resources of multiple angels and, therefore, can finance larger business ventures. Most angel networks invest in start-ups with capital requirements of less than 5 million dollars, with many focusing on investments between $100,000 and 1 million dollars. Angel investor networks tend to specialize, both geographically and by business type. For instance, there are angel networks that focus on technology, others who focus on energy, some that commit to a specific geographic region, and finally, some that are college alumni–based. Many angel investors and angel networks want to see the owner have skin in the game, and others also like to be the first stranger to the table, meaning they also want friends and family to invest before they do. In today's marketplace, the majority of angel networks are looking for at least a 10-time (10x) return on their investment based on the future sale of the business. Following are some important things to understand if you are going to pursue funding from individual angel investors or an angel network.

- Angels and angel networks often expect to earn a return on their investment equal to at least 10x their initial investment. This return is usually calculated based on the business being sold in the future (five to seven years down the road). Angels expect this high rate of return since an estimated 9 out of 10 new ventures don't achieve their targets.
- Have a detailed business plan, investment memorandum, five-year cash flow *pro forma* with return on investment metrics, and a "pitch deck" (PowerPoint) for your business.
- Make sure that your pitch deck addresses the following: the opportunity or problem that your business venture will address; the business solution you are proposing; the market demand (potential clients and/or members) for your solution and/or offering; the team behind the business (qualifications and experience); how as the owner and operator you will market and sell your offering; your exit strategy; the revenues and cash flow projections for the first five years; the total investment being requested; the funds already contributed (e.g., personal, friends, and family) and the key investment criteria (e.g., return on capital, return on assets, and estimated pre- and post-money valuations).
- Most angel networks have a screening process that involves a series of presentations where you compete against other entrepreneurs and new business owners seeking seed capital. In many instances, you will have 6 to 10 minutes to present and 5 to 10 minutes to respond to questions.
- If an angel or angel network chooses to invest in your vision, they will want to begin with a term sheet that details the terms of their investment, including their ownership stake in the business, their level of participation in the business's annual profits, their level of participation in the net proceeds of a sale of the business in the future, and a guaranteed liquidation amount (amount of money they are guaranteed if the business sells).

☐ *Venture Capital.* Venture capital represents money provided by institutional investors who seek to invest in start-ups with long-term growth potential and have the ability to generate high returns. Venture capital firms refer to this as seed capital. Venture capital firms are not individuals or a network of angel investors; instead, they are professionally managed firms that oversee investments for large investors (individuals, pension funds, businesses, etc.). Venture capital firms are investing other people's money, not their own, so their expectations are quite different than those of angel investors. Most venture capital firms will want some form of control of your business, including a seat on your board, an ownership position, and most importantly, participation in the profits, and finally, a guaranteed return. Venture capital firms tend to invest in ventures with capital needs of over 5 million dollars, and frequently, much larger. Venture capital firms, because they are investing in new businesses, tend to seek higher rates of return than private investors or even private equity firms. Similar to angels and angel networks, venture capital firms tend to focus on a specific area of investment, such as energy, technology, or healthcare. In recent years, venture capital firms have moved away from funding start-ups and handed the mantle over to angels and angel networks, instead focusing on early-stage businesses with a proven business model and cash flow and a need for growth capital.

> **Venture capital firms are investing other people's money, not their own, so their expectations are quite different than those of angel investors.**

❏ *Private Equity.* Private equity is a source of capital from high-net-worth individuals and institutions (e.g., pension funds) that are typically managed by private equity firms whose responsibility it is to invest these funds in business opportunities that will generate a highly favorable return for the investors. Private equity funds are typically invested for a period of three to five years. Typically, a private equity firm is looking to achieve at least a 20 percent internal rate of return for the investors in the fund, which equates to a doubling of the initial investment over a five-year investment period. In some instances, the investors in a fund managed by a private equity firm seek rates of return closer to 30 percent. Private equity firms focus on funding underperforming business with a significant upside potential based on the proper infusion of capital and management expertise. In the health/fitness club business, private equity has fueled the growth of the industry over the past two decades, providing the financial resources and management expertise to fuel the growth (organically and through acquisitions) of many of the largest and most successful club companies in the industry, including leading companies such as 24 Hour Fitness, LA Fitness, Bay Clubs, Equinox Fitness, and Orange Theory.

> A bank loan is probably the most prevalent form of funding for new business owners and entrepreneurs other than personal equity and possibly investments from friends and family.

❏ *Bank Debt.* Bank debt, otherwise known as a bank loan, is probably the most prevalent form of funding for new business owners and entrepreneurs other than personal equity and possibly investments from friends and family. Because banks are regulated, they tend to be very careful in their lending practices. When looking for a bank to finance its business, a club should attempt to find a bank that defaults on no more than 0.5 percent of its loans. In other words, it makes the right financing decision 99.5 percent of the time. Some things every small business owner should know about bank lending are as follows:

- For banks, loans are an asset, which means that every loan application is reviewed very carefully. Since the recent recession of 2008–2009, most banks have intensified their scrutiny of loan applications.
- Banks look for individuals, partnerships, and businesses with good credit ratings.
- Banks expect to see a business plan that has reasonable assumptions, reasonable budget projections, a qualified leadership team (management expertise and experience), and detailed value of the collateral that will be put up to secure the loan (the collateral must hold value to the lender).
- Banks expect full disclosure from the company to which they are going to make a loan.
- Banks will normally apply covenants to a loan. Covenants help protect the bank's investment in the loan. These covenants can be restrictive (e.g., requiring a specific ratio of earnings to debt, ratio of earnings to interest payments, capital replacement approval, etc.). In turn, if the business breaks the covenants, the bank can demand immediate payment of the debt balance, or take over control of the assets of the business, and even sell the business if necessary.
- Banks prefer that the owner(s) of the business have equity in the company. For new businesses, banks like to see one dollar in equity for each dollar being lent. For mature businesses that have a track record of success and can

be secured with real estate, banks will normally loan out four to five dollars for each dollar of equity (in other words, owners are required to provide 20 percent to 25 percent equity to secure the loan). For example, if a club wanted to take out a loan for $2,000,000, it would need to put up $400,000 to $500,000 in equity. Since the recent period of economic turmoil that began in 2008 and subsided in late 2011, banks have often asked owners to put up a larger share of equity, and in many cases, have not even considered approving a loan unless the shareholders have at least 30 percent equity in the business. Many venture capital and private equity groups are able to secure debt with as little as 15 percent equity, particularly when the debt can be secured by hard assets. In almost all instances, banks prefer that the shareholders put up some form of collateral, typically real estate. Referred to as a collateralized loan, this type of a financial arrangement is much easier to obtain than a non-collateralized or non-secured loan.

- In the past, most banks liked the debt-to-EBITDA ratio of the business to fall between three and four (i.e., a club's total debt should not exceed four times its EBITDA). For example, if a club has an EBITDA of $1,000,000, its total debt should not exceed $4,000,000 and should fall between 3 and 4 million dollars. If its debt exceeds four times its EBITDA, then the club would be considered as heavily leveraged, which places a financial strain on the business, not to mention exposes it to the danger of not complying with the bank covenants for the loan. Since the most recent global financial crisis, many international banks have tightened up the debt-to-EBITDA ratio requirements, with lenders often restricting the debt-to-EBITDA ratio to 2.5.
- Cash-flow (or non-collateralized) loans are loans that banks provide that are not secured by real estate. In these instances, banks tend to limit the amount of the loan to a total that does not exceed 50 percent of the value of the assets of the business (a value that is often determined by a multiple applied to the club's EBITDA).
- The bank expects the club to educate it on both the industry as a whole and on the club's business model.
- In the case of small independent operations, such as fitness studios, the bank will tend to require full financial disclosure of any stockholders or partners with 20 percent or greater ownership in the business. Furthermore, these owners will often be required to sign a personal guarantee for the loan amount being pursued. Banks typically frame the interest rate for loans against LIBOR (London Interbank Offered Rate). LIBOR is the interest rate at which banks can borrow funds from other banks. The rate is set each day, based on a multitude of financial indexes, in particular interbank deposit rates for larger institutions. Typically, a large multinational business can get a loan rate that is three to five points above LIBOR, although since the recession of 2008 to 2011, many banks have offered loans at two or three points above LIBOR. As of January 2017 the one-year LIBOR rate was 1.7 percent, compared to being as high as 3.4 percent just prior to the market crash in September of 2008. It is a common practice for most start-up clubs to obtain equity through private investors and then raise the balance of the funds needed through debt. Larger multiple-club operations, on the other hand, usually utilize private-equity investment firms to raise the equity and even source the debt.

> The approach of choice for club operators or studio operators is a small business loan from a local bank that is guaranteed by the U.S. Small Business Administration.

The most popular form of lending pursued by small business owners and entrepreneurs, and definitely the approach of choice for club operators or studio operators is a small business loan from a local bank that is guaranteed by the U.S. Small Business Administration (SBA). The terms of an SBA loan are typically negotiated between the owner and the lender, and therefore, the specific terms of a loan will depend on negotiations between the lender and the borrower. Following are some important things to know about SBA backed loans:

- The SBA only provides loans to a legal business entity, not an individual, and therefore, eligibility requirements are based on the business, not the owner(s).
- The most important eligibility criteria for an SBA loan include: the business must operate for a profit; must be small as defined by the SBA (as a retail or service business revenues cannot exceed $2.5 million to $21.5 million, depending on the service); leverage other assets first, such as personal funds or investments from friends and family; use the loan funds for sound business purposes and not be delinquent on any existing debt. It should be noted that the SBA has far more criteria spelling out who is ineligible for an SBA loan.
- The interest rate on an SBA loan is negotiated between the lender and the borrower and is subject to certain maximums established by the SBA. The actual maximum interest rate is based on a base rate and an allowable spread.
- The SBA charges an additional fee to guarantee a loan and the amount is calculated based on both the amount of the loan and the loan's maturity.
- The SBA guarantees a percentage of the total loan amount. For example, loans of under $150,000 are guaranteed up to 85 percent of the loan amount, while loans above that amount are guaranteed up to 75 percent of the loan amount up to a maximum of $5 million.
- An SBA backed loan can be used to fund construction, equipment, inventory, and operations.
- An SBA backed loan must be fully secured. In those instances where the borrower does not have sufficient collateral (e.g., personal or business assets) to secure the loan, as long as all other conditions are met, the SBA will still guarantee the loan as long as all available collateral is secured.
- The SBA requires personal guarantees from all owners of the business who have greater than a 20 percent stake in the business, and can request personal guarantees from those with less than a 20 percent stake in the business. This particular requirement can often derail loans as some owners, usually outside investors, don't want to expose their personal assets.
- Most lenders will require owners to provide 20 percent and 40 percent equity before extending an SBA backed loan. Therefore, for a club owner who may be seeking a 3 million dollar loan, the bank will expect at least $600,000 of equity to be contributed.

Crowdfunding: A Non-Traditional Source of Capital

Crowdfunding is rooted in the convergence of social connectivity, investing democratization (i.e., anyone can invest), cloud-based technology, and government regulation. In 2012, the passage of the JOBS Act (Jumpstart Our Business Start-Ups) added an exponentially more powerful environment for the introduction of additional approaches for crowdfunding, opening the doors for both accredited and non-accredited investors to invest in the dreams and business solutions of entrepreneurs. Clifford Holekamp, Senior Lecturer of Entrepreneurship at Washington University, offers a very succinct description of the appeal and popularity of crowdfunding in today's new economy. He said, "The real reward of crowdfunding investors isn't financial—it's the opportunity to participate. Helping an entrepreneur achieve their dreams, and being a part of a company that changes its industry—or maybe even the world—is exciting and personally rewarding. Everyone should have the freedom to make a difference with their dollars."

According to the most recent global statistics, $34.4 billion was raised in 2015 using crowdfunding platforms. In 2015, experts estimate crowdfunding platforms will generate more capital than venture capital. According to a 2015 article that appeared in Entrepreneur online, approximately 41 percent of all funds raised through crowdfunding platforms are used to launch a small business.

Crowdfunding today is not unlike the "wild west" of the past. Today, entrepreneurs can attract capital through five different crowdfunding approaches, each uniquely different, and in most cases not nearly as well-regulated as more traditional means of raising capital. The five crowdfunding approaches are donation-based crowdfunding, reward-based crowdfunding, debt-based crowdfunding, equity-based crowdfunding, and royalty-based crowdfunding.

> Crowdfunding today is not unlike the "wild west" of the past.

- ❏ *Donation-Based Crowd Funding.* Donation-based crowdfunding—and its sibling, reward-based crowdfunding—first arose in 2003 with the introduction of ArtistShare, a donation-based funding platform designed to help raise funds for musicians seeking to digitally publish their recordings. Donation-based platforms focus on helping individuals, as well as small business raise capital by appealing to a common and compelling sense of purpose and passion, in many instances an altruistic one. Some have even referred to donation-based crowdfunding as charity crowdfunding. Individuals who donate to a campaign or project on a donation-based crowd funding platform do not receive a tangible benefit for their contribution, rather they receive a very intangible, yet potent benefit: knowing they are making a difference by helping someone achieve their vision. Today, the largest crowdfunding platform in the world is donation-based site GoFundMe, which in 2014 raised approximately 470 million dollars from its 6 million-plus donors. According to a variety of published articles, donation-based crowdfunding and its sibling sites offering rewards-based crowd funding are successful in raising the entrepreneur's targeted funds 54 percent of the time.

❑ *Rewards-Based Crowd Funding.* Reward-based funding platforms, which evolved from donation-based platforms, are presently the most popular globally, including leading sites such as KickStarter that launched in 2008, as well as Indiegogo and RocketHub. Rewards-based funding platforms operate similarly to donation-based sites, extending fans, friends, and followers the opportunity to contribute to a project that inspires them, leveraging the intangible benefits that accompany having contributed to the achievement of an entrepreneur's dreams and passions. Rewards-based sites one-up the donation-based sites by offering tangible benefits to sweeten the pot and generate additional buzz and participation. The top four crowdfunding sites (donation- and reward-based) based on contributor traffic are GoFundMe, Kickstarter, Indiegogo, and teespring. One example of the fundraising power exhibited by these crowdfunding sites is illustrated by the $440 million that KickStarter was able to raise for entrepreneurs in 2014 from its base of over 3 million contributors.

❑ *Debt-Based Crowed Funding.* Leave it to the financial markets to develop a lending solution that sources the vast wealth of the crowd. Introduced in 2006, debt-based crowd funding, also known as crowd lending or peer-to-peer (P2P) lending, has emerged as a highly viable approach to source growth capital for individuals and businesses. P2P differs from its siblings in the crowdfunding arena in two distinct ways. First, P2P is not a funding source for start-ups, it is only available to businesses (small to large) with a proven financial track record (meaning the business has shown it can generate a profit and pay bills), and second, it does not offer contributors equity, just a guaranteed return on their investment. P2P offers entrepreneurs a fast track for raising growth capital to expand their business. For example, a fitness studio owner who has achieved success with their first studio might consider P2P lending as a means to raise growth capital to open a second studio or develop a franchise model.

P2P lending offers entrepreneurs access to unsecured loans with more favorable terms (rates vary based on the level of risk associated with the loan) than a typical bank loan, meaning potentially lower interest rates and better loan covenants. Furthermore, P2P lending opens up lending investments to investors, accredited and non-accredited, who are passionate about supporting your business venture in return for receiving a guaranteed rate of return on their investment. Like any lending establishment, P2P lending platforms require potential borrowers to be vetted before their offer can be shared with the crowd. For example, Lending Club, the largest P2P platform, indicates it approves approximately 10 percent of the loan applications it receives.

According to CrowedCrux.com, a website focused on the crowdfunding industry, the leading P2P sites include: Lending Club (has sourced over $9 billion in loans since inception in 2007), Prosper ($3 billion in loans handled since its inception in 2006), Funding Circle (the leading online marketplace focused on small business with over $1 billion in loans provided for small business since inception), and Upstart.

- *Equity-Based Crowd Funding.* In 2011, as Barack Obama was campaigning for the passage of the JOBS (Jumpstart our Business Startups) Act, he was quoted as saying, "Right now entrepreneurs are already using crowdfunding to raise hundreds of thousands of dollars in pure donations—imagine the possibilities if these small-dollar donors become investors with a stake in the venture." What President Obama was referring to was equity-based crowdfunding, the newest player in the financial crowd-sourcing field. The JOBS Act of 2012 (in particular Title IV, Regulation A+) opened the door to an entirely new world for capital raises to fund start-ups and fuel rapid growth for early stage businesses. During the first quarter of 2015, firms raised $662 million in capital using crowdfunding platforms. According to Eric Smith, Director of Data Analytics at Crowdmetric, equity crowdfunding is expected to double on an annual basis as more investors and potential investors get to know about it.

  Equity-based crowdfunding allows Angels, also known as accredited investors (individuals with a net worth exclusive of their primary dwelling of $1 million or annual income of $200,000 or greater for the previous two years), and non-accredited investors to contribute funds to a business venture in return for equity in the business (become shareholders). This is dramatically different from donation- or rewards-based campaigns in which the contributor receives no equity, only good feelings and possibly some swag. One might think of equity-based crowdfunding as a global cloud-based angel network. Equity-based crowdfunding has opened the door for everyone to become a business investor and get in on the ground floor of a potentially lucrative business venture. For entrepreneurs, equity-based crowdfunding can introduce their business's value proposition to thousands, if not millions of potential investors—accredited and non-accredited. Some of the leading equity-based crowdfunding sites include CircleUp (targets small businesses), CrowdCube (UK-based platform), MicroVentures, Wefunder, and Fundable.

  Under Title IV of the JOBS Act, there are two tiers that apply to investment raises that reach out to non-accredited investors: Tier I and Tier II. Tier I is for capital raises seeking under $20 million USD, while Tier II is for capital raises between $20 million and $50 million. Tier I offerings have fewer restrictions placed on them than Tier II offerings; consequently, experts in the financial world expect Tier II crowdfunding to dominate the landscape because of its fewer restrictions for the entrepreneur.

  Title IV also places a limit on what non-accredited investors can contribute, which is a maximum of 10 percent of their annual income/net worth on an annual basis. These limits are intended to protect the non-accredited investor while affording them the opportunity to invest in start-ups and early-stage businesses.

  Equity-based crowdfunding comes with a cost that in many instances can exceed the capacity of entrepreneurs wishing to raise capital. The filing requirements make it necessary to bring on board both a CPA and attorney experienced in filing the proper investment documentation. The cost of meeting these filing requirements can range from as little as $10,000 to as much as $100,000. Consequently, many investment experts claim that unless an entrepreneur is seeking to raise at least $60,000, equity-based crowdfunding is not viable investing option.

> Equity-based crowdfunding has opened the door for everyone to become a business investor and get in on the ground floor of a potentially lucrative business venture.

Equity-based crowdfunding is risky. Typically 1 in 10 investments made in a start-up venture are considered successful (based on the typical Angel requirement of a 10x return on their investment). Consequently, equity-based crowdfunding investors run as great a risk as the entrepreneur.

❑ *Royalty-Based Crowdfunding.* Royalty-based crowdfunding represents a new twist on an old approach to investing where in return for investors putting up the equity to fund a venture, they receive a portion of future sales (royalty). Royalty-based crowdfunding offers investors an opportunity to share in the revenue performance of the venture, in essence allowing investors to capture a greater return as a venture's revenues grow. The benefit to the entrepreneur in this instance is they don't have to forfeit equity in the business, allowing them to maintain 100 percent ownership. The potential downside of this approach is that for a given period of time, the entrepreneur will be sharing a percentage of their gross sales with their investors (royalty purchasers). Some of the leading royalty-based crowdfunding sites include EquityNet, Quirky, RoyaltyClouds, and TubeStart.

In an article that recently appeared in CrowdFundBeat, the author shared some insights garnered from her interview with well-known financier Arthur Lipper. Some of the highlights include:

- Entrepreneurs are likely to see investors seeking longer-term royalties, ranging from 10 years to 20 years to help reduce the overall percentage of the businesses revenue to the royalty purchaser. If higher percentages are offered, then the duration of the holding can be lessened.
- Investors will likely be seeking out ventures with an aggressive growth model (at least 10 percent annually) and which offer at least payment of a 20 percent internal rate of return over the course of their holding.
- Investors are likely to seek royalty payments in the range of 5 percent to 10 percent of sales, but the specific percentage will be based on a variety of factors, including the perceived viability of the venture and the length of the royalty payment.
- Like equity-based crowdfunding, there are regulations that entrepreneurs will need to comply with in order to present their offering to crowdfunding investors.

Buying and Selling a Health/Fitness Business

The health/fitness club industry is a dynamic enterprise in which clubs and club companies are bought and sold regularly. One approach pursued by individuals who are considering entering the business is to acquire an existing club. In that regard, for a club that wants to grow its business, acquisition may be a suitable option, rather than building a new club. On the other hand, if investors (or an individual) want to cash out of the business or to become part of a larger business by being the seller rather than the acquirer, then selling the club may be appropriate. Among the key factors that should be considered when buying or selling a club business are the following:

❑ *Selling a Club.* If owners decide to sell their club, they need to understand some of the basic factors that apply to the sale process, including:

- Most clubs are valued by applying a multiple to the club's EBITDA, which results in a measure that is referred to as the enterprise value of the business. For clubs that are in a leased space, that multiple can range from two times EBITDA to as high as six times EBITDA. In the majority of instances, it will likely be in the range of four to five times the club's EBITDA. For example, a club that has an EBITDA of $500,000 would be valued at two to two and a half million dollars. Clubs that are freestanding and own the land on which they are located will have a projected value that ranges from three times its EBITDA to six or seven times its EBITDA. In the majority of instances, its enterprise value will be five to six times its EBITDA. In just the past two years, several acquisitions have taken place at multiples approaching 8x EBITDA, similar to what occurred prior to the recession of 2008. In other words, a freestanding club with an EBITDA of $500,000 would be valued at $2.5 million to $3.0 million. In most cases, the EBITDA that is used to project a club's value is what is termed "trailing EBITDA" (i.e., the EBITDA for the most recent trailing 12-month time period and not for a specific financial year).
- Even after a club's enterprise value is estimated using the multiple of EBITDA, the seller should be aware that buyers will deduct the value of the liabilities from the calculated EBITDA value before determining its equity value (e.g., purchase price), especially if they are buying the business and not its assets. For example, if a club has an EBITDA of one million and liabilities of $1,500,000, then the buyer will likely value the club at five times its EBITDA minus the liabilities, or a projection that is determined by first multiplying one million by five, and then subtracting $1,500,000 to derive a calculated equity value of $3,500,000.
- If someone sells a club, the preference of most individuals is to sell the business and therefore release themselves from the liabilities of the business. The buyer, more often than not, will want to buy the assets at the mutually agreed upon price, while the seller remains responsible for the club's liabilities.
- If the seller owns the land on which the club sits, the seller should consider holding onto the land and selling the business, and then leasing the land to the new owner. This approach enables the seller to generate more cash out of the sale. For example, if a business is valued at five million dollars (of which the asset value of the land is one million), an individual might sell the business for $4.5 million, but then lease the land to the new owner for $100,000 a year.
- Sellers should make sure that they complete their own due diligence before selling and have an accurate recording of their assets, liabilities, and EBITDA for the past three years, etc.
- Sellers should have an attorney involved and possibly a broker.

Prior to the onset of the 2008 economic recession, several health/fitness clubs generated a final enterprise value at EBITDA multiples in excess of nine. For example, 24 Hour Fitness was reported to have received a purchase price equivalent to 9.5 EBITDA when a controlling interest in it was sold to Forstmann Little. Similarly, Equinox was reported to have

> Clubs that are freestanding and own the land on which they are located will have a projected value that ranges from three times its EBITDA to six or seven times its EBITDA.

received over 11x its EBITDA when it was sold to Related Properties in 2005. Since the recession, buyers have not been offering nearly as large multiples, with most acquisitions in the industry taking place for multiples between three and five times EBITDA. In the summer of 2014, 24 Hour was sold by Forstmann Little for a reported multiple of seven times EBITDA, which represents a considerable difference in the valuation of the business from when they purchased it at a reported 9.5 times multiple back in 2006.

❏ *Buying a Club.* If their goal is to buy a club, then the individuals who are considering purchasing the business should make sure that they understand certain basics of buying a club business, including:
  - Buyers should perform their due diligence and audit the books and operations in their entirety. They should also make sure the accuracy and authenticity of the accounting is correct by having an independent audit made of the club's financial statements. Finally, they should make sure that they are fully aware of any liabilities that the business might have, in particular, any hidden account payables or legal suits against the existing club.
  - Most clubs in leased spaces will sometimes sell for two to five times their EBITDA, with four times more likely. Clubs that are freestanding will usually sell for between three and six times their EBITA, with a range of four to five times most likely. More often than not, sellers try to start at the high end of the price range, while buyers typically start at the low end and then work up.
  - If possible, buyers should only purchase the business assets, based on the cash flow value, rather than the business itself. When individuals purchase the assets of a business, they are acquiring both the short-term and long-term assets of the club, as well as purchasing the owner's equity. What they don't buy and don't really want are the liabilities.
  - When purchasing a club, the buyers should make sure that the debt they finance does not exceed three times the trailing EBITDA.
  - If the individuals purchasing the debt decide to buy the entire business rather than just the assets of the business, they should then make sure to deduct the liabilities from the enterprise value when determining the club's final equity value. In addition, it is important that both parties come to agreement on the EBITDA multiple that will be used to calculate the enterprise value.
  - The buyers should remember that if they purchase a club that sells annual membership contracts, that when they purchase the assets and cash flow of the business, they might not be receiving the expected level of dues if the previous owner collected the annual dues before the sale. If the buyers know that a club collects annual dues, then they need to consider lowering the price that they are willing to pay for the business or ask for consideration for those dues already collected in the asking price. All too often, buyers end up purchasing a club that does not produce dues for a considerable period of time because of such a scenario.
  - The buyers should retain the right to retain or dismiss employees of the former club.

Leasing and Sale Leasebacks

For most first-time club owners and operators, as well as the majority of existing club operations, leasing space for their club is a common practice. Leasing is usually the option most operators choose, especially since obtaining the land to build a freestanding club is often difficult to find and too expensive to purchase. In most situations, leasing requires less upfront capital. In turn, the club has less of a need to assume debt. On the other hand, on occasion, situations exist where independent and multiple-club operators actually purchase land and build a freestanding club under one company and then lease it back to the actual operating-club entity. By the same token, some clubs will take the land and building they own and sell it to an investor, with the agreement that investor will turn around and lease the building space back to the club operator (a practice often used by LA Fitness and as of the fall of 2014 it is a strategy being considered by Lifetime Fitness to enhance its market value). Such a practice is called a sale-leaseback and is often used to raise capital. Leasing can involve several factors, including:

- As a rule, leases have minimum time requirements. In most urban markets, the landlords of class A and class B buildings look for a minimum time period of 10 years, while in suburban settings, especially strip-mall centers, leases will usually be for five-year periods at a minimum. Prospective tenants should look for a five-year lease with an optional five-year extension period. If they are confident in their business model, then they should consider a 10-year lease. In some instances, a start-up may be able to secure a two- or three-year lease, but there will be a premium applied to the lease rate in such instances.

- Most leases can be negotiated to include clauses that allow tenants to renegotiate their lease rates at a predetermined timeframe within the lease. It is a prudent business owner who makes sure to negotiate this stipulation as part of their lease. A common practice would be to have a window of time for renegotiation in the second or third year in a five-year lease and the fifth year in a 10-year lease. This negotiating practice could also be employed to establish time periods for extending leases.

- Some landlords will offer a straight lease, which means that the tenant only pays the lease rate and the approved common area maintenance costs (CAM), but does not pay utilities and property tax. This type of lease is less common in today's market because of the high upfront costs and the carrying costs that many real estate owners assume. The more common lease is a triple-net lease, which is a contracted arrangement where the tenant is responsible for the lease, CAM costs, utilities, and property taxes on the space. Accordingly, prospective tenants should make sure that they know what type of lease is being offered and what the costs will be for each type.

- Most leases have a base rate that varies by building type (class A, class B, class C, strip mall), by location, and, of course, by market demand. In most markets, strip-mall space will carry base lease rates of between $12 and $25 a square foot. In urban markets, the base lease rate can range from as low as $20 a square foot for undesirable space (basement or concourse space) to $500 a square foot for desirable retail space. The most common

> Club operators should try to keep their base rent under $30 a square foot or less than 15 percent of their club's expected revenues.

range is between $30 and $70 a square foot. All factors considered, club operators should try to keep their base rent under $30 a square foot or less than 15 percent of their club's expected revenues.

- Tenants should know what their CAM costs will be. While in most leased spaces, it will range from five to eight dollars a square foot, there are buildings in some cities, such as Chicago and New York, where the CAM rates can reach as high as $15 or more a square foot.
- Most landlords provide tenants with a tenant-improvement allowance (TI) when the tenant moves into a space. As a rule, it is common for these allowances to run between $15 and $25 a square foot. In most instances, tenants will have the option of negotiating a higher TI allowance, especially if they are willing to pay a higher lease rate. For individuals who are having trouble raising capital to build the space, negotiating with the landlord to provide higher TI allowances, in exchange for higher rent, can prove helpful. In some instances, a landlord may actually pay for the entire costs of finishing out a tenant's space in return for a higher rental rate.
- If tenants are paying utilities either as part of their lease or separately, they should make sure that they request separate metering of the utilities for their space. Most landlords prefer to bill their tenants for the cost of their utilities. At the same time, a few landlords will add some overhead and profit to the actual utility costs that they pass through to their tenants.
- Tenants should make an effort to have their HVAC operated separately from the buildings they lease. In many cases, landlords have set times during which they turn their building's HVAC on and off. Turn-off times are normally based on the operating hours of a typical business. As such, all factors considered tenants who occupy buildings in which they have independent access to the HVAC for their space and have HVAC, which is independently metered, are better off. In the event that the club's space is tied into the building's HVAC, the tenant should be aware that they would probably need to negotiate after-hours access to the HVAC, which will typically result in higher costs to them.
- Tenants should establish a good relationship with the landlord and the landlord's representatives. Furthermore, they should make it a practice to meet with their landlord's representatives on a monthly basis.
- Tenants should know the details of their lease. Many leases require landlords to provide a certain degree of maintenance on tenant spaces. On occasion, some landlords will try to downplay this factor if they can, especially if their tenants have a relatively large space and pay a lower lease rate. Accordingly, tenants should always be fully aware of all of the conditions in their lease.
- In some instances, landlords may be willing to provide tenants with several months of free rent. Tenants should understand, however, that landlords recover these "lost" revenues in the actual rent that they subsequently charge them. As a rule, individuals who are starting a club would be wise to try and negotiate between six months and a year's free rent as part of their lease. The extent of the period of free rent is dependent upon the length of the lease and what they pay for rent, with those who have higher rents and longer leases receiving a longer period of time before their rent kicks in.

A sale-leaseback is another method that individuals employ to acquire space for their business. In a sale-leaseback, the club owner/operator will sell their property and building to another investor who then leases the space back to the club owner/operator for the business. This strategy is often used by club operators who wish to raise capital for expansion or renovation purposes. In early 2014, California Family Fitness used this strategy so it could focus on expanding its business. One of the primary benefits of this strategy is that it allows club owners to pull their equity out of the assets and use it for growing their business. In fact, several major club companies, such as LA Fitness, Lifetime Fitness, and 24 Hour Fitness have all participated in sale-leaseback arrangements for one or more of their clubs. In the fall of 2014, the shareholders of Lifetime Fitness were discussing creating a REIT (Real Estate Investment Trust) where the building an property owned by Lifetime Fitness would be spun off into the REIT and the property leased back to the Lifetime Fitness operating entity. This is a takeoff on the sale-leaseback strategy that can potentially offer shareholders greater returns on their investment.

> One of the primary benefits of a sale-leaseback is that it allows club owners to pull their equity out of the assets and use it for growing their business.

Reflections

For many club operators, raising capital to start or expand their business, along with the many nuances involved in buying, leasing, and selling, are not competencies that they typically master. By obtaining a better understanding of these complex business activities, club owners and managers can more effectively prepare themselves to deal successfully with them when the situations arise.

Part Four: The Business of Developing and Managing a Health/Fitness Business

PART 5
Staffing Issues in the Health/Fitness Facility Industry

Chapter 19
The People Factor: Employees in the Health/Fitness Industry

Chapter 20
Building and Leading a Successful Team

The People Factor: Employees in the Health/Fitness Industry

19

"Always treat employees exactly as you want to treat your best customers."

—Steven Covery

Chapter Objectives

The health/fitness business is a people-intensive industry. According to IHRSA's *2015 Profiles of Success*, the average health/fitness club employed 12 full-time employees and 22 part-time employees (a decline from 2014) with an average payroll approaching 42 percent of revenues in 2014. For health/fitness clubs under 20,000 square feet and fitness-only clubs, models that are more likely to reflect the majority of health/fitness clubs, the average club employed four full-time staff and five part-time staff, respectively, with an average payroll range equivalent to 35 percent to 40 percent of revenues. Why share all this? To point out the critical importance of staff to creating and sustaining the experiences that clients and members expect, and to highlight the fact that with this reliance on staff to deliver our offering comes a reasonably hefty price tag: a cost that typically consumes 40 percent to 50 percent of club's revenue.

One of the most frequently heard comments in the health/fitness facility industry is that its employees are the heart of the business, the fuel that drives the engine. It is the employees, and in many instances the independent contractors—both full-time and part-time, that deliver the services, create magic moments for the clients, and foster the relationships that are so vital to a club's or studio's success.

This chapter initially begins by defining the differences between an employee and an independent contractor, as well as detailing the differences between an exempt and a non-exempt employee. Next, it provides an overview of the various positions in the industry and the role each position has in delivering the club's experience. Then, it outlines the compensation norms and educational expectations for each of these industry positions. Finally, it concludes by reviewing the various organizational structures that independent clubs and multiple-club groups utilize in operating their business.

> One of the most frequently heard comments in the health/fitness facility industry is that its employees are the heart of the business, the fuel that drives the engine.

Employees vs. Independent Contractors

Similar to the separation between church and state, the lines between employees and independent contractors represent a challenge for the health/fitness club industry. All too often, clubs decide to have independent contractors provide a portion of their service delivery, not knowing that they are actually creating an employer-employee environment. It is critical, however, that club operators clearly understand the difference between an employee and an independent contractor.

The fundamental differences between an employee and an independent contractor are quite significant. State and federal laws are very adamant about businesses adhering to the policies concerning the separation of employees and independent contractors. Clubs that attempt to pay people as independent contractors, but treat them as employees, open themselves to potential fines from the government, not to mention lawsuits filed by contractors, or staff. If the club identifies someone as an independent contractor, but that individual is characterized by any of the criteria identified in the employee column in Figure 19-1, then that person is an employee and must be treated as such.

Employee	**Independent Contractor**
Working schedule is established and monitored by the club.	Establishes their own schedule, with no direction from the club.
Is expected to abide by employee policies and rules, including wearing any club-mandated uniform.	Is not required to adhere to employee policies and rules, other than what is stipulated in their contract.
The club sets the fees and rates for all services delivered by the employee.	Sets their own fees and rates for the services they provide.
Is required to clock-in (record arrival and departure) for all hours worked.	Records and tracks own hours and maintains a record of those hours.
Must be paid overtime for all hours worked in excess of 40 hours each week and be paid overtime for hours worked during any club recognized holidays (e.g., Christmas, New Years, Thanksgiving, etc.).	Does not receive overtime pay or holiday pay.
Is eligible for all club-sponsored benefits (e.g., medical, dental, 401K, liability insurance).	Is not eligible for club-sponsored benefits; instead, is responsible for providing their own benefits.
Is required to complete all employee hiring requirements, including, if required, the mandated interview process, the completion of a job application, the completion of an I-9 Employment Eligibility Verification form, submitting to a background check, participating in any mandated employee training program, attending all mandated employee meetings, etc.	Is not required to participate in any employee-mandated hiring and training programs other than what may be stipulated in their contract. Must provide a completed W-9 form before being paid.
Receives a W-2 at year-end; the club pays a portion of the employee's social security and Medicare taxes.	Receives a 1099 at year end and is responsible for paying the social security and Medicare taxes. Must also complete a W-9 on an annual basis.
Receives wages and commissions via a payroll check.	Receives payment through a vendor check.

Figure 19-1. Selected differences between employees and independent contractors

In the event your club's business model is reliant on retaining independent contractors, rather than hiring employees, following are several critical points you need to address, among them:
- Make sure you have a legally valid agreement, signed by both you and the independent contractor. The agreement should set forth the terms, conditions, and fees associated with the working arrangements.
- Make sure the contractor completes and signs a W-9 form before being retained. If the contractor is renting access, it is still wise to obtain a completed W-9. The W-9 should be completed on an annual basis.
- Make sure the contractor provides evidence of professional liability insurance. If they don't have insurance, don't retain them. Ideally, you would want the contractor to list the studio as an additional insured.
- If the contractor will be providing coaching and instructional services (e.g., group exercise instructor, personal trainer), then require evidence of certification from a nationally recognized certifying agency. You should also require evidence that they are currently certified in AED/CPR.
- Require the contractor submit an invoice for every payment.
- If the contractor will be renting access to the studio (a practice used by many studios), you will want to include these terms in the agreement. If the contractor is renting access, the contractor will not invoice the studio; instead, the studio will invoice the contractor.
- Make the agreement includes the requirement that the independent contractor provide you with evidence of being insured.

Exempt vs. Non-Exempt Employees in the U.S.

Another potential minefield for club operators involves whether an employee should be treated as an exempt or a non-exempt employee. The determination as to which employees can be considered exempt or non-exempt is established by the Federal Labor Standards Act (FLSA). An exempt employee, according to FLSA, is a professional who falls into one of the seven categories as highlighted in Figure 19-2, along with meeting certain other tests established by the FLSA. A non-exempt employee is any employee who does not meet the FLSA requirements. In 2004, federal legislation was passed by congress and subsequently signed by the President that applied tougher rules to the issue of overtime pay, extending overtime eligibility to certain exempt positions at lower pay levels, and extending additional overtime opportunities to hourly non-exempt employees. Historically, the health/fitness club industry has tried to skirt the regulations and create exempt positions for positions that are actually non-exempt, in an attempt to avoid paying overtime. Figure 19-2 provides a basic overview of the key attributes that delineate exempt employees from non-exempt employees.

Exempt	Non-exempt
Must supervise an enterprise department or sub-department.	Does not have supervisory responsibilities as primary function of the job.
Falls into one of six categories classified as exempt (executive, professional, administrative, computer employee, outside sales, highly compensated).	Does not meet FLSA criteria for exempt status.
Must be paid a salary of at least $455 a week ($23,660 annualized).	Performs manual labor.
Must supervise at least two full-time employees or the equivalent of.	Is paid an hourly rate, as well as time-and-a-half for overtime work and holidays.
Must have the authority to hire or fire.	
Must use discretion and independent judgment in performing their job, if the employee is administrative.	

Figure 19-2. FLSA categories for determining if an employee is exempt or non-exempt

Full-Time and Part-Time Employees

Along with an employee's status as either exempt or non-exempt, the determination of an employee's status as either full-time or part-time represents an additional hurdle for many small business operators. The regulations that determine an employee's status as either full-time or part-time are established by the federal government. The rules say a part-time employee must work less than 1,000 hours annually; the equivalent of 17.5 hours a week if they worked every week of the year. Fortunately, the "test" is based on the annual hours and not the weekly hours. As a result, a part-time employee could actually work as many as 29 hours a week, but only if they did seasonal work. Figure 19-3 highlights some of the differences between full-time and part-time, as well as the benefits associated with each classification.

Employment Status	Criteria	Benefits and Drawbacks for Employer
Part-time	• Cannot work over 1,000 hours in a calendar year. • As of 2014, federal law stipulates that part-time status requires the employee to work less than 30 hours a week or 130 hours a month.	• Reduces payroll and payroll-related costs for the employer. • Employer does not have to extend business-sponsored benefits. • Employees may lack commitment to the business and their job. • Employees likely to have less education and experience than full-time employees. • More likely to experience employee absenteeism.
Full-time	• Employee who works more than 1,000 hours in a calendar year. • As of 2014, federal law establishes a full-time employee as anyone who works on average more than 30 hours a week or more than 130 hours a month.	• Employees likely to be more experienced. • Employees likely to be more committed to their job. • Employees must be extended the opportunity to participate in any business-sponsored benefit program. • As of 2014, the business must provide employer-sponsored healthcare coverage to all full-time staff.

Figure 19-3. Differences between full-time and part-time employees

Permanent and Temporary Employees in Europe

In many European nations, as well as in Russia, employees can be classified as either permanent or temporary. Permanent employees are typically given an employment agreement that details the specific performance requirements of the job. A permanent employee is entitled to all the benefits that the employer provides, as well as being authorized to receive any government-mandated privileges and/or requirements (e.g., maternity leave duration, vacation time duration, holidays, social taxes, etc.). In some nations, such as Russia and Spain, an employee with permanent status has government-mandated rights that make it extremely difficult for the employer to remove that person from that individual's position.

An employee classified as temporary, on the other hand, has limited employment rights, and can be removed from the employee's position with limited-to-no notice. Furthermore, temporary employees in many European nations are not entitled to many of the benefits received by permanent employees. It is common for businesses in both European nations and in Russia to make use of temporary contracts whenever possible, because doing so can reduce their labor costs and makes it easier to reengineer their organization, if needed.

The Position Players in Health/Fitness Facilities

The health/fitness club industry requires a diverse array of talent to deliver the experiences that members desire, expect, need, and deserve. As such, clubs must have employees who have an appropriate blend of social/relationship skills and technical expertise. Because the services that clubs provide cover such a broad spectrum of experiences, a vast pool of talent with expertise in a broad range of services is required. Figures 19-4 through 19-6 detail the key positions in the industry and offer a brief synopsis of the responsibilities of each of those positions.

As the figures illustrate, the health/fitness club industry involves a multiplicity of positions. While the various positions in these figures are detailed in general terms and responsibilities, club operators can decide for themselves whether to develop positions that are consistent with the aforementioned descriptions or make adjustments in the various job specifications and define the positions in slightly different ways.

Clubs must have employees who have an appropriate blend of social/ relationship skills and technical expertise.

Position	Description
General manager	Oversees the entire operations of a club, with responsibility for all aspects of the club, including membership, accounting, and all operational departments.
Operations manager	Usually found in large club operations. Supervises the operating departments (front desk, house maintenance, pro shop, pools, etc.).
Sales manager	Usually found in larger clubs. Responsible for managing the sales staff and the sales efforts.
Fitness director	Oversees the employees and activities of the fitness department, which includes personal training, fitness floor, and group exercise.
Tennis director	Oversees the employees and activities of the tennis department, often including programming, pro shop, and related tennis activities.
Maintenance director	Found in most clubs. Oversees both maintenance and housekeeping employees and activities. In some clubs, also has responsibility for locker rooms and grounds.
Food and beverage director	In clubs with a food and beverage function, oversees all aspects of the food and beverage operation, including the employees and activities of the kitchen and dining areas.

Figure 19-4. Selected examples of typical exempt positions in the health/fitness club industry

Position	Description
Activity/program director	Found in larger clubs. Responsible for coordinating all club activities and programs and the employees involved in those endeavors.
Youth director	In clubs with extensive youth programming. Oversees the employees and activities involved in the youth department.
Personal-training director	A mainstay of clubs with large personal-training programs. Oversees the personal trainers and personal-training program.
Group-exercise director	Normally a part-time position, but in large clubs is often a full-time position. Oversees the group-exercise instructors and programs.
Aquatics director	In clubs with a large aquatic program. Oversees the pool and aquatic employees and the aquatic programs and activities.
Controller	In clubs with large accounting departments. Oversees the accounting department employees and the activities of the accounting department.

Figure 19-5. Selected examples of club positions that could be either exempt or non-exempt employees in the health/fitness club industry employees in a particular geographic area

Position	Description
Aquatic/swim instructor	Provides swimming instruction for members and guests on individual and group basis.
Personal trainer	Provides fitness instruction and coaching to members for a fee. Can be individual or small group training.
Fitness instructor	Provides supervision of the fitness floor, general orientation of members to the fitness centers' equipment and programs, and some personal instruction.
Group-exercise instructor	Teaches group-oriented exercise and fitness programs for members and guests.
Front-desk staff	Works the front desk. Greets members, monitors usage, answers phones, disseminates club information, and schedules appointments for club services.
Accountant/bookkeeper	Handles the basic accounting functions at clubs, including payroll, billing, accounts payable, and accounts receivable.
Maintenance/housecleaning	Provides cleaning, housekeeping, and general maintenance for the club. In many clubs, also handles the basic laundry functions as well.
Locker room	In clubs with large locker rooms, provides the general care and housekeeping of the locker rooms, but also greets members and delivers services, such as shoe shines, laundry, etc.
Child care/nursery	Provides supervision of the youth areas, including the nursery activities, but not licensed day care.
Tennis professional/instructor	Provides individual and group tennis instruction to members and guests. Also supervises leagues, mixers, camps, etc.
Activity instructors	Specialized professionals who provide individual or group instruction/coaching in their respective areas, including the martial arts, gymnastics, squash, racquetball, etc.
Massage therapists	Are professionals who are licensed by the state to provide massage therapy. Can also provide other spa services covered by their training and licensing.
Estheticians	Are professionals who are licensed to provide spa services such as manicures, pedicures, and facials.
Food-and-beverage service staff/waiters	Provide service to members and guests in the food-and-beverage area. May include waiters and bartenders.
Kitchen staff/cooks	Provide the cooking services.
Pilates/yoga instructor	Specialized instructors with advanced certifications to instruct Pilates and yoga on either an individual or group basis.
Lifeguard	Provides supervision of the pool and aquatic areas. Responsible for member/guest safety. May also have basic pool operational responsibilities.

Figure 19-6. Selected examples of non-exempt positions in the health/fitness club industry

Offsite Position Employees in Multiple-Facility Operations

With the continued growth of the health/fitness club industry, multiple-club operators represent close to 50 percent of the industry at the present time. The positions of accountability in these multiple-club operations are somewhat similar to those that exist in independent clubs at the club level. On the other hand, when the offsite support of these clubs is considered, the dynamics of employee accountability differ considerably. For example, most multiple-club operations usually allocate between three and eight percent of their total revenues, although in some instances it may amount to as much as 10 percent of total revenues, to non-club or offsite overhead positions. Figure 19-7, while not inclusive, presents an overview of the offsite positions that most commonly exist in multiple-club operations.

Compensation for Various Positions in the Health/Fitness Facility Industry

The degree to which a club can attract and retain great employees is, in large part, dependent upon the package of compensation and benefits it provides. Figures 19-8 through 19-10 illustrate the median compensation levels for both exempt and non-exempt positions in the health/fitness club industry based on data from IHRSA.

With regard to exempt club employees, most of these individuals are paid a base salary and receive variable incentive compensation. The variable incentive portion of the compensation tends to be position-specific. For example, in instances involving personal trainers, sales staff, tennis instructors, and spa therapists, compensation can often be composed entirely of commission (i.e., a percentage of the revenues that they generate) or involve an incentive-driven bonus (i.e., a fixed amount for achieving a designated performance target), while those individuals who are serving in exempt-level positions (e.g., managers, fitness directors, spa directors, etc.) are likely to experience a variable-based compensation package that encompasses 10 percent to 50 percent of their total compensation, based on their achieving designated performance metrics. The variable incentive portion normally consists of either a commission-based incentive (e.g., often used for such employees as the sales representatives, tennis directors, fitness directors, etc.) or a bonus, based on achieving predetermined performance targets (e.g., normally targeting individuals such as the CEO, manager, front desk manager, controller, etc.). Ideally, all exempt employees should have a compensation package that includes both a base salary and variable incentive compensation. Those exempt employees who are in sales-related positions, such as individuals working in the membership, tennis, or fitness areas of the club, should have a variable incentive compensation that is tied to their sales performance.

With regard to non-exempt employees, most of these employees are paid an hourly wage, with very few being eligible for variable incentive compensation. Three categories of non-exempt employees in the industry are typically paid on a commission structure: personal trainers, massage therapists/estheticians, and racquet/tennis professionals. These positions are considered commissioned,

Position	Description
Chief Executive Officer (CEO)	The CEO is the leader of the company and responsible for establishing the strategic direction of the company, serving as the public face of the company, involved with the company board, and often actively engaged in the new business development of the company. The CFO, CDO, CIO, and possibly one other position will report to the CEO.
Chief Operating Officer (COO)	The COO position and the position of president are often one in the same. The president/COO takes responsibility for overseeing all aspects of the day-to-day operations of the business, with direct leadership over the levels of management supporting the clubs.
Chief Financial Officer (CFO)	The CFO is responsible for the financial aspects of the business, including cash management, budgeting, financing, financial reporting, etc. The CFO also works closely with the financial stockholders of the business.
CMO (Chief Marketing Officer) (Vice President or higher position)	The majority of multiple-club operations have an individual who oversees the marketing and sales efforts of the company. This individual will normally provide strategic direction to the company's marketing and sales efforts and guide the systems used in marketing and sales.
Director of Human Resources (Vice President or higher position)	This individual will normally oversee all aspects of the company's human capital, including employee recruitment and selection, employee development and training, employee benefits, employee resources, etc.
Chief Information Officer (CIO) (Senior Vice President or higher position)	The CIO is responsible for the technology systems and support in the company. This position is involved in both the strategic direction of the company as it relates to technology, but also the oversight of all the employees who support the technology needs of the business.
Chief Development Officer (CDO) (Senior Vice President or higher position)	The CDO is responsible for all aspects of new business development. In many multiple-club operations, this position oversees new business, acquisitions, leasing, and construction.
Regional Operations Director or Vice President of Operations	Multiple-club operations that have a large number of clubs typically assign a freestanding manager who has direct responsibility for the operations of a set group of clubs. Normally, the regional position will oversee between 6 and 12 clubs, with the mangers of the clubs reporting directly to that position.
Regional Membership Sales Director	The regional membership salesperson usually reports directly to the vice president of operations (the regional operations director) and indirectly to the director or vice president of marketing and sales. This position is responsible for sales management for a designated group of clubs, including supporting all corporate initiatives, as well as assisting in the recruiting and training of club sales staff.
Regional Controllers	The regional controller normally reports to either the CFO or the vice president of operations. These individuals are responsible for supporting the club's accounting and bookkeeping staff, as well as assisting in financial reporting for the respective regions of clubs.

Figure 19-7. Selected examples of exempt offsite positions in multiple-club operations

because the services provided directly drive incremental revenue, which, in turn, is directly impacted by the sales performance of the individual employee. Figure 19-11, based on data from the *IHRSA 2017 Industry Compensation and Benefits Survey*, details the average commissions for personal trainers and sales staff in the health/fitness club industry.

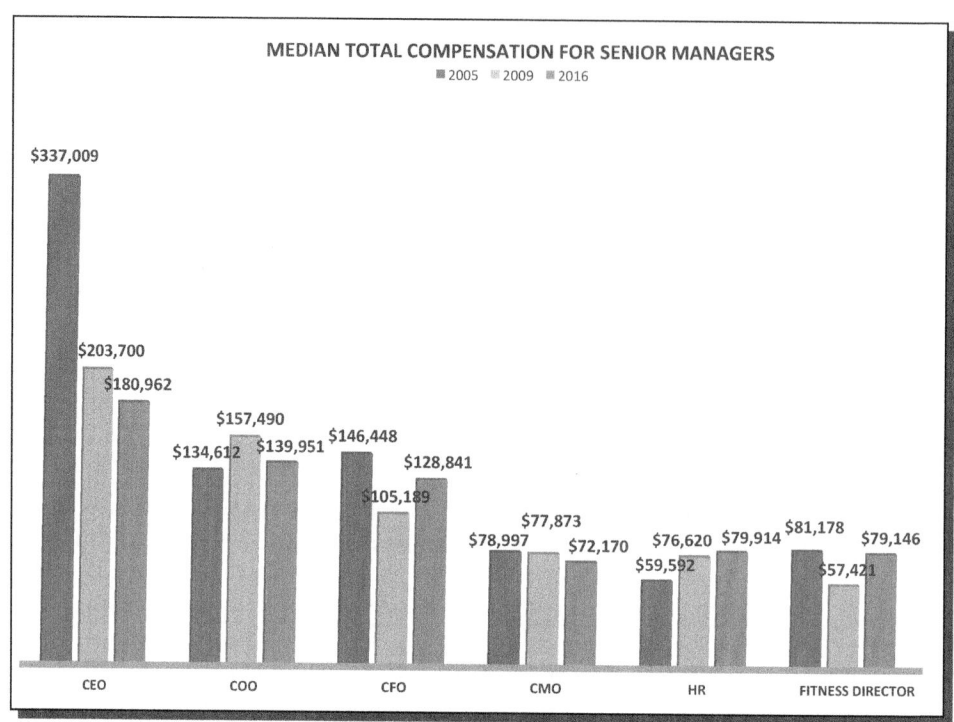

Figure 19-8. Median total compensation for corporate senior managers

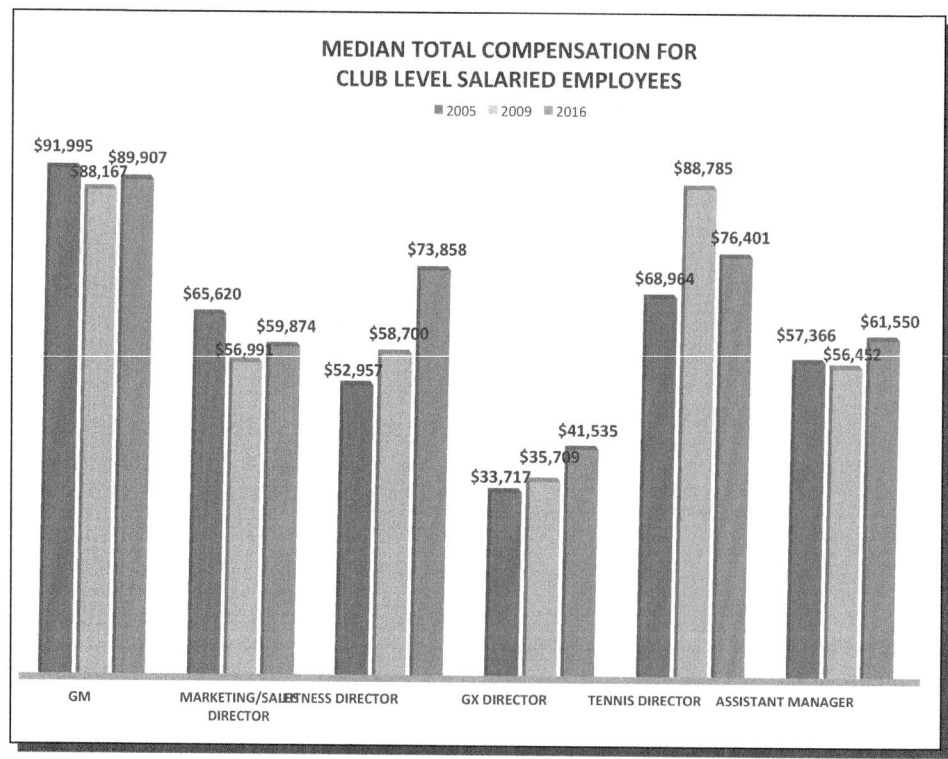

Figure 19-9. Median total compensation for salaried club employees

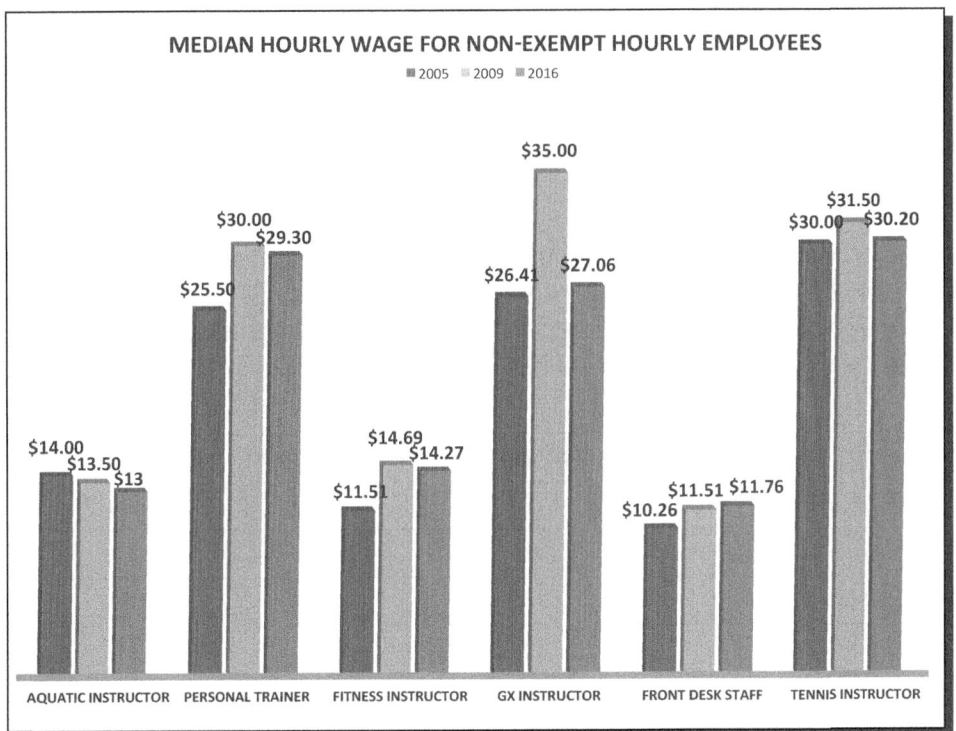

Figure 19-10. Median hourly rate for club level hourly employees

Position	Basis of Commission		Amount of Commission	
	% Revenue	Set Fee	%	Fixed
Personal trainer	54%	17%	50%	$25
Sales staff	36%	38%	22%	$37

Figure 19-11. Average commissions in the health/fitness club industry for personal trainers and sales staff (2009)

Although IHRSA did not collect data on the compensation level for either massage therapists or estheticians, the International Spa Association (ISPA), in its *2009 U.S. Spa Compensation Survey* reported the following information concerning the compensation of these particular positions:

- On average, 71 percent of the massage therapists earn between $20,000 and $50,000 annually, with 38 percent earning between $30,000 and $50,000. These earnings are based on the therapists working full time. It should be noted that the average massage therapist earns a commission equal to 40 percent to 60 percent of the massage fee.
- On average, 64 percent of the estheticians earn $20,000 to $50,000, while the earnings of 40 percent range from $30,000 to $50,000. Estheticians are paid a commission that is similar to that earned by massage therapists.

As a rule, the compensation package that a club offers its employees is based upon a number of factors, including the club's geographic location, its market position, and, most importantly, the level of education and experience it expects its employees to have.

Benefits Provided in the Health/Fitness Facility Industry

As discussed previously, benefits are second only to wages in terms of their ability to attract top-performing employees. The primary benefits offered by most club operators include: medical, life insurance, dental, vision, short-term disability, long-term disability, Section 125 plan, employee discounts for services, paid vacations, and educational reimbursement. Some clubs also include additional benefits in the benefits package for their employees, such as domestic-partner insurance and child-care assistance. Figures 19-12 and 19-13 detail several of the major benefits that are offered to both exempt and non-exempt employees in the health/fitness club industry based on data from 2016.

Benefit	Fully Paid	Partially Paid	Not Provided
Medical – employee	11%	80%	9%
Medical – family	5%	64%	31%
Life insurance	39%	20%	41%
Dental insurance – employee	15%	58%	27%
Educational assistance	5%	54%	42%
Employee discounts	33%	57%	10%
Section 125 plan	5%	30%	65%

Figure 19-12. Average benefits for exempt employees

Benefit	Fully Paid	Partially Paid	Not Provided
Medical – employee	5%	60%	36%
Medical – family	0%	49%	51%
Life insurance	23%	13%	64%
Dental insurance – employee	5%	44%	52%
Educational assistance	0%	45%	55%
Employee discounts	28%	51%	21%
Section 125 plan	2%	25%	74%

Figure 19-13. Average benefits for non-exempt employees

As a rule, the health/fitness club industry is not as generous with benefits as other industries are, either at the management level or the hourly, non-exempt employee level. As Figure 19-12 illustrates, at the management level, life insurance, medical benefits, and employee discounts are the most commonly offered fully paid benefits in the club industry, while dental benefits and educational assistance are next in line. For non-exempt, hourly employees, Figure 19-13 shows that the most significant, fully paid benefits that the industry provides to this particular group of employees are medical insurance and employee discounts.

Education and Skills Required of Health/Fitness Professionals

The health/fitness club industry is a somewhat unique business when it comes to the required educational and experience competencies of its employees. Some of the positions in the industry that were described earlier in this chapter require a relatively high level of academic qualifications (manager, accountant, fitness director), while others place more focus on the more non-traditional forms of education, such as certification and licensure (personal trainer, group exercise instructor, massage therapist). Still other positions involve a greater emphasis on work experience. The degree to which health/fitness club operators establish high academic/certification or experience standards will determine, to a large extent, their position in both the marketplace and the mindset of the customers that they are attempting to serve. Figures 19-14 and 19-15 provide an overview of the average level of education possessed by specific positions in the industry.

Position	High School	Associate's	Bachelor's	Master's	PhD
Manager	12%	6%	64%	12%	0%
Sales manager	12%	18%	59%	6%	0%
Fitness director	4%	4%	72%	4%	0%
Group exercise director	29%	10%	43%	3%	0%
Tennis director	20%	0%	53%	0%	0%

Figure 19-14. Average level of education in the U.S. health/fitness club industry—exempt positions (2016)

Position	Bachelor's	Certifications			
		ACSM	ACE	NASM	NSCA
Personal trainer	40%	49%	60%	46%	40%
Fitness instructor	16%	18%	25%	14%	13%
Group exercise instructor*	16%	16%	52%	8%	8%
*46% of group exercise instructors have AFAA certification					

Figure 19-15. Average level of education in the U.S. health/fitness club industry—professional non-exempt positions (2016)

It is evident that, for most exempt positions, the health/fitness club industry places a relatively high degree of importance on having at least a four-year college degree. As Figure 19-14 illustrates, at least 50 percent to 70 percent of club level exempt professionals (e.g., manager, sales manager, fitness director, assistant manager, etc.) have either a four-year degree or higher. The highest level of education in the industry is possessed by those employees who serve as either managers (19 percent have masters degree or higher) or fitness directors (6 percent have masters degree or higher). On the other hand, with regard to the non-exempt professional positions that provide members with instruction in fitness, recreation, or sports-related activities, the existence of a college degree in these employees falls dramatically. Less than 20 percent of fitness instructors and approximately 40 percent of personal trainers in the U.S.

> In many European and South American nations, instructors and trainers are required to have a four-year college degree.

have attained a four-year degree. It should be noted that in many European and South American nations, instructors and trainers are required to have a four-year college degree.

Education and Skills Required of Fitness Instructors, Group-Exercise Instructors, Personal Trainers, and Wellness Coaches

While many positions require minimal competency requirements (e.g., front desk, housecleaning, locker room staff), when it comes to the staff who are responsible for coaching, instructing, and educating clients (e.g., instructors, trainers, allied healthcare professionals), there is a significantly higher expectation. According to the American College of Sports Medicine's (ACSM) *Health/Fitness Facility Standards and Guidelines, 4th edition*, health/fitness professionals such as fitness instructors, personal trainers, group exercise instructors, and wellness coaches must have an appropriate level of professional education, work experience, and/or certification. Therefore, it is important that studio operators are clear about what is meant by an appropriate level of professional education, work experience, and/or certification.

❑ Professional Education

Education can take many forms. Education can be formal, such as that provided by accredited educational institutions (e.g., high schools, junior colleges, four-year colleges, graduate schools) or informal (e.g., non-accredited seminars and workshops). Education, like experience, is also influenced by the period of study, and the level of coursework the individual participates in. For example, ACSM indicates that a four-year degree in a fitness or related field is recommended for roles such as fitness director, fitness instructor, and personal trainer, and that at the minimum these professionals should have a two-year degree. While ACSM's standards provide a baseline from which operators can make their decisions, they don't provide details as to what competency requirements might be most appropriate for certain roles. One point which will help club operators make the right decision in regards to the proper educational levels for fitness staff is as follows:

- A four-year degree from an accredited institution provides an individual with a much stronger foundation in the areas of anatomy, biomechanics, motor function, nutrition, and physiology. These foundational elements allow fitness professionals to make more informed decisions in regards to how a specific instructional recommendation may impact a client's initial response, as well as their long-term progression. For example, a personal trainer interested in working in the medical fitness arena would need to have a two-year degree, while a clinical fitness instructor/trainer would require a four-year degree (refer to the Medical Fitness Association's Standards and Guidelines for Medical Fitness Center Facilities). In terms of academic preparation, an individual with a master's degree in exercise science, fitness, or health promotion has a stronger academic foundation in the field than someone with an undergraduate degree, and in turn a professional with a four-year college degree has a stronger academic foundation that someone with no degree. If a club's instructors and trainers will be working with clinical populations (e.g., people with health risks, physical limitations, disease states), then a four-year degree would appropriate; if your clients are primarily a young healthy population, then having a four-year degree would not be as important.

❑ Professional Certification

Certification—like its cousins, registration and licensing—represents a proven and recognized approach by which professionals demonstrate they have obtained a level of competency (e.g., blend of formal education and experience) necessary to effectively perform their job. Most positions in the healthcare profession, including those in complementary and alternative medicine (CAM), require state licensing or registration (e.g., acupuncturist, athletic trainer, massage therapist, chiropractor, nurse, physical therapist, respiratory therapist, occupational therapists, physician, and pharmacist). Fitness professionals are engaged in delivering services that are part of the healthcare continuum (e.g., prescribing exercise for people with risk factors, disabilities and diseases, providing post-rehabilitation exercise programs, and lifestyle coaching), yet no formal system of licensing or registration is currently required either on the national or state levels in the U.S. It should be noted that as of year-end 2015, eight state legislatures had bills pending or inactive that addressed the issue of personal trainer licensing and/or registration.

> No formal system of licensing or registration for fitness professionals is currently required either on the national or state levels in the U.S.

Since registration and licensing of fitness professionals seems to have reached a standstill from a national perspective (the industry continues to fight proposed legislation for licensing or registration of fitness professionals), certification has evolved as the most viable solution for fitness professionals, club operators, and the public. If developed and executed properly, certification demonstrates that an individual has the necessary level of competency to perform their job responsibilities. Unfortunately, not all certifications are created equal, nor do they all adequately measure a professional's level of competency. In 2006, IHRSA adopted a position statement indicating that IHRSA clubs should retain only personal trainers who have received certification from an organization whose certification procedures and practices have received third-party approval (e.g., accreditation) such as the National Commission for Certifying Agencies (NCCA), the accreditation arm of the Institute of Credentialing Excellence (ICE). Figure 19-16 provides a list of 15 organizations that offer NCCA-accredited certifications for either personal trainers or related health/fitness professions. Of the 15 organizations listed in Figure 19-16, three offer an accredited certification other than for personal trainer.

Organization	Accredited Certifications
Academy of Applied Personal Training Education (AAPTE)	Personal trainer
American College of Sports Medicine (ACSM)	Personal trainer, health fitness specialist, clinical exercise specialist, and registered clinical exercise specialist
American Council on Exercise (ACE)	Personal trainer
Cooper Institute (CI)	Personal trainer
International Fitness Professionals Association (IFPA)	Personal trainer
International Sports Science Association (ISSA)	Personal trainer
National Academy of Sports Medicine (NASM)	Personal trainer
National Commission for Health Education Credentialing (NCHED)	Health education specialist
National Council for Certified Personal Trainers (NCCPT)	Personal trainer
National Council of Strength and Fitness (NCSF)	Personal trainer
National Exercise and Sports Trainer Association (NESTA)	Personal trainer
National Exercise Trainers Association (NETA)	Personal trainer
National Federation of Professional Trainers (NFPT)	Personal trainer
National Strength and Conditioning Association (NSCA)	Personal trainer and certified strength and conditioning specialist
Training and Wellness Certification Commission (TW-CC)	Personal trainer

Figure 19-16. Accredited certifications

Some key points that will assist studio operators make the right decision when it comes to which certifications are acceptable are as follows:

- *What does the certification allow the fitness professional to do?* A certification means that the holder has demonstrated competency to perform the activities of a specific job (e.g., personal trainer, group exercise instructor, and health and fitness specialist). Therefore, operators need to determine which competencies are being measured by the certification. For example, industry personal trainer certifications currently do not measure competency in nutritional counseling, prescribing exercise for those with physical disabilities, or prescribing exercise for those recovering from an injury or illness. Until recently, these certifications also did not measure professional competency in the area of lifestyle coaching. As a result, just because you hire a certified personal trainer, it does not mean they are qualified to perform lifestyle coaching or prescribe exercise for those with physical disabilities of special health concerns.
- *Is the certification approved by an accredited third-party organization such as NCCA?* If the certification is not accredited (see Figure 19-16) by NCCA or a similar agency, then chances are their certification does not accurately measure the competencies that these professionals will be expected to demonstrate.

- *Is the certification current?* All certifications, especially those with third-party accreditation, require that the certification holder maintain a certain level of continuing education to maintain their certification. As a result, it's critical that you verify certification status on an annual basis.
- *Do they have current CPR/AED certification?* The various fitness certifications require that the professional have AED/CPR certification. Remember that AED/CPR certification must be renewed every two years. As a result, operators need to verify that their fitness professionals' AED/CPR certification is current.

❑ Professional Experience

In their standards, ACSM indicates that in addition to education and certification, professional experience is a critical determinant of a fitness professional's competency. In their 4th edition of their standards, ACSM provides general recommendations on the amount of experience they believe is sufficient for fitness professionals serving in a variety of roles. In most instances, the recommendations range from 100 hours to six months for entry-level fitness professionals, with three years of experience recommended for fitness professionals in leadership roles. The rationale behind these recommendations is that even with the proper education and certification, having experience under the watchful eye of another seasoned professional can help an individual acquire greater insight and competency in their respective field of expertise. In other healthcare fields, professionals have to earn a certain number of hours, or even years of experience prior to sitting for their licensing or registration. Following are some key points operators should consider when it comes to assessing the experience levels of their fitness staff:

- *How much experience is important?* While ACSM has provided some general guidelines on how much work experience is acceptable, this is really a decision for the operator. Typically, the more experience a professional has, the more likely they are to have attained a greater level of competency in their respective field.
- *Who is their experience with?* Experience for the sake of experience means nothing, unless that experience has been obtained under the coaching and mentoring of a qualified fitness professional. For example, wouldn't it speak more to a fitness professional's competency if they had one year of experience working under the tutelage of a certified and degreed fitness professional (e.g., fitness director, personal trainer) than if they had one year of experience working as a trainer in an unsupervised facility?
- *Can you verify the experience?* Dig into the resumes of all prospective employees. Search them out on LinkedIn or Facebook. Validate their certifications with the organizations that provided them. Degrees and certifications can be fudged on a resume, so taking the extra time to confirm what a candidate presents you is critical.

> In addition to education and certification, professional experience is a critical determinant of a fitness professional's competency.

Organizational Alignment and Structure in Individual Health/Fitness Facilities

It is important that independent club operators utilize and understand the various types of organizational structures that can effectively sustain accountability throughout the organization. The organizational structure a club chooses to employ is critical to establishing the flow of accountability and information that is essential if it is to achieve and maintain the desired level of profitability. Toward that end, an appropriate organizational structure helps to clarify the role of each employee, both in terms of personal and team responsibility. Figures 19-17 and 19-18 illustrate two different organizational structures that an individual club could utilize. Figure 19-17 depicts an organizational structure for a purely fitness club, while Figure 19-18 portrays a structure for a multipurpose club that offers racquet sports and aquatics.

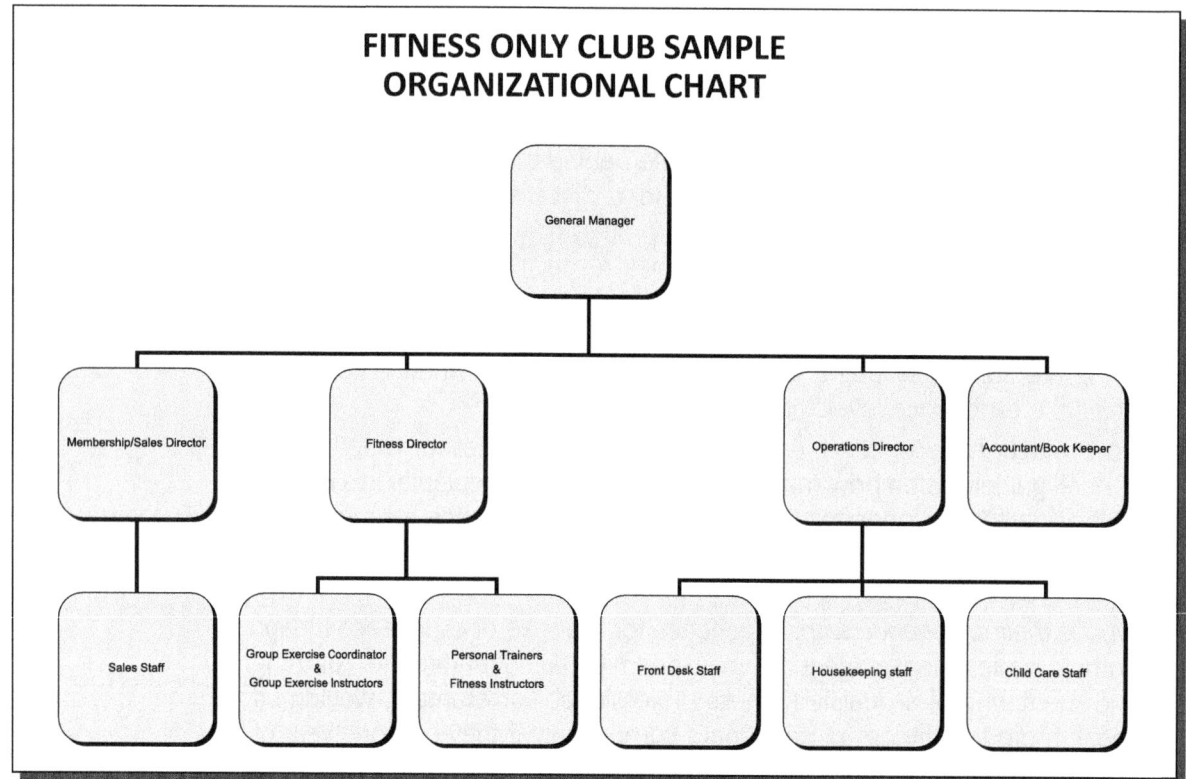

Figure 19-17. A sample fitness-club organization chart

The examples in Figures 19-17 and 19-18 are representative of the most common organizational structures that are utilized by individual health/fitness clubs. It is important to consider the following three critical success factors when designing a club's organizational structure:

- *Drive Accountability Close to the Member by Maintaining a Flat Organizational Structure.* In other words, the number of organizational layers between the member and the manager should be kept at a minimum. In the two aforementioned organizational structures, there are instances when the customer is only two layers away from the manager (sales) and

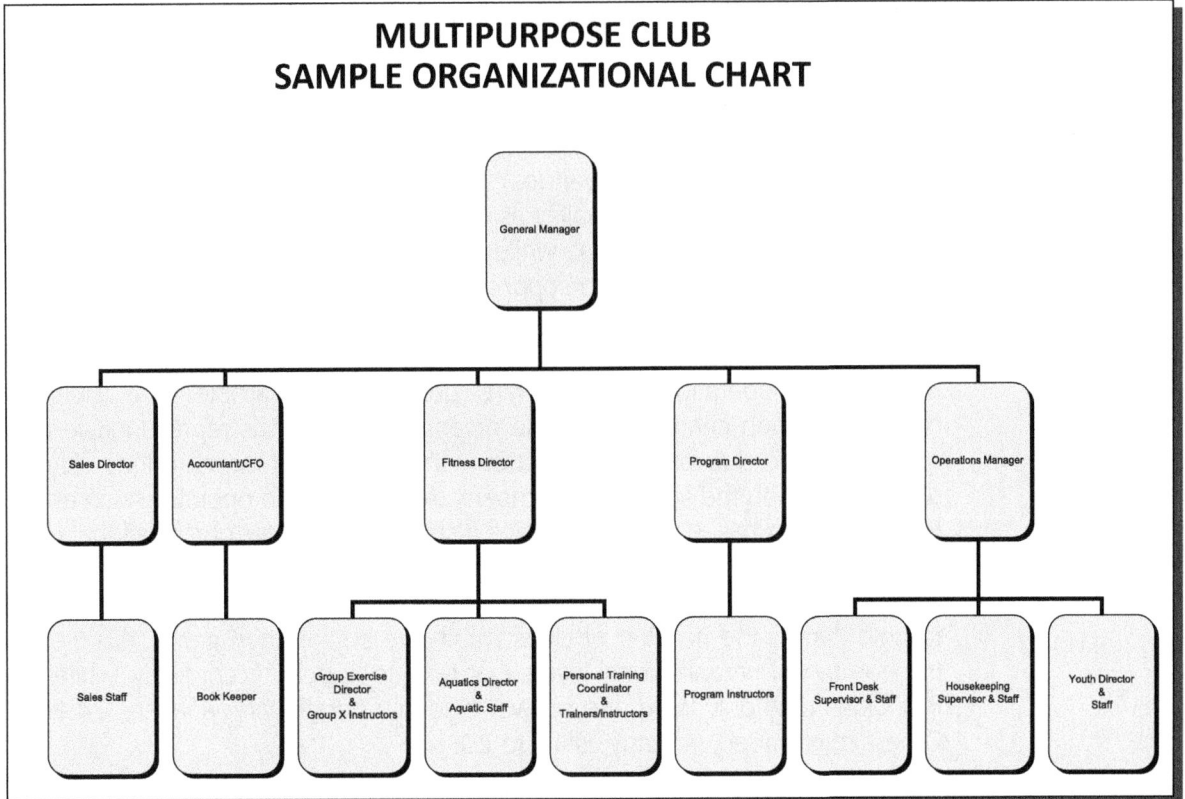

Figure 19-18. A sample multipurpose-club organization chart

other instances where the member is three layers away (personal trainers). All factors considered, the flatter the club's organizational chart, the closer the club brings accountability to the member. To achieve this objective, the club's employees need to be fully empowered.

- *Limit Direct Reports for any Supervisor.* Research in organizational management has determined that supervisors can be most effective if they have no more than six to eight direct reports and preferably less. If the club has a structure that requires leaders/supervisors to have too many direct reports, then it will find that these leaders/supervisors are far less effective in creating a high-performing, empowered environment for their direct reports.
- *Don't Create Titles; Create Accountabilities.* All too often, club management creates organizational positions to provide reward and recognition for employees. While this practice might seem like a good idea, an organizational structure should be built around the roles and the accountabilities needed to drive the club's success. As a result, all factors considered, it is often better to create fewer positions rather than more.

If club operators take the aforementioned three factors into consideration, they will find it easier to create an organizational structure that supports their business objectives, without placing excessive financial and communicative strain on the organization.

Organizational Alignment and Structure in a Multiple-Facility Operation

For multiple-club operations, the alignment of organizational accountabilities and positions is a sensitive issue. Since the cost of offsite overhead in a multiple-club operation can place a significant strain on club earnings (between three and eight percent of revenues), a need exists to create an organizational structure that brings accountability as close to the club employees as possible and at the lowest possible cost, while also providing the logistical and strategic resources that are essential to support the operations of each club. The three critical success factors previously detailed for establishing the organizational structure for a single club also apply to the organizational structure of a multiple-club operation. Figure 19-19 provides an example of a multiple-club organization chart. This sample organizational chart is representative of a typical multiple-club operation, with only the number of direct reports varying, depending upon the size of the company. A multiple-club operator, such as the Bay Clubs, that has 10 clubs, will have a smaller and flatter organizational chart than either a company, like Lifetime Fitness, that has over 100 clubs, or a much larger company, like 24 Hour Fitness, that has over 400 clubs. It is important to note that as the number of clubs within the organization grows, the greater the number of organizational layers that tend to appear. Accordingly, while the Bay Clubs may only have one or two regional operational managers, 24 Hour Fitness might need as many as 15 to 20.

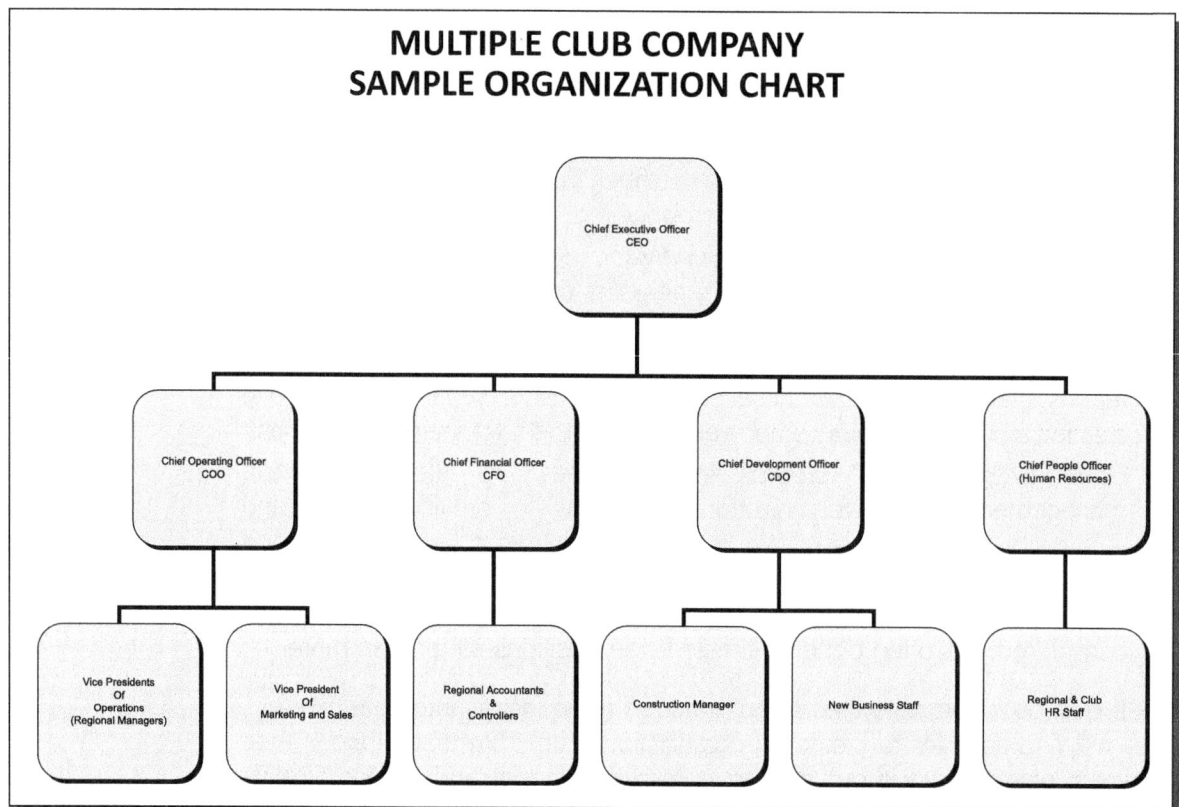

Figure 19-19. A sample multiple-club organizational chart

Reflections

As was stated at the onset of this chapter, employees and independent contractors represent the single-most important and costly asset the health/fitness club business has. As presented in this chapter, there are numerous regulations and processes that govern how you establish and manage your workforce. Understanding these regulations and processes, and acting responsibly to ensure they are executed properly, is an essential skill required of all management professionals in the health/fitness club industry.

Employees and independent contractors represent the single-most important and costly asset the health/fitness club business has.

20 Building and Leading a Successful Team

"It is teamwork that remains the ultimate competitive advantage. Both because it is so powerful and so rare"

—Patrick Lencioni, *The Five Dysfunctions of a Team*

Chapter Objectives

According to the article "The Service-Profit Chain," co-authored by Leonard Schlesinger, profit is driven by great service to the customer, which, in turn, is driven by a great employee team that is the recipient of great internal service from management. In that regard, this chapter examines the process of creating an exceptional health/fitness club team. Initially, the four Es of developing an extraordinary team are discussed. Next, the role of recruiting and selecting team players is reviewed. Then, the underlying principles and concepts attendant to effective leadership are detailed. Finally, the chapter addresses two very important issues: determining job descriptions and developing compensation agreements that provide an incentive for high-performing team players.

The Four Es of Building a Great Team

> The process of building a great employee team is one of the most important responsibilities that management has.

The process of building a great employee team is one of the most important responsibilities that management has. In his book entitled *The Five Dysfunctions of a Team*, Patrick Lencioni is quoted as saying; "It is teamwork that remains the ultimate competitive advantage, both because it is so powerful and so rare." Consequently, for club operators whose desire is to be the best, teamwork becomes an important focus. The process of team development is neither an easy undertaking nor a short one. Rather, it is a task that requires an understanding of the critical stepping-stones that need to be laid in order to build a strong team foundation and provide the basic roots that are needed for a continual evolution and empowerment of the team. The four Es are a relatively easy-to-remember tool that outlines four key steps in the team-building process. In order to be better prepared to build a great team, it is essential for club managers to be aware of and sensitive to the key factors attendant to the four Es: expectations, equipping, encouragement, and evaluation.

❏ *Expectations—Setting the Course for the Team.* The club's first step in building its team of employees is to establish clear expectations for both individual and team performance. Without clear expectations, individuals and teams will not have the direction that they need to be successful. Among the components that are essential for creating clear expectations in that regard are the following:

- *Provide each team member with an introduction to the club's core values and philosophies.* These values and philosophies serve as the core foundation of the decision-making process. Families, relationships, cultures, and businesses should have a set of common values that each member respects and lives by. If the club wants its team to be strong, it must ensure that the team is values-oriented. In their book, *Karaoke Capitalism*, Jonas Ridderstrale and Kjell A. Nordstrom are quoted as saying, "Values are magnets, and magnets attract." Therefore, every great team needs to be built around a set of compelling and attractive values.

- *Provide each team member with a job model, a copy of the club's organizational chart, and a listing of each individual's personal annual performance goals.* The job model should detail the specific accountabilities of the employee's position, as well as the manner in which that position interacts with the other members of the team. In addition, all employees should be given a copy of their personal performance goals that are updated on at least a six-month cycle. Collectively, these documents should help eliminate any confusion or misunderstandings concerning each person's accountabilities as either an individual or a team member. The organization chart should help clarify each team player's role and how the team members should interact with each other and work as a single, functioning unit.

- *Have a clear set of employee policies and rules.* While policies and rules can be relatively brief in scope, they play an essential role as a means of helping communicate the expectations of the business concerning employee and team behavior. Together with the club's core values, they set the framework for the behavior of the team.

- *Provide each employee with a personal development plan.* The personal development plan is a relatively simple tool that helps an employee to establish a path for professional development. By helping each employee set a course for such growth, the club is facilitating the team's overall development and, at the same time, creating a succession plan that will have team members ready to take on new roles when and if needed.

- *Have regular meetings of the team.* Team meetings are critical to setting and supporting the club's expectations. These meetings should be viewed as an opportunity to reinforce expectations, share achievements, reinforce values and purpose, and create new directions. They are also a time to build team trust.

- *Develop new tools to share the club's expectations with the team.* Newsletters, videos, weekly line-ups, and web pages for employees are all methods that can be employed to share the expectations and the performance achievements of a team with its members.

❏ *Equipping the Team Through Education and Growth.* The second step in building a great team is to provide an environment that equips the members of the team to successfully undertake and fulfill the club's expectations. Too many businesses mistakenly assume that once their expectations have

> Every great team needs to be built around a set of compelling and attractive values.

been defined, their employees will proceed to successfully achieve them. In reality, the process is not automatic. Rather, club owners and operators should provide the members of their teams with the resources that they need to meet both theirs and the team's expectations. This process is commonly referred to as "equipping the team" and includes the following:

- *Institute an internal formal-education system for all employees.* In this instance, a formal educational program refers to a standardized program that educates all of a club's employees on its values, philosophies, policies, traditions, and basic operating systems. Every new employee and even the tenured employees should go through a formal education system that constantly updates the employee's knowledge of the club's business and expectations. At ClubCorp, this system was called Star Education. All employees were expected to complete the Star Education Program and become certified in their assigned specific area of responsibility. At the Russian Fitness Group, the company has a training director who assists the company and various department supervisors in developing and implementing educational programs that can help facilitate the professional development of the employees.

- *Establish an external continuing-education program for the enhancement of each team member's technical, sales, and people skills.* Beyond its own education system, the club should develop and implement a system that affords its employees the opportunity to pursue continuing education that can help them advance their technical skills, sales skills, and people skills. For fitness employees, this process could involve several measures, such as bringing in outside speakers to discuss technical topics, offering scholarships or shared funds that would enable the fitness professional to attend industry-sponsored workshops, etc. For employees in other areas of interest, this undertaking could involve such steps as bringing in sales trainers or individuals to speak on customer service. The key point to note in this regard is that educational efforts, such as these, can play an important role in developing a strong team.

- *Provide the tools that employees need to do their jobs.* One of the biggest mistakes that club operators can make is to set expectations for their team and then not provide the tools that their employees need to get the job done. In this instance, tools refer to the assets/resources that are essential to completing a particular task. For example, if a piece of equipment is needed to do a job, that resource is provided. By the same token, if a job requires access to certain information, then that information is made available. All factors considered, the most powerful and valuable tool that a team can have is information. Accordingly, the club should ensure that its employees are able to access the information that they need to be able to do their job.

- *Open the communication lines.* Club management should make sure that the club has an open communication process that allows its employees to ask questions of management and share comments with management. The process should also make it relatively easy for management to share ideas, results, and feedback with its employees. As a rule, the greater the degree to which these lines of communication are opened up, the better the flow of information and resources will be between the team and management.

Chapter Twenty
Building and Leading a Successful Team

- *Walk the talk.* The axiom that leaders should act in a manner that is consistent with what they espouse has been around for a long time. Many club employees feel that one of the most important tools that the club has to equip them to perform their duties is to know that management is willing to perform those same responsibilities.

❑ *Encouragement—The Fuel of Champions.* The next step in building a great team is to create an environment that encourages employees to take ownership in their own and their team's performance. Such an environment should also reward the club's employees when certain process and outcome goals are achieved. Encouragement is normally a blend of strategies, including:
  - *Have a formal employee-recognition program.* Formal recognition programs are an effective method for fostering an environment of reward and encouragement. The focus of a formal employee-recognition program should be to reward employees for performing in a manner that is consistent with the club's core values and delivering upon the team's expectations. At ClubCorp, this program was called Star Recognition, and they rewarded employees on the basis of how well they delivered on the company's values and philosophies. At the Russian Fitness Group, they had several awards that recognize employees, including the "Legends" award to recognize those employees whose efforts over the long haul had a significant impact on the success and reputation of the organization. Other clubs undertake efforts that attempt to provide a similar level of recognition, for example employee-of-the-month programs, employee-of-the-week programs, etc. Some key elements of an employee-recognition program include:
    - ✓ The program should focus on objective measures so that it is consistent from one employee to the other.
    - ✓ The program should be designed to encourage employees to deliver on the values and standards of the business.
    - ✓ The program should have employee ownership, such as an employee committee that oversees its conduct.
    - ✓ The rewards provided by the program should be relevant to the employees, not merely what management feels that the employees would value.
    - ✓ The delivery of the program should be consistent.
  - *Leaders must be cheerleaders.* According to Ken Blanchard, in his best-selling book, *The One-Minute Manager*, management should catch employees doing things right. As a rule, the best encouragement that employees can receive is the personal recognition that comes from a leader recognizing their efforts and providing them with a thank you and job well done. When employees talk about encouraging environments, they often speak about the personal recognition that they receive from their managers/leaders. In the 80s and 90s at ClubCorp, Robert Dedman, Sr., the company founder and chairman, made a habit of writing personal notes to company employees, thanking them for their efforts. These notes were treasured by those employees who received them. Accordingly, leaders should make it a habit to walk the club, looking for employees who are doing great things and then letting those employees know how much

> Formal recognition programs are an effective method for fostering an environment of reward and encouragement.

their efforts are appreciated. Another key factor is to make sure that other employees see the encouragement provided by management.

- *Have recognition meetings.* Another valuable tool that the club can utilize to provide encouragement is to hold open meetings with its employees, during which the results of the club's performance are shared and discussed. At the Russian Fitness Group, quarterly meetings were held at which the employees whose contributions made a difference in the attainment of company goals were recognized and honored. Sharing the results in an open setting and letting the employees know how much the club values their efforts creates an open and honest team environment, which is a critical factor in encouraging employees to do their best.
- *Avoid finger pointing.* One of the easiest approaches to creating an environment of encouragement is to foster a workplace that does not condone finger pointing and blaming. Instead, it fosters a workplace focus on solutions. In that regard, leadership should cultivate an environment where employees are not afraid to make mistakes. Rather, employees should be willing to take risks and should have a sense of ownership toward addressing key issues, because they realize that no blame will be placed as long as they act in a professional manner.

> Leadership should cultivate an environment where employees are not afraid to make mistakes.

❑ *Evaluate the Expected.* The final step in the four "E's" is evaluation. If the club wants its employees to succeed both individually and collectively, it needs to establish an evaluation system that measures what is expected of its employees and provides constructive feedback for their continuous growth. Among the key evaluation tools that a club should consider in this regard are the following:

- *Create objective performance evaluations for each employee.* Each employee should have a performance evaluation that is tailored to the specific performance goals set forth in their job model. The evaluation tool should be specific to each employee and include the measurement of both the personal goals and team goals in which the individual employee has a role.
- *Evaluate at least twice a year.* Performance evaluations are most effective if they are done at least twice annually. The longer the club waits between performance evaluations, the less likely it will be able to create a link in the employee's mind between what the club expects and what feedback is being provided to each employee.
- *Make it a habit to evaluate daily.* Leaders need to actively engage in the evaluation process by walking around the club. If they observe behavior that warrants their feedback, the best time to provide comments of any kind is to do so immediately.
- *Create a business scorecard.* To help facilitate the team's performance, leaders should develop a club business scorecard that every employee can understand. This scorecard should be to help assess team performance, as well as communicate recognition and education. The scorecard can be incorporated as part of every meeting to either recognize the team or educate it. The scorecard should be more than a financial tool. Rather, it

should help evaluate the performance of the club's employees against the core values and standards of operation of the business.

- *Never let performance go without recognition, education, and follow-up.* If the club's managerial staff sees good performance, they should make sure that the individual or team is recognized and rewarded. By the same token, if they see performance that falls below their expectations, they should acknowledge the performance misstep; educate the employee involved about how to improve it, and then follow-up to make sure that the individual's performance has changed appropriately.

Recruiting and Selecting the Business's Team

One of the biggest challenges in any business, and in particular the club industry, is building a great team. Before the aforementioned four steps to building a great team can be undertaken, however, the club needs to have the right people as employees. As Jim Collins states in his seminal text, *Good to Great*, it begins by getting the right people on the bus, and from there determining where to go. Therefore, the easiest way to build a great team is to hire great employees, a practice approach that requires a systematic approach to recruiting and selecting the best available employees to serve on the team. In this regard, the following factors apply:

> The easiest way to build a great team is to hire great employees.

Recruitment

- ❑ *Develop a Hiring Model and Posting for Each Position.* The first step in recruiting is to create a model of what the employee profile should be. A hiring model is a shortened version of the job model that identifies the values, attitudes, and skills expected for each position.

- ❑ *Place the Postings/Models in the Appropriate Areas.* When the club is ready to recruit, the club should make sure that it places its hiring models/posting with the right lead sources, including:
  - Local two-year and four-year colleges can be excellent sources of employees. If the club is looking for fitness staff, it should contact the college's kinesiology department. On the other hand, if it is looking to hire swim instructors, it should get in touch with the coach of the college's swim team.
  - The ad seeking new employees should be posted on the appropriate career-center websites for the respective specialty areas. For example, when the club is seeking to hire fitness staff, the websites of ACSM, ACE, NSCA, and IHRSA would be excellent sources. If massage and spa employees were wanted, the club should contact any institution/entity that might be aware of individuals who would accommodate the club's needs, such as the local massage schools, the American Massage Therapy Association, etc.
  - The club should consider creating a career center on its website. Companies, such as 24 Hour Fitness, ClubCorp, Equinox Fitness, Fitness First, Lifetime Fitness, and Virgin Active, have developed their own recruitment sites, as have some independent clubs, such as the Eastbank Club in Chicago, and Gainesville Health and Fitness in Gainesville, Florida.

> Many of the top club companies in the industry offer internships.

- *Develop Internship Programs With Colleges.* Possibly the best recruiting tool is to develop an internship program with local colleges and high schools. By creating internships, the club can provide learning opportunities for those students who have an interest in fitness and health and, at the same time, give the club a chance to evaluate each intern's potential as a future employee. In fact, many of the top club companies in the industry offer internships. These companies report finding that their best employees often are those individuals who have previously served in internships. IHRSA has developed an internship manual that clubs can utilize to help implement a successful internship program.

- *Recruit From Other Service Industries.* If a club is seeking people who have a servant's heart and understand how to work within a hospitality/service business, it should consider recruiting from similar hospitality businesses. The recruiter should carry business cards and, if and when they observe a worker whose performance aligns with the club's culture, hand the worker a card and invite that individual to visit the club. Over the years, I have personally made it a habit to leave my business card with those employees of other organizations whom I feel represent the type of employee we wanted in our company.

Selection

- *Compare Applications and Resumes to the Hiring Model.* The first step that a club should take when deciding who to hire is to compare every application and resume, via a checklist, with its hiring model. Clubs can subsequently rank the applications and resumes by how closely they align with the hiring model. Performing this step allows the club to limit the number of candidates it takes to the next step of the selection process. Clubs can employ this method to identify those applicants who most closely reflect their hiring model.

- *Use Multiple Interviews.* Every candidate under consideration should go through a series of interviews. The first interview should be conducted by the immediate supervisor, though in larger organizations, it may be a human resource professional. This initial interview should focus on uncovering the basic values, beliefs, attitudes, and skills of the applicant. It is essential that during this first interview that you identify the candidate's "cultural fit" with the organization (alignment with the club's values and philosophies). This first interview can be conducted using a structured interview format and checklist. While most initial interviews are conducted in person, a growing trend is to conduct the first interview over the phone, over Skype, Google +, or even in a virtual environment, such as Second Life. If the candidate fits the culture and meets the expectations of the first interview, then a second interview should be conducted with multiple members of the team, using a structured format. The second interview should be more detailed than the first and should focus on role-play situations, based on predetermined questions that are designed to be value indicators of success in the club business. If the candidate gets through the second interview successfully, then the third interview should be conducted in a team format with several members of the team present. This interview can be more free-flowing than the other two, because its primary focus is to determine if an appropriate fit exists between the team and the applicant.

- ❑ *Consider an Industry Profile.* Many club operators employ personality and job-profile surveys that are designed to help compare the candidate's personal profile against the known attitudes and attributes of a successful employee. These profiles, typically used with senior-level employees, are usually available through human-resource organizations and private companies that are focused on profiling employees. As a rule, these profiles measure such key attributes as leadership, communication, teamwork, work ethic, relationship skills, etc. By comparing the profile of a candidate with the standardized profile of a top-performing employee, the club can obtain a better reading of the candidate's potential for success.

- ❑ *Only Hire From the Top of the List.* After completing all of the aforementioned steps, the club should develop a list of potential candidates, with the best candidate placed at the top and the others ranked in a priority order. Leaders should make an effort to let their team help compile the rankings. Once the rankings are completed, they should initiate the selection process by contacting the candidate at the top of the list.

Leadership

Leadership has been a topic of discussion for decades. Henry Kissinger, former U.S, Secretary of State may have summed it up the best when he said: "The task of a leader is to get people from where they are to where they have never been." In both large business organizations and small businesses, one of the most common concerns is their perception that they don't have enough great leadership. In fact, this issue is often ranked as the number one perceived weakness in most organizations. Over the years, teachers, scholars, and philosophers have attempted to provide a variety of definitions for leadership and have put forth a seemingly endless abundance of theories on what it takes to be an effective leader. One factor that seems to be a common thread among all the definitions and theories on leadership is that organizations that want to be successful need leaders at all levels of the organization. This section is not intended to provide a detailed description of leadership or any particular style of leadership. Rather, its primary goal is to present an overview of what leadership is, how leadership impacts the club business, and how every employee of a club, from fitness instructors to managers, can develop the basic attributes of leadership.

Organizations that want to be successful need leaders at all levels of the organization.

- ❑ *The Role of Leaders.* The primary responsibility of leaders is to determine the culture and goals of the business and help establish an environment in which every employee takes ownership in living the culture and achieving the goals. John Quincy Adams, the sixth President of the U.S., said: "If you actions inspire others to dream more, learn more, do more and become more, you are a leader." Realistically, an effective leader might be defined as an individual who is able to influence the passion, vision, and commitment of others in order to channel the efforts and talents of individuals who

are going separate directions into a cohesive team of employees who are functioning as a single unit. Among the roles that leaders most often assume in an organization, such as a health/fitness club, are the following:
- To establish a compelling vision and culture for the business. This role is most often assumed by the primary club leader (e.g., owner or manager). The vision and the culture serve as the foundation for the success that the business achieves.
- To communicate the culture and vision of the club every day. This role should not just involve the club's top leader, but also every employee who interacts with and has responsibility for the behavior of another employee.
- To develop a team of employees who will take ownership in a common vision and goal by seeing how working together benefits both the individual and the team.
- To demonstrate trust in their team and, in return, gain the respect and trust of their team.
- To build consensus when appropriate, but also to make tough decisions when they are needed.
- To see themselves as servants for their team by providing a vision, the support, and the resources that their team needs to achieve the club's vision and goals.
- To set the course, provide guidance along the way, remove barriers, build bridges, leverage talent, recognize the need for change, and hold people and teams accountable for their actions.
- Challenge the status quo by seeking to identify and execute business strategies that can enhance the efficiency and quality of their business.

❏ *The Qualities of Leaders.* Great leaders who can take on the aforementioned roles and successfully execute them often exhibit certain basic qualities, including:
- *Dare to be different.* Daring to be different involves capitalizing on whatever is unique about the individual in such a way that it positively impacts the business. Having attributes (e.g., passion, creativity, vision, imagination, etc.) that can be leveraged to the advantage of the business are an important trait of all leaders.
- *Emotional intelligence.* Great leaders have the ability to sense what is occurring in the business environment around them. This instinct does not emanate from the ability to analyze the impact of relevant numbers on the situation. Rather, it involves having the ability to sense the soft data and the emotions of the people and then being able to interpret that information to the benefit of the organization. Leaders with emotional intelligence are sensitive to the emotions of their staff members and are able to openly discuss these emotions as they relate to the work environment. Emotional intelligence also requires the ability to listen without prejudice, to hear what is actually being communicated.
- *Empathy with strength.* Great leaders have the ability to communicate through their actions to their employees that they care about them. Empathetic leaders demonstrate genuine care about the members of the team and are legitimately interested in the work that their employees do.

> Great leaders have the ability to communicate through their actions to their employees that they care about them.

This empathy evolves not only from respect and trust, but also from the ability to deal with each employee in an honest and ethical manner.

- *Are not afraid to be vulnerable.* Great leaders realize that all other factors being equal they can enhance the level of trust in the organization by being willing to show their weaknesses to other individuals in the organization. Revealing weakness involves the ability to let their team know that they are willing to take accountability for their actions and behaviors, rather than hiding them. Exposing their own personal limitations also enables leaders to surround themselves with people whose strengths can counterbalance the weaknesses exhibited by the leaders. In other words, leaders who are willing to lay bare their weaknesses are not threatened by the strengths of others. Instead, they are able and prefer to utilize the strengths of others to strengthen the team.
- *Manage systems, not people.* Leaders understand that people manage themselves. Leaders understand that their job is to create and support systems that enable people not only to manage themselves, but also to achieve the expectations set forth for them by the business. A leader ensures that systems are in place that will allow the goals of the business to be accomplished and then empowers employees to leverage those systems for the benefit of the organization.
- *Let the people lead.* Leaders understand that if, figuratively, they get out of the way and let the members of the team lead, then everyone will be successful. Lao Tzu, a famous Chinese philosopher said this about leaders: "Bad leaders are those whom the people revile, great leaders those whom the people praise and great leaders are those whom the people say, we did it ourselves." In other words, effective leaders are able to get everyone to take ownership of the business. They are also able to establish a work environment that enables the individual skill-sets of each employee to link together. In essence, each employee becomes a leader of the team's other employees, with each person headed in the same direction. As such, the process involves creating leadership disciples.

> Leaders understand that if, figuratively, they get out of the way and let the members of the team lead, then everyone will be successful.

❑ *Characteristics of Great Managers.* Great managers build great teams and produce great results. As a rule, great managers in the health/fitness facility industry possess the following characteristics:

- *They plan for success.* One attribute that all great managers have is that they have a plan for success at their club. In other words, they develop a comprehensive plan that identifies specific objectives for their business, including quantitative benchmarks for such areas as membership growth, revenue growth, expense control, people development, marketing, community development, and facility enhancement. Each objective is stated in relatively simple terms with clearly definable, measurable targets and is subsequently communicated to all members of that person's team. The plan includes a detailed financial budget that delineates specific financial targets for each aspect of the business. As such, great managers leave nothing to chance.
- *They know their numbers.* Great managers always seem to know their facility's numbers. In other words, they know what the budgeted targets are

for every possible area of importance in their club and are aware of how well their facility is doing with regard to these key parameters on a daily, weekly, and monthly basis. Want to know what their club's membership retention level is—just ask them. Want to know what their facility's payroll percentage is—just ask them.

- *They are coaches and educators.* One of the most notable characteristics of great managers is how much time that they spend with their "people." The employees of great managers tend to speak very highly of them, particularly how they have helped them grow both professionally and personally. These manager-coaches make sure that all of their employees know the club's business plan, ensure that employees know they care about them, and expend substantial time teaching and counseling their employees. Great managers educate, motivate, and inspire their employees.

- *They get their hands dirty.* Great managers are someone who will do any job in the club, whether it is working the front desk, teaching a class, or cleaning the locker room. They do not see themselves as being above the fray. Whatever the situation, they are willing to "get their hands dirty." It is not that they spend a lot of time performing a particular task; rather it's that they do the job when it is needed, the way it should be done. In the process, they set the perfect example for their staff.

- *They have great relationships with the members.* When members stop by the manager's office or approach that person on the floor to converse, that manager probably has a positive relationship with the club's members. Great managers tend to make it a practice of getting close to the membership and building trust between the club's management and its members. In that regard, they try to learn (and remember) the members' names and get somewhat knowledgeable about the members' families. They express sincere interest in the members—particularly how each member is doing in the club, how well the facility is treating the person, etc.

- *They have an open door.* Individuals who want to know if the club has a great manager should just go to the manager's office. Great managers have an open-door policy in which they maintain an environment that encourages employees and members alike to approach them about their concerns—good or bad. Those managers who try to hide behind their office door have neither the courage nor the wisdom to fulfill their assigned role. Confident, successful managers, on the other hand, do not set such barriers. Rather, they make every effort to ensure that their club's members and employees know that they are there to support them and assist them.

- *They are sponges for learning.* Great managers make it a habit to continually expand their horizons. They are aware of the need for lifelong learning. They make a commitment to establish an organization with a suitable environment for group learning. They accept the value of critical thinking. They understand that learning is reciprocal. They exhibit a number of characteristics, including a thirst for relevant knowledge concerning the industry and their organization, a desire to learn, and a willingness to be teachable.

- *They are salespeople.* Great managers seem to have an affinity for selling—not the hard-core approach to selling, but rather the understanding that every relationship is an opportunity for selling. These managers build upon their relationships with other people to identify opportunities to make their members aware of the fact that the facility has offerings (services, programs, and products) that they may need. Managers who are salespeople are able to create an environment that encourages every employee to see themselves as a "salesperson." Great managers emphasize the point that sales is about identifying the needs of the members and then providing a service that fulfills that need.

- *They are passionate.* Anything worth doing is seldom achieved without passion. In that regard, great managers are incredibly passionate about the health/fitness club business. In a very real sense, passion is the lubricant of their success. They have the ability to exercise sound judgment, control their emotions, be passionate about what they do, and be aware of the tremendous value of a physically active lifestyle.

> **Great managers are incredibly passionate about the health/fitness club business.**

- *They know the competitors.* Great managers know their competition. They know everything about them, from their facilities to the way that they program their clubs. They subscribe to one of the basic principles highlighted in Sun Tzu's Art of War, which essentially states, "Keep your allies close and your enemies even closer." A tendency exists among some managers to criticize and belittle their competitors. Rather, they should learn from them and take advantage of their good ideas.

❑ *The Situational Leadership Model.* For the first-time supervisor or manager, the responsibility of leadership can be overwhelming. While the attributes detailed in the previous sections are essential to great leadership, a person who is new to the obligations that leadership entails cannot develop and refine all of those qualities overnight. For those novice leaders, the model of situation leadership, as presented in Ken Blanchard's best-selling book, *The One Minute Manager and Leadership,* can be an excellent tool. Blanchard's model of leadership reviews the following four styles of leadership and details how they can be applied with different employee populations:

- *Directive leadership.* This style of leadership is most effective when undertaken with new employees, as well as with other employees whose knowledge of the job (i.e., skill level/technical expertise of job) and its expectations are relatively low and their desire to achieve is high. The leader needs to provide direction to these individuals concerning how the job should be performed. This direction might be presented in several formats, including checklists, regular meetings, teaching, goal setting, etc.

- *Coaching leadership.* This style of leadership is most effective when utilized with those employees who have garnered a relatively strong understanding of the job and whose level of desire or passion may have waned slightly. As a rule, these individuals are usually more tenured employees who have yet to achieve an empowered status, as an outgrowth of their skill, passion, and understanding of the job. With these employees, the leader should listen to the employee, be supportive of the employee's efforts, and if needed, provide the direction or goals for the job to get done.

- *Supportive leadership.* This style of leadership is usually employed with employees and teams of employees who have the knowledge, experience, and an understanding of what needs to occur in the workplace. With these employees, the leader must listen, support, and facilitate change. This style is not about giving direction; rather, it involves facilitating interaction and supporting the employees, and only stepping in if needed.

- *Delegating leadership.* This style of leadership is appropriate for use with employees and teams who are knowledgeable, experienced, focused, and passionate. With these employees, the leader is focused on providing an environment of trust and handing over the reigns of leadership. This type of leadership involves fully empowering employees and letting them lead.

It is important to understand that each style of leadership is applicable to every employee. While it might appear that the needs of each employee would dictate that a specific style of leadership be utilized, it is far more likely that each employee will require each of these styles at different times over the course of their employment. Occasions will arise when an employee or team needs to be directed, while at other times, those same individuals will need to be coached, supported, or delegated. It is the role of the leader to know which style to use and when to use it. This responsibility can involve several factors, including emotional intelligence, empathy, and being open to and in touch with the work environment.

Developing Job Descriptions and Compensation Agreements for Employees

As previously discussed, one of the keys to building a team is providing each employee with a job description (model) and a compensation agreement. These two documents are two of the most critical tools in establishing expectations, offering encouragement, and providing evaluation. In reality, the job description and compensation agreement are not documents, as much as they are living roadmaps for the employee.

- ❏ *Building the Job Model.* The job model is a roadmap for the employee, because it points out the expectations that the club has for a particular job (position) and details how that job interacts with the other members of the team. Building a job model involves the following steps:
  - *Begin with the job overview.* The first part of the job model is a simple paragraph that summarizes the primary responsibilities and accountabilities of the job. This narration should be clear and direct.
  - *Identify whether the position is exempt or non-exempt.* The job model should detail how the various positions in the club are to be categorized. For example, a fitness director would be an exempt position, while a personal trainer would be a non-exempt position.
  - *List the essential accountabilities of the job.* The essential accountabilities of the position involve the top five behaviors/areas for which the employee will be held accountable. Collectively, these factors should reflect the big picture. For example, employees might be held accountable for their department achieving its annual budget target for revenues.
  - *List the secondary accountabilities.* Secondary accountabilities involve those areas/behaviors over and beyond the aforementioned essential accountabilities for which the club will hold the employee accountable.

These areas are not tasks; rather, they are areas of accountability. For example, employees might be held accountable for completing their work schedule each week.
- *Identify the reporting lines.* This factor involves clarifying whom employees report directly to, whom the employees have indirect reporting responsibility to, and whom they supervise (if anyone). For example, an employee might report to the operations manager, but is expected to work with the fitness director when needed, and is responsible for the personal trainers.
- *Identify the physical requirements of the job.* This stipulation is an OSHA requirement. It involves identifying the specific physical tasks, such as lifting, walking, etc., that a particular job requires.
- *Identify the educational expectations for the position.* This measure refers to the fact that the club should provide a listing of any educational requirements for the position, such as certifications, licenses, etc.

Several examples of job models that are employed in the health/fitness club industry are included in the appendix of this book.

❏ *Building the Compensation Agreement.* Every employee should receive a written compensation agreement, in addition to a copy of the job model for their position. A compensation agreement is a non-binding understanding of the compensation that will be provided for performing the duties expected of a specific position, rather than a contract for employment. On the other hand, it should be noted that in many European countries, the compensation agreement is actually a contract of employment. The compensation agreement should be consistent with the accountabilities of the job and spell out in detail for the employees exactly how they derive their personal earnings. Building a compensation agreement can involve several critical elements, including:

- *Non-exempt hourly employees:*
  ✓ Identify their hourly wage and share with them the changes in that rate for overtime and holiday work.
  ✓ Identify what benefits they are eligible for as a non-exempt employee.
  ✓ If employees are being paid by commission only, make sure that the commission structure is completely outlined and provide a sample template so that they can see how the compensation process works for them.
  ✓ For employees who are paid by commission, also include a second hourly rate that can be applied for holidays and vacations.
- *Exempt employees:*
  ✓ Identify their base salary. This step should be communicated in terms of the club's standard pay period and also be outlined in an annualized amount. For example, the employee will receive a base salary of $2,000 every two weeks equal to $52,000 annually.
  ✓ Identify any incentive or variable pay, based on performance. Make sure that employees understand clearly how their variable or incentive pay will be given. For example, employees have the potential to earn $10,000 each at year-end if they achieve 100 percent of their revenue

> Every employee should receive a written compensation agreement, in addition to a copy of the job model for their position.

goal. Furthermore, they will receive a percentage of the $10,000 that is proportional to the percentage of the revenue goal they achieve (e.g., $5,000 for reaching 50 percent of the assigned goal, etc.).
✓ Identify all benefits provided, including vacation, education allowances, medical, profit-sharing, etc.

Reflections

To paraphrase the quote shared earlier in this chapter, teamwork represents the ultimate competitive advantage because of its power to drive extraordinary results. Building on this premise, great organizations are the consequence of great teams that have an extraordinary leader at the helm. Building great teams does not happen by accident, it requires great leadership and a disciplined approach to recruiting, hiring, developing, coaching, encouraging, and supporting people.

> Great organizations are the consequence of great teams that have an extraordinary leader at the helm.

PART 6
Facilities and Equipment in the Health/Fitness Facility Industry

Chapter 21
Health/Fitness Facilities

Chapter 22
Fitness Equipment for the Health/Fitness Facility Industry

Courtesy of Essenza Architecture

Health/Fitness Facilities 21

"A great building must begin with the unmeasurable, must go through measureable means when it is being designed and in the end must be unmeasurable."

—Louis Kahn, architect

Chapter Objectives

The health/fitness industry, whether a large multipurpose facility or an intimate boutique studio, is heavily dependent upon its facilities for driving business profitability. In the case of many operators, the facility is positioned as the competitive differentiator. This chapter presents an overview of the facilities that compose the majority of health/fitness clubs. The chapter initially reviews the various types of facilities. The chapter then discusses the areas that typically are found in these types of facilities. The chapter continues by examining the design and construction process for health/fitness club facilities, including providing examples of cost guidelines for construction. Finally, the chapter provides several examples of various facility designs.

> The health/fitness industry is heavily dependent upon its facilities for driving business profitability.

Types of Health/Fitness Facilities

The International Health, Racquet & Sportsclub Association in its 2015 industry data survey, the *IHRSA Profiles of Success*, separates facilities into two generic categories: fitness-only and multipurpose. In the association's *2016 Health Club Consumer Report*, it looks beyond these two categories and introduces for the first time boutique fitness clubs, facilities designed to serve a niche audience with a uniquely targeted environment. While these categories enable the various kinds of facilities to be grouped into three primary types of facilities, each of these major categories can be separated into even greater detail, based on the actual business operated in the facility:

❑ *Fitness-Only Facilities* (called Gym-Only in Europe). Fitness-only facilities are defined as those clubs that have facilities that provide space specifically for the pursuit of fitness activities. These facilities typically consist of activity-specific areas for cardiovascular equipment, resistance-circuit equipment, free-weight equipment, and group-exercise studios, as well as common areas, such as locker rooms and reception areas. Fitness-only facilities typically range in size from 3,000 square feet (280 meters) to as large as 40,000 square feet (2,800 meters), depending upon whether they include group-exercise studios, and how large the local market is. Based on the average membership for a fitness-only club, as reflected in IHRSA's 2015 research, these fitness-only facilities provide approximately 9 square feet (just under one square meter) per member. In fact, several of the leading operators in the fitness-only segment actually provide as few as 2.5 to 3 square feet per member.

Some of the leading global industry players whose focus is providing fitness-only facilities include:

- *Planet Fitness, U.S.* Planet Fitness is one of the leading global gym operators in the high-volume, low-priced business segment (dues under $10 a month). The Planet Fitness model is a pure fitness-only operation, with relatively small locker rooms, a reception area, and expansive equipment areas. A Planet Fitness facility will typically range in size from 15,000 to 20,000 square feet.
- *24 Hour Fitness, U.S.* 24 Hour Fitness began as a fitness-only company and, over the past decade, has expanded its product offering to include a range of multipurpose facilities (Sport, Super Sport, and Ultra Sport). A significant number of its existing facilities are still fitness-only operations (Active). These facilities are typically less than 30,000 square feet and offer both a gym and group-exercise studios.
- *Equinox, North America and UK.* Equinox is the premier operator of high-end premium fitness facilities in the U.S. with over 90 properties. The majority of Equinox's facilities are fitness-only, though with the acquisition of the former Sports Club/LA facilities they now operate luxury multipurpose facilities. Equinox's fitness-only facilities tend to range in size from 25,000 to 40,000 square feet.
- *Anytime Fitness, global franchise.* Anytime's typical franchise model is a 3,000 to 5,000 square foot, fitness-only facility.
- *McFit, Germany. McFit,* which like Planet Fitness operates in the high-volume, low-price (budget) segment of the fitness industry, offers a fitness-only facility. McFit facilities are typically fitted out at around 12,000 to 25,000 square feet and do not include group exercise.

Fitness-only facilities are commonly found in strip malls, office buildings, residential buildings, and corporate wellness and fitness programs.

❏ *Boutique Fitness Facilities.* Boutique fitness facilities are designed to serve a niche audience with a uniquely targeted environment. While boutique fitness studios have been around for over a century, only since 2010 have they grown into an influential segment of the club industry. Boutique fitness facilities can range in size from as small as 1,000 square feet (91 square meters) to as large as 15,000 square feet (1,360 square meters). In a 2016 study conducted by the Association of Fitness Studios (AFS), it discovered that approximately 73 percent of boutique studios were less than 5,000 square feet (455 square meters) and 33 percent were actually smaller than 2,500 square feet (228 meters). In a 2016 study of boutique fitness studios

> While boutique fitness studios have been around for over a century, only since 2010 have they grown into an influential segment of the club industry.

conducted by AFS, the average boutique studio occupied 3,813 square feet. In the majority of instances, these boutique facilities will fall between 2,000 and 5,000 square feet (180 to 455 square meters). The most prominent types of boutique fitness facilities include:

- *Yoga studios.* The majority of yoga studios are independent studios, but in recent years there has been a proliferation of corporately owned yoga chains and yoga franchises. Some of the more well-known multi-unit yoga studios include Pure Yoga owned by Equinox and based in New York; Yoga Works, a chain of approximately 25 yoga studios operated in California and the Northeast corridor of the U.S., and Core Power Yoga, based out of Denver, Colorado, with more than 100 studios throughout the U.S. According to AFS's 2016 research, approximately 2 percent of studio owners indicated their primary discipline was yoga.

Yoga studio with yoga wall, ACAC, Charlottesville, VA

- *Pilates studios.* The vast majority of private Pilates studios are owned and operated by individuals. The largest operator of Pilates studios is Club Pilates, a franchise model that presently has over 170 studios operating throughout the U.S. Another large operator is IMAX Pilates with over 25 franchise locations. According to AFS's 2016 research, approximately 4 percent of studio owners indicated their primary discipline was Pilates.
- *Barre studios.* Barre studios have evolved as one of the leading boutique fitness facility concepts over the past several years. While yoga studios were initially the primary domain of individual entrepreneurs, Barre studios have since grown through a franchise model. The largest barre franchise operation in the U.S., with approximately 300 locations, is Pure Barre out of South Carolina. Another well-known barre franchise is the Bar Method with approximately 72 locations in the U.S., and Barre Code with approximately 28 locations.

- *Cycling studios.* Over the past decade studios dedicated purely to cycling have evolved, such as the ever-popular Soul Cycle in New York, owned by Equinox, which operates 80-plus studios across the country, Flywheel, a cycling franchise with approximately 40 locations throughout the U.S, and cycling franchise CycleBar with just over 100 locations in the U.S. According to AFS's 2016 research, approximately 4 percent of studio owners indicated their primary discipline was group cycling.

Group cycling studio, City Club, Fort Worth, TX

- *Free-weight gyms.* Free weight gyms remain an important niche in the boutique segment of the health/fitness club industry. These gyms typically provide a relatively large free-weight area, a reception area, and locker rooms. Free-weight gyms have become less prevalent over the past few decades, as they have evolved into offering other forms of exercise equipment.
- *Personal-training/small group training studios.* Personal training/small group training studios represent the largest single segment of the boutique fitness facility market. Personal training studios are composed primarily of resistance, cardiovascular, functional training spaces, and stretching areas. Some might have reception desks and locker rooms or changing rooms. According to AFS's 2016 research, approximately 42 percent of studio owners indicated their primary discipline was personal training. In IHRSA's *2016 Health Club Consumer Report*, 15 percent of health/fitness facility users indicate they frequent personal training/small group training studios.
- *Cross training/boot camp/HIIT studios.* The cross training/boot camp/HIIT studios have emerged in the past five to seven years as possibly the strongest segment of the industry after yoga studios. These facilities vary in focus, some offering a structured high-intensity interval-style workout such as the studios operated under the Barry's Bootcamp and Orange Theory franchises, to others offering a more eclectic functional experience such as the facilities operated as Crossfit affiliates or Iron Tribe Fitness franchises.

- *Express facilities.* These facilities are designed to offer a quick and efficient workout, typically a 30-minute circuit. These facilities, such as Curves for Women and Ms. Sporty in Germany, typically have a small open area for equipment, a small reception area, and in some cases, changing facilities. These facilities tend to occupy less than 3,000 square feet of space, with many express clubs being less than 1,000 square feet.

❑ *Multipurpose Facilities.* Multipurpose facilities are defined as clubs that offer fitness facilities and one or more recreational spaces, such as racquet courts, pools, gymnasiums, spas, and outdoor recreational areas. The typical multipurpose facility will range in size from 45,000 square feet to 80,000 square feet. Based on data reported in the publication, the IHRSA *2015 Profiles of Success*, the average multipurpose club provides approximately 14 square feet (1.3 square meters) per membership, approximately 30 percent more space per membership than offered by fitness-only clubs. Similar to what occurs in the fitness-only market, some multipurpose clubs, such as those operated by Lifetime Fitness or LA Fitness, provide as little as 5 to 10 square feet per membership. The largest single multipurpose club in the U.S. is the member-owned Multnomah Athletic Club, located outside Portland, Oregon, at over 550,000 square feet. Just behind Multnomah in terms of size is the Eastbank Club in Chicago at 450,000 square feet. Some of the other massive multipurpose clubs in the U.S. include the Rochester Athletic Club in Rochester, Minnesota at over 200,000 square feet; and Red's in Lafayette, Louisiana, at over 185,000 square feet. Some of the leading global industry players that focus on providing multipurpose facilities include:

- *Bay Clubs.* The Bay Clubs (formerly Western Athletic Clubs) operates 11 premium and luxury multipurpose clubs throughout California..
- *David Lloyd Leisure Clubs.* David Lloyd operates 89 clubs throughout Europe, most of which are large-scale multipurpose clubs, with gyms, spas, racquet courts, and pools.

Fitness area view rendering, U.S.

> Lifetime Fitness is the biggest operator of large multipurpose clubs in the U.S.

- *Lifetime Fitness.* Lifetime Fitness is the biggest operator of large multipurpose clubs in the U.S., with over 110 properties. The typical Lifetime Fitness facility ranges in size from 110,000 to 120,000 square feet.
- *Companhia Athletica.* Companhia Athletica operates 13 premium multipurpose clubs in Sao Paulo, Brazil, most of which are over 40,000 square feet.

Several sub-categories of multipurpose clubs exist, including racquet courts only, pools only, gymnasiums only, clubs with tennis courts, and clubs with a blend of each type of activity area. The majority of multipurpose clubs have fitness facilities, racquet courts, gymnasiums (sometimes referred to as sport courts), pools, and in some instances, tennis courts. Some multipurpose facilities also have outdoor facilities, such as outdoor pools, ball fields, and even team-building venues. The largest multipurpose clubs tend to be those with tennis facilities, gymnasiums, and outdoor facilities.

Multipurpose facilities are typically located in suburban settings, due to their space demands and the lower cost of land. Since late 2010, 24 Hour Fitness has established a standardized multipurpose club model of 45,000 square feet, which closely approximates the size of a standard LA Fitness facility, a company that has suburban multipurpose clubs that tend to range in size from 45,000 to 65,000 square feet.

The Various Spaces Found Within a Health/Fitness Facility

This section presents a brief overview of the most common spaces found in health/fitness clubs (fitness-only and multipurpose). A description is provided of each area's function, space requirements, and any critical design or construction requirements. For ease and clarity of understanding, the discussion of the areas is separated into physical-activity areas and service areas.

Primary Physical-Activity Areas

- ❏ *Aquatic Areas.* The aquatic areas of a facility can serve multiple functions, ranging from lap swimming and exercise classes to full-scale aquatic entertainment and recreation centers. A number of aquatic spaces are commonly found in clubs, including lap pools, therapy pools, and recreational pools:
  - *Lap/fitness pools (47 percent of settings offer).* These pools are designed primarily for individuals who want to pursue fitness swimming, commonly referred to as lap swimming, but can also be used for other activities, such as water-exercise classes and swim lessons. The typical lap pool in clubs will be 25 yards long (75 feet) and 15 yards wide (45 feet and six lanes) and will be four to five feet deep at its deepest. Lap pools that are going to be used for swim meets must have both a depth of at least seven feet at one end of the pool to accommodate surface diving and lane widths of seven feet (2.15 m). In fact, many of the lap pools that were built before 1980 have depths of 10 to 12 feet and can be used for board diving. The current trend among many of the lower priced multipurpose clubs is to build lap pools between 60 and 75 feet in length and provide only three

Aquatic zone rendering, World Class Zhukovka, Moscow, Russia

or four lanes for lap swimming. The larger multipurpose clubs often install regulation short-course competitive pools in their facilities that are either 25 m (international) or 25 yards (domestic) in length and have eight lanes of 2.15 m (7 feet) width. Most lap pools are built with gunite or stainless steel, though fiberglass structures also exist. The surface of these pools is plaster, stainless steel, or tile. Most clubs keep the water temperature in their pools between 78 degrees and 86 degrees Fahrenheit. Starting in 2013, pools that have over 300 linear feet of edge were required to provide two ADA accessible entries to the pool.

- *Therapy pools.* Therapy pools are designed primarily for group classes and therapeutic exercise. These pools may be as small as 20 feet wide by 20 feet long or as large as 40 feet wide by 60 feet long. The average size of therapy pools in the club industry is approximately 1,500 square feet. With a depth that typically ranges from 2.5 to 5 feet, these pools are designed to be handicap accessible. The materials used to construct these pools are similar to those employed with lap pools. The water temperature in most therapy pools is kept between 86 degrees and 92 degrees Fahrenheit.
- *Recreational pools or aquatic parks.* Recreational pools are the newest trend for indoor multipurpose facilities. These pools are designed to accommodate various types of recreational activities (wading, swimming, sliding, splashing, etc.). The most common features of recreational pools are zero-depth entry (sloping from deck level to the desired depth), water slides, wave features, splash pads (sprays, fountains, and similar), lazy-river features, and non-traditional shapes. These pools can have two to three times the area of a typical lap pool. Lifetime Fitness offers both indoor and outdoor recreational pools in many of its facilities, each of which is composed of areas for water slides, splash pads, and general recreational aquatic activity. In fact, a few clubs in the industry have recreational pools that occupy as much as 5,000 square feet of pool surface area and an additional 5,000 square feet of deck surface. Most of these pools have

starting depths of zero feet and normally go no deeper than four feet, unless the pool has water slides, in which case, additional depth levels are usually required by local codes. The water temperature in most recreational pools is kept between 82 degrees and 86 degrees Fahrenheit.

Many of the newer multipurpose facilities, such as those of Lifetime Fitness, headquartered in Minnesota, or some more established multipurpose facilities such as the Atlantic Coast Athletic Clubs in the Mid-Atlantic region, have aquatic environments that include two or more of these aquatic spaces. For additional information on the types of pools offered in the industry, refer to Chapter 27, which has a section dedicated entirely to aquatics.

❑ *Fitness Areas (called Gym Areas in Europe).* The fitness areas in most clubs include four primary zones to house the fitness and exercise equipment of the club. The typical gym space may range in size from 1,500 square feet (e.g., Anytime Fitness, Snap, etc.) to over 10,000 square feet (e.g., Eastbank Club, Lifetime Fitness, etc.) and include as many as 400 to 500 pieces of equipment. As a rule, these spaces involve the cardiovascular zone, the resistance-circuit zone, the free-weight zone, functional training zone, and the stretching zone:

Fitness floor, Megatlon, Buenos Aires, Argentina

- *Cardiovascular zone.* The cardiovascular area houses the club's cardiovascular equipment, including treadmills, elliptical machines, mechanical stair climbers, and stationary bicycles. Cardiovascular areas normally allocate between 40 and 50 square feet of space per piece of exercise equipment (the typical manufacturer space recommendation for a piece of equipment). On average, the club's cardiovascular area occupies between 1,000 and 5,000 square feet, depending upon the size of the fitness area. These areas are typically located in relatively open spaces, with indirect fluorescent lighting and durable floor surfaces. Usually, the floor surface in this area is either carpet or rubber (e.g., Everlast, Mondo, or Softpave). In Europe, many clubs have wood flooring in the cardiovascular area. Many of the clubs provide an entertainment system as part of their cardiovascular area, such as the systems manufactured by Broadcast Vision or Cardio Theater. One of the newest industry trends in this regard is to provide individual viewing screens for each piece of cardiovascular equipment, a practice that all manufacturers currently follow. As a rule, the club's cardiovascular areas require sufficient airflow (measured in cubic feet a minute—CFMs) to maintain a temperature range of 68 to 72 degrees Fahrenheit and a relative humidity level of under 50 percent, based on the expected head load.

- *Resistance-circuit zone.* The resistance-circuit area in a club normally holds the selectorized-resistance machines, such as those manufactured by companies such as Cybex, Free Motion, Life Fitness, Matrix, Precor, Technogym, Keiser, and Hoist. As a rule, these areas allocate between 40 and 60 square feet of space per machine, based on the manufacturer's requirements. The average health/fitness club has one or two resistance circuits, each of which has 10 to 12 machines per circuit and occupies approximately 600 to 800 square feet per circuit. It is a common practice in the industry for a club to have one circuit dedicated to those members who wish to follow a dedicated circuit and another circuit that is devoted to the serious weight-training members. Some of the larger clubs, such as the Gainesville Health and Fitness Center, located in Gainesville, Florida, and Lifetime Fitness, provide several circuits of resistance equipment.

  Most resistance-training areas are commonly located in wide-open spaces, with a rubberized floor surface. A few club operators use carpet or wood, instead of a rubber surface. Most of the newer facilities also provide some form of audiovisual entertainment in this area. Most resistance circuit areas also have at least one wall with mirrors so that members can check on their posture and mechanics while exercising. These areas require sufficient air circulation (CFMs) to maintain a temperature range of 68 to 72 degrees and a relative humidity level of under 50 percent.

- *Free-weight zone.* This area of the club houses the free weights and the plate-loaded weight machines. The free-weight area is similar to the resistance-circuit area, in that it requires 40 to 60 square feet per piece of equipment and a rubber floor surface. The size of this area varies from club to club, depending upon the amount of equipment provided. Some clubs only devote a few hundred square feet to this area, while others allocate over 5,000 square feet of space to it (e.g., LA Fitness, Red's, East Bank Club, etc.). It is a common industry practice for the free-weight areas to have one or more mirrored walls so that members can monitor their mechanics and posture while training. These areas require sufficient CFMs to maintain a temperature range of 68 to 72 degrees and a relative humidity level of under 50 percent.

- *Functional training zone (46 percent offer according to 2016 fitness trend survey conducted by ClubIntel).* Starting around 2010, functional training zones emerged as one of the most important training areas in fitness centers, in particular among boutique fitness studios. The functional training

> One of the newest industry trends is to provide individual viewing screens for each piece of cardiovascular equipment, a practice that all manufacturers currently follow.

zone serves as the focal point for conducting boot camp, cross-training, and functional training activities. The typical functional training zone ranges from 400 to 2,000 square feet, but in some clubs, such as the Eastbank Club in Chicago and Red's in Lafayette, Louisiana, the space dedicated to functional training can exceed 5,000 square feet. These functional training areas typically are open spaces with rubber floor surfaces that house equipment such as kettlebells, medicine balls, suspension training apparatus, plyometric benches, balance boards, stability balls, and related training accessories. Like the other training areas, the functional zones require indirect lighting and sufficient CFMs to maintain a temperature range of 68 to 72 degrees and a relative humidity level of under 50 percent.

- *Stretching area (46 percent offer according to 2016 fitness trend study conducted by ClubIntel).* Over the past decade, a number of clubs have made stretching areas an integral part of their physical-activity space. While no specific design parameters currently exist for stretching areas, it is a common practice for facilities to allocate between 200 and 800 square feet to these areas. The stretching area is usually a quiet area that utilizes exercise mats for a floor surface. Some more progressive clubs actually build stretching platforms with privacy walls. The temperature for this area is normally the same as for the other fitness spaces, although in an ideal environment, it should be slightly warmer to facilitate the dynamics of stretching.

A recent trend in the design of fitness areas involves the creation of specific zones, separated by low walls or other partitions, so that instead of massing all the equipment together, facility operators can offer smaller, less intimidating zones that include no more than 12 to 15 pieces of equipment. Life Fitness, a leading manufacturer of exercise equipment, has developed what it calls the Journey system, which is a concept that provides club operators with a custom-designed floor plan that separates a gym floor into distinct zones of equipment, that are often based either on the equipment in the zone or the interests of the members.

❑ *Group-Exercise Studios (82 percent of clubs offer according to 2015 IHRSA data).* The group-exercise area is a space designed to provide a suitable environment for offering group-exercise and fitness activities (note: these areas were formerly called aerobic-exercise studios). The group-exercise space in a club can be as small as one multipurpose studio or as extensive as four or five studios with dedicated functions. The most common group-exercise studio spaces are multipurpose, group cycling, Pilates, and yoga:

- *Multipurpose studio.* The multipurpose studio provides space to offer the majority of group-exercise activities, such as step classes, sculpt classes, resistance classes, stretch classes, yoga, and group cycling. Because such studios serve multiple activities, their design must accommodate the variety of activities performed in the allotted space. As a rule of thumb, these studios should allocate between 40 and 60 square feet of space per user, with an average of 50 square feet per user being the norm. Some high-volume facilities allocate as few as 20 square feet per member. Typically, multipurpose studios in clubs range in size from 1,000 to 4,000 square feet. These rooms most commonly have a cushioned wood floor (i.e., a floor with a shock-absorbing sub-layer, plywood underlayment, and solid wood surface). Two of the leading manufacturers of these floors are Conner Flooring and Robbins Sports Surfaces.

Another typical requirement for a multipurpose studio is to have mirrors on at least two adjacent walls. The multipurpose studio should also have its own thermostat to control airflow and temperature, with the temperature range during class set between 68 and 72 degrees and a relative humidity of less than 50 percent. When these classes are not in session, these rooms may seem cold. The multipurpose room should also have lighting as standard equipment that can be adjusted to different levels, depending upon the needs of the class.

- *Group-cycling studio (45 percent offer according to 2016 trend survey conducted by ClubIntel)).* The group-cycling studio is designed for the specific demands of group cycling. As a rule, this room requires 20 to 50 square feet per cycle, although some clubs offer far less space. The ideal floor surface for this studio is either wood or rubber, with rubber floors being the most common. Some clubs carpet the area, but this practice is not recommended because of the high level of perspiration that is generated in these studios. These studios should have at least one wall with a mirror, normally the wall behind the instructor. These studios should also have adjustable lighting as well, since many instructors like to vary the lighting levels to establish certain mood states during class. With the advent of free-standing cycling studios such as SoulCycle and Flywheel, many clubs—particularly larger fitness-only and multipurpose facilities—have begun to theme their group-exercise studios in an effort to establish a unique environmental experience. The group cycling studio should have its own thermostat to control airflow and temperature, with the temperature range during class set between 68 and 72 degrees (some studios actually set the temperature lower to accommodate the high heat load generated when classes are packed) and a relative humidity of less than 50 percent. When classes are not in session, these rooms frequently feel cold. The industry trend in the past few years has been to combine the group-cycling studio with the multipurpose studio, rather than devoting a separate space to this activity.

Group exercise studio, Lakeshore Athletic Club, Broomfield, CO

- *Pilates studio.* The Pilates studio, a relatively new addition to the group-exercise area of most clubs, should be designed to accommodate the unique requirements of group and private Pilates training. This room requires approximately 60 to 80 square feet per user, primarily due to the equipment that is used. These rooms may have a wood, rubber, cork, or even carpeted floor surface. Instructors like to have a studio with at least two mirrored walls. Like the other group-exercise studios, this room requires adjustable lighting and a separate thermostat for temperature control. The Pilates room normally has a higher temperature range than either the group cycling or the multipurpose studio. As a rule, most Pilates exercisers prefer to work out in rooms in which the temperature is over 70 degrees. Normally, the temperature is set in most Pilates studios between 72 and 76 degrees Fahrenheit.

Pilates room, Buenos Aires, Argentina

- *Yoga studio (42 percent offer according to 2016 trend survey by ClubIntel).* Yoga, according to research conducted by IHRSA in 2015, is the most popular form of group exercise in the club industry. In some clubs, yoga comprises over 50 percent of all class offerings. Because of the unusual space demands of yoga, a separate studio is often required. Many of the newest club facilities in the industry have established standard yoga studios. The yoga studio requires between 50 and 75 square feet per user. The floor surface for the yoga studio can be wood, rubber, or carpet, with wood floors being the most common. Regardless of what material is used for the floor of the yoga studio, the surface must be firm and level to accommodate the postures and movements of yoga. Like the other studios, at least one wall should be mirrored. Many of the newer studios also offer a yoga wall, which accommodates special props such as anchors, straps, and ropes that are used in the practice of Iyengar-style yoga, while others go as far as providing special ceiling anchors and cloth hammocks for the performance of anti-gravity or aerial-style yoga. Yoga studios require adjustable lighting. The yoga room normally has a higher temperature range than the other studios, with most users preferring temperatures over 70 degrees. Typically, the temperature in most yoga studios is somewhere between 72 and 85 degrees Fahrenheit. The practitioners of Bikram-style yoga or one of its spinoffs, such as hot yoga, often turn the temperature in the studio between 85 and 105 degrees Fahrenheit (note: all factors considered, this is not a healthy environment for exercise), thereby requiring special insulation and heating elements be incorporated into the design of the space.

Yoga and barre studio, Exhale, New York, NY

❑ *Racquet Courts.* Racquet courts are as varied in their design and function as are the games that are played on them. The types of racquet courts that are most frequently found in health/fitness clubs are racquetball courts, squash courts, and tennis courts. In addition to these court areas, some clubs also have some of the less-commonly used court areas, such as court tennis, paddle tennis, badminton, and platform tennis.

• *Racquetball courts (41 percent of clubs offer according to 2015 IHRSA data).* In the past two decades, racquetball has been far less popular than it was when it achieved its pinnacle of participation in the 1970s and early 1980s. A racquetball court is typically used for racquetball, although it can also be utilized for activities such as handball and walleyball. A regulation racquetball court is 20 feet wide by 40 feet long (800 square feet) and 20 feet high.

Racquetball courts usually have a suspended wood floor and walls composed of panels of a compressed wood material, unlike the courts that were built in the early days of the sport's infancy, which were often constructed with plaster walls or wood-panel walls. The typical racquetball court floor should be refinished on a regular basis. Most racquetball courts have a back wall that is composed of glass, although some clubs have courts that are fully enclosed by compressed panels or plaster, with only a rear door providing visibility within. Racquetball courts require separate air circulation control due to the volume of the space and the temperature and humidity requirements for that space. Under normal conditions, the court temperature should be between 60 and 68 degrees Fahrenheit. One common mistake that is often made in the construction of racquetball courts is failing to allow the wood-floor materials to acclimate to the indoor environment before laying them (e.g., a 7- to 10-day acclimation period is recommended). The lighting of a racquetball court should allow for at least 40 to 50 foot candles at floor level.

- *Squash courts (20 percent of clubs offer according to IHRSA 2015 data).* Over the past 10 to 15 years, squash has grown in popularity to the point it has overtaken racquetball as an indoor racquet activity in many clubs. Squash courts originally could be grouped into two categories—North American courts and International courts. The North American courts were the primary playing surface in the United States, while the International courts were the primary playing surface throughout the rest of the world. Since the early 1990s, the International game has been adopted as the accepted version of squash. As a result, the North American courts are no longer built.

    The World Squash Federation (WSF) has established that an International singles court be 21 feet wide by 32 feet long (672 square feet), with a ceiling height of 20 feet. The International doubles court is slightly larger with dimensions of 25 feet wide by 32 feet long (in some instances the WSF allows the doubles court to be 27.6 feet wide). The court surface in an International court is unfinished hardwood. The walls and ceilings can be a compressed-wood panel system, plaster, wood, or a sand-filled, panel wall system. At the present time, most courts developed in recent years employ the compressed-wood panel system, although the sand-filled panel system is the surface of choice for serious squash players. Squash courts are similar to racquetball courts in their lighting and air circulation requirements. In that regard, they ideal temperature range is 59 to 68 degrees and lighting levels of at least 40-foot candles.

    While the International court is the preferred court area for squash, many clubs still have either North American courts or converted racquetball courts as their squash-court area. The North American court, which is 18.5 feet wide and 32 feet long, requires a completely different game and ball and offers a somewhat less-than-satisfactory-playing space for the game of squash.

- *Tennis courts (12 percent of clubs offer indoor courts and 15 percent outdoor courts according to IHRSA 2015 data).* Tennis is the most popular court sport in the U.S., with over 23 million participants. Tennis is somewhat different than the other racquet-court games, because it offers players multiple playing surface options, as well as variable playing environments—ranging from outdoors to indoor-climate controlled to somewhere in between. A regulation tennis court requires a total square footage of 7,200 square feet, with the court area being 120 feet long by 60 feet wide. The actual court area (where the ball is in play) is 36 feet wide (doubles area) and 78 feet long, with a court surface that extends 12 feet to either side of the playing area and 21 feet to either end of the playing surface (note: a singles court is only 27 feet wide). If the playing area is an indoor court, it requires a ceiling height of at least 24 feet, and preferably 38 feet high.

Chapter Twenty-One

Health/Fitness Facilities

Clay tennis courts, Vilas Club, Buenos Aires, Argentina

A tennis court surface can be grass, clay, or hard-court. Grass is predominately an outdoor playing surface and is not very common in North America. Grass surfaces require considerable care and produce a relatively faster game of tennis. Clay is also a predominately outdoor playing surface, although it can be used on indoor courts. The Mayfair Racquet and Fitness Clubs in Toronto, Canada, for example, have indoor clay surfaces. A clay surface can be red clay or green clay. The brand name of the most common type of clay is Har Tru. Clay courts require constant care, including watering, raking, taping, and resurfacing. Clay courts offer an outstanding playing surface for older adults because they tend to place less physical strain on the player's joints and slow the game down. Hard courts are the most common playing surface in the United States and is best suited for outdoor courts. Hard courts can be either blacktop or a synthetic surface that has been laid over a concrete foundation, which is the most common type of hard court. Tennis courts can also have surfaces that use either carpet or artificial turf. In reality, neither material is utilized as a court surface, as a rule, in North America, although many indoor courts in Europe (primarily in England) employ such coverings. The ideal lighting environment for tennis is to provide at least 50 foot-candles of light at the net surface (for competitive play, 75 to 100 foot-candles are preferred), using one of the following light sources: metal halide, halogen, or even fluorescent. If the courts are located in a climate-controlled environment (i.e., heating and cooling provided), then the air temperature of the courts should be maintained between 52 and 62 degrees Fahrenheit.

- *Gymnasiums/Sport Courts (17 percent of clubs offer according to IHRSA 2015 data).* The gymnasium is a multipurpose area in which a host of recreational sports can be conducted. The most common activities offered in the gymnasium are basketball, volleyball, badminton, group-exercise classes, and youth-oriented activities. Depending upon the club and the market in which it is located, a variety of less common activities can also be programmed in the gymnasium, including such activities as roller hockey, roller skating, and indoor soccer. Since the primary function of a gymnasium is normally for basketball, most facilities design and build their gymnasiums to accommodate the space requirements of basketball, which has parameters that are more than sufficient for activities, such as volleyball and badminton.

The standard practice for clubs that desire to offer a full array of activities in the gymnasium is to build the space in accordance with the American collegiate-sized court, which is 94 feet long and 50 feet wide, with a recommended 10-foot perimeter around the playing area of the court (7,980 square feet). Another option is to build the gymnasium to North American high-school dimensions, which are 84 feet long by 50 feet wide, with a 10-foot perimeter around the playing area of the court (7,280 square feet). On the other hand, because of the aforementioned relatively large space requirements, some clubs develop courts that are comparatively smaller, usually 60 feet long by 40 feet wide, with a minimum perimeter distance of three feet (3,036 square feet). These smaller courts are primarily used for basketball and volleyball.

The gymnasium typically has a suspended wood floor that is comprised of a cushioned or suspended sub-floor structure, with a hardwood floor surface (maple, beech, etc.). Clubs also have the option of installing a rubber-floor surface on the floor of the gymnasium court, which is less expensive than wood-floor systems.

When a gymnasium is built, the standard practice is to mark the floor surface for basketball and volleyball, and sometimes for badminton. Most gymnasiums have six basketball hoops, so that games can be played either full-court or half-court. The recommended lighting levels in the basketball area are similar to indoor tennis courts, with somewhere in the neighborhood of 40 to 50 foot-candles at the floor surface.

Service Areas

While the main spaces found in health/fitness clubs are physical-activity areas, service areas are also essential. Service areas are those physical spaces that are used by members for non-physical activity. It is critical that a club provides an appropriate number, as well as a mix, of service areas. The most common types of service spaces in a club are locker rooms, child-care areas, day spa/massage areas, and reception-and-greeting areas.

❏ *Locker Rooms.* The most heavily used area in most facilities, locker rooms, are provided in the vast majority of health/fitness clubs (many boutiques, budget clubs, and express clubs do not offer locker rooms). It is estimated that on average, members may spend as much as 25 to 50 percent of their time in the locker rooms. Locker rooms can serve several purposes, including providing an area for members to relax, network, and change their clothes before and after working out. Most clubs offer lockers, wet areas, rest-room facilities and relaxation amenities in this area.

- *Lockers.* In the health/fitness club industry, three distinct approaches exist concerning providing locker facilities. Some clubs have day-use lockers that members can access at no charge; others offer lockers that can only be rented, and finally, some clubs offer a blend of both alternatives. The most common scenario for a club is to provide day-use lockers. The most desirable feature of this practice involves the fact that the club only needs to provide a sufficient number of lockers to accommodate the expected number of users expected to use the facility during any given time period. For example, a club might have 4,000 members, and might expect that approximately 1,000 members a day (25 percent of its membership) will utilize the facility. In all likelihood, no more than 10 percent of the membership will be present in the club during any given two-hour time period. In other words, because no more than 400 members would need lockers, the club would only require 400 day-use lockers in the facility. Most economy clubs and middle-market clubs prefer this approach. Clubs operated by companies, such as 24 Hour Fitness, LA Fitness, and Town Sports International leverage this approach for providing lockers. In some of the budget clubs (e.g., Planet Fitness, Blink, and Crunch), the locker rooms afford far fewer lockers, since the majority of their members come already attired to work out.

    Renting lockers is a practice that higher-priced clubs (i.e., premium and luxury clubs), serving a more affluent member base, employ. These clubs build lockers and offer members the opportunity to rent the lockers on a monthly, semi-annual, or annual basis. As a rule, this scenario involves having the club provide enough lockers to accommodate at least 70 percent of the expected membership. For example, if the club has 2,000 members, it needs to provide approximately 1,400 lockers. The Houstonian in Houston, Texas; Bay Clubs in California; and the ClubCorp sports clubs are examples of health/fitness companies that utilize this particular approach to providing lockers. On the other hand, some facilities offer both day-use locker areas and rentable locker areas. The recent trend is to create "executive-locker areas," which are separate areas in the club with full-size rentable lockers (e.g., Eastbank Club, Chicago and Bay Clubs, California).

    The actual lockers are offered in a variety of sizes. The most common size for day-use lockers is 36 to 42 inches tall, 12 to 15 inches wide, and 20 inches deep, while the size of rentable lockers can vary from simple 12 inches by 12 inches by 20 inches locker spaces to full-size 72 inches by 15 inches by 21 inches lockers. The dimensions of lockers are influenced by cost, the space available, and the type of market being served. Most lockers are composed of solid wood, wood laminate, or a polyvinyl material.

    The final element of the locker puzzle is the actual locking mechanism. A variety of options exist. For day-use lockers, the primary options include keyed locks, card/coin locks, digital keypad locks, and digital locks that use an imbedded chip. Those clubs that rent lockers tend to go for combination locks or digital keypad locks, with the newest approach involving locks that are controlled by computer chips and exist on a network, such as those produced by Gantner Technologies

A recent trend is to create "executive-locker areas," which are separate areas in the club with full-size rentable lockers.

Wet wellness area rendering

- *Wet areas.* The wet areas encompass both the showers and the wet-amenity spaces, such as the sauna, the steam room, whirlpools, and cold plunge. The number of showers that a club needs depends on the number of users that it expects to have. Some clubs have as few as one or two showers per locker room (e.g., budget clubs), while other clubs have several dozen per locker room. While no standard quantitative measure exists for determining the number of showers that a club should have, a basic guideline is to provide one shower in each locker room for every 250 to 500 members of the facility. For example, if a club has 2,000 members, it should have at least four to eight showers per locker room. The typical shower is at least nine square feet and is constructed with a surface of tile or other solid material (e.g., granite, stone).

  The amenities normally offered in the wet area include a sauna (69 percent of clubs offer), a steam room (50 percent of clubs offer), and whirlpools (56 percent of clubs offer). The sauna is the most favored feature because of its popularity among both men and women and its relatively low installation cost. The typical sauna occupies approximately 80 to 150 square feet and is constructed of wood. Two recent trends involve the introduction of infrared saunas and wet saunas that are a blend of sauna and steam. A steam room, on the other hand, is more popular among men than women. A standard steam room takes up between 100 and 200 square feet and is built similar to a shower. The whirlpool requires considerable space and dollars to install, which are the primary reasons for whirlpools not being located in more clubs. As a rule, whirlpools are constructed of fiberglass, stainless steel, or concrete. A few clubs, such as Stonecreek Club and Spa in Covington, Louisiana also offer a cold plunge. The preferred temperature range is 40 degrees to 46 degrees Fahrenheit, though in the U.S. the preferred temperature range is 50 to 55 degrees Fahrenheit.

It is important to note that both men and women prefer the aforementioned wet amenities only in their own locker rooms, although a number of international clubs (e.g., Germany, England) offer these amenities in a common wet area. Industry-compiled data from the U.S. indicate that individuals do not like or use coed wet-amenity spaces very often. In some international clubs, wet areas will also integrate unique water-therapy amenities, such as Turkish baths, snow rooms, and stone therapy pools.

- *Relaxation areas.* A number of health/fitness facilities include relaxation areas as part of their locker-room offerings. Among the more popular relaxation areas are lounges, nap rooms, and massage rooms. Lounges are usually found in locker rooms that provide rental lockers, because they serve as an area in which members can relax before heading out. Nap rooms exist in many of the higher-end club facilities that cater to an affluent member demographic. Massage rooms are the most common relaxation-area amenity, since most clubs do not have separate spa facilities.

- *Restroom facilities.* Every locker room has restroom facilities. As a rule, the quantity of restrooms in a particular area or club is normally determined by the existing building codes and the occupancy levels expected in the space.

❑ *Child-Care and Children's-Service Areas (21 percent of clubs offer a children's-only section according to IHRSA 2015 data).* Traditionally, facilities that offered nurseries and dedicated children's centers were not the norm. At the present time, however, such spaces are becoming an integral part of many clubs. A nursery is an area that is dedicated space for providing basic children sitting or care—not licensed day care. In most states, specific guidelines exist for these spaces. In that regard, two of the most common regulatory stipulations are children cannot be left in these areas for more than a couple of hours and their parents/guardians must be on the club's premises. These rooms may be as small as 100 square feet or as large as 15,000 square feet (e.g., Lifetime Fitness). In most instances, these spaces include a small area for cribs and playpens, an area for games and activities, and an area for television. In some clubs, these spaces are separated by age group in an effort to provide dedicated space to specific age categories.

A dedicated children's area is a space in which services and activities (beyond simply offering nursery services) are provided, such as arts and crafts, recreational games, nap-and-rest areas, and even birthday parties. The Bay Club in Redwood City, CA, for example, has over 10,000 square feet in its children's area, including a small gymnasium, an arts and crafts area, a game area, and a nursery area. Lifetime Fitness offers approximately 15,000 square feet in many of its clubs specifically for a children's area. The Belair Athletic Club, in Belair, Maryland, operated by Wellbridge of Denver, Colorado, has a separate building just for children's services, while the Boston Sports Club in Wellesley, Massachusetts has a dedicated children's area of over 5,000 square feet. In all of these facilities the focus is on providing a space that is safe for young people. As a rule, these spaces typically have rubber flooring, no edges, no mirrors, and no breakable materials that could otherwise harm a child. Finally, most state laws require a separate children's restroom that is handicap accessible.

> Massage has grown increasingly popular over the past decade, as have day spas, in the health/fitness club environment.

- ❏ *Spa and Massage Facilities (10 percent of clubs offer spa facilities according to 2015 IHRSA data).* Massage has grown increasingly popular over the past decade, as have day spas, in the health/fitness club environment. The space allocated to either massage or spa services ranges drastically in the health/fitness club industry. Some clubs offer one room for massage, while other clubs, such as the Houstonian in Houston, Texas or the Village Health Club and Spa at Gainey Ranch, which is operated by DMB Sports in Phoenix, Arizona, offer full-blown spas that encompass in the neighborhood of 15,000 square feet. Many of the larger premium and luxury club chains, such as Lifetime Fitness (e.g., LifeSpa) and the Bay Clubs, offer a branded spa facility in each of their clubs. The most common spaces in a day spa include:
  - *Massage rooms.* The standard massage room is at least 90 square feet, preferably 100 to 120 square feet. A massage room will normally have a wood floor or other floor surface that is both attractive and easily cleaned (a carpet is not a good choice). These rooms typically have indirect lighting on dimmer switches to control the light levels and are constructed with soundproofing to reduce noise from entering the room. As a rule, most massage rooms also have both a sink and a storage space.
  - *Facial rooms.* Typically, the facial room (a room for providing facial and basic skin care services) shares space with the massage room, since both involve the same basic design and construction. Facial rooms can often be as large as 150 square feet in order to accommodate the space required for a separate shower.
  - *Wet-treatment rooms.* Wet-treatment rooms are areas that are normally used for body scrubs and body wraps. As such, these activities involve considerable moisture. The room should be at least 150 square feet, have floors and walls that are impervious to water, and have a shower and sink. On occasion, these rooms are utilized for Vichy showers, hydrotherapy treatments, and related water treatments, all of which require additional plumbing.
  - *Pedicure space.* The typical pedicure space requires an operational area of between 50 and 60 square feet. This area should have a floor that is impervious to water (e.g., be constructed of tile or a similar material) and have drainage that accommodates the small footbaths that commonly are a part of the newest pedicure stations.
  - *Manicure space.* The manicure space requires an operational area of between 40 and 50 square feet. This space should be open, rather than enclosed to promote the social element of the experience. Preferably, the floors of this room should be either wood or another hard surface that is easily cleaned.

  In addition to the aforementioned facility spaces in a spa area, the spa facilities in many clubs also include a relaxation area that allows customers to sit and relax before and after receiving a treatment. In fact, many of the larger spas also offer reception areas and have separate relaxation areas for men and women. Ideally, a club-based day spa should be designed to be between 1,400 and 2,000 square feet—collectively, a space that would accommodate a relaxation area, four to eight treatment rooms, two to three manicure and pedicure stations, and a small retail area. For additional insights on club-based spas, refer to Chapter 25.

Chapter Twenty-One

Health/Fitness Facilities

Lobby, Pfitzenmeier Sport & Wellness, Schwetzingen, Germany

- *Reception-and-Greeting Areas.* The reception-and-greeting area is one of the most important spaces in the club. This area is the first internal space in the club that members see when they arrive and the last space that they see when they leave. Accordingly, this space should be designed and constructed to provide a positive impression and to facilitate the immediate needs of the members and guests who are entering and leaving the facility. In most clubs, the reception area (i.e., the front-desk area) serves as the entry point for the club and is designed to accommodate such essential functions as security, member greeting, appointment scheduling, phone answering, and information dissemination. Some larger clubs often have a separate area that is dedicated to scheduling appointments and answering the phones. The reception area normally occupies 400 to 2,000 square feet and includes a desk and a small lounge space. As a rule, this area often has some of the most aesthetically pleasing features in the club, including stone or wood floors, wood or solid surface desks, and attractive low lighting.

- *Other Facility Areas.* Besides activity and service areas, most clubs also have operational spaces that are used to support the operational and administrative functions of the business. Examples of such spaces include offices for the key staff, the laundry room, and storage area(s). In most clubs, the amount of space allocated to offices is 80 to 100 square feet per office, with the typical facility providing offices for accounting, membership sales, the manager of a club, and the key department heads. In most facilities, the total space that is allocated to offices does not exceed 1,000 to 1,500 square feet. The typical laundry (two washers, two dryers, and circulation space) ranges in size from 150 to 250 square feet. Storage space is often the area that receives the least amount of attention in the design phase of developing the club, and yet is the most needed area when the facility finally opens. Since the typical club design allocates 10 to 15 percent of the facility's total space to circulation, at least 25 percent of that area should be allocated to storage.

The Design and Construction Process

Whether the endeavor involves building a new health/fitness facility, expanding an existing facility, or just renovating some space, it is important to understand the basics of the design and construction process. Understanding this process can help club owners/operators avoid many of the pitfalls and expenses that often occur during these processes.

❑ *The Design Process.* The design process occurs in several stages, which if carried out in their proper sequence, will help ensure that the facility is properly designed. One of the first steps that every club operator should take is to hire a licensed architect to design any facility additions, expansions, or renovations. In most cases, an architectural firm will charge a fee, ranging from as low as six percent to as high as 12 percent of the total construction costs for the design work. The average rate is seven to nine percent. With small jobs, some architectural firms will charge their clients a higher rate than normal, simply because certain services are required on all jobs. It is recommended that owners enter into one of the standard agreement forms between an architect and owner, as provided by the Architectural Institute of America (AIA). As a rule, the design process involves several phases, including:

- *Programming phase.* The programming phase is primarily an internal process in which the club team identifies its specific program and activity needs for the spaces they want in the facility. Most architects will ask to meet with the team and conduct a review of the club's program plan so that they have a clear understanding of what the team believes is needed in the space that will be designed. This phase is usually part of the schematic-design phase for most architects. The key for the club team is to be as specific as possible concerning what their needs will be with regard to facility space.
- *Schematic-design phase.* This phase of the design process involves the architect taking the programming information and combining it with the field work of the architect that has been undertaken to that point to identify a preliminary floor plan and "appearance" for the facility space. During this phase, the architect normally takes pictures of existing spaces, performs field measurements, asks for existing plans, and meets with local authorities about special regulations and zoning issues. The architect uses this information to prepare a preliminary floor plan and some sections (vertical representations) of the design that are then shared with the club team. This process normally can take from two to six weeks, depending upon the size of the project. The cost for this phase normally ranges from 10 to15 percent of the overall architectural fee.
- *Design-development stage.* During this stage, the architect, using feedback from the club team on the schematic design, prepares a more complete set of plans. During this phase, the architect utilizes the services of structural,

electrical, and mechanical engineers, as well as those of soil engineers and surveyors, if needed. The goal of this stage is to provide the owner with a set of plans that offers substantial detail on each space, including the basic electrical, plumbing, mechanical, and structural work. During this stage, the architect also provides the owner with additional details on the space dimensions and elevations of the facility. Upon the completion of this stage, it is essential that the club owner/operator reviews the plans and provides input. Once this stage has been concluded, many architects then obtain initial cost estimates for the work that is to be performed so that they can get an initial estimate of the approximate cost of the planned project. The cost of this phase can range from 15 to 25 percent of the overall architectural fee.

- *Construction-document stage.* During this stage, the architect takes the design development plans and the feedback that has been received from the club and local authorities to prepare a full set of construction documents. Most top architectural firms usually meet at least once during this phase with the owner to give the club owner an additional opportunity to review the plans, which are usually at 90 percent of completion at that point. During this phase, the architect completes a full set of construction documents, which contain details on all aspects of the project. The architect also works closely with the local authorities at this point in the process to address all use and permit requirements so that finished plans can be submitted for building permits. At the completion of this stage, the architect and club owner normally meet one final time to make sure all plans are correct. At the end of this stage, the architect, at the owner's direction, then forwards the design plans to at least three general contractors for bidding documents. The bidding process normally takes approximately 30 to 45 days to complete, at which time, the owner should receive three cost estimates (bids) from the general contractors. The cost for this phase is the balance of the architectural fees already paid subtracted from 85 percent of the total estimated design cost.

- *Construction-administration stage.* This phase includes the architect's involvement in the bidding process and the selection of the general contractor (which is typically undertaken with the club owner), as well as the architect's efforts during the construction process. During construction, the architect reviews and approves all general contractor submittals for work, approves all changes recommended by the contractor, reviews pay applications, and checks the progress of work through inspections at each phase of construction. Subsequently, in concert with the owner, the architect completes the final punch list and approves the final conditions of the construction. The cost for this phase of services is normally 15 percent of the overall design work.

❑ *The Construction Process.* The construction process begins once a general contractor has been selected and hired. The selection of the contractor should be based on several factors, including bid price, references, and experience with similar projects. It is important to note that accepting the lowest contractor's bid does not always lead to the best work or even the

> The construction process begins once a general contractor has been selected and hired. The selection of the contractor should be based on several factors, including bid price, references, and experience with similar projects.

lowest price once the project has been completed. Once the decision has been made to hire a particular contractor, the club owner should consider and be sensitive to the following factors, all of which can impact the job:

- *Be aware of the fact that contractors have a fudge factor in their price.* General contractors base their submitted bid on cost estimates that they have received from sub-contractors. Most sub-contractors double their costs in order to arrive at their bid price. In turn, the general contractor applies a 20 to 100 percent profit margin to each sub's bid price. Furthermore, the general contractor includes a line item for general conditions in their bid, which consists of their cost to supervise the job, along with another line item for profit and overhead that normally runs from 5 to 15 percent of the total cost from all bids. In other words, the final bid price that the club owner receives from the contractor usually has another 15 to 25 percent of wiggle room for price negotiation.

- *Get a contract.* Club owners should utilize one of the standard agreements from the American Institute of Architects (AIA), such as a lump-sum agreement, with the contractor. These agreements provide considerable protection for the owner. Such an agreement should address all details of the project, including the payment schedule, change orders, pay applications, liability insurance, performance criteria, etc. The owner should consider including deadlines and penalties in the agreement to cover situations in which the contractor fails to finish a particular part of the project on time, as well as for cost overruns. It is critical that the contract stipulate that between 5 and 10 percent of the contract price is held out of each payment (referred to as a contingency), until after the final punch-list work is completed. The contract should also require the contractor to provide evidence of liability insurance (it is important that the owner is listed on the contractor's insurance as co-insured) and, if the contractor is from a relatively small company, evidence of bonding.

- *Limit change orders.* Change orders occur when a contractor has to perform work that is not reflected in the original construction documents. As a rule, contractors charge a premium for change orders (typically a 20 percent profit premium). Once a change order has been received, the contractor obtains a bid from a sub-contractor for the work involved in the change order and adds a premium of at least 10 percent to the bid (note: the degree of mark-up that is permissible can be specified in the contract). Change orders occur most often because owners want to make changes during the construction phase or the architect and owner have not clarified the plan documents. As a result, it is critical that the plans are reviewed by all parties involved so that no misunderstandings exist and that the owner is aware of the fact that any changes to the plan once construction begins will involve additional costs. Finally, all change orders should be submitted to the architect for approval before any work mandated by the change order can begin or be paid for.

- *Review all pay applications in detail.* Contractors submit a pay application for work performed each month. The pay application provides a detailed listing of all divisions of work and the percentage of work completed for each category. The amount to be paid is based on the work completed. On each application, the contractor lists the contract price, the amount paid

> It is critical that the plans are reviewed by all parties involved so that no misunderstandings exist and that the owner is aware of the fact that any changes to the plan once construction begins will involve additional costs.

to date, the balance, the amount due, and the retainage held out. The pay application should be reviewed and approved by the architect first and then by the owner to ensure that the work that has actually been completed corresponds with the figures shown on the pay application and that no extra costs are included.

- *Conduct regular meetings with the contractor.* The owner and architect should meet regularly with the contractor during the course of construction. In most cases, these meetings are held once a month, while on smaller jobs, they might be scheduled once a week. These meetings should focus on a review of all work, change orders, and pay applications. These meetings should also include an inspection of the job site.

- *Get partial and full lien waivers.* A lien waiver is a form that says that the contractor has received payment for the work completed and that all subcontractors and parties have been paid for their work. When a contractor submits a pay application, lien waivers should be turned in at the same time that correspond to the amount of work completed and the amount of the work paid for by the club owner. This process ensures that a lien is not placed on the business if a sub-contractor claims that they have not been paid for work that they performed. The final lien waiver should be submitted when all of the work has been completed.

- *Conduct a punch list.* After the contractor completes the job, the owner, architect, and contractor should walk through the job and complete a punch list. The punch list identifies any work that either has been performed in an unsatisfactory manner or work that still needs to be done. The punch list ensures that the work is completed to the satisfaction of the owner. Once the punch list is completed, the contractor is paid the retainage fees that have been held out during the course of each pay application.

- *Obtain the warranties and owner's manuals.* At the completion of a construction project, the contractor is obligated to provide the owner with an operator's manual on each product that was utilized in the project (e.g., carpet, HVAC, lighting, floor surfaces, etc.). The operator's manual provides the owner with resources that might be useful with any product-related problems that might subsequently arise with the construction. The standard practice for contractors and their subcontractors is to provide a one-year guarantee on all work and products, commencing from the time the project is completed. Before making a final payment to the contractor, the owner should obtain these warranties from the contractor.

- *Be aware of the fact that under certain circumstances, the contractor can be removed from the job.* If the owner uses a standard AIA agreement, that agreement includes a section that spells out the owner's right to remove the contractor, select another contractor, and let the new contractor finish the job, using the original contractor's equipment. This stipulation can be important, because some small contractors start out relatively strong and then fade as the project moves forward.

Costs Associated With Design and Construction

Some general cost guidelines for design and construction exist that can be useful in determining the scope of a project, including:

> The total cost for all design work can run as high as 14 to 15 percent of the overall construction costs.

- ❑ *Design Costs.* As discussed previously, an architect's costs can run from as low as six percent to as high as 12 percent of total construction costs. The fees of structural engineers, mechanical engineers, and electrical engineers are all included in this expense. Among the items that are not included in the architect's fees are the costs attendant to landscape design, civil engineering, acoustical engineering, surveys, and other specialty work. Collectively, the total cost for all design work can run as high as 14 to 15 percent of the overall construction costs.

- ❑ *Construction Costs.* Most construction is priced on a unit basis, either in linear feet, square feet, or some other basic unit of measurement.
  - *Overall construction costs.* The cost per square foot can vary considerably, depending on the facility's level of finish. The average cost for building a shell (i.e., site work, foundations, bringing in utilities, and building a frame) normally runs approximately $75 to $150 a square foot, depending on the region of the country. The national average would be in the neighborhood of $100 a square foot, depending on the local conditions. The balance of construction after the shell has been completed is considered finish work (i.e., plumbing, electrical, HVAC, surfaces, etc.). The cost range for this stage varies considerably, based on finish levels, with costs as low as $50 a square foot to as high as $200 to $300 a square foot in some geographical areas. The national average for this kind of work would be in the neighborhood of $75 to $125 a square foot. For example, if a freestanding facility was being constructed in a state like Florida or Texas, it might cost from $150 to $175 a square foot, whereas the cost of that same facility in California or New York might be between $300 and $400 a square foot.

Examples of Health/Fitness Facility Designs

The schematic designs, isometrics, and renderings illustrated in this section are intended to showcase some of the unique elements discussed in the previous sections of this chapter.

Chapter Twenty-One

Health/Fitness Facilities

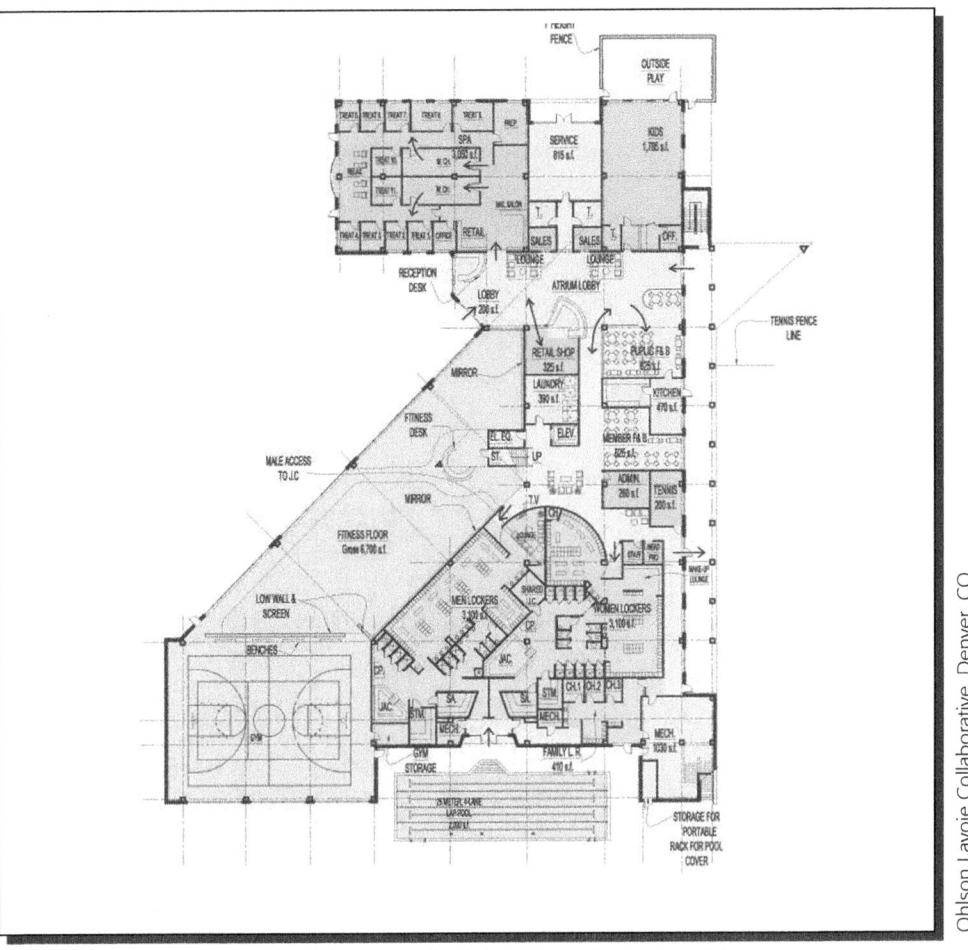

Schematic plan (first floor) of Stonecreek Club & Spa, Covington, LA

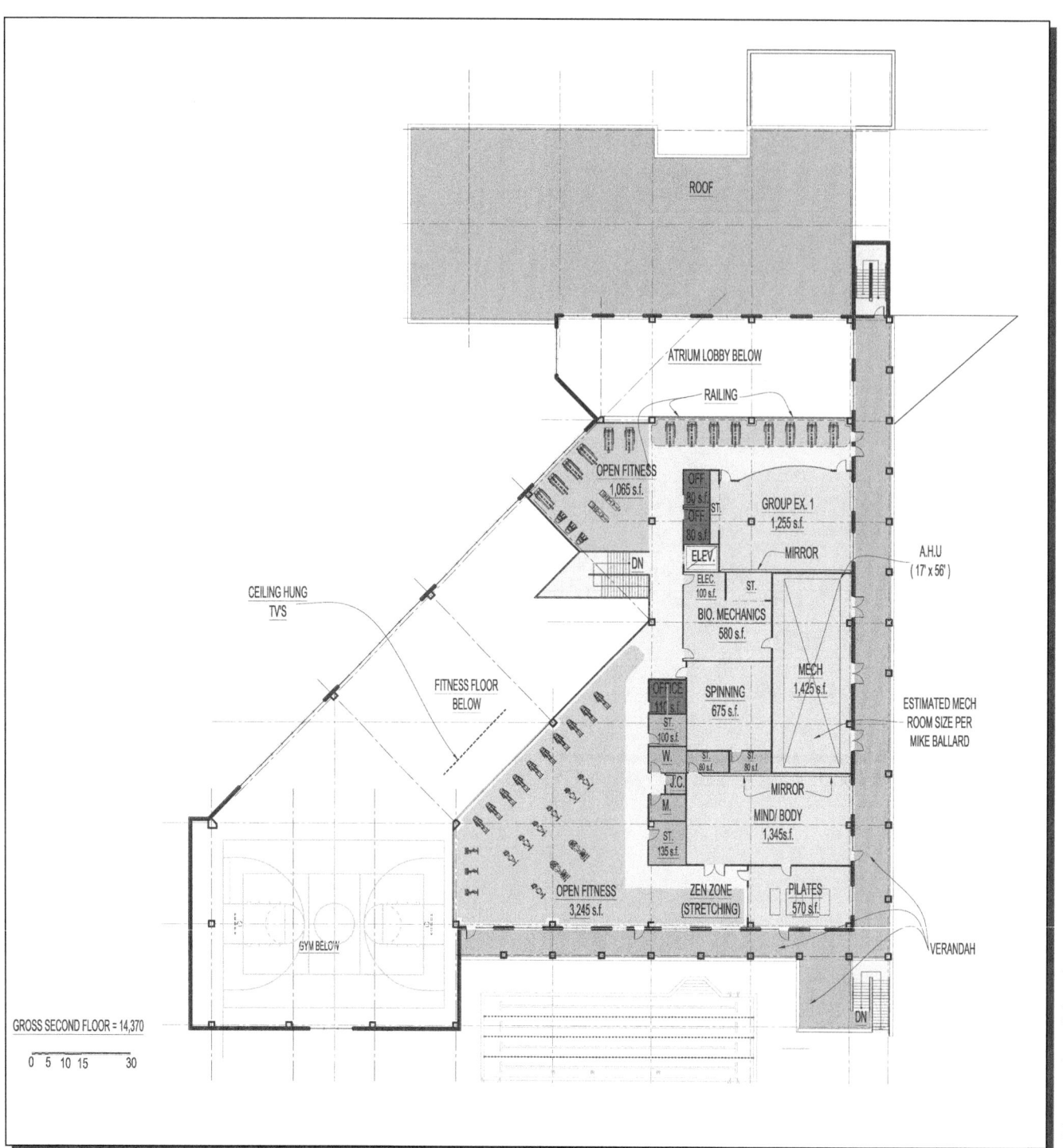

Schematic plan (second floor) of Stonecreek Club & Spa, Covington, LA

Chapter Twenty-One

Health/Fitness Facilities

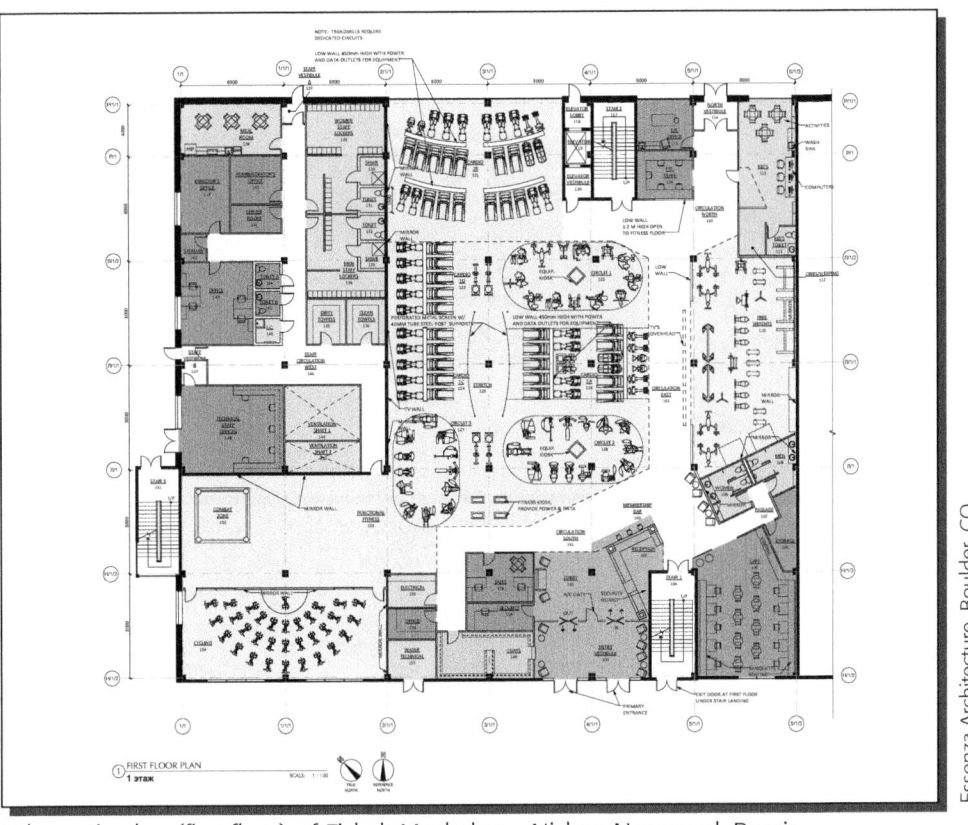

Schematic plan (first floor) of Fizkult Meshchera, Nizhny Novgorod, Russia

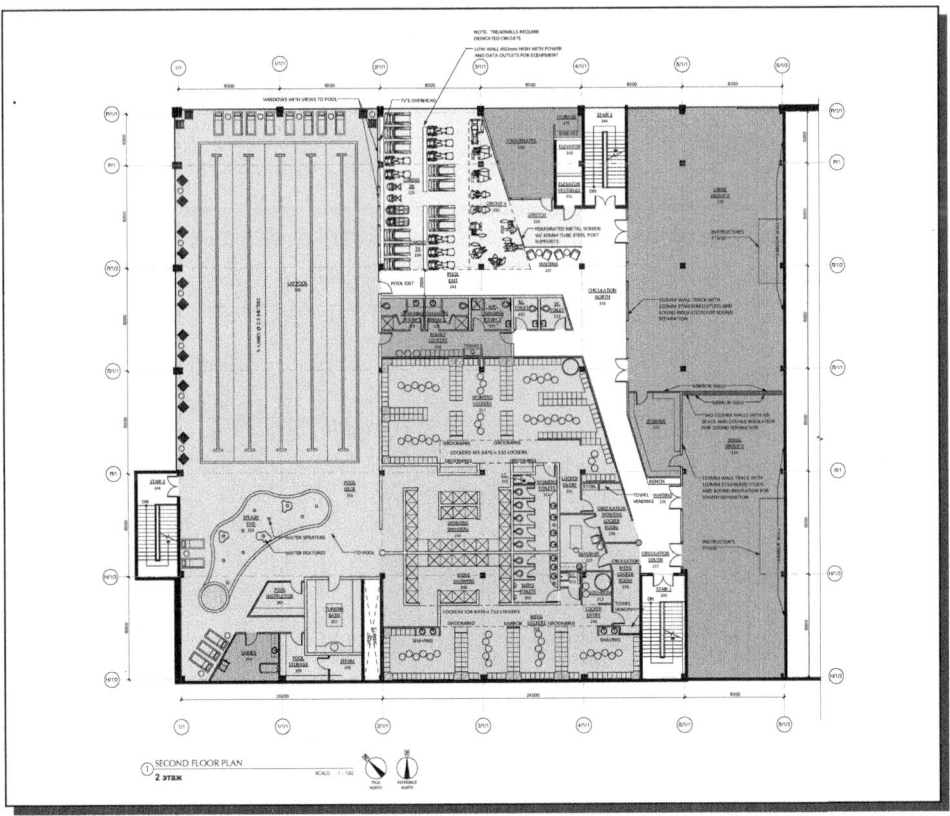

Schematic plan (second floor) of Fizkult Meshchera, Nizhny Novgorod, Russia

Part Six

Facilities and Equipment in the Health/Fitness Facility Industry

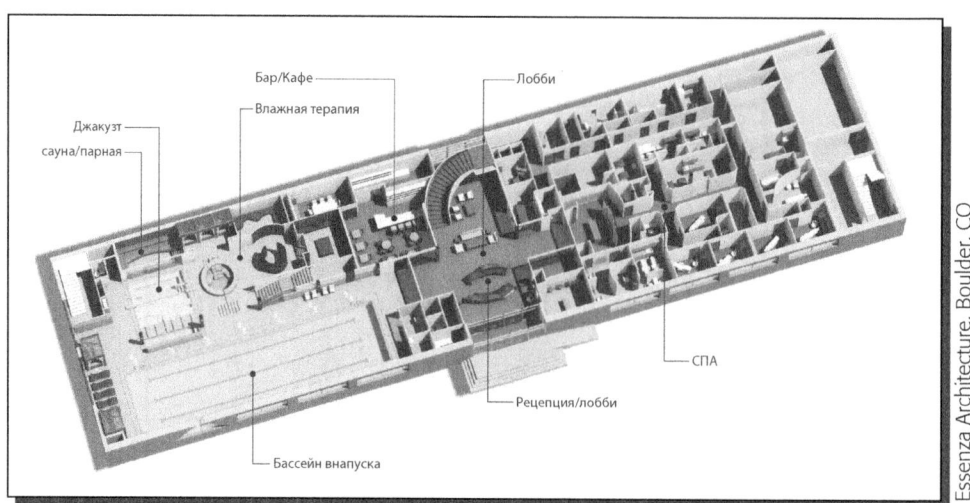

Isometric floor plan (first floor) of World Class Zhukovka, Moscow, Russia

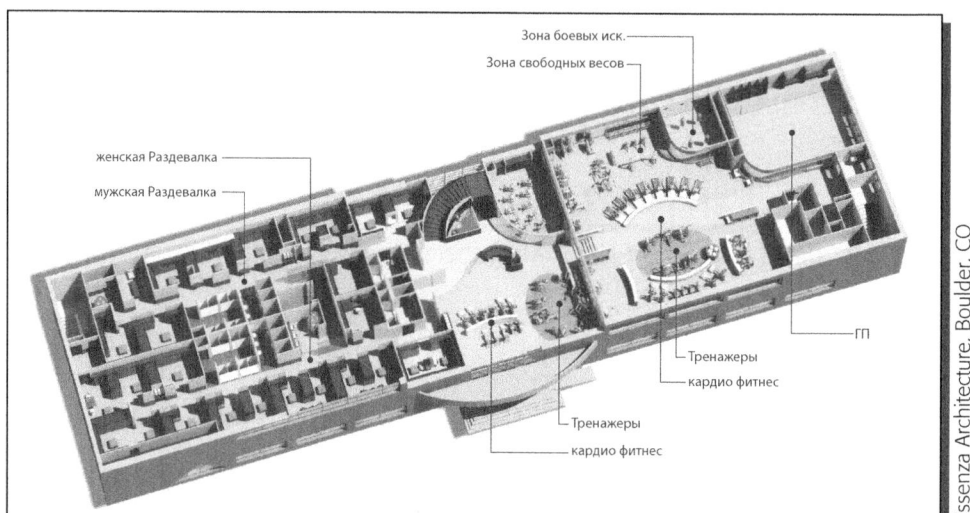

Isometric floor plan (second floor) of World Class Zhukovka, Moscow, Russia

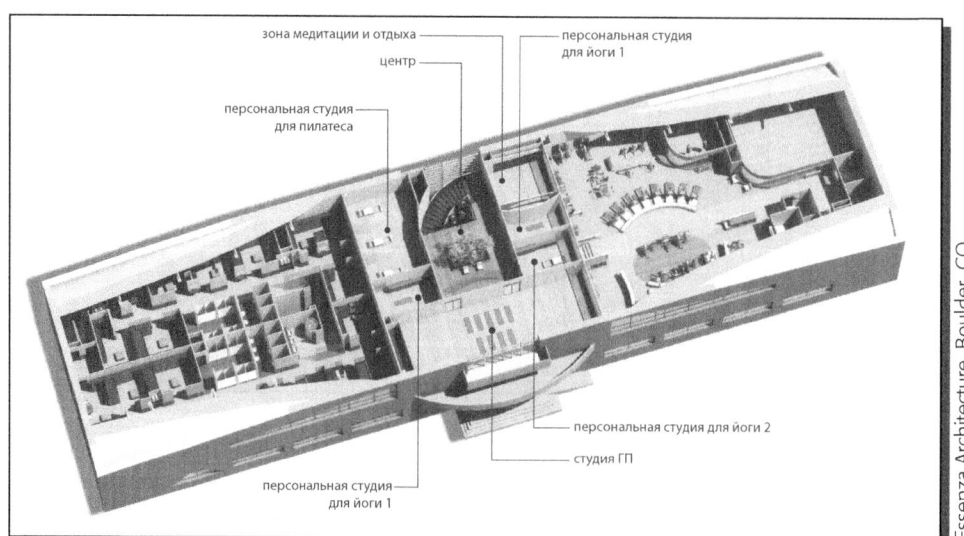

Isometric floor plan (third floor) of World Class Zhukovka, Moscow, Russia

Reflections

The proper design of a fitness center is imperative to its future success. Operators who fail to understand the needs of their members and clients, along with the projected member load, are likely to experience issues going forward. It is imperative that club operators begin the design process by exploring the needs of the membership. Once an understanding of the member demand has been obtained, it's important to have professionals familiar with fitness center design assist you in determining the scope of the facility. The design should not only accommodate expected demand, but should offer the ability to adapt the space to accommodate additional demand in the future.

> **The proper design of a fitness center is imperative to its future success.**

22 Fitness Equipment for the Health/Fitness Facility Industry

"When future archaeologists dig up the remains of California, they're going to find all those gyms their scary-looking equipment, and they're going to assume that we were a culture obsessed with torture."

—Douglas Coupland

> The typical health/fitness club spends 1.5 percent of annual revenues investing in new fitness equipment.

Chapter Objectives

The health/fitness club industry is capital-intensive, with facilities and equipment encompassing the majority of that capital outlay. According to industry research, as reflected in IHRSA's publication, *Guide to Lenders and Investors*, most newly built clubs expend approximately $15 to $25 per square foot on fitness equipment. It is not uncommon, however, for the cost of fitness equipment to run as high as $30 per square foot, especially in fitness-only facilities. This initial investment in equipment is compounded by the need for club owners to reinvest in equipment on an annual basis to stay current with equipment trends in the industry and to deal with the depreciation and wear on existing equipment. According to IHRSA's *2015 Profiles of Success*, the typical health/fitness club spends 1.5 percent of annual revenues investing in new fitness equipment. For a club that generates $5 million in revenues, this amounts to $80,000 each year. This chapter reviews the basic categories of fitness equipment in the industry, the leading equipment manufacturers, and the costs associated with the equipment, including a brief discussion of the pros and cons of purchasing versus leasing. The chapter is not intended to delve into great depth on this subject; rather, it is designed to provide a basic overview of the key factors attendant to the equipment end of the industry. As such, the information is grouped and reviewed according to the major equipment categories in the industry, including cardiovascular equipment, resistance-circuit equipment, free-weight equipment, cardiovascular-entertainment equipment, and other types of equipment that are frequently required in the health/fitness club industry.

Cardiovascular Equipment

Cardiovascular equipment exists in nearly all health/fitness clubs and is second only to free-weight equipment in terms of its availability and popularity in the industry. Although cardiovascular equipment has been around since the 1870s (when the Curtis indoor rowing machine was first introduced in clubs), it has only been since the 1970s that it has been accorded such a prominent role in the marketing and programming of clubs.

❑ *Historical Overview.* The first pieces of cardiovascular equipment that were utilized in the club industry were stationary indoor rowing machines, the first of which was the Curtis rowing machine introduced in 1871 by William Curtis, a founding member of the New York Athletic Club. During the late 1800s and early part of the 1900s, rowing machines, such as the Curtis rowing machine, Kern's & Laflin rowing machine, and those rowing machines that were marketed and sold by A.G. Spaulding and Narragansett Machine Company, represented the primary form of indoor cardiovascular conditioning equipment in clubs. In 1932, the Exercycle, invented by Gordon Berg, became a part of the club industry. In the process, it became the second most popular indoor cardiovascular training machine (after rowing machines). The first commercial treadmill (Quinton treadmill) was a relatively large machine that was developed by Robert Bruce (who is relatively well-known in some circles for devising the Bruce protocol) and Wayne Quinton. In the 1960s, the Pacemaster treadmill, developed by Bill Staub and Kenneth Cooper, M.D., was introduced, a machine that was followed shortly thereafter by the Trotter treadmill in the early 1970s.

In 1968, the Lifecycle was invented by Keene Dimmick. Six years later, in 1974, Ray Wilson purchased the rights to the Lifecycle and, along with his first employee, Augie Nieto, introduced it to the club industry. As the first mass-produced electronic piece of cardiovascular equipment, designed specifically for the health/fitness club industry, it subsequently became the benchmark for all future developments in the industry. The Lifecycle established itself as one of those brands that become virtually synonymous with the product type. Fairly or not, all indoor exercise cycles, at one time or another, have been called Lifecycles. The Lifecycle subsequently gave rise to other early brands of indoor electronic cycles, such as Biocycle and Universal. During the late 70s, treadmills began to have a presence in the health/fitness club market through models built and sold by companies such as Pacemaster, Quinton, Marquette, and Trotter. Since then, treadmills have blossomed into the largest segment of cardiovascular equipment in the industry, a segment that is dominated by companies such as Life Fitness, Matrix, Precor, Star Trac, and Technogym. According to IHRSA's 2015 *Health Club Consumer Report*, treadmills are the most popular type of fitness equipment among consumers.

The next landmark type of cardiovascular equipment to hit the industry was the development of StairMaster machines in 1984. To many industry observers, StairMaster evolved into the industry equivalent of the Lifecycle in the 80s and early 90s. The developmental evolution of cardiovascular equipment continued in the mid-1990s when in 1995, Precor introduced the first elliptical machine. Subsequently, the Precor EFX became the StairMaster of the previous decade.

During the 1970s, a number of other types of cardiovascular equipment were also popular, including the Nordic Track cross-country ski machine, the Cybex upper-body ergometer, and the Concept II Rower. The late 1980s

> The first pieces of cardiovascular equipment that were utilized in the club industry were stationary indoor rowing machines.

and early 1990s also witnessed industry efforts to expand the types and features of "cardio" equipment. Some of these machines, such as the Reebok Sky Walker, had an early, but not lasting, impact on the industry. At the present time, cardiovascular equipment continues to evolve, as manufacturers incorporate new technology and improved mechanics and as the public looks for even better/newer exercise tools.

❑ *Categories.* Cardiovascular equipment can be grouped into the following major categories: elliptical machines, stairclimbers, recumbent and upright bicycles, adapted movement machines, and treadmills. In addition to these major categories, a few, less-prominent categories exist, such as rowing machines, upper-body ergometers, and cross-country ski machines.

• *Elliptical motion trainers (19 percent to 38 percent of club members use and 67 percent of facilities offer).* Elliptical machines have been the fastest growing category of equipment in the health/fitness club industry over the past decade. Since their introduction by Precor in 1995, they have become the second most popular form of cardiovascular machines in clubs. Elliptical trainers reflect an evolution in how the industry looks at cardiovascular exercise. These machines exert load forces on the body similar to those imposed on an individual's musculoskeletal system while walking and running, but with significantly less impact. These machines also feature technology that allows for integrated upper-body movement with lower-body movement. At the present time, elliptical machines are available both with and without upper-body movement arms. The industry leader in this type of equipment is the Precor EFX. Companies such as Life Fitness, Star Trac, Matrix, Cybex (Arc Trainer), Octane, and Technogym also manufacture well-received models of elliptical machines. Most of the elliptical machines currently available in the market offer heart-rate technology, integrated entertainment technology (e.g., touch screen LED screens and are compatible with most smartphones and tablets), and accessories for holding items, such as water bottles and reading materials. The average retail cost of a commercial-grade elliptical machine ranges from $4,000 to $7,000 per machine.

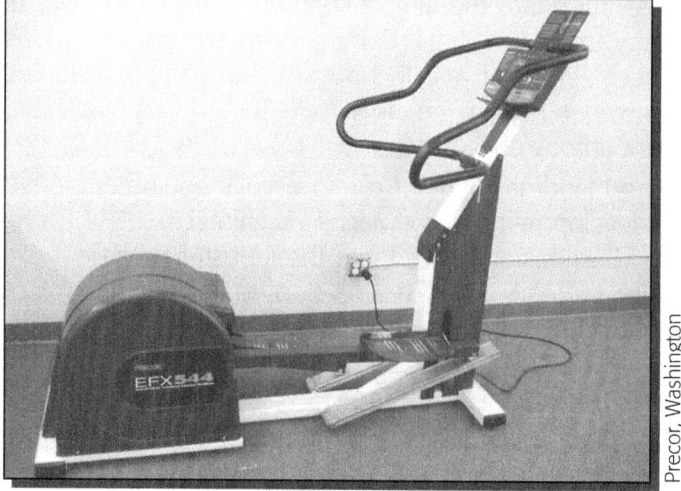

Precor EFX 544 elliptical machine

- *Stairclimbers (7 percent to 29 percent of member use and 57 percent of clubs offer).* Mechanical stairclimbers have lost much of their market share since the introduction of the elliptical trainers. Once the highest volume seller in the industry, stairclimbers currently rank behind treadmills, elliptical machines, and bicycles in terms of their popularity among health/fitness club users. StairMaster Sports/Medical Products, Inc. (a company that is part of the Nautilus Group), which developed and manufactured the first mechanical stairclimbing machine, remains the industry leader in this equipment category. Several other companies, such as Life Fitness, Star Trac, Precor, Technogym, and Cybex, also produce stairclimbing machines that are popular in the industry. The first model of a stairclimbing machine that Stairmaster produced (originally called the Gauntlet, but subsequently renamed as the Stepmill), which featured a series of stairs that actually rotated, is often still the piece of cardiovascular equipment of choice among those individuals who either would like to engage in a particularly intense workout or see a direct correlation between the exercise afforded by revolving stairs and a personal activity interest (e.g., outdoor climbing). This particular type of stairclimbing apparatus has made a comeback in the past five years as several of the leading manufacturers have begun producing their own version of the machine since the patent rights have expired. The technology involved in mechanical stairclimbing has not changed all that much since these machines were first introduced. Some of the newer stairclimbing machines feature heart-rate monitor technology, entertainment technology and Internet connectivity, as well as offer soft pedals and accessories to hold water bottles and reading materials. The average retail price for a commercial-grade stairclimber ranges from $3,000 to $6,000.
- *Recumbent and upright bicycles (10 percent and 16 percent of members use, respectively, while 64% and 61% of facilities offer, respectively).* Upright bicycles were the first type of cardiovascular equipment that was introduced to the club market. Within the industry, they remain popular among club users. Recumbent bicycles, the more popular of the two types of bicycles (recumbent and upright), were introduced in the industry in the late 1980s and early 1990s, to ostensibly serve an older demographic. Bicycles are third in popularity, behind treadmills and elliptical machines, among current facility users. The current trend in the technology for both types of bicycles is to provide lower starting workloads, heart-rate feedback, fully adjustable seats and pedals, self-adjusting workloads based on heart-rate response, and integrated entertainment technology, including Internet connectivity. The leading manufacturers of bicycles include Life Fitness, Star Trac, Precor, and Technogym. The average retail price for either a recumbent or upright bicycle ranges from $2,500 to $4,000.
- *Treadmills (37 percent to 50 percent of members use and 71 percent of facilities offer).* Treadmills are the single-most popular piece of cardiovascular equipment in the industry and involve the largest expenditure for cardiovascular equipment by clubs. According to IHRSA's most recent consumer research, between 37 percent and 50 percent of all health club members (dependent on age group) use a treadmill. As previously discussed, the first treadmills offered to the club industry were models developed by Quinton, Pacemaster, and Trotter, each of which was

Between 37 percent and 50 percent of all health club members (dependent on age group) use a treadmill.

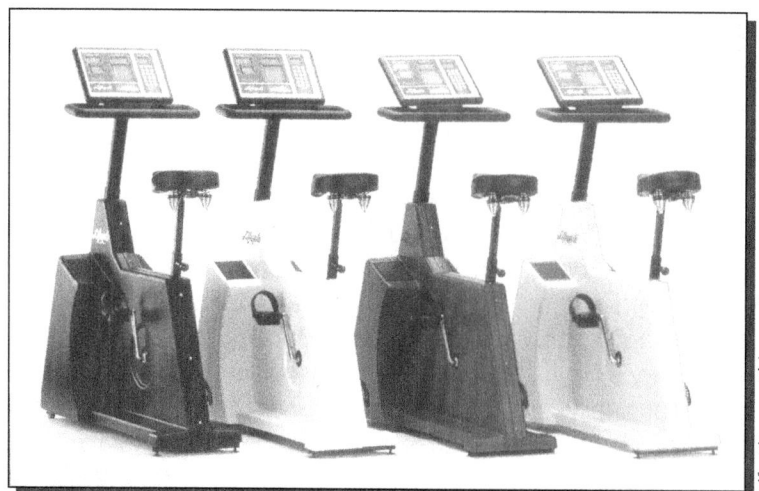
Lifecycle 2000

relatively large and cumbersome to use. Over the years, treadmills have become the cardiovascular modality of choice for many club members. Much of their popularity can be attributed to the evolution of technology, often based on research into the mechanics of human motion, which is featured in most treadmills. For example, almost every treadmill now offers some form of soft deck (shock-absorbing surface), programmable features, controllable speed that ranges from less than 1 to 15 mph (some as high as 20 mph), adjustable grades (negative-degree grade to as high as a positive 50-degree grade), contact and remote heart-rate monitoring, integrated audiovisual entertainment, Internet connectivity, accessories for holding items, such as water bottles and reading materials, and, on occasion, fans for "cooling" the individual who is using the machine. The leading manufacturers of commercial-grade treadmills are Life Fitness, Matrix, Precor, Cybex, Technogym, and Woodway. Some smaller companies, such as True, and Sport Art, also produce treadmills. The average retail price of a quality commercial-grade treadmill ranges from $5,000 to $10,000.

- *Adaptive movement machines/cardio-cross trainers (7 percent of members use)*. In the early part of the 21st century, several manufacturers introduced a new category of cardiovascular equipment, one of which was an offshoot of the elliptical and total-body training machines introduced in the late 1990s by companies such as Precor and Life Fitness. These new machines leveraged the popularity of the elliptical trainer by establishing adapted movements that were similar to those of an elliptical trainer, but which also provided a different modality for the user. The first adaptive movement machine was the Arc Trainer, which was introduced by Cybex. The Arc Trainer provided users with both upper- and lower-body movement that followed a semi-arched or elliptical-type movement through the lower body. One of the Arc Trainer's unique features is that it allows the user to be "suspended" in air while performing the movement. The second adaptive movement machine to hit the market with a bang was the Cardiowave from Technogym. The Cardiowave, released in 2005, simulated the movement of ice skating or uphill Nordic skiing. Interestingly, back in the 1990s, Nautilus introduced an ice skating simulator that had provided a similar movement pattern. The

Cardiowave's unique design allows users to develop several physical attributes, including cardiovascular endurance, lower-body muscular endurance, and lower-body muscular strength. In 2007, Precor released a machine called the Adaptive Motion Trainer (AMT). The AMT provides users with three distinct movement patterns—stepping, elliptical training, and running. The AMT allows the user to adapt their stride length and mobility patterns to simulate one of the abovementioned movements.

Selectorized/Variable Resistance Equipment

According to the published report, the *IHRSA 2015 Profiles of Success*, selectorized/variable-resistance equipment is found in 52 percent of all facilities. According to IHRSA's 2016 *Health Club Consumer Report*, approximately 36 percent of all members (depending on age category) use these machines. A recent global fitness trend study reported that 57 percent of facilities offered selectorized resistance machines. In reality, almost all traditional clubs offer some form of variable-resistance equipment, while boutique studios tend to shun the use of variable-resistance machines (only 15 percent report using selectorized resistance equipment according to a 2016 Association of Fitness Studio benchmarking report). Variable-resistance or selectorized-resistance equipment encompasses strength-training equipment that utilizes weight stacks and pulley mechanisms to provide resistance to movement, while the user typically assumes (and maintains) a set position. The primary advantage of this type of resistance exercise is that it provides a safe and efficient strength-training modality, while reducing the level of exercise anxiety and the perceived need for demonstrable fitness prowess that some individuals experience.

❑ *Historical Overview.* Resistance-training machines, in one form or another, have been in existence for more than 150 years. The first such resistance machines, which look similar to today's modern resistance machines, were developed in the 1860s by Dr. Gustav Zander. Dr. Zander developed over 27 different mechanical machines that featured graduated levers, springs, weights, and pulleys to create variable resistance. His machines included a number of devices, such as the pull-down machine, the abdominal punching machine, and the torso resistance machine.

> Resistance-training machines, in one form or another, have been in existence for more than 150 years.

In the 1880s, another industry legend, Dudley Allan Sargent, director of the Heminway Gymnasium at Harvard, invented the first variable-resistance pulley machines. Over time, Sargent created more than 30 distinct machines, including the chest pulley system and abdominal pulley system. By the late 1880s, Sargent's pulley systems could be found in gymnasiums around the country and were being replicated by several other equipment companies, such as A.G. Spalding.

The selectorized resistance machines that currently exist in the health/fitness club industry originated in the late 1950s, as a result of the efforts of Harold Zinkin, Sr. to develop the first Universal machine. Zinkin's equipment featured a single-training unit that had multiple-exercise stations, each with its own weight stack. These early machines employed a system of levers to move the weight stack and provide resistance (Universal called it dynamic-variable resistance). As a rule, Zinkin's machines were somewhat limited by the fact that they had an uneven distribution of the resistance load at different points in the range of motion. Until the 1970s, however, Universal and Paramount were the preferred choices of the industry where it involved the purchase of resistance-training machines.

In 1970, Arthur Jones revolutionized the equipment manufacturing and club industries with the introduction of Nautilus machines. Nautilus machines featured variable resistance, made possible by the use of a cam that controlled the level of resistance afforded to the user. The cam allowed the resistance offered by the machine to vary based on the fulcrum's (mechanical movement arm) position on the cam while the machine was being used. Concurrently, the concept of "strength curves" was introduced into the mindset of many club members. According to Nautilus, one of the most desirable features of its equipment was the machine's capacity to provide resistance to the user that is applied in a manner that is consistent with the normal strength curve of the user's muscles. Another selling point for Nautilus machines was their ability to isolate specific muscle groups while exercising. Nautilus also featured mechanisms that allowed users to adjust their seat position and body position while exercising, which is designed to enhance both the mechanical efficiency and effectiveness of their exercise bout. Nautilus advocates adhered to a prescription and training concept that involved performing one set of each exercise to near muscular fatigue, doing each repetition in relatively slow motion (e.g., four to six seconds each), and placing equal or greater emphasis on the eccentric portion of the exercise movement (versus the concentric phase).

The Blue Monster by Nautilus

Eventually, Nautilus was followed by a new group of equipment manufacturers, such as Eagle (later to become Cybex), Body Masters, and Icarian, among others, who led the effort to expand the technology involved in variable-resistance machines. For example, by the early 1980s, Eagle had entered into the market for variable-resistance machines and captured much of the demand for such equipment. Cybex and many of the resistance equipment companies that followed improved on the original Nautilus design by creating lighter machines that required less space, employed airplane cable or Kevlar belts instead of chains, offered additional color options, and were aggressively marketed at a lower-price point to the industry.

While the number of variable-resistance equipment manufacturers grew over the years, no new innovations hit the industry until 1978 with the introduction of Keiser pneumatic machines. The Keiser machines involved a new, innovative concept—the use of air pressure to create resistance. This feature provided exercisers with greater flexibility in adjusting either the level of resistance or speed. Subsequently, companies, such as Hydra Fit, introduced a line of resistance-training machines that were powered by pneumatic cylinders, while others developed machines that employed water as a means to adjust the level of resistance. At the present time, Keiser is one of the few manufacturers of resistance machines that do not employ a weight stack.

The next stage in the evolution of resistance-training machines occurred in the early 1990s, when several manufacturers introduced computerized-resistance training (e.g., Powercise, Life Circuit) machines. These machines employed electromagnetic forces (controlled through computer chips) to produce resistance. The most noteworthy feature of these machines was their ability to adjust the resistance level, based on the user's strength that day, as well as memory of how the user had performed on the previous workout. This approach to resistance training did not catch on with consumers and disappeared from the industry within a few years.

At the end of the 1990s, Ground Zero, later renamed Free Motion, developed a line of functional resistance-training equipment, featuring pulleys that enable users to exercise in a variety of positions and planes. The efforts of Free Motion have since given rise to an entire manufacturing segment in the industry attempt to design and produce functional resistance-training machines.

❑ *Categories.* Variable-resistance equipment can be grouped into three distinct categories: fixed-position weight stack, functional fitness-based weight stack, and alternative resistance.
  • *Fixed-position based weight stack.* This category encompasses over 80 percent of the market for variable-resistance equipment. This type of machine provides resistance through the use of cams or other pulley-based systems that are attached to weight stacks. These machines enable users to perform a specific exercise movement in a fixed position that isolates one or two muscle groups. The basic design of these machines provides a high degree of user safety since most of the postural and mechanical alignment errors that can occur in more functional exercise are eliminated. Another benefit category of variable-resistance equipment is the ability to set up circuits of the machines that allow a user to perform movements for each of the major muscle groups by exercising on 8 to 12 machines that have been arranged in a circuit. Most of these machines also allow personalized position adjustments to accommodate multiple body types, as well as

> Fixed-position based weight stack equipment encompasses over 80 percent of the market for variable-resistance equipment.

feature more aesthetically pleasing designs. A host of manufacturers of this type of equipment exists in the industry, including Life Fitness, Cybex, Technogym, Nautilus, Precor, Paramount, Star Trac, and Matrix The average retail price for a complete circuit of 12 machines is approximately $30,000 to $40,000, with each piece ranging from $2,500 to $5,000 in price.

- *Functional fitness-based weight stack.* This category of variable-resistance equipment has evolved from having a relatively small role in the club industry to being a major focus of variable-resistance equipment manufacturers. At the present time, all of the leading manufacturers of variable-resistance equipment offer machines in this category. This type of equipment is based on the two primary concepts. First, muscles don't contract in isolation. Rather, a synergy of contraction occurs during exercise, involving agonist, antagonist, and stabilizer muscle groups. Second, the body does not function in an isolated or a fixed position. Instead, the functional performance of movement requires both balance and posture. Accordingly, the design of these machines features pulley and cable systems that allow users to adjust their position and angle of movement, as desired. Furthermore, these machines often require that users perform the movement in a standing or similar position—where the body is not fixed in a set position, thus incorporating an element of balance in the exercise. The manufacturing leader in this area is Free Motion Fitness, although additional companies, such as Life Fitness, Cybex, Precor, Star Trac (Human Sport), and Technogym (Kinesis), among others, have developed their own models of this equipment. These machines range in cost of approximately $2,500 to $6,000 each, with a complete circuit of 12 machines retailing in the neighborhood of $30,000 to $40,000.

> Alternative-resistance machines are similar to the fixed-position, weight-stack equipment except that they utilize a resistance source other than weight stacks.

- *Alternative resistance.* Alternative-resistance machines are similar to the fixed-position, weight-stack equipment except that they utilize a resistance source other than weight stacks. These machines operate on the same basic principles as the other two basic categories of variable-resistance equipment (i.e., most of these machines provide isolated movements, with the user set in a fixed position). The leader in this category is Keiser, which manufactures a line of equipment that uses air resistance. Keiser has been able to attract a relatively strong following in some segments of the industry, based on the ability of air resistance to allow for loads light enough for the weakest individual and loads in excess of what the strongest human could lift. Keiser has also capitalized on the fact that its equipment nearly eliminates placing undue load forces on the joints, which makes it a very suitable resistance-training modality for older adults. Other manufacturers exist that use alternative forms of resistance, such as water, air, and hydraulics. On average, these machines retail for between $3,000 and $5,000 per machine and for approximately $30,000 to $40,000 for a complete 12-station circuit.

Free-Weight Equipment

Free-weight equipment has been around longer than any other form of exercise equipment. According to the publication, the *IHRSA 2015 Profiles of Success*, 83 percent of all clubs indicate that they offer free-weight equipment, thereby making it the most popular type of exercise equipment in the health/fitness club industry. IHRSA's 2016 *Health Club Consumer Report* shows, depending on the individual's age, that between 23 percent and 32 percent of members regularly use free weights (e.g., barbells and dumbbells), making it the fourth-most popular form of equipment among consumers.

> Free-weight equipment has been around longer than any other form of exercise equipment.

❑ *Historical Overview.* Free-weight equipment has been around for well over two thousand years. The first piece of free weight equipment introduced to physical culturists was dumbbells (originally called halteres when they were introduced during the Greek period of 300 to 700 BCE), followed shortly thereafter by the medicine ball. The kettlebell was introduced around 1700. By the mid-1800s, globe barbells and dumbbells (bells were filled with either sand or metal pellets that were loaded to the end of a bar), also became popular, along with Indian clubs.

Milo Barbell, founded by Alan Calvert in 1902, was the first company to commercially produce free-weight sets. These early free-weight sets allowed the user to easily change weights and brought free-weights into gyms and homes throughout America. During the early years of the health/fitness club industry in the late 1940s, most free-weight equipment consisted of barbells, dumbbells, and benches built by individuals for their gyms. The free-weight equipment industry underwent its first major thrust in popularity with the introduction of the York barbell in the late 1930s. Developed by the legendary Bob Hoffman, the York Company purchased the assets of Milo Barbell and proceeded to create an entire market for barbells, dumbbells, and free-weight benches. In fact, until the late 1980s, York was one of only a few companies that made free-weight equipment.

The popularity of free-weight equipment received a substantial boost in popularity in the late 1980s and early 1990s, when research began to document and reinforce the enumerable benefits of strength training for all segments of the population. As a result of the impetus for resistance training that was provided by this research, companies began to expand into the free-weight market. Among the manufacturing companies that were at the forefront of this effort were Cybex, Icarian, and Body Master. By the turn of the 21st century, nearly every major exercise equipment manufacturer offered full lines of free-weight plates, benches, and accessories.

One of the biggest developments in the history of the free-weight industry occurred in 1989, when Hammer introduced plate-loaded resistance equipment. Hammer machines featured the functional advantages of free-weight movements, combined with the advantages of variable-resistance, weight-stack equipment. Initially, Hammer developed a significant following in both colleges and professional sports, before gaining in popularity in the club industry. Hammer's prime engineer was none other than Gary Jones, son of Arthur Jones, the creator of Nautilus. As of 2013, approximately 60 percent of clubs reported offering plate-loaded equipment.

The most recent attempt at innovation in free-weight technology has been the introduction of weight plates with holes for easier grasping. Free-weight equipment has evolved from an exercise tool primarily targeted at bodybuilders to the resistance-training modality of choice for many average consumers.

❑ *Categories.* Free-weight equipment can be grouped into three primary categories: barbells and dumbbells, benches and support machines, and plate-loaded equipment.
  - *Barbells and dumbbells.* Barbells and dumbbells have evolved very little since they were first introduced. At the present time, most barbells involve Olympic-style bars and plates that have ball-bearing sleeves that allow the weights to revolve around the end of the bar. The most innovative change in barbells in recent years has been the introduction of plates (technology first introduced by Iron Grip) that have holes that allow the user to more easily grasp the plates.

Power rack, La Palestra, New York, NY

Dumbbells have also not evolved all that much over the last century. Two changes that have occurred in dumbbells, however, are the use of rubber-plate coatings that have been put on the plates to protect them and the presence of more ergonomic handles that have been developed. Another change has been the use of kettlebells, which have become quite popular in the past few years. First used in the early 1700s by Russian strongmen, kettlebells are large metal balls with a fixed handle on top. The leading manufacturers of barbells and dumbbells are Ivanko and Iron Grip. The retail cost of barbells varies, with most commercial grade Olympic-style bars retailing for between $150 and $500 dollars, while plates cost between $.30 and $1.00 per pound. The cost of solid dumbbells ranges from less than $.30 a pound to over $1.00 a pound, depending on the actual weight (e.g., heavy dumbbells cost less per pound).

- *Benches and support machines.* Benches and support machines comprise the largest segment of the free-weight product line. These products range from simple Olympic style flat benches for performing bench presses to power racks and Smith machines. Each bench and accessory is designed to be used with barbells and dumbbells. The variety of products in this category is substantial and includes such items as adjustable incline benches, flat benches, decline benches, leg- press machines, Smith machines, power racks, cable-crossover machines, curling benches, T-bar rowing machines, calf machines, 45-degree back benches, and abdominal benches. The leading manufacturers of this product segment include Life Fitness, Cybex, Technogym, Precor, Star Trac, Matrix, and Gym 80. These benches and machines have wide-ranging retail prices. For example, most benches retail for between $400 and $900 each, while larger machines, such as power racks and Smith machines, cost in the range of $1,000 and $4,000 each.
- *Plate-loaded machines.* Plate-loaded equipment is the most recently developed type of free-weight equipment, having only been around since 1989. Plate-loaded machines involve a hybrid piece of equipment that allows the average health/fitness club user to experience some of the benefits of free weights, while simultaneously receiving the advantages that variable-resistance equipment can provide, such as enhanced safety and the ability to exercise isolated muscles. Plate-loaded equipment enables users to perform a variety of fixed-position (isolated exercise movements) and functional based movements (exercises that involve closed-chain movements). The leading manufacturer of this type of free-weight equipment is Hammer (owned by Life Fitness), although other companies, such as Cybex, Precor, Technogym, and Star Trac, also offer plate-loaded machines. The majority of plate-loaded machines retail for between $1,000 and $3,000, with only a few pieces ever exceeding $3,000 in cost.

Cardiovascular Entertainment Equipment

Cardiovascular entertainment equipment involves a system of apparatus that is employed in concert with cardiovascular-exercise equipment (e.g., indoor cycles, treadmills, elliptical machines, stairclimbers, etc.) that allows individuals to watch televised images while they work out. Such a system can accomplish several goals, including: enable individuals to disassociate from the perceived effort to exercise, help mask general feelings of fatigue, enliven the workout, make the exercise bout more interesting, etc.

❏ *Historical Overview.* Assumptions concerning how to "entertain" individuals while they are exercising changed substantially when Tony DeLeede introduced Cardio Theater to the health/fitness club industry in 1991. Before Cardio Theater, the entertainment efforts of most clubs were strictly limited to background music systems that played soundtracks from either licensed programs, such as Musak, or from radio stations. Prior to Cardio Theater, a few clubs set up televisions in their cardiovascular areas and tuned them to established stations so that members could watch and listen to television while they trained. The constraints of these various efforts became quite apparent when Cardio Theater developed a system that allowed users to tune into the television or music station of their choice through a special control that is mounted on the equipment on which the individual is exercising. The popularity of Cardio Theater led to the development of other audiovisual entertainment systems, including one produced by Broadcast Vision. The effort was further advanced when two companies, E Zone and Net Pulse, developed personal viewing systems that were attached to each piece of equipment. Net Pulse created individual kiosks for each piece of equipment that allowed users to surf the net or tune into their favorite television station. E Zone established a system, featuring small viewing screens that could be mounted in front of each piece of equipment and allowed users to view television stations, listen to CDs, or listen to music stations. E Zone also introduced personal headsets that enabled users to navigate throughout the club and continue listening to the station to which they were tuned. By the beginning of the 21st century, both E Zone and Net Pulse experienced problems with their business models and basically disappeared from the cardio-entertainment industry. Subsequently, both Broadcast Vision and Cardio Theater developed personal viewing systems that have been incorporated into their offerings. Starting in 2005, many equipment manufacturers began integrating personal viewing systems (PVS) into their equipment design. The first to leverage this approach was Life Fitness. The development of integrated personal viewing systems continues to evolve and currently includes systems that offer touch-screen technology, HD LED screens, MP3 compatibility, and streaming from the Internet.

❑ *Categories.* Cardio-entertainment systems are offered in three distinct categories: personal viewing systems, interconnected audiovisual systems, and personal tuner audiovisual systems.

- *Personal viewing systems (PVS).* Personal viewing systems involve individual LCD screens (13 inches to 15 inches) that are either mounted in front of each piece of equipment and are connected to an integrated audiovisual network or integrated into the control panel of the equipment. Each user is able to tune into the station to which they want to watch or listen, using either a control module that is mounted on the equipment or through touch-screen technology that is integrated into the control panel of the equipment. As a result, users have their own personal entertainment system while exercising. As of 2010, most manufacturers of cardiovascular equipment offer models that include fully integrated entertainment systems that are compatible with the newest media devices, such as iPhones, iPads, etc. The price of PVS ranges between $1,000 and $1,500 per unit, with the newest integrated systems adding as much as another $1,500 to $2,000 per piece of cardiovascular equipment.
- *Interconnected audiovisual entertainment systems.* These systems integrate wall/ceiling-mounted televisions with audio and video channels that are connected through a transmitter and equipment-mounted control boxes. Users can utilize the control box to select a channel that corresponds to either a television station or an audio channel. These systems have a varied number of channels (e.g., 4, 8, or 16) that allow users to select from a variety of audiovisual options. These systems feature headsets that users connect to the equipment-mounted control boxes. Most of the systems are wireless, but a few clubs employ hard-wired systems. The leading

manufacturers of these systems are Broadcast Vision and Cardio Theater. The cost of these systems varies, based on the number of televisions, the number of channels on the system receiver, the number of control boxes needed, whether a DVD or video deck is provided, and whether wiring is needed. The control boxes retail for between $140 and $200 each, while an 8-channel receiver ranges in price between $1,300 and $1,500. A club that has 50 pieces of cardiovascular equipment might expect to spend in the range of $20,000 to $30,000 for a full system. One of the biggest challenges facing clubs that have these systems is the ongoing need to replace headphone jacks that are damaged through the constant placement and removal of user headsets.

- *Personal tuner audiovisual systems.* These systems are similar to the aforementioned integrated systems, except that they do not involve having control boxes on the equipment. These systems require that all televisions are set to specific, unused FM frequencies. This feature enables users to bring their own personal audio machine to their workout and tune into the frequency that corresponds to the television station they want to watch. Users can also tune into their favorite radio station. Many clubs prefer these systems, given that they involve less upfront expense and do not cost as much to operate, because they don't include equipment-mounted control boxes.

Other Frequently Required Equipment for Health/Fitness Facilities

As discussed previously, the health/fitness club industry is a capital-intensive business, especially from an equipment perspective. The majority of the capital spent on equipment is expended in one of the aforementioned four categories. Nonetheless, some relatively smaller categories also exist that can play an important role in the delivery of the health/fitness club experience, including:

- ❑ *Functional Fitness Accessories.* With the explosive growth of functional training, cross-training, and high-intensity interval training, an entirely new segment of equipment has taken hold in the industry, in some cases representing a significant investment for many clubs. Today, functional training equipment is separated into two distinct categories: traditional and non-traditional. According to a recently released global fitness industry trend report, 79 percent of facilities offer traditional functional equipment. Examples of traditional functional equipment include balance boards, the Bosu ball, medicine balls, stability balls, and exercise tubes. The same survey found 72 percent of facilities indicated they offer non-traditional functional training equipment such as kettlebells, battling ropes, sleds, tires, sandbells, and sandbags. Suspension training apparatus (such as offered by TRX) is a third category of functional training equipment. According to the abovementioned survey, 63 percent of facilities offer suspension equipment. Since 2013, traditional and non-traditional functional fitness accessories have been among the fastest growing fitness equipment segments. Some of the leading suppliers of functional fitness accessories include Perform Better, Power Systems, Rage, and Spri.

Since 2013, traditional and non-traditional functional fitness accessories have been among the fastest growing fitness equipment segments.

> Although whole-body vibration training equipment is popular in Europe and South America, as of 2014, it had not established much traction in the U.S. market.

❏ *Whole Body Vibration Machines (WBV).* Whole-body vibration training, sometimes referred to as acceleration training, was initially introduced to the club industry in 2001 by Power Plate, a European-based company. Whole-body vibration training equipment involves the transfer of an alternating mechanical wave from a vibrating platform to the tissues of the body. The transfer of these alternating mechanical waves from the machine platform to the body's tissues results in the creation of physical and neural overloads, which then lead to muscular and soft-tissue adaptation. The advocates of this style of training promote its ability to create improvements in muscular tone and conditioning in relatively brief bouts of activity. Although WBV equipment is popular in Europe and South America, as of 2014, it had not established much traction in the U.S. market. According to an industry trend report conducted by ClubIntel in 2016, only 7 percent of clubs indicate having whole-body vibration equipment. The two leading brands of WBV equipment are the Power Plate and the iTonic, distributed by Free Motion. It should be noted that many exercise scientists remain somewhat skeptical of this particular form of training.

❏ *Pilates Equipment.* Pilates equipment has slowly evolved into a significant equipment category with the expansive growth of Pilates programs. Pilates equipment consists of reformers, trapezes, ladder barrels, towers, Wunda chairs, combo chairs, and step barrels and arcs, as well as some additional pieces of accessory equipment. The majority of Pilates equipment purchased by clubs falls into the category of personal reformers (e.g., a single-user reformer that can be used in an individual or group setting), which is the primary piece of equipment employed in both personal-Pilates training and group-Pilates training. The leading manufacturers of Pilates equipment are Balanced Body, Peak, and Stott. The cost of Pilates equipment varies from item to item, brand to brand, and model to model. For example, the average retail price for studio reformers ranges between $3,000 and $4,500 each, with the classroom-designed reformers, such as Balanced Body's "Allegro Reformer," retailing for around $2,500. Another popular piece of Pilates equipment, the Cadillac (which is also referred to as the "Trapeze") ranges in price from $5,000 to $6,000, depending on the accessories purchased with it. (Note: The Cadillac is a Pilates table with a series of attached overhead implements.). Another piece of Pilates equipment that has taken hold in the health/fitness club industry is the Tower, a freestanding unit that allows individuals to perform some of the movements typically done on a Cadillac.

❏ *Spa Equipment.* As day spas have evolved into a noteworthy profit center for many clubs in the health/fitness club industry, the market for the equipment utilized in day spas has grown substantially. An incredible variety of equipment is needed to operate a successful spa, including:
  • *Massage tables.* Massage tables range from fixed tables to adjustable tables, including hydraulic-driven adjustable tables. The price of a massage table ranges from $800 to $1,200 if it is self-adjusting and closer to $2,200 to $4,000 if it is hydraulic.
  • *Facial tables.* Facial tables are similar to massage tables, except that they also have armrests and backs that enable users to be elevated so that they

can be placed in a partially seated position. The cost of these tables ranges from $1,200 to $4,000, depending on the features desired.
- *Manicure tables.* The typical manicure table includes all the storage that is needed for the manicure products. A high-quality manicure table retails for between $900 and $1,500.
- *Pedicure stations.* The most popular pedicure stations include a number of features, such as a custom chair with armrests and a separate footbath/whirlpool. These stations retail for between $4,000 and $6,000. Some pedicure stations are also available that employ portable footbaths and chairs, rather than the more first-rate features. These stations cost approximately $2,000 less than the more upscale models.
- *Facial Stations.* A facial station encompasses a variety of devices necessary for performing basic facials, such as a magnifying light and rotary brush. A quality facial-station system retails for around $2,500 to $5,000.

Examples of other equipment that is often employed in spas include hot wax units, paraffin baths, thermal heaters for hot packs, Vichy shower units, hydrotherapy tubs, scotch hoses, massage chairs, wet tables, and aromatherapy diffusers. Purchasing spa equipment can be a somewhat difficult task, since no single manufacturer makes all of the items needed to operate a day spa. Some companies, such as Living Earth Crafts and Golden Ratio, provide a variety of tables and accessories, but not the full line of spa equipment. A few companies, such as Universal and Takara Belmont, distribute spa equipment from a variety of different suppliers.

Because the equipment industry is an ever-changing, fast-evolving enterprise, health/fitness club professionals need to stay abreast of the changes that occur if they want to be knowledgeable about essential equipment-related factors. IHRSA annually produces a publication, *FIT* (Fitness Industry Technology), that provides an overview of the various equipment categories and a listing of the various equipment suppliers. Several industry-related magazines (including *Athletic Business, Club Industry, Club Solutions,* and *Recreation Management*) also publish editions that detail the equipment that is utilized in the health/fitness club industry. (Note: A list of the leading manufacturers of health/fitness equipment in the industry is included in the appendices of this book.) One of the best ways to stay abreast of changes in equipment is to attend one of the major industry tradeshows, such as Club Industry (typically held in October), Athletic Business (held in either November or December), IHRSA (usually held in March), and FIBO (held in Germany every April).

Purchase or Lease Equipment

As previously stated, outfitting a health/fitness club with new equipment can range from $15 to $30 a square foot. As a result, a typical health/fitness facility might have to spend between $300,000 and $1,000,000 on exercise equipment. Because this expense can often represent a significant financial hurdle for owners, leasing becomes a viable alternative to acquisition and later depreciation. Many of the most successful club operators (e.g., LA Fitness, 24 Hour Fitness, etc.) often choose to lease their equipment rather than purchase it, which enables them to save the initial investment that would be required if they had purchased it. The following list provides a brief overview of the pros and cons associated with either leasing or purchasing equipment.

- ❏ *Purchasing Equipment*
  - Pro:
    - ✓ Outright ownership of the equipment
    - ✓ Able to depreciate the equipment on financial statements
    - ✓ Not at the mercy of leasing companies
    - ✓ Causes club owners to have a greater "stake" in the business and a resultant commitment to making the business work (they cannot walk away as easily from the business)
  - Con:
    - ✓ Initial up-front investment can be overwhelming and consume a significant amount of start-up funds
    - ✓ Equipment depreciates in value as an asset (loss in asset value)
    - ✓ Clubs are often less likely to invest in new equipment in coming years

- ❏ *Leasing Equipment*
  - Pro:
    - ✓ Eliminates up-front investment
    - ✓ Allows cost of equipment to be spread over several years
    - ✓ Provides opportunity to upgrade equipment more readily and remain current with industry equipment trends
    - ✓ Owners can step away from leases in the event of financial challenges
  - Con:
    - ✓ Increases the cost of equipment due to interest payments to leasing company
    - ✓ May require club to have leases with more than one company

Reflections

Fitness equipment represents a significant investment for club operators. Fitness equipment, along with the club facilities, programs, and staff, is one of the four legs of the industry's general business model. With the possible exception of fitness programs, no other element of the industry model is influenced more by fitness trends, and consequently, club operators must remain current with the latest equipment advances.

> Many of the most successful club operators (e.g., LA Fitness, 24 Hour Fitness, etc.) often choose to lease their equipment rather than purchase it.

Other Health/Fitness Facility Models

PART 7

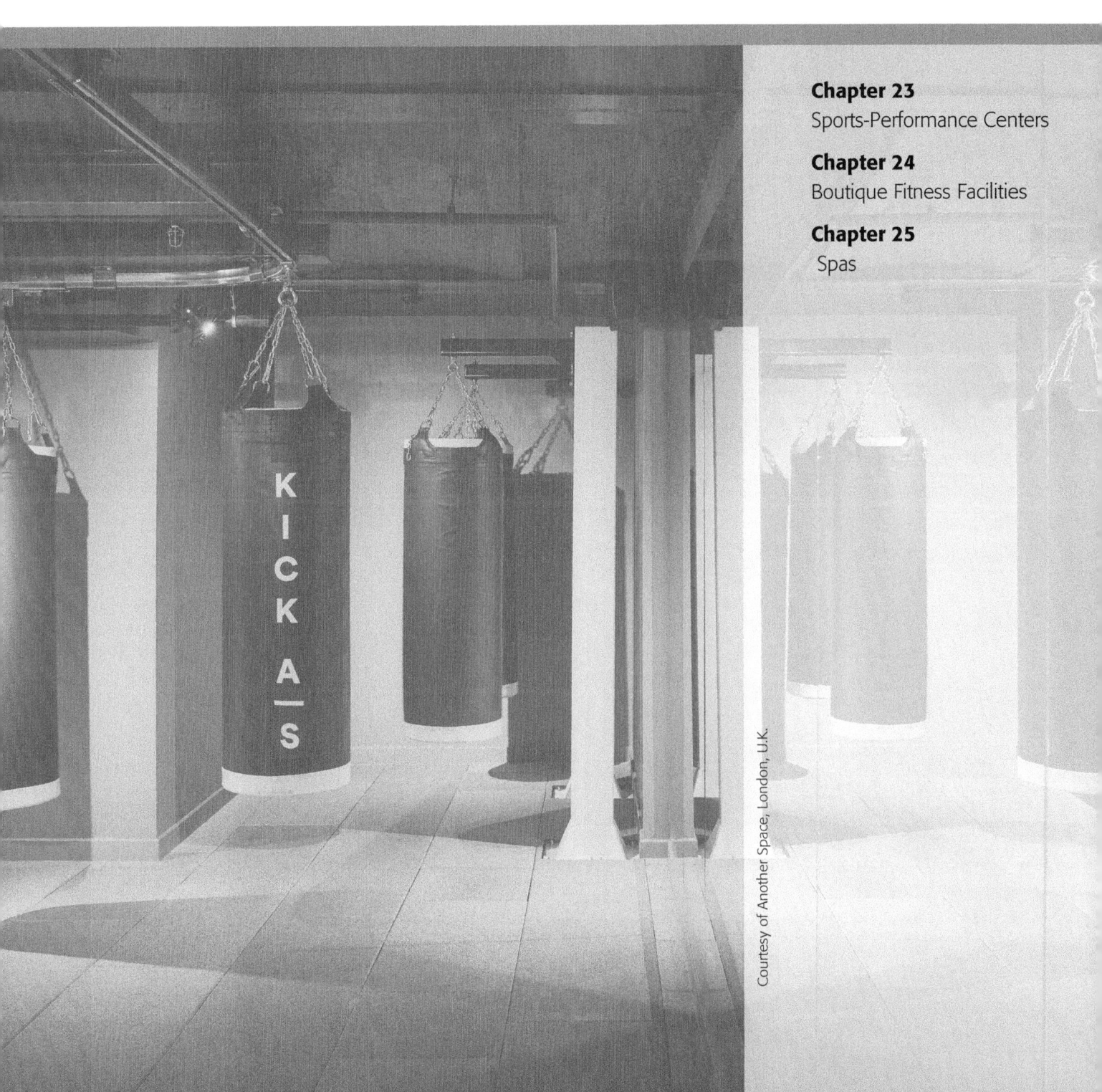

Chapter 23
Sports-Performance Centers

Chapter 24
Boutique Fitness Facilities

Chapter 25
Spas

Courtesy of Another Space, London, U.K.

Sports-Performance Centers

23

"Good, better, best. Never let it rest. Until your good is better and your better is your best"

—Tim Duncan, NBA MVP

Chapter Objectives

Over the past decade or so, sports-performance programming and sports-performance centers have become new elements in the health/fitness facility experience offering. Since sports-performance centers are such a new arena of programming for health/fitness facilities and because relatively little has been written about them, this chapter provides an overview of this niche industry, which has increasingly become an important component of the overall club industry product mix.

Introduction to the Sports Performance Training Market

The sports-conditioning and sports-performance industry is a relatively young industry, having its roots in the early 1990s. The industry can trace its roots to the expansive growth in youth and adult sports participation that began in the late 1980s and early 1990s.

Within the context of health/fitness clubs, sports-conditioning and sports-performance training involves the modalities, protocols, and programs that focus on enhancing an individual's ability to perform in athletic-related activities at a peak level, while encountering the challenges and stresses inherent in either a competitive or a recreational sports environment. Such performance training is also designed to serve as a mechanism for reducing the risk of injury due to sports participation. As a rule, sports conditioning and performance training provides movement modalities, protocols, and programs that are designed to enhance sport-specific attributes, such as acceleration, agility, balance, core stability, power, recovery, speed, and strength. In addition, because documented evidence shows that corporate executives and homemakers sometimes experience stresses equal to or exceeding those of competitive athletes, the value of sports-conditioning and sports-performance centers for aiding those target groups has helped lead to a further expansion of this industry segment. According to IHRSA's latest *Health Club Consumer Report*, approximately 2 percent of health club consumers indicate they are members

> The sports-conditioning and sports-performance industry can trace its roots to the expansive growth in youth and adult sports participation that began in the late 1980s and early 1990s.

of sport-specific training facilities or sports performance boutiques, equivalent to 1.2 million members.

The sports performance industry represents a crossover of two more established industries—the health/fitness club industry and the healthcare/physical therapy industry. The influence of the health/fitness club industry is reflected in programs such as agility training, core conditioning, speed training, and strength training, which are fitness-based modalities. In addition, the use of certified personal trainers, pay-as-you-go packages, and monthly fees can also be traced back to the health/fitness club industry. Finally, the franchising model being employed by many of the sports-performance center operators is very similar to the model used in the health/fitness club industry. The healthcare industry (in particular, the physical therapy industry) has also influenced the practices of those in the athletic and sports-performance business. Because many sports-performance centers feature programs and services that are dependent upon the expertise of certain healthcare professionals, among them physical therapists, physical-therapy assistants, athletic trainers, chiropractors, and nutritionists.

The Primary Forces Driving the Sports Performance Training Market

Participation in organized sports has grown significantly since the mid-1990s, both for youth between the ages of 6 and 17 and for adults, ages 35 and older. According to a report released by Sports Marketing Surveys in 2013, overall participation in sports, fitness, and related physical activities for 2012 among individuals over the age six represented 33 percent of the population. In this same report, it showed that between 28 percent and 63 percent of adults, depending on generation (i.e., Baby Boomers, Generation X, and Generation Y), participated in either individual sports, team sports, or outdoor sports, while as many as 66 percent engaged in fitness sports. In a research report released in 2008 by the National Council on Youth Sports, it indicated that approximately 44 million young people participated in youth sports activities, 66 percent of whom were boys and 34 percent of whom were girls. In 2013, a report generated by the Sports and Fitness Industry Association showed that 21.5 million youth between the ages of 6 and 16 played on sports teams. Finally, in a research report published in 2009 in the *Journal of Physical Activity and Health*, the researchers reported that approximately 25 percent of adults participated in sports activities.

Youth Sports Participation and What Lies Behind It

According to the most recently available data on sports participation from the Sports and Fitness Industry Association, approximately 21.5 million boys and girls between the ages of six and 17 participated in organized and team sports in 2012. In the Sports and Fitness Industry Association's *2013 Topline Report*, it shows among Generation Z (youth born after the year 2000) that approximately 50 percent play individual sports, 53 percent team sports, and 63 percent outdoor sports. Figure 23-1 shows some general statistics regarding the types of organized sports in which Generation Z participates.

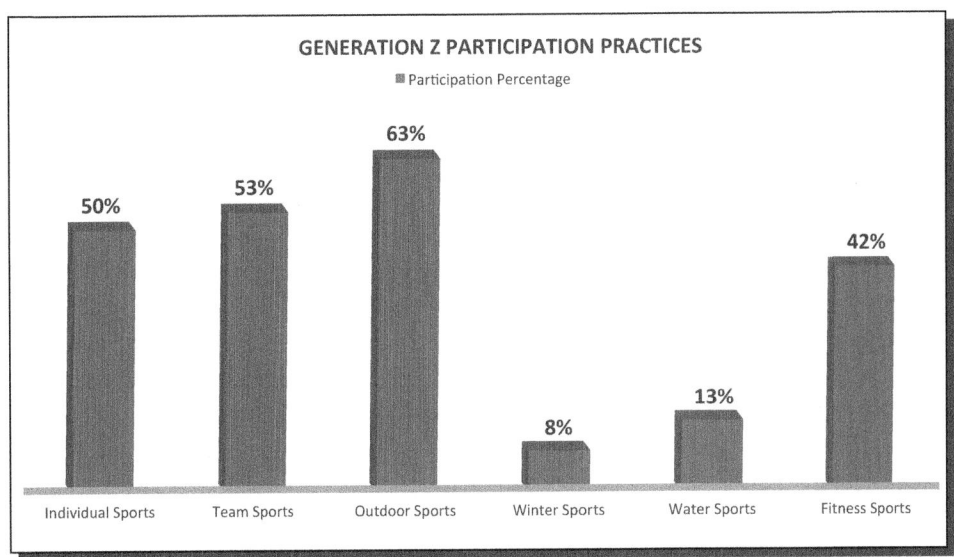

Figure 23-1. Generation Z sports participation practices

Sports participation among youth has been driven, in large part, by the parents of these young people. According to a recent survey conducted by sports-participation researchers, nearly 99 percent of parents surveyed indicated that they believed sports participation promotes physical fitness. This belief may be fueled, in part, by the mounting evidence that shows that over one-third of today's American youth are obese, and nearly 50 percent of today's youth are overweight. Furthermore, several recently conducted studies indicate that youth-sports participation may fulfill a number of important developmental needs for youth, including:

- Sports participation is fun and provides instant gratification for the child.
- Sports participation fulfills the "affiliative" need of youth, which involves such factors as friendship, sense of belonging, and social connection.
- Sports can provide physical exercise, which can promote improved health.
- Sports can help youth with the development of self-esteem, self-confidence, and positive social values.

According to the National Association for Sport and Physical Education (NASPE), participation in organized sports and fitness activities is particularly important for middle school-aged youth (e.g., ages 10 to 14). NASPE-sponsored research shows that recreational and organized sports participation improves motor skills, physical fitness, physical and social growth, and self-esteem for middle school-aged youth. While many experts in the field of child development differ on which of these four drivers of sports participation are actually critical factors, the resulting outcomes are evident. Youth are currently far more likely to be actively engaged in at least one organized sports activity. In fact, it is the Association's position that all middle school-aged youth should, at least, have the opportunity to participate in organized sports and physical activity.

A strong indicator of youth sports-activity participation can be traced to population demographics. According to research, 33 percent of parents who enroll their youth in organized sports activities have household incomes in excess of $75,000 annually. In addition, the parents of youth engaged in organized sports are far more likely to have a college education, be a white-collar professional, and have two family members in professional careers. If the data on youth-sports participation is closely examined, a hypothesis could be made that youth-sports participation is partially a result of an affluent, competitive, and results-driven adult population that seeks to provide its children with experiences that simulate the competitive and results-driven world of which they are a part. Another indication of the growth in sports participation is reflected in data released several years ago by the National Federation of State High School Associations that show enormous increases in the number of students actively engaged in high school sports. It is interesting to note that Texas, at the time the report was released, had over 740,000 students involved in organized school sponsored sports, which is 70,000 more than California, the second most active state, and over twice as many as New York—the third most active state for high school sport participation.

The burgeoning youth sports-participation market is not the only driver in the growth of sports performance based training programs and centers. Parents also see sports-performance conditioning as a way to provide their children with a competitive edge, as well as a means of increasing the chances that their children will receive a college scholarship and even have professional sports careers.

Colleges and universities have also contributed to the growth of specialized athletic and sports conditioning. Most colleges and even some high schools currently employ certified sports conditioning specialists (e.g., individuals certified by the National Strength and Conditioning Association). As this practice has evolved at the college and university level, it has created an ever-increasing demand at the high school and junior high school level for similar programs. This push has subsequently manifested itself in individuals as young as six years of age. Many coaches and parents believe that specialized training that focuses on improving agility, balance, quickness, speed, and strength can help youth perform better, which in turn, will have a positive impact on age-group recognition, and the possibility of receiving a college scholarship and/or having a professional sports career. The desire to have youth excel at their given sport activity at earlier and earlier ages is a significant and important driver of the demand for sports-conditioning and performance programs.

Preventing Sports-Related Injuries in Youth

Approximately 3.5 million children under the age of 18 receive medical treatment each year for sports-related injuries. Most of these injuries are attributed to collisions, falls, and overexertion. Overuse injuries account for nearly 50 percent of all sports injuries at the middle and high-school level (ages 11 to 18). Interestingly, 55 percent of all school injuries are related to sports participation, of which 62 percent occur during practice. The majority of these injuries are typically treated in sports-medicine clinics, rather than in hospitals.

Football generates the greatest number of sports injuries among youth. As can be seen in Figure 23-2, however, football is by no means the only sport that results in significant levels of injury to American youth. When the date is broken down further, youth between the ages of six and 14 account for 40 percent of all hospital-reported sports injuries. From the ages of six to nine, girls are the most frequently injured, while boys between the ages of 10 and 14 are most often injured and most seriously injured.

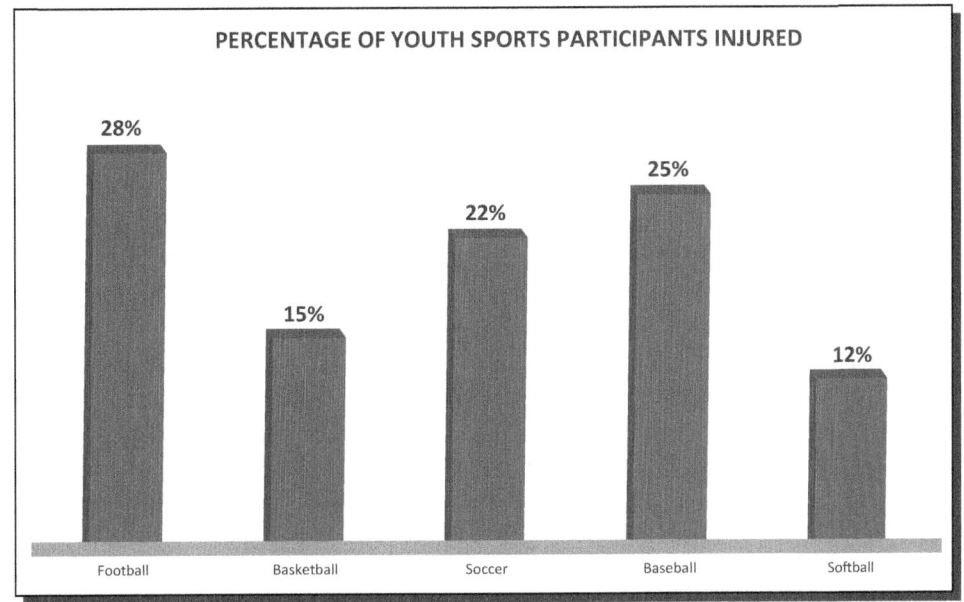

Figure 23-2. Youth sports with the highest incidence of sports injuries

The Role of Sports-Conditioning Programs for Youth

According to a policy sheet written by the American Academy of Pediatrics (AAP), youth-sports injuries can be reduced when several important steps are taken, including:

- Matching the skills of the child to the demands of the particular sport
- Providing proper physical conditioning for the child before they participate
- Grouping children by skill level
- Ensuring that youth receive a physical exam before participating

Sports-conditioning and performance centers can play a critical role with two of the AAP recommendations. First, these centers can be involved in matching the specific demand of a sport to the skills and maturation level of the child. Second, these centers can provide the proper conditioning programs for reducing the likelihood of injury due to inadequate physical preparation.

In addition to being able to play a role in injury prevention, sports-performance programs and centers can play an important role in helping a child recover from a sports injury and helping prepare them for a safe reintroduction to their sport. Finally, sports-performance programs and centers can play an important role in building the basic components of fitness that allow for enhanced sports performance. By employing scientifically based steps for safely developing such athletic-related attributes as agility, speed, strength, and core stability, these programs can assist young people in reaching new performance heights in a relatively risk-free and time-efficient manner.

It is important to note that according to data in the publication, the *IHRSA 2015 Profiles of Success*, approximately 5 percent of health/fitness club memberships are held by youth under the age of 18. Accordingly, sports-performance centers are fulfilling a market niche that other health/fitness programs have generally been unable to capitalize on to this point.

Adult Sports Participation

As discussed previously in this chapter, a large number of adults participate in fitness and sports activities. While adults in Generations Y and X remain the two most active adult populations, Baby Boomers (adults born between 1946 and 1964) remain active in sports activities. According to the aforementioned *Sports Fitness Industry Association Topline Report*, between 27 percent and 33 percent of Baby Boomers participate in individual and team sports, and 62 percent participate in fitness sports. The largest segment of sports participation among adults is in fitness sports, activities such as resistance training, walking, group-exercise classes, etc. Figure 23-3 provides an overview of adult sports participation based on the *Sports Fitness Associations Topline Report* for 2013. Researchers believe that several significant factors have contributed to this growth in fitness and sports participation, including the desire for older adults to feel and look younger, the desire of individuals to prevent major illness as they age, the desire of people to enjoy activities that they enjoyed when they were young adults, and the desire of individuals to remain active throughout their life.

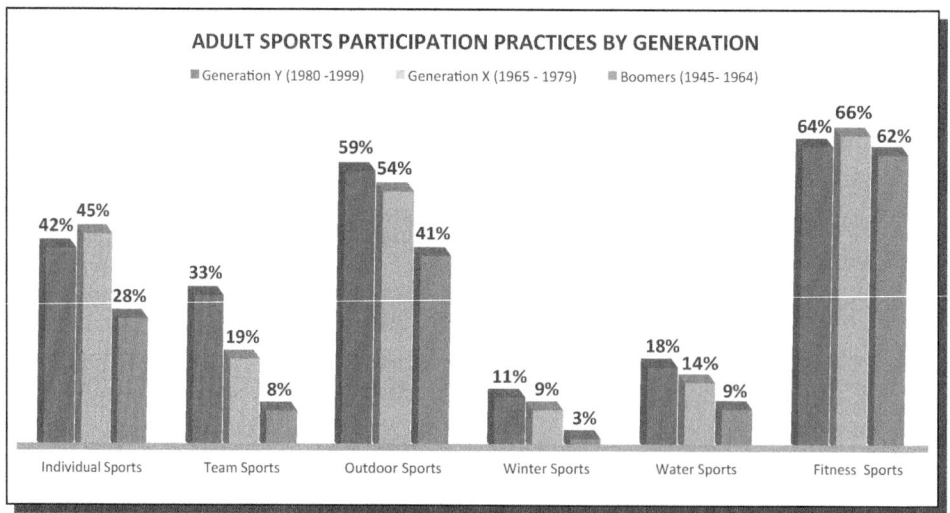

Figure 23-3. Adult sports participation practices

Unfortunately, as many of these adults begin participating in fitness and sports activities for the first time in years, they experience a higher incidence of discomfort and injury. According to the research, Baby Boomers generate a more significant number of sports injuries than any other segment of the population. From 1991 to 1998, sports injuries among baby boomers increased by over 33 percent. Even more alarmingly, for adults over the age of 65, the number of sports injuries during this time period increased by 54 percent. The majority of the sports injuries in these adult populations can be attributed to such factors as muscle imbalances, a lack of flexibility, problems with balance and agility, core strength weakness, and improper preparation for the targeted sport activity.

The Role of Sports-Conditioning Programs for Adults

Based on the data reviewed in the previous section, sports-conditioning programs can fulfill several important roles for the adult population, particularly for baby boomers.

- Because adults should have access to a trained professional who understands the physical limitations of aging and the demands placed on the musculoskeletal system, as people age, physical therapists and certified-fitness specialists in this arena may be the most qualified individuals to fulfill this responsibility.
- Programs that focus on agility, balance, and core strength are critical to allowing older adults to safely and enjoyably participate in fitness and sports. These are factors in which most sports-conditioning programs specialize.
- Reducing the risk of injury and providing services that assist in the road to recovery from injury are important to active older adults. These are roles that sports-conditioning programs can play.
- For the older adult whose desire it is to continue engaging in competitive sports and activities, the conditioning expertise provided by sports-conditioning programs can be critical.

Overview of the Sports Conditioning Industry

In existence since the early 1990s, the sports-conditioning industry is currently evolving from an entrepreneurial industry, led by independent single-business operators and single-franchise operators, to a maturing industry, led by franchise organizations and larger corporately owned businesses. The most dominant players in this particular market are Velocity Sports, based in Georgia; Athletic Republic (e.g., formerly Frappier Acceleration Training), based out of North Dakota; and D1 Sports, based in Tennessee. Velocity presently has over 50 franchised locations in the United States, while Athletic Republic has franchised its program to over 160 locations in the United States, making it the leading sports-performance center franchise in the world. D1 Sports, which is the newest player in the industry, now operates over 30 facilities throughout the U.S. In addition to these market-leaders, several other business models have arisen in the past five to ten years, including EXOS, formerly Athletes Performance Center's for Athletic Performance (CAP), High Impact Training (HIT), Competitive Athlete Training Zone (CATZ), and Parisi Speed School. The Parisi Speed School, which has emerged as a major player in the market by focusing its efforts on the health/fitness facility industry, currently has over 75 club-based programs in operation around the United States, making it the second largest sports-performance center franchise in the U.S.

> The sports-conditioning industry is currently evolving from an entrepreneurial industry, led by independent single-business operators and single-franchise operators, to a maturing industry, led by franchise organizations and larger corporately owned businesses.

A Profile of the Market for Sports-Conditioning Programs in Health/Fitness Facilities

The primary market for sports-conditioning programs in the health/fitness club industry can be described as follows:

- Middle school–aged boys and girls (e.g., 10 to 14 years old). This group may comprise as much as 50 percent of the total audience in many markets.
- High school–aged boys and girls (e.g., 15 to 18 years old). This group may comprise approximately 20 percent of the audience.
- Youth-aged boys and girls (e.g., 6 to 10 years old). This group comprises approximately 10 percent to 15 percent of the audience in most markets.
- College and professional athletes (e.g., 18 and older individuals who participate in high-level amateur or professional competition). This group might comprise as much as 5 percent to 10 percent of the audience, depending on the specific market that exists in a particular geographic area.
- Recreational adult athletes (e.g., individuals over the age of 18 who engage in athletic endeavors that are recreational in nature). Depending on the specific market, this audience might range from 5 percent to 15 percent of the total.

One of the top predictors of sports-performance center success is based on the estimated number of student athletes (e.g., athletes in middle-school and high-school sports) who reside within a 20-minute driving distance of the site location. Sports-participation statistics indicate that approximately 55 percent of high school students and an estimated 30 percent of all middle-school students participate in some form of sport activity. According to antidotal research from the leading franchise operators, one meaningful benchmark for success is based on having an eligible student-athlete population of at least 1,500, and preferably 4,000, within the desired market area. Based on this antidotal data, the ideal market should have a student population of 12,000. Some unpublished research indicates that sports-performance centers are found to attract between 3 percent and 5 percent of the eligible youth population between the ages of 10 and 18, who reside in households earning over $75,000 annually.

A second important predictor of success in the sports-performance center segment of the industry is based on the average household income of the targeted demographic area, especially those served by the identified schools. Households with an average income in excess of $75,000 are the most attractive market, since one-in-three of these households will have youth involved in sports participation.

Sports-Performance Center Metrics

In general, the sports-performance industry does not publish benchmark metric data. The data that is available is based on a survey of a small sample of successful operators. As a result, the metrics presented in this section may not be statistically valid, but are reflective of what several operators in the business produce.

Sports-performance centers range in size from 1,000 square feet to over 20,000 square feet, with the majority ranging in size from 3,000 to 5,000 square feet.

Sports-performance centers range in size from 1,000 square feet to over 20,000 square feet, with the majority ranging in size from 3,000 to 5,000 square feet. A typical center tends to have between 20 and 90 clients a month, with the months of May, June, July, and August being the busiest. Unpublished research indicates that between 50 percent and 60 percent of client traffic in these centers is attributed to these four months of the year. On an annual basis, the average center sees about 500 clients over the course of the year. Client traffic is generated through a blend of private- and small-group training (e.g., less than six clients) and larger-group sessions (e.g., 12 to 20 clients). The majority of sports-performance centers offer training packages ranging in duration from 8 sessions to 26 sessions, with packages of 20 sessions being the most popular. A typical training package of 20 sessions might cost between $400 and $1,000 dollars, with an average package price of approximately $700. Furthermore, the average annual revenue per client is just over $600, and the average revenue per client visit is slightly over $25. As such, from a health/fitness club industry perspective, the revenue generation capability of sports-performance centers is in the neighborhood of $100 per square foot per year.

The Essential Components of a Sports-Performance Center

- *Facility.* As previously discussed in this chapter, the average free-standing sports-performance center ranges in size from 3,000 to 5,000 square feet. Centers located within an existing club environment might range from as small as 800 square feet to as large as 10,000 square feet. Red's, a large multipurpose club based in Lafayette, Louisiana, recently opened a free-standing performance center called MIT (maximum intensity training) which occupies approximating 10,000 square feet. The typical free-standing facility could include one or more of the following components:
  - Indoor running track (20 to 60 yards)
  - Sport court
  - Indoor sport-turf surface

- Open space for functional equipment (e.g., ladders, cones, hurdles, medicine balls, running cords, plyometric boxes, etc.)
- Treadmills (e.g., super treadmills that go as fast as 25 miles per hour with grades exceeding 20 percent)
- Resistance equipment (both circuit and free-weight oriented)
- Custom plyometric equipment
- Locker rooms
- Classroom for athlete assessment (physical testing and videotaping and viewing)

❑ *Equipment.* Most, if not all, of the existing sports-performance centers utilize the following equipment and accessories:
- Plyometric benches and boxes
- Hurdles
- Ladders
- Cones
- Bands, tubes, and cords
- Chutes and sleds
- Weighted vests
- Super treadmills
- Resistance equipment (e.g., free weights, functional plate-loaded, and selectorized)
- Medicine balls
- Stability balls
- Balance boards
- Foam rollers
- Kettlebells
- Customized floor surfaces (e.g., rubber track, indoor turf, etc.)

On an annual basis, the average sports-performance center sees about 500 clients over the course of the year.

- *Conditioning Concept.* The majority of sports-performance programs focus on a blend of training modalities that concentrate on the development of acceleration, high-end speed, agility, core stability, power, movement mechanics, and neuromuscular coordination. Among the techniques featured in these efforts are active stretching, plyometric training, hyper-speed training, and power training with resistance and body weight, balance training, and cord training.

- *Program Packages Built Around Either a Specific Sports Theme or a Particular Age Group-Oriented Need.* In this regard, age-group programs are normally offered for youth 6 to 11, 12 to 18, and adults. The most commonly themed programs are targeted at speed development, jumping development, or sport-specific training protocols targeted at a particular activity, such as football, basketball, baseball, soccer, volleyball, hockey, etc. The most successful performance programs appear to be driven by a focus on acceleration, speed, and power production. Among sports, football tends to represent the largest audience, although the most involved athletic endeavor can vary by market.

- *Packages Bundled by the Number of Sessions Offered.* Typical package durations range from 8 sessions to 26 sessions. Many of the national sports-performance programs offer guaranteed performance-improvement results, if a certain number of sessions are attended.

- *Small-Group Personal Coaching Sessions.* A majority of the sports-performance programs feature scheduled sessions that involve groups, ranging from two to a dozen athletes. Although numerous programs offer customized personal-performance training, it is not the primary business driver. Most scheduled sessions last between 60 to 90 minutes.

- *Team Field Programs.* Many of the leading national programs offer structured conditioning programs for teams (e.g., youth teams, middle-school teams, high-school teams, etc.). These programs are made available in a variety of formats, ranging from one day to several weeks. As a rule, most of these programs are conducted at a team's location.

- *Sports-Performance Camps and Academies.* During certain times of the year, many sports-performance centers offer specialized camps (e.g., one day to two weeks) that are targeted at a specific sport or skill (e.g., basketball, soccer, jump, speed, etc.).

- *Certified Trainers.* The franchised programs require staff to go through both online, video, classroom, and hands-on training before delivering their programs. In most cases, the programs have a prerequisite that the trainer must have an undergraduate degree in exercise science, athletic training, or physical therapy. In addition, many programs employ staff members that possess a master's degree. Among the numerous health/fitness industry certifying organizations, NSCA and NASM certifications appear to be the most frequently seen in the sports-conditioning arena.

- *Software-Based Monitoring.* It has become a standard operating practice for the programs to use software to design and monitor the programs for the athletes.

Marketing Sports-Performance Centers

Marketing, especially grass roots marketing, is critical to the development and operation of a successful sports-conditioning and performance center. As previously discussed in this chapter, the primary audiences for such services are youth at the middle school and high school levels. As a result, club operators must develop an effective marketing strategy that enables it to attract these young athletes. Among the strategies that have proven successful in reaching this particular target audience are the following:

- Advertisements in local papers and magazines
- Contacting the local schools and talking with the coaches
- Conducting in-service training clinics for coaches
- Conducting workshops and seminars for parent groups
- Conducting testing and one-day trial programs for the local middle-school and high-school coaches
- Contacting and working with the local youth-sport leagues. Getting involved with the coaches and parents groups associated with these programs.
- Getting involved with the local booster and sport-league associations
- Sponsoring sports teams in the community
- Aligning with local college or professional athletes/teams. Getting a local professional and/or college team/athlete to be a spokesperson for the center.
- Interactive websites and social media pages.
- Contacting local physician groups and physical-therapy groups that see kids with sports-related injuries
- Direct mail or email blasts to local youth-sports team organizers, parent groups, and coaches. Most direct mail is followed by phone calls and visits.

An Overview of Several Leading Sports-Performance Operations

- ❏ *Athletic Republic.* Athletic Republic, formerly Frappier Acceleration, was founded in 1990 by John Frappier, an exercise physiologist and established expert in the area of training athletes. The Athletic Republic business model was developed around specialized exercises, exercise protocols, and equipment which have benefits that have been documented through research to have a positive impact on sports performance. Rather than creating a franchise business model, Frappier initially established a licensing model that allowed local entrepreneurs to purchase a license for his program and then incorporate it into a business model, which they could adapt to their local market. In 2006, the company went to a franchise model and, a year later, changed its name to Athletic Republic. Over the past 15 years, over 100,000 athletes at 165 Athletic Republic licensed facilities have completed at least one level of the program. The Athletic Republic model consists of the following elements:
  - Eight trademarked pieces of training equipment (e.g., treadmill, plyometric leg press, etc.) to support the program modules
  - Multiple-stage acceleration program modules that are designed to accommodate mechanics, neuromuscular coordination, anaerobic and

aerobic conditioning, muscle physiology, and posture. Modules are available in individual and group formats.
- Facility spaces ranging from 2,500 square feet to 7,500 square feet
- Custom software program for athlete testing and monitoring
- Video-analysis system using custom software
- The primary target audience is middle school-age student athletes.
- Sessions are conducted in either a private or group format, with groups ranging from two to eight athletes.
- Single-session pricing varies from $25 to $40.
- Packaged programs vary in length from eight sessions to 25 sessions.
- Specialized training and certified staff who deliver the programs.

❑ *Parisi Speed School.* The Parisi Speed School was initially developed in 1993 with a free-standing sports-performance and personal-training center (initially operated with a Frappier license). Parisi opened a second center in 1998. By 2005, Parisi had a total of four locations. In 2005, Parisi went forward with the development of a franchise model that allowed health/fitness facilities to franchise a Parisi Speed School. As of 2014, there were over 75 Parisi franchise locations. Parisi is most noted for its work in preparing athletes for the annual NFL combine. The Parisi business model consists of the following elements:

> **The Parisi Speed School is most noted for its work in preparing athletes for the annual NFL combine.**

- Three custom-program levels that are designed for three distinct athlete groups (Fast, Fit, and Fun for 7- to 11-year-olds, Total Performance for 12- to 18-year-olds, and Reach Peak for elite athletes over the age of 18).
- Speed camps
- NFL combine program
- Team training newsletter and program
- Video store, with tapes for training various level athletes
- A space of at least 2,500 square feet
- Utilizes existing ground-based equipment and has affiliations with vendors for functional equipment and treadmills.

❑ *Velocity Sports Performance.* Velocity Sports was founded in 1999 by Loren Seagrave, an internationally recognized track and field coach who specialized in training student-athletes. After opening his first center in Atlanta, Seagrave saw the potential of bringing his new model of performance training to other markets and retained specialists in franchising to assist him. Since its inception, Velocity has grown to approximately 50 franchises across the U.S. The Velocity business model consists of the following elements:
- 8,500 to 15,000 square feet of total pace (some facilities are as large as 30,000 square feet)
- 7,500 to 12,000 square feet dedicated to sports conditioning
- Indoor turf field, indoor basketball court/sport court, 60-meter track, weight room, and lockers
- Basic conditioning accessories (e.g., bands, cones, ladders, plyometric benches, etc.)

- Structured programs for different levels of athletes, both individual and group
- A primary target audience of 12- to 16-year-old student athletes (e.g., encompassing approximately 60 percent of its market share)
- Packaged programs of 12, 18, and 24 sessions, with each session lasting 90 minutes
- Sessions conducted in a group format, with the number of athletes per class ranging from 2 to 10
- An average session cost of $25 to $35. The packaged programs range from $444 for a 12-week package to $1,275 for 75 sessions. Franchises may differ in their pricing.

❑ *D1 Sports.* D1 Sports was founded in 2003, and in the past decade has grown to over 30 locations throughout the U.S. One of the unique business approaches used by D1 is to bring in local business partners (investors) for each location who are former or current professional athletes. This approach has enabled them to create considerable buzz in each of the markets where they conduct business. For example, one of its first investor partners was Peyton Manning. The D1 business model consists of the following elements:
- They have investor partners in each market who are professional athletes.
- They partner with local medical and/or physical therapy groups in each of their markets.
- They focus on athlete-based group training built on a balanced conditioning approach that incorporates a dynamic warm-up, speed, agility and quickness training, strength training, and core and flexibility conditioning.
- They offer structured programs for three primary groups: scholastic (youth), adult, and elite athletes. Each program is composed of several levels.

Reflections

The sports performance business has emerged in recent years as a viable offering for the health/fitness club industry. As presented in this chapter, youth and adult sports participation continues to grow and with it the demand for training programs specific to the needs of those engaged in sports. The sports performance training industry has emerged as a viable business model over the past decade, and more recently, has experienced growing demand from health/fitness club operators. Sports performance training programs offer an excellent opportunity to engage youth populations that previously represented a challenging market segment for the club industry. Club operators whose business model is built around serving a family market might want to consider exploring the addition of a sports performance training program to their existing business model.

Boutique Fitness Facilities

24

"No matter what or whom we're talking about, from movies to chiropractors to books to financial planners, the consumer hankers after specialization."

—Susan Friedman, author of *Riches in Niches*

Chapter Objectives

Starting around 2010, the health/fitness industry was shaken by a new and highly disruptive business model known as boutique fitness studios or, as some in the industry reference them, micro-gyms. The boutiques brought to market an entirely new value proposition, one predicated in large part on providing a highly personalized, niche program driven and socially enlightened fitness experience. When boutiques first made noise, the industry ignored it, brushing aside their rumblings, thinking they were nothing more than a consumer fad. By 2016, boutiques had become the mouse that roared, and in doing so they, along with budget clubs, became the two largest disruptive business models in the health/fitness club industry. According to data presented in IHRSA's *2016 Health Club Consumer Report*, approximately 35 percent of health club consumers (Figure 24-1) indicated they belonged to or visited a boutique fitness studio.

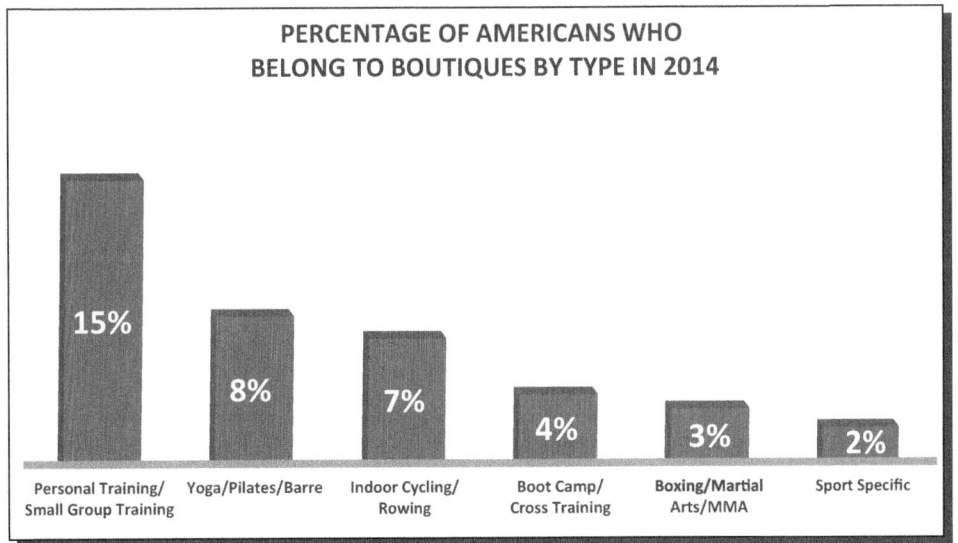

Figure 24-1. Percentage of Americans who belong to boutiques by type in 2014

This chapter will explore the phenomena of boutique fitness studios, or micro-gyms. The chapter will begin by taking a look at some of the most prevalent boutique fitness studios that are presently operating around the globe. Next, the chapter will explore some of the unique dynamics of the boutique space. Finally, the chapter will provide insights into the power of the boutiques and why they have become such a disruptive force in the health/fitness club industry.

Types of Boutique Fitness Offerings

Boutique fitness facilities are as varied as the interests of their customers and the passions of their owners. Boutiques can range in size from as small as 1,000 square feet (91 square meters) to greater than 10,000 square feet (1,000 square meters). In a 2016 study conducted by the Association of Fitness Studios (AFS), the group discovered that approximately 73 percent of boutique studios were less than 5,000 square feet (455 square meters), and 33 percent were actually smaller than 2,500 square feet (228 m) (Figure 24-2). In a later study conducted by AFS in 2016, they found the average boutique studio to occupy 3,800 square feet. So what are some of the unique and disruptive business models that comprise the boutique segment?

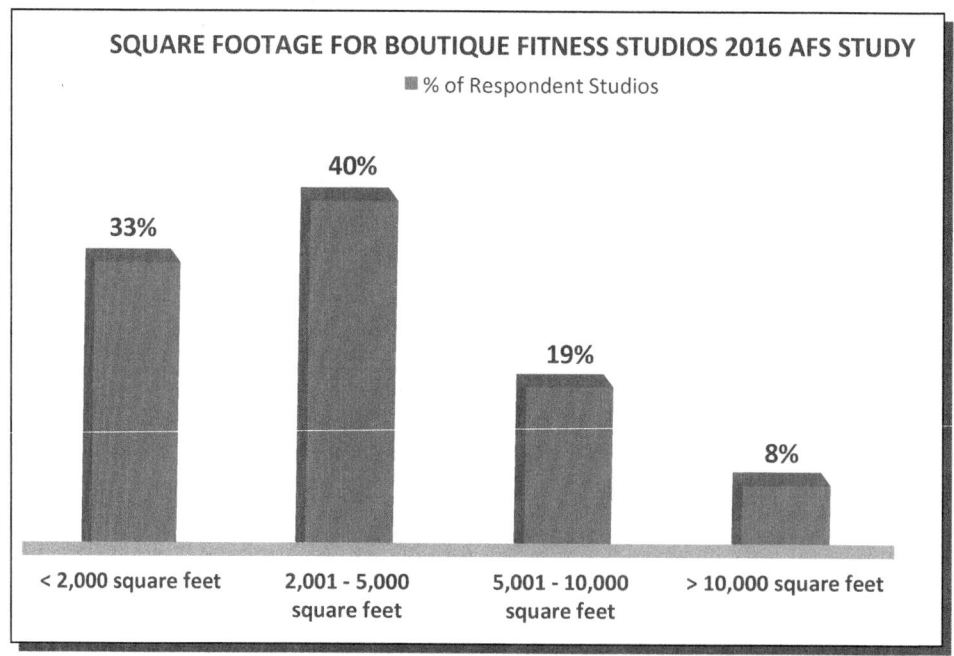

Figure 24-2. Square footage for boutique fitness studios 2016 AFS Study

- ❏ *Yoga Studios.* According to a survey conducted by the Association of Fitness Studios (AFS) in 2016, approximately 2 percent of boutique studio owners indicated they operated a yoga studio (Figure 24-2). According to IHRSA's *2016 Health Club Consumer Report*, 8 percent of consumers (Figure 24-1) indicated belonging to a yoga/Pilates/barre studio. The vast majority of yoga studios are independent studios, but over the last few years there has been an emergence of corporately owned and franchise yoga chains. Some of the more well-known multi-unit yoga studios include Pure Yoga owned by Equinox and based in New York; Yoga Works, a chain of approximately 30 yoga studios operated in California and the Northeast corridor of the U.S., Core Power Yoga, based out of Denver, Colorado, with over 100 studios throughout the U.S., Bikram franchise studios with hundreds of locations around the globe; and Antigravity Yoga franchised and licensed studios with well over 50 locations globally. Yoga studios come in a variety of forms, including:

- Antigravity yoga studios (developed by Christopher Harrison) and some of its many knock-offs that offer suspended or aerial style yoga movements.
- Bikram yoga studios, which offer the founder's unique style of yoga comprised of standard positions performed in temperatures exceeding 100 degrees Fahrenheit.
- Singular-style yoga studios that focus on one form of yoga such as Ashtanga, Hatha, Iyengar, power, and Vinyasa.
- Multi-discipline yoga studios that offer multiple styles of yoga.

❏ *Pilates Studios.* The vast majority of private Pilates studios are owned and operated by individuals, with few if any being large multi-studio business that are either corporate-owned or franchised. According to AFS's 2016 research, approximately 4 percent of boutique studio owners indicated their primary offering was Pilates. As shared earlier, approximately 8 percent of consumers indicate being a member or user of a yoga/Pilates/barre studio. One of the larger multi-unit Pilates organizations, with approximately 25 franchise locations around the U.S., is IMX Pilates. In addition to IMX, other Pilates franchises include Club Pilates with over 170 locations and WundaBar Pilates with six locations.

❏ *Barre Studios.* Over the past five years, barre studios have evolved as one of the leading boutique fitness facility concepts. Barre studios appear to have started as individually owned and operated business, but in just a short period of time have evolved into larger multi-group businesses under a franchise umbrella. In just the past few years, several prominent barre studio franchises have emerged, among them Pure Barre, with approximately 300 locations in the U.S., Bar Method with an estimated 72 locations in the U.S., Barre Code with approximately 28 locations, and Physique 57 with nine locations. Barre studios have their origins in the Lotte Berk Method that was brought to the U.S. in the 1970s and is still offered in the UK under the Lotte Berk name.

❏ *Cycling Studios.* Over the past decade, studios dedicated purely to cycling have evolved, such as the ever-popular Soul Cycle in New York, owned by Equinox which presently operates over 80 studios across the country; Flywheel, a cycling franchise with approximately 40 locations throughout the U.S.; and CycleBar, a cycling franchise with over 70 locations. According to AFS's 2016 research, approximately 4 percent of studio owners indicated their primary discipline was group cycling. According to IHRSA's *2016 Health Club Consumer Report*, approximately 7 percent of consumers indicate they belong to a cycling/rowing studio.

> Personal training studios represent the largest single segment of the boutique fitness facility market.

- *Free-Weight Gyms.* Free-weight gyms remain an important niche in the boutique segment of the health/fitness club industry. These gyms typically provide a relatively large free-weight area, a reception area, and locker rooms. Free-weight gyms have become less prevalent over the past few decades, as they have evolved into offering other forms of exercise equipment. No statistics were available as of the writing of this book as too how many boutique free-weight gyms exist.

- *Personal Training/Small Group Training Studios.* Personal training studios represent the largest single segment of the boutique fitness facility market. As brought forward in IHRSA's *2016 Health Club Consumer Report*, 15 percent of American health club consumers indicate they are members of a personal training/small group training studio (Figure 24-1). According to AFS's 2016 research, approximately 42 percent of studio owners indicated that their value proposition is built around personal training (e.g., private training and small group training). Personal training studios are composed primarily of resistance, cardiovascular, functional training spaces, and stretching areas. In many instances, personal training studios also offer small group training.

- *Cross-Training/Boot Camp/HIIT Studios.* The cross-training/boot camp/HIIT is the fourth most popular studio based on IHRSA's *2016 Health Club Consumer Report*, with approximately 4 percent of all health/fitness consumers indicating they frequent these studios. These facilities vary in focus, some offering a structured high-intensity interval boot camp-style workout such as the studios operated under the Barry's Boot Camp franchise (approximately 18 franchise locations globally) and Orange Theory franchise (over 500 franchises open at the end of 2016), to others offering a more eclectic functional and high-intensity training experiences such as Crossfit affiliates (over 12,000 global affiliates) or Iron Tribe Fitness franchises (70 franchises awarded as of 2016). Collectively, these cross-training/boot camp/HIIT studios may be the second largest segment of the boutique market.

- *Multi-Disciplinary Studios.* These are studios whose owners don't attach themselves to any one specific form of training and might incorporate a blend of training modalities such as personal training, boot camp classes, HIIT classes, and yoga. According to AFS's 2016 study, approximately 25 percent of respondents indicated they operated a multi-disciplinary studio. Examples include Defined Body and Mind, a U.S.-based franchise that offers yoga and cycling, and Another Space, a UK studio that integrates cycling, HIIT, and yoga.

- *Boxing/Martial Arts Fitness Studios.* These are studios whose training protocols are built around the combative arts (e.g., boxing, karate, mixed martial arts). According to the aforementioned 2016 study by IHRSA, 3 percent of consumers indicate they are members of a boxing/martial arts studio. Most are independently owned and operated, but like the other boutique models highlighted in this chapter, franchise models have emerged as one of the leading means by which this form of fitness training studio has grown. Two of the most established boutique fitness franchises in this segment include 9Round Fitness with over 700 franchise locations round the globe, and Title Boxing Club (over 130 franchises opened and awarded).

❑ *Express Facilities.* These facilities are designed to offer a quick and efficient workout. Some express studios such as Curves (over 3,000 franchises) and Ms. Sporty based in Germany (over 300 franchise locations) are focused on offering a 30-minute circuit, while others such as the Exercise Coach (over 25 franchise locations) offer a highly personalized, high-tech and effort-focused system that can be done in under one hour a week. These facilities, rather than serving a specific exercise niche, are more focused on offering a time-efficient, effective, and integrated fitness program.

Boutique Studio Dynamics

In 2013, the Association of Fitness Studios (AFS) was established to provide a singularly focused organization to support the rapidly growing boutique fitness studio market. One of the charges that AFS took on was to explore the breadth and dynamics of the industry in order to more effectively serve the needs of this quickly growing health/fitness industry segment. In 2014, 2015, and 2016, the association conducted its first benchmarking studies of the boutique fitness industry. Some of the highlights of those two surveys are as follows:

- The average boutique fitness studio was 3,813 square feet (Figure 24-3). Approximately 33 percent of studios were less than 2,000 square feet, while an additional 40 percent were between 2,001 and 5,000 square feet. All told, 73 percent of all studios reported being less than 5,000 square feet, while 27 percent exceeded 5,000 square feet. These numbers clearly show that boutique fitness studios require a minimum of space in which to operate when compared to the standard health/fitness club models. In essence, studios are agile business platforms that allow them to operate within a small footprint and, consequently, they can go where most typical health/fitness facilities can't.

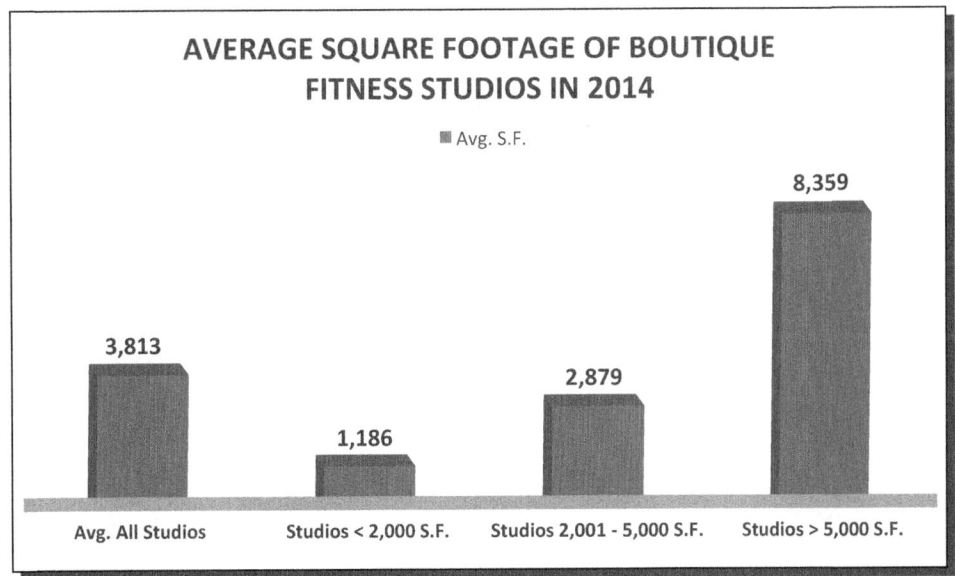

Figure 24-3. Average square footage of boutique fitness studios in 2014

Ezia Performance Center, San Diego, CA

- In 2016, the average number of members and/or regular clients served by a boutique fitness studio was 288, with studios between 5,001 and 10,000 averaging 410 members, and those studios over 10,000 square feet having on average 790 members (Figure 24-4). On average, fitness studios allocate 13 square feet per member. It appears from this data that the vast majority of studios serve fewer than 200 members/clients, making them less of a threat to big box clubs on an individual basis, but when considered collectively they are a formidable group that could easily extract 10 percent to 20 percent of a big-box operator's members. These numbers also support the premise that boutiques serve a very targeted and niche audience.

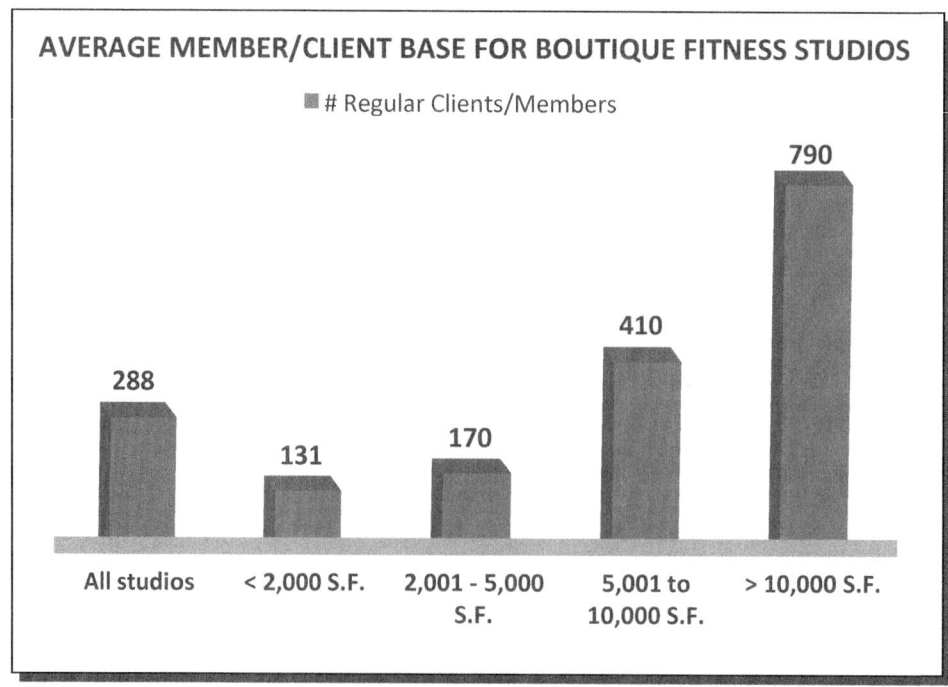
Figure 24-4. Average member/client base for boutique fitness studios

- As seen in the previous section, the variety of studio models available to consumers is as diverse as the interests of consumers and the passions of the proprietor. While 42 percent of respondents to the AFS survey indicated their primary focus was to offer personal training, barre, cycling, dance, group exercise, HIIT, small group training, and other niches were well represented.

- In 2015, the average revenue generated by a boutique fitness studio was $297,468 (Figure 24-5), the equivalent of $77 per square foot. The average EBITDA margin for boutique fitness studios in 2015 was 24 percent. The greatest source of revenue for the studios came from memberships with an average of 72 percent, while the second largest contributor was personal training/small group training, which on average generated between 30 percent and 60 percent of total revenues. The two largest expense items for boutiques were staffing, which consumed 63 percent of revenues, and rent, which consumed approximately 21 percent of revenues.

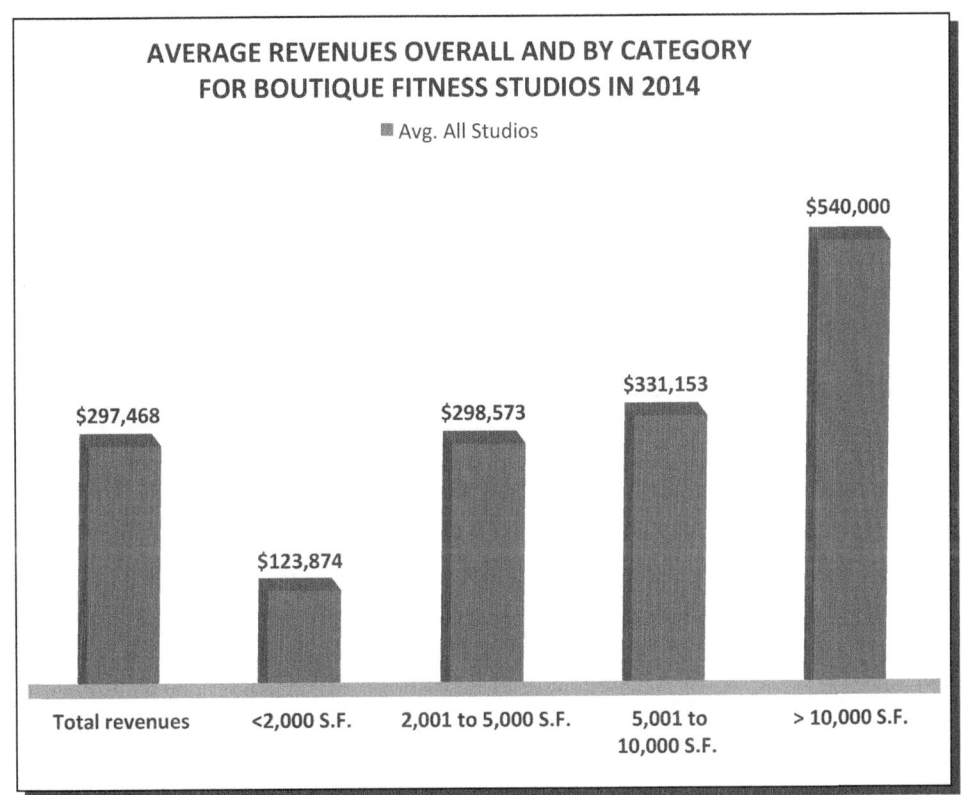

Figure 24-5. Average revenues overall and by category for boutique fitness studios in 2014

- Of the studio operators that responded, 50 percent indicated they have five or fewer instructors and/or trainers. Another 10 percent of respondents indicated they had between 6 and 10 instructors and/or trainers. Among the survey respondents, nearly an equal number of respondents indicated that their staff were either employees or independent contractors. Interestingly, these numbers—especially when it comes to the number of trainers—do not vary dramatically from some of the big-box players. What this does tell you is that the ratio of staff to members/clients is high, meaning that members receive a considerable amount of personal attention.

- In the AFS data, the average price charged for an individual training session was approximately $70. In regards to small group training, the AFS data shows that among those who responded the average price charged was $34. When it comes to the price for engaging in a group exercise class, the average price reported by boutiques was $24. Based on the aforementioned numbers and data from the traditional health/fitness club segment, it appears that boutiques charge more than big-box clubs for individual and small group training, as well as for group exercise classes.
- In 2015, for those studios that offer group exercise classes using a subscription model (unlimited monthly classes for a set fee), the average reported price charged was $95 a month. For the studios who offered unlimited privileges to small group training classes, the average price charged was $137 a month. It should be noted that some boutique group exercise studios, in particular barre studios, charge well in excess of $325 a month for unlimited classes, and some studios offering small group training charge as much as $300 a month.
- When it came to marketing, the vast majority of studio operators indicated they had a limited marketing budget, on average spending 3 percent of revenues on marketing. Interestingly, just over 75 percent indicated that their primary means for reaching out was social media, while 85 percent indicated word of mouth was their most significant lead generator. Internet marketing and email marketing were also heavily used. It would appear that boutiques rely heavily on the loyalty of their existing clients, but also understand the significance of using the Internet, especially social media, to reach their respective audiences.

FNS Training Center, Santa Clara, CA

The Power of Boutiques

So what is the power that these boutiques exert that causes such consternation to traditional health and fitness club operators and such loyal and passionate support from consumers? While not all-inclusive, the research, as well as industry experiences, points to five powerful elements that appear to be the magic elixir for the present success of boutique fitness studios. These five elements include the following:

- *Exerciser-centric.* Boutique studios speak to the interests and passions of their audience in a way that a something-for-everyone club doesn't. If you love the burn of barre, get an endorphin high from sun salutations, dream about the farmer's walk, or fantasize about getting your Polar to max out, then the centricity that boutiques offer is far more appealing, not to mention more alluring than having to navigate the loneliness of a facility that speaks to everyone vaguely and no one specifically.

- *Clan-centric.* Throughout the history of mankind, people have gravitated to be a part of a community or group that shares the same passions, interests, and beliefs (the actual definition of a club). Being part of a tightly knit clan builds personal confidence, offers mutual support, and removes the hassle of having to deal with people whose interests and passions don't align with yours. A great example of this is the fanatical base of Crossfit members (or as the Urban Dictionary defines them, Crossfitters). Like any great clan, they have their own culture and their own language.

Viking Power Fitness, Greenfield Village, CO

- *Community-centric.* In today's globally connected environment, consumers (and in many cases, businesses) have lost touch with their local community. In times gone by, small businesses that were part of the community garnered the love and loyalty of their consumers. These independent owners tend to provide a consumer experience that is more intimate, where trusting relationships are formed, similar to being part of a family. People inherently feel more connected to and supportive of the small guy who is part of the community. A great example of this community-centric phenomenon is the "locally grown" push by grocers, Whole Foods being one of the industry leaders in this quickly emerging trend. Locally grown—or in the case of a boutique fitness studio, being locally trained—tends to foster a sense of trust that larger health and fitness facilities don't engender.

- *Passion of the owner and ownership.* This is a two-headed monster that can be incredibly powerful and persuasive. First is the passion of the owner for what they do, in particular their approach to fitness. Consumers, clients, and members can instinctively sense when the owner is passionate about their training philosophy. A passionate owner is inspirational, not unlike an aphrodisiac for exercise. A great example of this is Todd Durkin (of Fitness Quest 10 in San Diego), who exudes passion and inspiration. Second, ownership means it's theirs, not yours. Ownership trumps employment every time, and consequently there is nothing the owner won't do to bring their business to life. It is like being a parent.

- *Personalized not commoditized.* Our world has become commoditized. In the club industry, despite what some in the industry might believe, most clubs look, feel, and act the same. Today's consumer, heavily influenced by the Millennial Generation, does not want to be just another sale, another number; they want to be seen and treated as individuals. Boutiques offer consumers a chance to be seen and heard, to have their goals identified, their supportive needs met, their achievements recognized. Boutiques give consumers a true sense of being cared for, of being appreciated, and of being valued. It should be noted that the primary consumer of the boutique experience are adults from the Millennial Generation, from where approximately 40 percent of all boutique consumers germinate.

The five aforementioned power elements are heavily influenced by the changing cultural, economic, and social landscape of the globe. The boutiques have harnessed the power that exists in these cultural phenomena and created business models to build upon them.

Reflections

While small in stature, the boutique market as a collective market segment has emerged as a powerful disruptive force in the health/fitness club industry by attracting members away from the existing industry business models. The boutiques have literally captured the moment, leveraging the changing interests and dynamics of the global human environment. By creating offerings that are highly personalized, socially and culturally relevant, and nimble, boutiques are disrupting the health/fitness club landscape, forever changing the way consumers purchase fitness and operators run their businesses.

> Boutiques have literally captured the moment, leveraging the changing interests and dynamics of the global human environment.

Spas

25

"Listen to your body. The quality of your communication matters."

—Natalie Geld

Chapter Objectives

Day spas have not always been such an important component of the club industry. As early as the mid-1990s, most club operators would have questioned the wisdom of devoting financial resources to build and operate a day spa. On the other hand, at the present time, many club operators are aware of the value of a day spa in serving the needs of the marketplace and helping to grow the club's overall operating revenues. According to IHRSA's *2015 Profiles of Success*, approximately 10 percent of surveyed clubs had day spas and another 4 percent offered a hair and beauty salon. In this chapter we will present an overview of the day-spa business as it applies to the successful operation of a spa within a health/fitness club. This overview addresses several factors attendant to the spa business and club spas in particular, including:

- Defining the types of spas that exist, particularly those in the health/fitness club industry
- Describing the individuals who like to engage in the spa experience and how understanding these populations can assist in operating a spa for a particular type of club
- Detailing the basic facility and equipment needs of a successful club spa
- Identifying the basic program and service elements needed for a successful club spa
- Discussing the most effective approaches to marketing a club spa
- Reviewing several of the key issues involving spa staff

> Many club operators are aware of the value of a day spa in serving the needs of the marketplace and helping to grow the club's overall operating revenues.

General Spa-Industry Data

At year-end 2013, the International Spa Association (ISPA) reported that there were an estimated 20,180 spas in the United States, up 1 percent from year-end 2012 and slightly down from 2009, when there were an estimated 20,600 spas. According to ISPA's research, the spa industry generated a total of $14.7 billion in 2013, representing an increase of close to 20 percent since 2009, when the industry generated $12.3 billion in revenue. Overall, spas experienced 164 million visits in 2013, an increase of 4 million visits when compared to just a year earlier. Based on this data the average spa experienced slightly over 8,100 visits in 2012, the equivalent of 22 visits each day. The average revenue per visit in 2013 according to ISPA's data was $89. According to the *ISPA 2008 Global Consumer Study*, among active U.S. spa goers, 82 percent utilized day spas in 2008. Besides the U.S., only England, Japan, and Singapore had as many as 65 percent of spa goers frequent day spas during that time frame. It is interesting to note that according to this 2008 consumer study of spa goers that U.S. spa patrons ranked third in terms of average annual spending on spas at $537 annually, trailing Singapore residents who spend $937, and the approximately $850 annually spent by Italians who use spas.

According to the publication, the IHRSA *2015 Profiles of Success*, 10 percent of health/fitness clubs in the U.S. and Canada have day spas, and approximately 4 percent offer hair and beauty salons, while 47 percent of clubs indicate they offer massage and 14.2 percent claim to offer spa treatments. One could interpret from these statistics that more clubs offer spa-related services than actually have spaces dedicated to the delivery of these services. From a financial perspective, the 2015 IHRSA report indicates that on average, club spa services contributed 3 percent of a club's total revenues.

The Spa Landscape: Definition and Description

To many individuals, a spa represents a retreat from the world; a place where they can escape from their normal daily regimen and pursue activities that they believe will help to enrich their lives. According to the International Spa Association (ISPA), spas have been in existence for centuries, and possibly in one form or another for millennium. The original concept of a spa was derived from retreats that had hot springs and provided treatments that involved the use of these soothing hot-mineral springs, many of which were felt to have medicinal qualities. The original concept for spas emanated from baths filled with hot mineral waters that were believed to be beneficial for the body. Over the years, however, spas have evolved substantially, resulting in spas moving well beyond the original notion of hot-mineral baths.

Spas provide several services, including massages, facials, body wraps, manicures, pedicures, salon services, yoga, meditation, nutrition counseling, and exercise classes. The introduction of these multiple services into the spa environment has spawned numerous spa concepts. According to ISPA and as reflected in Figure 25-1, several primary types of spas exist, including:

❏ *Medical Spas.* Medical spas are spa facilities that provide services that are medically focused. These services encompass therapeutic and rehabilitative treatments (e.g., therapeutic massage, exfoliation, detoxification, botox treatments, collagen injections, liposuction, chemical peels, microdermabrasion, hair removal, etc.) that are integrated with more conventional medical services. According to the *ISPA 2010 U.S. Spa Industry Study*, medical spas represented approximately 8.7 percent of the total spa market, putting them third behind day spas and resort/hotel spas. As of 2013, medical spas have emerged as the second largest type of

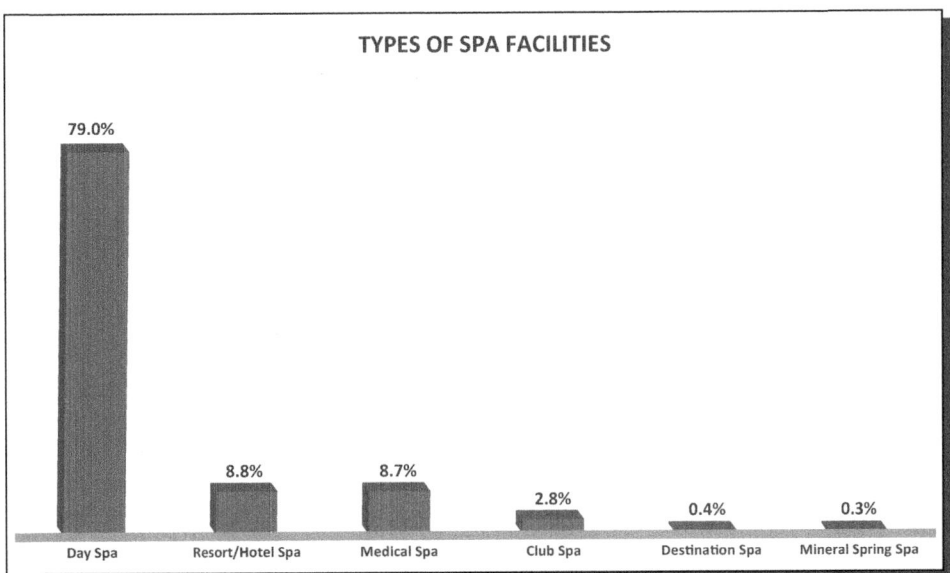

Figure 25-1. Types of spa facilities

spa, with day spas being the only industry segment that is larger. As Baby Boomers continue to age and demand increases for wellness and medical spa services, medical spas are likely to see their ranks continue growing.

❏ *Resort/Hotel Spas.* Resort/hotel spas are spa facilities that are located in either a hotel or resort setting. The primary focus of these spas is to provide basic spa services (e.g., sauna, steam, whirlpool, massage, facials, and related treatments) for hotel and resort guests. Resort spas, as compared to hotel-based spas, offer an incredible array of spas services, including body treatments, facials, manicures/pedicures, massage, and various wet-therapy modalities. According to the *ISPA 2010 U.S. Spa Industry Study*, resort/hotel spas are the second largest segment of the industry, representing 8.8 percent of the total spa market.

❏ *Destination Spas.* Destination spas are spa facilities that are located on resort properties that offer a complete destination experience. These spas fully engage the visitor in a spa experience that includes such endeavors as dining, exercise, and spa treatments (e.g., massage, body wraps, facials, pedicures, hot mineral baths, etc.), among others. These spas usually bundle their services into packages that involve designated time periods. According to ISPA's research, destination spas represent less than one-half of one percent of the total spa market in the United States. One of the legendary destination spas in the U.S. is Canyon Ranch.

❏ *Mineral-Springs Spas.* Mineral-springs spas are spa facilities that offer spa services that incorporate the use of onsite sources, such as natural minerals, and naturally heated water and seawater, which are employed in hydrotherapy treatments. According to ISPA's 2010 survey, less than one-half of one percent of the total number of spas that exist in the United States marketplace are mineral-spring spas. Mineral spring spas are far more prevalent in Europe, especially in Germany.

> **Approximately 79 percent of the spas in the United States are classified as day spas.**

❑ *Day Spas.* Day spas are spa facilities that focus on delivering easily completed spa services (e.g., hair, manicures, pedicures, facials, massage, etc.) that can be experienced in periods of 30 minutes to one day in length. Most day spas are located in affluent urban and suburban markets that serve individuals who want to have a spa experience without having to leave their community. Approximately 79 percent of the spas in the United States are classified as day spas. The largest operator of day spas is franchisor Massage Envy Spa with over 1,000 facilities throughout North America.

❑ *Club Spas.* Club spas are day-spa facilities that are located within health/fitness clubs that focus on providing basic spa services, such as massage, facials, manicures, sauna, steam, etc., to club members and guests. According to ISPA's research, club spas represent 2.8 percent of the entire spa industry. If you took IHRSA's most recent data on health/fitness clubs, which shows a total of 32,500 clubs in the U.S., and then multiplied it by the percentage of clubs indicating they have a day spa facility, it would represent approximately 1,000 club-based spas in the U.S. Among club-based spas, those housed in private clubs (member-owned country clubs, athletic clubs, and social clubs) appear to be growing the fastest. This segment of the club spa industry has its own association, the Club Spa and Fitness Association.

As the aforementioned review of the various types of spas indicates, the spa industry affords individuals multiple opportunities to immerse themselves in the pleasant environment afforded by spas while also experiencing the healing power afforded by various spa treatments. One of the underlying themes among all of these spa offerings is the fundamental focus on providing an experience that can help enrich the individual's life.

Spa Consumer Profile

In 2004 and 2006, ISPA-sponsored research that was designed to identify the characteristics of the individuals who use spas identified three primary profiles for spa consumers: periphery spa consumers, mid-level spa consumers, and core spa consumers.

❑ *Periphery Spa Consumers.* Periphery spa consumers are individuals who tend to be impressed by well-operated spas and whose primary expectations concerning the spa involve indulging in cosmetic services that make them feel special and look beautiful. These consumers are price-sensitive and tend to prefer the more superficial spa services (e.g., cosmetic or physical body). As a rule, they want to experience pleasurable and light spa services. These consumers are not into the wellness and spiritual aspects of spa services; rather they prefer massages, facials, and manicures. This consumer group is the predominant segment for which club-based spas should develop and target their facilities and services.

❑ *Mid-Level Spa Consumers.* Mid-level spa consumers are people who tend to view going to spas as more of a wellness experience. These individuals want to achieve an emotional encounter, as well as experience the cosmetic and physical-body services that the periphery spa consumer typically pursues.

These individuals prefer the isolation of a treatment room, seeking services such as massage, skin treatments, and body treatments. These consumers tend to be price-sensitive when the more esoteric services are involved. They are not as sensitive about price when it comes to less arcane services, such as massage, manicures, and facials. These consumers are interested in the therapist's credentials. In most instances, this group is a secondary market for club spas. Individuals who comprise this group also want to be able to customize their experience.

❏ *Core Spa Consumers.* Core spa consumers are individuals who have "adopted" the spa lifestyle. They tend to view the spa experience as being an essential part of their overall wellness routine. These consumers place a high level of importance on the entire spa experience, not just the actual treatment. They measure the spa experience, starting with their arrival, and continuing through the treatment that they receive and concluding when they depart. All factors considered these individuals are the most demanding of the consumers who utilize the services of club spas. As a rule, they prefer not to interact with periphery and mid-level consumers. While individuals in this group will use a club spa, they also tend to expect to receive services and achieve experiences that are counter to the largest audience for the services offered by club spas. These customers want to customize their experience.

With regard to spas, the club industry has the greatest opportunity to be successful when they provide spa experiences that appeal primarily to periphery spa consumers and to mid-level consumers to a lesser degree. As such, the group of core spa users is relatively small. In reality, if that group is targeted, it will often drive away the other two consumer audiences.

According to the *ISPA 2010 U.S. Spa Industry Study*, approximately 80 percent of all spa goers are women. In their 2008 Global Consumer Study, ISPA indicated that the two largest age-driven demographic segments for spa goers were those individuals over the age of 55 and those people between the ages of 18 and 34. Over 50 percent of spa consumers are married, while 57 percent are employed full-time or part-time. The average household income of a spa consumer, based on ISPA data from 2006, was $72,000 annually (it should be noted that this was almost identical to the average household income of the average health/fitness club member during the same time period). In essence, the demographic profile of a spa consumer closely parallels the demographics of health/fitness club members, with one notable exception—women are more likely to be spa consumers than club members.

A Profile of Why Consumers Use Spas

Industry research shows that spa consumers at all levels indicate that they have three primary rationales for using a spa: indulgence, escape, and work.

❏ *Indulgence.* The most self-centered of the reasons for using a spa, indulgence is the primary driver for periphery consumers and a secondary driver for mid-level consumers. Accordingly, it is the factor that clubs should focus on when they design their spas. When consumers refer to indulgence, they often inject such talk by mentioning such factors as fun, playfulness, decadent, pampering, heavenly, joy, enjoyment, and personal time. As a rule, women, more than men, are willing to indulge themselves. Indulgence is highly dependent on household cash flow. In that regard, when the expendable income level of peripheral and mid-level consumers declines, they are less likely to engage in indulgent activities. The most common spa services that are categorized as indulgent are massages, facials, aromatherapy, body scrubs, and thermal treatments.

❑ *Escape.* Escape is the primary driver to use a spa for those consumers who are not engaging in spa services merely as a means to an end. In this instance, escape refers to achieving an experience that allows consumers to remove themselves from the everyday occurrences of life. This process entails a blend of mind and body factors. Escapist experiences involve spa treatments that create an environment that is characterized by a sense of calmness, respite, tranquility, seclusion, etc. This driver is likely to be one of the major reasons why mid-level or core consumers utilize a spa. The most common escapist spa experiences include body scrubs, body wraps, aromatherapy, and hydrotherapy.

❑ *Work.* Work is a driver for using a spa that is grounded in the desire of individuals to make improvements in themselves, whether it is to look better, feel better, or balance their life. Mid-level consumers and core consumers are more likely to be driven to utilize spas by work than either indulgence or escape, because they tend to see spas as being a more integral element in their overall lifestyle. This may be one of the drives now fueling the growth of the medical spa market.

Spa Visit Motivators

In the *ISPA 2008 Global Consumer Study*, researchers looked at the various "motivators" that generate traffic for a spa. In the U.S., the three primary reasons consumers visit a spa are first, to relax and relieve stress, second, to be pampered, and finally, to enhance overall health and well-being. When it comes to actually having an enjoyable and uplifting spa experience, consumers indicate that the leading factors are: a stress-free environment, the expertise of staff, and the overall atmosphere of the spa.

It should be emphasized that the aforementioned factors for influencing consumer spa behavior fluctuate based on the nation of origin, but, in general, the leading influencers remain similar. As to what actually drives spa consumers to the door of a spa, in the U.S., the top three drivers were referral from a friend (45 percent), an offer of complimentary products or bonus services (38 percent), and the recommendation of a healthcare professional (30 percent). These three motivators vary considerably from nation to nation. For example, in France, the opportunity to receive a complimentary product or bonus service is the leading motivator (45 percent), while in Australia; a gift certificate (60 percent) is the most likely factor to drive spa traffic.

Spa Facilities and Features

According to the ISPA 2010 U.S. Spa Industry Report, the average day spa occupies 2,655 square feet and has 6.6 treatment rooms. The typical club spa can encompass one or more types of treatment spaces, including massage rooms, facial rooms, multipurpose-treatment rooms, wet-treatment rooms, manicure and pedicure spaces, relaxation space, and reception area/retail space. Research conducted by the Club Spa and Fitness Association (CSFA) showed that the average spa in a private club had three multipurpose treatment rooms and six salon stations. It should also be noted that one of the most recent trends in spa facilities is the inclusion of rooms where couples can receive massages, facials, and wet treatments (approximately 38 percent of spas offer couple treatment rooms according to ISPA data). Each of the various types of treatment spaces in spa facilities has its own unique features.

❑ *Multipurpose-Treatment Rooms.* Multipurpose-treatment rooms are available in 62 percent of spas, while 67 percent of spas offer massage rooms. As noted above, the average number of treatment rooms in a private club spa is three. Body treatments and massage services are the predominate treatment offered by day spas, with 94 percent offering body treatment services and 88 percent massage services. From a consumer perspective, 81 percent of U.S consumers take massage, while facial services are the third most popular treatment, with 42 percent of consumers receiving a facial. As a result, multipurpose rooms need to be designed to accommodate the delivery of a variety of spa-related activities, including massage services, body treatments, and facials. These rooms typically range in size from 120 to 150 square feet. Couples rooms are usually larger—150 to 200 square feet. As a rule, multi-purpose treatment rooms include:

Old World treatment room, Boca West Country Club, Boca Raton, FL

- Indirect lighting that is controlled through dimmer switches
- Floor surfaces that are easily washable and provide cushioning for the therapists. The best surfaces are soft vinyl floors or treated wood floors. Some surfaces, such as tile, are relatively easy to clean, but are not good for the therapists. On the other hand, carpeting can be difficult to keep clean. Recently, the use of cork as a flooring surface has grown in popularity.
- Built-in sound systems that can be controlled by the therapists
- Built-in millwork that includes a hard counter surface, sink, storage spaces, and retail-display cabinetry
- Wall surfaces that can easily be cleaned, as well as being able to help provide a soothing environment
- Individual room thermostats that can help maintain the proper air temperature
- Added sound attenuation construction to reduce transmission of sound

All factors considered, multipurpose treatment rooms are the most important spaces in the club spa, because they are in areas in which peripheral spa consumers are most likely to engage in spa services. The typical treatment room accounts for 52 percent of spa revenues, according to data from the spa industry.

❏ *Wet-Treatment Rooms.* In the spa industry, the average wet-treatment area consists of one to two rooms (18 percent of spas have rooms for Vichy showers and 16 percent for hydrotherapy). Wet-treatment rooms are utilized primarily for spa treatments that involve the use of water. Among the treatments that are performed in these rooms are body wraps, body scrubs, and hydrotherapy treatments (16 percent of spas have hydrotherapy space), which involve such implements as hydrotherapy tubs, Vichy showers (18 percent of spas have space for Vichy showers), Scottish hose (less than 2 percent of spas have space allocated for the Scottish hose), etc. In the U.S., approximately 22 percent of spa services are wet treatments (body scrubs, wraps, hydrotherapy, etc.). These rooms typically range in size from 150 to 200 square feet, while rooms for couples are closer to 250 square feet. As a rule, these rooms include:

- Indirect and direct lighting, both on dimmer switches
- Floor and wall surface that is water resistant and easy to clean. The most suitable surface for the floors and walls is tile (e.g., ceramic or porcelain). At the least, the walls in these areas need to have a four-foot wainscot of tile. Custom vinyl surfaces can also be used, in lieu of tile.
- Built-in shower and additional water faucet fixtures. The additional fixtures can be used for hydrotherapy tubs or Vichy showers.
- Floor drains
- Built-in sound systems that can be controlled by the therapists
- Built-in millwork that includes a hard counter surface, sink, storage spaces, and retail-display cabinetry
- Added sound attenuation construction to reduce the transmission of sound

Because wet-treatment rooms appeal primarily to mid-level and core consumers, they are not essential to the successful operation of a club spa, but rather are a nice element to add if the space is available.

> Because wet-treatment rooms appeal primarily to mid-level and core consumers, they are not essential to the successful operation of a club spa, but rather are a nice element to add if the space is available.

❑ *Salon Spaces (e.g., Hair, Manicure, and Pedicure Spaces).* The hair, manicure, and pedicure spaces require a more social and open atmosphere than do the multipurpose and wet- treatment rooms, which need to be private. According to CSFA, the average private club spa has six salon stations. These spaces not only are designed to provide manicures and pedicures, but also to facilitate social interaction between the therapists and customers. These spaces typically include the following features:

- *Pedicure space* (in the spa industry, the average pedicure space has three stations):
  ✓ Approximately 40 to 60 square feet per pedicure station (chair, foot bath, and therapist chair)
  ✓ Floor and wall surfaces which are water resistant and easy to clean. The most suitable surface for the floors and walls is tile (e.g., ceramic or porcelain). At the least, the walls in this area should have a four-foot wainscot of tile. Custom vinyl surfaces can also be used in lieu of tile.
  ✓ Floor drains
  ✓ Soft, yet bright, lighting
  ✓ Built-in sound systems that can be controlled by the therapists
  ✓ Dedicated negative exhaust system to help pull fumes out of the space

Spa pedicure space, Atlantic Club, New Jersey

- *Manicure space* (in the spa industry, the average manicure space has four stations):
  ✓ Approximately 30 to 50 square feet per manicure station (table and two chairs)
  ✓ Floor surfaces that are either carpet or a solid material (e.g., vinyl, wood, or tile)
  ✓ Lighting that is soft, yet bright
  ✓ Built-in sound systems that can be controlled by the therapists
  ✓ Dedicated negative exhaust system to help pull fumes out of the space

- *Hair station.* A hair station includes space for both styling and shampoo. Typical features include:
  - ✓ 35 to 40 square feet for a styling station and another 35 to 40 square feet for shampooing. If both services will be offered in a common space then a space of at least 70 square feet will be required
  - ✓ Floor and wall surfaces that are water resistant and easy to clean. Surfaces such as tile, vinyl, and water-repelling wood surfaces are suitable.
  - ✓ Lighting that is soft, yet bright
  - ✓ Built-in sound systems where the therapists can control the music selection as well as the level of sound
  - ✓ Dedicated negative exhaust system to help pull fumes out of the space
  - ✓ Dedicated 110 volt 20 amp circuit for primary needs

  Individuals consider hair services, as well as manicure and pedicure services as both an indulgence and work. In the past few years, blow dry bars have emerged as the newest salon station trend. Accordingly, the services offered in these spaces tend to appeal equally to core spa consumers and peripheral spa consumers. In the U.S., manicures and pedicures are the second most frequently used spa services, with 45 percent of spa goers receiving one or both of these treatments. It should be noted that the manicure and pedicure business is highly competitive as numerous salons dedicated to these services exist in every town. Club-based spas should view these spaces as being somewhat less essential than multipurpose treatment rooms, possibly more as an ancillary spa service.

❑ *Relaxation Space.* A relaxation space is most commonly found in club spas that have more than six treatment rooms. The relaxation room serves as a transition space between the treatment rooms and the rest of the club, an area in which the client is allowed to relax prior to entering a treatment room, or wind down after a treatment, before returning to the locker room or leaving the spa. Some of the larger club spas have both a men's and a women's relaxation area. As a rule, these rooms typically range in size from 100 to 400 square feet and include the following features:
- Soft floor surfaces (e.g., carpet or wood with throw carpets)
- Indirect soft lighting
- Sound attenuation construction that facilitates a quiet environment
- Millwork with display cabinets, hard-surface countertops, and built-in refrigerators
- Built-in sound system

  Relaxation rooms appeal mostly to core spa consumers and, as a result, are not an essential element when developing club spas. On the other hand, if the club wants to appeal to core consumers, then relaxation rooms are a must.

❑ *Reception Area/Retail Space.* A reception area/retail space is not normally incorporated into the design of most club-based spas. These spaces, which provide a separate entry and retail space specifically for the spa, are normally not required, unless the club spa is designed to drive a large non-member level of business. This space normally consists of a reception desk, retail

> In the U.S., manicures and pedicures are the second most frequently used spa services, with 45 percent of spa goers receiving one or both of these treatments.

displays (e.g., wall-mounted cabinets, floor displays, etc.), and a soft-seating area. This space typically features:

- Wood, granite, or similar hard surface flooring
- Extensive millwork with retail displays
- Indirect soft lighting
- Custom wall treatments and furniture
- Sound system

In addition, if the club spa has more than four treatment rooms, then a separate storage/preparation room and employee break room should be provided. Such an area can be used for several purposes, including storing the various treatment supplies, preparing the treatment materials, and serving as a location for therapists to relax.

Spa Space Requirements

A club spa can be simply as small as a single multipurpose treatment room or as large as a 20-room, full-service facility. The typical fitness club has between one and four treatment rooms, with two treatment rooms being the norm (compared to an average of 6.6 treatment spaces in a day spa, and three in a private club spa). A few club companies, such as Lifetime Fitness, the former Sports Club/LA, Village Health Clubs and Spas, and the Bay Clubs offer spas that encompass anywhere from 6 to 20 treatment rooms, while other club operations have spas that consist of over 20 rooms (e.g., Exhale). In the private club sphere there are spas that have as many as a dozen treatment rooms and a dozen salon stations. When developing a club spa, facilities should evaluate several factors, including the following:

- *Internal Market Demand.* How many current club members would be interested in using spa services? Typically, a club that serves either a family market or a predominately female market will have greater demand for spa services. Anecdotal data from the club industry indicates that between 5 percent and 10 percent of a facility's members will use spa services on a regular basis, with some luxury club operators reporting usage levels that are slightly higher. For example, if a club has 3,000 members, it could expect that approximately 300 of those members will become active spa goers.
- *External Market Demand.* How large is the non-member market, and what type of traffic can be generated? Many club operators report that in mature club spas (spas open a few years), approximately 50 percent of their business comes from non-members, while in the beginning club members may encompass 70 percent to 80 percent of the client base.
- *Target Audience.* Which spa consumer group will be the club's desired audience? Will you create a day spa that has more appeal to the periphery market, or will you try to incorporate a balanced approach that offers something for each of the spa consumer profiles?
- *Available Space in the Facility.* What space is available for renovation or conversion to spa-related services? You don't want to put yourself in a situation where you have to make accommodations to the physical space that might result in a negative experience for the members.

> Many club operators report that in mature club spas (spas open a few years), approximately 50 percent of their business comes from non-members, while in the beginning club members may encompass 70 percent to 80 percent of the client base.

> It is important to treat the development of spa as a business investment and not pursue its development without considering the financial implications.

- *Costs of Development.* What will it cost to develop a spa, and what will be the expected return on the investment? It is important to treat the development of spa as a business investment and not pursue its development without considering the financial implications.

While no actual club-industry averages exist for how many rooms should be incorporated into a club spa, a list of the general guidelines on how to proceed in this regard includes the following:

- Provide a minimum of one treatment room/station per 1,000 memberships and a maximum of two to three treatment rooms/stations per 1,000 memberships. For example, if the club has 3,000 memberships, it should have between three treatment rooms and six treatment rooms.
- For club spas that have fewer than four treatment rooms, all of them should be designed as multipurpose treatment areas. If a facility has more than four treatment rooms, it should consider providing one wet-treatment room (only if its intent is to appeal to mid-level and core consumers). In most instances, a club spa will never need more than one wet-treatment room.
- The club spa should include relaxation space if the facility has at least six treatment rooms and the decision has been made that the spa is going to target core spa consumers. If the spa facility wants to attract a relatively large number of women, the club should consider having both a women's and a men's relaxation room.
- As a rule, manicure and pedicure areas normally never have to exceed two stations each, unless the club is offering a full-service spa that attempts to appeal to all levels of spa consumers. In the event that the club has a full-service spa, the number of spaces for pedicures and manicures depends upon the assumed traffic level.
- Depending on the number of specialized rooms (e.g., treatment areas, manicure/pedicure spaces, and relaxation rooms) that are included in the club spa, the typical club spa facility ranges in size from 600 to 2,000 square feet. It should also be noted that the median free-standing day spa in the United States is 2,655 square feet, according to statistics provided by ISPA.

Spa Equipment

The variety and quantity of equipment in a club spa is dependent upon the services provided by the spa and the facility spaces that exist. Figure 25-2 presents a list of the basic equipment requirements in the various types of club-spa areas.

Spa Service Offerings

The three leading service offerings in the U.S.-based spa industry are massages (81 percent), manicures/pedicures (45 percent), and facials (42 percent). From a revenue perspective, massage/bodywork treatments drive approximately 32 percent of spa revenue, and skin treatments, including facials, account for approximately 25 percent of revenue, followed by retail sales, which generate 12 percent of revenue and manicures/pedicures, which contribute 8 percent of revenue (refer to Figure 25-3).

Multipurpose Treatment Room
- Massage/facial table (adjustable)
- Therapists stool
- Bolster pads
- Stone heater and stones
- Warmers for oils and lotions
- Hydro collator
- Paraffin heater/ bath
- Facial system (rotary brush, vapo-steamer, vacuum/spray, high-frequency galvanic stimulator, and magnifying lamp)
- Towel-heater cabinet
- Sterilizer/autoclave
- Mixing bowls
- Blankets and sheets

Wet Treatment Room
- Wet/dry table
- Vichy shower unit
- Hydrotherapy tub (optional)
- Heat lamp
- Hydro collator
- Mixing bowls
- Paraffin heater/bath
- Shower
- Step stool
- Therapist stool

Manicure/Pedicure Space
- Manicure table
- Task chairs
- Pedicure chair with footbath
- Nail-drying station
- Foot spa
- Pedicure stool
- Paraffin heater/bath
- Storage cart

Relaxation Room
- Soft seating (sofas and chairs)
- Coffee table
- Magazine racks
- Refrigerator
- Cabinets for retail displays and storage
- Dispenser system for drinks

Figure 25-2. Equipment options for a club spa

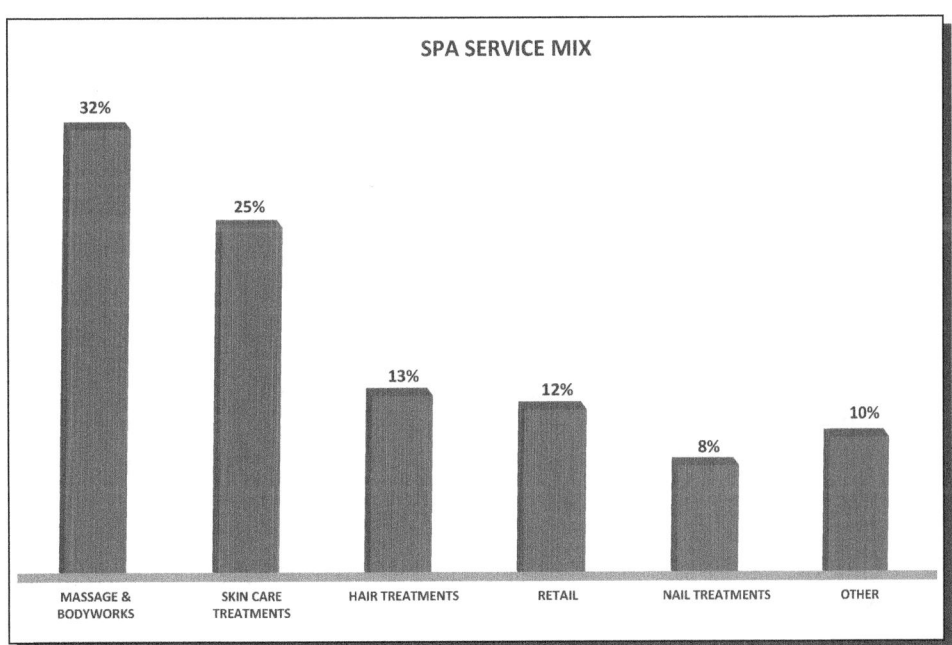

Figure 25-3. Spa service mix

The services that a club spa provides depend upon several factors, including the market it intends to serve (periphery, mid-level, or core), the space it has available, and its overall revenue and profitability goals. Industry research indicates that club spas should focus most on those consumers who

> Providing massage, manicure/pedicure, and facial services should be a top priority for clubs with a spa.

are seeking indulgences (first) and escapes (second). As a result, providing massage, manicure/pedicure, and facial services should be a top priority for clubs with a spa. Since 10 percent to 20 percent (12 percent on average) of spa revenues typically come from retail sales, clubs should also consider allocating space to this function.

- ❏ *Massage Services* (offered by 80 percent of spas). Massage encompasses a vast array of treatments, ranging from soothing massage modalities to therapeutic modalities. The most frequently offered massage services include:
  - *Swedish massage* (offered by 94 percent of spas that offer massage). A gentle relaxing massage modality that focuses on enhancing circulation and relaxing the musculature.
  - *Sports massage.* A more therapeutic massage modality that centers on addressing specific sport/activity-related issues. This type of massage tends to involve deeper massage, designed to release deep tension and break up scar tissue.
  - *Trigger-point massage.* A modality based on Asian massage techniques that focus on applying pressure to specific trigger points to release tension. While this type of massage can be painful at first, it is excellent as a therapeutic modality.
  - *Hot-stone massage* (offered by 90 percent of spas that offer massage). A modality that employs pre-heated stones, placed along the musculature, to help release tension. The stones are moved periodically to other areas of the body's surface.
  - *Aromatherapy massage* (offered by 85 percent of spas that offer massage). A modality that involves the use of aromatic oils, in combination with Swedish massage techniques. Some individuals consider this type of massage to be both relaxing and therapeutic.
  - *Thai massage.* Thai massage blends manipulation and massage while the recipient is positioned on in a variety of yoga-like postures on a mat. The recipient typically wears loose clothing during the treatment. A typical Thai massage can last two hours and exposes the recipient to a variety of static and rhythmic pressures and manipulations.
  - *Reflexology* (offered by 78 percent of spas that offer massage). Reflexology involves the application of focused pressure to specific points and regions of the feet and hands that correspond to and are associated with various organs and body systems. By applying pressure to these different regions, the therapist is able to trigger an effect in another part of the body. For example, applying pressure to the tips of the toes can have a beneficial influence on the frontal sinuses, while applying pressure to the base of the toes can have a favorable impact on the eyes or ears.

  In addition to the aforementioned massage techniques, a host of more esoteric techniques exist that vary in popularity, depending upon the facility's geographic location. These activities include such techniques as bamboo massage and shiatsu. Most massage treatments involve time periods ranging from 25 to 90 minutes.

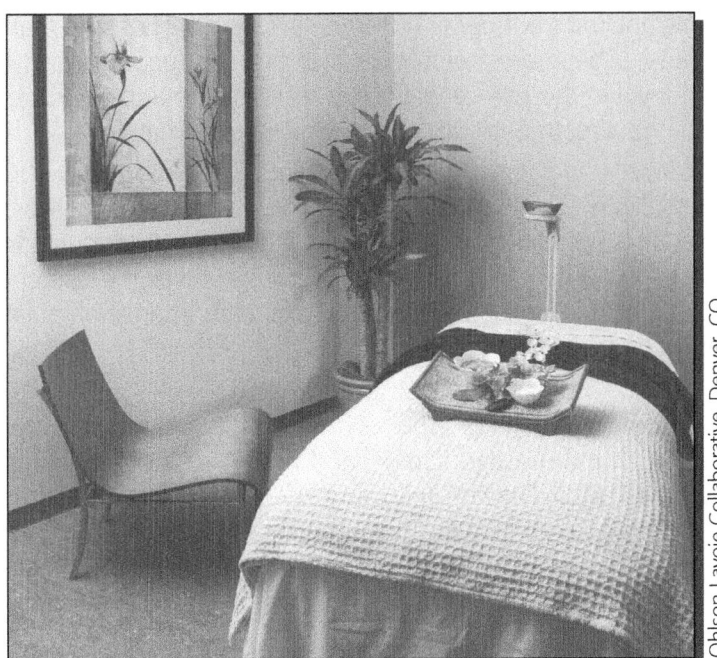

Spa room, Lakeshore Athletic Club, Broomfield, CO

❑ *Facial Services.* Facials involve a combination of treatment applications, including exfoliation, detoxification, hydrating, and massage. The most common type of club-spa facials encompass the use of special lotions to exfoliate the skin, followed by gentle massage, and finally, the application of lotions to hydrate the skin. Recently, day and club spas have begun to utilize microderm abrasion and other medical spa services to provide a more thorough exfoliation of the skin surface. It is common for spas to provide special names for their various facial treatments, based on the lotions and techniques used, for example, executive facials, spa facials, European facials, eye-contour treatments, acne treatments, back facials, facial peels, fruit-based facials, facial masks, make-up applications, etc.

❑ *Body Treatments and Wet Treatments.* Body treatments and wet treatments are services that the majority of club spas provide in their wet treatment rooms. The body treatments normally involve some use of water, while wet treatments (as the term implies) directly incorporate the use of water. The most frequently offered body and wet treatments include the following:

- *Body scrubs* (offered by 74 percent of spas that offer body treatments). Body scrubs are treatments that involve the use of brushes, sponges, and/or lotions to exfoliate the targeted skin surface. Some of the most common types of body-scrub treatments are deep-sea salt scrubs, body polish, essential oil scrubs, Turkish body scrubs, and fruit-based body scrubs.

- *Body wraps* (offered by 72 percent of spas that offer body treatments). Body wraps are treatments that involve wrapping the entire body or a segment of the body with special products, such as seaweed or mud. These treatments focus on both detoxification and exfoliation. Examples include herbal wrap, mud wrap, essential oil wrap, spirulina wrap, silk wraps, etc.

- *Hydrotherapy tub treatments* (offered by 13 percent of spas that offer body treatments). These are treatments that are conducted in a hydrotherapy tub and involve the use of water jets to stimulate and massage the body. Hydrotherapy treatments can also incorporate aromatic oils.
- *Vichy shower and Scottish hose treatments.* The Vichy shower involves the use of multiple water jets to massage the body. In most cases, the client is prone on a wet table while the Vichy treatment is conducted. A Scottish hose is a more intense water treatment that involves the use of a powerful water jet that is sprayed on the body to create intense stimulation of the skin and underlying body tissues.

❑ *Other Services That Club Spas Can Offer.* In addition to certain basic services, such as massage, facials, and body treatments, club spas should also consider providing the following services, based on the audience to which they are attempting to appeal:
- Manicures
- Pedicures
- Waxing (a fast-growing service-treatment segment)
- Paraffin treatments for the hands and feet
- Cosmetic application (assisting clients in the proper use and application of cosmetics)
- Spray-on tanning
- Blow drying

One of the newest service trends in the spa industry is to offer shorter treatment sessions. Because the time demands of consumers have intensified, spa operators have developed new treatment approaches that involve durations of 30 minutes or less. Not only do these shorter treatment sessions accommodate consumer time restraints, they also provide consumers with an opportunity to spend less on their treatments.

Spa Retail

According to research conducted by ISPA, a well-designed and -operated retail shop can generate 10 percent to 12 percent, and sometimes as much as 20 percent of a spa's revenue. Depending upon the scope of your club's spa, the retail operations may be facilitated out of a dedicated spa retail space or integrated into the club's existing retail operations. Some keys to a successful and profitable spa retail program include:

❑ *Select spa products that align with the needs and wants of the members.* Before deciding on what spa products to carry in your retail shop, consider opening a dialogue with your members in regards to what they would like to see. This dialogue could involve individual discussions with members, focus group sessions, or possibly a survey.

- *Focus on one or two product lines.* Once you have identified the product lines that have the highest level of appeal for members (e.g., holistic, organic, botanical, French, Swiss, etc.), narrow your final selection to one or two lines and three at the most. By staying with fewer lines, you will be able to garner greater wholesale discounts from the supplier, but will also be able to carry a larger inventory of the products members prefer. Another added benefit of limiting your product lines is that suppliers will often provide ongoing education and training for your staff on how to leverage their products for various treatments. Many of the leading spas in the U.S. focus on offering one primary line of spa products (e.g., Anantara, Body Bliss, ESPA, Eminence Organics, Mandara, Natura Bisse, Phytomer, and others), and a second niche line that speaks to their brand.

- *Incorporate your spa retail products into your treatment protocols.* Members will be more inclined to purchase products they have experience with, especially if they are products your professionals use and recommend. Consequently, you want to make sure your spa staff is comfortable with the products selected for your retail shop and, furthermore, that they have received training from the supplier in the use of these products.

- *Create appealing retail displays to showcase your products.* A retail display needs to appeal to all the senses: visual, olfactory, auditory, and touch. You want to immerse your members in the experience, and consequently you need to appeal to multiple sensory receptors. One important element in this regard is to make sure your members have to pass through the retail area on their way into and out of the spa.

- *Create retail displays in each treatment room.* Every treatment room should have a small display area that features the spa products offered by your spa. These in-room displays should feature the products used in the treatments. Having the retail product on display in the room also makes it easier for the therapist to sell the product to the member/client before they ever leave the room.

- *Empower and incent your spa staff to sell your retail products.* Spa-goers are more inclined to purchase a product if their therapist recommends it. Consequently, you want your spa staff to be trained in how to sell your retail products (thus the reason for a retail display in each room) and also incentivized to make the sale. Leading spas offer their therapists a commission on every spa product they sell.

- *Offer trials.* Next to the recommendation of a trusted therapist, having the opportunity to physically experience a spa product is the most valuable approach to generating sales. As a result, your spa retail operation needs to offer members sample products they can trial either at the spa itself or at home. For example, you might offer members small samples to take home with them, or you could have feature days when you offer trial treatments using your products.

Many of the leading spas in the U.S. focus on offering one primary line of spa products, and a second niche line that speaks to their brand.

> *Offering gift certificates (especially around the holidays) can generate significant sales of retail products.*

❑ *Leverage gift certificates and rewards.* Research conducted by ISPA, as well as empirical data from top spa operators, shows that offering gift certificates (especially around the holidays) can generate significant sales of retail products. Another highly successful approach to generating sales is to offer members a rewards or loyalty program that allows them to earn discounts on products as they spend more.

❑ *Price your product to make a profit and move.* Your product supplier will provide you with a suggested retail price on their product, typically representing a 100 percent mark-up. Therefore, if you purchase a skin care product for $20 a bottle, the suggested retail will be $40. Some destination spas and high-end day spas mark-up their products more than 100 percent. The typical mark-up for spa products will be in the neighborhood of 100 percent, allowing you to have a projected cost of sale equal to 50 percent before accounting for inventory turn or incentives paid to your therapists. That said, sometimes by lowering the margin you can enhance sales volume, and while the margin on each product might decline slightly, overall net profit will increase. Another key element about pricing relates to discounting. While you may initially mark up your product 100 percent, most successful retail operators establish markdown timelines that allow them to reduce the retail price based on the time the inventory sits on the shelf.

❑ *Manage product inventory.* No matter how successful you are at selling spa products, if you don't manage your inventory, you can easily lose everything you make. In the retail world, they speak of inventory turn, which is how frequently a business turns over its inventory. The more frequently you turn your inventory, the more profitable you will be. According to an article that appeared in ISPA's Pulse magazine in 2006, a good inventory turn for spa retail is three to four times annually. The higher your inventory turn, the fresher your product, the lower your cost of sales, and the higher your profit margin. In an article published in DAYSPA magazine, the author quotes Charles Compton, president of retail consulting firm Mars Solutions who indicates that you want to have no less than three month's sales inventory on hand and no more than six months. To properly turn your inventory you want to not only limited the number of lines you offer, but also identify an approved list of items you will carry and a minimum quantity that you will carry for each of these items. Next, you want to establish a par stock, which is the level of inventory you want to carry before having to order new product. Your par stock levels are based on multiple factors, including forecasted sales cycles and how long it takes to receive shipment on new orders For example, if you know it will take three weeks to receive shipment on a new order, then you will want to make sure that when your inventory drops to one month's forecasted sales that you place your new order, thereby insuring you receive new product before your inventory runs out.

❑ *Know what sells best, and apply your focus to these products.* Every spa retail operation will have products that fly off the shelf and others that appear to establish roots. To enhance profitability, focus on learning what those top sellers are and making those more available, and concurrently, learn what products tend to establish roots on the shelves and find a way to remove those from the line-up.

Spa Financial Parameters

The price that club spas place on their services depends upon many factors, including the geographic region in which the spa is located, the club's initial investment in the spa facility, the target audience, the surrounding demographics, and the role the spa plays in the club's overall business strategy. Clubs should always conduct the proper market research before establishing the services that they will offer and the prices that they will charge for those services. Club-based spas, on average, offer their services at a lower price point than day spas, resort/hotel spas, and destination spas. If the club is trying to grow the business and appeal to periphery spa consumers, the price points for its services must be carefully considered, since this group of consumers is extremely price sensitive. According to the ISPA 2010 Spa Industry Study, the average price of a spa treatment was $83, with a massage going at $85, a facial at $91, body treatments at $95, and nail service (manicure/pedicure) at $42. Figure 25-4 illustrates the general ranges for several of the most common club-spa service price points. Figure 25-5 shows the average pricing for a variety of spa services in the private club arena, which in most instances closely parallel the average pricing seen in ISPA's data for the spa industry.

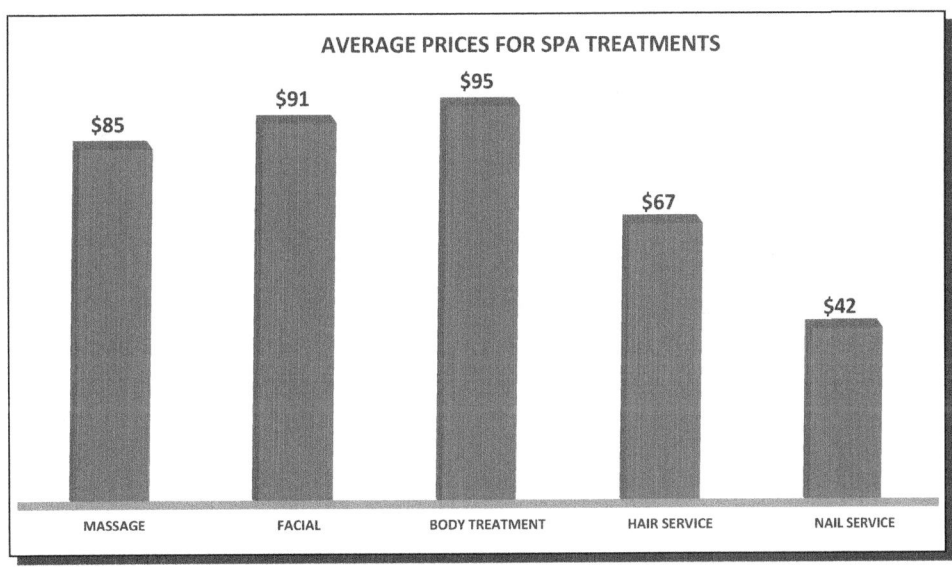

Figure 25-4. Average price for spa treatment (2009)

According to 2010 ISPA research, the average freestanding day spa generated $490,000 in 2009 with average revenue per square foot of $185 and average revenue per employee of nearly $35,000. Based on these metrics, a day spa could expect to generate close to $75,000 per treatment room annually. Data from CSFA shows that the average treatment room in a private club spa generates $50,000, while the average salon station generates $25,000. As such, the average club spa might expect to generate between $3,000 and $5,000 a month per treatment room and $1,000 to $3,000 a month per manicure/pedicure station.

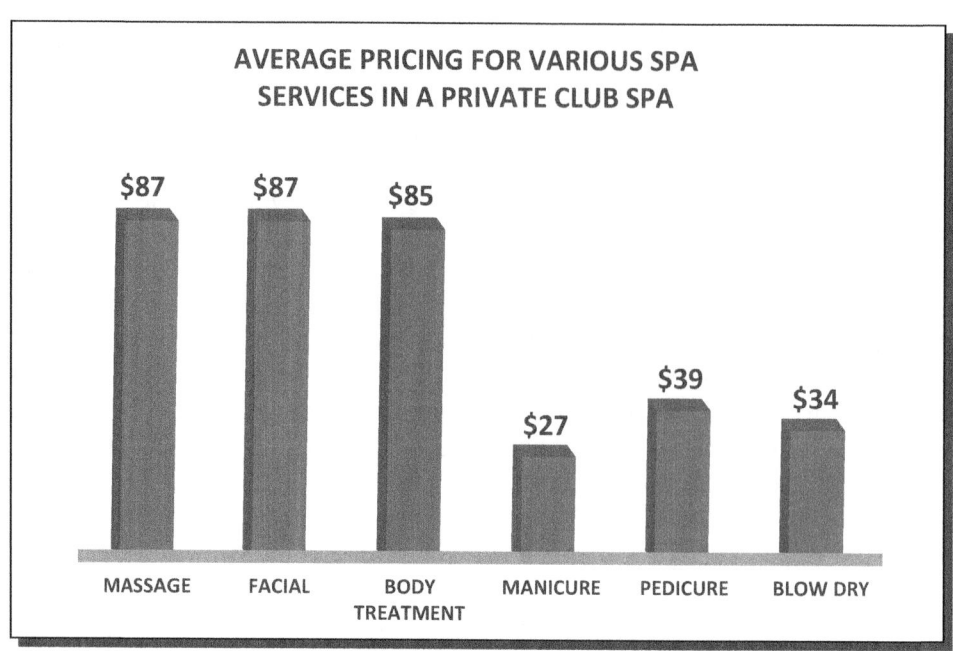

Figure 25-5. Average pricing for a variety of spa services in the private club arena

In 2009, the profit margins of spas varied significantly. Approximately 20 percent of spas reported a profit margin exceeding 20 percent, while 23 percent reported profit margins of between 10 percent and 20 percent. Unfortunately, 27 percent of day spas actually lost money in 2009. According to IHRSA's *2015 Profiles of Success*, the average profit margin for club-based spas was 25.2 percent, with some spas reporting profit margins as high as 36 percent. As the data shows, a club spa can on average generate a considerably higher profit margin than a free-standing spa. This is most likely because the club-based spa does not have the same expenses associated with its operation as a free-standing spa, in particular, rent and utilities. The primary expense for a club-based spa would be employee compensation, which, according to ISPA, represents on average 47 percent of revenues and in 38 percent of spas, represents over 55 percent of total revenues. Accordingly, a well-operated club spa should experience profit margins ranging from 20 percent to 30 percent of revenues.

Marketing the Spa

The marketing efforts of a club spa depend, in large part, on the audience that the club is attempting to attract. Ideally, a mature club spa should pull 50 percent of its clients from the club's existing membership base and 50 percent from non-members who either reside or work within the locale of the club's primary market. This duality of markets requires a club to pursue two distinct approaches to marketing. First, it must establish a marketing approach that effectively draws members from its target market. Second, it must develop a marketing strategy that attracts non-members to the spa without impacting any sense of overall exclusivity of the club that the facility might be attempting to establish. Club operators who view the spa as a prospecting source for membership often incorporate efforts to promote the spa to non-members as part of their overall membership marketing campaign. Several successful strategies can be employed to help market club-spa services, including:

❑ *Strategies Used to Market the Spa to Members:*
  - *New-member coupons.* When individuals first become a member, many clubs provide them with a coupon for either a complimentary spa service or a spa service at a discounted rate. Clubs that offer a discount rate should quote the discount in absolute dollars, rather than percentages. According to 2010 ISPA data, 63 percent of spas offered first-time users a discount.
  - *Club displays.* Some of the best efforts to market the spa involve internal spa displays that touch the various senses, by incorporating visual, auditory, touch, and olfactory elements.
  - *Spa demonstrations.* Clubs can program monthly or even weekly demonstrations that offer members the opportunity to experience the club's spa services on a complimentary basis. For example, the club's complimentary spa offerings could include five-minute chair massages, one nail manicure, aromatherapy, etc. According to research conducted by ISPA, receiving complimentary products and services, or add-ons to existing services is one of the top three drivers of day-spa usage.
  - *Special classes.* Many clubs have found that offering special classes, such as massage classes for couples or classes in skin care, can help introduce members to the club's spa services.
  - *Posters/flyers.* The use of custom-designed posters and flyers that are displayed in appropriate areas of the club can also help bring attention to the club's spa services.
  - *Member spa-appreciation programs.* Generating additional business from existing clients is often as important as bringing in new clients. One means of generating repeat spa business is to leverage the loyalty of existing clients by offering member appreciation and loyalty programs. In 2010, 60 percent of spas offered special incentive programs to generate additional traffic from existing clients.
  - *Member referral programs.* According to the *ISPA 2008 Global Consumer Study*, the leading global driver of spa visits was referral from a friend (45 percent of spa-goers). As a result, implementing some form of a program around member/client referral would seem critical to a club-based spa's success. According to 2010 industry data, 64 percent of spas in 2010 offered incentive programs for members and clients who referred others.
  - *Special-event invitations.* Special days and holidays (such as Valentine's Day, Mother's Day, birthdays, etc.) represent great opportunities for attracting members to the club's spa services. Clubs can send special invitations and gift certificates to their members during these time periods to help attract them to the spa.

> Some of the best efforts to market the spa involve internal spa displays that touch the various senses, by incorporating visual, auditory, touch, and olfactory elements.

Moonstone couples treatment room, Broken Sound Country Club, Boca Raton, FL

- *Spa brochures.* Producing an attractive spa brochure that can be displayed in the club, as well as distributed to the membership, can be another excellent marketing tool.
- *Spa website.* Developing a website for the spa that is directly linked to the club's website can be helpful by providing a source of updated information on the spa's services (e.g., spa menu) and should allow for online scheduling of appointments for the spa.
- *Social media sites.* With the recent advent of social media sites as marketing venues, club spas should consider creating special Facebook and YouTube pages to promote their spas services. Social media sites offer a unique and highly effective means of sharing client and member testimonials about a club's services, as well as providing a means to provide greater education about the facility's spa services.

❑ *Strategies Used to Market the Spa to Non-Members:*
- *Spa brochures.* Producing an attractive spa brochure that can be distributed to the market via direct mail and retail displays can be an excellent marketing tool.
- *Direct-mail invitations/certificates.* Targeted direct-mail invitations, email blasts, and gift certificates can be employed to attract non-members to the club spa.
- *Spa fairs.* Special massage events, involving local businesses or local community groups, can be conducted that can provide targeted consumers with a sampling experience of the club's spa services.
- *Special-event invitations and coupons.* Special days and holidays, such as Valentine's Day, Mother's Day, Father's Day, Christmas, birthdays, etc., represent great opportunities for attracting non-members to the club's spa services. Clubs can send special invitations and gift certificates to targeted non-member audiences during these time periods that are designed to help draw them into the spa.

- *Member-sponsor program.* Clubs can develop a sponsorship program that rewards members for inviting non-members to the club to engage in spa services. For example, each time a member brings in a non-member, the member could be given a special discount or a credit against the normal price for spa services. According to ISPA, approximately 64 percent of spas offered referral incentive programs in 2009.
- *Spa website.* Clubs can create a spa website that is linked to the club's primary website. This spa site can provide updated information on services and allow online appointment scheduling of the spa's services for non-members. If feasible, the website could also be linked to search engines for spas.
- *Social media sites.* With the recent advent of social media sites as marketing venues, club spas should consider creating special Facebook and YouTube pages to promote their spas services to the public. Social media sites offer a unique and highly effective means of for sharing client testimonials about your services, as well as providing a means to provide greater public education about your spa services.

In addition to the aforementioned strategies concerning the most effective approaches for promoting a club's spa services, clubs can also employ less-targeted marketing approaches, such as newspaper ads, magazine ads, and radio spots, to make non-members in the marketplace aware of the spa-related offerings in their facilities.

Spa Staff

According to 2012 data released by ISPA, the spa industry employs a total of 343,600 people, of which 44 percent are employed on a full-time basis and 56 percent on a part-time basis. In addition, approximately 14 percent of all spa staff is considered independent contractors. ISPA research from several years back indicated that the average day spa had 14 employees, of which 5.7 were full-time employees, 5.7 were part-time, and 2.7 were contracted providers. On average, spas spend 47 percent of their revenues on employee-related expenses, with 38 percent of spas allocating over 55 percent of their revenue to employee-related costs, and 16 percent allocating over 65 percent of revenues to employee-related costs. According to ISPA data, the typical spa director earns between $30,000 and $75,000 annually, with 38 percent earning between $30,000 and $50,000 and 22 percent earning between $50,000 and $75,000 annually. The average spa technician earns between $20,000 and $50,000 annually (64 percent), while less than 3 percent earn over $75,000 annually.

Club operators have two basic options concerning the most effective approach for staffing their spa. They can either hire employees (full-time or part-time) to operate the spa (approximately 80 percent of workers are either full-time or part-time employees according to ISPA) or recruit independent contractors to do the job (approximately 20 percent of workers). The benefits and limitations of these two options are reflected in Figure 25-6. Once the decision has been made to utilize either employees or independent contractors, the next decision that has to be made involves the make-up of the staff and the compensation that should be accorded to each of the designated positions. The most common job roles in a club spa, the accompanying compensation ranges, and the job skill requirements for those positions are shown in Figure 25-7.

Employees		Independent Contractors	
Benefit	**Downside**	**Benefit**	**Downside**
• The club has control of schedules, hours, pricing, and services. • Employees will blend with the overall club culture. • Employees will likely take more ownership in connecting the spa with the rest of the club. • Performance-based compensation can be established that supports spa and club goals.	• Added costs related to benefits • Possibly not as recognized in the community	• No payroll or payroll costs involved • Ability to use well-known business operator from the community • Costs are more directly tied to revenues generated; no downtime costs. • Potentially lower operating costs	• Less likely to have an integration of the spa with the club • The club has limited control of services and pricing. • The club has potentially less opportunity to generate revenues.

Figure 25-6. Benefits and downsides of hiring employees vs. using independent contractors in a club spa

Some of the larger club spas, in addition to having a spa director, spa therapists, and estheticians, also have receptionists. For most club spas, the receptionist's responsibilities can easily be filled by other staff members during times when they are not performing treatment sessions.

Reflections

Club spas offer club operators a unique opportunity to monetize their existing membership base, as well as attract new prospects to the club. According to research provided by IHRSA, 10 percent of spas have dedicated day spas, which contribute on average 3 percent of the club's revenues with an average profit margin of nearly 23 percent. As the U.S. population continues to age (e.g., Baby Boomers) and the demands on an individual's time increases, a club spa that provides a refuge for personal indulgences and escapes will remain as both a valuable revenue source and an effective tool to enhance membership retention for health/fitness clubs.

Position	Compensation	Competency	Role
Spa director (normally in club spas with greater than four treatment rooms)	Base salary range of $18,000 to $40,000, plus commission on retail sales (two to five percent) and commission on total spa gross revenues or net revenues. Therapists are paid a commission on any treatment sessions they perform.	College degree or spa experience; either licensed massage therapist or licensed esthetician preferred.	Supervises the spa and is responsible for all aspects of the spa's operation. In smaller spas, this individual also performs treatments.
Massage therapist	Commission for services ranges from 35% to 60% of revenue generated. Range of 40% to 50% is most common. Base wage of six to eight dollars an hour during administrative times.	Licensed registered or certified by the state in massage therapy (varies by state); previous work experience.	Performs all massage treatments and also can do other body treatments, such as body scrubs, body wraps, etc., if they have undergone the appropriate training.
Spa therapist	Commission for services ranges from 35% to 60% of revenue generated. Range of 40% to 50% is most common. Base wage of six to eight dollars an hour during administrative times.	Licensed as a massage therapist or esthetician preferred. No licensing is required in most states for those individuals who conduct body wraps, scrubs, etc., if they have undergone the appropriate training.	Performs the body treatments and wet treatments, except does not do any massage or facial work; appropriate training in modalities required.
Esthetician	Commission for services ranges from 35% to 60% of revenue generated. Range of 40% to 50% is most common. Base wage of six to eight dollars an hour during administrative times.	Licensed by the state as an esthetician; previous work experience.	Performs all manicures, pedicures, and facials; can also conduct body-treatment sessions if they have undergone the appropriate training.

Figure 25-7. Club spa staff positions, compensation, and credentials (based on research conducted by ISPA)

Part Seven

Other Health/Fitness Facility Models

Part 8

Business Operational Practices in the Health/Fitness Facility Industry

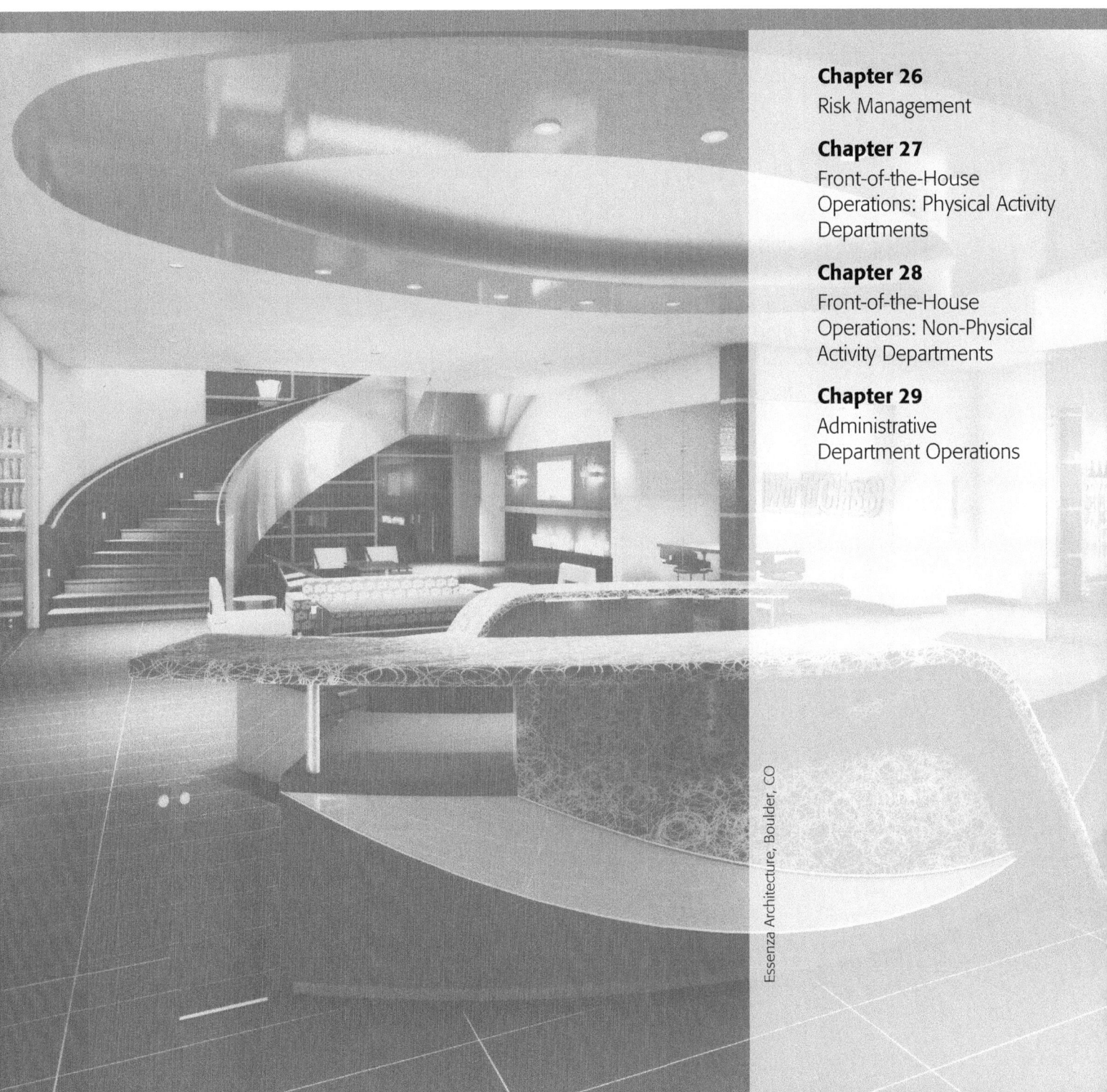

Chapter 26
Risk Management

Chapter 27
Front-of-the-House Operations: Physical Activity Departments

Chapter 28
Front-of-the-House Operations: Non-Physical Activity Departments

Chapter 29
Administrative Department Operations

Risk Management 26

"Anticipate the difficult by managing the easy."

—Lao Tzu

Chapter Objectives

It is usually not until an accident happens or a lawsuit is filed that health/fitness club operators realize the value of a well-designed *risk management* program. For many operators in the health/fitness club industry, the term risk management conjures up visions of policies and practices that interfere with their ability to do what they do best: help people achieve their fitness goals. Nothing could be further from the truth. Risk management is vitally important to any business, and for club and studio operators it can make or break their business.

Risk management refers to the policies and practices that a business puts in place to help reduce and/or eliminate the risk of an employee or client experiencing an event that could result in harm to the individual (employee or customer) or expose the business itself to liability and financial loss. This chapter reviews the most critical risk-management practices and factors that clubs should address in order to provide an environment that presents the lowest possible risk to the employees, members, and business.

> Risk management is vitally important to any business, and for club and studio operators it can make or break their business.

Risk Management Practices to Reduce Employee and Business Risk

Clubs should consider a number of key practices, policies, and systems when managing their business risk as it applies to their employees, and ultimately to their members, including:

❑ *Background Checks for Specific Employee Populations.* Most of the employees in the health/fitness club industry are actively involved in providing personalized experiences that can expose not only themselves, but also the club, to considerable risk. Numerous club personnel such as personal trainers, massage therapists, fitness instructors, and swim instructors, among others, typically work closely with members in a one-on-one environment, where the chance of a risk-related situation occurring exists. Some club employees, such as child-care workers, swim instructors, summer camp instructors, tennis instructors, etc., are in even more potentially risk-vulnerable positions, because they work closely with young adults and children. The key point that should be emphasized is that clubs should seriously consider doing criminal background checks on every employee who comes into personal contact with the members to ensure that each individual member of the staff has no prior record of unsavory behavior that might expose other employees, members, or guests to harm. For example, a simple criminal background check can be performed by an outside agency, or complimentary online platform such as CheckPeople.com, backgroundchecks.com, or DMV.org to determine whether an employee has a past criminal record. In addition to those individuals who work closely with people, any employee who is responsible for handling money on a regular basis should also be a serious candidate for a background screening.

As such, numerous businesses, including many in the health/fitness club industry, conduct annual background checks of those employee populations who present the greatest risk, such as those who meet the aforementioned criteria. It is important that if a club performs background checks, it should make its employees aware of its practices, policies, and procedures in this regard.

❑ *Drug and Alcohol Pre-Employment Screening.* The use of alcohol or drugs can impair an employee's judgment, which, in turn, could ultimately expose other employees or members to harm. Accordingly, drug and alcohol pre-employment screening is recommended for individuals employed in certain positions, such as those that require the handling of dangerous equipment, working with minors, or dispensing of alcohol. Such testing can help reduce the risk of an employee being impaired while acting on behalf of the club. Clubs should also consider testing other employees, such as bartenders, servers, housekeepers, engineering staff, locker-room attendants, and even fitness instructors. By law, drug and alcohol pre-employment screening cannot be conducted without the permission of the individual who will be tested. As such, clubs must give their employees (actual and prospective) the option of whether to participate in the screening program. Fair or not, many businesses will view the refusal of an individual to undergo testing as a negative factor with regard to that person's worthiness as an employee.

❑ *Ensure That Employees Have the Right Credentials to Perform Their Job.* The health/fitness club industry has numerous positions that require specific licensing, registration, or certification. In that regard, clubs can limit their risk by ensuring both at the time of an individual's employment and during the course of employment that each employee's credentials are valid and current. If a person who holds a particular position that requires special education, training, registration, or licensure is found to be lacking, that club may be exposing itself to considerable financial risk. Among the positions in a club where an individual's credentials should be checked at the time of employment or contract signing and thereafter on an ongoing basis are the following:

- *Massage therapists.* In the majority of states, massage therapists must be either licensed or registered to practice. Accordingly, clubs should ask all of their massage therapists for a copy of their license or registration documents (as appropriate) at the time of their employment and ensure that these are maintained.
- *Estheticians.* Estheticians are employees/contractors who provide selected spa services, such as manicures, pedicures, facials, and hair styling. Because these employees must be licensed, similar to massage therapists, clubs should obtain evidence of licensure upon employment.
- *Dieticians/nutritionists.* Many clubs offer nutritional counseling and related dietary advice. A registered dietician is a professionally trained individual who is recognized as having the education and qualifications needed to counsel and prescribe a nutritional plan. If the employee or contractor is not a registered dietician, then the club is exposing itself to an increased risk of liability.
- *Personal trainers and instructors.* At the present time, no established national standard or law exists concerning the required qualifications for a personal trainer or exercise instructor. The American College of Sports Medicine, in its highly regarded text—*ACSM's Health/Fitness Facility Standards and Guidelines, 4th edition* indicates that fitness professionals involved in counseling, instruction, and physical activity supervision have an appropriate level of professional education, work experience, and/or certification. The standards state that the appropriate professional certification must have third-party accreditation from a nationally recognized certifying agency [e.g., National Commission of Certifying Agencies (NCCA)] or from an institute of higher education whose curriculum has received accreditation from the Commission on Accreditation of Allied Health Education Programs (CAAHEP). Examples of third-party accredited certifications for trainers include, but are not limited to, those offered by ACE, ACSM, and NSCA. As of 2014, eight state legislatures had introduced legislation to compel personal trainers to be either registered or licensed, though none had passed. If a personal trainer does not have the appropriate certification, the club is exposing itself to greater risk.
- *Lifeguards.* In all states, lifeguards are required to have advanced lifesaving and water safety certification. Employing lifeguards without those credentials would expose a club to a substantial risk in the event of an accident.
- *Physical therapists.* Physical therapists must be licensed in the state in which they practice. As a result, it is imperative that any physical therapist you employ or retain provide evidence that they have a valid license to practice.

Besides ensuring that employees and contract labor possess the appropriate credentials, clubs should be aware of exactly what actions these individuals are legally permitted or qualified to perform. For example, a personal trainer is not qualified or legally recognized as someone who can prescribe either supplements or rehabilitative exercises. Likewise, a personal trainer cannot diagnose a member's health status. Similarly, massage therapists are not legally qualified to perform therapeutic treatments using massage, unless they have the appropriate credentials. Clubs can avoid these issues by making sure that their job descriptions and employee policies clearly clarify such matters.

Besides ensuring that employees and contract labor possess the appropriate credentials, clubs should be aware of exactly what actions these individuals are legally permitted or qualified to perform.

❑ *Handling Hazardous Chemicals and Materials.* The health/fitness club industry is a field in which many of its employees are exposed to materials that the Occupational Safety and Health Administration (OSHA) considers dangerous. Club positions, such as housecleaners, lifeguards, locker-room attendants, maintenance staff, and fitness staff, among others, are occasionally exposed to hazardous chemicals and materials. These chemicals and materials include items such as cleaning agents, paints, and lubricants. For example, employees who work in closed areas where air circulation is inadequate, particularly in locations where sanding, drilling, or similar activities are occurring, can suffer undue exposure to particle matters. To comply with OSHA guidelines and reduce the level of risk involving the handling of hazardous chemicals and materials to their employees, clubs should undertake the following actions:

- Ensure that the material data sheets (MDS) for every chemical and agent used in the club are posted in a visible location for all employees to view. Clubs who have an intranet site for employees should also consider posting these MDS documents online.
- Provide an MDS binder for all employees/contractors to review. Confirm that these individuals have viewed the information and understand the issues, usually by having them sign a designated sheet.
- Store all chemicals and agents in secure locations. Make sure that these materials are stored off the floor and in an area that is off-limits to the members. These storage areas should have locks in order to prevent their access by unauthorized individuals. In addition, only those staff who have received the proper training in the handling of these agents should be allowed access to these secured storage areas.
- Provide regular training in the proper handling of hazardous chemicals and materials. This training should include a combination of direct hands-on training as well as video content that can be viewed online.
- Make sure to provide employees with the proper protective apparel, e.g., protective gloves, aprons, face masks, respirators, etc.

❑ *Handling Body Fluids.* The health/fitness club industry is a field that exposes its members and employees to various bodily fluids. In fact, almost every individual who works in the industry can come into contact with bodily fluids, thereby being exposed to the resultant risk of blood-borne pathogens. Too many club operators fail to realize that even the handling of towels involves an increased risk of exposure for employees and members to the problems that can arise from handling bodily fluids. As a result, an increased risk to the business itself exists in such circumstances. Among the key steps that every club can take to minimize their risk in this area are the following:

- Provide training for employees. Make sure that employees are taught how to handle bodily fluids. In this regard, OSHA provides training materials, as do many other organizations. Many of these training resources can be accessed online.
- Provide literature for employees on the handling of bodily fluids.
- Make sure employees who are handling towels, cleaning, or picking up papers wear gloves (surgical-style gloves). Employees who have to handle bar soap or razors should be provided with latex or similar type of gloves.

- Have a system within the club for the disposal of items that contain bodily fluids. If the club provides razors for members' use, it should have a biowaste container for their disposal. If the club washes the towels that are utilized in the facility, it should use bleach, which will help kill most of the pathogens that are carried in bodily fluids.
- If blood is visible, clean it immediately with bleach or similar agent, and do not let employees or contractors handle it without the proper protective apparel.

❏ *Have a Staff Safety Program.* Clubs that want to reduce their level of risk involving their practices, policies, and procedures and the costs associated with those factors need to provide worker safety programs that address the key safety issues inherent in each job. Many of the costs and liabilities incurred by clubs result from not having a safety program in place that provides the proper education to employees and contractors about the risks of each job and how to prevent them. For example, massage therapists, tennis instructors, and group-exercise instructors experience more work-related injuries than any other positions in the health/fitness club industry. The key point that should be emphasized in this regard is that a club must establish clear guidelines concerning certain positions and job responsibilities, for example, setting limits on the time a therapist can perform massage during a given schedule or placing strict boundaries on the number of classes that instructors are allowed to teach. A sound employee-safety program addresses several factors, including:

- Making sure that every job description identifies the tasks and activities of that job that may expose an employee to an increased risk of being injured (e.g., fitness instructors can be exposed to lifting and moving heavy objects, while massage therapists can be open to incurring chronic repetitive motion injuries). Having the employee sign off that they are aware of these job-related parameters and risks is important.
- Providing ongoing educational programs on worker safety. These can be conducted as group sessions or offered online.
- Establishing a reward program for safety that recognizes organizational and employee actions that increase the safety level of the work environment.
- Making sure that all accidents or incidents are immediately reported and documented and that appropriate action is taken to deal with the incident.

❏ *Have the Appropriate Insurance Policies.* Clubs should maintain the appropriate types and the proper amounts of insurance in order to minimize their level of risk in the work environment and help protect both the physical and intellectual assets of their business. In this regard, club operators should carry the following types of insurance:

- General liability insurance. Every club should have a general liability insurance package that provides at least one million dollars in coverage per occurrence and up to three million dollars of total coverage. General liability insurance covers most incidences of negligence or accidents.
- Professional liability insurance. Professional liability insurance is one key type of insurance that many fitness businesses fail to provide. Certain positions—such as personal trainers, group-exercise instructors, and

Professional liability insurance is one key type of insurance that many fitness businesses fail to provide.

massage therapists—should be covered by professional liability insurance. This insurance covers issues involving professional competency. Although most clubs do not have this type of insurance, they should. Several of the professional associations in the industry (e.g., ACE, ACSM, NSCA, etc.) offer professional liability insurance-coverage packages, which members of those associations can obtain. If you retain contractors to provide the club's professional services (e.g., personal training and massage therapy), then these individuals should be required to present evidence of professional insurance coverage before the commencing with work.

- Worker's compensation insurance. Clubs should consider establishing a worker's compensation program for their employees, especially if they have individuals who are performing jobs that expose them to injury and loss of work. In many states (e.g., California), such a program is required.
- Property insurance. Although property insurance covers the physical assets of a business, this type of insurance can be another key element in managing a club's risk, particularly its risk of financial loss if something happens (damage or loss) to its property or other physical assets.
- Business interruption insurance. Business interruption insurance provides clubs with insurance against revenue loss due to unforeseen circumstances. For example, if a club has to close for a month due to fire damage, this insurance would protect their revenue stream during the time they are closed. A great example of how valuable this type of insurance is was brought forth during Hurricane Sandy when it flooded lower Manhattan. Those clubs that had business interruption insurance were able to get through the three-plus months of down time that occurred during the recovery, while many of the clubs without business interruption insurance went out of business due to the loss of revenue.

Essential Risk Management Practices to Reduce Member/User and Business Risk

Effectively managing the level of risk to which members are exposed is important to clubs for at least two reasons. First, having sound member risk-management practices can help provide a safer facility environment for the members and help reduce their chances of being injured or suffering other health-related problems. Second, properly managing the risks that members encounter in a club's facility can help reduce the likelihood of litigation directed to the club that can drain the financial resources of the business. In that regard, several policies, practices, and systems exist that clubs can utilize to reduce the level of risk for their members.

❑ *Pre-Activity Screening.* One step every fitness business can take to enhance client safety and reduce risk is to make sure every member and club guest has completed a pre-activity screening. According to the most recent editions of *ACSM's Health/Fitness Facility Standards and Guidelines* (4th edition released in late 2011) a club must provide pre-activity screening for its members and users. Pre-activity screening should involve, at the minimum, screening for basic health risks (e.g., coronary-risk factors, orthopedic issues, history of health problems). There are a host of proven tools, such as the Par-Q or a simple medical history questionnaire.

❑ *Medical Clearance.* Clubs that utilize pre-activity screening tools should also have a system by which those individuals who are identified as having an increased risk due to their health profile either are referred to a physician for medical clearance before engaging in physical activity or if they refuse to obtain a physician's release (for whatever reason), are required to sign a waiver or other legally drawn up form, indicating that they have decided not to obtain clearance from a physician and, as a result, are releasing the club from any liability associated with their participation in any physical-activity offering of the club.

The medical release can be as simple as a one-page document that is forwarded by the club to the member's physician or provided to the member to personally take to their physician. The medical-release form should clearly indicate that the member has been identified as being at an increased risk of incurring an injury or health-related problem if the individual participates in a physical-activity program and that by completing and signing the form, the physician is clearing the member to participate in physical activity. The release should allow physicians to provide any recommendations they may have concerning the individual's participation in physical activity. An example of a medical-release form is included in the Appendices.

❑ *Waiver of Liability.* A waiver is a legal document that members/users sign, indicating that they are aware of the risks associated with their participation in a physical-activity program that involves the club's facilities, programs, and services and that they knowingly accept full responsibility for their decision to participate in such offerings and are releasing the club from any and all responsibility for their participation. A waiver should be prepared by an attorney and should address the following:
- The facilities, programs, and services that the member has access to and might use to pursue a program of physical activity.
- The risks involved in engaging in physical activity, including and up to the risk of a cardiac event or even death.
- A statement that the member is aware of the risks involved, that the club has explained those risks thoroughly, and that the member is willing to accept those risks.
- The member's willingness to accept all responsibility for their participation in light of the information they have been provided and that they are accepting complete responsibility for their actions and releasing the club from any and all liability associated with their decision.

The use of a waiver should be standard practice for every club in legal jurisdictions that allow the use of a waiver. There are states in which a waiver will not be upheld in court, but in most instances, a waiver provides a significant degree of protection for the business. Ideally, all members/users should complete and sign a waiver form upon joining a club. *ACSM's Health/Fitness Facility Standards and Guidelines*, 4th edition indicates that waivers should be a standard practice for health/fitness club operators. (Note: Some recent court rulings have upheld a plaintiff's right to legal action even when a waiver has been signed.)

> The use of a waiver should be standard practice for every club in legal jurisdictions that allow the use of a waiver.

- *Emergency-Response System.* Having an appropriate emergency-response system is an essential factor in the effort to establish a safe environment for members and employees, as well as a sound risk-management practice. In that regard, health/fitness clubs must develop emergency response systems that help ensure that their members have the highest reasonable level of safety. An emergency-response system should encompass several key elements, including:
  - Local healthcare and/or medical personnel should be solicited to help develop the emergency-response system that the club utilizes. Most emergency-medical services are willing to assist a club in developing an emergency-response program. Clubs can also pay for the services of a qualified person, such as a physician, registered nurse, or certified emergency-medical technician, to help guide the development of their program.
  - The club's emergency-response system should address the major medical emergency situations that might occur, such as heart attacks, strokes, orthopedic-related injuries, accidents, etc., as well as non-medical emergencies, such as fires and natural disasters.
  - The club's emergency-response system should detail explicit steps or directions concerning how each emergency situation should be handled, including the roles that should be played by first, second, and third responders to an emergency. In addition, the emergency-response system should specify the locations of all emergency equipment (e.g., AEDs and first aid kits) and all emergency exists.
  - The emergency-response system should be fully documented and kept in an area that can be easily accessed by the club's staff. Many clubs place their emergency response policies and systems online so employees can more easily access them. In addition, the emergency-response system should be reviewed with each employee on a regular basis.
  - The emergency-response system should be physically rehearsed by everyone (e.g., employees and contractors) involved at least twice annually.
  - The emergency-response system should incorporate the use of an automated external defibrillator (AED) and cardiopulmonary resuscitation equipment (both of which are covered in greater detail in a later section of this chapter).
  - The emergency-response system should address the availability and location of first-aid kits within the club.
  - The emergency-response system should identify an on-site coordinator for the program (the employee who is responsible for the club's overall emergency readiness).

- *Signage.* Clubs can reduce their level of business risk and concurrently help create a safer physical activity environment for their members by developing signage that is posted in appropriate locations that communicates to its members those areas of the club that involve a potentially substantial risk to an individual's health and safety. This signage should indicate the risks involved and include information that can lessen the member's risk if they respond appropriately to the information provided to them. Detailed information on developing proper signage for the health/fitness club industry is available from the American Society for Testing and Materials (ASTM) in its *Standard Specification of Fitness Equipment and Fitness Facility Signage and Labels (F1749-02)*. The key areas of a health/fitness facility that should have signage include:

- *Cold plunges, sauna, steam room, and whirlpool.* Each of these areas presents a real danger to members and users because of high temperatures, low temperatures, excessive humidity, or possibly the combination of more than one of these elements. Saunas, steam rooms, and whirlpools due to their high temperatures and humidity can easily result in individuals experiencing hyperthermia, heat exhaustion and heat stroke, loss of consciousness, or death. In certain instances, especially in saunas and steam rooms, the possibility of serious burns also exists. Cold plunges, which have recently become popular features in many health/fitness facilities, present a similar level of risk, but for different reasons. In cold plunges, where temperatures can be as low as 4 degrees Celsius (39 degrees Fahrenheit), users can experience hypothermia in a matter of minutes. Beyond these consequences, users who have preexisting medical conditions can be at risk just by partaking in the use of these areas. Signage in each of these areas should include:
  - ✓ Information about the temperature range to which the user will be exposed
  - ✓ A warning about the increased risk of hyperthermia (or in the case of a cold plunge, hypothermia), if too much time is spent in any of these facilities
  - ✓ A warning about specific populations that should avoid exposure to these areas unless they have their physician's approval, such as those individuals with high blood pressure or coronary artery disease, women who are pregnant, members on vasodilator medications, etc.
  - ✓ A warning to cool down after exercise, preferably for a period of at least 10 minutes before entering these areas
  - ✓ Guidelines on what constitutes a reasonably safe time period for individuals to utilize these areas
  - ✓ A warning about not entering the pool if the individual has an open wound
- *Aquatic areas.* Most state and local health departments require certain signage be posted in the pool areas. These signage requirements are designed to protect users from exposure to risky behavior. Among the key elements that are normally indicated in pool signage are the following:
  - ✓ A warning about not running or playing on the pool deck
  - ✓ A warning about deck surfaces being slippery when wet
  - ✓ A warning about no diving
  - ✓ Information about food not being allowed around the pool
  - ✓ Information that no supervision or lifeguard is present (if the pool is not required by law to have lifeguards)
  - ✓ Information about not entering the pool immediately after eating
  - ✓ Information about showering before entering the pool
  - ✓ A warning about not entering the pool if the individual has an open wound

> The fitness floor, with its abundance of equipment, presents risks that many members and guests are unfamiliar with.

With regard to signage for aquatic areas, club operators should be familiar with the local laws and regulations to ensure that their facilities are in full compliance with all the legally required signage expectations.

- *Enclosed racquet courts* (e.g., handball, racquetball, and squash). Clubs should provide signage that indicates that individuals should wear appropriate eye protection when using the courts.
- *Fitness floor.* The fitness floor, with its abundance of equipment, presents risks that many members and guests are unfamiliar with, and if they have opted not to receive an orientation, are most likely to be completely unaware of. Therefore, facility operators have a duty to provide signage that clearly communicates to their members and guests the risks associated with the general fitness areas and provide instruction on how to avoid those risks. Examples of signage in these areas might include:
  - ✓ Recommendation to have a spotter present when performing certain free-weight exercises (free-weight area)
  - ✓ Recommendation to get instruction or guidance from a fitness professional before embarking on an exercise program
  - ✓ Recommendation to stop exercising if the individual experiences dizziness, pain, or unusual discomfort
  - ✓ Instructional signage that helps enhance the safety level of a particular piece of equipment
  - ✓ Signage indicating that a piece of equipment is out of order
  - ✓ Recommendation to read the labels and operational instructions provided on all equipment prior to using it

  In addition to signage on the fitness floor that focuses on the aforementioned information and warnings, clubs should also provide either perceived-exertion charts or target heart-rate charts so that members/users can monitor their level of exertion while exercising.

- *Hazardous conditions signage.* Hazardous conditions signage is general signage that warns members/users of any unusual risk attendant to a particular physical condition or practice at the club. For example, these signs should be used in situations such as:
  - ✓ When equipment is out of order, and the club wants to make its members aware that the equipment is out of use
  - ✓ When floors are wet, and the club wants to make its members/guests aware of slippery conditions
  - ✓ When a condition exists, such as damaged walking surfaces, loose impediment, or a related condition that would increase the risk to the club's members and guests
  - ✓ When repairs or construction are being performed and the club wants to warn its members and guests of specific dangers or locations to avoid

❑ *Preventative Maintenance Schedules and Audits.* One of the best practices that clubs can adopt for increasing member and guest safety and reducing their business risk is to implement preventative maintenance procedures that are audited on a daily and/or weekly basis. The majority of accidents in the health/fitness club environment occur because club operators fail to execute basic preventative maintenance procedures and provide the necessary inspection of these procedures. Among the core practices that a club can execute in this regard are the following:

- Employ cleaning and preventative maintenance checklists for all fitness equipment. Clubs should ensure that its equipment is maintained on a daily, weekly, and monthly basis. This endeavor should include checking all bolts, checking all cables, checking for loose parts, cleaning surfaces, etc.
- Adhere to daily, weekly, and monthly schedules for cleaning all areas of the club.
- Utilize checklists for performing preventative maintenance of lights, plumbing, and HVAC.
- Make sure to follow the manufacturer's guidelines concerning the care of equipment. In that regard, clubs should have operator manuals for each piece of equipment in the facility.

The most critical factor is to have a system in place to verify compliance with the aforementioned, prescribed checklists. Many club operators employ supervisors to conduct regular audits of their maintenance procedures and practices. When audits are conducted, it is important to make sure the audit is documented, and the results are kept on file.

In the past few years, firms have emerged that provide outsourced assistance with monitoring and caring for fitness equipment. These firms offer real-time, cloud-based software applications that monitor the use and condition of equipment and provide notification when equipment is in need of routine or emergency maintenance. Among the many firms that provide this type of support service for health/fitness facilities, the most recognized are Fitness EMS (www.fitnessems.com) and Fiix (www.fiixsoftare.com).

❑ *Incident Reports.* Incident reports are standard forms that a business completes whenever an accident or incident occurs on its property. For health/fitness clubs, it should be standard practice to complete an incident report each time an accident or safety-related event occurs at the club. The purpose of the incident report is to obtain the necessary information attendant to a particular event, such as the nature of the event, time of the event, witnesses, extent of any injury resulting from the event, response of the club to the incident, etc. This information can be extremely important for situations involving insurance, litigation, and responding medical agencies.

Automated External Defibrillators (AEDs)

❑ *Overview.* Every fitness facility that cares about the safety and well-being of its clients should have an emergency response system (EMS). An EMS is designed to provide a club's staff with a structured process that will allow them to consistently and properly respond to an emergency event that takes place in the studio. One of the most important emergency response protocols for a fitness facility to establish involves incidents involving sudden cardiac events. In these situations, the American Heart Association (AHS) and the American College of Sports Medicine (ACSM) have emphasized the importance of fitness facilities having a Public Access Defibrillation program (PAD).

> One of the most important emergency response protocols for a fitness facility to establish involves incidents involving sudden cardiac events.

Public Access Defibrillation (PAD), a term coined by the AHA, refers to emergency response protocols involving the use of an automated external defibrillator (AED) in a public setting, including in fitness facilities. AEDs are computerized devices that enable a layperson with minimal training to administer a potentially lifesaving intervention to individuals who experience sudden cardiac arrest (SCA). AEDs are devices that can be employed in an emergency situation to detect a life-threatening cardiac arrhythmia and then administer an electrical shock that can restore the heart's normal sinus rhythm. AEDs represent the third step in the American Heart Association's (AHA's) renowned "chain of survival"—after calling 911 and administering early CPR.

The AHA reports that research shows that the delivery speed of defibrillation, as provided by an AED, is the major determinant of success in resuscitative attempts for ventricular fibrillation (VF) cardiac arrest (the most common type of cardiac arrest). Survival rates after VF decrease 7 to 10 percent with every minute delay in defibrillation. A survival rate as high as 90 percent has been reported when defibrillation is administered within the first minute of collapse, but decreases to 50 percent at five minutes, 30 percent at seven minutes, 10 percent at 9 to 11 minutes and two to five percent after 12 minutes.

Those communities that have incorporated AEDs into their emergency systems have achieved significant improvements in the survival rates for those individuals who have experienced cardiac events. In the state of Washington, for example, the survival rate increased from 7 to 26 percent, whereas, in Iowa, the survival rate increased from 3 to19 percent. Some public programs have reported survival rates as high as 49 percent with prompt administration of an AED. The American Heart Association is a strong proponent of having AEDs as accessible to the public as possible. The use and application of AEDs in a public setting is detailed in the American Heart Association's *2004 AED Implementation Guide and its 2010 Guidelines for CPR and ECC*.

As of January 2010, 11 states had passed AED legislation, as it pertains to health/fitness facilities (Arkansas, California, Illinois, Indiana, Louisiana, Michigan, Massachusetts, New Jersey, New York, Oregon, and Rhode Island). In addition to these states, several local districts—Suffolk County, NY; Weston, Florida; and Montgomery Country, Maryland—have passed legislation requiring health/fitness facilities to have AEDs. Similar legislation requiring clubs to have AEDs is also pending in Wisconsin. Only four states have legislation that accommodates unstaffed fitness facilities.

The movement toward requiring an AED in health/fitness facilities received strong support in 2007, when the American College of Sports Medicine, in the 3rd edition of *ACSM's Standards and Guidelines for Health/Fitness Facilities*, indicated that an AED must be a part of every health/fitness facility's emergency response plan. The standard has since been updated, and the most current standards for the integration of a PAD program in a health/fitness facility are set forth in the 4th edition of *ACSM's Standards and Guidelines for Health/Fitness Facilities*. Among the U.S. health/fitness club companies that have adopted that standard are ClubCorp, Dallas, Texas; Sport and Health, Washington, DC; Midtown Athletic Clubs, , Chicago, Illinois; Town Sports International, New York, New York; Wellbridge, Denver, Colorado; Equinox Fitness, New York, New York; and the Bay Clubs, San Francisco, California. A recently released trend study commissioned by ClubIntel showed that approximately 63 percent of all health/fitness facilities had AEDs, while closer to 70 percent of traditional commercial facilities had AEDs.

❑ *Guidelines for Implementing an AED Program in a Health/Fitness Club:*
- Every site with an AED should make an effort to get the response time from collapse to defibrillation to five minutes or less.
- AEDs that are located in the club facility should ideally be within a 1.5-minute walk of a potential collapse site. A responder should be able to reach an AED within a 1.5-minute walk time. With today's portable AED systems, this has been made considerably easier.
- The FDA requires that a physician must prescribe an AED before it can be purchased. The AHA strongly recommends that a physician, licensed to practice medicine in the community, should provide the oversight of the facility's emergency system and the role of AEDs in that system. In most cases, the company from which the AED is purchased will assist the club with identifying a physician to provide these services, or will include those services with the purchase an AED. Physician oversight refers to:
  ✓ Prescribing the AED
  ✓ Reviewing and signing off on the emergency plan
  ✓ Witnessing at least one rehearsal of and providing a written report of such events
  ✓ Providing standing orders for the use of the AED
  ✓ Reviewing documentation of any instances when the emergency plan is initiated and the AED is used
- A club's emergency plan and AED plan should be coordinated with the local emergency medical services (EMS) provider (the product provider normally does this step). Coordinating with the local EMS provider refers to:
  ✓ Informing its local EMS provider that the club has an one or more AEDs
  ✓ Informing its local EMS provider of the location of each AED in the club's facility
  ✓ Working with the local EMS provider in providing ongoing training of the club's staff in the use of the AED. In many instances, the AED provider offers this service.
  ✓ Working with the local EMS provider to provide monitoring and review of AED events
- The AHA's Emergency Cardiac Care Committee, as well as numerous international experts, encourages a skills review and practice sessions with the AED at least every six months with regular practice drills every three to six months recommended.
- The AED should be monitored and maintained to the manufacturer's specifications on a daily, weekly, and monthly basis. All results from those

efforts should be recorded. AEDs currently on the market provide this capability through an automated process, where the information is actually uploaded to the cloud.

- All incidences involving the administration of an AED must be recorded and then reported to the physician who is providing oversight. It should be noted that the HIPPA (Health Insurance Portability and Protection Act) does not allow medically sensitive information to be released to anyone other than the medical director.
- Each club should have an AED program coordinator who is responsible for all aspects of the facility's emergency-response plan and the use of the AED, as outlined in *ACSM's Health/Fitness Facility Standards and Guidelines*, 4th Edition.
- All employees who are likely to be involved in a situation in which they might have to administer an AED should complete a program in basic life support (BLS) and AED usage from an accredited training organization. The two most recognized organizations in this regard are the American Heart Association (AHA), which offers its Heart Saver CPR/AED training and certification, and the American Red Cross, which offers separate courses in CPR, AED, and First Aid training. Numerous local and national organizations, including the American Council on Exercise (ACE), facilitate either AHA or ARC courses in the administration of an AED and CPR. These programs involve a minimum of four hours of direct-contact training. Because certification in these areas lasts for two years, employees should be required to complete such training on an every-other-year basis.
- A club should have at least one employee on duty at all times who is currently trained and certified in CPR/AED administration. Ideally, more than one such trained and certified employee should be on duty at all times.
- Four special situations exist involving the use and application of an AED that the club should be familiar with and which should be reviewed during the initial AED training of the club's employees:
    - ✓ AEDs should not be used in or around water. Because electricity takes the path of least resistance, it should not be used in or near puddles of water (e.g., shower, steam room, whirlpool, etc.) or in the rain. If necessary, the patient should be moved and dried off before attaching the AED.
    - ✓ The American Heart Association, in its 2010 *Guidelines* that include references to emergency cardiac care, and the Pediatric Life Support Task Force (PALS) of the International Liaison Committee on Resuscitation, in its 2002 position paper, both indicate that an AED can be used on children under eight years of age when no sign of circulation exists. In these instances, the electrical shock should be delivered in a pediatric dose using pediatric pads.
    - ✓ External factors, such as clothing, jewelry, medication patches, and too much hair on the chest, could interfere with the AED effectiveness, and as a result, these items should be removed. Furthermore, if the individual has excess moisture build-up on the body (e.g., perspiration), this will need to be removed as well. Prep kits with towels and razors are normally included with the AED and can assist in the removal of these items.

- ✓ Some individuals may have implanted internal devices, such as pacemakers and defibrillators. These devices create a small prominence under the skin. If such devices are detected, the individual using the AED should make sure that the pads are not placed directly over these devices, because they may block the flow of energy.

❑ *Guidelines for Locating AEDs in a Health/Fitness Club Facility:*
- A critical step in the standard of care for use of an AED is the need to locate the AED where it can easily and rapidly be accessed in the event of a cardiac event. According to the AHA, this factor refers to the fact that an AED must be reachable within 1.5 minutes by a responder and must be applied in three to five minutes from the onset time of a cardiac event. Accordingly, the club must consider these two time-related factors, when determining how many AEDs are needed and where they should be located in the facility.
  - ✓ Clubs should determine which locations in the facility could be most easily accessed within a 1.5-minute walk. The average person who is walking at four mph can cover a distance of approximately 350 feet a minute, which translates to a distance of approximately 525 feet (175 yards) in 1.5 minutes.
  - ✓ For clubs that have tennis facilities, the most suitable location in the tennis area for an AED would be the reception or reservation desk. If the desk cannot be reached in 1.5 minutes from some courts, then a second AED may be required and located at a second site. In most instances, a club with fewer than 20 courts will probably need only one AED, whereas a club with more than 20 courts might consider at least two AEDs. The highest risk areas in a health/fitness facility are normally the racquet courts, the steam, sauna and whirlpool areas, and the locker rooms.
  - ✓ For clubs that offer fitness facilities, the most suitable location to locate an AED would be at the front desk. If any portion of the fitness facility cannot be accessed from the desk in 1.5 minutes, then at least one additional AED may be required and located at another appropriate site. Clubs that have two floors should consider positioning an AED on each floor. Other than the front desk, an AED might also be located in the exercise area, pool, or locker rooms. As a rule, the highest risk areas in an athletic facility are the locker rooms (where the steam, sauna, and whirlpool areas are located), the fitness center, group-exercise studios, and racquet courts.
- Make sure to secure the AED. The best option is to have the AED locked in a secure wall-mounted cabinet. If the cabinet is in a location where opening with a key would delay response time, then the cabinet should be left unlocked. Recently, many facilities have been using portable AED kits that allow staff and members to more readily access and then transport to the site of an incident.
- Make sure to indicate the location of all the clubs AEDs. Make sure you have signage that indicates the location of the AED. Typically, this would involve a sign located in proximity to the AED cabinet, but it may also involve directional signage in those areas more remote from the AED locations.

> An AED must be reachable within 1.5 minutes by a responder and must be applied in three to five minutes from the onset time of a cardiac event.

- Consider having an AED notification system. This is an automated alarm system that notifies the local EMS whenever the AED is removed from its cabinet.

The key point that must be emphasized when deciding where to position AEDs in a facility is to ensure that every AED can be easily accessed by anyone. In other words, the AED should be positioned in an open location that has limited traffic congestion, rather than locked or placed in a closet or other area that cannot be easily accessed.

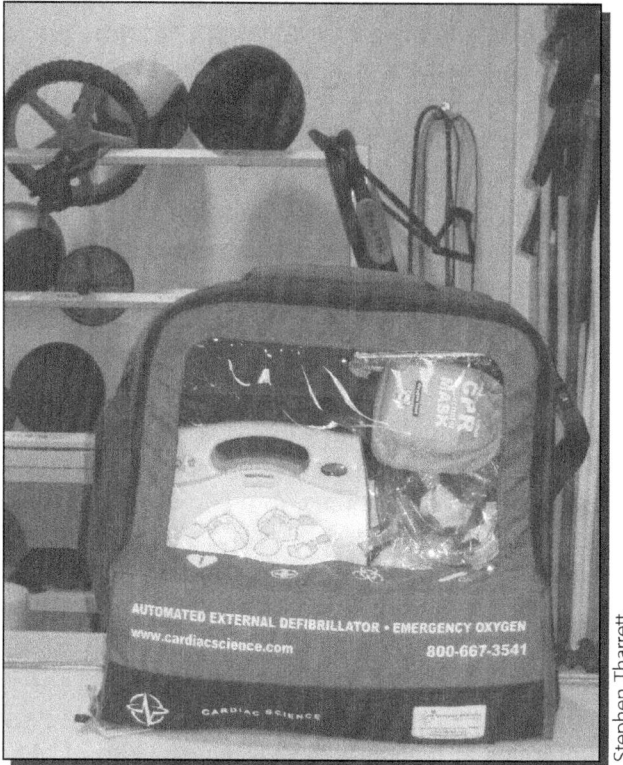

Recently, many facilities have been using portable AED kits that allow staff and members to more readily access and then transport to the site of an incident.

Reflections

Risk management is good business and, unlike many other operating practices, it has a material impact on several fronts, including member health/safety, member satisfaction, employee health/safety, employee productivity, membership retention, and profitability. For many operators, risk management frequently takes a back seat to sales, programming, retention, finance, and even cleanliness. The consequences of such behavior could have a deleterious impact on the success of the business, not to mention endanger employees and members. Consequently, operators need to take risk management seriously, and make it a routine part of their operating practices.

Front-of-the-House Operations: Physical Activity Departments

27

"Efficiency tends to deal with things. Effectiveness tends to deal with people."

—Author unknown

Chapter Objectives

Health/fitness clubs are successful because of many factors, including their operating practices. Operating practices are those administrative policies, practices, procedures, and systems that enable a club to deliver its products and services that foster memorable member experiences and drive financial profitability. This chapter examines the "best" industry practices involving front-of-the-house operations (e.g., departments whose employees regularly interact and engage with clients and members) as they pertain to the most common physical activity areas in a health/fitness facility. These front-of-the-house physical activity departments include the fitness department, aquatics department, and racquet/tennis department. Not intended to be all-inclusive, the chapter reviews the most critical practices (i.e., the "best" practices) that club operators should address in their operations.

Defining an Operating Practice

Operating practices can be most easily defined as administrative policies, practices, procedures, and systems that enable and empower employees to deliver the club's products and services to its members as consistently as possible. Operating practices range from the policies governing scheduling appointments to the practice of conducting new member orientations. The more formalized these operating practices are, the easier it is for the club to consistently deliver its products and services. The health/fitness facility industry has numerous well-thought-out and proven operating practices. As a result, no one best method for operating a club exists. Instead, there are benchmarks or best practices that can help clearly define what health/fitness facility operators should do in order to run their business successfully. The most successful club operators divide operations into two important components: standards and systems. The operating standards are the minimum expectations that a club has for the delivery of a practice. These expectations provide a basic action framework for the staff. The systems are the tools that the staff can employ to meet the established standards or expectations.

> No one best method for operating a club exists. Instead, there are benchmarks or best practices that can help clearly define what health/ fitness facility operators should do in order to run their business successfully.

Fitness Department (Fitness and Group Exercise)

The fitness department is primarily responsible for making sure that each member and guest of the club is able to engage in a physical-activity program in a safe and effective manner. Although much of what this department does revolves around programming and risk management, a few operating practices are critical to the achievement of its goals, including pre-activity screening, fitness assessment, orienting new members/guests to the fitness facilities, exercise prescription and training, on-the-floor supervision, and equipment care and maintenance.

> Clubs should establish policies and practices that ensure that each member/user is offered a pre-activity screening prior to participating in a physical-activity program.

❑ *Pre-Activity Screening.* The purpose of pre-activity screening is to identify the physical and behavioral factors that will influence the member's/user's ability to participate safely in a physical-activity program. As presented in Chapter 26 on risk management, the industry standard is for every member and/or guest to be offered a pre-activity screening. Clubs should establish policies and practices that ensure that each member/user is offered a pre-activity screening prior to participating in a physical-activity program. The two most common pre-activity screening tools are the Par-Q (physical-activity readiness questionnaire) and the medical history questionnaire (MHQ).

• *Par-Q.* The Par-Q is a simple, self-administered, one-page written instrument that screens for coronary-risk factors and identifies individuals who are at an increased risk of having a cardiovascular incident with the onset of moderate-to-vigorous physical activity due to their present coronary health status. The Par-Q was developed over 30 years ago as a basic, straightforward tool for identifying coronary heath risks. If the member completes this form, that individual can easily be identified as a person who has any risks that would require further assessment from a healthcare professional. If the club administers the Par-Q, then the staff can easily identify those individuals who will require further assessment from a healthcare professional or more careful guidance with their physical-activity program. This tool is designed to be used by both lay people and fitness professionals. Since the Par-Q is a self-administered screening instrument, some clubs have chosen to post the Par-Q on a wall in the club entry or fitness area so that all visitors have the opportunity to read it and make their own determination. There are also some big-box clubs that have incorporated the Par-Q into their membership application materials, both print and digital.

• *Medical history questionnaire (MHQ).* The MHQ is a more complete screening tool than the Par-Q and is expected to be administered by a qualified fitness professional. A MHQ allows a club not only to identify coronary health risks, but also to uncover other health-related issues that might compromise the member's/user's ability to exercise safely. The MHQ can come in a variety of formats, ranging from a short form that seeks information on the most basic health-related issues to a form that elicits information concerning past exercise patterns and related lifestyle behaviors. The results of a MHQ should be interpreted by a qualified fitness professional.

Clubs should determine which of the screening tools will work best for them. Once a tool is identified, the club should then establish a process by which each new member of the club completes the pre-activity screening assessments.

❑ *Fitness Assessment.* Assessing the members' level of fitness is a practice that clubs should consider undertaking. All factors considered a fitness assessment may not be appropriate for every member. Primarily, fitness assessments should be used with those club members for whom additional information is needed to properly design their exercise program or for those members/users who want to establish benchmarks for monitoring their body's responses to physical activity. Clubs should have a system in place that provides a clear path concerning which members/users should be channeled into the fitness-assessment process. Fitness-assessment systems tend to vary considerably and can include any or all of the following elements:

> Clubs should have a system in place that provides a clear path concerning which members/users should be channeled into the fitness-assessment process.

- *Cardiovascular assessments.* Cardiovascular assessments can be as simple as a three-minute step test or as complex as a physician-supervised, graded exercise test. Most clubs typically employ either a step test or a sub-maximal exercise test using a bicycle ergometer to evaluate a member's level of cardiovascular fitness. A recent innovation has been the introduction of metabolic carts, such as the Cardio Coach manufactured by Korr Medical Technologies, that are used to measure metabolic capacity (VO_2max) while the member exercises on either a treadmill or bicycle.

- *Muscular strength and endurance assessments.* The industry benchmarks for assessing muscular strength and endurance are component-specific tests, such as a grip-strength test, one-minute sit-up test, 1RM or 10RM test with specific exercises, or timed push-up test. On the other hand, a few clubs utilize sport-specific tests to evaluate the muscular strength and endurance levels of their members.

- *Flexibility assessments.* The most common flexibility assessment is the sit-and-reach test. A number of clubs use a goniometer to measure joint-specific ranges of flexibility for the trunk and limbs.

- *Body-fat assessment.* Body-fat assessment may be the fitness measurement that is most desired and used by members. The assessment tools for this factor range from simple circumference measurements to skin-fold measurements with calipers to underwater weighing for more exact determination of body fat. In recent years, some clubs have opted to use bioelectric-impedance devices and technologically advanced apparatuses, such as the Bod Pod (www.bodpod.com), to assess body-fat levels. The most recent innovation in body-fat assessment involves body-scanning devices such as those produced by Styku (www.styku.com) and Fit3D (www.fit3d.com).

- *Metabolism.* With the recent focus on the nation's obesity epidemic, many clubs have started to employ more health-oriented assessments, such as those that measure an individual's overall resting metabolism and caloric expenditure. The newest approach for measuring whole-body caloric expenditure involves a technique called indirect calorimetry, using devices such as ReeVue by Korr and Microlife's BodyGem and MedGem handheld units. Information generated by these indirect calorimeters can be used to provide better guidance with regard to weight-management efforts.

- *Functional movement screenings.* With the advent of functional training and similar exercise regimens, clubs have introduced assessment protocols into their overall assessment procedures. Functional movement screenings look at an individual's posture, muscle imbalances, and muscular movements to ascertain the types of movements they can perform safely and where there may be a need to prescribe corrective exercise movements for the individual.

A club can offer other assessments to its members, depending on the level of sophistication the club wants to achieve. More detailed information on both pre-activity screening and fitness assessment is available in the most recent edition of *ACSM's Guidelines for Exercise Testing and Prescription* (10th edition) and the *ACE Personal Trainer Resource Manual*.

❏ *Fitness and Physical-Activity Orientation.* It is essential that every club has a system in place to orient each new member to its fitness and exercise facilities. The primary goal of this orientation process is to ensure that all members/users have the information and guidance that they need to safely use the club's facilities to pursue a program of physical activity. Some club operators design their orientation process to provide members/users with a brief introduction to their facilities and equipment, while other club operators view the orientation process as an opportunity to fully engage every new member into the club. Within the industry, clubs take several approaches to the orientation process, including the following:

- *Small group orientations.* Many clubs schedule group orientations, which involve having new members attend a 30- to 60-minute session that is facilitated by a fitness professional. These sessions typically provide an overview of the club's equipment, a sample exercise program for working out with the equipment, and a brief explanation of how to use the equipment. Not only are these sessions designed to get new members started on the right foot, so to speak, they are also intended to introduce them to other services the club offers. In the higher-end clubs, these small group orientations may also include an overview of other departments and an introduction to other services offered by the facility.

- *Individual orientations.* An individual orientation is a more personalized approach that is employed by some clubs. An individual orientation allows a new member to spend time, one-on-one, with a fitness professional who provides a more personalized introduction to the club's fitness facilities and services. In some instances, these sessions feature a single 30- to 60-minute appointment, while in other clubs, they are offered as a series of 30- to 60-minute sessions. The extent of these individual sessions might range from a tour of the fitness facilities and overview of the equipment to a complete exercise prescription and multiple personal-training sessions. The trend among many of the larger club operations (e.g., 24 Hour Fitness, Town Sports International, Equinox, etc.) is to offer new members a three-session, personal-training package at an introductory rate as a means of orienting them to the club's fitness facilities.

- *Self-directed orientations.* Over the past few years, several health/fitness operators, such as McFit based in Germany and The Gym Group in England, have moved toward self-directed orientations that utilize web-based software applications. In these clubs, members are directed to a website or internal kiosk, where they can view an orientation program and receive an initial exercise program to follow in the club. As such, in the next 5 to 10 years, this approach may become the orientation process of choice for many club operators.

❑ *Exercise Prescription and Personal Training.* The process of providing members with an exercise prescription and personal-training session may be the most effective approach for integrating new members into the club and getting them started toward achievement of their fitness goals. Over the last decade, clubs have moved away from the tendency to provide each new member with an exercise prescription. Instead, they have focused on promoting personal training. This trend, while a positive step for those individuals who can afford to utilize personal training (according to IHRSA's 2016 Health Club Consumer Report, 12 percent of club members engaged in at least one personal training session during the previous year), creates a situation in which other members might be left without the guidance that they need to be successful with their physical-activity program. All factors considered, wise club operators should provide both of these systems for their members, given the fact that they build on and enhance each other's effectiveness and can help increase the overall level of member/user participation in the club's fitness offerings.

- *Exercise prescription.* An exercise prescription is a personalized-exercise plan that is based on the needs of the individual. An exercise prescription takes into account several factors, including the member's health status, the person's level of inactivity/activity, and the individual's related lifestyle behaviors. Properly designed, it should serve as the foundation for a sound exercise and lifestyle program. Ideally, all members should receive a personalized exercise prescription that is documented for them on either an exercise card or within one of the many cloud-based fitness tracking software programs. The exercise prescription should then be used to provide personalized fitness instruction from a qualified professional. The process of providing new members with an exercise prescription often involves having someone from the fitness staff initially takes the member through the exercise program at least once. After the initial session(s), the fitness staff should monitor the member's progress and, if needed, develop a revised program for the member. One of a club's primary goals should be to establish an exercise roadmap for members to follow and then to check their progress on a regular basis, ideally each quarter. Recently, many clubs have chosen to cloud-based applications that make it easier to construct and monitor a member's exercise prescription.

- *Personal training.* All factors considered personal training is more of a program than an actual operating practice. Nonetheless, personal training is an important system that clubs should incorporate into their operations. In recent years, personal training (individual and small group) has developed into one of the leading sources of incremental revenue for the health/fitness club business. The original focus of personal training was to provide members with the opportunity to work closely with a fitness professional who could provide them with a personalized exercise prescription and ongoing direction and inspiration. As brought forward earlier in this chapter, approximately 12 percent of health/fitness facility members try personal training at least once, and approximately 4 percent engage in personal training at least 20 times a year. Currently, many club operators (e.g., Equinox, 24 Hour Fitness, Bay Clubs, Virgin Active, etc.) have sophisticated systems for introducing new members to personal training.

The process of providing members with an exercise prescription and personal-training session may be the most effective approach for integrating new members into the club and getting them started toward achievement of their fitness goals.

❏ *Fitness-Floor Supervision.* The process of supervising the fitness floor is an operational practice that can lead to improved membership retention, enhanced level of revenue, and a safer club environment. Fitness-floor supervision refers to the process of having the club's fitness staff regularly walk the fitness floor to assist members with their exercise programs and to answer any questions members may have about their fitness programs. According to the most recent edition of ACSM's Health/Fitness Facility Standards and Guidelines, clubs should have at least one fitness professional on duty at all times who is dedicated to supervising the fitness floor. Accordingly, clubs should have a floor-supervision system that ensures that a fitness professional is always available to assist members on the fitness floor. The activities involved in fitness-floor supervision may include one or more of the following:

- Answering questions for members who are having issues or challenges with their exercise program.
- Correcting members with their exercise technique, when appropriate.
- Teaching new exercises to members, if appropriate, to replace ones that they are currently performing.
- Checking the status of the equipment to make sure it is working correctly.
- Greeting new members.
- Promoting other services and programs of the club.
- Checking exercise cards and redesigning exercise programs.
- Providing towels or water to the members.
- Reinforcing the fact to members that they are exercising in a safe environment

Over the past few years, clubs have focused more heavily on offering personal training and have deemphasized the practice of maintaining a strong floor-supervision presence. One of the difficulties with this approach is that personal training typically reaches only 5 to 20 percent of the membership, while supervising the fitness floor can touch the needs of far more members. It is interesting to note that one of the primary complaints of members on the fitness floor, based on industry-based, member-retention research, is the lack of attention they receive and the difficulty of obtaining assistance from fitness staff without having to pay for it. The key point that must be emphasized is that clubs that focus on establishing a process for providing supervision of the fitness floor can reap substantial rewards, in terms of both member satisfaction and membership retention.

> Clubs that focus on establishing a process for providing supervision of the fitness floor can reap substantial rewards, in terms of both member satisfaction and membership retention.

❏ *Equipment Care and Maintenance.* Another critical operating practice that the fitness department must have is an established system for monitoring and caring for the equipment on the fitness floor. By monitoring the condition of the equipment, the fitness department can help provide a safer and more convenient exercise environment. The process of monitoring and caring for the equipment should be a standard element of every fitness department's operating practices. In that regard, clubs should establish daily, weekly, monthly, and annual checklists for monitoring and caring for the equipment on the fitness floor. These checklists can serve as a means for the club to audit its equipment and ensure that all equipment is ready for use by the members. Almost without exception, all equipment manufacturers provide care and maintenance guidelines for their equipment. Figures 27-1 and 27-2 detail some of the important monitoring and care activities for fitness equipment.

Equipment	Daily Care	Weekly Care	Monthly Care	As Needed
Variable-Resistance Equipment	• Clean frames with mild soap and water. • Clean upholstery with mild soap and water.	• Check all cables and bolts and tighten as needed. • Check moving parts and adjust as needed.	• Lubricate the guide rods with lightweight oil.	• Repair and/or replace pads. • Replace cables if needed.
Free-Weight Benches and Accessories	• Clean frames with mild soap and water. • Clean upholstery with mild soap and water.	• Check all cables and bolts and tighten as needed. • Check moving parts and adjust as needed.		• Repair and/or replace pads. • Replace cables if needed.
Dumbbells and Bars	• Clean off bars with a dry cloth.	• Check all screws and bolts and tighten as needed.	• Use lightweight oil on a cloth to remove any rust.	• Repair and/or replace broken bars and dumbbells.

Figure 27-1. Care and maintenance guidelines for resistance equipment

Aquatics Department

Pools have evolved over the last 50 years to become an integral programming and revenue source for the health/fitness club industry. When once pools were seen as a necessary evil whose only value was to enhance membership sales, today's health/fitness club operators see aquatic environments as an integral part of their value proposition.

Equipment	Daily Care	Weekly Care	Monthly Care	As Needed
Bicycles and Recumbent Bicycles	• Clean off control panel with a damp cloth. • Clean off seats with mild soap and water. • Clean housing with mild soap and water.	• Check equipment diagnostics on the control panel for any warnings or indications of problems. • Check all screws and bolts and tighten as needed. • If positioned on a carpet, vacuum underneath.	• Remove housing covering the bike and clean out any dust or lint.	• Refer to manufacturer's guidelines.
Elliptical Trainers and Stairclimbers	• Clean off control panel with a damp cloth. • Clean housing and pedals with mild soap and water.	• Check equipment diagnostics on the control panel for any warnings or indications of problems. • Check all screws and bolts and tighten as needed. • If positioned on a carpet, vacuum underneath.	• Remove housing covering the elliptical or stairclimber and clean out any dust or lint.	• Refer to manufacturer's guidelines.
Treadmills	• Clean off control panel with a damp cloth. • Clean housing with mild soap and water.	• Check equipment diagnostics on the control panel for any warnings or indications of problems. • Check all screws and bolts and tighten as needed. • If positioned on a carpet, vacuum underneath.	• Clean belts using a damp cloth. • Check belt/deck surface and lubricate as needed. • Check rollers and adjust if they're out of alignment.	• Replace belts if warranted. • Replace deck surfaces if diagnostics indicate. • Refer to manufacturer's guidelines.

Figure 27-2. Care and maintenance guidelines for cardiovascular equipment

Types of Aquatic Facilities in Health/Fitness Clubs

Among the various types of aquatic environments a health/fitness club can offer, the following are the most prevalent.

❑ *Lap/recreational pools.* These pools are designed primarily for individuals who want to pursue fitness swimming, commonly referred to as lap swimming, but can also be used for other activities, such as water-exercise classes, swim lessons, triathlon training, and swim team. The typical lap pool in most private clubs will be 25 yards (75 feet) long and 15 yards (45 feet and six lanes) wide, and will be four to five feet deep at its deepest. Lap pools that are going to be used for swim meets must have a depth of at least seven feet at one end of the pool to accommodate surface diving and lane widths of seven feet (2.15 meters). In fact, many of the lap pools that were built before 1980 have depths of 10 to 12 feet and consequently can be used for board diving, though in today's risk management climate, having diving boards can be a risky and expensive proposition. Many private clubs that have successful swim teams often install regulation short-course competitive pools in their facilities that are either 25 meters (international) or 25 yards (domestic) in length and have eight lanes of 2.15 meters width. As of 2013, pools that have over 300 linear feet of edge were required to provide two ADA accessible entries to the pool, rather than the single one that was required in the past.

- *Therapy pools.* Therapy pools are designed primarily for group aquatic exercise classes and therapeutic exercise. These pools may be as small as 20 feet wide by 20 feet long or as large as 40 feet wide by 60 feet long. With a depth that typically ranges from 2.5 to 5 feet, these pools are designed to be handicap accessible. The materials used to construct these pools are similar to those employed with lap pools.

- *Leisure/waterpark-style pools.* Leisure/water park-style pools are one of the newest trends for private clubs. These pools are designed to accommodate various types of leisure style activities (wading, swimming, sliding, splashing, etc.). The most common features incorporated into these pools include:
  - *Zero-depth entry.* This represents a design feature where the pool entry gradually slopes from deck level to the desired water depth.
  - Water slides. First introduced in water parks, pool slides come in all sizes and shapes and allow users to slide into the pool, sometimes on a tube or on their own.
  - *Splash pads.* Splash pads are a popular feature for young children as these areas typically have only a few inches of water over a soft base and offer exciting features such as water sprays and water features.
  - *Lazy rivers.* These aquatic features are intended to simulate a river or stream and have a moving current. Users can float along these features on inner tubes or similar flotation devices.
  - *Wave pools.* This is a special feature that can be incorporated into a leisure pool. It uses a machine to artificially generate waves that simulate being in the ocean.

Fundamental Operating Practices for Aquatic Environments

The aquatics department requires strict attention to operating standards and systems. Much of this requirement stems from the fact that state and local health departments regulate the practices that are employed to operate commercial and public pools. Although not intended to cover every operating practice that is required to operate a pool environment, this section reviews the key operating practices and practices that are essential for the safe operation of an aquatics department, including:

The aquatics department requires strict attention to operating standards and systems.

❑ *Monitoring and Controlling Pool Chemistry and Temperature.* Maintaining the proper chemical balance in the pool is a crucial factor in member/user safety, not to mention a strict requirement of most state and local departments of public health. Some health departments mandate that pool operators monitor and record pool chemistry and temperature at least three times a day, while others only require such monitoring once daily. In addition to monitoring the chemistry and temperature levels in the pool, most health departments have established guidelines for what constitutes appropriate chemical levels. The four primary chemical levels that should be monitored and maintained are:

- *Chlorine or bromine level.* Most private and commercial pools use either chlorine or bromine as the chemical agent to sanitize their pools (chlorine and bromine are EPA-registered sanitizing agents). Chlorine, the most frequently used chemical, is added to the pool in several ways. The two most frequently used approaches to pool chlorination involve the introduction of free chlorine into the pool in either tablet form (calcium or lithium) or in liquid form. When chlorine is introduced using one of these two methods, the free available chlorine (FAC), the sanitizing agent, combines with chemicals given off by the body to form chloramines, which in turn cause skin and eye irritation, as well as the "chlorine aroma" that is typically associated with a pool environment. The formation of chloramines depletes the water of free chlorine, requiring operators to regularly monitor add chlorine, and on occasion shocking the pool with high doses of chlorine to achieve the proper balance of chlorine for sanitation purposes. In either instance, the chlorine level is controlled through automated systems that maintain the free chlorine level in accordance with industry standards and/or public health codes. According to the ANSI/APSP standards, FAC should be kept between a minimum of one part per million (1 ppm) and not exceed four parts per million (4 ppm). The newest automatic chlorination systems offer cloud-based software applications that allow club operators to manage the system from anywhere.

Over the past decade, salt-water pools have emerged as a preferred method of pool sanitation. With a saltwater system, the system's generators continuously break down the salt and generate free chlorine ions, eliminating the formation of chloramines, and therefore the typical pool aroma and the skin irritation issues typically associated with chlorine. According to both the ANSI/APSP Standard and the National Spa and Pool Institute (NSPI), the minimum level of free chlorine should be 1 ppm. With regard to user safety and comfort, the level of free chlorine should not exceed 4 ppm. Because chlorine is a highly dangerous chemical, the staff should take considerable care whenever they handle it.

> Over the past decade, salt-water pools have emerged as a preferred method of pool sanitation.

While bromine is used less frequently than chlorine, many individuals consider it to be a more effective and user-friendly chemical than chlorine. Bromine is colorless and odorless and, as a result, is not as irritating to the pool user. The aforementioned standards and recommendations indicate that bromine levels should normally be maintained between 1 ppm and 8 ppm, with the most appropriate levels being between 2 ppm and 3 ppm. Most modern pool systems monitor the chemical levels and adjust them automatically, based on the requirements established by the operator. Despite new technologies that monitor and adjust pool chemistry automatically, it is still highly recommended for pool operators to hand-monitor the chlorine and bromine levels in the pools themselves.

While law mandates that operators must use one of the aforementioned EPA-registered sanitizing agents (chlorine and bromine), operators can supplement their use with either an ozone sanitization system or ultraviolet light system. In cases where clubs use these supplemental sanitizing approaches, they must still maintain the required levels of either chlorine or bromine.

- *Total alkalinity.* The alkalinity level is another important factor that should be monitored at least once daily. Alkalinity level, along with calcium hardness and pH level, influences water clarity, and therefore swimmer safety. The ANSI/APSP standard for the total alkalinity level is between 60 and 180 ppm. NSPI indicates that when a chlorine system is employed, those levels should ideally be between 80 and 100 ppm and between 100 and 120 ppm when bromine is used.
- *Calcium hardness.* The ANSI/APSP standard for calcium hardness dictates a minimum level of 150 ppm and a maximum level of 1,000 ppm.
- *pH (percent hydrogen).* The recommended standard for pool pH is 7.4, with a range of 7.2 to 7.8 being the standard established by ANSI/APSP. If the pH falls below 7.2, then the pool water is becoming too acidic, and if it rises above 7.6, it is becoming too basic. Changes in a pool's pH level can be an indication that a chemical imbalance exists.

In addition to monitoring and maintaining the aforementioned chemical levels, pool operators should also monitor and control the temperature of the pool. According to industry practices, the temperature of the pool should be maintained within plus or minus two degrees of the temperature that is appropriate for the circumstances in the pool during the course of the day. The proper temperature for a pool depends on the activities that are being performed in the pool. While no universal standard exists, Figure 27-3 details temperature guidelines that are consistent with policies and practices in the industry.

Despite new technologies that monitor and adjust pool chemistry automatically, it is still highly recommended for pool operators to hand-monitor the chlorine and bromine levels in the pools themselves.

United States Water Fitness Association by Activity	Temperature Recommendation (Fahrenheit)	USA Swimming by General Activity	Temperature Recommendation (Fahrenheit)
Competitive and serious lap swimming	78 to 82 degrees	• Competitive swimming • Adult aerobic lap swimming • High-intensity aquatics exercise	82 degrees or less
Recreational swimming	82 to 86 degrees	• Learn-to-swim • Moderate intensity aquatics exercise • Low-intensity lap swimming • Recreational swimming	86 to 88 degrees
Aquatics exercise (intense)	78 to 82 degrees	• Aquatics therapy • Learn-to-swim for children	90 to 92 degrees
Arthritis exercise	Above 83 degrees	• Aquatics therapy • Learn-to-swim for preschool	95 degrees
Prenatal	Above 84 degrees		

Swimming lessons (beginners):
  Preschool
  3 to 5 years
  6 to 13 years
  Adults
	
	88 to 94 degrees
	86 to 90 degrees
	84 to 86 degrees
	85 to 89 degrees		

Figure 27-3. Suggested water temperatures (United States Water Fitness Association and USA Swimming)

- ❏ *Cleaning the Pool and Filters.* Next to monitoring and maintaining the pool chemistry, cleaning the pool is the second most important day-to-day operating practice that clubs should systemize. All pools use filter systems to remove particulate matter from the water. By removing particulate matter, the filter system allows operators to maintain the clarity and safety of the water environment. Typically, a pool will use one of the following filtration systems:
- *Sand filters.* Sand filters use sand to filter the water, in most instances capturing particles as small as 20 microns. Most sand filter systems will clog up over time as a result of the accumulation of particulates. When the filter becomes clogged, the pressure in the system rises, which in turn can cause the system to back-up and push particulate matter back into the pool. Consequently most sand filters need to be back-washed on a weekly basis and during peak periods of usage, on a daily basis.
- *Diatomaceous Earth (D.E.) filters.* D.E. filters use fossilized exoskeletons of tiny diatoms to filter out particles; in essence, they are using organic matter to serve as a filter. D.E. filters can extract much smaller particles than a sand filter, often as small as 3 microns, and consequently allow for the greatest water clarity. D.E. filters are costlier to maintain than a sand filter due to the cost of regularly replacing the organic matter and replacing internal elements of the filter. Like sand filters, D.E. filters also require backwashing.
- *Cartridge filter.* Cartridge filters are self-contained units that are cost-effective and energy-efficient. A cartridge filter has similar filtering capability

to a D.E. filter, which means it can produce greater water clarity than a sand filter. Cartridge filters do not require backwashing, which is a time-consuming activity; instead, the filters can be removed and hosed down two to three times a year. Cartridge filters typically need to be replaced every few years.

Clubs should establish a cleaning checklist that is audited on a daily, weekly, and monthly basis to ensure that all basic cleaning functions are undertaken as scheduled. Figure 27-4 provides a general overview of the most critical cleaning practices for commercial pools, each of which should be an integral part of a club's pool-operating practices.

Cleaning Activity	Comments
Vacuuming the pool	Pools should be vacuumed daily, using either built-in vacuums or automatic vacuum systems. The best time to perform vacuuming is at closing to allow for the appropriate interlude (at least five hours) to pass before allowing members to use the pool.
Cleaning skimmers	This practice is only required in pool systems that use skimmers. Most modern pools use gutter systems. In busy pools, this task should be done on a daily basis.
Cleaning the walls and tile	If the pool surface is paint, vinyl, or fiberglass, then the cleaning should be done with a nylon brush. This process needs to be done at least monthly and more often in pools with heavy usage. In addition, the scum line should be cleaned on a regular basis, using a soft brush or cloth.
Backwashing the filter	Backwashing needs to occur on a regular basis. In very busy pools, this step can be as often as once a day, but more likely will need to be done weekly. The frequency of backwashing normally is based on the guidelines of the filter manufacturer and type of filter employed (sand, diatomaceous earth, or cartridge). A pressure rise of 5 psi is often an indicator that a filter needs to be backwashed.

Figure 27-4. Key pool-operating practices

- ❑ *Emergency and Safety Preparation.* The pool facilities are among the most likely areas of a club to experience incidents that place members and guests in harm's way. As a result, clubs should implement operating systems that allow for the safest possible environment for members and users. The previous chapter presented an overview of basic emergency preparedness factors, measures that are especially important in the pool area. Beyond these basic emergency-preparedness steps, clubs should also consider standardizing and executing the following pool-specific emergency and safety practices:
- *Posting all appropriate signage, per local and state codes.* This signage should address several key elements, including showering before entering the pool, not running on the pool deck, no diving, notices on pool depth, communications on pool supervision or lack thereof, the location of emergency/safety equipment, and information on contacting assistance.
- *Making sure that the proper safety equipment is positioned at poolside, and communicating its location to staff and members/users.* Most local and state governments have specific requirements concerning safety equipment in the pool area. Far too often, these requirements are insufficient. The proper safety equipment for a pool includes:

- ✓ First aid kit
- ✓ Automatic external defibrillator (AED)
- ✓ Spinal board
- ✓ A 25-foot rope attached to a ring buoy
- ✓ Shepherd's crook
- ✓ Extension poles (at least one)
- ✓ Eyewash station
- ✓ Blankets or similar wrap

- *Providing the necessary supervision and oversight of the pool area.* The regulations governing the supervision of aquatic environments fall under the authority of the state and/or local health department, and as a result are not uniform from state to state. For example, most (if not all) states require lifeguard supervision for wave pools and those with water slides, while the typical recreational pool may or may not require the presence of a lifeguard. In those instances where state regulations do not require a lifeguard be present, there is usually a mandate to provide signage indicating a lifeguard is not present. While the best operating practice is to provide a lifeguard during all hours that a pool is in operation, in those regions where one is not required, clubs should establish a monitoring system that ensures reasonable oversight of the pool area. Examples of such a system could include the following steps:
  - ✓ Using video equipment and monitors
  - ✓ Having supervisory staff do a walk-through of the pool every hour that the pool is open to members and guests
  - ✓ Using volunteer lifeguards during peak hours
  - ✓ Posting signage indicating the level and type of supervision that is available during aquatic operating hours. Most, if not all States require pool operators to provide such signage when lifeguards are not present to provide supervision.

- *Conducting weekly safety audits.* Clubs should develop an audit checklist that addresses such factors as safety equipment, pool chemistry, pool cleaning, and supervision, and is used to perform an audit on a weekly basis to make sure that the appropriate safety procedures are being taken, for example:
  - ✓ All pool chemicals are stored in a safe and secured area. The chemicals used in pool care should be stored in a dry area, off the floor. Many of the chemicals used in pool care are highly volatile if they come in direct contact with moisture or other chemicals. The storage area should be secured, as well as only be accessible to authorized staff (e.g., staff trained in the handling of pool chemicals such as a certified pool operator).
  - ✓ All members/users sign in. A highly recommended operating practice is to have every member/user sign in and out when using the pool. Limiting access to the pool area to authorized individuals can be a life-saving measure.

Tennis Department

The tennis department, like the other aforementioned departments, can also benefit from having structured operating systems that can help ensure the consistent delivery of a safe and enjoyable experience. Administering the tennis department often involves many of the same operating practices that other front-of-the-house departments employ. Several operating practices exist that are somewhat specific to the circumstances attendant to the tennis department, including:

- ❑ *Cleaning and Maintenance Practices.* In order for members to have a relatively safe and enjoyable experience with the club's tennis facilities, certain cleaning and maintenance practices are necessary. Above and beyond the normal cleaning practices that a club conducts, these steps include:
  - *Checking light levels and adjusting them as needed.* The light levels at net height should be at least 40 foot-candles, preferably closer to 75 foot-candles (professional competitive level play often requires illumination levels as high as 125 foot-candles). If the club has indoor courts, it should establish a practice of regularly monitoring light levels and replacing bulbs whenever the light levels fall below the minimum recommendation. As a rule, every few years, the light ballasts will need to be replaced.
  - *Cleaning the courts surfaces of debris.* Cleaning the court surfaces of indoor hard courts typically involves vacuuming the courts at least once a day to remove ball fuzz. For outdoor hard courts, this task entails vacuuming or blowing off the courts on a regular basis, while for clay courts, it involves sweeping and watering the courts. Regardless of the type of court-playing surface or the method used to clean that surface, the key goal is to remove any loose impediment that could interfere with play or present a potential danger to the members/users.
  - *Check the nets for damage and tension levels.* Nets with holes should be repaired or replaced, and nets at the improper height should be adjusted.
  - *Inspecting and repairing court surfaces.* Because hard courts often crack, they can present a danger to the member/user. Clay courts can have low spots or areas of hardening that can also present a danger. Accordingly, clubs should regularly inspect the court surfaces and make any appropriate repairs.

- ❑ *Scheduling Court Reservations.* Every club should establish operating policies and practices regarding the scheduling of tennis-court time. These policies and practices should be understood by the staff and clearly communicated to the club's members. Examples of reservation and scheduling practices and policies include:
  - *Establishing limits for court time.* Most indoor courts normally schedule time in one-hour blocks, while outdoor courts employ 90-minute blocks.
  - *Establishing advance reservation limits.* Clubs should set limits concerning how far in advance members/users can reserve a court. Most clubs in the industry permit reservations to be made up to one week in advance.
  - *Establishing matchmaking services.* Many clubs develop practices that allow the club to arrange matches for members in those instances when the facilities are provided with sufficient notice.

Every club should establish operating policies and practices regarding the scheduling of tennis-court time.

- *Establishing a requirement for the basic information needed to reserve a court.* As a rule, this requirement involves obtaining several pieces of information, including name, member number, number of players, etc. This practice is very similar to front-desk operations. Like front desk operations, most clubs use a cloud-based court reservation system that automatically captures the necessary information.
- *Establishing permanent court-time policies.* Some clubs provide their members with a permanent court time, which refers to the practice of giving members the same reservation time slots each week. This practice requires careful consideration to ensure that too many members of the club are not precluded from playing because other members are assigned the most desirable time slots.

❑ *Programming Functions.* Sound programming is the essence of a successful tennis program. The most successful tennis operators establish specific operating practices that govern their facility's approach to programming. In turn, these practices enable members to actively participate in those tennis programs that most interest them. Examples of operating practices often employed in the industry involving tennis programming include:
- Establishing and distributing an annual program calendar and booklet.
- Having a matchmaking policy and detailed steps that should be taken for matchmaking to occur.
- Having registration forms for each tennis program available in areas that members/users can easily access.
- Posting the guidelines and rules pertaining to each program. This step can involve employing a variety of tools, such as websites, Facebook page, newsletters, or printed program handbooks for members.

Reflections

It is important to note that a club's practices for front-of-the-house operations are not exclusive of other club practices, involving such diverse elements as programming, service delivery, and marketing. In many instances, what might be considered service delivery might actually be an operating practice, or what is considered programming could also be viewed as operations. Accordingly, the operating practices reviewed in this chapter involve those policies, practices, and systems that were not previously detailed in other chapters.

Front-of-the-House Operations: Non-Physical Activity Departments

28

*"Efficiency tends to deal with things.
Effectiveness tends to deal with people."*

—Author unknown

Chapter Objectives

Health/fitness clubs are successful because of many factors, including their operating practices. Operating practices are those administrative policies, practices, procedures, and systems that enable a club to deliver its products and services that foster memorable member experiences and drive financial profitability. This chapter examines the "best" industry practices involving front-of-the-house operations (e.g., operational departments within a facility where the staff and clients regularly interact) for the two major non-activity areas of a facility: the front-desk department and the child-care department. Not intended to be all-inclusive, the chapter reviews the most critical practices (i.e., the "best" practices) that club operators should address in their operations.

Defining an Operating Practice

Operating practices can be most easily defined as administrative policies, practices, procedures, and systems that enable and empower employees to deliver the club's products and services to its members as consistently as possible. Operating practices range from the policies governing scheduling appointments to the practice of conducting new member orientations. The more formalized these operating practices are, the easier it is for the club to consistently deliver its products and services. The health/fitness facility industry has numerous well-thought-out and proven operating practices. As a result, no one best method for operating a club exists. Instead, there are benchmarks or best practices that can help clearly define what health/fitness club operators should do in order to run their business successfully. The most successful club operators divide operations into two important components: standards and systems. The operating standards are the minimum expectations that a club has for the delivery of a practice. These expectations provide a basic action framework for the staff. The systems are the tools that the staff can employ to meet the established standards or expectations.

> The more formalized the operating practices are, the easier it is for the club to consistently deliver its products and services.

Front-Desk (Reception) Department

The front-desk department at the majority of health/fitness clubs has four primary responsibilities: welcoming members and guests, scheduling appointments, answering phones, and disseminating club information. The degree to which the club is successful at each of these responsibilities is dependent to a great extent on the operating practices it has implemented.

- ❑ *Welcoming Members and Guests.* The practice of greeting members is especially important in the club business because it sets the tone for each member's or guest's overall experience in the club. Successfully greeting members and guests depends on several factors, such as being able to make contact with each member/guest and calling them by name. It also requires being aware of their arrival and monitoring their access to the club. As a result, most club operators establish baseline policies and practices that are designed to drive the greeting process. Examples of some of the most effective operating practices or systems include:
  - *Membership identification system.* The majority of clubs require members to provide evidence of membership upon entry to the club. Typically, this is done by presenting a membership ID, most often a card. Not only does requiring members to present their ID enable the staff to ensure that each visitor to the club is a member, more importantly, it provides a means for personally identifying and greeting each member by name. Some clubs ask their members to show their card to front-desk staff, while others require members to swipe their card, either by passing it through a card reader or across a scanner. Fingerprint identification has also emerged as a cost-effective and high-security approach to identifying members and guests when they enter the facility. 24 Hour Fitness uses fingerprint scanning devices in all 400-plus of its properties. In Germany, instead of swiping the card, members place either their card or other object containing a computer chip against a device that can register the information present on the chip. The most recent approach used in the U.S. is to provide a membership identification application for smartphones that individuals can show when entering the facility. In Brazil, many clubs take fingerprint scans, while in Turkey a few clubs use either an eye/retina scan or other biometric scanning device to monitor member entry. These various identification systems usually drives a screen on the front-desk computer that displays basic information on the member, including the individual's name, the last time the person visited the club, the individual's activity interests, etc. If the visitor is an invited guest, clubs require the presentation of an authorized guest pass that identifies the name of the guest, the dates the guest pass is valid for, and the name of the club member or staff person who authorized the guest pass.

    The most important policy for clubs with regard to greeting members is to have standards concerning their expectations on how members should be greeted. At ClubCorp, for example, one basic standard was to greet each member by name within 10 seconds of their arrival. Another standard was to stand and smile when greeting a member or guest. On one hand, ClubCorp's standards set the framework for its employees, while, on the other hand, the actual systems for performing standard-related tasks, such as collecting cards, swiping cards, etc., were the practices that allowed the standard to be met at ClubCorp.

- *System for monitoring member and guest access.* Monitoring the access of members and guests is different than greeting them. Monitoring refers not only to being able to identify who is using the club, but also making sure that whoever is using the club is not exposing the club to any undue liability. The most critical step in monitoring access to the club is identifying if the visitor is a member or guest and whether that person is authorized to have access privileges. The majority of clubs utilize technology to accomplish this step. Numerous software applications now exist (e.g., Aphelion, CSI, Jonas Fitness, Motionsoft, Twin Oaks, and iGo Figure) that provide software which allows staff to verify a member or guest's status, using existing databases that are stored in the software or on the cloud. Most of these monitoring systems have applications that can be downloaded to a smartphone and used whenever a member or guest visits.

  The monitoring process is important for several reasons. For example, it helps make sure that the club's facilities are made available to only those individuals who have paid for the privilege. It also provides a means to know who is in the club at any given time (an important factor from a risk-management perspective). In addition, it enables the club to determine overall club usage, information that can later be used to make other operating decisions. Knowing who is in the club can become extremely valuable in the event of an emergency or if someone needs to contact that individual. For those clubs that do not use software, the next best practice is to employ a sign-in log. A sign-in log involves having each visitor, member, or guest sign their name and list the time of their entry to the club.

  Another operating practice involved in monitoring is to ensure that each non-member/guest has completed a pre-activity screening instrument and has signed a waiver (if appropriate) within the past 12 months. According to *ACSM's Health/Fitness Facility Standards and Guidelines, 4th Edition*, all club users must undergo pre-activity screening. Completing this requirement at the time of a person's entry to the club makes the most sense.

❑ *Scheduling Appointments.* In most health/fitness clubs, the front-desk staff has the responsibility of making all reservations and appointments, including court reservations, appointments for personal training or massage sessions, class registrations, and event sign-ups. In some of the larger clubs, these functions are often handled by a separate reservation desk (e.g., East Bank Club, Chicago; Bay Clubs, California; Lifetime Fitness, Eden Prairie, Minnesota and Telos Fitness, Dallas, Texas). In the last few years, many operators have gone to online real-time, cloud-based scheduling and reservation systems such as those offered by software companies such as Mind Body, CSI, and Motionsoft. These new online reservations tools, whether cloud-based or an app for customers' smartphones, afford clients and members incredible flexibility and also reduce the demand placed on facility staff. Whether your club uses a cloud-based scheduling platform, mobile application, or handles reservations through a front desk or sports desk, standards and practices for performing those duties should be established.

> Online reservations tools, whether cloud-based or an app for customers' smartphones, afford clients and members incredible flexibility and also reduce the demand placed on facility staff.

- *Scheduling standards.* To ensure that the scheduling of appointments and reservations is handled properly, basic standards need to be established concerning what constitutes an appropriate reservation. In that regard, some of the key standards might include:
  - ✓ *Having a set restriction concerning how far in advance appointments can be scheduled.* In most clubs, this standard can range from one day to as far as a month in advance. Within the industry, for example, some tennis clubs limit their reservations to seven days in advance, while others allow reservations to be made only one day in advance. The key is for the club to identify the appropriate time limit during which its membership can schedule appointments in advance. If a club is using a cloud-based or mobile platform for scheduling, then it can build those restrictions into the system.
  - ✓ *Having a cancellation/no-show policy.* The most successful club operators establish clear cancellation and no-show policies concerning reservations and appointments. Such policies help establish clear value for the club's services and also help provide flexibility to accommodate other members and guests. A common practice in the industry is to have a 12-hour cancellation policy. In other words, those appointments that are cancelled more than 12 hours in advance result in no charge, while those that are terminated with less than 12 hours notice involve some form of penalty charge. A no-show policy involves establishing some type of consequence if an appointment does not show. For example, the club might charge a $10 fee for no-shows.
  - ✓ *Specifying the information to be collected.* It is critical that clubs establish a standard concerning what information should be obtained when scheduling an appointment or reservation. Typically, this would involve getting the member's name, membership number, and contact information. For example, at ClubCorp, when an appointment is made for a tennis court, the staff must get the member's name, the member's membership number, the time and date of the appointment, the court the reservation is for, and the staff person who made the appointment. In addition, the ClubCorp staff person who made the reservation/appointment had to initial the reservation. With today's cloud-based and mobile reservation systems, this information is automatically collected.
  - ✓ *Having a procedure that confirms appointments and reservations.* Another essential standard is to develop and adhere to a firm practice of confirming all appointments. Some club operators require their staff to send a confirmation e-mail 24 hours in advance of the appointment, while others have one of their employees reconfirm the appoint by calling the individual who made the appointment. Again, with today's cloud-based and mobile systems, automatic reminders can be generated in compliance with club policies.
- *Scheduling systems and practices.* As of 2014, many clubs have gone to cloud-based or mobile application scheduling and reservation systems. A few clubs remain that employ a paper reservation and scheduling system. These systems utilize pre-designed appointment books or reservation sheets that enable the necessary appointment information to be

documented for each reservation and appointment. The cloud-based and mobile portals provide incredible flexibility, since they allow members to schedule appointments and reservations through their own computer or smart phone, but also allow the club's staff to book reservations through the club's computers. Not only do these cloud-based and mobile systems allow appointments to be made more quickly, they also have the capability of printing out daily appointment and reservation sheets for the staff, as well as sending reminder emails and text messages directly to the member. Supplier companies, such as those mentioned previously for club check-in, have all developed either good web-based, scheduling software or mobile portals. While no documented studies have been published regarding the frequency of using the web-based programs, empirical evidence exists that indicates between 10 and 50 percent of members schedule appointments through web-based programs, with the percentage likely to increase as these web-based systems become more prevalent.

❑ *Answering Phones*. For most independent club operators, the front desk is the location where all phones are answered and information from those calls is processed. Many larger clubs have a separate department (some larger companies have call centers) that is dedicated to answering the phone. The most recent trend in the club industry has been to automate the phone answering system (VOIP) so that callers never speak to a staff person; instead, calls are handled through a voicemail system. Those clubs that still view answering the phone as a primary responsibility of the front desk should establish standard practices for answering the phone. Examples of the more critical standards in this area include:

- *Specifying the number of rings before answering the phone*. At ClubCorp, for example, all phones must be answered within five rings. The key is for each club operator to establish a standard for this issue that is appropriate to the club.

- *Specifying the greeting*. Clubs should identify a standard way in which the phone should be answered by every staff person, for example, "Hello, this is the Racquet Club, Mary speaking, how may I assist you?" Customer research indicates that it is very important for a business to answer the phone in a welcoming manner. Accordingly, clubs must establish clear standards concerning how the phone will be answered.

- *Specifying how callers should be put on hold or forwarded and, if necessary, how messages should be taken*. Every club should have a standard practice concerning how calls should be forwarded and how callers should be put on hold. For example, at ClubCorp, callers are never left on hold for more than 30 seconds, before being given the opportunity to speak with a staff person. In this instance, the primary goal is to make sure that callers know that their needs are being taken care of in a prompt manner. With regard to forwarding calls, clubs should also have a set policy concerning this practice. As such, the club standard might involve requiring the staff person who answered the phone to contact the requested staff person to notify that individual of the phone call before forwarding the call. If the staff person is not in, the outside caller should be informed and asked if that person wants to leave a message. Each club can establish its own

> The most recent trend in the club industry has been to automate the phone answering system (VOIP) so that callers never speak to a staff person; instead, calls are handled through a voicemail system.

policies concerning how to handle phone calls. However, if the club wants to provide great service, it should establish clear standards in this regard. Similar to forwarding calls and putting the caller on hold, when it comes to taking messages, clubs should ensure that they have a standard format for taking messages. At ClubCorp, the front-desk staff is expected to get the name of the caller, the time and date of the call, the name of the person the call is for, and to initial the message. With the advent of VOIP (voice over Internet protocol), many clubs have automated answering systems that automatically forward calls and take messages. One of the downsides to VOIP technology is the absence of a human voice answering the call.

❑ *Disseminating Club Information.* Another key responsibility of the front-desk staff is to disseminate information about the club. Front-desk staff is often expected to share important information about the club, either over the phone or in person. Accordingly, clubs should establish standards and practices for handling the dissemination of information at the front desk. Examples of basic standards and practices in this regard include:

- *Establishing what information can be disseminated.* Most clubs like to have their front-desk staff provide general information about club programs and events. On the other hand, front-desk staff should never be required to give out membership information or employee/member information. Accordingly, club operators should develop a clear set of standards and/or practices that clarify the information that can be provided through the front desk.
- *Making the information accessible.* Once the club has established what information may be distributed through the front desk, it then becomes the club's responsibility to make that information easily accessible. For example, at some clubs, the front-desk staff are provided with binders that include information on:
  ✓ Quarterly events and program calendar
  ✓ Monthly newsletters
  ✓ Group-exercise class schedules
  ✓ Basic club information (e.g., the location, operating hours, and general description of the club's facilities, programs, and services)
  ✓ Daily information (e.g., what is scheduled to occur that day at the club)
  ✓ Club phone numbers
  ✓ Names of department heads
  ✓ Emergency procedures and information
  ✓ Club policies and rules

  In the last few years, clubs have begun to push information through their websites, Facebook pages, Twitter pages, in-club kiosks, and customized smartphone applications. As a result, front desk staff members in these facilities are not the primary information distributors. Instead, they are expected to guide members and guests to the appropriate information resource.

Child-Care Department

Many health/fitness clubs provide a child-care department (according to IHRSA's *2015 Profiles of Success* approximately 47 percent of surveyed clubs offer a nursery and 21 percent offer a children-only section) that could reasonably be considered as short-term "babysitting" for parents who are participating in activities at the club. These "babysitting" services differ from both licensed day care, which requires state licensure, and youth programming, which involves the delivery of organized and structured activity programs for children. Several policies and practices are very critical to the safe and successful operation of a child-care department, including:

- ❏ *Hours of Operation.* Clubs should inform their members when the child-care services will be available. Within the industry, these schedules can vary from club to club. For example, in some urban clubs, the hours that child-care services are available are scheduled around specific programs or times of the day, while in many of the suburban clubs that target the family market, these services are provided during the entire day.

- ❏ *Age Groups.* Clubs should make it crystal clear what age groups can be handled by the child-care department. Most clubs don't normally permit children below the age of six months or above the age of eight years to participate in their child-care programs. Many family-oriented clubs offer separate child-care areas for different age groups, such as a room for children who range in age from six months to 18 months, another for those from 19 months to three years, yet another for kids from three years to five years, and one for those from six years to eight years old. Every club should establish clear policies in this area. Many clubs also develop activity areas within the facility that are designed specifically for those children who are over the age of eight, but who are not yet teenagers (individuals who are often referred to as "tweeners").

- ❏ *Drop-Off and Time-Limit Policies.* Definitive guidelines concerning drop-off and time-limit stipulations are among the most important child-care policies and practices that a club can establish. Since most states have strict restrictions governing the amount of time and extent of child-care services, clubs must be aware of the relevant regulations involving those matters so that they don't find themselves delivering a service that requires state licensure. For example, most states place restrictions on a club's drop-off policies if the facility offers "babysitting" services. Examples of key, specific issues that should be addressed in this regard include:

  - *Time limit.* In most states, the maximum time a child can be left in an environment, such as a child-care area in a health/fitness club, is four hours, before licensing is required. To be on the safe side, many clubs limit the hours that they will "watch" a child to two or three hours.

  - *Parent's presence.* Because of state requirements, clubs must require that parents be on the premises at all times when their children are in the child-care area. As a result, clubs should communicate this fact to their members. Furthermore, clubs should make sure that the members indicate their presence when they sign their children in. The only time a parent does not need to be on the club property is when a child is registered for a club program that has defined parameters, such as a one-week summer camp or school holiday camp. In many states, conducting camps and academies where the parents are not present on the property requires the club to

Definitive guidelines concerning drop-off and time-limit stipulations are among the most important child-care policies and practices that a club can establish.

obtain a special license. From a safety (as well as a liability) perspective, the club should not allow any children under the age of 12 to be on club property unless the parent is present. If for any reason the club allows the parent/legal guardian to leave the property while the child is still on the premises, they need to ensure that they are in compliance with all applicable laws and regulations. For example, in Texas, a club must request an exemption from the Texas Department of Family and Protective Services if they are going to conduct activities where the child will be under the care of the club when the parents are not present.

- *Sign in and sign out.* A standard practice in most clubs is to require the parents or guardians to sign their children in and out of the child-care area. This practice usually involves having the parent/guardian sign their name, identifying their child's name, note (in writing) the time of the drop-off, and indicate which part of the club they will be in. If the parent chooses to have someone other than themselves pick the child up, when they sign in, they must provide that person's name and a means of identification for that person. At the time of signing out, the parent must present themselves, sign a sheet indicating the time they picked the child up, and note their relationship to the child.

❑ *Services Provided.* It is critical that every club spell out in detail what services are provided in the child-care area and how the children will be handled. In that regard, the following should be addressed:

- *Food.* Clubs should establish a policy concerning the provision of food for children in the child-care area. Some club operators require that parents/guardians furnish all of the food and beverages that their children consume while in the child-care area, whereas others adopt policies that indicate that they will provide water, crackers, etc. for the children. All factors considered the prudent approach for a club is to have a policy that requires the food to be provided by the parents or guardians.
- *Restroom practices.* Restroom policies are a very sensitive issue for clubs and parents. With some children still in diapers, clubs must have a policy regarding the changing of diapers. The safest approach is to state that the club will not change diapers and will notify parents in the event that a diaper has to be changed. Clubs also should have a policy that clearly states what the policy will be when an older child needs to use the restroom. In these circumstances, some clubs require that the parent/guardian handle the situation. Other clubs have a policy that mandates that an adult of the same gender must accompany the child to the restroom entry and stand outside the restroom while the child is using the facility. This latter approach involves a higher level of risk from a liability perspective. Another option involves the fact that many child-care areas currently have a separate children's restroom that cannot be locked from the inside. In these facilities, a child can use the restroom, while the child-care staff maintains supervision of the child without direct contact or interference. Some clubs conduct criminal background checks on all staff members who work in the child-care area (a prudent recommendation for any club operator) and share the fact that these individuals have satisfactorily cleared their background checks with the parents who bring their children to the club. Another very

important part of any policy concerning the child-care area is to have a sheet that the parent or guardian must sign, indicating how they want the club to deal with this issue while their child is in the club's care.
- *Activities.* Clubs should include in their child-care policies what activities are provided for children while they are in the care of the club, for example, arts and crafts, computers, video games, nap time, etc. These activities should be spelled out very clearly for parents/guardians.

❑ *Registration and Enrollment.* Every club should have a policy regarding what information should be obtained the first time that a child is left with the child-care department. In most instances, this step would involve:
- *Obtaining medical/health information.* Clubs should obtain a basic medical background on each child, including any allergies, medical-health issues, special-handling instructions, name of the child's physician, etc.
- *Getting family-background information.* Each parent/guardian should provide certain background information, such as their names, contact information (phone, e-mail, etc.), whom to contact in an emergency, etc.
- *Waiver or release.* Each parent/guardian should sign a waiver or release indicating that they are aware of the club's policies and practices and concur with them. The waiver/release sheet should include specific space that can be used to document any special requests of the parent concerning the child. It should be noted that in many parts of the U.S., courts do not recognize waivers that parents have signed on behalf of their children.
- *Special instructions.* Each club should have a form that allows the parent/guardian to identify any special requirements or practices they want addressed with their child.

❑ *Staff-to-Child Ratio.* If the club offers licensed day care, it is legally required to abide by certain child-to-staff ratios. These ratios vary, depending on the age of the children. Even though most clubs do not offer licensed day care, it is still important that all clubs have policies that address the ratio of staff-to-children in their child-care areas. While clubs should determine what is best for them concerning this factor, the following guidelines illustrate some of the practices that exist in the industry:
- Children under age two: no more than three children per adult.
- Children two to five: no more than five children per adult.
- Children five to eight: no more than six to seven children per adult.

❑ *Medical Situations.* It is extremely important that the club has a policy for handling any medical situations involving children in the child-care area. The two most important issues in this regard are handling children who are sick and their parents want to leave them in the child-care area and responding to a medical situation that arises while a child is under the care of the child-care department. In the case of a child being ill, clubs should have a firm policy concerning whether children who are ill can be left in the child-care area. Most clubs do not allow children who are ill to be left in the child-care area. This particular policy, while strict, helps prevent other children from catching an illness from the sick child. All factors considered it is a well-advised policy to have in place. In the event of medical emergencies, the

> It is important that all clubs have policies that address the ratio of staff-to-children in their child-care areas.

club should have a clear policy concerning what to do that is communicated to all staff and members. A critical part of that policy or practice should be to contact the parent or guardian immediately in the event of any emergency. Another key element of such a policy should be to have a signed form that indicates how the parent wants any emergency to be handled, if they cannot be reached immediately and the emergency requires prompt action.

Reflections

It is important to note that a club's practices for non-physical activity front-of-the-house operations are not exclusive of other club practices, involving such diverse elements as programming, service delivery, and marketing. In many instances, what might be considered service delivery might actually be an operating practice, or what is considered programming could also be viewed as operations. Accordingly, the operating practices reviewed in this chapter involve those policies, practices, and systems that were not previously detailed in other chapters.

Administrative Department Operations

29

*"Efficiency is doing things right;
effectiveness is doing the right things."*

—Peter F. Drucker

Chapter Objectives

The previous two chapters presented an overview of the basic operating practices and systems that are important to front-of-the-house departments (e.g., front desk, child-care, fitness, aquatics, and racquet/tennis). This chapter examines the "best" practices for administrative (or as they are commonly referred to, "heart-of-the-house") operations. Administrative operations encompass supporting areas of the club that may directly serve the members and users, or possibly may support the activities of staff serving in front-of-the-house roles. The most common administrative operations in health/fitness facility industry include locker rooms, laundry, housecleaning, and accounting. This chapter provides a detailed review of the key operating practices and systems for each of those departments.

Locker Rooms

The health/fitness club industry has a diverse array of locker-room offerings and operations. For example, some clubs have small changing rooms with a few day-use lockers and a couple of showers (e.g., budget clubs and express clubs), while others have locker rooms offering large changing areas with day-use lockers and basic amenities (e.g., LA Fitness and 24 Hour Fitness), and finally, facilities featuring full-scale locker rooms that include such conveniences as rental lockers, laundry services, and a full array of amenities (e.g., Bay Clubs and Equinox Fitness). As a result of this diversity of offerings, the operating practices involving locker rooms tend to vary from club to club. This section on locker rooms initially presents an overview of basic locker-room operating models and then examines the key practices that clubs should adopt to facilitate operations in their locker rooms.

> The operating practices involving locker rooms tend to vary from club to club.

❑ *Types of Locker Rooms.* There are four basic types of locker rooms. The first type of set-up for locker rooms is the basic model that involves a changing area with day-use lockers (users bring their own locks), shower areas, and restrooms. Locker rooms in this category offer no towel service (although some clubs provide towels for a fee) or any type of amenity, such as soap or shampoo. Some of the European "budget" club operators, such as McFit in Germany and the Gym Group in England, charge a fee for the use of their showers. In most instances this type of locker room is typically found in clubs that have a lower dues structure (e.g., normally under $25 a month), such as U.S chains Blink, Crunch, Fitness Evolution, and Planet Fitness.

The second type of locker room (this structure is the most common in the industry), consists of locker rooms that have changing areas with day-use lockers (the lockers have day-use access with cards, keys, digital locks, computer chips, or personal locks), showers, restrooms, sauna, steam and/or whirlpool (usually a combination of these), and several basic service amenities, such as towels, soap, and shampoo. This type of locker room arrangement typically exists in clubs that have monthly dues structures that range from $40 to $100 a month, such as U.S. chains 24 Hour Fitness, LA Fitness, Lifetime Fitness, and Town Sports International, as well as global operators, such as Virgin Active, England.

The third type of operating structure for locker rooms, which appear mostly in premium and luxury clubs, such as U.S. operators Equinox Fitness, the Bay Clubs, Wellbridge, and Midtown Athletic Clubs, entails locker rooms that include changing areas with both day-use lockers and rentable lockers (a combination of card access, chip card access, and keyed locks), showers, restrooms, sauna, steam and/or whirlpool (usually all three are provided), a full line of amenities, such as towels, soap, and shampoo, and services, such as laundry and shoe shines.

The fourth type of locker room operating structure is available in some of the top luxury clubs and club companies in the industry, such as the Houstonian, Houston, Texas; ClubCorp, U.S.; Bay Clubs, California. This "executive" premier locker-room space includes premium lockers (i.e., full-height, rentable lockers), private showers, separate sauna, steam room and whirlpool, uniform and laundry service, shoe shines, lounges, coffee services, and more.

Each of the aforementioned operating structures has its advantages and disadvantages. On one end of the continuum is the simple locker-room structure that requires minimal to no staffing and work to maintain and brings in no incremental revenue (unless the limited funds generated by towel and shower fees are counted). On the other end of the continuum is the full-service locker room that involves considerable staffing and work to maintain, but concurrently produces significant revenue streams (for example, a few of the aforementioned luxury club operators generate as much as $500,000 annually from their locker rooms).

❑ *Operating Practices for the Locker Room*
- *Cleaning and care of locker rooms.* According to research conducted by Roper Starch for IHRSA earlier this century, members see cleanliness as one of the critical factors in choosing a club. This attribute becomes even more crucial when it comes to women, since they tend to see cleanliness as far more important than men when choosing to join or remain a club member. Since locker rooms typically have the most traffic of any area in the club (statistics indicate that members spend between 25 and 50

> Members see cleanliness as one of the critical factors in choosing a club.

percent of their time in the locker room), the value of maintaining the locker room in tip-top condition is heightened. Accordingly, club operators should establish a system that ensures that their facility's locker rooms are well maintained and clean at all times. Figure 29-1 illustrates the most important areas of cleaning in the locker room.

Daily Activities	**Bi-monthly**	**Monthly/Quarterly/Annually**
• Remove trash and replace liners	• Completely clean mirrors and glass surfaces	• Refill air fresheners and dispensers (monthly)
• Refill paper dispensers	• Clean all hard surfaces by scrubbing with a machine or similar brush	• Clean grout lines in showers (monthly)
• Refill all soap and related dispensers	• Clean and disinfect showers, steam room, sauna, and whirlpool completely	• Clean carpets with bonnet-style cleaner (quarterly)
• Dust all surfaces with a lint-free cloth	• Clean and dust all HVAC grills and vents	• Extraction clean carpets (annually)
• Spot clean all mirrors and glass surfaces	• Clean light fixtures	• Wash down all walls (annually)
• Spot clean locker surfaces, doors, and all exposed hardware	• Empty and clean out all dispensers	
• Clean and disinfect sinks, commodes, and urinals	• Empty and clean out all waste repositories	
• Clean and disinfect sauna, steam room, and whirlpool	• Clean and polish all wood surfaces	
• Vacuum carpets		
• Dust-mop or sweep wood surfaces		
• Wet mop and disinfect hard-floor		

Figure 29-1. Locker room cleaning and care chart

- *Maintaining the sauna, steam room, and whirlpool.* It is important that clubs that offer one or more of these amenities should care for and monitor these areas on a regular basis. Accordingly, clubs should establish a system of standardized practices to help maintain these areas. Examples of standardized practices for the sauna, steam room, and whirlpool include the following:

  ✓ Sauna:
  - Monitor the temperature in the sauna every couple of hours and maintain it between 160 and 170 degrees Fahrenheit.
  - Make sure that a working clock and thermometer are present at all times in the sauna area.
  - Clean and disinfect the surfaces daily.
  - Check the room every couple of hours to make sure no member is in harm's way.
  - Pick up all loose papers in the room.
  - Post appropriate signage regarding the precautions that members should take before entering and using the sauna (refer to the chapter on risk management for additional information).
  - Have a mechanism in place to shut down the sauna if the room's temperature rises too high.

> Clubs should establish a system of standardized practices to help maintain the sauna, steam room, and whirlpool areas.

✓ *Steam room:*
  - Monitor the temperature in the steam room every couple of hours and maintain it between 100 and 110 degrees Fahrenheit.
  - Make sure that a working clock and thermometer are present at all times in the steam room.
  - Clean, disinfect, and scrub the steam room's surfaces, floors, and walls daily.
  - Make sure that a source of cold water is available in the steam room.
  - Check the steam room every couple of hours to make sure that no member is in harm's way.
  - Pick up all loose papers in the room.
  - Post appropriate signage regarding the precautions that members should take before entering the steam room (refer to the chapter on risk management for additional information).
  - Have a mechanism in place to shut down the steam room if the room's temperature rises too high.

✓ *Whirlpool:*
  - Monitor the temperature in the whirlpool every couple of hours and maintain it between 102 and 105 degrees Fahrenheit.
  - Monitor the pool chemistry (pH and chlorine levels) at least twice a day and maintain the proper balance (ph 7.2 to 7.4 and chlorine 1 ppm to 4 ppm)
  - Make sure that a working clock and thermometer are present in the area of the whirlpool at all times.
  - Empty and clean the whirlpool daily, including cleaning the scum line along the top edge of the whirlpool.
  - Check the whirlpool every couple of hours to make sure that no member is in harm's way.
  - Remove any unwanted containers that might be adjacent to the whirlpool.
  - Post appropriate signage regarding the precautions that members should take before entering the whirlpool (refer to the chapter on risk management for additional information).
  - Have a mechanism in place to shut down the whirlpool if the temperature in the whirlpool rises too high.

- *Locker assignments and usage.* As discussed previously, lockers are handled in one of three ways in most clubs. The first method allows members/users to bring their own locks to use with available lockers. The second option permits members to use available lockers, but requires the utilization of either an access card (usually the individual's membership card), token, key or touchpad. The third approach involves renting the lockers and providing the member/user with a combination for the locker or a card containing a chip that opens the locker. Among the more important practices that apply to each of these systems are the following:

- ✓ *Available lockers, with the user's padlocks:*
  - ▷ Provide signage at the front-desk area, inside the locker room, and inside the lockers that indicate that the club is not responsible for items that the member leaves in the lockers.
  - ▷ Have a daily system in which the staff removes padlocks that remain on lockers at closing each evening.
  - ▷ Have a system in place where the staff removes any items remaining in the lockers at closing each evening.

- ✓ *Available lockers, accessed with a card, key, digital lock, chip card, or token:*
  - ▷ Provide signage at the front-desk area, inside the locker room, and inside the lockers that indicate that the club is not responsible for items that the member leaves in the lockers.
  - ▷ If members have to obtain the access card, key, or token from the club, have a system for requiring the user to leave personal identification or other item as collateral for the access item. The club employs this collateral to help motivate individuals to return the access tool before leaving the club.
  - ▷ Have a system in place where the staff checks the lockers at closing each evening and removes any remaining items.
  - ▷ Have a system in place that enables the staff to open the lockers if members lose their key or access card/token.

- ✓ *Rented lockers, accessed with a combination or digital code:*
  - ▷ Provide signage at the front-desk area, inside the locker room, and inside the lockers that indicates that the club is not responsible for items that the member leaves in the lockers.
  - ▷ Provide a system that ensures that each member registers for a locker. This step requires a process of obtaining specific information from the member, assigning a locker and combination, and initiating charges for the locker. Software applications are now available to handle this process.
  - ▷ Provide a system to audit/monitor the rented and un-rented lockers each month to verify occupancy and charged fees.
  - ▷ Provide a system that allows members to forego their commitment to rent a locker. As part of this system, the club must have a method for ensuring that those lockers are not in use and have a process to make sure that the combination on all resigned lockers is changed before a locker is rented to another member.
  - ▷ Have a system in place where the staff checks the lockers after a resignation and removes any items that remain in the locker.
  - ▷ Have a system in place that enables the staff to open the lockers if members forget their combination.

- *Dispersing and handling amenities.* As discussed previously, many locker room operational set-ups offer various amenities to club members. In this instance, the most commonly provided amenities are towel service,

> **The most commonly provided amenities are towel service, basic personal-care items, shoe shines, and uniform services.**

basic personal-care items, shoe shines, and uniform services. Clubs should establish standardized systems for each of these practices to ensure that they are handled in a consistent, appropriate manner. These operational practices can address the following key factors:

✓ *Personal-care items.* Two of the items most frequently provided by clubs are soap and shampoo. Other personal-care items that some clubs offer include conditioner, body lotion, hair spray, shaving cream, and razors. With regard to personal-care items, the following operational practices can help ensure an orderly dispensing system:

- Establish a practice of having the staff check all dispensers before each high-activity period and make sure that all dispensers are filled.
- Establish a par-stock inventory practice. This requires the club to have the staff sign out and identify the quantity of items they remove from the inventory and place in the locker rooms. This process helps ensure that clubs do not fall low on their inventory and helps control potential inventory theft.
- Establish consistency in the types of personal-care items that the facility provides. Many members perceive changes in personal-care items, especially if they are perceived as lower quality, among the most disturbing actions that clubs can take.

✓ *Towels.* Towels are among the most worthwhile amenities that a club can offer its members. At the same time, if a club does not handle the disbursement of towels properly, it can present one of the greatest operating challenges that the staff might experience. The type of towels offered will depend on the dues structure and market position of the club. Clubs with lower price points normally offer import towels that weigh between six and eight pounds to the dozen, while clubs serving a more affluent demographic normally provide domestic towels that range in weight from 10 to 14 pounds to the dozen.

- Establish a system for distributing towels. Some clubs, for example, distribute towels at the front desk and require users to pay for them, while other clubs leave the towels out in the locker rooms and allow members to use as many as they desire. The tendency for clubs that leave the towels out in the locker rooms is to charge higher dues.
- Establish a system to monitor towel usage. If the club distributes towels at the front desk, this practice can also serve as a system for monitoring or controlling towel usage. Clubs that leave towels out in the locker room, however, should perform regular weekly inventory counts to maintain better control of their towels. These clubs should consider placing an abundance of towel bins in the locker-room areas to encourage members to leave the towels that they use in the club.
- Establish a system where the staff monitors the locker rooms every few hours to pick up towels and replenish the supply of towels.

✓ *Shoe shines.* In many of the higher-end clubs (e.g., ClubCorp, Midtown Athletic Clubs, Houstonian and Bay Clubs), shoe shines are an important locker-room amenity. Some of these clubs provide shoe shines purely as a value-added service, while others see it as a source of added incremental

> If a club does not handle the disbursement of towels properly, it can present one of the greatest operating challenges that the staff might experience.

revenue. From an operating perspective, several key practices should be developed with regard to offering a shoe-shine service, including:

- ▷ Establish a process for members/users leaving their shoes. Some clubs require that members take their shoes to a designated shoe-shine area, while others have members leave their shoes in front of their lockers, where the staff picks them up and returns them.
- ▷ Establish a fee system for the members, where the members either charge the shoe-shine service to their membership or pay the locker room staff directly. In a few facilities, the service is provided on a complimentary basis.

✓ *Uniform service.* Providing uniforms (workout shorts, shirts, socks, and supporters—if needed) in the locker room has become an increasingly popular amenity, especially in urban clubs, clubs that serve a corporate market and luxury clubs. Two distinct approaches exist with regard to offering uniform service. In one scenario, some clubs provide and wash the uniforms of members and employees (e.g., ClubCorp). The other option involves clubs allowing their members (and in some cases, employees) to use their own workout apparel, which the club washes and cares for them. Both of these approaches require that clubs should establish practices that help ensure that this amenity is provided (delivered) in an appropriate manner. In that regard, the following steps can facilitate the process:

- ▷ Establish a detailed delivery process if the club supplies the uniforms. Some clubs, for example leave the uniform items on shelves for members to select. In this situation, members wear the uniform and afterwards drop the used uniform in a bin to be washed. Other clubs issue each member a uniform and uniform bag. This practice involves having the member wear the uniform and afterwards place it in a bag that is left in a bin for washing. The bag is subsequently returned to the member's locker.
- ▷ If the club washes the member's/user's personal workout apparel, establish rules and processes governing this practice. In this regard, clubs should specify what workout apparel the club will wash and whether the club will assume responsibility for any lost apparel (except for very unique circumstances, clubs should not be responsible for lost apparel). The club should also develop a system for handling personal workout apparel (e.g., the club provides laundry bags for members to use).
- ▷ Establish a policy that limits the club's responsibility for replacing lost or damaged uniforms (e.g., one uniform per member per year if the club provides the uniform).

Laundry

Laundry operations exist in approximately 50 percent of health/fitness clubs in the industry. As a rule, they are a standard service in those clubs that serve a more affluent member demographic. The laundry department's sole responsibility is to handle the laundry needs of the club, ranging from washing towels only to cleaning an array of items, such as towels, uniforms, sheets,

Laundry operations exist in approximately 50 percent of health/fitness clubs in the industry.

table covers, etc. Although a few clubs employ outside laundry services for their towels and related items, the cost of these services and the quality of the towels normally provided by them does not always serve the best interests of either the club or the members. While laundry operations are not very complicated, if the right systems are not in place, clubs will likely discover that the laundry can cause far more difficulties than expected, particularly with regard to member satisfaction. Accordingly, clubs should standardize the most basic laundry practices to ensure that difficulties do not arise. Among the key practices involving the laundry are the following:

❑ *Have the Right Equipment.* If the club is going to have a laundry, it is essential that the facility has the equipment that the staff needs to handle the laundry demands of the club, for example, commercial-grade washer extractors and dryers. Most clubs will find that they need a minimum of one 50 to 60 pound washer extractor for every 1,500 memberships and twice that (100 to 120 pounds) in dryer capacity for every 1,500 memberships if they do towels only. If the club provides laundry service for uniforms, then the aforementioned equipment requirements will apply for every 1,000 memberships. In addition to an appropriate number of washers/extractors and dryers, clubs should have automated dispensing systems (machines that mix the cleaning agents and dispense them at the right time and in the right combination in the washers). Several companies, such as Ecolab, manufacture these systems.

❑ *Establish Task-Oriented Checklists.* Many clubs assign the responsibility of handling the laundry to the housecleaning department or earmark the duties involved to all staff members. Other clubs, such as the East Bank in Chicago or the Houstonian in Houston, have dedicated laundry staff. Figure 29-2 presents a list of those operational practices that should be established (and monitored through task-oriented checklists) to effectively manage the laundry.

Activity or Task	**Frequency**
Clean out dryer filter	After each drying cycle
Check cleaning-fluid levels for the washer	Before each load is put in
Adhere to recommended guidelines concerning specific number of items that can be placed in either the washer or dryer	Count before each load and the machine is started
Clean out behind washers and dryers	Daily
Follow cleaning and drying instructions, per manufacturer guidelines	Adhered to with each load
Fold towels and uniforms (clubs should outline their expectations)	After each load
Inventory towels	Daily, weekly, and monthly

Figure 29-2. Recommended operational practices involving the laundry

Housecleaning

The cleaning and care of the overall facility is often one of the most overlooked elements of club operations. According to industry research sponsored by

IHRSA, the cleanliness of a facility is one of the most important factors that influence a person's decision to either join or remain a club member. Despite its importance to the consumer, the need to keep the facility clean and well-maintained is frequently neglected by club operators. In fact, cleaning the facility should not occur either by accident or as an afterthought. Rather, it should be a by-product of an established system of formalized practices that the club adheres to on a routine basis. Figures 29-3 through 29-5 provide an overview of the cleaning requirements for several of the key areas in a health/fitness club, including the fitness center, the group-exercise studios, gymnasium, racquet courts, tennis courts, offices, lobby and circulation areas, and massage rooms. (Note: cleaning guidelines for locker rooms and pools are not covered in these figures because they have been addressed in previous chapters.)

Facility Area	Cleaning Activity	Frequency
Fitness Floor	Remove trash	Daily
	Dust all horizontal surfaces	Daily
	Clean and disinfect vinyl pads on equipment	Daily
	Clean and disinfect equipment frames	Daily
	Vacuum carpets and clean stains	Daily
	Spot-clean mirrors	Daily
	Wash and disinfect hard-floor surfaces, including all rubber-floor surfaces	Daily
	Clean HVAC vents	Bi-monthly
	Clean light fixtures	Bi-monthly
	Vacuum and clean under all equipment	Bi-monthly
	Fully clean mirrors and glass surfaces	Bi-monthly
	Clean carpets	Quarterly or annually
	Clean wall surfaces thoroughly	Annually
Group-Exercise Studios	Remove any trash	Daily
	Dry mop wood floors	Daily
	Dust all horizontal surfaces	Daily
	Spot clean mirrors and glass surfaces	Daily
	Clean mirrors thoroughly	Daily
	Wet mop wood floors	Weekly
	Wash and disinfect rubber floor surfaces	Daily
	Clean HVAC ducts	Bi-monthly
	Clean light fixtures	Bi-monthly
	Clean the audio equipment	Bi-monthly
	Wash the solid-surface walls	Quarterly to annually
	Refinish wood-floor surfaces	Annually

Figure 29-3. Cleaning guidelines for fitness and group-exercise facilities

Facility Area	Cleaning Activity	Frequency
Gymnasium	Remove trash	Daily
	Dry mop and dust floors	Daily
	Dust all horizontal surfaces	Daily
	Spot clean all glass surfaces	Daily
	Clean all glass surfaces thoroughly	Weekly
	Tack/wet mop the wood floors	Weekly
	Clean HVAC filters	Bi-monthly
	Clean light fixtures	Bi-monthly
	Refinish wood floors	Every two years
Racquet Courts	Remove trash	Daily
	Dry mop and dust floors	Daily
	Dust horizontal surfaces	Daily
	Spot clean walls and glass surfaces	Daily
	Remove ball marks	Daily
	Tack or damp mop the floors	Weekly
	Thoroughly clean glass surfaces	Bi-monthly
	Clean HVAC vents	Bi-monthly
	Clean light fixtures	Bi-monthly
	Refinish floors (squash should be left unfinished, but sanded)	Annually
Tennis Courts	Remove trash	Daily
	Sweep/vacuum indoor hard courts	Daily
	Blow outdoor courts to remove debris	Daily
	Roll dry outdoor hard courts after rain	Daily
	Sweep courts and brush lines for clay courts	Daily
	Water clay courts	Daily
	Scrape dead material on clay courts	Weekly
	Patch low spots on clay courts	Weekly
	Jet broom and sweep hard courts	Weekly
	Pressure wash hard courts	Bi-annually
	Recondition clay courts (add surface material)	Semi-annually to annually
	Replace tape on clay courts	Every two to three years
	Resurface hard courts	Every three to four years
	Resurface clay courts	Every three to four years

Figure 29-4. Cleaning guidelines for gymnasiums, racquet courts, and tennis courts

Facility Area	Cleaning Activity	Frequency
Lobby and Circulation Areas	Remove trash	Daily
	Vacuum carpets	Daily
	Clean off walk and mats in lobby areas	Daily
	Wet mop hard-surface floors (granite, tile, etc.)	Daily
	Buff hard surfaces	Daily
	Dust horizontal surfaces	Daily
	Clean and polish furniture	Daily
	Clean and polish mirrors, sconces, etc.	Bi-monthly
	Clean light fixtures	Bi-monthly
	Clean HVAC vents	Bi-monthly
	Clean carpets	Quarterly to annually
	Strip and refinish wood floors	Annually
Massage Rooms	Remove trash	Daily
	Vacuum carpeted floors	Daily
	Dust horizontal surfaces	Daily
	Remove all soiled linen	Daily
	Clean and disinfect beds, tables, etc.	After each client
	Clean and polish furniture	Daily
	Wet mop the floors if wood or tile	Daily
	Clean light fixtures	Bi-monthly
	Clean HVAC vents	Bi-monthly
	Clean carpets	Annually
Offices	Remove trash	Daily
	Vacuum carpeted areas	Daily
	Dust horizontal surfaces	Daily
	Clean and polish furniture	Daily
	Wet mop the floors if wood or tile	Daily
	Clean light fixtures	Bi-monthly
	Clean HVAC vents	Bi-monthly
	Clean carpets	Annually

Figure 29-5. Cleaning guidelines for the lobby, massage rooms, and offices

Accounting

Accounting operations are a sub-set of the financial management practices that were reviewed earlier in the book. As was noted, financial management encompasses a club's financial structuring and the types and kinds of reports the facility uses to monitor its overall financial performance. Accounting operations, on the other hand, are the processes, policies, and practices that the club employs to ensure that the money is handled in an appropriate manner, both on the revenue and the expense side. These processes, policies, and practices can normally be grouped into four distinct categories: accounts payable, accounts receivable, payroll functions, and financial reporting. Club operators have several resources available that can help them set up their accounting practices, including GAAP (generally accepted accounting practices) principles in the U.S. and IFRS (international financial reporting standards) in global markets, each of which are an accepted set of accounting principles, standards, and procedures that most (if not all) companies employ to compile their financial statements. In the United States, GAAP is administered by the Financial Standards Board that is headquartered in Norwich, Connecticut.

❑ *Accounts Payable.* Accounts payable refers to the policies and practices that govern how the club/facility pays its vendors and employees for services. Because accounts-payable practices focus on managing and making payments to the club's outside vendors, they are an integral element of controlling expenses. Figure 29-6 lists several of the most relevant accounts-payable practices that clubs can adopt to assist them in managing their finances.

Accounts Payable Practice	Description/Purpose
Expense reports	The expense-report process requires employees to complete an expense report with accompanying receipts for all business-related expenses. The reports should be approved by a supervisor before payment.
Check requests	The check-request process requires department heads to complete a form requesting any check for payment of a service provided by a vendor. This form is usually approved by the manager before a check can be issued.
Purchase orders	A purchase-order system requires that before any items are ordered, the items desired be priced beforehand and put on a purchase order for approval. Once approved, the items can be purchased. The purchase order then serves as a check-and-balance mechanism against the packing slip and invoice from a supplier.
Par-stock inventory system	Every supply the club uses and every item/product sold should have a par-stock that is inventoried regularly. A point-of-sale software system typically does this for retail operations, but clubs need their own system for supplies.
Check and invoice approval and payment	To provide better control, each club should have a process that requires at least two signatures on a check request or invoice before a check is cut. Furthermore, every check should be reviewed against the invoices and signatures by someone other than the accountant or bookkeeper before it is released.

Figure 29-6. Accounts payable practices

CHAPTER TWENTY-NINE
Administrative Department Operations

❑ *Accounts Receivable.* The accounts-receivable accounting operation involves the policies and practices that pertain to the billing and collection of funds from anyone (e.g., members) who uses the club's services. The primary focus of the accounts-receivable accounting function is to ensure that the club receives all monies that are due for the services and benefits provided to anyone by the facility. Figure 29-7 illustrates several of the most relevant accounts receivable practices that clubs utilize to assist them in managing their finances.

Accounts Receivable Practice	Description/Purpose
Monthly member billing	Creating the monthly member statements if the club bills its members directly or if an EFT process is used making sure all EFT drafts are correct.
Daily charging activities	Applying all member charges to their member accounts in the event the club allows members to charge services on their membership account.
Monthly EFT and charge handling	Most clubs use electronic funds transfer to bill and collect member payments. Accounting needs to correctly set-up each member's account for proper billing and collection.
Bank reconciliation	This practice falls into both a payable and a receivable function, because it involves the daily undertaking of reconciling the books to make sure all deposits and debits are accounted for and that the bank account is liquid.
Accounts receivable collection	Accounting has the responsibility of monitoring the club's accounts that are outstanding and making sure all past-due funds are collected. This involves 30-, 60-, and 90-day policies and practices that are focused on prompt collection of all past-due funds.

Figure 29-7. Accounts receivable practices

❑ *Payroll Functions.* Payroll functions refer to the policies and practices governing a club's handling of all compensation and benefits involving both employees and independent contractors. The main focus of payroll activities is to ensure that employees and contractors receive the proper compensation for the services they have rendered. Figure 29-8 details several of the most relevant payroll-related practices that clubs employ to assist them in managing their finances.

Payroll Practice	Description/Purpose
Time sheets/time cards/time clock	Every club should have a system in place to set employee schedules, have the employees check-in, monitor the hours that employees work, provide reports on time worked, overtime hours, etc.
Preparing payroll and contractor checks	Involves preparing the payroll and contractor checks, and using the time-card and time-sheet information.
Monitoring overtime, vacation, and personal time	Most accounting departments are involved in monitoring overtime hours, vacation pay, and personal pay. In addition to monitoring, accounting handles all distributions of compensation related to those factors.
Employee benefits administration	Most accounting departments are responsible for the appropriate enrollment of employees in the club's benefit programs and handling the activities related to those benefits.

Figure 29-8. Payroll practices

❑ *Financial Reporting.* Financial reporting refers to the policies and practices that are involved in monitoring the club's overall financial performance. Financial reporting may also include activities that relate to the preparation of a club's budget and monitoring the facility's actual adherence to the budget (financial-wise). Figure 29-9 presents an overview of several of the most relevant financial-reporting practices that clubs can use to assist them in managing their finances.

Financial Reporting Practice	Description/Purpose
Daily sales sheets	Daily sales sheets allow clubs to monitor the total sales each day. A daily sales sheet encompasses a tally of each sale that occurs that day. The daily sales sheet should reflect each sale, what it was for, the amount of the sale, the category of sale, whether it was cash or charge, etc.
Daily, weekly, and monthly financial reports	Clubs should have specific reports that can help them better understand their finances, including daily sales report, daily payroll report, weekly/monthly profit-and-loss statement, weekly/monthly balance-sheet report, weekly/monthly accounts-payable report, weekly/monthly accounts-receivable report, and monthly fixed-asset report.
Budget and forecast tools	Every club should have an annual budget for each department, as well as quarterly forecast reports for each department that reflect the expected revenue and expense outcomes of operations. Accounting is normally responsible for preparing and printing these reports, in conjunction with management.

Figure 29-9. Financial reporting practices

Reflections

Heart-of-the house operations are a critical element of the overall formula for success in the club business. Since quite often these functions don't directly touch the member, operators may place less emphasis on them, thinking that the front-of-the house operations are all that matters. As this chapter points out, heart-of-the-house operations require as much planning and executional detail as front-of-the-house operations if a club wants to achieve industry-leading levels of profitability.

PART 9
Overview of the International Health/Fitness Club Market

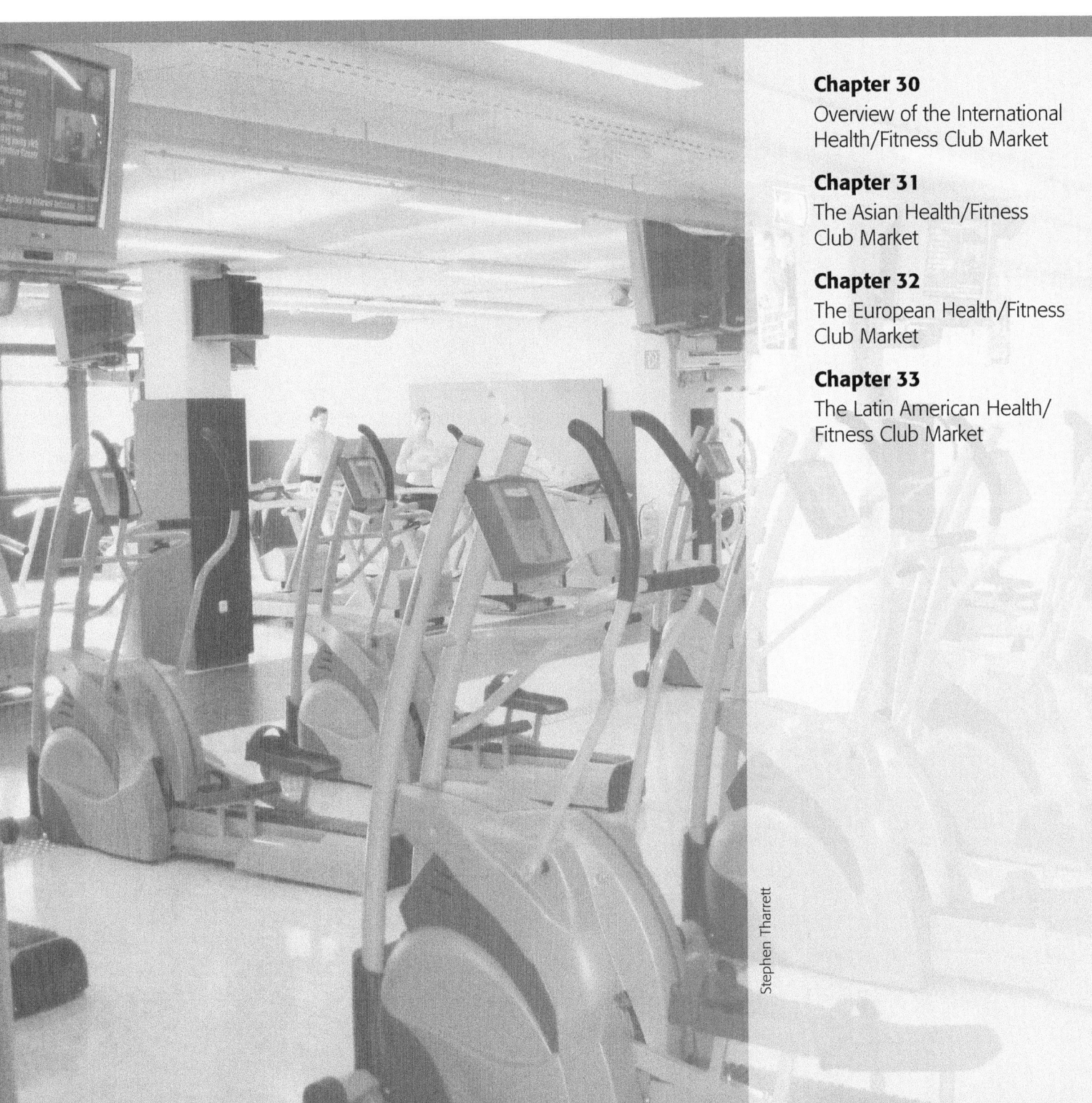

Chapter 30
Overview of the International Health/Fitness Club Market

Chapter 31
The Asian Health/Fitness Club Market

Chapter 32
The European Health/Fitness Club Market

Chapter 33
The Latin American Health/Fitness Club Market

Overview of the International Health/Fitness Club Market

30

"It used to said that when the U.S. sneezed, the world caught a cold. The opposite is equally true today."

—Larry Summers, former Secretary of the Treasury

Chapter Objectives

Understanding the dynamics of the international market can help facilitate a greater understanding of the competencies involved in managing and leading a successful health/fitness club business. As of 2015, the global health/fitness industry was an $81 billion industry, serving nearly 187 million members in over 186,000 different clubs. In 2004, the first year IHRSA reported global industry numbers, 33 percent of all clubs presided in the U.S. where just over a decade later the U.S. club industry represented slightly less than 20 percent of the global market. In 2004, the U.S. club market generated approximately $15 billion in revenues, which represented 38 percent of global revenues, where just over a decade later, the U.S. club industry's revenue haul had declined to 32 percent of total industry revenues. Over the decade spanning from 2004 to 2014, U.S. club revenues grew by 51 percent, while the global market's revenues grew by more than 100 percent. The bottom line, while the U.S. market experienced approximately 50 percent growth in revenues over the past 10 years (equivalent of a 4.23 percent CAGR), the rest of the global industry grew by 129 percent, or the equivalent of 8.66 percent CAGR, more than double the growth experienced in the U.S. market.

Looking at the world market for fitness, it can be said that the top five markets account for approximately 49 percent of the total number of health/fitness facilities (U.S., Brazil, Germany, Mexico, and Argentina) and over 50 percent of the global industry revenue (U.S., United Kingdom, Germany, Japan, and Spain). This chapter presents a basic overview of the international health/fitness club market that includes not only a brief history of the international health/fitness club industry, but also a discussion of the current dynamics of the market. Chapters 31, 32, and 33 delve into the Asian, European, and Latin American markets in greater detail.

> While the U.S. market experienced approximately 50 percent growth in revenues over the past 10 years, the rest of the global industry grew by 129 percent.

Historical Perspective

- *The Early Years.* Similar to the domestic U.S. market, private clubs (particularly athletic-oriented clubs) evolved in the international arena in the 1800s. One of the earliest health/fitness clubs to open in Europe was Turnverein, opened in 1811, which was operated by Frederick Jahn. In 1848, Hippolyte Triat inaugurated Gymnase Triat in Paris, France, which was a club dedicated to men in pursuit of physical culture. In addition to these two landmark clubs, the Lille Athletic Club, Lille, France, was started in 1885 by Edmond Desbonnet; the Vienna Athletic Club, Vienna, Austria, commenced operations in the 1880s; the Athletic and Cycling Club of Saint Petersburg, Russia was opened in the 1880s; the London YMCA, England, opened for business in the 1880s; and Louis Durlacher, also known as Professor Atilla, started his famous gym in Belgium also in the 1880s. These early clubs were predominately oriented toward men and provided a physical-activity environment that was based on gymnastics, sport, and martial arts (e.g., boxing, wrestling, etc.). In addition, these clubs introduced the world to organized group exercise, along with the use of barbells and dumbbells.

The Lille Athletic Club in Lille, France, founded by Edmond Desbonnet in 1885

The earliest United Kingdom clubs were organized around social relationships and athletic endeavors, such as court tennis, cricket, squash, snooker, and lawn tennis. One of the first facilities in this regard was the All-

England Lawn Tennis and Croquet Club, which was founded in 1868 and began operations in 1877, just outside London. The Fitzwilliam Lawn Tennis Club in Dublin, Ireland, which was founded in 1877, lays claim to actually operating as a club before the aforementioned All-England Club. In the late 1880s, the London YMCA began operations. It was one of the first clubs in England to offer exercise classes and a fully equipped gymnasium. These facilities were representative of the earliest form of recreational sports-driven clubs (e.g., multi-purpose sports clubs) that subsequently were developed in the United Kingdom. With a strong social component, these facilities provided men with the opportunity to engage in physical activity. The programming focus in these clubs tended to involve either physical-culture activities (e.g., physique improvement, combat sports, and acrobatics) or court sports (e.g., court tennis, squash, tennis, etc.). As such, these early European efforts led to the development of America's first social/athletic clubs, such as the Olympic Club in San Francisco, California and the New York Athletic Club in New York, New York. Subsequently, the concept of social/athletic was also exported to Asia by expatriates, thus creating this type of club in Hong Kong and other major Asian markets.

❑ *The Modern Era.* The birth of the modern era of the international health/fitness club industry occurred in Europe about twenty years after Vic Tanny introduced America to the modern health club. (Note: The modern era is defined as the period during which health/fitness clubs became part of the culture and opened their doors to the general public to provide a means of improving physical health, generally speaking, after World War II.) One important delineating factor of the modern era with regard to the global market was the formation of companies dedicated to operating multiple clubs to serve the fitness and sports needs of the marketplace. In 1967, Keiser Training became the first German company to emerge as a multiple-site operator. About this same time period, health/fitness clubs also began to take root in Japan and somewhat later in other Asian countries. In fact, several organized health/fitness club operations were established throughout Asia during the 60s and 70s. Clark Hatch International opened its first club in Tokyo in 1965, and over the next few decades, would go on to operate over 100 clubs throughout Asia. Central Sports, which opened in 1969 and The People Company, which started in 1973, have since become two of the largest club companies in the world. However, it wasn't until the late 1970s and early 1980s that health/fitness clubs became a significant business venture in the international arena. It is interesting to note that this scenario coincided closely with the consequential changes that were occurring in the United States marketplace.

In the early 1980s, club groups, such as Archer Leisure, Vardon Leisure, David Lloyd Leisure in the United Kingdom, and DIC in Japan, entered the market, followed a few years later by health/fitness industry groups, such as G&P Gockel in Germany, Health and Racquet in South Africa, and Living Well in the United Kingdom. During the same period, the health/fitness club industry also began to take off in a number of other segments of the international market, including Spain, Sweden, Norway, Italy, and the Netherlands. The 1980s also ushered in the beginning of large-scale operators, which in turn drove the international industry.

The real renaissance of the health/fitness club industry internationally occurred in the 1990s. The international health/fitness club market exploded during this decade, with England, Germany, France, South Africa, and Japan experiencing the most significant growth. Figure 30-1 illustrates the enormous growth that occurred in the various international markets over the past decade.

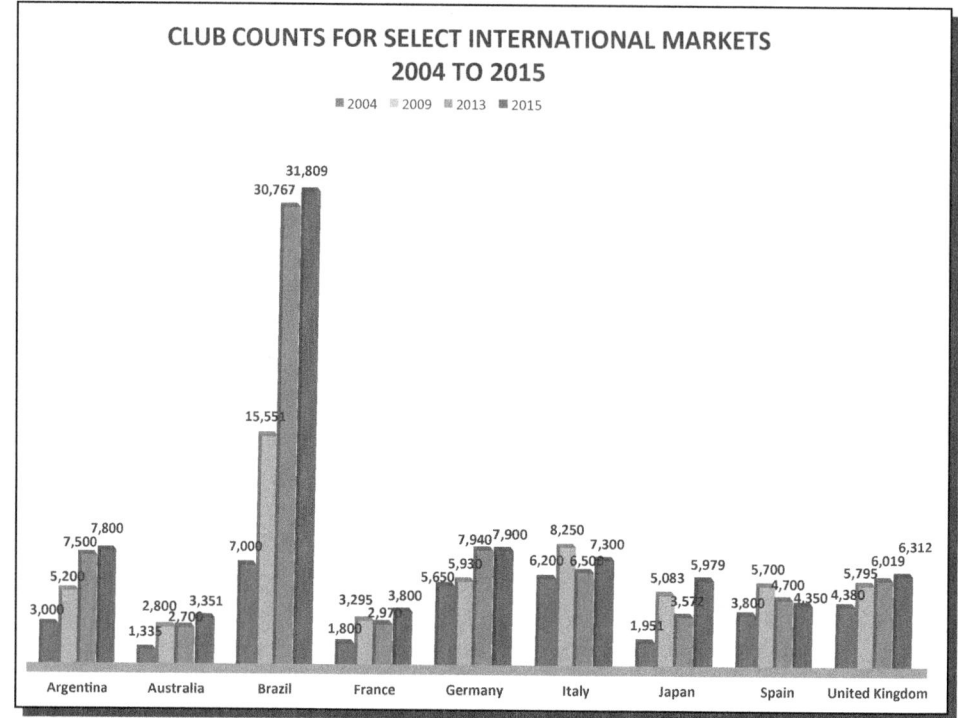

Figure 30-1. Sample global club count (2004–2015)

In the 1990s, the United Kingdom was the center of attention in the international health/fitness club market because of the explosion of quality facility operations in England, such as David Lloyd Leisure, Esporta, Holmes Place, Cannons, Dragons, and LA Fitness. These various operations featured business models that took British consumers by storm and created an incredible buzz in the financial markets. David Lloyd Leisure was sold to Whitbread for approximately $350 million dollars, which, at the time, involved a high multiple of earnings and became the benchmark that the financial markets in England employed to judge the other up-and-coming health/fitness club operations. Besides David Lloyd, companies such as Cannons, Holmes Place, Esporta, and Fitness First, also went public in the late 1990s and were very well received by Britain's financial markets.

During the later half of the 1990s several of these businesses traded at 30 to 40 times earnings, far in excess of the four to eight times earnings multiples that were the norm in the United States. One of the most unique factors about the British market, other than the incredible multiples on earnings, was the fact that they did not experience the price wars and discounting practices that had plagued the United States (in 2017, however, this situation is not the case). During this period, the market in the United

Kingdom focused on establishing quality benchmarks and avoiding the price markdowns and strong sales tactics that the U.S. industry experienced during its early years. In addition, British clubs were able to work closely with England's national health insurance group to create several important synergies for the market.

During this period, British clubs could be grouped into three basic categories, based on price and amenities. Clubs, such as Fitness First and LA Fitness, were what would be termed in the U.S. domestic market as affordable and convenient fitness-only facilities. Focused primarily on fitness-related activities, this group of facilities operated smaller, well-outfitted ventures that were both convenient and affordable to the masses, particularly to single individuals. In contrast, a number of British health/fitness operations, such as Esporta, were structured on a larger multipurpose-club model, one that targeted families, and provided slightly more amenities and services at a higher price. In the United States, such a facility would be called a mid-price level, family-fitness club. The third type of facility focused on the high end of the market. This group featured full-service, multipurpose clubs that offered both great programming and exceptional service. These high-end operations emphasized an appropriate blend of fitness, recreation, and social interaction (e.g., David Lloyd Leisure, Cannons, Holmes Place).

During the 1990s, the health/fitness club industry also began to thrive in other European countries, such as Germany, Italy, Belgium, France, Sweden, and South Africa. For example, a French company, Compagnie Gymnase, grew to 116 clubs by the mid- to late-1990s. A significant portion of Compagnie Gymnase's clubs were subsequently sold to Club Med, which, in turn, branded them as Club Med Gyms. A chain in South Africa, Health and Racquet, reached over 60 clubs by the mid-to-late 1990s. Eventually, this chain expanded into both Europe and Australia (under the brand name Healthlands). However, because of legal and financial problems, it had to divest of its holdings. At the present time, the former Health and Racquet clubs in South Africa and Europe are operated by Virgin Active, which had created its own unique brand of health/fitness clubs during this same period.

> During the 1990s, the health/fitness club industry began to thrive in European countries such as Germany, Italy, Belgium, France, Sweden, and South Africa.

In markets such as Germany, Italy, Spain, and Sweden, several smaller multiple-club companies opened their doors and brought a number of innovative (for their respective areas) programming emphases to their respective markets. For example, Keiser training opened small clubs in Germany that focused entirely on delivering a resistance-training environment. 24 Hour Fitness made its presence in the international market by purchasing several facilities in the Scandinavian region (e.g., Denmark, Norway, and Sweden). At one point, 24 Hour Fitness had approximately 70 clubs in the Scandinavian region. Subsequently, these clubs were sold to Nordic Capital and became a part of the SATS club group, a publicly held company of over 100 clubs.

During the late 1990s, Fitness First, based in London, seized a dominant position in the Australian market, by purchasing the clubs that were formerly operated by Health and Racquet of South Africa (e.g., Heathlands). Starting with approximately 15 clubs, Fitness First grew its Australian club's holdings to over 70 strong. Before Fitness First entered the Australian market, most of the health/fitness clubs down under were either small independent operators with less than 10 clubs or community swimming centers that were operated by the local government bodies. In an attempt to emulate Fitness First's success in Australia, a second major player in the industry, Fernwood, a women's-only chain, emerged in Australia. During the early part of the 21st century, a third major player emerged in the Australian market: Zest.

Since the 1990s, Japan has strengthened its dominant position as a commanding factor in the international health/fitness club industry. At the present time, three companies—DIC, Central Sports, and Konami (formerly, the clubs operated by the People Company)—operate close to 25 percent of the health/fitness facilities in the Japanese marketplace and generate close to 40 percent of the total revenue produced by clubs in the market. These Japanese operations feature facilities that provide exceptional fitness, group-exercise, and swimming programming. Swimming is an extremely popular activity in Japanese clubs, as is group exercise.

During the 1990s, the Asian market (exclusive of Japan) was primarily driven by small fitness centers that were located in hotels and residential developments. One of the first individuals to recognize the opportunities that existed in Asia was Clark Hatch, who has since opened over 100 clubs in markets such as Singapore, Hong Kong, Malaysia, Thailand, and the Philippines, most of which, if not all, are associated with hotel properties. During the later half of the 1990s, some U.S. entrepreneurs also decided to enter the larger Asian markets. For example, California Fitness, founded by Ray Wilson, became one of the first health/fitness club chains to enter Hong Kong. In fact, its first facility reached over 12,000 members in its first year of operation. Another organization that established a presence in Asia was 24 Hour Fitness, which created a subsidiary that operated those aforementioned California Fitness clubs. In addition to 24 Hour Fitness, Fitness First (based in London) and Gold's Gym and Bally's (from the U.S.) made significant inroads into the emerging Asian market. Currently, the prevailing approach to the Asian market seems to be franchising, a philosophy espoused by Fitness First, Anytime Fitness, and Gold's Gym, all of which have made strategic moves into the Asian markets. In India, the largest operator is a locally based company.

Similar to Europe and Asia, Latin America also witnessed the emergence of the health/fitness club market in the 1980s, with the opening of Companhia Athletica and Runner/SA—both in Brazil. These two firms, while still operating in Brazil, are no longer the largest operators. Since 2001, IHRSA has been involved as a cosponsor of Fitness Brazil, one of the largest global conferences for health/fitness club owners and operators. In 2004, three years after Fitness Brazil launched, Mercado Fitness, a Latin American fitness convention based in Buenos Aires, Argentina, was introduced. These two events, both in existence for more than 10 years are a reflection of the industry's growth over the past decade.

> What was once considered primarily a U.S. industry has developed into an international industry, one in which North America—particularly the United States—is just another player in a global marketplace.

By 2015, the international markets represent approximately 64 percent of the total membership base and approximately 68 percent of the gross revenues in the global health/fitness club industry. In other words, what was once considered primarily a U.S. industry, has developed into an international industry, one in which North America—particularly the United States—is just another player in a global marketplace. Figure 30-2 presents a quantitative overview of the international industry from a revenue perspective, showing the changes in revenue from 2004 to 2015.

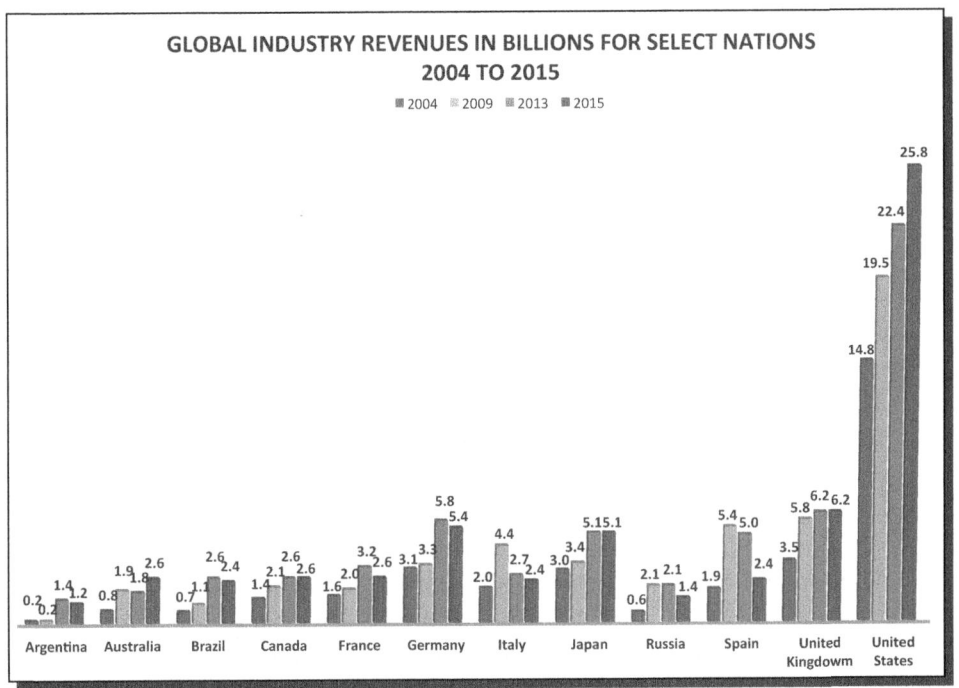

Figure 30-2. Global industry revenues by select nation

❏ *The Future.* In 2006, IHRSA reported that, with regard to the global marketplace, one of the goals of the health/fitness industry was to reach 120 million club members by the year 2010, with 50 million in the United States and 70 million in the various international markets. As of 2015, health/fitness clubs worldwide had an estimated 186 million members, with approximately 55 million in the United States and 131 million internationally. What once seemed a lofty goal for the global health/fitness club industry had been achieved, and, in the case of the international market (i.e., non-U.S.), has been exceeded. As of year-end 2015, the global industry had reached nearly 187 million members.

The future of the international health/fitness club industry appears to be as promising as its past. In that regard, the following trends should have a substantial impact on the growth of the international marketplace over the next decade:

• *Club Consolidation and Strategic Acquisitions.* The health/fitness club industry in the United Kingdom and mainland Europe has stagnated over the past several years, with the total number of clubs in the UK, Italy,

Germany, Sweden, etc. remaining relatively flat and revenues declining since 2013. This situation is due in part to the global economic downturn that started in 2008 and extended well into 2012, the emergence of budget clubs that generate less revenues, as well as the consolidation that has occurred in many markets (e.g., England, Germany, Netherlands, etc.). The rapid expansion in the European industry that occurred in an earlier part of this century caused many clubs to reach a point where further growth in their home markets was a challenge, and expansion outside their local markets would lead to in further challenges to the profitability of the overall organization. As a result, several European based companies, such as Fitness First, retrenched in their core markets (UK and Germany) and sold off assets in less-profitable markets (e.g., Spain, France, Italy), while others actively pursued consolidation in strategic markets. Virgin Active in the UK acquired both Holmes Place and Esporta in the UK, resulting in it more than doubling its base of clubs. Health City, based in the Netherlands, acquired over 100 Fitness First clubs in several European markets (France, Italy, and Spain). Fitness First, once the largest player in Europe, has sold off all its European assets and recently sold its remaining UK assets to another firm. As of 2015, budget operator Basic-Fit, who only a decade earlier had no clubs, is now the largest player in Europe, followed by budget operator McFit in Germany, who also didn't exist in 2004.

- *Development of New Business Models.* In the last five years, a new business model has taken Europe by storm, and currently seems to be taking hold in other nations across the globe. The key element of this new business model is the development of "budget" clubs. Budget clubs are differentiated from other club business models by the following attributes: low price that is typically half of the average market price, pure gym models (no pools, no group-exercise studios, no saunas, etc.), limited-to-no staffing, limited-to-no amenities (no towels, pay for showers, etc.), 24-hour access most, if not all, days of the week, and a heavy reliance on technology for servicing the customer (e.g., use of technology for everything from signing up people for membership to providing exercise prescriptions). Three of the leading players in this emerging business segment are McFit, based in Germany, Basic-Fit operated by Health City with its main offices in the Netherlands, and the Gym Group, based in the United Kingdom. McFit currently operates close to 240 clubs in Europe with the majority located in Germany. The Gym Group, which opened its first club in 2008, has grown to 74 clubs as of 2016. Basic-Fit, which received a large investment in late 2013, now has more than 400 facilities in four European countries. The budget club model represents the fastest growing segment of the industry in Europe and the U.S., and is now emerging in other markets such as Asia and Latin America. Besides budget clubs, the boutique fitness studio market is beginning to take hold in Europe as it has in the U.S.

- *Emerging Franchise Models.* Franchising has become one of the newest trends in the global fitness market. Curves started the international love affair with franchise models, and over the past few years, several other firms have leaped on the opportunity. Anytime Fitness, a fitness-only club model based out of the U.S. with approximately 3,000 franchises globally, has made significant inroads into Asia, Latin America, and Europe. Viva Fit, a women's-only group, based out of Portugal, currently operates over 40 franchises in Portugal and Spain, but has now established franchises in Asia and the Middle East. Mrs. Sporty, a German-based women's-only chain, has over 400 franchise locations in Europe.

- *An Emerging Global Middle Class: Market Penetration Opportunities.* At the present time, the international market, as a whole, only penetrates approximately three percent of the eligible world population. While the level of penetration in Western Europe is higher, ranging from around 4 percent to approximately 19 percent, the overall European average (approximately 7.5 percent and 8 percent in the EU) is still well below the 18 percent level that exists in the United States. In Eastern Europe and Russia, the levels of market penetration range from less than 1 percent to a high of 3 percent. In the Asian and South Pacific markets, penetration rates range from less than 1 percent to over 12 percent, with large markets, such as China, India, and Indonesia, reaching between 1 percent and 3 percent of the eligible market. These statistics reflect the fact that a huge opportunity exists to provide a product that can tap into these relatively underserved and emerging middle-class markets. One of the challenges will be creating a workable model that fits within the cultural and financial conditions attendant to each specific country. For example, in the United States, the average annual club dues—as a percentage of per capita income—are approximately 2.2 percent. In contrast, in Europe, the average annual dues as a percent of per capita income are similar at just over 2 percent. In Eastern Europe and Asia, dues represent an even larger percentage of the average citizen's household income.

  In order to make fitness more accessible in the global marketplace, two factors have to happen. First, many of these markets have to see a continued growth of a middle class, with expendable income growing. At the present time, the middle class is defined by the World Bank as earning between $10 and $20 a day (under $5,500 annually), while Goldman Sachs, in a report released around 2011, believes it should be defined as earning between $6,000 and $30,000 a year (it should be noted that in developed nations, middle class encompasses between $17,000 and $70,000 annually and in the U.S., between $20,000 and $100,000 a year). According to various sources the global middle class will add two billion people over the next 20 years. The question becomes, what incomes must be present for the emerging middle class to afford a club membership? Second, clubs will need to create new business models that can attract the emerging middle class and then will need to be prepared to change that offering as the per-capita income of people grows. The new budget clubs sprouting up in Europe and around the globe appear to represent a viable approach to penetrating this emerging global middle class. What is known is that since the definition of middle class varies by market, the models that operators develop must also diverge in order to appeal to those respective markets.

- *Tackling a Growing Health Problem.* With regard to obesity, the global marketplace is confronted with similar challenges. In the last decade, the level of obesity has increased in every country, in both genders, and

> The international market, as a whole, only penetrates approximately three percent of the eligible world population.

across all age groups, races, and types of backgrounds, to a point where it is currently a worldwide epidemic. In fact, obesity represents one of the two most significant global opportunities for the health/fitness club industry to have a meaningful impact on the health of the planet. Leveraging this opportunity will require close cooperation between club operators and the various global political institutions.

- *Growing Older.* Statistics indicate that the population of the world is aging. In fact, the over-50 population is projected to be the largest segment of the world's population over the next decade, with countries such as the U.S., Japan, Italy, Germany, and England having a significant portion of their population over the age of 50. It is predicted that by the year 2050 there will be approximately two billion global citizens age 60 and older. The efforts that international clubs undertake to target this market will, in large part, determine their financial success in the coming decade.

- *Growing Up.* The under-30 population (i.e., the Millennial Generation) may represent the biggest challenge for the health/fitness club industry. Possibly, the most globally influenced group of individuals in the history of mankind because of the world to which they have been subjected (e.g., mass media, Internet, smart phones, social media, etc.), this relatively young population has been raised on fast foods, video games, and sedentary living, as well as the addictive and celebrity fantasy realm of social media and ever-evolving technology. Millennials are responsible for the rapid growth of boutique fitness studios, a business model that may emerge as the preferred business model for the next few decades.

- *Moving Toward the Establishment of "Clans."* The global marketplace is fusing. Borders are being eliminated by the Internet and social media. News and information are becoming readily available 24/7, due to modern technology. This intent-driven fusion of global cultures has also seen an emergence of clans, niches, and cult brands. People, while becoming connected to a larger population of global citizens, are also seeking out relatively small groups that reflect their specific interests and desires. In the future, the global club industry's growth will depend on the ability of operators to morph from "karaoke" operators to businesses that are able to fulfill the needs of specific audiences (e.g., clans, micro-audiences, niches, etc.) and create what one modern business guru defines as "cult" brands.

Reflections

The health/fitness industry is no longer the U.S. market's to lead. The global health/fitness industry, led by operators in established markets such as the UK, Germany, and Japan, along with operators in emerging markets such as Brazil, Argentina, India, and China, have taken the helm so to speak in expanding the size and scope of the health/fitness industry. While the U.S. market is still perceived by many in the global marketplace as the industry leader, that role is slowly changing, and within the next decade industry leadership may just emerge from outside the U.S.

(Note: Additional information on the global health/fitness club marketplace is readily available from IHRSA.)

The Asian Health/Fitness Club Market

31

*"It says something about the new global economy
that USA Today now reports every morning
on the day's events in Asia."*

—Lawrence H. Summers, U.S. economist

Chapter Objectives

This chapter provides an overview of the Asian health/fitness club market and the implications this information holds for the health/fitness industry in Asia and throughout the world. Following the introduction, a closer look at the dynamics of the Asian health/fitness club industry is taken, including some of the differences that exist between Asia and other global club markets. The chapter features ideas, insights, and information on the opportunities and challenges that may arise for Asian health/fitness club operators over the next decade.

Overview of the Asian Market

The Asian continent is comprised of 48 separate countries that have an estimated combined population of 4.42 billion people, equivalent to 61 percent of the world's population. The 48 nations that make up the continent of Asia include countries, such as China, India, Japan, South Korea, Georgia, Cambodia, Azerbaijan, Afghanistan, Singapore, and Thailand, to name a few. In fact, three of these Asian nations—China, India, and Indonesia—are among the six largest in the world and have a combined population that approaches 3 billion people. The enormity of Asia may be hard to visualize until it is compared to the total population of Europe, which is approximately 742 million, North America, which is just over 349 million, and Latin America, which has approximately 430 million people. The Asian market is nearly four times as large as the next largest market, Europe, and over eight times larger than the North American market.

According to the IHRSA *2016 Global Report*, there are an estimated 31,011 clubs in the 14 Asian-Pacific countries surveyed in the study. These 31,011 clubs serve an estimated population of 17,356,000 members or approximately three tenths of a percent of the entire Asian population. Of course, the IHRSA data only applies to the 14 countries surveyed, rather than the 48 countries that make up Asia. Even when the population of these 14 countries is taken into consideration, the health/fitness club industry in Asia has still penetrated less than one percent of the entire Asian population. In contrast, Europe has over

> The Asian market is nearly four times as large as the next largest market, Europe, and over eight times larger than the North American market.

51,000 clubs that serve approximately 7 percent of the population, and the United States has just over 36,000 clubs that service approximately 19 percent of the population. This cursory review suggests that Asia is an extremely fertile territory for the development of the health/fitness club industry. The most significant challenges for the health/fitness club industry in Asia are knocking down government-built barriers to a free-market economy and identifying ways to provide a health/fitness club experience to relatively large populations of people with limited economic resources.

Overview of the Health/Fitness Club Industry in Asia

❏ *Clubs, Members, and Penetration.* As indicated in the previous section, the Asian health/fitness club market is comprised of approximately 31,000 clubs, clubs that serve approximately 17,400,000 members and generate total annual gross revenue of approximately $14.5 billion (U.S.). Figures 31-1 and 31-2 illustrate the number of clubs and revenue contributions of the various nations in the published report, the IHRSA *2016 Global Report*, which included the Asian market. The data clearly shows that the Asian market is in its infancy, given that the total number of clubs and the total estimated revenues generated by facilities on this continent are significantly below those of Europe, Latin America, and North America. As a reflection of its relative state of infancy, the entire Asian market is smaller than that of Brazil (e.g., based on club count).

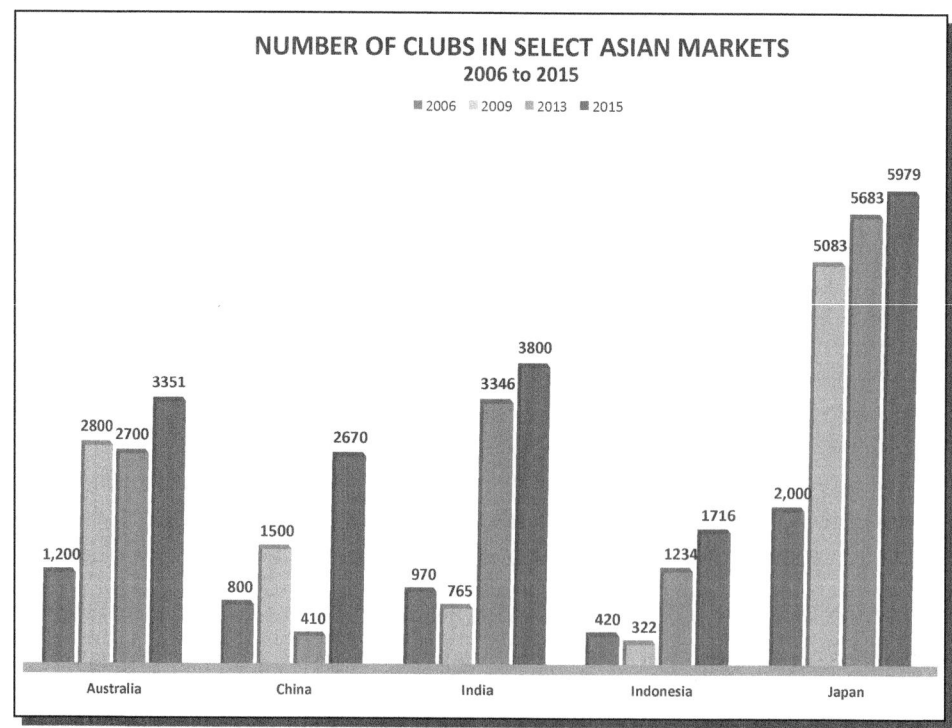

Figure 31-1. Number of clubs in various Asian markets (2006 to 2015)

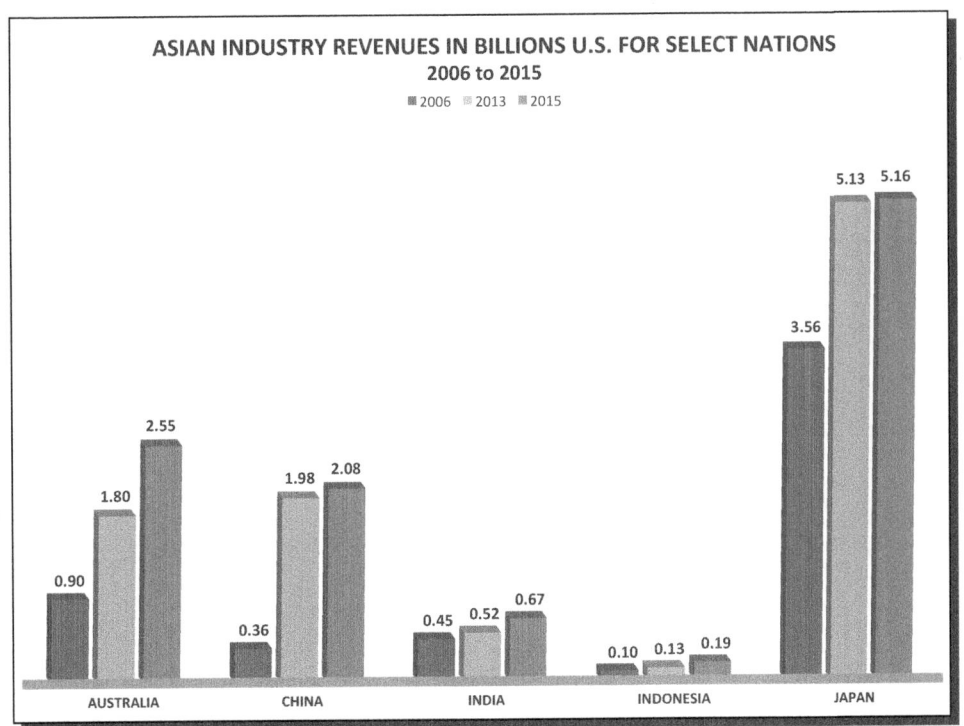

Figure 31-2. Asian industry revenues (2006 to 2015)

While the Asian market, as a whole, may be considered in its infancy, nations, such as Japan and South Korea, represent an entirely different dynamic. These two nations more closely align with the health/fitness club markets in Europe and North America. As of 2015, South Korea and Japan account for 41 percent of the clubs in the Asian market, with Korea accounting for 22 percent and Japan accounting for nearly 19 percent of all of the clubs in Asia. When revenue contributions are considered, Japan alone contributes 37 percent of the total revenue generated by clubs in Asia, with Australia now the second largest market by revenues, accounting for 18 percent of the markets reported revenues. Over the past few years, Australia has been the most actively growing market in Asia from a revenue perspective.

A final, somewhat telling statistic about both the maturity of the health/fitness club industry in Asia and its potential for future growth is the data on market-penetration. As a whole, the Asian health/fitness club industry has penetrated less than 1 percent of the eligible population, which, when compared to Europe at 7 percent and North America at approximately 17 percent, indicates a significant upside (refer to Figure 31-3 for the estimated penetration percentages for the various nations in Asia as of 2013). The most successful market, in terms of market penetration, is South Korea, with an estimated 7.9 percent penetration, followed by Japan, with a 3.1 percent penetration of the market. Interestingly enough, Japan, which operates approximately 19 percent of the clubs in Asia and generates 37 percent of the market's total revenue, has only been able to reach 3.1 percent of its population.

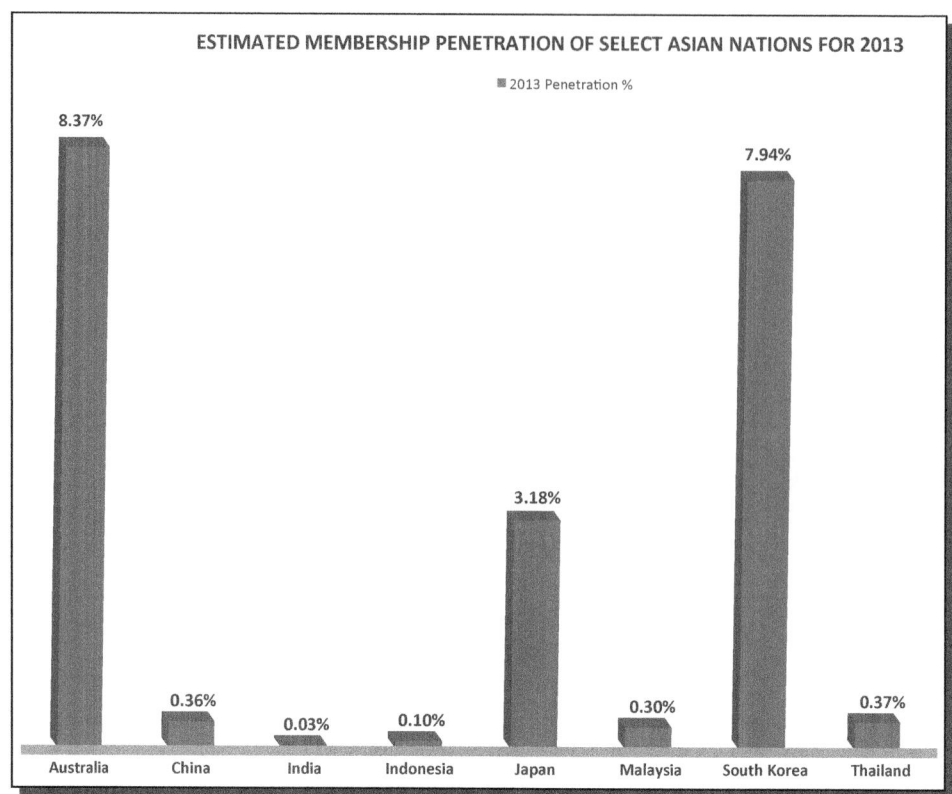

Figure 31-3. The Asian health/fitness club market—membership penetration rates by nation

In Asia, the average monthly dues for a health/fitness club ranges from a low of $24 a month in India to $79 a month in Vietnam (*IHRSA 2008 Asia Pacific Market Report*). Comparatively speaking, the average monthly dues in the majority of Asian markets are considerably lower than the averages for both Europe and the U.S. For example, the lowest average monthly dues in Asia are $24 in India, which closely aligns with the lowest average dues in Europe (Romania at 20 Euros). At the other end of the pricing spectrum, Vietnam has the highest average monthly dues seen in Asia at $79, which is nearly identical to Switzerland, which has the highest monthly-dues average in Europe at $81.

Figure 31-4 provides an overview of the average dues pricing for the 12 nations included in the *2008 IHRSA Asia Pacific Market Report*. While the monthly dues prices for clubs across the various Asian nations approximates those of Europe and North America, the actual cost of membership as a percentage of annual per-capita income is significantly higher in Asia than either Europe or North America. The percentage of per-capita income allocated to annual health/fitness club dues ranges from a low of approximately 2.2 percent in Japan to just slightly over 36 percent in Vietnam. These percentages are considerably higher than the average dues that exist in both Europe and North America. For example, in Europe, average annual dues run around 2 percent of per-capita income, while in the U.S. the average is also in the neighborhood of 2 percent of per-capita income.

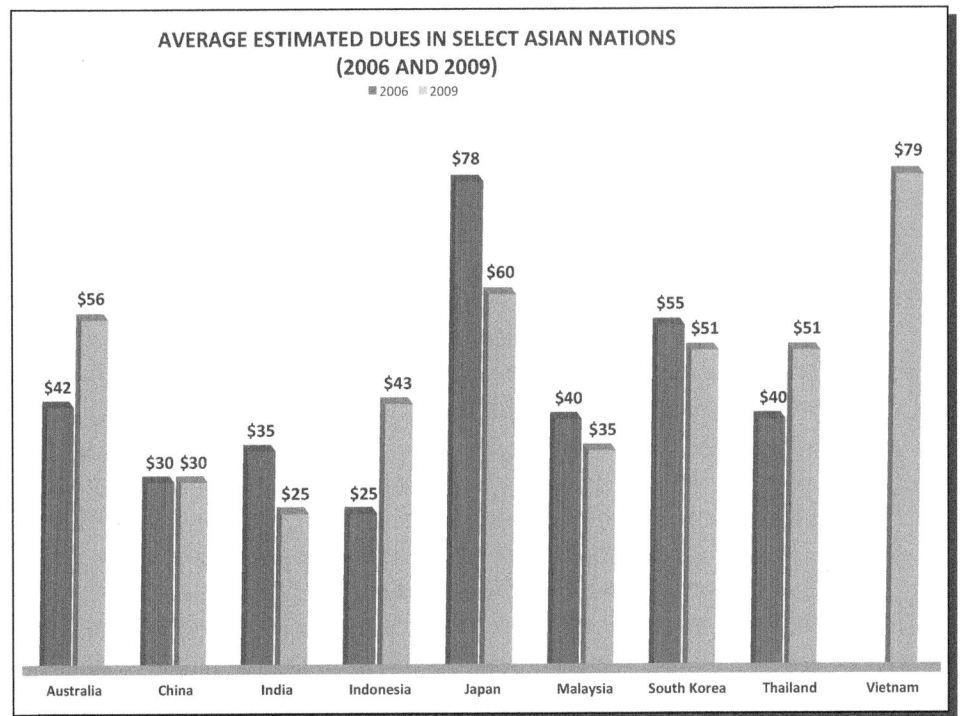

Figure 31-4. Average estimated monthly dues in various Asian nations (2006 and 2009)

The reasons for these unique and wide-ranging variances in market penetration, membership pricing, and overall industry size for the various Asian nations can be traced back to several possible factors, including:

- *Disposable income of the populace.* Per capita earnings across Asia tend to be significantly lower than in either Europe or North America. Hong Kong, Japan, Singapore, South Korea, and Taiwan are the only nations where the per-capita income exceeds $20,000 (U.S.) annually (excluding Asia nations that are located in the Middle East). Only Japan, Singapore and Taiwan have average per-capita income levels at or above $28,000 (U.S.) annually. In contrast, Europe and North America have average per-capita incomes of $30,000 U.S. and over. What may be even more telling is that China and India, the two most populous nations in the world, and two of the globe's fastest emerging economies (China is now the second largest economy, after the U.S.), have average per-capita incomes of under $6,800 (U.S.) and $1,499 (U.S.), respectively (World Bank data from 2013), on an annual basis. When the fact is considered that the middle class has been defined in some quarters as $10 to $20 a day, and by others as between $6,000 and $30,000 annually, the per capita incomes for China and India indicate that the average citizen is really not in a position to afford a fitness club, even a budget club. When the per-capita incomes are so low, it is easy to understand why the Asian operators have had less success penetrating the market than operators in Europe and the Americas. In those nations where the per-capita income approaches European and North American levels (e.g., Hong Kong, Japan, South Korea, Singapore, and Taiwan), club operators have experienced more success.

- *Cultural factors.* Cultural traditions definitely impact the ability to rapidly grow the Asian market. For example, in China, Hong Kong, and Taiwan, many older adults still practice martial arts in the parks and use this as their basic form of physical activity. As such, this segment of the older population does not perceive the same need for joining a health/fitness club as older adults in Europe and North America do. In many Asian cultures, physical work and activity are a natural part of their day, and, in many cases, these people expend more calories during the course of the day than do many active health/fitness club users in either Europe or North America. The health/fitness club market in many of the Asian nations (e.g., with the exception of Japan and South Korea) is primarily the fitness environment of choice for the young and the affluent populace.

- *Industry longevity.* The Asian market is relatively new when compared to the markets in either Europe or North America, although the Japanese health/fitness club market has been in existence since the mid-1960s. In fact, the leading Japanese companies, such as Central Sports and Konami, opened for business in the late 1960s and early 1970s, which places them in the same approximate timeline category as the most mature operators in Europe and North America. Clark Hatch, a company that manages over 100 facilities throughout Asia, most of which are located in hotels, entered the Asian market in 1965 nearly 20 years later than Vic Tanny introduced the modern health club to the U.S. As a consequence, the health/fitness club industries in Japan and Taiwan had a significant edge over other Asia nations when it came to establishing a foothold for their businesses.

  On the other end of the spectrum, the health/fitness club industry is relatively new to countries such as China, India, and Malaysia. In these countries, the industry has been around for less than 20 years and, in many cases, less than 10 (e.g., it should be noted that in many Asian nations, member-owned athletic clubs that serve expatriate populations and the very affluent have been in existence for decades). From a historical viewpoint, compared to both the European and the U.S. club industries, the early development years for the Asian health/fitness club industry have been relatively slow. Once a strong foothold has been established in a given country, however, the industry has taken off.

- *Domestic operators.* One of the factors that has driven the growth and success of the health/fitness club industries in North America and Europe has been the passion and determination of domestic entrepreneurs. When the industry is grown organically (i.e., local business entrepreneurs take the lead in developing the club business), the industry is far more likely to achieve faster growth. In China, India, and Japan, local entrepreneurs launched the health/fitness club industry (e.g., Central Sports, Konami and Renaissance in Japan). As a result of these pioneering local operators, their businesses and the industry in their respective countries have been able to grow in a manner that is similar to health/fitness clubs in Europe and North America. Besides the aforementioned examples, most of the Asian market has either been developed by either expatriate companies (i.e., companies whose headquarters are based outside of Asia) or been grown by local entrepreneurs using expatriate franchises (i.e., local business operators who purchase an international franchise). An examination of the various markets in Asia shows that many of the leading companies in that area of the world are expatriate-branded companies (e.g., Anytime Fitness, World Gym, Fitness First, and Gold's Gym).

While each of the various business models provide an excellent brand for local owners to build on, the consumers in those markets still perceive these brands as foreign brands, and, in many instances, do not trust them. The perception of being foreign can be a particularly difficult hurdle to overcome in the international market, especially in Asia. All factors considered, as more local businessmen and women begin taking the lead in developing their own organic brands, at that point, the industry in the many undersized markets throughout Asia will begin to prosper.

Membership Characteristics

Data pertaining to the general membership characteristics of the Asian market are not as readily available as they are for North America and Europe. While the age, gender, and general-usage demographics of club members in Europe and the U.S. have been published by IHRSA in its various reports (e.g., the *2013 IHRSA European Market Report and the IHRSA 2015 Profiles of Success*), no such data concerning Asia has been released. Based on anecdotal evidence gleaned from personal observations by the author made during visits to Asia and information obtained from conversations with a few of the leading health/fitness club operators in the respective Asian markets, certain membership features of these markets can be formulated. In that regard, a list of key observations about the membership characteristics of the Asian market includes the following:

- In Japan, the gender profile of membership leans toward women. While an exact percentage is not available, it is estimated that the gender blend of the Japanese market closely parallels that of several European nations and the United States, with women comprising in the neighborhood of 50 percent to 55 percent (and possibly higher) of the market. From a usage perspective, group fitness and swimming are among the most popular activities in the clubs. Japanese club consumers are more accepting of technology as part of the club experience than their counterparts in the U.S.

- In China, the membership base swings heavily toward a younger age demographic, similar to several European countries, where the 18 to 34 age group (e.g., Millennials) is the largest segment. Prior to 1995, the Chinese market was essentially made up of a few hotel-based clubs and expatriate private clubs. Only in the last decade does the industry really take off, in large part due to the introduction of foreign franchise models. As a result, health/fitness club membership in China, which formerly were the domain of the affluent, have only recently become attractive to the rapidly emerging young middle class. Group-exercise classes are extremely popular, and similar to both North America and Europe, women are the predominant participants in these programs.

> Many of the leading companies in the Asian market are expatriate-branded companies (e.g., Anytime Fitness, World Gym, Fitness First, and Gold's Gym).

The Leading Players in the Asian Health/Fitness Club Market

When the Asian market is viewed on a nation-by-nation basis, it is evident that in each of these national markets, a small number of health/fitness club companies hold a considerable share of the overall club market. For the nations profiled in the *IHRSA 2008 Asia Pacific Market Report*, the top five club companies in those nations control anywhere from 1 percent of the market to 33 percent of the market, with nine of those nations having over 10 percent of their market controlled by the top five companies, and four of those nations (Australia, Japan, Singapore, and Taiwan) having over 20 percent of the market controlled by the top five companies. In fact, the top players in Singapore and Taiwan control more than 30 percent of the market.

In contrast, among the nations in the European Union, in only five nations, do the top five companies hold greater than 10 percent market share. In the U.S., the top five players hold less than 4 percent of the total market. What these numbers clearly indicate is that in the various Asia nations, more so than in either the European nations or the U.S., the market has been, and possibly will continue to be, influenced and controlled by a small segment of relatively large and highly successful operators.

The Asian continent is quite different than either the European continent or the North American continent when it comes to the total market share being controlled by the major club companies. In Asia, approximately 7.4 percent of the club market is held by seven companies while the remaining 92.6 percent is held by smaller national companies and independent operators. Figure 31-5 shows the size of four of the largest homegrown club companies in Asia. In comparison, for data from the same time period, the top seven club companies

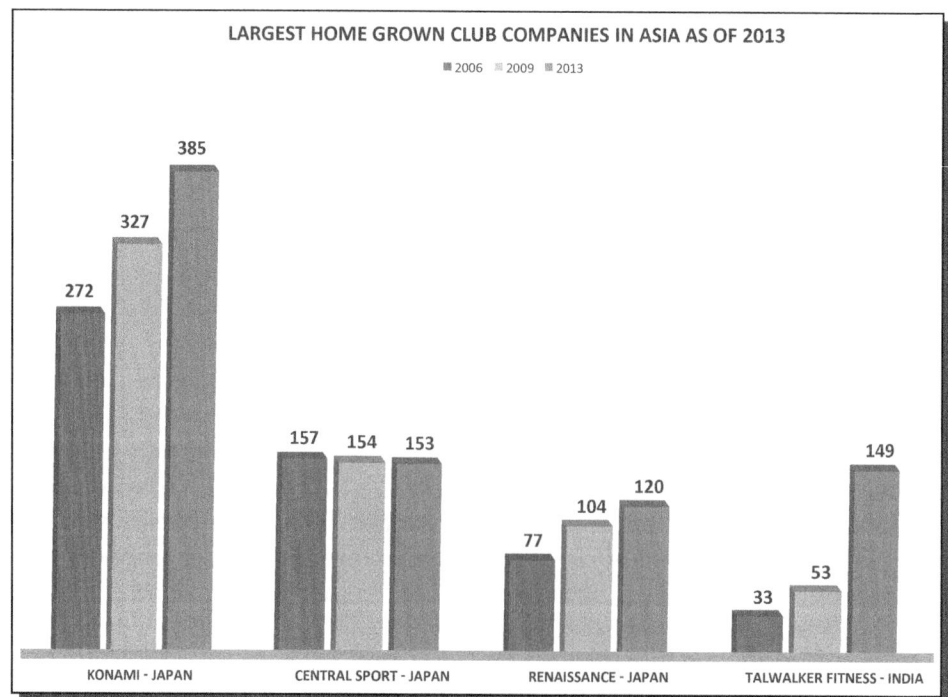

Figure 31-5. Largest homegrown companies in Asia (2013)

in Europe controlled approximately 2 percent of the market, while in the United States the top seven club companies controlled approximately 4 percent of the market. This data suggests that a small number of highly successful club companies can play a significant leadership role in shaping the trends and practices in both a single nation and across the entire Asian market.

The largest player in Asia, both with regard to the number of clubs it operates and the revenue it generates, is Konami, with 385 clubs and 2013 revenues of approximately $788 million (U.S.). The second largest player in Asia is Central Sports, with 153 clubs and 2013 revenues of approximately $484 million (U.S.). In comparison, the largest player in Europe with revenues of approximately $1 billion (U.S.) is Virgin Active. In the U.S., the three largest players are LA Fitness with estimated revenues exceeding $1.5 billion (U.S.), 24 Hour Fitness, with reported revenues of approximately $1.3 billion (U.S.), and Lifetime Fitness with revenues of approximately $1.3 billion (U.S.). What this data indicates is that the top two players in the Asian market, while not as large as the top players in Europe and the U.S., are still highly successful.

The Asian market has not encountered the same level of merger and acquisition activity as its European counterparts or the large influx of private equity that club operators in both Europe and North America have experienced. The Asian environment for mergers or acquisitions does not seem as opportunistic as it is in Europe and North America. Some of the smaller nationally based operators (i.e., local ownership, not foreign) have utilized equity infusion from Asian-based firms and investors to help foster their organic growth. As of yet, private-equity firms have not been involved in the Asian market to the degree that they have been in the European and North American markets. While the private-equity side of the Asian market is significantly less active than the markets in Europe and North America, the presence of publicly listed Asian operators is quite similar. The three largest Japanese companies—Konami, Central Sports, and Renaissance—are all publicly listed. In the U.S., Town Sports International and Planet Fitness are the only publicly listed companies, while in Europe, SATS and Pure Gym are publicly listed.

Opportunities and Challenges for the Asian Market

❑ *Opportunities*
- *Market penetration.* As an industry in its infancy, with the exception of the Japanese, South Korean, and Taiwanese markets, the Asian club industry has an incredible future ahead of it. As the statistics show, with less than 1 percent of the Asian market served by health/fitness clubs, the opportunity for new business development is immense. In fact, in both China and India, whose combined population approaches 2.6 billion, the opportunities are enormous. These two nations are among two of the four largest expanding markets in the global economy (e.g., part of the BRICS, along with Brazil, Russia, and South Africa). Imagine the opportunities for club operators if market penetration in these countries were even to approach 3 to 5 percent; then take these penetration percentages and expand them across the entire Asian continent.

> • *Attracting investment capital.* As the economies in Asia continue to develop and with the rapid expansion of the emerging middle class, its citizens will likely realize greater economic freedom, including more discretionary income. As the economic landscape improves, investors will want to capitalize on the opportunity to bring the health/fitness club experience to an audience that hereto has never had the ability or the inherent desire to join a health/fitness club.

❏ *Challenges*
> • *Economic clout.* The most significant hurdle for the Asian market involves the economic conditions and earning power of its citizens. In many Asian nations, there is a very small population of affluent citizens and a very large group of poor citizens as measured by the Gini index, a measurement of income inequality. Until a larger segment of the Asian population achieves the Western definition of middle-class status, the health/fitness club industry in that area of the world will have a difficult time achieving rapid growth. In nations, such as China and India, a rapidly emerging middle class exists, which, in part, is driving the current growth in those markets.
> • *Cultural barriers.* In many Asian nations, membership in a health/fitness club is not part of the cultural tradition. Those citizens who parallel the baby boomer generation in the U.S. do not see the same value in club usage as the baby boomers in the U.S. and Europe. In addition, cultural traditions around family, gender, and physical-activity practices are all potential hurdles that the industry will need to overcome if it is to achieve the same popularity that it has experienced in Europe and the U.S.
> • *Organic growth.* As occurred in Europe and the U.S., when local business leaders take the lead in developing the industry, the industry prospers far more significantly than it does when foreign companies take the lead. In that regard, the primary challenge for the Asian health/fitness club market is to follow the lead of companies such as Central Sports, Konami, and Renaissance in Japan. These companies were neither developed nor operated by foreign companies. As a result, they have been able to garner greater brand trust with the citizens of their respective nations. The challenge for the Asian market, which is also an opportunity in waiting, is to look toward organic growth fueled by investment from local investors versus allowing so much foreign franchising and management.
> • *Talent availability.* Finding adequate personnel to staff and manage a health/fitness club is a global challenge, not just an issue facing Asia. Nonetheless, in order for the industry to achieve significant growth, the operators in Asia will have to identify and execute strategies to quickly develop fitness professionals who can step in and manage a club.

Reflections

Asia is the largest geographic populace in the world. This continent represents approximately 60 percent of the world population. Japan and China are already global economic powers, while India and South Korea are becoming or may already be considered global economic powers. The combination of populace size and growing economic clout suggest a market that, in the next 20 years, may become the largest health/fitness club market in the world. The Asian club market is an emerging and dynamic business environment that is being shown the way to responsible growth by excellent operators, such as Central Sports, Konami, and Renaissance among others. In several countries, such as Japan, South Korea, Singapore, and Taiwan, the industry is well-established and serves as a template for entrepreneurs in other Asian markets who wish to build successful and profitable health/fitness club empires. If the current trends continue for the next 10 to 20 years, little doubt exists that Asia will emerge as a global leader in the health/fitness club industry.

If the current trends continue for the next 10 to 20 years, little doubt exists that Asia will emerge as a global leader in the health/fitness club industry.

32 The European Health/Fitness Club Market

"Europe's strength is its diversity, not its uniformity."

—Sir John Harvey Jones, British author and ICI chairman

Chapter Objectives

This chapter provides an overview of the European market and the implications that this data holds for the health/fitness club industry in Europe and for the industry in the rest of the world. The chapter then examines the dynamics of the European health/fitness club industry, including review of the primary differences that exist between the European health/fitness club market and the North American club market, particularly the U.S. club market. The chapter offers ideas, insights, and information on the opportunities and challenges that may arise for European health/fitness club operators over the next decade.

Overview of the European Market

Europe is a continent of 58 nations, with an estimated population of 742 million people, equivalent to approximately 10 percent of the world's population. The 58 nations of Europe range from Gibraltar, with approximately 30,000 residents, to Russia, with a population of over 143,000,000. In comparison, the North American market, consisting of only two nations (the U.S. and Canada), has an estimated population of 349 million, the equivalent to 4.8 percent of the world population. When viewed in this perspective, Europe represents a market that is over two times as large as that of North America. As these numbers indicate, Europe is an important and influential player in the current and future development of the global health/fitness club industry. In fact, the European health/fitness club industry in 2015 generated approximately $30 billion U.S. (EUR $26.7 billion), which is approximately $1 billion U.S. more revenue than was generated by the industry in North America (U.S. and Canada). In fact, Europe is the largest fitness market in the world. According to the *2016 European Health and Fitness Market Report* prepared by Europe Active and Deloitte, there are an estimated 51,200 clubs on the European continent. These facilities collectively have approximately 52.4 million members

> Europe is the largest fitness market in the world.

or 7 percent of the continent's population. In contrast, North America has approximately 42,336 clubs, representing an estimated 61 million members or 16.7 percent of the total population. From an absolute quantitative perspective, Europe has 25 percent more clubs than North America, 14 percent more members, and yet the market penetration in Europe is only 42 percent of that in North America. This comparative statistic represents both a unique challenge and an incredible opportunity for European health/fitness club operators. The challenge for Europe is to achieve levels of membership penetration that are comparable to those in the North American market. It should be noted that several nations (e.g., nations, such as the Netherlands, Norway, and Spain) already have achieved penetration rates that approach those seen in North America. The opportunity for Europe is that if it is able to achieve the same penetration rates as those that occur in North America, then the number of health/fitness club members in Europe could nearly triple to approximately 130 million. Furthermore, the revenues flowing to the health/fitness club industry in Europe would also increase proportionally which would result in revenues growing from the current 2015 estimate of just over $30 billion (U.S.) to over $90 billion (U.S.).

Overview of the Health/Fitness Club Industry in Europe

❑ *Clubs, Members, and Membership Penetration.* As indicated in the previous section, the European health/fitness club market is comprised of over 51,200 clubs and 52.4 million members that generate gross revenues of approximately $30 billion (U.S.) annually. One of the more unique features of the European market is the level of maturity and sophistication that exists across the continent. Several nations, such as the United Kingdom, Spain, Sweden, Netherlands, and Norway, have already achieved market penetration levels that approach those seen in the U.S. market, while concurrently, emerging Eastern European nations, such as Estonia, Hungary, and Poland, have market penetration rates that are comparable to developing nations in Asia and Latin America. Figures 32-1 through 32-3 provide a visual perspective of these dynamics by showing the number of clubs, the number of club members, and the membership-penetration rates, respectfully, for select European markets. What these figures clearly indicate is that in many of the Western European nations (e.g., Netherlands and United Kingdom), health/fitness club membership is as much a part of the daily routine for citizens as it is in the United States. In Eastern European nations, on the other hand, the health/fitness club industry is in its infancy. One last insight is the impact that the recent economic recession in Europe, where in nations such as Italy, the Netherlands, and Spain the member levels and member penetration percentages have declined since 2009.

In many Western European nations, health/fitness club membership is as much a part of the daily routine for citizens as it is in the United States. In Eastern European nations, on the other hand, the health/fitness club industry is in its infancy.

PART NINE   *Overview of the International Health/Fitness Club Market*

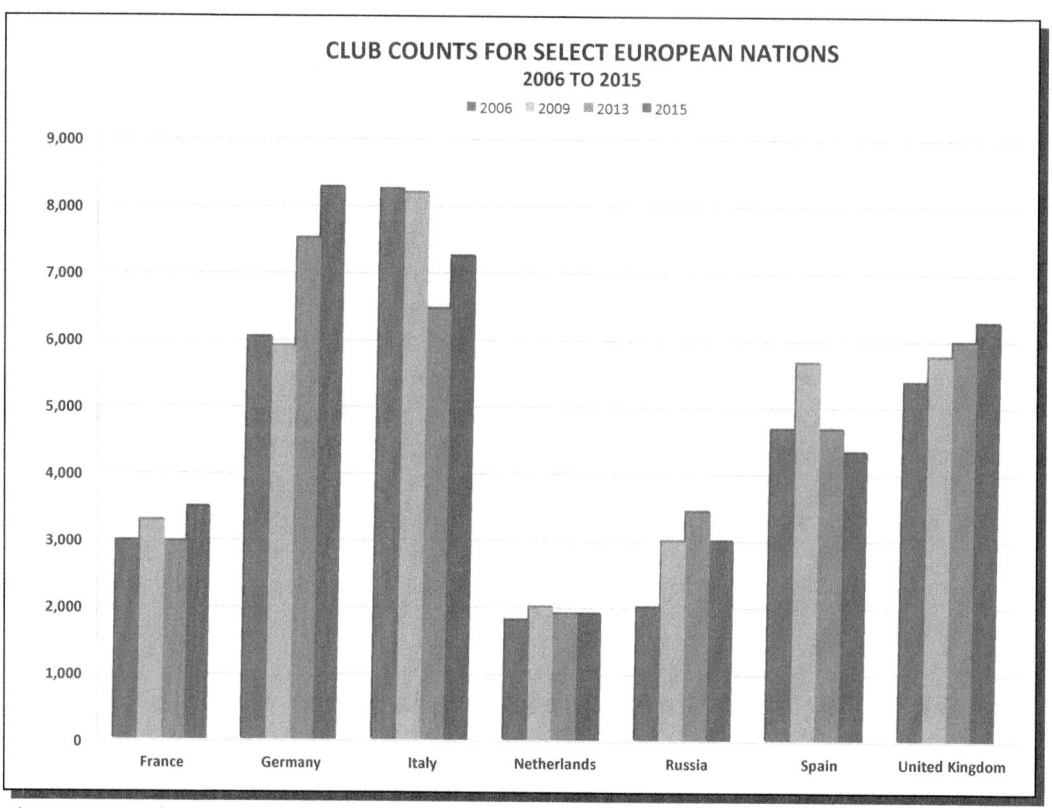

Figure 32-1. Club counts for Europe (2006 to 2015)

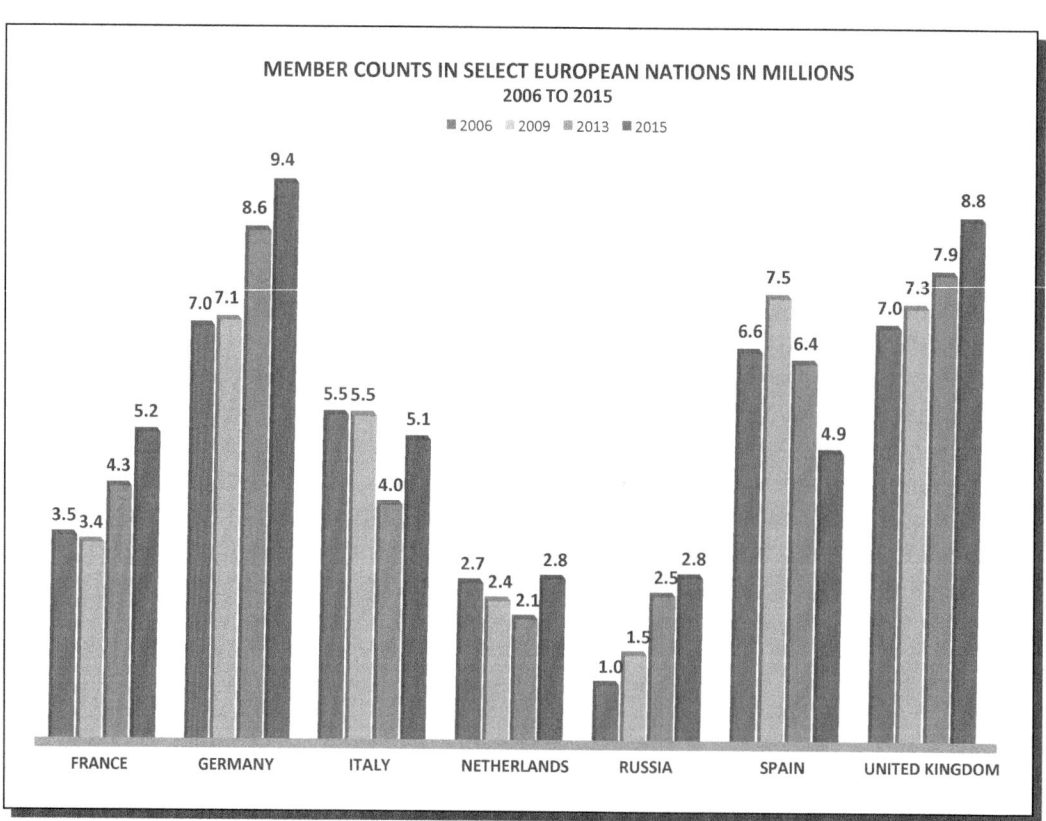

Figure 32-2. Member counts in European nations (2006 to 2015)

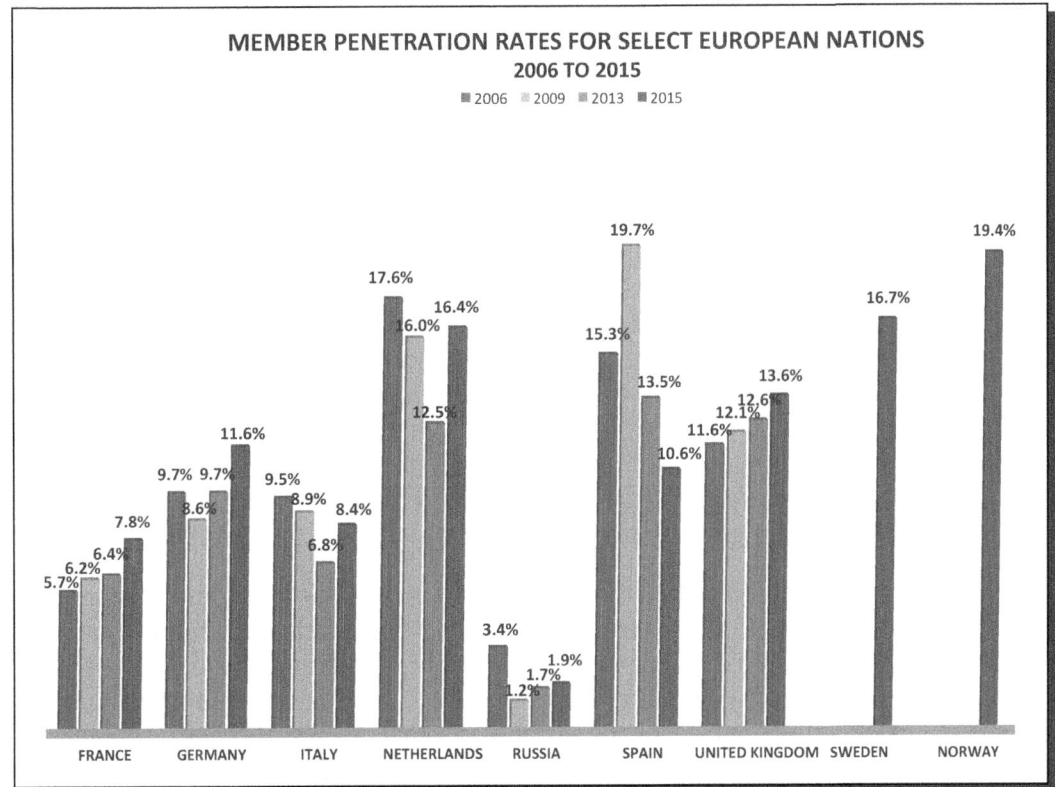

Figure 32-3. Market penetration rates in select European nations (2006 to 2015)

The European nation with the largest number of clubs as of 2015 was Germany with 8,332 clubs, followed closely by Italy with 7,300 health/fitness facilities, and then the United Kingdom with just over 6,312 clubs. Germany can also lay claim to having the most health/fitness clubs members with just over 9.5 million, with the UK a close second at 8.8 million. It should be noted that nations such as Italy and Spain have seen a decline in the number of clubs and members since the last large-scale survey completed in 2009, most likely the result of the floundering economies in these two nations. As industry insiders have come to understand in the United States, the most important measure of the health/fitness club industry's success is not the total number of members, but the percentage of residents within a market who have adopted the health/fitness club lifestyle. Based on this dynamic, Norway has the highest market-penetration level, having attracted approximately 16 percent of the market for memberships, followed closely by Denmark and Spain, each of which has been able to attract over 13 percent of its population as members.

A number of factors affect the dichotomy in club membership penetration across Europe, including the economic environment, the enormous difference in sports-culture, the level of professionalism of the club operators, and the organization of the industry. With regard to the latter dynamic, many countries do not yet have a well-organized, regionally based association of either health/fitness club professionals or facilities. With regard to the economic environment in Western Europe, a free market economy has existed for centuries. As a result, many citizens in these countries have sufficient expendable income to put toward club memberships. The average per-capita income, per the *IHRSA 2013 European Health Club Report*, ranges from 13,617 Euros (Russia) to 61,355 Euros (Luxemburg), which if converted to U.S. dollars would be similar to the income ranges that exist across the various states in the U.S.

In the European Union (a consortium of 28 of the 58 European nations), the average adjusted gross disposable per-capita income is approximately 20,145 Euros, equivalent to $26,678 U.S. This figure is approximately 65 percent of the per-capita income of Americans. Eastern Europe's free-market economy is newer, and therefore these nations have lower per capita income. In fact, in many cases, free-market economies in these nations is less than 20 years old. As a result, economic conditions are evolving, a situation which results in a polar economic climate (e.g., affluent and poor populations) and a slowly emerging middle class. As the middle class continues to evolve in Eastern Europe so will membership levels in health/fitness clubs.

In Europe, as of 2015, the average monthly health/fitness club dues was 44 Euros ($50 U.S.) with a large variance across nations, ranging from a low of around 36 Euros (approximately $41 U.S.) in Portugal and Spain up to an average of 70 Euros (approximately $80 U.S.) in Switzerland (refer to Figure 32-4 for a comparison of average monthly dues by European countries). The average monthly dues prices shown in Figure 32-4 include the value added tax (VAT) that club members must pay on top of the quoted dues price (VAT is a form of taxation that is similar to the sales tax that some municipalities in the U.S. place on health/fitness club memberships and ranges from 8 percent to 25 percent across Europe).

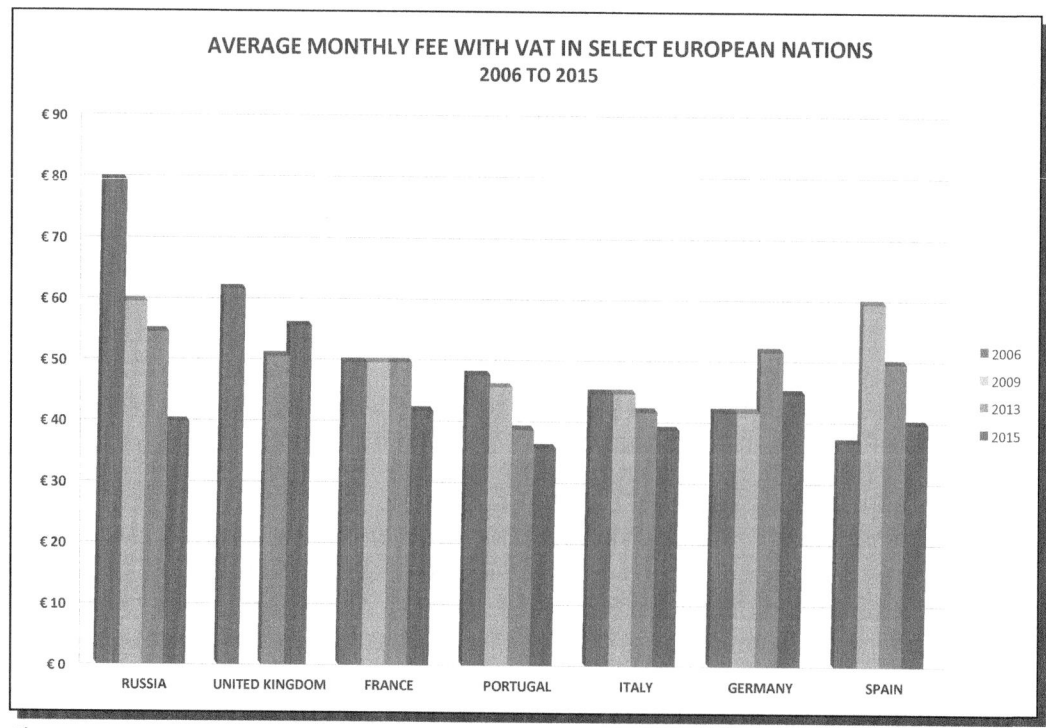

Figure 32-4. Average monthly dues in euros for select European nations (2006 to 2015)

Comparatively speaking, the average monthly dues paid by most Europeans for a health/fitness club membership represents a similar percentage of per-capita income to the U.S. For example, in the U.S., according to the publication, the IHRSA 2016 Health Club Consumer Report, the average amount paid for monthly dues for a health/fitness club in the U.S. was $54 (or $648 annually). This figure represents approximately 2.1 percent of the average real per-capita income for a U.S. citizen. In comparison, the average dues in Germany are equal to 2 percent of GDP per-capita income, in England they are equal to 2.1 percent of GDP per capita income, and in Russia are equal to slightly over 4.8 percent of GDP per-capita income (refer to Figure 32-5 for national comparisons as of 2013). This single measure indicates that in Europe, the average citizen spends slightly more of their income on membership compared to Americans, but the gap is lessening when compared to nearly a decade earlier.

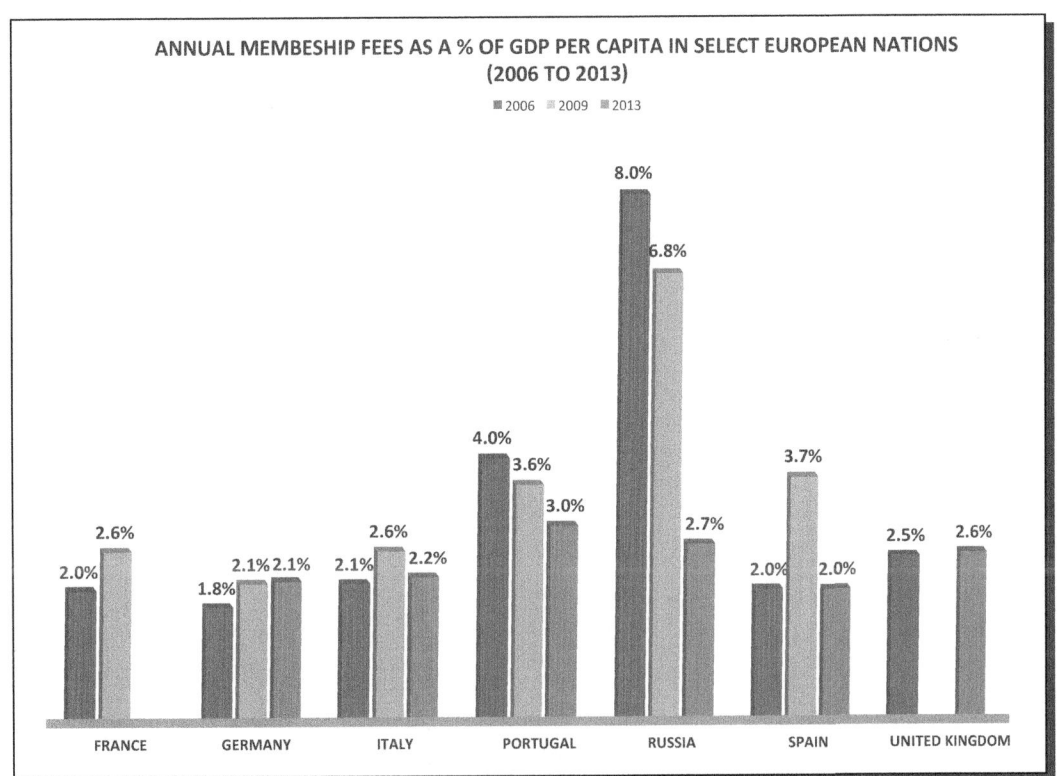

Figure 32-5. Annual dues as a percentage of GDP per capita income in select European nations (2006 to 2013)

Three factors impact the competitive atmosphere, and in particular club pricing, for the health/fitness club industry in Europe. One is the strong development of local-authority (i.e., city/village operated) fitness facilities in countries like the UK and Spain, where a large portion of the market is public and costs are kept low. Second has been rapid growth of budget-clubs, which charge half or less the dues price of the average health/fitness club. Among the leading budget-club operators in Europe are McFit/High5, in Germany, Pure Gym in England, and Basic-Fit based in the Netherlands, but with clubs in several European markets. The budget-club segment, while emerging in Germany in the late 1990s, has only become as a significant club segment since 2008, which coincidently coincides with the onset of the recession in Europe.

❑ *Membership Characteristics.* In Europe, gender involvement in the health/fitness club experience varies widely. In many cases, it is significantly different than what exists in the U.S (refer to Figure 32-6 that is based on 2006 data). For example, in the U.S, according to the publication, the *IHRSA 2016 Consumer Health Club Report*, approximately 51 percent of club membership is composed of women. In Europe, while the overall average for gender participation across all nations is comparatively close to that of the U.S., the mix by nation is considerably different. In France and Italy, for example, 66 percent and 58 percent of club members, respectfully, are women, while in Germany approximately 50 percent of members are female. In Spain and the United Kingdom, statistics indicate that approximately 53 percent and 54 percent of members respectively are female. It should be noted that the European data is based on data from a decade earlier than the U.S. data.

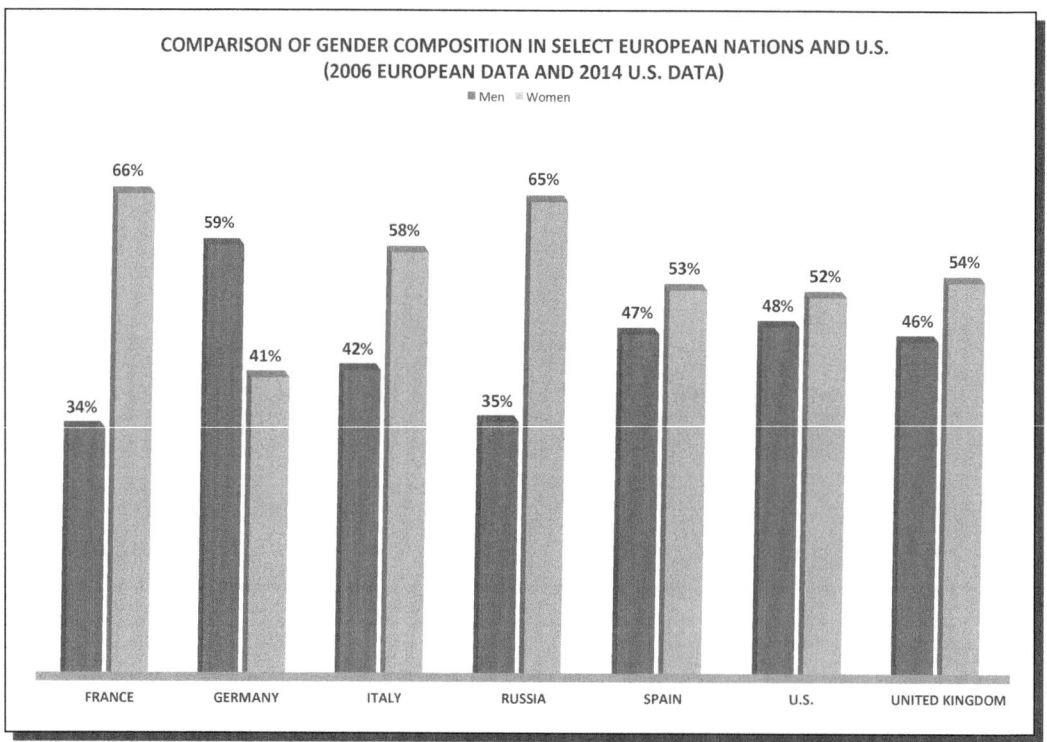

Figure 32-6. European health/fitness clubs: gender balance in membership

Such differences in gender participation could logically be expected to play a significant role in driving the design, marketing, and programming of European health/fitness clubs, given that club operators must offer an experience that is appealing to the largest user audience. Not surprisingly, some of the gender differences actually play a significant role in the club's product offering. For example, in France and Italy, where 6 out of 10 club members are women, group exercise is far and away the most popular activity (e.g., 69 percent and 65 percent of users participate).

In Germany, a completely different dynamic exists. For example, in Germany, club membership is almost evenly distributed between men and women, which is different than it was over a decade earlier when men actually represented nearly 60 percent of the market. Despite having an equal number of men and women, strength training appears to be the most popular form of club activity in Germany (e.g., 87 percent of activity). Similar to the U.S., Europeans exhibit activity tendencies based on gender, with men and women almost equally involved in cardiovascular training (50 percent men and women), men more inclined toward strength training than women (56 percent men and 44 percent women), and women significantly more involved in group fitness than men (27 percent men and 73 percent women).

Exterior, Fitness First, Frankfurt, Germany

In Europe, the largest demographic segment of club membership is driven by adults 18 to 34 years old (36.5 percent), with the second largest population of members coming from those 35 to 54 (34.9 percent). This age demographic is similar to the current U.S. club mix, in which 26 percent of members come from the 18 to 34 age group, and 34 percent come from the 35 to 54 age group. Interestingly enough, Europe has a larger portion of its members come from the over-55 population than the U.S., with Germany and Italy having the oldest demographics in Western Europe. (Figure 32-7 provides an overview of the age demographics for select European nations, based on 2006 data.) The aforementioned described age demographics vary considerably, when the data for some of the European nations is examined closely. For example, in Germany, 53 percent of memberships are driven by the 18 to 34 age demographic, while in Italy only 11 percent of memberships are derived from this same demographic category. Although no specific rationale was put forth in IHRSA's data on these varying demographic swings in membership penetration, it is quite possible that some of the following factors might come into play:

- The nearly equal penetration of the 55-plus demographic in both Europe and the U.S. possibly speaks to the fact that for baby boomers, regularly scheduled exercise is still a new lifestyle phenomenon. In many Eastern European nations, penetration into this demographic category is further impacted by the fact that this generation of Eastern Europeans has not had an equal opportunity to exploit the financial rewards of a free-market economy.
- The high penetration of the 18 to 34 age demographic in Europe parallels what the U.S. experienced back in the 1980s when having an exercise and club membership was primarily the domain of the younger population (in the U.S., it's now moving back in that direction). In Europe, this phenomenon might exist for a couple of reasons. First, this is an age in which younger individuals are likely to be most interested in a person's physical appearance and athletic accomplishments. Second, this generation, which is very technologically savvy, has been exposed through the Internet and social media to the trends in fitness, something that their parents were not afforded.
- Penetration of the 35 to 54 age demographic, as well as the over 55 age bracket, is the same in Europe as it is in the U.S.

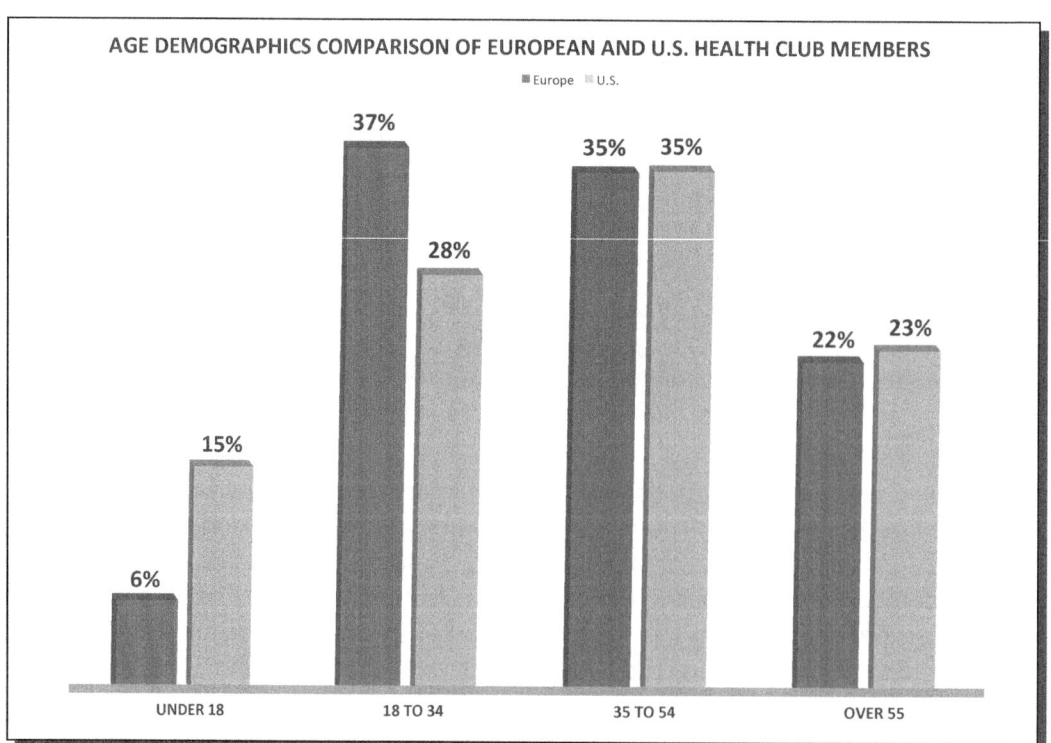

Figure 32-7. European and U.S. health/fitness clubs: age demographics of membership

The Leading Players in the European Health/Fitness Club Market

The European health/fitness club market, particularly in those nations represented by the European Union, has similar parallels to the U.S. market, when it comes to the role of leading health/fitness club operators. While the European industry is still the domain of the independent, entrepreneurial club operator, significant changes have occurred over the past 10 years that reflect a growing trend for commoditization and consolidation among club operators. According to the *2016 European Health and Fitness Market Report*, the leading club operators (based on the number of health/fitness clubs) in each of the European nations represent anywhere from 2.5 percent of the market (Italy) to 43 percent of the market (Sweden). Figure 32-8 provides an overview of the market share of the leading players in several European markets according to the *2016 European Health and Fitness Market Report* prepared by Europe Active and Deloitte. Over the next 5 to 10 years, this trend will continue, as equity capital continues to find its way into the European club market, and many of the leading club operators pursue a consolidation strategy aimed at leveraging core strengths in specific markets.

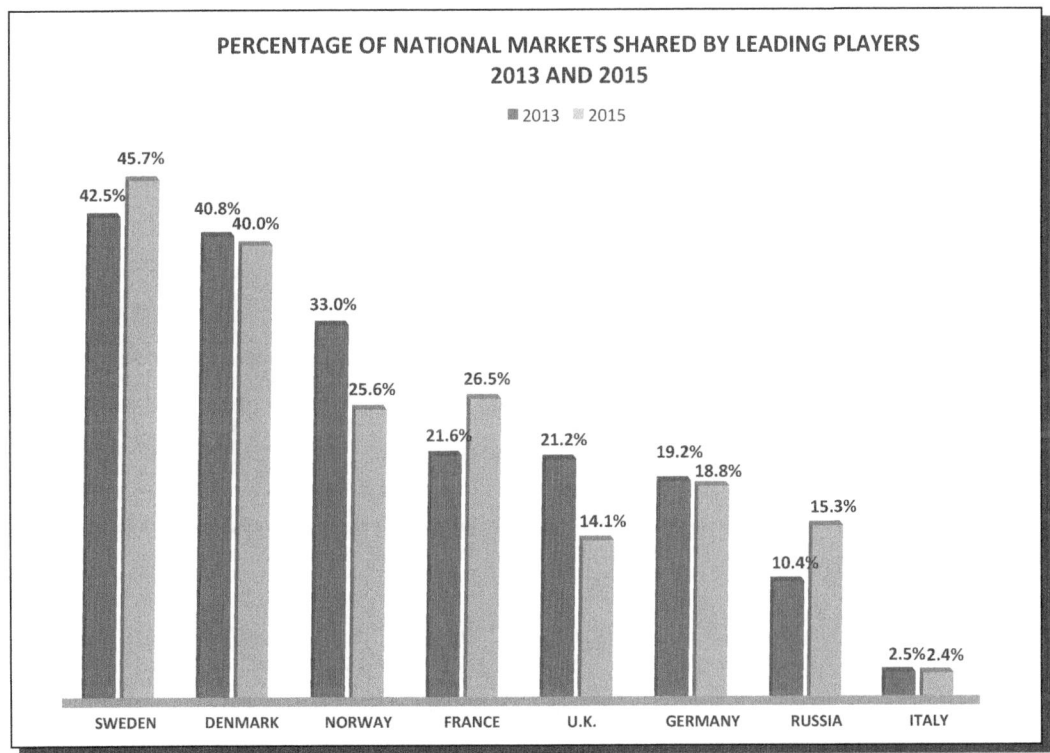

Figure 32-8. Percentage of national markets under control of leading club operators in 2013 and 2015

What may be more significant than the influence of the leading operators in each nation is the influence of the top 20 companies in Europe. This group represents over 9 million members, approximately 17 percent of the total health club members in Europe. The largest operator in Europe from a revenue perspective is Virgin Active, which generated 468 million Euros (or approximately

$554 million U.S.) in 2015, with David Lloyd Leisure not far behind with 460 million Euro (or $525 million U.S.). The highest revenue producing budget club operator in 2015 was McFit/High5, who reported generating approximately 268 billion Euro (or just over $306 million U.S.). The largest operator in Europe based on the number of members served in 2015 would be budget club operator McFit, with just over 1.4 million members. Figure 32-9 offers a visual representation of some the largest European club operators based on member count for YE 2015. Since 2015, the landscape has changed considerably with the emergence of leading budget club operators such as Basic-Fit, Pure Gym, and Clever Fit. In 2013, only McFit had a membership count that fell in the top ten, but in 2015 the top three operators by member count are all budget club operators (i.e., McFit/High5, Basic-Fit, and Pure Gym).

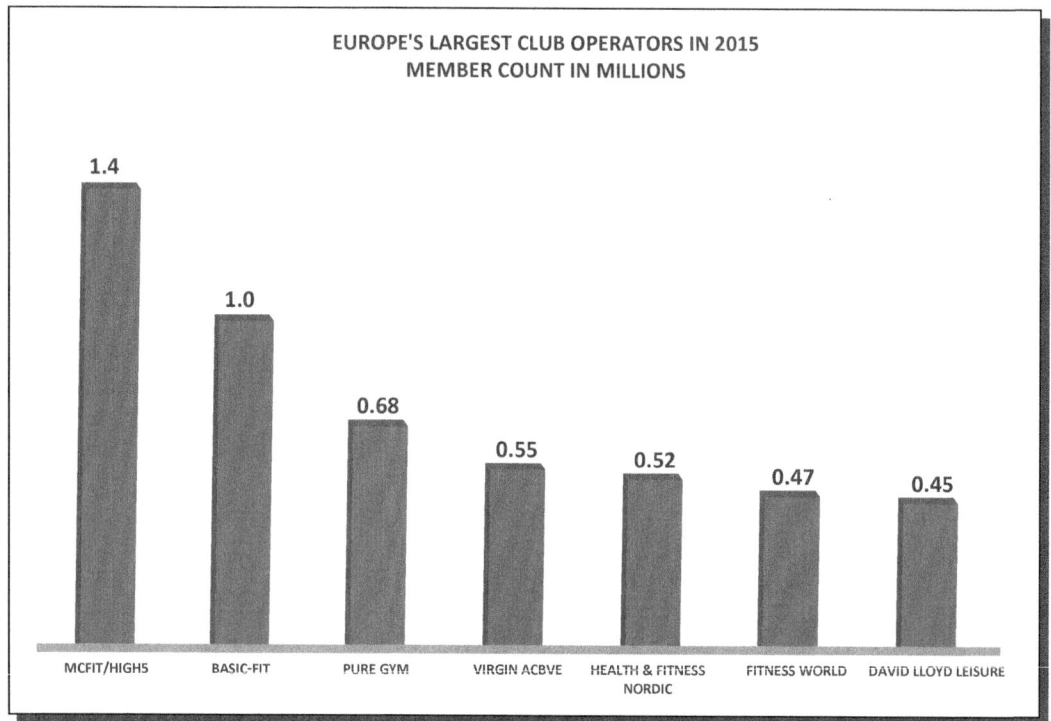

Figure 32-9. Largest European club companies by member count

The consolidation and commoditization of the European market has been driven primarily through an influx of private equity and large-scale mergers. Some of the most significant transactions since 2013 include:
- Purchase of INJOY by GMZ German Holding in 2014
- Budget club operator Basic-Fit's purchase from Health City by 3i Group plc in 2013
- Merger of SATS, Fresh Fitness, Elixia Nordic, and Metropolis in 2013 funded by Health and Fitness Nordic
- Purchase of David Lloyd Leisure by TDR Capital in 2013

The outcome and advantages of these various mergers and acquisitions is at least three-fold. First, many of the mergers have brought together the top players in their respective market niches, thus giving the purchaser significant advantages in cost efficiencies, market pricing, and possibly more importantly, in market presence and top-of-mind awareness with the consumer (for example, McFit's purchase of a portion of Fit24, Health City's purchase of over 100 Fitness First clubs, and Virgin Active's acquisition of 55 Esporta clubs). Second, many of the mergers have enabled the purchaser to enter new market niches, thus allowing it to assume a leading position in more than one market segment (for example, Virgin Active's purchase of Holmes Place and Esporta has enabled it to be a player in the premium and high-end premium segments). Third, the acquisition of a club business by a non-industry player with a desire to grow their investment can fuel significant organic club growth (e.g., David Lloyd Leisure in the UK, and Basic-Fit of the Netherlands).

Relaxation area, Pfitzenmeier, Schwetzingen, Germany

While the primary outcome of consolidation, commoditization, and private equity infusion in the European club market is larger and more powerful players that can influence industry-pricing activities and consumer perceptions of the industry (for example, in the U.S., big-box players, such as 24 Hour Fitness, LA Fitness, Planet Fitness, and Lifetime Fitness, have a substantial impact on both consumer perceptions and club pricing), there are other valuable outcomes that can occur for the industry as a result of private equity infusion, particularly the development of key market niches, such as the following:

❏ *Creation of budget-club brands.* In Germany, McFit has carved out a very successful niche as a convenient and inexpensive brand. At under 20 Euros a month and with over 230 locations throughout Europe, it is one of the feel-good stories in the European health club industry. McFit's model, which involves having limited staffing (usually one or two staff members per club), leveraging technology (members join on-line or through club kiosks, providing all club information through in-club kiosks and the Internet, facilitating exercise advice and member communication through the Internet, and gaining entry through the use of imbedded chip cards), offering limited amenities (members actually have to pay to take a shower and have to purchase drink and food through vending machines), and renting space in secondary locations, has allowed the company to generate, on average over 6,000 members per club and achieve EBITDA margins of over 35 percent. Another great story in the budget segment is the success of Health City's Basic-Fit clubs (recently purchased by the private equity group 3i Group), which were introduced around 2006 and have since grown to 400-plus clubs in Europe. Building on the business model established by McFit and Basic-Fit, other operators in Europe have exploited the power of this business model, including: Pure Fitness and Clever Fit in Germany; The Gym Group, Pure Gym, and Fitspace in the UK; Fresh Fitness in Denmark, and Fitness Hutt in Spain. This rapidly growing segment of the club market in Europe has placed strong downward pricing pressure on the rest of the industry, causing many operators who formerly operated in the affordable fitness segment to rethink their value proposition.

Kiosks, McFit, Munich, Germany

❑ *Creation and expansion of premium brands.* In the UK, Virgin Active's acquisition of Holmes Place, a premium brand in the United Kingdom, and more recently Esporta, has allowed Virgin Active to expand and broaden its brand's presence in the premium segment. For example, many of the Holmes Place and Esporta clubs have been repositioned as Virgin Active Classic clubs, which operate in the premium- and luxury-market segments. In just the past few years, Equinox Fitness out of New York has opened a club in London, adding an entirely new dynamic to the premium and luxury segment of the industry.

❏ *Expansion across national borders.* In the past, many European operators have found it difficult to take their brand to another European nation and operate clubs successfully and profitably. The merger-and-acquisition approach enables club operators to reach across borders and leverage the local talent of an acquired organization to expand their brand's market reach in new national markets. Health City, which formerly dedicated itself to serving its core markets in the Netherlands, has expanded into other markets, such as Spain, through its purchase of Fitness First clubs in those markets. Virgin Active has recently used an acquisition strategy to expand its presence in England, as well as in other European markets, such as Italy.

Opportunities and Challenges for the European Health/Fitness Club Industry

❏ *Opportunities*
- *Market penetration.* The overall European market has a membership penetration rate that currently runs at approximately 7 percent of the population. While some countries (such as the Netherlands, Spain, and Norway) have achieved or even exceeded the membership penetration rates that approach those that exist in the U.S., as a continent overall, a huge opportunity for membership growth exists in Europe. According to the IHRSA 2010 European Health Club Report, if those nations within the EU whose penetration percentages are below the EU average were able to bring their market-penetration levels up to the average, it would entail nearly 4,500,000 new members and generate new revenues of nearly 2.3 billion Euros. For operators and investors, this situation is an enormous opportunity.

Fitness floor, Gym Group, London, England

- *VAT.* The value added tax (VAT) is a significant issue in many, if not most, of the European nations. The cost impact of VAT to club members in Europe is far greater than sales taxes on club memberships in the U.S. In over a dozen European Union nations, the VAT runs over 20 percent, with Denmark and Norway having the highest VAT at 25 percent. Through the Brussels-based European Health and Fitness Association, now called Europe Active, and IHRSA Europe, club owners have a unique opportunity to leverage their combined voice with the political leaders of the EU to reduce the VAT burden on the health/fitness club industry. If this goal can be achieved, then the result will be a more affordable club experience for the members, which, in turn, would help increase market penetration and grow industry revenues.

  Portugal provides a great example of how VAT can positively and negatively impact the club industry. After the turn of the 21st century, club operators in Portugal were able to get the VAT on club dues reduced to 5 percent, a significant reduction from the former VAT rate. When the VAT tax reduction was put in place, clubs did not reduce their pricing, and as a result, a greater portion of revenue flowed to the bottom line of each club business. In 2011, the government pushed the VAT on membership up to 23 percent. Since most club operators could not increase their prices that significantly, the portion of revenues flowing to their bottom line dropped significantly. In those cases where an operator tried to increase the membership price to offset the increased VAT, consumers responded by not purchasing as many memberships. One operator indicated that the added VAT tax drove as much as 30 percent of the clubs out of business. This example shows both the challenge and the opportunity inherent in VAT policy. If club operators, through the efforts of their European and national associations can get governments to reduce the VAT load, it can have a significant impact on the profitability and growth of the industry.

Free weights, World Class Zhukovka, Moscow, Russia

- *Obesity pandemic.* Unfortunately, the obesity epidemic that has occurred in the U.S. has also "spread" across Europe. Similar to the U.S., the growing trend in obesity among both adults and children is fueling an increase in lifestyle diseases throughout the continent of Europe. According to data shared in IHRSA's 2013 European Health Club Report, 52 percent of the European population is overweight, while 17 percent of European Union citizens are considered obese. This obesity pandemic represents an outstanding opportunity for European club operators to take the lead in their respective communities and serve as facilitators of obesity-prevention and weight-reduction programs. If club operators are able to establish greater credibility as resources and destinations for fighting the obesity pandemic, a surge in club membership growth is quite likely.
- *Staff professionalism.* One of the most important steps that European club operators can undertake to enhance their standards and the quality of their services is to employ educated and certified staff. In that regard, Europe Active, formerly the European Health and Fitness Association has introduced the very successful REPS program in the UK and in the rest of Europe under the name EREPS, which is a web-based, European-wide register for certified fitness professionals. In the past five years, Europe Active has released standards that address the competencies and education of fitness instructors and personal trainers.
- *Healthcare.* European operators, like their counterparts in the U.S., have the same opportunity to establish a strong presence in the healthcare continuum. In England, UK Active has already made inroads interacting with the healthcare industry by working with one of the country's primary healthcare insurers. Similar efforts are now occurring in other countries in Europe. If the industry is able to make significant inroads in this arena, it will have a huge impact on the health/fitness club industry's growth in Europe. For instance in the Netherlands, one of the leading groups is ACHMEA, a healthcare-insurance company that owns a national chain of 32 health clubs. In the UK, Cannons (65 clubs) was acquired by Nuffield Hospitals in late 2007, and as a result, a new club brand, called Nuffield Health, was introduced. Nuffield clubs have positioned themselves as a "wellness" and health-promotion group, rather than just a chain of fitness clubs. It is also interesting to note that in Switzerland, about half of the members in the health/fitness club industry receive a subsidy from their health-insurance company. Furthermore, the European Commission has created a think tank called the EU Platform on Diet, Physical Activity and Health, which is charged with working with private industry to develop specific action-plans to combat lifestyle diseases. Representing the fitness industry on this Platform, Europe Active committed to promoting a healthier Europe. As such, if the industry is able to make significant inroads in this arena it will have a huge impact on the industry's growth in Europe.

❏ *Challenges*
- *Commoditization.* The club industry, particularly in the EU, is experiencing incredible merger and acquisition activity. While this situation offers some outstanding opportunities, it also presents the industry with some potentially

critical challenges. As clubs continue to merge or be acquired, the tendency is to move more and more toward a commodity-business model and further away from a personalized business offering. Club memberships are different than most retail and service sector experiences. Often, they are unique to a particular geographic region. As such, club operators will need to be cognizant of these subtle but important factors. If the industry moves too fast or too heavily into the commoditization arena, it will potentially sacrifice its ability to create personalized-business models that will enable it to reach into untapped markets. European operators need only look at the U.S. market to see the basic challenge that is inherent in this model.

- *Pricing.* As the top players in the European health/fitness industry continue to expand their reach and influence, the challenge of pricing will raise its ugly head. Larger companies will begin to leverage their operating efficiencies and marketing clout by using price discounts to wage war on their competitors. Furthermore, with the booming growth of budget clubs that offer memberships for under 20 Euros a month, and in some cases lower than 15 Euros a month (now the fastest growing segment of the industry), pricing pressure on the market has increased. The impact of budget clubs, as well as the pricing power of the very large operators, could be devastating to clubs, both small and large. Already in the UK, pricing, which was not an issue at the turn of the century, has become a topic of serious discussion among club operators. Again, European operators should learn from the experiences of the U.S. market to find an approach to deal with this potential challenge to their profitability in future years.

Reception and front desk, Intenso, Darmstadt, Germany

- *Leadership talent availability.* One of the biggest challenges any industry faces is finding the appropriate amount and blend of management and leadership talent, especially when it is experiencing exponential growth. As the number of clubs grows so will the demand for appropriately educated and trained management personnel. In the U.S., the health/fitness club industry faces a significant challenge in finding the appropriate leadership and management talent that will allow it to continue experiencing significant profitable growth. Similarly, club operators in many European markets are already beginning to face this challenge. The key to overcoming this challenge is to develop industry-based systems and practices to fuel the internal growth of leadership and management talent.

- *Industry representation.* Unlike the USA, where the commercial health/fitness club industry is represented by one national association (IHRSA) as well as numerous regional associations, Europe remains fragmented. In fact, many countries do not have a national association (e.g., Russia), or in some instances, the industry associations are operated under a profit umbrella. Perhaps, more importantly, the industry has only recently obtained the needed representation at the political level in Europe, with Europe Active (formerly EHFA). Europe Active's offices in Brussels have given the European industry a boost in its efforts to navigate the political landscape and to gain traction on several agenda items that are important to the continuing success of the industry. Beyond Europe Active, only a few countries have managed to establish organizations that can provide assistance in tackling the political and governmental hurdles that face the industry (for example UK Active in the UK, which has been around for over 20 years, has done an outstanding job representing the interests of the club industry in the UK).

- *European economy.* The economy in several European nations has been slow to rebound from the recession that first arose in 2008. Nations such as Greece, Ireland, Italy, Portugal, and Spain acquired incredibly high debt-to-GDP ratios, which resulted in economic assistance from the EU and ultimately tighter economic policies. These economic factors have influenced the entire EU, and as seen in the data, the club industry in some of these nations has suffered. The recent Brexit vote, which has the UK stepping out of the European Union, may have further impact on the European economy and consequently the performance of the European fitness industry. The future growth of the industry will be heavily influenced by how quickly the economy improves.

Reflections

The European health/fitness club industry is possibly the most unique club-related industry in the world. On one end of the spectrum, the European industry is at a level of maturity that rivals and possibly exceeds that of the U.S., with large, professionally run organizations that continue to attract members and investors. On the other end of the spectrum is an industry in its infancy, one trying to establish itself in emerging economies that are still in the process of defining their economic models. What is known, however, is that as a whole,

> The European health/fitness club industry is possibly the most unique club-related industry in the world.

Europe has more clubs, more club members, and generates greater revenue than the North American market.

Europe has more clubs, more club members, and generates greater revenue than the North American market. The success of the European industry in the immediate future is likely to be more dependent on the government of the European Union and the respective nations than on anything else, as they combat the lingering impact of the recession and the burden of heavy taxation.

The Latin American Health/Fitness Club Market

33

*"Since economies in the process of organization lack
resources to dynamize themselves ... it is the right to
accept the aid of all who want to run with us the risks of the
marvelous adventure that is progress."*

—Roberto Campos, Brazilian economist

Chapter Objectives

This chapter provides an overview of the Latin American market and the implications that this information holds for the health/fitness club industry in Latin America and throughout the world. The chapter then takes a closer look at the dynamics of the Latin American health/fitness club industry, including some of the differences that exist between this particular club market and other global club markets. Finally, the chapter reviews the opportunities and challenges that may arise for Latin American health/fitness club operators over the next decade.

Overview of the Latin American Market

The Latin American market is comprised of three distinct segments—Central America, South America, and the Caribbean. In total, Latin America is home to approximately 597,526,000 people, with approximately 8 percent of the entire population of the world. Latin America is the third largest global market after Asia and Europe. Population-wise, Latin America is 20 percent smaller than the European market and approximately 71 percent larger than the North American market.

Latin America is the third largest global market after Asia and Europe.

Central America (2013 estimates) has approximately 193 million residents, while South America has an estimated 404 million residents. Brazil, with approximately 201 million residents, is the largest nation in Latin America and is home to just over 32 percent of the total population of Latin America, and 48 percent of the South American population. Mexico, with an estimated population of approximately 118 million residents, is the second largest nation in Latin America and is home to nearly 20 percent of Latin American residents. Brazil and Mexico together represent 52 percent of the Latin American population.

According to the *IHRSA 2016 Global Report*, which looked at 16 of the 28 Latin American markets, there were an estimated 55,809 clubs, more than in any other global market, and 9 percent larger than the next largest club market, Europe. It is interesting to note that Brazil, with an estimated 31,809 clubs, has the second largest health/fitness club market in the world. In fact, only the U.S. club market (36,180 clubs) is larger. Brazil, based on the *IHRSA 2016 Global Report*, has 57 percent of the total club count in Latin America, and is second only to the U.S., with regard to a single nation's dominance of a regional market.

The 55,809 health/fitness clubs in Latin America serve an estimated population of 16 million members or approximately 2.5 percent of the entire population (based on the 16 Latin American countries studied). In contrast, the Asian health/fitness club market serves less than 1 percent of its population, the European health/fitness club market serves approximately 7 percent of its population, and the North America health/fitness club market serves approximately 17 percent of its population.

Overview of the Health/Fitness Club Industry in Latin America

❑ *Clubs, Members, and Penetration.* As indicated previously, the Latin American health/fitness club market, based on data from the 16 countries studied, is comprised of approximately 55,809 clubs, and approximately 15,719,490 members, which generates annual revenues estimated at 65.9 billion (U.S.) annually. Figures 33-1 and 33-2, based on data from the *IHRSA 2016 Global Report*, provide a visual overview of the number of clubs and the club members for several Latin American nations. The data demonstrates that the Latin American health/fitness club market, when compared to the club markets in Europe and North America, is still in its infancy (e.g., based on total club count and membership-penetration levels). At the same time, the health/fitness club market in nations, such as Argentina, Mexico, and Brazil, more closely approximate the level of industry maturity (e.g., based on club

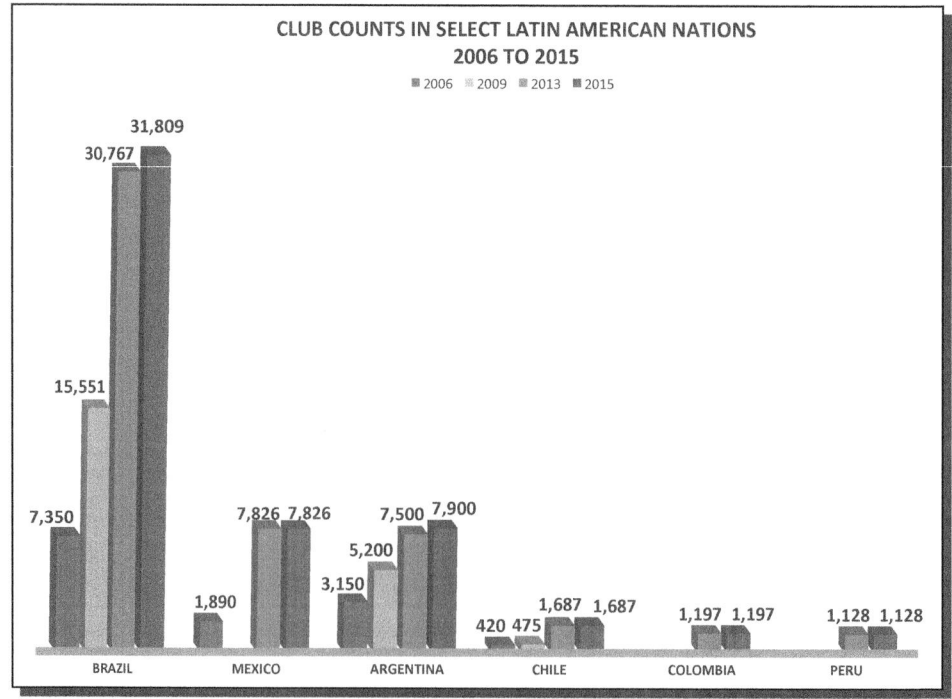

Figure 33-1. Club counts in various Latin American nations (2006 to 2015)

counts and membership levels), as seen in markets, such as Germany, Japan, and the United Kingdom. The health/fitness club market in a few of the urban centers of Latin America, such as Buenos Aires, Argentina; Mexico City, Mexico; and Rio de Janeiro and Sao Paulo in Brazil, rival the sophistication and maturity of health/fitness club markets, such as London, Tokyo, and New York.

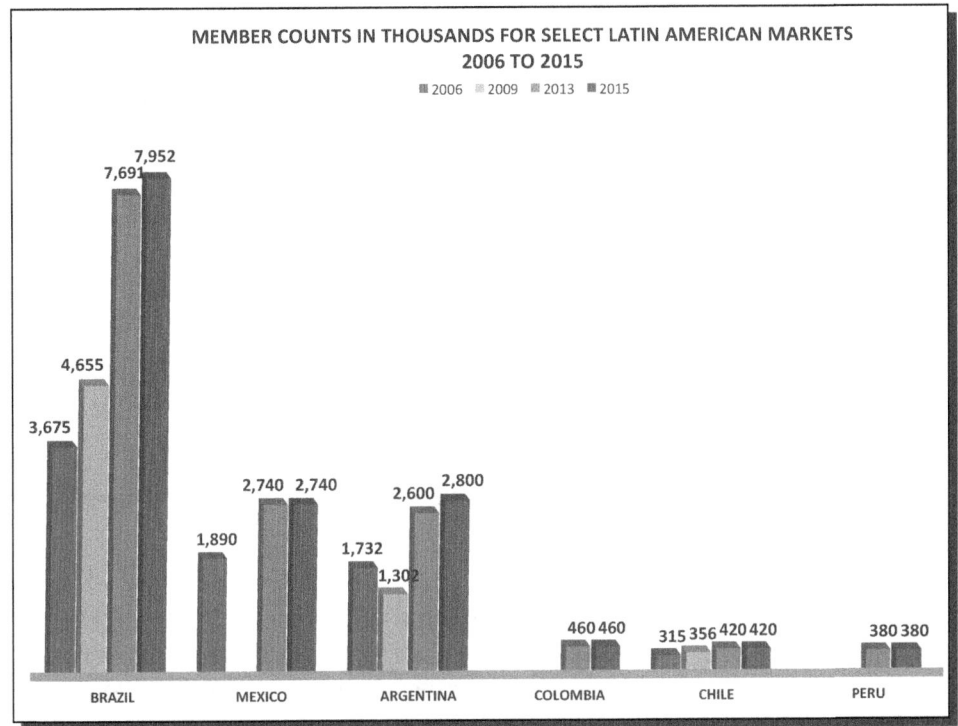

Figure 33-2. Health club member counts in various Latin American countries (2006 to 2015)

Brazil accounts for approximately 57 percent of the number of health/fitness clubs in Latin America as reported in the *IHRSA 2016 Global Report*, while Mexico and Argentina account for another 15 percent and 14 percent respectively of the market. When industry revenue contributions are considered, Brazil contributes approximately 41 percent of the total revenue generated by Latin American health/fitness club operators, as reported in the 2016 IHRSA data. In contrast, the revenue generated by clubs in Argentina and Mexico represent approximately half that amount at 20 percent and 25 percent respectively of the Latin American market.

When estimating the health/fitness club industry's growth potential in a market like Latin America, it is critical to look at data on market penetration. The Latin American health/fitness club industry has penetrated less than 3 percent (refer to Figure 33-3 for penetration percentages for the various nations in Latin America) of the eligible population (e.g., based on the nations included in the *IHRSA 2016 Global Report*s). When compared to Europe's market penetration of 7 percent and North America's at slightly over 17 percent, these statistics indicate that a large upside for growth exists in Latin America.

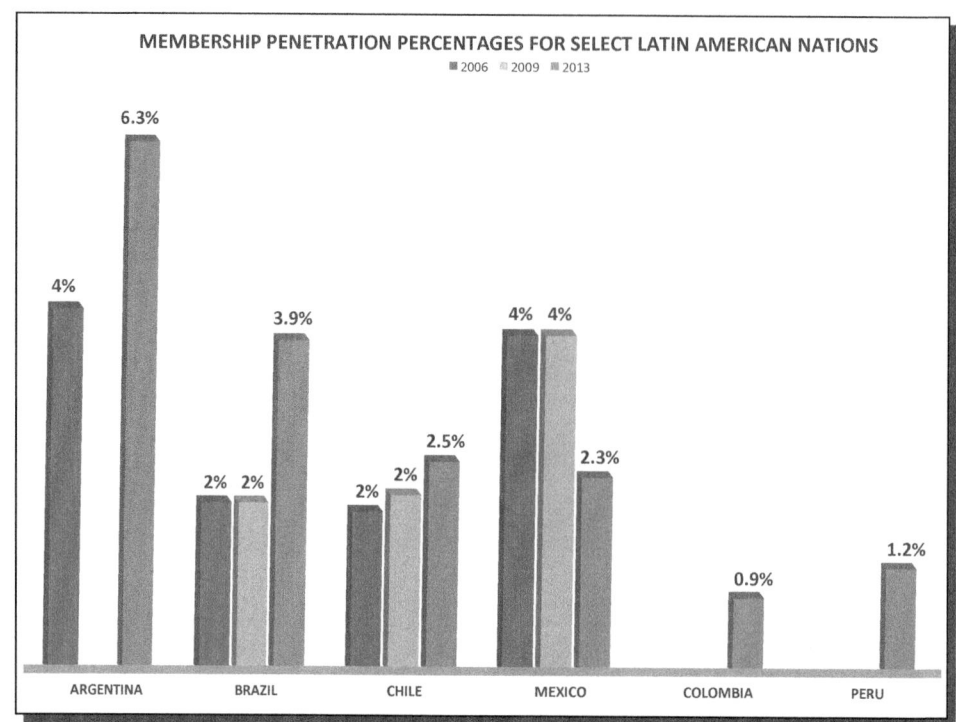

Figure 33-3. Market penetration percentages in select Latin American nations based on 2013 data

Argentina's membership penetration numbers (6.3 percent) most closely resemble the rates seen in many of the European markets, but considerably less than the leading international markets, which have greater than 10 percent membership penetration. The second most successful market at attracting its citizens for membership has been Brazil at 3.9 percent, followed by at Chile at 2.5 percent penetration and Mexico at 2.3 percent penetration. In comparison, most of the other Latin American nations appearing in IHRSA's 2016 report have achieved membership penetration percentages under 2 percent. These market-penetration levels fall considerably below most European nations, and just slightly higher than most of the Asian nations.

IHRSA has accumulated statistical data on the average monthly dues rates in Asia, Europe, and North America, but not for the Latin American market. As a result, specific statistical metrics on dues pricing are unavailable for the various Latin American countries.

Among the possible reasons to explain why the Latin American health/fitness club market achieves lower levels of market penetration than club operators in Europe or North America are the following:

- *Disposable income of the populace.* GDP per-capita earnings across Latin America averages $11,770 (U.S.) and ranges from a high of approximately $29,594 (U.S.) in Trinidad and Tobago to a low of $1,600 (U.S.) in Haiti. The three largest health/fitness club markets of Argentina, Brazil, and Mexico have GDP per-capita respectively of $18,200, $16,426, and $14,551 (U.S.), respectively, which is approximately half of what it is in the leading European markets. According to the Organization of Economic Cooperation and Development (OECD), Latin America has one of the most unequal distributions of income in the world. According to the World Bank, the Gini index (a measure of income inequality) for nearly all of Latin America is among the highest in the world. Argentina, Brazil, Chile, Colombia, and Mexico, for example, all have indexes approximating 50, which is higher than what is seen in most other global markets. Since per-capita incomes are so low and income distribution is quite unbalanced, it is somewhat easy to understand why Latin American operators have had less success than their North American and European counterparts penetrating the populace. In essence, these Latin American operators are limited to a viable economic audience that represents anywhere from 10 percent to 20 percent of the total population. If viewed from this perspective, the membership-penetration levels of the health/fitness club industry in the Latin American are very respectful.

Fitness floor, Megatlon, Buenos Aires, Argentina

- *Education levels.* According to global statistics, Latin America has a lower than average level of education among its populace. While the region boasts some outstanding institutions of higher learning, the general population is not as well educated as the residents of either Europe or North America. According to industry statistics provided in the publication, the IHRSA 2016 Health Club Consumer Report and other industry-based studies, one of the best predictors of health/fitness club membership is education level (in the U.S., a college education or higher is an excellent predictive demographic for club membership). As a rule, the higher a nation's educational attainment, the higher the level of market penetration for club membership. All factors considered the educational demographics of the Latin American market are not as suitable for attracting club memberships, when compared to the education demographics of regions such as North America and Europe.

- *Industry longevity.* The Latin American market is relatively new when compared to the markets in either Europe or North America. The Brazilian health/fitness club market has been in existence since the mid-1980s, with Runner S/A beginning operations in 1983 and Companhia Athletica opening in 1985. In Mexico, the industry has been in existence for just over 40 years, with Organizacion Britania opening its doors to the public in 1970. While industry players, such as Companhia Athletica, Runner S/A, and Organizacion Britania, have been in business for nearly as long as the leading club operators in Europe, Japan, and North America, the majority of club operators in Latin America have been in business for less than 20 years, and, in many cases, for less than a decade. As a result, health/fitness clubs are still a relatively new industry in Latin America. As industry longevity increases, the public's awareness of it will also increase, thus fueling the industry's growth.

Fitness floor, Companhia Athletica, Sao Paulo, Brazil

❑ *Membership Characteristics.* Data pertaining to the general membership characteristics of the Latin American club market are not as readily available as they are for North America and Europe. While the age, gender, and general-usage demographics of club members in Europe and the U.S. have been published by IHRSA in various reports (e.g., the IHRSA 2008 and 2010 European Market Reports and the IHRSA 2016 Health Club Consumer Report), no such data has been released with regard to Latin America. Based on personal observations on visits by the author to the Latin American market and conversations with a few of the leading club operators in the respective markets during those visits, the following points can be made about the membership characteristics and activities of the Latin American club market:

- In Brazil, as well as in Argentina and Mexico, the typical health/fitness club member has a similar per-capita income and household income as his counterparts in Europe or North America. This situation is, in part, the result of a dues-pricing policy that is affordable to only a certain market demographic.
- It appears that the general age demographics of a Latin American health fitness club member more closely parallels the age statistics reflected in Europe and North America more than those of Asia. In North America, the 34 to 45 age demographic is the largest, while the 18 to 34 age demographic is slightly larger in Europe. It could be argued that the same demographic groups represent the top audiences for membership in Latin America.

Additional information about the Latin American market can be obtained by contacting the International Health, Racquet & Sportsclub Association, based in Boston, Massachusetts.

The Leading Players in the Latin American Health/Fitness Club Market

The Latin American market has begun to look similar to the Asian, European, and North American markets, with regard to the role that the key industry players have in influencing the overall health/fitness club market. The reason for this has been the infusion of private equity funding behind some of the more prominent players and consequently an expansion of their footprint. Among the largest players in Latin America are: Bio Ritmo/Smart Fit, Brazil with 290 clubs (includes its Smart Fit brand of budget clubs); Body Tech, Colombia with 141 clubs; Body Tech, Brazil with 96 clubs; and Sport City, Mexico with 41 clubs. From a revenue perspective, the largest operators as of YE 2015 include: Bio Ritmo/Smart Fit with an estimated $218 million (U.S.); Body Tech, Brazil with revenues of $137 million (U.S.), and Body Tech, Colombia with approximately $125 million (U.S.).

Crossfit, Buenos Aires, Argentina

While these statistics are impressive, they pale in comparison to the leading club companies in Asia, Europe, and the U.S., where companies such as Virgin Active of the UK, 24 Hour Fitness of the U.S., and Konami of Japan all operate well in excess of 250 clubs, and all have revenues approaching or in excess of $1 billion (U.S.). In these other global regional markets, especially in Europe and North America, numerous club companies either operate in excess of 100 clubs and/or generate club-based revenue exceeding $200 million (U.S.) annually.

When the Latin American market is viewed on a nation-by-nation basis, in only a few instances are there one or two dominant industry operators, an indication that these markets are still extremely fragmented. The most dominant player from a market share perspective may be Body Tech in Colombia, which has an estimated 8 percent of the clubs in Colombia (based on data available at the time of publication) and generates almost two-thirds of the industry revenue. The Latin American market appears to consist of brands with outstanding reputations, but much less dominance from a market share perspective, including such well-recognized and influential brands as Companhia Athletica, Brazil; Bio Ritmo/Smart Fit, Brazil, Runner/SA, Brazil; Megatlon, Argentina; Body Tech, Brazil; Sport City, Mexico and Sportlife in Chile. Another interesting point that can be made about health/fitness club operators in Latin America is that, until recently, the leading club brands have stayed within their own national markets and have not attempted to expand their operations into adjacent national markets, such as has occurred in Europe and some of the Asian nations. Bodytech of Colombia was one of the first Latin American operators to cross borders, having opened or acquired clubs in Chile, Ecuador, and Peru. Recently, Smart Fit, a budget club franchise owned by Bio Ritmo, has franchised budget clubs in other Latin American markets such as Mexico.

Pool lobby, Ecofit, Sao Paulo, Brazil

The Latin American market has not experienced the merger and acquisition activity that has occurred among its European counterparts, or the large influx of private equity that has fueled the incredible growth of some club operations in Europe and North America. The environment for mergers or acquisitions does not seem as opportunistic, at least at this point in time, as they are in Europe and North America. Interestingly though, private equity firms have begun investing in the industry, which in time will fuel the growth of the industry.

Opportunities and Challenges for the Latin American Market

❑ *Opportunities*
- *Increased market penetration.* As an industry in its infancy, the health/fitness club industry in Latin America has an incredible future ahead of it. As the statistics show, with approximately 2 percent to 6 percent market penetration in the leading Latin American markets (e.g., Argentina, Brazil, Chile, Mexico) served by health/fitness clubs and less than 2 percent in the other national markets of Latin America, the opportunity for new business development is immense. Brazil and Mexico, both with well-developed health/fitness club markets, are only penetrating between 3 percent and 4 percent of a combined population, approximating 314 million people. If the market penetration of just these two markets increases to the average level of the European market (e.g., 6 percent penetration), the total membership base in Latin America would increase by nearly 3 million members. Imagine the opportunities for club operators if market penetration in these countries, as well as the other Latin American nations, were to approach 5 percent penetration levels.
- *Consolidation.* The Latin American market, possibly more than any other global regional market, is ripe for consolidation. With only two companies operating in excess of 100 clubs, the industry is ripe for consolidation. Consolidation is a by-product of merger and acquisition activity, which, in turn, is driven by the influx of private equity into the market. The recent success of Body Tech of Colombia in acquiring smaller operators with private equity capital may be a sign of things to come. Attracting private-equity investment is also a great opportunity for the Latin American market.

❑ *Challenges*
- *Economic clout.* The most significant hurdle for the Latin American market involves the economic conditions and earning power of its citizens. As discussed previously, the majority of Latin American citizens don't have the financial resources to make club membership a part of their day-to-day routine. Until a larger segment of the population achieves the economic equivalency of middle-class status, the health/fitness club industry in Latin America will have a difficult time achieving rapid growth. Over the past few years, Brazil has emerged as a growing global economic power, and nations such as Argentina, Chile, and Mexico have seen the economic power of its citizens elevate, it may lead the rest of Latin America into a more prosperous economic environment.

The Latin American market, possibly more than any other global regional market, is ripe for consolidation.

- *Education.* As detailed previously, the overall education level of many Latin Americans is below that of their counterparts in markets of other regions, such as Europe and North America. Health/fitness club membership penetration parallels the education level of the market, and as a result, one of the challenges that operators in Latin America face is finding a means to bring fitness education to the market.
- *Talent availability.* Finding, identifying, and hiring talented staff is a global challenge, not just a challenge for Latin America. Nonetheless, in order for the industry to achieve significant growth, health/fitness club operators in Latin America will have to establish results-driven strategies to quickly develop fitness professionals, who can step in and manage their clubs.
- *Government policies.* In many Latin American nations (Argentina and Brazil, for example), the government imposes a high cost of doing business, ranging from high taxes, unfavorable employment laws, regulations that make it difficult to obtain bank financing, the high cost of capital, and burdensome business start-up practices.

Reflections

While Latin America is the third largest geographic populace in the world, this continent encompasses only approximately 8 percent of the world's population. Brazil, the largest nation in Latin America and currently the most dominant economically, was until its recent economic slide in 2016, recognized as one of the three emerging global economic giants, along with China and India. This combination of populace size and growing economic clout suggest a market that may in the next 20 years be one of the leading health/fitness club markets in the world. The Latin American health/fitness club market is an emerging and dynamic one that is being fueled by the efforts of several excellent operators, including Body Tech (Brazilian and Colombian businesses), Bio Ritmo, Companhia Athletica, Megatlon, Sport City, and Sportlife.

In Argentina, Brazil, and Mexico, the club industry is well established and serves as a template for entrepreneurs in other Latin American markets who wish to build successful and profitable club companies. In addition, the growth of industry publications, such as *Mercado Fitness*, based in Argentina, and *Fitness Business Brazil*, and the continuing development of large industry meetings directed toward health/fitness professionals, such as those organized by Fitness Brazil and Mercado Fitness, are two of the factors helping to spur the spread of the health/fitness club industry across the Latin American continent.

PART 10
The Future of the Health/Fitness Facility Industry

Chapter 34:
The Future of the Health/Fitness Facility Industry

The Future of the Health/Fitness Facility Industry

34

"The future is like a corridor into which we can see only by the light coming from behind."

—Edward Weyer Jr.

Chapter Objectives

The health/fitness club industry is an evolving entity, both domestically and internationally. While it is more of an accepted part of the American culture and lifestyle than it was 40 years ago or even a decade ago, the industry remains somewhat susceptible to the whims of changing demographics, trendy popular culture, and macroeconomic conditions. Several factors involving these demographics, popular culture, and the global economy may have a significant impact on the club industry over the next two to three decades. The more clubs are aware of those factors and respond accordingly, the more the industry will be able to sustain continued growth and profitability across the various markets. This chapter details seven important demographic, cultural, and macroeconomic trends and the potential impact these trends will have on the future of the health/fitness club market.

Seven Important Demographic and Cultural Trends That Will Shape the Future of the Health/Fitness Facility Business

1. The Age Wave: Baby Boomers and Echo Boomers (Millennial Generation)

The first three to four decades of the 21st century will be impacted significantly by two age-related demographic trends. The first factor is the aging of the Baby Boomers, 74 million U.S. adults and over 600 million global adults as of 2017 who were born after 1946 and who, collectively, are the wealthiest population in the world (e.g., hold 70 percent of U.S. net worth and 80 percent of all money in savings and loan banks). Baby Boomers represent an aging and affluent generation of "me"-oriented adults, seeking to age gracefully and live healthy for as long as they can. This population is willing and able to spend the money necessary to strive for their goals (e.g., Baby Boomers hold 70 percent of U.S. disposable income and represent 40 percent of total consumer spending). This demographic wave also represents the largest population segment in several nations, such as the U.S., England, Germany, Italy, and Japan. Over the next two decades in the U.S., Baby Boomers will see their U.S. ranks shrink from

> Several factors involving demographics, popular culture, and the global economy may have a significant impact on the club industry over the next two to three decades.

its present level of 74 million to fewer than 45 million. According to global statistics, it is estimated that by 2050 there will be approximately 2 billion people age 60 and older.

The second factor is a population referred to by demographers as the Echo Boomers, or Millennial Generation, a group of young adults who were born after 1981 and prior to 2000. At 88 million strong, millennials are the largest demographic population in the U.S, and the world. The Millennial Generation in the U.S. is expected to increase from its present level of 88 million to 96 million over the next two decades. This group grew up in the era of technology, social media, and multi-tasking. Millennials are attuned to the environment, are computer savvy, socially connected via the Internet, are social collaborators, and possibly more significantly are rebelling against many of the institutions created by the Baby Boomers. Lastly, Millennials currently represent 28 percent of all consumers spending, a percentage that will jump dramatically over the next two decades, and will receive over $40 trillion in wealth transfer over the same time period.

According to global demographers, nations can be classified into one of four core age profiles, based on the percentage of their population that is under the age of 30 (Millennials): very young (66 percent of the population under age 30), youthful (60 percent of the population under age 30), transitional (between 45 percent and 60 percent of the population under age 30), or mature (less than 45 percent of the population under age 30). To a degree, these classifications indicate that the very young, youthful, and even transitional markets are very strongly influenced by the Millennial wave, while nations that have substantial transitional and mature markets are more heavily influenced by baby boomers. It is interesting to note that all of North America, Europe (including Russia), and Australia have substantial mature populations, in which baby boomers have a significant influence with regard to purchasing behavior and other trends. On the flip side, most of Asia, Latin America, and Africa feature markets that can be defined as being very young, youthful, and in a few cases, transitional. In those markets, the Millennials are the dominant demographic influence.

The potential business implications for the health/fitness club industry of serving two diverse demographic populations, such as Baby Boomers and Echo Boomers, may include:

❑ *Implications Driven by the Baby Boomer Population:*
- Exercise for health and well-being will take center stage. While baby boomers want to extend their lifespan, more importantly, they want to enjoy life as long as they can. This population wants to age gracefully. Research shows that Baby Boomers feel nine years younger than their chronological age. As the saying goes, 60 has become the new 40!
- Programming will need to focus on creating results for those with growing physical limitations and increased disease states. Programming will need to focus on addressing mobility, as well as movements that foster enhanced functional capabilities.
- Health/fitness professionals will need to be educated in working with individuals who have special conditions (e.g., arthritis, diabetes, heart

disease), with a focus on creating exercise progressions that accommodate the interests, needs, and goals of those with health-related problems.
- Member service will become essential to the overall member experience, as aging and affluent members seek more personalized face-to-face encounters.
- Medical oriented services will have to merge with fitness as the lines between them blur.

For example, medical spa services (e.g., Botox, liposuction, and microderm abrasion) and physical therapy services will likely become an essential component of many health/fitness clubs.

❑ *Implications Driven by the Millennials:*
- Clubs will need to incorporate innovative programs and services that entertain, inspire, and challenge, not to mention encompass seamless virtual platforms. Member blogs, virtual personal-training sites, mobile applications that engage the member, and virtual communication will become necessary in attracting this generation. Social media sites, such as Facebook, Instagram, Snapchat, Twitter, and YouTube, will become essential tools in reaching out to this population.
- Entertainment will take on greater importance, since Millennials need and want to be entertained when they exercise. As a result, clubs will need to redefine entertainment, since Millennials connect entertainment to technology, and in most instances mobile technology.
- Clubs will need to re-think how they deliver the club experience, because Millennials prefer to be involved in the service-delivery process, or as researchers describe it, collaborative engagement with the brands they purchase from.
- Coaching skills will become a critical part of management's arsenal, since employees from this generation respond less favorably to baby-boomer management techniques, such as, "do it or else," and instead prefer to work in highly collaborative environments.
- Boutique offerings will become more popular as the Millennials pursue their individual interests and pursuits and the desire to connect with their unique tribe.

2. The State of Health: A Shifting Paradigm

In just the past decade, the world has seen an exponential increase in obesity and the many negative health conditions that are attendant to obesity. According to the World Health Organization (WHO), in 2014 more than 13 percent of the world's adult population was obese and 39 percent of the world's adult populations are overweight. Most of the world's population live in nations where being overweight and obese is more likely to kill people than being underweight. Finally, the WHO says that in 2014, 41 million children under the age of 5 were overweight or obese. According to healthcare professionals, it is believed that for the first time in the history of mankind, children will die at a younger age than their parents. The increasing role of technology in the world has created a generation of adults who move less, eat more, and as a result, experience significantly higher rates of obesity and obesity-related disorders, such as diabetes, heart disease, and cancer. The fact that the healthcare system is broken only exacerbates the situation. Built on a model of expensive treatment, rather than inexpensive prevention, the healthcare system is overtaxed, and in many cases, not within the financial reach of the average person. These factors present both a challenge and an opportunity for the health/fitness club industry. The potential business implications of a changing state of health in the health/fitness industry may include:

- Fitness providers must establish greater credibility with the healthcare industry in an effort to be perceived as an essential provider of preventative health services.
- Fitness programming will need to evolve into specialized niches for various special populations, such as arthritic, obese, diabetic, and COPD, among others.
- Fitness professionals will need to expand their educational horizons and become better educated in subject matter related to healthcare. Basic fitness certifications will become an outdated notion of the past, as the credentials of fitness professionals will align more with those of other healthcare professionals, such as physical therapists and nurses.
- Alternative and complementary medicine will slowly emerge as an entirely new and profitable programming segment for many health/fitness clubs.

3. The Wealth Gap and Income Inequality

According to a variety of leading economic sources, approximately 1 percent of adults hold 40 percent of the world's wealth, while another 50 percent of the population has another 1 percent of the world's wealth. In addition, approximately 10 percent of adults hold 85 percent of the world's wealth, which means that the remaining 90 percent hold only 15 percent of the globe's wealth. Regionally, the U.S., Japan, China, England, and Germany hold over 50 percent of the world's net worth. Since the mid-90s, the disparity between those who have money and those who don't has continued to grow. This trend of wealth inequality is not limited to the U.S.; rather, it is an international trend. Most of the nations in Latin America, and many in Europe and Asia, have serious income inequality issues. According to recent government data, over 45 million Americans are classified as being below the poverty line. This growing disparity represents a significant challenge to those in the health/fitness club industry worldwide. On one hand, the industry must balance between its need to appeal to a larger audience of prospective members, many of whom have little disposable income, while on the other hand depending to heavily on the wealthiest segment of consumers because of the need to operate profitably and compete with multiple new competitors for a small fragment of the population that has enough wealth to spend liberally on its services. The enormity of this challenge can easily be seen in the data from the U.S. health/fitness industry, where the income demographics of club members are even more skewed than the U.S. population as a whole. The same can be said for member income demographics in other nations. The potential business implications of wealth disparity in the health/fitness club industry may include:

- Owners and operators will need to create new business models that will provide an appealing and results-oriented environment for those individuals with relatively low levels of discretionary income. While the emergence of budget clubs may be one answer to this situation, it is not likely the only one. Budget clubs, until recently, did not focus their efforts marketing toward lower income brackets and instead focused on attracting members away from more expensive club models by locating in affluent markets. Budget club operators of the future will need to rethink this strategy, especially if the industry as a whole wishes to attract a larger segment of the world population.

- Clubs may have to adapt their current business model to accommodate a new delivery model that focuses on providing club-like experiences over the Internet and through less expensive virtual environments (e.g., free-to-play gamification models involving downloadable or streaming fitness content). Because the use of virtual-training environments will continue to evolve, club operators will need to find a way to employ these non-traditional training platforms to reach out to new audiences.

- Clubs may need to adapt to becoming resource centers that provide fitness and physical activity outside their physical facilities. Appealing to the less affluent will require a less asset-oriented approach. Smartphones and other "high-tech wearables" will become the means by which fitness advice and guidance is delivered to those with less expendable income.

- Owners who understand how to deliver transformational experiences that have been built on a foundation of authenticity will be able to create niche business models that are appealing to the most affluent, and thus generate significant profitability by serving a relatively small, but affluent, audience. The recent emergence of boutique fitness studios might represent the beginning of this approach to offering more transformational experiences to those who can afford it.

4. Globalization: The World Is Now One

The 21st century is an era of cultural fusion, one in which physical borders alone no longer allow individuals to be protective of their independent cultures. Technology has shrunk the world and, in many cases, erased many of the cultural borders and protections of the past decades. At the present time, countries and cultures have fused together in a mesh of economic and popular culture. As indicated by the title of Thomas L. Friedman's landmark book, *The World is Flat*, the globe has become significantly more fused, and as a result, most business and cultural phenomena can literally impact the entire world within minutes. A great example of this snowball-like impact of a globally fused business and cultural environment was the economic recession in 2008 that began in the U.S. and eventually touched the entire world, some regions which are still recovering from it 8 years later. This fusion of cultures means that the communities served by health/fitness clubs are no longer represented by a singular audience, but instead consist of multiple audiences—each with its own set of unique preferences and traditions.

According to the *IHRSA 2016 Global Report*, less than 40 percent of all health/fitness club members reside in the U.S. While the U.S. still has the

The communities served by health/fitness clubs are no longer represented by a singular audience, but instead consist of multiple audiences—each with its own set of unique preferences and traditions.

largest number of clubs and members, its domination of the industry is slowly losing out to a global encroachment of outstanding club operators and a global market that is more aware of the value of fitness. The potential business implications for a global health/fitness industry may include:

- Industry best practices will continue to emerge from several markets, such as Asia, Europe, and Latin America. Industry trends will no longer be the sole domain of U.S. clubs, but instead will represent a blend of fused ideas from many nations (for example, the explosion of Zumba or the introduction of electrical muscle stimulation (EMS) training).
- Individual communities served by health/fitness facilities will continue to see a more diverse membership, made up of people who speak different languages and, more importantly, have different values and interests. Clubs will need to expand programming and find niche programs that appeal to various global audiences. Already in parts of the U.S. (California, Texas, and Wisconsin, for example), club operators are finding they have to introduce new programs to satisfy the cultural needs of its contingency.
- Clubs will begin considering niche markets, based on cultural background. As a result, new social communities, or tribes, will be created around physical activity. In turn, a club targeted toward specific ethnic and cultural communities will not be far behind. This may be a domain for boutique operators.
- Fitness professionals will seek opportunities around the globe, thus changing the dynamics of employee recruitment. Global players will be forced to compete for the best talent in the health/fitness club industry.

5. Green: Reconnecting With Nature

The 21st century has evolved into a time of environmental consciousness. Individuals and businesses have become more conscious of the need to protect the world's natural resources. Global warming and dwindling energy sources have created a sense of urgency in the global mindset to think and act in a manner that protects, rather than scavenges, the environment. Automakers are building and selling hybrid vehicles with lower emissions and greater energy efficiency. Developers are creating more "green" buildings—buildings that are constructed with sustainable and renewable products and that are more energy efficient. Suddenly, it is "cool" to think and even act "green." Corporations now speak a mantra of environmental consciousness in the hopes of appealing to the ever-growing consumer audience who wants all things "green." The Millennial generation, the second largest demographic population on the planet, is as green focused as any other generation and, as the largest population on the planet, is pushing the world toward a green future. The potential business implications for going "green" in the health/fitness club industry may include:

- Clubs will need to consider the use of environmentally friendly products for cleaning their facilities, as consumers demand less use of environmentally unfriendly, cleaning products.
- Clubs will need to incorporate sustainable products in their new construction and renovation. Renewable woods, bamboo, cork, recycled glass, solar power, recycled rubber, and reclaimed rain water will become essential

elements in the design and construction of health/fitness clubs. At Ecofit in Brazil, the club harnesses both reclaimed rain water and solar energy to power its club.
- Clubs will need to be seen as supporters of the "green" push in their communities. At Ecofit in Sao Paulo, Brazil, the club provides recycling containers, in which members can deposit paper, glass, metal, and even technology equipment will later be recycled.
- Clubs will need to provide programming that helps their members connect with the environment in a manner that allows them to feel they are one with nature, and just as importantly, doing something to help the environment.
- Clubs will need to move away from equipment that is energy inefficient and move toward equipment that places fewer demands on the environment.

6. Narcissistic Capitalism and Karaoke Innovation

Narcissistic capitalism refers to a highly selfish and self-serving form of capitalism that is all about "me" or in the case of global economics, a small clan of investment bankers, private-equity houses, and private investors. In narcissistic capitalism, making money is both the end and the means. It is also a situation in which ethics take a back seat to integrity. The global economic meltdown of 2008, 2009, and 2010 was, in large part, due to this narcissistic approach to generating wealth in an ethically challenged manner. It would appear that the lessons of the recession have not had much of an influence on this highly evolved form of autocratic-style capitalism.

An excellent example of the aforementioned narcissistic phenomena is the acquisitions of several health/fitness club firms during the middle of the last decade. During the first five to six years of the 21st century, PE firms purchased club companies for large multiples (equivalent to 8 to 12 times EBITDA), and funded the purchases with high levels of debt (i.e., interest-coverage ratios that were less than 1.5). These highly leveraged deals resulted in some businesses declaring bankruptcy, others selling for a loss, many dramatically restructuring their debt and organizational structures, and, in some cases, the purchaser holding on to the investment longer than desired because they could not sell the business for at least the purchase price.

In their book, *Karaoke Capitalism*, authors Jonas Ridderstrale and Kjell A. Nordstrom speak about a business environment in which innovation has given way to replication. Rather than create new business models, business leaders are recycling and putting a new skin on old ideas; just look at the rapid growth of franchise business models. The authors claim that this karaoke mindset is slowly creating a commoditized world, one in which businesses are becoming more like physical commodities than unique business models that focus on the needs of consumers. In the past 5 to 10 years, the health/fitness facility industry has seen an influx of highly leveraged venture capital enter the industry. This influx of highly leveraged capital has resulted in the creation of numerous large and successful club models that essentially all look alike (e.g., LA Fitness, 24 Hour Fitness, Virgin Active, Planet Fitness, Lifetime Fitness, Orange Theory, etc.). The demand for high returns and rapid growth from investors has

> In the past 5 to 10 years, the health/fitness facility industry has seen an influx of highly leveraged venture capital that has resulted in the creation of numerous large and successful club models that essentially all look alike.

helped the industry become more commoditized, rather than more unique. Among the potential business implications for the club industry of this growing commoditization are the following:

- Well-capitalized and well-leveraged club companies will bring about further consolidation of the industry, both domestically and globally. Like Walmart in the retail sector, one of these well-capitalized club companies could further drive the pricing wars in the years to come. In England, Virgin Active was able to purchase two other club operators, as a result of Virgin Active's capitalization and the overleveraged position of the companies that they purchased.
- Overleveraged companies will either be sold at well below initial shareholder value or declare bankruptcy, in order to alleviate much of their debt. An example is the recent sale of 24 Hour Fitness for an EBITDA multiple considerably less than what it was purchased for six years earlier.
- Entrepreneurs will seek out new niche markets by creating unique business models that hold little value to the large commodity players (e.g., boutique fitness studios). Entrepreneurs will perish if they are unable to create unique business models that target markets that are less appealing to the commodity players.
- Fitness professionals will need to become fluent in the culture and language of business. Fitness professionals will need to become as well-versed in business as they are in fitness.
- The industry will need to find a balance between growing the bottom line and creating an environment that provides clients with a transformational and results-oriented experience.

7. Technology: The Antithesis of Activity

Over the past decade, technological advances have evolved so rapidly that the world seems to change as fast as technology innovates. The growth in portable electronic communications (e.g., smart phones, hand-held computers and tablets, satellite-based broadband networks, etc.), the evolution of virtual worlds and social networking sites, and the continued growth in virtual reality games that enable individuals to do more by physically doing less is creating an entirely new business and operational framework for the health/fitness club industry. While technology has given the world many wonderful and helpful tools, it has also created a society that is less inclined to be physically active and interpersonally engaging. As technology continues to evolve at lightning speed, people will have less reason to be active and even less reason to interact with others in a face-to-face environment. The founders of Google have even said they see a time when people never have to leave their house or take a step. As a result, individuals will be able to travel across nations virtually, but may not be able to walk across the street without the help of an AED and wheelchair. Among the potential implications of the technological boom for the health/fitness club industry are the following:

- Clubs may need to create virtual environments to supplement their physical environments (e.g., virtual group classes and personal training). Marketing and even basic programming may begin in the virtual world in an effort to draw interest in the physical world. Facebook, Instagram, Snapchat, Twitter,

and YouTube will be a part of every club's lexicon, and in a few years, operators will ask how they ever operated without them.
- Virtual exercise programming may become as important as in-club personal training is currently. Getting members started through virtual personal training may lead to new clients for in-club personal training and programming. In reality, members can currently leverage great personal training and nutritional tools on their computer or smart phone. In time, virtual exercise programming will evolve into virtual and augmented reality platforms.
- The use of technology to monitor and communicate with members will free up staff to work more directly with those members who need personal attention and instruction. Eye scans and facial recognition for member check-in, fingerprint or chip entry to lockers, web-based and mobile scheduling for programs, cloud-based fitness tracking and real-time communication with members may become essential to the successful club of the future.
- Entertainment, especially for the Millennials, will require the creative use of technology.

Reflections

No one can accurately predict the future, including that of the health/fitness club industry. The real key to success for club owners and operators over the next two decades will come from understanding the demographic and cultural forces driving the world, understanding the rich history of the industry, and creating innovative solutions that build on that understanding. A quote from an unknown author may have summed it up best by saying, "It appears that when we first gaze into our past, we elongate our future." This chapter has attempted to view the recent past through a discussion of current and emerging trends, with the hope that the information presented can be utilized to elongate the future of the health/fitness club industry.

PART TEN   *The Future of the Health/Fitness Facility Industry*

PART 11
Case Studies and Operator Insights From the Health/Fitness Facility Industry

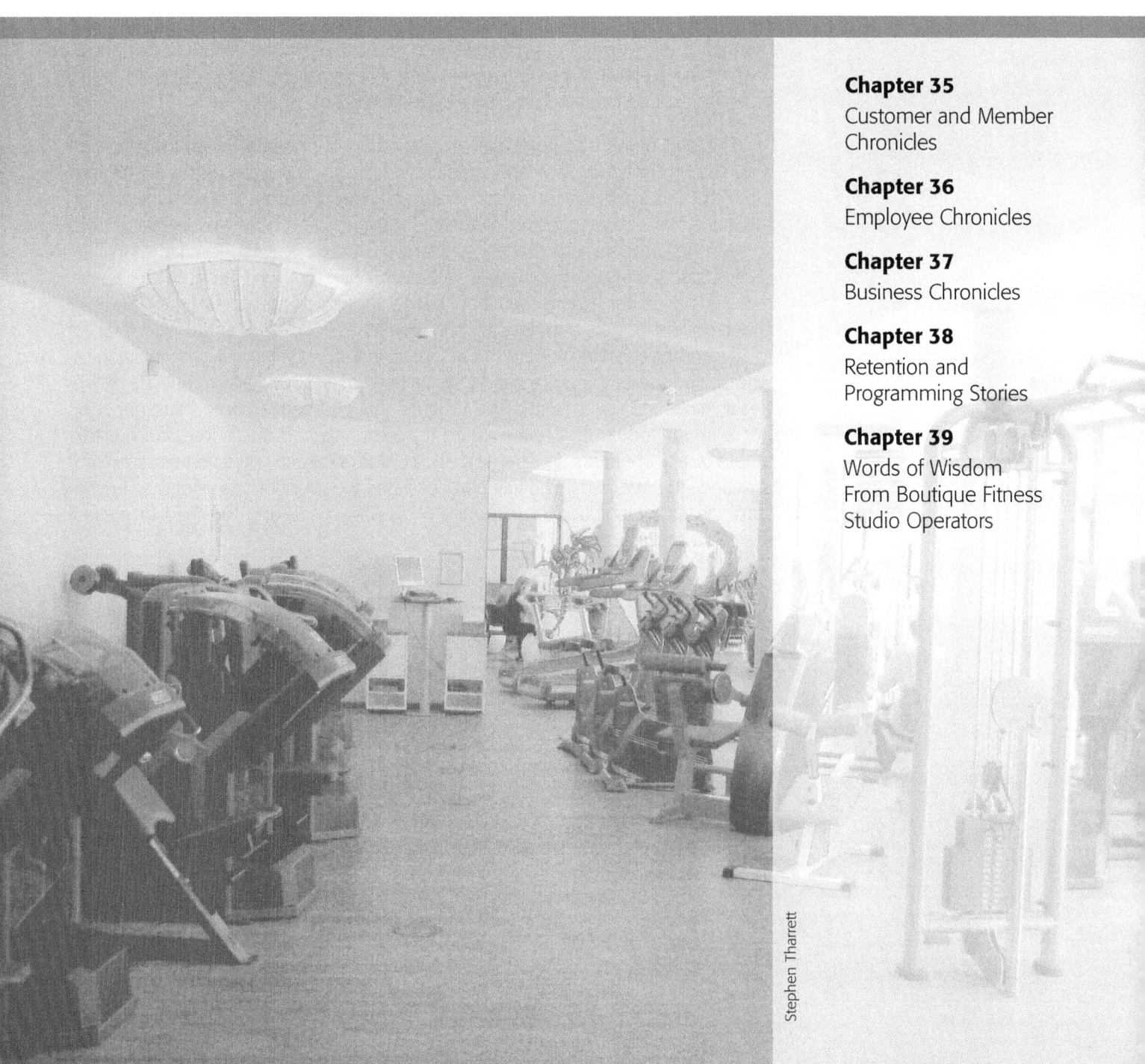

Chapter 35
Customer and Member Chronicles

Chapter 36
Employee Chronicles

Chapter 37
Business Chronicles

Chapter 38
Retention and Programming Stories

Chapter 39
Words of Wisdom From Boutique Fitness Studio Operators

My first manager called it, "baptism by fire." He was referring to the leadership and management scenarios that occur in the health/fitness industry that are not taught in textbooks. Later in my career, I decided that his primary point was that the only way to really learn management and leadership is by dealing with the unique and unexpected situations that often transpire when working with members and employees. Most first-time managers and leaders enter their new roles armed with a rudimentary understanding of the basic principles of financial management, leadership, programming, sales and marketing, member/customer relations, and employee relations. In reality, such basic competencies will only carry a person so far in business. Individuals who want to operate a great club—one that is known for its outstanding member/customer service—must be prepared to lead and manage during challenging and unexpected circumstances. Addressing these events in an appropriate manner is an ever-evolving process that can benefit from continual nurturing. Among the steps that can be undertaken in this regard is to study and learn from the experiences and problem-solving efforts of others.

This part of the book provides a compilation of operator-driven insights and case studies, which provide an incredible wealth of on the job wisdom. The first three chapters in this section recap several of the most demanding and challenging situations that actually occurred in the club business and how seasoned and not-so-seasoned leaders and managers dealt with them. The fourth chapter in this section offers stories by experienced fitness operators who excel in delivering rewarding member experiences that engage and enrich members' lives. The final chapter offers insights from leading boutique fitness operators about what it takes to succeed as an entrepreneur in the fitness industry. Collectively, the individuals who shared their experiences and insights have over 300 years experience in the health/fitness facility industry. The insights and experiences they share are real, not textbook fodder, but real wisdom from experienced and successful health/fitness facility operators. In Chapters 35, 36 and 37, each management scenario is defined in three parts. The first part describes the event or scenario; the second summarizes the solution or response of management; and the third discusses the event and solution.

The primary objective of Part 11 is to provide an opportunity to share the wisdom of those who have entered the trenches of the health/fitness facility industry and come out victorious.

Customer and Member Chronicles

35

*"Customer service is just a day in, day out
ongoing, never ending, unremitting, preserving,
compassionate, type of activity."*

—Leon Gorma, CEO, L.L. Bean

Chapter Objectives

The situations recounted in this chapter focus on events and experiences involving the customers and members of health/fitness clubs. Each of these stories represents a unique situation that required extraordinary leadership and management.

Sun Wars

❑ *Scenario.* In the mid-80s, a high-end club located in the northeast had just completed an extensive renovation. Serving approximately 2,000 memberships with an average household income in excess of $200,000 annually, the club had a fitness center, group-exercise studios, locker rooms, dining area, pool, and sun deck.

The new fitness director had just been hired. One of the first stories he heard from his colleagues concerned the "sun wars" that were occurring on the club's sun deck, which was located eight stories above street level. He was told that over the past few summers, members had hit each other, stolen others' items from the sun deck, and thrown lifeguards in the pool—all in an effort to get one of the 30 lounge chairs that were located on the sun deck. Rather than take these stories at face value, the new fitness director decided to observe the actions of the club's members and staff. Since the sun deck did not officially open until Memorial Day, the fitness director felt that by observing events in the spring, he might be able to gain a better idea of what was really happening. After a couple of sunny weekends, the fitness director observed a litany of troubling events, including one of the facility's lifeguards being hit and thrown into the pool, member's clothes that were hanging on lounge chairs being thrown off the deck, members pulling each other's hair as they pulled each other off lounge chairs, members yelling at each other when they thought it was time for them to have a lounge chair, and verbal and physical threats being made against staff by members.

> Over the past few summers, members had hit each other, stolen others' items from the sun deck, and thrown lifeguards in the pool—all in an effort to get one of the 30 lounge chairs that were located on the sun deck.

❏ *The Solution.* The fitness director met with his senior-level department heads and a few members to try to identify a possible solution that would eliminate the dangerous situation and, hopefully, produce a mutually satisfactory outcome for all involved. After considerable discussion, a solution was proposed that included the following elements:

- A reservation system for lounge chairs was developed that would allow members to reserve a specific chair up to seven days in advance.
- Each lounge chair would be marked with a number and a corresponding reservation card, and a chair-reservation book would be prepared for the summer and kept at the front desk.
- A sun deck map was devised that showed the location of the lounge chairs.
- A $10 charge to reserve a chair for a two-hour time period would be implemented.
- A cancellation and no-show policy would be instituted. If someone failed to cancel their chair reservation at least 24 hours in advance or if they did not show to claim their reservation, they would be charged the full amount for their lounge chair.
- The reservation, which had to be made in person or over the phone, could be made no earlier than seven days in advance.
- A concierge would be provided for the deck and would circulate every couple of hours with the reservation sheet to verify reservations and to pass out complimentary beverages.
- Details about the chair-reservation program would be communicated to the members, approximately two months before it was set to begin. Such efforts would include such steps as sending a personal letter to each member, placing posters up in conspicuous locations in the facility, putting notices in the club's member newsletter, and having the staff speak to the members they know.

When the chair-reservation program was first introduced to the members, the club received considerable feedback from the membership, most of which was not very flattering. And yet, one week before Memorial Day, all of the lounge chairs had been reserved, and a waiting list had been created. Over the course of the first summer, the chairs were 100 percent booked each weekend in two-hour time slots, with a waiting list of at least 10 people each weekend. By the July 4th weekend, the club had introduced food-and-drink service. During the first summer of the program, only one argument ensued. As a result, the club's members and staff did not have to deal with all of the fights and disorder that had previously existed. Another positive by-product of the new policy was the fact that the club generated approximately $1,000 to $1,500 in revenue each weekend.

❏ *Discussion.* The aforementioned scenario is an example of a club not listening to its membership and understanding that a membership need existed that was not being addressed with an appropriate service-delivery process. The members wanted to see and feel the sun, a goal that was not so easily attained in this northeastern market. The members also needed to know that once they had a spot on the sun deck, that someone could not just walk up and take it. In essence, it was a basic supply-and-demand situation that had evolved into a member/customer relations headache for the club and, in the end, had led to a considerable degree of member/customer outrage. The proposed solution worked for the following reasons:

- The staff took the time to talk with members and staff, as well as observe the situation before attempting to identify a solution. Because the club got everyone involved in the situation in its efforts to understand the attendant circumstances, those individuals took ownership of the subsequent solution.
- The solution leveraged the supply-and-demand issue and provided the facility's customers and members with the opportunity to get what they wanted on a relatively exclusive basis.
- Value was created where it did not exist before. By putting a time limit on the use of a chair, setting a price for the service, and requiring reservations, the club had established a value for the sun deck.
- The club communicated its intentions sufficiently in advance so that it could address any concerns that might arise well before the program went into place.
- The club took a dynamic approach to the solution by continually offering new services to the members.

In reality, other possible solutions to the situation existed, including closing the deck, incorporating a reservation system but not charging for it, selling the chairs for the season, etc. Ultimately, the solution that was implemented achieved its desired goal of preventing more fights. It also resulted in an unexpected benefit—additional revenue and cash for the club.

Odor Eaters

- *Scenario.* This situation occurred in the mid-90s and involved a high-end club that was located on the west coast. The club had 2,500 memberships and provided full-service amenities. One of the unique services of this club was that all of the members rented lockers ($25 a month), which included access to such amenities as laundry service and shoeshines. Each individual paid an initiation fee of $1,000 to join this facility and $100 monthly dues to maintain their individual membership.

    The fitness director, who had responsibility for the locker rooms and the fitness areas of the club, was approached by several members complaining about one of the club's most prominent constituents. Their grievance involved the fact that this particular individual had a very distinct aroma about him, both when he exercised and in the locker room. In fact, several of the complaining members stated that they would resign their membership if the offensive odor problem was not resolved. These members made it clear who the offending member was and that they did not want it to be known that they had complained. His pungent aroma made it difficult not only for other people to be on the exercise floor at the same time with him, but also (and possibly worse) to be in the locker room area around his locker.

His pungent aroma made it difficult not only for other people to be on the exercise floor at the same time with him, but also (and possibly worse) to be in the locker room area around his locker.

> The offending individual was an important member who spent a considerable amount of money in the club.

❑ *The Solution.* Understandably, the fitness director was very concerned. He was fully aware of the fact that the offending individual was an important member who spent a considerable amount of money in the club. He also knew that the club could not afford to lose the other members. The effort to identify a possible solution to this problem involved the following steps:

- He talked privately with the members who had complained in an attempt to get a better handle on the issues. He also told them that he would be taking action on their concerns.
- He spoke with his staff to get additional information on the situation. In addition, he checked out the offending member's locker during after-hours.
- He subsequently contacted the offending member by phone and asked if there was a time that they could meet. A meeting was set up in one of the private offices of the club. During the meeting, the fitness director told the individual about the other club members' concerns. The fitness director then asked the individual to express his feelings about the issue. The member was upset and wanted to know who was complaining. The fitness director replied that he understood the member's hurt feelings and that he would like to work with him to resolve the issue.
- The member and fitness director agreed to take several steps, including the club would provide the member with free laundry service for his clothes and provide him with his own soap solution that he could keep in his locker. Furthermore, the club agreed that they would always check to make sure that the member's laundry was done, even if he did not leave it out for laundering.
- The fitness director got in contact with the members who had complained and informed them that he had talked with the member who had the odor problem and that a solution had been reached. He told them that he appreciated their bringing this matter to his attention and asked that they let him know if the proposed solution did not work to their satisfaction.

❑ *Discussion.* This scenario is one that will likely occur at some point in every health/fitness club, especially if the facility provides rental lockers. When a facility has a diverse membership that extensively utilizes the club's services during the hours that it is open, it can expect situations such as this to occur. While no "perfect" solution to this kind of situation and problem exists, the club in this scenario handled the circumstances in a professional manner. The aforementioned solution worked for several reasons, including:

- The manager took the time to gather information about the situation by talking to members and staff and by personally observing what was occurring.
- The manager made sure to let the members who were complaining know that he would address the situation and get back to them.
- The manager set up a private appointment with the offending member. During that meeting, as professionally as he could, he discussed the situation that had been brought to his attention. Furthermore, he asked the member how he felt about the issue and made sure that the member had the opportunity to express his feelings about the situation.

- The manager worked with the offending member to identify a solution that would be appropriate for everyone involved.
- The manager made sure to follow up with those individuals who had complained to thank them and let them know what actions had been taken. He also asked these members to feel free to contact him if the proposed solution did not seem to be working.

It is always difficult to share unfavorable news with members, especially when it is unflattering. Whether it is odor or any other difficult issue, it is important to remember that the privacy and feelings of everyone involved should always be accorded an appropriate degree of attention and respect. When dealing with such a situation, the manager should communicate openly, but with a sense of empathy. Managers who are open-minded, are good listeners, and demonstrate that they can be trusted, will likely elicit favorable responses from the members.

> It is important to remember that the privacy and feelings of everyone involved should always be accorded an appropriate degree of attention and respect.

Naked Man on the Loose

- ❏ *Scenario.* This scenario took place in an urban fitness club that was located along the northeast corridor. Open for just over 10 years, the club served a rather upscale market of business professionals who lived in the area.

  The club had just hired a new operations manager, who was experiencing his first week on the job. At the time, he was going through his initial training with the club's staff. On this particular day, he was training with one of the facility's sales directors. This particular sales director was giving a tour to a couple in their 40s. The operations director was tagging along to learn more about how to conduct a tour of the club.

  As the tour proceeded towards the locker-room areas (the men's and women's locker rooms were located across the hall from each other), a man suddenly ran out of the locker room completely naked and confronted the sales director. The member jumped up and down in front of the salesperson, prospects, and operations manager, shouting that someone was in the locker room rifling through lockers. He demanded that the situation be taken care of immediately, thinking nothing of the fact he was standing naked in front of a group of people—several of whom were complete strangers to him.

- ❏ *The Solution.* Within seconds of the man appearing naked and screaming at the sales director, the following actions took place:
  - The first step that the sales director took was to tell the member that the club's operations manager would be right in to address the situation.
  - The sales director then turned to the prospects and apologized to them for the member's behavior. She attempted to diffuse the awkwardness of the moment by casually mentioning that in this city anything was possible. The sales director affirmed that having a member of the club stroll the hallways in the nude was not a normal part of the sales tour. She added that the operations manager would address the member's issues and invited everyone to proceed with the tour.

- The operations manager immediately escorted the member into the locker room, and then contacted security to let them know that a stranger was in the club who was stealing from member's lockers.
- After making the call to security, the operations manager continued through the locker room and found the culprit. He tried to retain him, but he escaped to the freight elevator.
- Subsequently, security personnel captured the would-be thief as he left the freight elevator and contacted the operations manager to give him an update about the situation.
- The operations manager then met with the member who had originally seen the thief and let him know how the situation had turned out. Furthermore, he informed him that, in the future, it would be more appropriate if he would at least wrap a towel around himself before leaving the confines of the locker room.
- The operations manager then let the sales director know what had occurred so that she could communicate it to the prospects.

❑ *Discussion.* While having a naked member run out in front of everyone when a tour is being conducted is not likely to happen often, it does represent a situation that can be embarrassing for everyone involved. As such, it requires quick thinking on the manager's part. The staff involved in this situation handled it professionally. Their response and solution were effective because of several factors, including:

- The sales director maintained her calm and responded to the member's concerns at once by indicating that immediate action to address the situation would be taken.
- Exhibiting a professional presence, the sales director immediately apologized to the prospects. Her efforts to apologize also included a touch of humor that helped diffuse any tension that was present.
- The operations manager escorted the member back into the locker room and then immediately contacted security.
- The operations manager, after contacting security, searched for the thief and attempted to retain him until security personnel arrived.
- After the thief was apprehended, the operations manager contacted the sales director and gave her an update on the actions that had been taken. He also made sure to inform the member who had originally brought the matter to the club's attention.

Paying attention (listening), apologizing, taking action, and finally, following up are all critical steps in dealing with any member or customer issue that arises in the club. Furthermore, by maintaining a calm, professional presence, the team was able to put the member and prospects at greater ease.

Peace and Harmony During the Holiday Season

- *Scenario.* This scenario occurred in a small suburban fitness club in the southwest. The club was a fitness-only facility that served a corporate market. The club had been in business for several years at the time of the event.

    It was the holiday season, and the club was brightly decorated. The club, as was its usual practice each holiday season, was filled with the sounds of joyful holiday music. While most of the club's members enjoyed the holiday music, one particular member felt that it was inappropriate music to listen to while working out. All of a sudden, one member of the club started arguing with another member over the music that was being played. The manager noticed that these two individuals were arguing over the music and asked them to separate. The two members then retreated to the men's locker room. Subsequently, the manager heard from yet a third member of the club that the two men were now in a fistfight.

- *The Solution.* The manager immediately got hold of one of the male personal trainers and had him go into the locker room. The personal trainer separated the men and broke up the fight. The manager told the trainer to communicate to both of the individuals that the manager would like to meet with them. Subsequently, one of the combatants met with the manager, who explained to him that his behavior was completely unacceptable. Indignant, the member offered a series of excuses. Eventually, he was asked to leave the club by the manager and did. The other member was so angered that he just left the club without talking to the manager. Later on, the manager met with him the next time he was in the club.

- *Discussion.* In reality, disputes over music are not that rare. It is relatively amazing how something as simple as the choice of music can cause grown men to get into a fistfight. In this particular scenario, the manager handled the situation very well by taking the following steps:

- Terminating the argument on the exercise floor, and when it continued in another area of the club, having a personal trainer of the same gender enter the locker room and break it up.
- Talking with both of the combatants to let them know that their behavior was unacceptable.
- Requesting that the one recalcitrant member immediately leave the club.

    In almost every situation when a fight breaks out between members, the manager's best course of action is to break it up, ask the members to leave the facility, and schedule time to talk with each of the members at a later date about their behavior. In some instances, suspending a member from the club might be necessary.

> It is relatively amazing how something as simple as the choice of music can cause grown men to get into a fistfight.

With regard to music selection—a factor that causes problems more frequently than most would like to believe—clubs should establish a music policy that is made known to the members. By having a clearly communicated music policy, members are aware of what they can expect and are less likely to behave in an antisocial manner.

Beware of the Nose

❑ *Scenario.* This scenario took place in a fitness club that was located in an urban market in the deep-south. The facility served a reasonably high-end corporate membership. At the time of the incident, the club had been in business for over 20 years.

The situation involved a member of the club who ran on a treadmill a few times each week. Several of the club's members and employees complained about the member's behavior while he was using the treadmill. Their complaint involved the fact that every time the member ran on the treadmill, he would perform a "farmer's blow" (i.e., blowing his nose into his hands) and then would touch the treadmill. The fitness director was informed by both the staff and several members that they found the exerciser's disgusting behavior repulsive, to a point where no one wanted to work out in the same area of the club when this member was on the treadmill.

❑ *The Solution.* The fitness director decided to contact the member in question by letter. He felt that if he initially met with the member in person, he might embarrass that individual if the conversation was overheard by others. He sent the letter to the member's home. The letter detailed the member's unacceptable conduct and emphasized how important it was to keep the club clean and hygienic for all of the members. The letter indicated that his actions were insulting to other members and impacted the club's overall cleanliness. The member responded to the letter by contacting the fitness director personally and thanking him for sharing what he did and doing so in a confidential manner. Going forward, the member did not exhibit the offensive behavior any more.

❑ *Discussion.* It is not uncommon for some members to be disrespectful of the club and other members when it comes to hygiene. In this particular scenario, the fitness director handled the circumstances appropriately. As a result, the behavior came to a halt. Among the steps that enabled this situation to be dealt with successfully were:

- The fitness director contacted the member confidentially, thus helping to limit any possible embarrassment.
- The fitness director focused his efforts on addressing the offending behavior, not the member. He ensured that the member knew that his behavior was causing a problem for other members of the club. In essence, he "de-personalized" the issue.

> When an individual does something that results in unhygienic conditions and impacts the ability of other members to enjoy the club, it is the responsibility of management to address the issue with that member.

When an individual does something that results in unhygienic conditions and impacts the ability of other members to enjoy the club, it is the responsibility of management to address the issue with that member. To the extent possible, this effort should always be kept private to help prevent any embarrassment for the member. Furthermore, the endeavor should focus on the behavior of the offending individual and its impact on other members and staff, rather than making it a personal issue.

Clubs can help head off situations similar to these by having house rules that clarify how members should respect the club, other members, and employees and what behaviors are unacceptable. These rules can be very simple and shared with each individual through a member's handbook, a notice on the website, or other appropriate forms of media (e.g., signage, mailings, etc.).

To the Rescue

- ❑ *Scenario*. This scenario occurred in the mid-Atlantic region of the U.S. in a facility that was a well-operated multipurpose club serving a family market. In this particular set of circumstances, club management had become aware of a young woman who they believed had an eating and exercise disorder. Management had noticed that this individual, who was in the club almost every day, had become ever-increasingly emaciated over the last several weeks. Management believed that it had an obligation to become involved in the situation, but was not sure how to do so without overstepping its expertise or abusing the privacy and feelings of the member involved.

- ❑ *The Solution*. After considerable discussion among the senior leaders of the club, an intervention was identified that everyone agreed upon. As such, management decided to take the following actions:

  - They identified the club's resident registered nurse as the most appropriate staff person to open a dialogue with the young woman.
  - Management asked the nurse to open a dialogue with the young woman and request that she obtain a medical clearance from her physician before continuing with her use of the club.
  - Management decided that because they were asking the young woman to seek medical clearance, the club had to be prepared to provide emotional and financial assistance if it was determined to be warranted.
  - The nurse set up a private meeting with the member involved in the situation and informed her that the club would require her to obtain medical clearance before she would be allowed to continue using the club's facilities. At first, the young woman was defensive, but then became offended by the club's request.
  - After informing the young woman of the club's position, the nurse told her that the club was willing to lend her assistance, both financially and emotionally. Upon hearing this, the young woman's attitude changed dramatically, and she expressed her thanks. Subsequently, the young

> The nurse set up a private meeting with the member involved in the situation and informed her that the club would require her to obtain medical clearance before she would be allowed to continue using the club's facilities.

woman indicated that she was aware that she had a problem and had been struggling to identify a clinic or program that could meet her needs (note: her parents had previously washed their hands of the situation).

- Upon hearing the young woman's comments, the staff nurse researched the clinical options until she found a facility that seemed to offer what the young woman needed. Once the clinic was identified, the nurse and staff worked with the young woman to help her get accepted into the clinic's eating disorder program. Subsequently, after the young woman had been admitted to the program, she reported that she had a fear of travel since losing one of her favorite travel companions a few years earlier (e.g., a stuffed animal).
- The nurse proceeded to purchase a special travel companion for the young woman, which she presented to her prior to her departure to the clinic for the first time.
- The young woman made a commitment to the club to successfully complete her treatment program and to come back healthy.

❑ *Discussion.* This set of circumstances is one of the most challenging situations that management can face. The dilemma facing management involved several interrelated factors: the privacy of a member, the medical diagnosis (which is not the club's role), the endangerment of the member's health, and the self-esteem of the member. By any reasonable standard, determining an appropriate solution to this particular situation could have been very difficult. In this situation, however, management took several steps that led to a successful resolution of the problem, including:

- The staff met as a team and identified the steps that would be taken. Subsequently, the measures were perceived as a team solution, which is the best basis for attempting to resolve any situation.
- The staff person most qualified to deal with this particular issue (e.g., a registered nurse) was identified.
- The nurse spoke privately with the young woman and asked her to obtain medical clearance.
- The club expressed its willingness to provide assistance—both financially and emotionally—to the young woman.
- The club followed through on its commitment.

Collectively, the net effect of management's actions was a young woman who opened up about her problems and was able to make a commitment to pursue much-needed therapy.

Several points should be emphasized to anyone in a leadership position in a club who may be confronted by a situation like this in the future. First, clubs are not (and should not be) in the business of making medical diagnoses and must not assume that a member has a particular health problem unless the individual informs them or provides them with a note from a physician that informs them of that fact. Second, a club is obligated to seek medical clearance from any member or prospective member who has known risk factors that would increase that person's likelihood of experiencing a health or medical problem as a result of exercising. The key for a club, in this regard, is to make sure that it is consistent in how it applies the use of medical clearance to all of its members. Third, all factors considered, the facility should seek advice from its legal council before proceeding in situations like this. Fourth, when the club initiates dialogue with the member, it is best if it involves someone who already has a positive, trusting relationship with the member. Finally, the club should be prepared for the likely responses in such circumstances (e.g., denial of any problem, an expression of anger and hurt, and a refusal to obtain medial clearance).

I had two experiences with a member whom we believed had anorexia. In both instances, steps similar to the ones undertaken by the club in this scenario were initiated, with the exception that we talked with our attorney, and we had a physician (rather than a registered nurse) from our medical-advisory committee talk with the member. In both cases, the member was hurt and angered, and we ended up having to remove their membership.

The solution developed and successfully implemented by the club in this scenario is an excellent example of a management team that, through empathy and a commitment to its members, was able to turn a potentially perilous situation into a life-changing one for the member involved.

Cell-Phone Enforcer

❑ *Scenario.* This scenario took place in a mid-western multipurpose club that served a relatively affluent membership base of approximately 4,000 individuals. This particular club had a policy that disallowed camera phones in the locker rooms. One member of this facility was convinced that any individual using a cell phone in the locker room was actually taking pictures of him. Over a period of time, this particular member had become obsessed about cell-phone usage in the locker room and had decided to take it upon himself to be the club's enforcer with regard to camera phones and cell phones. The club's policy concerning this issue was clear. If a member notices that a camera phone is in use in the locker room, that person should contact management and allow staff to deal with the situation. Disregarding the club's policy, this member had begun accosting other members and verbally abusing any individual he saw with a cell phone in the locker room. When this member was approached by the manager on duty about his behavior, the abusive member verbally assaulted him.

❑ *The Solution.* The club management took the following steps to resolve the situation to the satisfaction of everyone involved:

- The operations manager contacted the member by phone to rationally discuss the concerns of other members and of club management in an attempt to reach a reasonable solution to the problem. The member responded by saying that the club should ban all cell phones from the club and that furthermore, he would physically accost any individuals whom he found with a cell phone.
- The executive director of the club then contacted the member and explained to him that his behavior was unacceptable. The executive director also informed the member that the club could not ban all cell phones

Most clubs have instituted policies that ban the use of camera phones in their facilities.

(even if it wanted to), because several of the members were physicians who might need to be reached. On the other hand, he indicated to the member that the club's policy did ban the use of camera phones and that if he noticed another member with one, he should please contact a member of the staff, and management would address the situation.

- Finally, the executive director informed the member that if he continued his verbal attacks on members that he would face expulsion from the club and possible criminal action.

❑ *Discussion.* Cell phones (camera phones in particular) have become a big issue in the club industry. Most clubs have instituted policies that ban the use of camera phones in their facilities. This particular situation arose possibly out of a member's safety concerns and his inability to clearly understand the club's policies. The member's subsequent actions were totally inexcusable and caused serious problems with the other members. The response of management in this situation was effective because of several reasons, including:

- The club had a senior manager talk directly with the member in a manner that did not embarrass him.
- When the member did not respond appropriately to the club's initial efforts to resolve the situation, a senior-level manager spoke with him in a private setting.
- That manager reinforced the club's policies concerning the use of both cell and camera phones and detailed the member's options involving situations that warranted attention. The senior-level manager also communicated his displeasure with the member's actions and informed him that if he continued, that the club would consider banishing him from the club.

When dealing with situations similar to this one, the club should do the following:

- Develop house rules and policies that address such issues and take steps to ensure that each member is aware of these rules and policies. Not only should these policies address the use of cell phones, they should also deal with other issues that are important to maintaining the club's atmosphere and sense of privacy. These rules should also detail guidelines concerning what actions management can take in the event that the policies are violated. For example, the club should have a policy that states that management maintains the right to expel any member of the facility if that individual blatantly ignores the policies and rules of the club.
- Consider having the most noteworthy policies, such as camera-phone rules, posted in the locker rooms and even inside the lockers. Ensuring that the members are fully aware of all key policies and rules of the club is important.
- Establish a hierarchy of management for responding to these types of situations.
- Ensure that all conversations with members concerning the possible violation of the club's rules and policies are conducted in private.
- Document the member's activities and the resulting actions of management concerning those activities and place the report in the member's file.

> **The club should have a policy that states that management maintains the right to expel any member of the facility if that individual blatantly ignores the policies and rules of the club.**

While prohibiting camera phones in the locker room is a good rule, this policy should apply throughout the club. Prohibiting the use of these phones in only one area of the facility can cause problems. All factors considered, it is better to preclude their use anywhere in the club. It should be emphasized that it is always advisable for a club to get its legal council's advice before establishing any policy concerning the use of camera phones in the facility.

Reflections

Delivering extraordinary experiences for members and guests involves a host of competencies that include empathy, emotional intelligence, tact, outstanding communication, and humility. In most instances, members and guests appreciate and value what you offer. Unfortunately, there are instances, where no matter what you do, you fail to meet the expectations of members. In some of these instances, members may feel you intentionally failed them, or in other situations, they believe they desire to be treated differently than everyone else, and not in a good way. This chapter was intended to provide examples of some unexpected and difficult situations that club operators have faced, and in doing so offer up insights on how these and other unexpected and uncomfortable situations can be successfully handled by club leaders.

> Delivering extraordinary experiences for members and guests involves a host of competencies that include empathy, emotional intelligence, tact, outstanding communication, and humility.

36 Employee Chronicles

"The way your employees feel is the way your customers will feel, and if your employees don't feel valued, neither will your customers."

—Sybil F. Stershic,
*Taking Care of the People Who Matter the Most:
A Guide to Employee-Customer Care*

Chapter Objectives

The scenarios related in this chapter involve situations that entail employee experiences in health/fitness clubs. Resolving them required both insight and thoughtful managerial acumen.

Health Hearsay

❑ *Scenario.* This scenario took place in a large upscale club during the mid to late 1980s, which was located in an affluent residential neighborhood on the east coast. At the time, the club had approximately 3,000 memberships, for which it charged approximately $120 a month for dues for a single membership. The club offered approximately 150 to 200 personal training sessions a week at an average cost of $40 each. These workouts were supervised by a group of eight personal trainers, two of whom conducted about 35 to 40 sessions each week.

One of the most popular trainers was a gentleman who had been in the personal training business for a considerable time period and had a reputation as being one of the best in his field. Subsequently, several female members approached the fitness director with their concerns about the trainer. They indicated that they thought the trainer had AIDS (because of a quite noticeable skin condition) and that he should not be allowed in the club. Within days, over 40 members had come to the fitness director and indicated that they had heard this particular employee had AIDS and asked what the club was going to do about it. Eventually, a number of the club's employees went to the fitness director and reported that they believed that this personal trainer had AIDS and should be dismissed from the club. In only a few short days, over 100 complaints about this individual had been received, all based on a similar rumor.

❑ *The Solution.* The fitness director decided to investigate the situation. His first step was to speak with the other employees and members, each in private.

Chapter Thirty-Six

During his talks with these individuals, he informed them that he wanted to initially determine whether a problem existed. If and when he discovered an issue that needed attention, he would address it as appropriately as possible. Subsequently, he took the following steps:

- He met with the manager of the facility to share with him what was occurring and asking for his guidance. The manager replied that he would talk with the club's legal counsel.
- The fitness director then had a private meeting with the personal trainer in question and informed him that some of the club's employees and members had expressed their concern that he might have a contagious virus. Although he was slightly offended, he assured the fitness director that he was fine and that he had a minor illness that was being treated, which posed no problem to others.
- The fitness director, taking the trainer at his word, went back to the manager and detailed their conversation. In addition, the fitness director met privately with the members and staff who had expressed their concern and told them that he had met with the personal trainer, that they had discussed the person's health, and that the rumor was false.
- Subsequently, the manager informed the fitness director that he wanted the trainer to see a physician and be screened for AIDS. The fitness director replied that although he personally felt that such a request was inappropriate, he would reluctantly ask the trainer to do as the manager wanted and get a note saying that he was healthy and not contagious. The manager then announced that the fitness director had no choice; either get the individual screened for AIDS or else.
- Consequently, the fitness director met privately with the physical trainer and told him that the club was willing to pay for him to visit a local physician, undergo a physical, and get a clearance note. Furthermore, he informed the trainer that this step would put the concerns of the members and management to rest. No mention was made of AIDS testing. The personal trainer consented and a physician's appointment was made for him.
- On the day of the appointment, the trainer was accompanied to the doctor's office by his direct supervisor at the club. When the trainer got to the physician's office, he received a physical, but was then asked to sign a sheet regarding undergoing a blood test for AIDS, a request that angered him a lot. He took the blood test, but immediately returned to the club.
- The fitness director then met with the personal trainer and his supervisor and discussed the events that had occurred. The fitness director apologized to the trainer for not telling him about the AIDS test beforehand. In reality, he said that he was very uncomfortable about the situation and wanted to avoid that issue if he could, but felt that there was no other way for him to handle it.
- After considerable discussion, the personal trainer and fitness director came to a mutually agreed upon resolution. The trainer would not come to work for a few days, so he could gather himself. Subsequently, however, the trainer would return for full duty.

> The fitness director had a private meeting with the personal trainer in question and informed him that some of the club's employees and members had expressed their concern that he might have a contagious virus.

- The blood tests indicated no evidence of AIDS, but did show a treatable virus that was affecting his skin. Medicine was provided to him, and his virus was successfully treated.
- The fitness director met with both the members and the employees who had lodged a complaint about the trainer's perceived medical condition. He informed them that the issue had been addressed and that the rumors were blatantly untrue.

❑ *Discussion.* This situation involved a very challenging employee issue that required total privacy. Unfortunately, the situation was not handled as well as it should have been. As a result, the trust of an employee was lost, and the integrity of a leader was negatively impacted. While eventually the matter was addressed to the satisfaction of those who were concerned with the medical condition of the personal trainer, it was not handled in an appropriate manner from the employee's perspective. In fact, the staff's actions could have exposed the club and fitness director to a lawsuit. Several key observations could be made regarding the situation and how it was handled, including:

- The fitness director responded appropriately at first by talking with his manager and collecting information from the concerned members and staff.
- The fitness director also acted in a responsible manner by speaking with the personal trainer in question and soliciting feedback from him.
- On the other hand, the fitness director should never have sent the employee to see a physician under false pretenses, no matter how much pressure was applied by senior management. Because his integrity and character were at stake, the fitness director should have taken a firmer position with senior management.
- Failing that, the fitness director should have been up-front (honest) with the trainer and should have asked him to please bring in a note from his physician that confirmed that he was not contagious. The fitness director should not have recommended a physician, unless asked to do so by the trainer. The choice of which physician to utilize should have been left to the trainer.
- Much earlier in the sequence of events, the fitness director should have informed the members that he had addressed the situation with the personal trainer and that it had been safely resolved. Furthermore, the matter (including the members' concerns, complaints, and accusations) should have been dropped at that point.

It cannot be overemphasized how important it is for managers to respect their employees and be truthful with them at all times, no matter how challenging or difficult the situation. Furthermore, managers must always respect the privacy of both employees and members and never do anything that might compromise their privacy. In addition, managers should address issues truthfully. Parsing the facts or their words is never the right approach for dealing with any situation. Managers should also remember that making the right decision is the proper course of action, even when doing so might cause them to lose their job. Finally, when dealing with members, managers

> Managers should remember that making the right decision is the proper course of action, even when doing so might cause them to lose their job.

should inform them that they have addressed the issue in a manner that they feel is appropriate. If the members don't feel comfortable with that, it is their problem. Managers should let the members deal with it, rather then try to go too far in appeasing them. A fine line always exists that managers should not cross when attempting to address issues that arise between members and employees.

A Lover's Quarrel

- *Scenario.* This scenario occurred in an urban racquet club that was located along the northeast corridor during the early part of the 1990s. Serving an upscale membership base, this facility provided fitness and racquet-sport services for its members.

    The situation involved a female assistant general manager with four years experience who was on duty at the time of the incident. This employee started her career at the front desk and, through hard work and stellar performance, had been promoted to her current position. Also on duty during the same shift was the front-desk concierge, who had been with the club for six months and had been, to that point, an exemplary employee. As happens with matters of the heart, both employees had recently begun seeing each other on a personal level.

    About 5:00 p.m. that day, during the club's prime time, the front desk was very busy. The desk was manned by the assistant general manager, the front-desk concierge, and two other staff personnel. In addition, at least 10 members were checking in at the desk at the time. All of a sudden, without any warning, the assistant general manager and the front-desk concierge began screaming at each other, a situation which quickly escalated into a full-scale battle. Subsequently, the front-desk concierge slapped the assistant general manager, who then punched the front-desk concierge in the head. The fight continued to escalate, with swearing, hissing, and the further threat of physical violence.

- *The Solution.* The manager and owner of the club almost immediately became aware of the situation and responded as follows:
  - The manager immediately separated the two employees and brought them into his office. He then scheduled meetings with each of them for the next day and sent both home for the rest of the day.
  - The manager first met with the assistant general manager and informed her of his dissatisfaction with the behavior that had occurred the prior evening and reiterated with her the type of behavior that was expected. He then suspended her for two weeks without pay.
  - The manager next met with the front-desk employee and conveyed his displeasure with the actions that had occurred the prior evening and shared with that individual the type of behavior that was expected of all club employees. The manager then told the front-desk employee what action had been taken against the assistant manager. The front desk employee got angry, indicated that this was not the end of the situation, and then proceeded to quit.

> All of a sudden, without any warning, the assistant general manager and the front-desk concierge began screaming at each other, a situation which quickly escalated into a full-scale battle.

❏ *Discussion.* Situations such as this one can happen in any business, including the club industry. When employees work together for extended periods of time, the possibility of romantic relationships occurring will increase. While most clubs have policies against employees having relationships with each other, it is still difficult, if not almost impossible, to prevent personal relationships from transpiring. In this particular set of circumstances, the manager handled the situation well by doing the following:

- Immediately separating the two employees and getting them into his office. The manager also did the right thing in sending both employees home separately, but only after scheduling meetings with each of them for the next day. It is important that after such an emotional event, both parties involved be given a cool-down period before meeting with each of them privately.
- Holding private meetings or counseling sessions with each employee was an appropriate next step. In the case of the assistant general manager, the two-week suspension provided a clear message as to the serious nature of the violation. On the other hand, it let the employee know that the manager valued her (she could have also been fired). The other employee quit before further disciplinary action could be taken.

To prevent instances such as this one from occurring, clubs should establish policies and practices that clearly communicate the expectations of the facility with regard to personal relationships between employees. Once instituted, those policies and practices should be enforced on a consistent basis. When it involves personal relationships between supervisors and employees, those policies and practices must be particularly explicit and straightforward. It is never a good idea for supervisors to have a romantic relationship with an employee who reports to them. If and when management becomes aware of a personal relationship between employees, especially those between a supervisor and employee, they should reiterate and reinforce the club's policy concerning such associations with each participant in the relationship. In most instances, when a relationship between a supervisor and an employee happens and management counsels these individuals, one of the following actions should occur:

- The supervisor and subordinate must agree not to see each other anymore.
- One of the two employees should be asked to leave; in most cases it will be the employee with less tenure and perceived value to the club.

By undertaking the necessary steps, a situation such as the one detailed in this scenario can be prevented. However, in the event it does, the actions taken by this manager provide an excellent template to follow.

Anyone Up for a Dip?

❏ *Scenario.* This scenario took place in a high-end club that was located in the southwest part of the country. The club offered a variety of sports and recreation-related programs. One of the club's most valued features was its outdoor swimming pool. During the outdoor season, the outdoor pool had a staff of six lifeguards, all between the ages of 18 and 20, and one head lifeguard, who was female. The manager of this operation had had great

Chapter Thirty-Six — Employee Chronicles

success with this team for the entire outdoor season. The pool closed each evening around 9:00 p.m.

Near the end of the outdoor season, the manager was returning from a dinner meeting with one of the members, at approximately 10:30 p.m. The manager was walking to his car in the lot when he heard some strange noises coming from the pool. Since the pool supposedly closed over an hour earlier, the manager decided to take a look. As he approached the pool, he heard laughing and loud noises, including some emanating from the club's head lifeguard. When he got up to the edge of the pool, his head lifeguard had swum up to the edge to greet him. There was a moment of silence, until the manager explained to her that everyone must get out of the pool. The head lifeguard did not move. Puzzled, the manager again asked the lifeguards to get out of the pool. All the lifeguards, with the exception of the head lifeguard, proceeded to get out at the other end of the pool. It was then that the manager noticed that his entire staff had been "skinny dipping." Dismayed, he turned away so the head lifeguard could leave the pool.

- *Solution.* Once the pool had emptied and the lifeguards had gotten dressed, the manager had them depart, but only after scheduling meetings with each of them for the next day. He then proceeded to clean up and close the pool area.

  The next day, he met with each of the lifeguards. He explained to them how disappointed he was with them and how inappropriate their behavior was. Because the club still had to serve the members, the option of dismissing the entire staff was not one that could be taken. Instead, after meeting with each individual, he wrote each one up for behavior unbecoming of staff. In addition, he spent extra time in counseling the head lifeguard. Finally, he spent the remainder of the outdoor pool season working evenings to make sure no further problems occurred.

- *Discussion.* It is not uncommon when dealing with a young staff (a common circumstance in the fitness industry), especially when the supervisors are young themselves, for foolish and inappropriate behavior to occur. In this situation, the staff demonstrated a lack of maturity, disregard for leadership, and disrespect to the membership. The manager dealt with the situation in a professional and satisfactory manner by performing the following steps:

- Clearing the pool upon noticing what was occurring
- Respecting the employees by not making a spectacle of them at that time
- Scheduling time to meet the next day with each individual and counseling them on their behavior
- Providing the employees with written warnings concerning their behavior that would go on their employee records
- Monitoring the actions of the staff after the event to ensure that such behavior did not occur in the future

  Had a need not existed to have the lifeguards on duty for the remainder of the outdoor pool season, the manager indicated that he would most likely

> Had a need not existed to have the lifeguards on duty for the remainder of the outdoor pool season, the manager indicated that he would most likely have dismissed all of the employees.

have dismissed all of the employees. From a professional perspective, it would have been wise to suspend the head lifeguard immediately. This step would have sent a relatively strong message to the other lifeguards. While it would have undoubtedly subjected the manager to a heavier workload, the end result of suspending the head lifeguard would have sent the message that the other lifeguards needed to hear.

As individuals in a position of leadership, managers sometimes need to make a strong statement about values, respect, and trust. Suspending or dismissing a supervisor who has demonstrated behavior that is totally inappropriate can be a necessary step in order to maintain long-term stability and respect among the rest of the team.

> Suspending or dismissing a supervisor who has demonstrated behavior that is totally inappropriate can be a necessary step in order to maintain long-term stability and respect among the rest of the team.

A Little Affair

❑ *Scenario.* This scenario took place in a suburban club that was located in the southwest. Designed to serve an affluent family market, the club provided a host of networking and social activities for the members. The facility's membership roster was small, and most of the members knew each other.

Late in the evening one day, the club was nearing the end of another successful member social event. Many of the members and employees in attendance decided to continue the party at a local pub. The manager decided to attend the after-hours event to make sure that nothing inappropriate occurred. The manager noticed that a senior member of the staff was receiving some flirtatious looks from one of the club's female members. The manager thought about the situation for a moment, but figured this employee was a top supervisor and the member was a married woman with children. He felt that he could go home and nothing would happen.

The manager arrived home around midnight and was immediately told by his wife that the security company had called and that an alarm had gone off at the club. The manager immediately returned to the club. When he arrived, he noticed two cars in the lot, one of which was the supervisor's car. The manager then went into the club and kept calling out to see if anyone was there. Hearing no response, he searched the entire club and found nothing. Just before departing, he decided to go to his office. Upon opening the door, he found his employee and the member in a very compromising position, both with blank stares on their face.

❑ *The Solution.* Once the manager had entered the room, the member pleaded with him not to tell anyone. The manager asked the member to leave and told her that he would meet with her the next day. The manager then had the employee get dressed, after which he read the employee the riot act. He told the employee he would meet with him the next morning.

The manager met with the member first. The member told her side of the story and pleaded for confidentiality. She promised not to place the club or the manager in that situation again. She did not want this to get out and end her marriage. The manager decided that it was in the best interest of everyone involved to keep this situation under wraps. The manager then met with the employee and explained to him that this event was to remain confidential and that he would not be dismissed because it would bring unwanted attention to the situation. On the other hand, the manager did share with him that if word did leak out, he would be immediately terminated. The manager took the time to explain the member's request for confidentiality to the employee. The employee apologized to the member and the manager.

While the manager indicated that he was not sure he did the right thing, he did feel, at the time, that it was important to protect the member. As a result, he did not punish the employee to the degree he might otherwise have.

- ❏ Discussion. As hard as it may be for some individuals to believe, employees and members occasionally enter into inappropriate relationships. When employees work closely with members and begin seeing each other in a social context, situations such as this scenario can arise. In this particular instance, the employee and the member both showed poor judgment—not just by having an affair, but consummating it on club property. The manager, in this instance, handled the situation as best he felt he could, given the fact that he faced a dual dilemma of having to discipline an employee and maintain the privacy of the member, both of which were critical factors. The manager's response dealt satisfactorily with the situation, particularly from the member's perspective, because he undertook the following steps:
- Once he came upon the employee and member together, he separated them and sent the member home.
- He immediately talked with the offending employee to make sure that he knew the gravity of the situation.
- He met privately with the member and kept the situation in total confidence. He maintained the level of trust that is essential in a situation of this magnitude.
- He met privately the next day with the employee and recounted the details of the meeting with the member. He further counseled the employee and gave him a warning that any leak of the information involving the situation would result in his immediate termination.

While the situation seemed to end reasonably well, the manager should have written the employee up and suspended him. While cause certainly existed to dismiss the employee, which would have been a perfectly appropriate response, a suspension would have worked just as well. With regard to the member, he could have suspended her from the club and asked her not to return. Since this member was married and had a family, the manager decided to focus his efforts to resolve the situation on the member's circumstances, rather than doing something that might cause further damage to her. Considering the social nature of the club and the family situation, this was a good decision. Had the member been single, the more appropriate option might have been to suspend her from the club.

Since this member was married and had a family, the manager decided to focus his efforts to resolve the situation on the member's circumstances, rather than doing something that might cause further damage to her.

Club managers should be aware of the fact that member-and-employee relationships can and will occur. Accordingly, it is important for clubs to have policies in place that make it clear that such behavior is unacceptable and inappropriate for employees. A club should also have house rules that address this type of situation from a member's perspective as well. Such policies should be reinforced regularly. If and when these policies are violated, the proper discipline should be administered.

Reflections

As the case studies in this chapter reflect, leading an employee team can frequently present unexpected challenges for which there is no clearly defined solution. Leadership is most often associated with fostering an inspiring business culture, building trust among a team of individuals, and coaching and mentoring that gets everyone to strive toward achieving the same goals. But what makes for a truly great leader is someone who can deal with the numerous and often complex human issues that arise when members of a team work together. Hopefully, this chapter provides aspiring leaders with insight in how to address some of these unexpected challenges.

> What makes for a truly great leader is someone who can deal with the numerous and often complex human issues that arise when members of a team work together.

Business Chronicles

37

"Even a mistake may turn out to be the one thing necessary to a worthwhile achievement."

—Henry Ford

Chapter Objectives

The situations detailed in this chapter encompass stories involving business-related circumstances. Resolving them required sound leadership and managerial skills.

Closing a Club and Gaining Fans

❑ *Scenario.* This scenario took place in a large multipurpose club that was located in the south. Approaching its 10th anniversary, the facility was recognized as the number one adult club in the marketplace and served a membership base of over 2,000 individuals. The building in which the club was located had been sold to new owners in the past year. The new owner had a reputation for demanding premium leases.

The club, which was part of a chain, had not funded all of the necessary capital improvements that it needed over the past several years. As a result, during its 10th anniversary year, the indoor pool experienced problems, causing it to empty into the tenant's space below it. In order to get the pool up and running, the club manager and regional manager sought a capital infusion of a couple of hundred thousand dollars to repair the pool. Concurrently, the new building owner was seeking to ignore the club's request for a lease extension and increase the club's base rent by 200 percent.

The manager and regional manager went before senior management asking for capital to repair the pool and for help with negotiating with the new landlord. While the club had contributed significant cash flow to the company in the past, the prospect of investing a couple of hundred thousand dollars and having the cost of the lease at least double caused senior management to make the difficult decision to close the club. Senior management informed the regional manager and manager that they had decided to close the club. Unable to change the minds of senior management, the regional manager and manager received permission to have a 90-day window in which to close the facility.

> The prospect of investing a couple of hundred thousand dollars and having the cost of the lease at least double caused senior management to make the difficult decision to close the club.

> Once the decision to close the club had been communicated to the regional manager and club manager, they went into action.

- ❏ *The Solution.* Once the decision to close the club had been communicated to the regional manager and club manager, they went into action. Among the steps that they took to address the club's closing were the following:
  - The regional manager and manager initially decided that the best course of action was to develop a strategy for closing the club that they would review with the senior staff before settling on a final plan.
  - The regional manager and manager met with the senior staff in a private setting and informed them that senior management had decided that the best course of action for the club was to close its doors. In this meeting, the regional manager and manager encouraged the senior staff to share their feelings concerning the situation. As a team, they then identified the best strategy for going forward.
  - Before communicating further with either the staff or members, the manager and regional manager determined the steps that would be undertaken to help ensure that both the members and employees ended up in the best possible situation, including:
    - ✓ The manager and regional manager would get each employee a severance package that paid that individual all accrued vacation and sick time, as well as one week's pay for every year worked for hourly employees and two week's pay for every year worked for salaried employees.
    - ✓ The regional manager would arrange job opportunities with other clubs within the company for the supervisory staff.
    - ✓ The manager would contact other local clubs to make special membership arrangements that would allow the club's members to transfer to these other clubs with full privileges and not have to pay for them for a specified period of time (the club would pay the dues for those members for that time period).
    - ✓ The manager and regional manager would arrange to sell the equipment in the club to help offset the costs of closing the facility.
    - ✓ The senior staff would take responsibility for developing a closing party and would designate a charity that would be the recipient of any funds that would be raised at the party.
  - Next, the regional manager and manager met with the entire staff. At this meeting, the regional manager shared the news about senior management's decision and stated the reason for closing the facility. At the meeting, all of the arrangements regarding compensation payments, new jobs, etc. were discussed. In addition, the plans for handling the membership were reviewed. Employees were given the opportunity to go to their new jobs immediately or remain with the club until it closed. Everyone chose to stay and get new jobs after the closing.
  - The regional manager and manager then met with a group of vocal and influential members of the club to share the news and seek their ideas on how best to communicate the closing to the entire membership. At that time, management told the group about plans for a closing party and the arrangements made with the other local clubs.
  - Management then informed the entire membership about the closing and what was going to occur. Initially, this communication was accomplished

through personal letters that were sent to each member and signed by the manager. Once the letters went out, special message boards were put up around the club for member viewing. In addition, the manager and the facility's senior staff met personally with each of the members that they knew. Their dialogue with these individuals included the following information:

- ✓ That there would be a special closing party on the final day. That they could bring a guest and that all entry fees ($20 a person) would go to a local charity.
- ✓ That the party would include a cash bar and a live band.
- ✓ That the club had made arrangements with other local clubs, and that representatives of those clubs would be available for the members to meet with and sign them up for memberships in those clubs.
- ✓ That the staff would do whatever they could to help members with the transition.

- Management, including the regional manager, kept their doors opened over the next 60 days for anyone who wanted help with a closing-related issue, assisting members with the transition, supporting employees with any problem that they might have, and preparing for the final closing.
- On the final day, the closing party was the highlight event. The staff worked the party so that members and guests could enjoy the party. A total of 2,000 individuals attended the party. In the process, over $10,000 was raised for charity. The party lasted for over five hours, and closed with a special funeral procession.
- The event featured celebrations and storytelling. A local TV station covered the event and collected stories from members. The next day, the by-line of the local station's nightly newscast was "local landmark closes."
- After the party, members called and stopped by to say how much they appreciated how the closing was handled and that they hoped that someday the club would return.

- ❑ *Discussion*. Closing a club is one of the most challenging tasks that leadership will ever face. Members and employees who have been involved with a facility for any period of time take a sense of ownership in the club. As a result, they often feel an incredible loss when a club closes. Accordingly, club owners and operators need to realize that closing a facility can be traumatic for both members and employees. How the club closes not only impacts the facility's relationship with its members and employees, but also the community. In this particular instance, the facility had been a great club for almost 10 years. The closing, although lamentable, was handled in such a way that the employees, members, and community all retained their sense of pride about the club. Among the keys to this particular closing's success were the following:

- Management took the time to initially communicate and discuss the event with the facility's senior staff. Concurrently, they solicited feedback from the staff regarding what would be the right way to close the club.
- Management informed members at various levels about the closing and made the process as personal as possible.

> Club owners and operators need to realize that closing a facility can be traumatic for both members and employees.

- Before meeting with the club's employees and members, management made sure that they would be able to answer any important questions that might come up during the meeting.
- Management made the closing a celebration and made it an event that demonstrated that the club was still an important part of the community by contributing proceeds from the closing party to a local charity.
- Management made arrangements for members and employees before the meeting in an effort to help lessen the shock of the closing.
- Management, staff, and members worked together until the end, instead of becoming adversaries.
- Until the very last moment, management's approach was to be upbeat and positive, to view the process of closing the club as a change, instead of an end point.
- If staff or members wanted to talk about the closing on a personal level, the manager and regional manager made themselves available, rather than hiding behind their doors.

While closing a club is not a frequent experience for managers, nonetheless, it is an experience that many managers will have. The ability to close a club, while maintaining the relationships and integrity of the club in the eyes of employees, members, and community, is a sign of exceptional leadership. One key lesson that can be learned from this particular scenario is that managers should never burn a bridge; instead, they should continue to build, since they never know when they might return.

Drive-In Fitness Anyone?

❑ *Scenario.* This scenario occurred in a suburban fitness club in the southwest. Located along a major thoroughfare, the club leased space in a corporate business park. The facility served a corporate market and had approximately 800 memberships. The club opened at 5:30 a.m. and closed at 9:00 p.m. on weekdays.

One night at approximately 1:00 a.m., the manager received a phone call from the building's landlord who informed him that a car had just driven through the exterior window of the club and was lodged in the fitness center. The manager immediately came to the club to find a car situated inside the club, with shattered glass everywhere. Not only had the car broken a significant portion of the exterior window, it had destroyed two offices and part of the fitness floor. Glass was strewn throughout the entire fitness area. Subsequently, the police arrived and had the vehicle towed out of the club.

❑ *The Solution.* Upon surveying the situation, the manager proceeded to take the following actions:
- The manager immediately contacted the staff who were scheduled to open the club the next morning at 5:30 a.m. to let them know what happened and discuss a plan of action.

- The manager showed up at the club prior to 5:30 a.m. the next day and met with the staff. The staff then made signs that explained what happened and what actions would take place.
- Subsequently, the manager and employees greeted the club's members as they arrived at the facility and directed them over to another club for their morning workouts (the manager contacted that club upon arriving to make arrangements for his club's members to use that facility at no cost to them).
- During the course of the day, members were greeted by the facility's staff and manager who informed them of the club's closing and let them know that they would have access to and privileges at another club during the clean-up period.
- The manager brought the entire staff into the club later in the morning, and everyone worked all day cleaning up the space. The building landlord also sent staff down to help clean up.
- The manager also contacted the club's insurance agent to get that process activated.
- The club was cleaned and open to members the next afternoon.
- For a couple of weeks, the club operated with plywood on several of its windows. Within 30 days, however, the window, carpet, and broken equipment were replaced.
- No members left the club as a result of the incident.

> **The manager and employees greeted the club's members as they arrived at the facility and directed them over to another club for their morning workouts.**

- ❑ *Discussion.* A car driving through the club is not a normal event. Obviously, had it occurred during the club's normal operating hours, serious harm could have resulted. The real challenges in this particular scenario were having to address the members' needs the next morning, get the club repaired, and make sure that staff was completely informed about the situation. Furthermore, an event such as this could have resulted in the loss of members. The club manager did an excellent job on short notice of ensuring that the members were taken care of in an appropriate manner. Among the key actions that helped resolve this situation were:
- The manager visited the site right away and surveyed the situation.
- The manager immediately contacted the club's opening staff to inform them of what happened and made sure that they had a plan upon arriving in the morning.
- The manager and staff got to the club early and greeted the members as they arrived, explained the situation to them, and got them access to another club.
- The manager made arrangements for the members to use another club at no cost to them.
- The staff, with assistance from the landlord, was able to get the club cleaned up and open within one day.
- The manager made sure that the club maintained communication with the members throughout the period of the incident.

  Situations such as the one recounted in this particular scenario cannot be predicted. If they arise, however, the critical factor is the ability of management to communicate with the members to lessen the shock and confusion that can accompany such an event and provide every possible opportunity for the members to pursue their fitness activities, with as minimal a level of disturbance as possible.

Now, Where Did You Say the Fitness Area Was?

- ❑ *Scenario.* The club involved in this scenario was located along the northeast corridor in a dense urban market. The club had been open for several years and had a membership of approximately 1,600. Recently, the club had decided to go through a $3 million renovation that would take approximately 12 months to complete. During the renovation, the facility's goal was to grow membership by at least 500. The club had also decided that during the course of the 12-month renovation, it would remain open for the members and keep its dues pricing unchanged.

- ❑ *The Solution.* Once the decision to renovate the facility and remain open during the renovation was made, the club's leadership team developed a game plan to tackle the process. In that regard, some of the most important actions that took place included:
  - The club had models and color floor plans of the renovation produced that could be used to share information with the members about the renovation process.
  - The club created a renovation calendar that provided approximate timelines for each phase of the renovation, including what areas of the club would be under construction, when these spaces would be worked on, and what changes in the facilities would occur during each stage.
  - The renovation calendar and pictures were included with a letter that was forwarded to each member. In addition, a notice on the club's plans for renovation was put in the newsletter. These communication efforts occurred approximately 90 days in advance of the start of the project and again at 60 days and 30 days prior to work beginning.
  - The club set up a renovation hub in the club that members could refer to every day regarding the status of the project. This hub had a model of the new club, pictures of the new equipment, copies of the renovation calendar, and a daily update poster that showed what was happening each day.
  - The staff had daily meetings and updates so they could communicate effectively with the club's members.
  - The locker rooms had to be switched on four occasions, with the women utilizing the men's lockers on one occasion, and during another period, the men and women using the locker rooms on alternate days. A special area for lockers was set up so that even during the time that radical changes were occurring in the location of locker rooms, the members always had a locker in which to store their items.
  - The club provided special treats and drinks each day to help ease any pain caused by the renovation efforts.

- When the exercise studios were closed, the club provided members with hard hats and held classes in the construction areas after hours. This step was facilitated by using special flooring that the staff could roll out on the concrete floors after the construction workers had left for the day.
- Special classes and programs were offered that provided members with the opportunity to exercise at times they might not otherwise have worked out.
- The manager and department heads made themselves available to the members in 12-hour shifts to address the members' complaints and deal with any other issues that they might have.
- Each time a phase of work was completed, the club held a relatively small celebration party.
- Each of these parties provided an opportunity for special instructors and celebrities to visit the club during those days on which the festivities were held in order to further enhance the experience.

After 12 months of renovation, the club's membership had increased from approximately 1,600, when construction began, to 2,400 at the time of completion. Furthermore, the member retention rate remained at the same level as it was prior to the renovation work.

❑ *Discussion.* One of the most challenging experiences that managers will encounter in the club business is operating a facility and serving the members during a period of major renovation. Clubs cannot afford to just close their doors during renovation, or they would lose their revenue stream from dues. Clubs have to find ways to continue operating at full bore and provide the same (or better) service during periods of renovation. Because the health/fitness club industry changes frequently, clubs will be challenged at one time or another with having to make a facelift—sometimes a major facelift. The key to successfully meeting such a challenge is whether the club can continue to operate and drive revenues during a period when members will be inconvenienced.

Club owners and operators who are involved with facilities that will be undergoing renovation must find a way to succeed at delivering their club experience under times of high duress. Without question, members will complain during renovation. At the beginning of the renovation efforts, most members will be excited about the changes that are occurring and tolerate the inconveniences that are being caused by the construction. As the construction wears on, however, usually at about six months, members will begin to complain and will become less accepting of any inconveniences that might arise. Concurrently, the staff will be challenged to have to provide satisfactory service under the most trying of circumstances. As members begin to complain more, the employees will be subjected to additional stress.

The aforementioned circumstances require extraordinary leadership if the club's renovation efforts are to proceed smoothly, with minimal disruption to the membership. In this particular scenario, club management did an outstanding job of turning a long renovation into a successful operation. Among the most critical steps that allowed management to be successful in this situation were the following:

Clubs have to find ways to continue operating at full bore and provide the same (or better) service during periods of renovation.

- Management created an entire game plan around the renovation that addressed the concerns of both members and staff.
- Management informed the membership well in advance what was going to occur and repeated efforts to communicate with the members throughout the process.
- Management created a communication center that provided daily updates concerning the renovation efforts.
- Management developed a series of newly created experiences that were designed to help take the members' and employees' minds off the actual renovation process.
- Management and staff undertook several activities (e.g., parties, social events, and special classes) that helped lend a measure of excitement to the renovation process.
- The employees pulled together under a common cause to help make the situation better for the members.
- Management provided additional support to the employees so that they, in turn, could take better care of the members during the renovation process.
- A club can do a number of things to help make a renovation, such as this one, relatively palatable to everyone involved. The key point that should be emphasized is that if the management and employees are able and willing to plan and act in an appropriate manner, the entire renovation experience can be somewhat rewarding for members and employees alike, rather than an unnerving, strife-filled struggle.

> Great managers are those who face unexpected and often challenging situations, and are able to identify and execute the right solutions.

Reflections

No matter how well a business plans, both for the expected and unexpected, there will be events that occur for which no plan exists. Great managers are those who face these unexpected and often challenging situations, and are able to identify and execute the right solutions. This chapter shared examples of several unexpected business occurrences and how the managers and leaders of these businesses handled them. The objective being to provide insight into how even the most uncomfortable and challenging business situations can be solved if approached with an open mind, empathy, humility, and discipline.

Retention and Programming Stories 38

"Stories translate information into emotion."

—Jonas Ridderstrale and Kjell A. Nordstrom,
Karaoke Capitalism

Chapter Objectives

The club stories presented in this chapter bring forward insight into how some of the industry's best and most innovative clubs approach member retention and programming. The content in this chapter was extracted from two books previously written by the author. The first, *Why People Join, Leave, and Stay with Health Fitness Clubs*, was co-authored with Paul Bedford, Ph.D. The second book, *101 Programming Strategies for Engaging Members in Health/Fitness Clubs*, was co-authored with Teresa J. Thomason. The chapter begins with a look at a few different approaches clubs have taken to engage their members and stage memorable experiences that enhance member retention. The chapter concludes with a few examples of different programs that leading clubs offer in an effort to enhance the value of membership.

Engaging Members Into the Club Life

❏ *Where Everyone Knows Your Name. Cambridge Group of Clubs, Toronto and Montreal, Canada.*

> The Cambridge Group of Clubs is a network of three clubs (Adelaide Club, Cambridge Club, and Toronto Athletic Club) that are based in Toronto, Canada. At the Cambridge Group of Clubs, its membership retention efforts revolve around three core fundamentals: properly introducing new members to its clubs, providing a socially supportive and interactive club environment, and focusing on the development of member relationships. This three-pronged approach to membership retention has resulted in retention rates that range from 71 percent to 82 percent.
>
> When a prospect makes the decision to join one of its three clubs, the first step that is taken, after the membership sign-up is completed, is to have a professional staff member take the new member through an extensive discovery-and-welcoming process. This discovery-and-welcoming process begins with a conversation, in which the staff member seeks to understand what the new member's personal interests and goals are, what their current

A three-pronged approach to membership retention has resulted in retention rates that range from 71 percent to 82 percent.

level of fitness is, and finally, identifying what support and assistance they will need to be successful. Once this initial dialogue is completed, a thorough orientation process is undertaken that includes introducing the new member to key staff and existing members, each of whom can provide assistance and support to the new member as the individual embarks on the club journey. The primary focus throughout this introduction is to demonstrate the club's genuine care and concern. As such, whatever time is needed is taken to make sure that the new member feels welcome in the club.

Another key element behind the retention success of the Cambridge Group of Clubs is based on the company's approach to creating an engaging physical environment that promotes social interaction between the members. In that regard, the club's social stages (casual lounges, food and beverage areas, etc.) are fundamental to bringing members together in a non-intimidating environment. When members are able to engage with each other in a non-intimidating physical environment, the development of personal relationships is promoted. This element moves a Cambridge Clubs' facility from being a gym to being a club. As a consequence, its members develop an emotional tie to their clubs.

Another underlying focus of the Cambridge Group of Clubs is to encourage its staff to be matchmakers of sorts. In that regard, an essential element of everyone's job is to introduce members to each other, as well as to staff. The company preaches that it is the responsibility of every employee to make sure that no member ever goes without a welcome and greeting, nor do they ever go without being introduced to another member of staff person. This attitude is a further effort on its part to bond members to each other and eventually to the club.

❏ *A Home Away From Home, Oase Health and Sport Club, Bochum, Germany*

After more than three decades of operations, the success of the Oase Health and Sports Club can be attributed to a number of reasons. One factor why the club has been so successful in reaching and keeping its members happy lies in the club's philosophy and policy of being the "second home" or "home away from home" for its members. That approach, and more importantly the club's promise to its members, is to establish a club atmosphere that reminds them of being at home.

> **Oase's ultimate goal is that when members think of not being at home, they think of coming to Oase.**

Oase's ultimate goal is that when members think of not being at home, they think of coming to Oase. Being part of city and community life for so long, Oase has established a reputation as the place to go in the community for individuals who are seeking either to lead an active lifestyle or to socialize with nice people in a great environment.

The average age among members is 47 years and it is not unusual to have three generations of the same family in the club at the same time. For example, a grandfather discusses the world with his friends in the Oase café, his daughter works out with friends in the facility's group-exercise studio, and her baby boy is being cared for in the Crèche. Engaging in an active life is an ageless pastime that knows no generational boundaries, a principle that serves all members of Oase well.

Oase undertakes a number of actions to foster the home-away-from-home environment. For example, its willingness to reinvest, rejuvenate, and upgrade the facilities to a standard that members expect at home (or higher) helps make its members feel comfortable from the start. In addition, a high level of quality and professionalism is expected from staff, with the result that its members are treated to the highest level of professionalism every time they visit the club. Oase also prides itself on outstanding staff-member communication. In fact, the resulting interaction among members and staff is a critical element of the club's success. The consequence of this focus on staff professionalism and staff-member interactions is a club in which the relationships between members and staff and between members and other members are exceptionally strong.

Oase also is actively involved in the community. For example, it has a seat on the Health Development Forum of the Chamber of Commerce. In addition, it has received an award as German Club of the Year. It is also renowned for its adherence to high educational quality standards in the health/fitness club industry on a European level. As such, collectively, its members take great pride in its actions.

Finally, Oase makes a concerted effort to understand, care for, and value the lives of its members, their families, and their friends. Its unrelenting passion and commitment to its members build a bond of trust and confidence between Oase, its members, and the community. As a club, it takes great pride in being the "second home" for its members.

❑ *Exceeding Member Expectations, East Bank Club, Chicago*

The primary business focus of the East Bank Club is to exceed the expectations of the members. This unrelenting focus on exceeding the anticipated outcomes of the members is built on a model that encompasses the following core elements:
- Delivering an extremely high level of service
- Offering an unsurpassed variety of programming, amenities, and services
- Providing an engaging club environment that provides members a multitude of ways to interact socially
- Offering a club environment that is energetic and exciting

Since the East Bank Club opened on December 15, 1980, the club's owners and management have been passionate about delivering exceptional member service. This maniacal focus on delivering exceptional member service has become a mantra for the more than 600 staff members, more than 50 percent of whom have worked at the club for five years or more and 30 percent of whom have worked at the club for 10 years or more.

A few years back, the club implemented an extensive service-training program that each staff member undertakes (new hires and current

> **A maniacal focus on delivering exceptional member service has become a mantra for the more than 600 staff members, more than 50 percent of whom have worked at the club for five years or more and 30 percent of whom have worked at the club for 10 years or more.**

employees). The service-training program ensures that all employees learn the skills necessary to professionally interact with members; resolve member service challenges or situations to the delight of members; and provide members with a memorable experience. In addition, the training program is designed to provide staff with an enhanced level of pride about where they work and the job that they perform.

East Bank offers more than 200 complimentary group-exercise classes each week, including yoga, Pilates, dance, strength conditioning, and aerobic conditioning. In addition, a host of other unique classes are tailored to the specific desires and interests of its members. Furthermore, the club offers an extensive array of "niche programs" for members, including tennis, aquatics, golf, triathlon, running, children's programs, and even kayaking on the Chicago River. The club offers programs suited for a wide array of interests and needs, ranging from new members and individuals just starting a fitness regimen to programs tailored for the most experienced athletes. Collectively, the club runs more than 450 programs and classes each week.

> Collectively, the club runs more than 450 programs and classes each week.

In addition to group classes, niche programs, and private training, the club offers programs and services that include a full-service salon and women's spa; a pro shop that doubles as a boutique fashion store; a gourmet deli with take-out items; and several unique specialty services, such as a car wash, dry cleaners, and physical therapy. Similar to its personal-training program, these services are priced reasonably in order to encourage member involvement.

The club works hard to create an environment that encourages and supports the development of relationships between members. Members befriend other members through the classes and programs that the club offers, as well as through casual interactions in the various social spaces in the club. The club also offers social networking on the club's website, which further enhances the ability of the members to connect with each other. The club holds regular social functions, ranging from small intimate events, such as Friday night tennis socials, to much larger functions, such as wine tastings that attract 300 or more people. The club's most attended social event and a club tradition is the annual Summer Sun Deck Party, which brings in more than 1,000 people. The club's social environment is further enriched through a thriving food and beverage operation. The food and beverage operations include Maxwell's at the Club, a sophisticated-but-casual upscale restaurant; a casual grill; a juice bar; a gourmet deli; and the Sun Deck Café, a restaurant located on the roof of the club (adjacent to two outdoor pools, a pool bar, and 20,000 square feet of lounge chairs and tables).

The club's owners and management are passionate about providing a five-star experience. This focus is targeted around an unrelenting commitment to quality—quality staff, quality services, quality equipment, and quality facilities. East Bank is a single-facility operation, which has meant that quality control is inherent. It is, in fact, the club's sole focus.

Programming That Makes a Difference

❑ *Aquatic Excellence, Red Lerille's Health and Racquet Club, Lafayette, Louisiana*

Brenna Suter is the aquatics director for Red's, a 200,000 square foot indoor health and fitness club based in Lafayette, Louisiana, whose aquatic facilities include: an indoor 25-yard, six-lane lap pool, indoor 25-yard three-lane lesson pool, an outdoor 25-meter, six-lane lap pool, an outdoor aquatic playground with slide, lazy river, splash park, and baby pool, and finally an indoor cold plunge. Brenna started off by saying, "Pools are an important part of the Red's membership experience. We have over 11,000 memberships and 18,000 members, and many, if not most, enjoy our aquatic environments. Our outdoor aquatic playground was built at the turn of the most recent decade in response to requests from our family members who wanted an outdoor area they could spend an entire day with their kids. Our outdoor and indoor lap pools in turn are used extensively for programming, and when not programed, they are constantly occupied by our members who compete in triathlons."

"Possibly our most popular aquatic programs are the Masters classes where we have four different Masters sessions: two in the morning, one in the afternoon, and one in the evening. Other popular aquatic offerings include: private swim lessons (adult, youth, and babies), Red's swim camp which offers basic stroke instruction for newcomers, kid's pool parties, wave classes (aquatic exercise classes), lifeguard classes, and swim team training." These programs are offered to members on a year-round basis. In addition to the regular year-round aquatic programs, the club also hosts special activities and holiday events. One of the things Red's does as part of its ongoing commitment to the local community is to make its pools available to one of the local high schools for swim team practice during the high school swim season. According to Brenna, "Red's takes great pride in being able to offer its members the best aquatic campus in town."

❑ *Fitness Tours, World Class Fitness, Moscow, Russia*

According to World Class Fitness's former CEO Irina Kutina, approximately 10 years ago members of several clubs expressed an interest in organizing sport tours involving a combination of sport activities (e.g., skiing, biking, etc.) accompanied by organized training from the company's personal trainers. "When the tours were first organized, the members actually organized them and invited our trainers to join them, paying the trainers' way and providing additional compensation for providing organized training. After the first couple of events, we decided that it would be better if our company organized and conducted the tours." According to Irina, what began as one single fitness tour in 2003 had by 2012 evolved into over 50 trips around the world, incorporating activities as diverse as bicycling, deep water diving, high mountain trekking, ice and rock climbing, water rafting, parachuting, and skiing. In 2012, the company organized 55 tours that attracted 480 clients, $380,000 in profit and 32 new members.

> What began as one single fitness tour in 2003 had by 2012 evolved into over 50 trips around the world.

World Class typically has one trainer for every 6 to 10 members, with the trainers providing group training sessions, as well as participating in the events with the members. To make things more interesting for the members, the trainers will conduct group training sessions, which include circuit training, core training, battle drills, obstacle courses, and team games. One of the outcomes of facilitating the tours has been the fostering of great relationships between the members and staff, as well as providing a means for numerous members to achieve goals they never before felt were achievable.

One of the most interesting and successful tours involved the Mont Blanc climbing competition in which a team of members achieved first place. The clubs' members spent six days in the mountains, acclimatizing, as well as receiving intensive training in sliding step skills, stepping down techniques, and working together as a team under extreme conditions. As a result of this training, the team was able to win the event. In 2011, the members and staff participated in a new extreme adventure entitled Seven Tops, which will take three years and involve climbing seven different mountaintops.

Irina says the Fitness Tours have generated an entirely new source of revenue for the company, as well as provided a means to attract new members. "The benefits of the Fitness Tours has extend far beyond the direct outcomes of the events, and extended into other areas of the business. We have seen an increase in individual and group personal training tied to these events, as well as greater demand for local sport activities, including our annual World Class Games which now attract well over 1,000 members."

❑ *Signature Group Classes, Sports Club/LA and Now Equinox*

According to the former national director of group exercise for Sports Club/LA, the company has always had a reputation in the marketplace for offering unique group exercise classes taught by some of the nation's leading instructors. Like other clubs located in large highly competitive urban markets, many of the company's top instructors also taught at other clubs, resulting in some popular classes being replicated by instructors when they taught at a competitor's club. The result of this instructor sharing was a lack of group exercise brand differentiation for the Sports Club/LA brand.

In 2010, the company determined that it needed to create its own signature classes. Management decided to have its instructors design the signature classes, and furthermore to allow the classes to only be taught at the company's clubs. By taking this approach, management felt it would provide its top instructors with a unique professional opportunity to leverage their talents, while also receiving recognition for creating one-of-a-kind classes that would be taught exclusively at Sports Club/LA locations.

The first signature classes offered by Sports Club/LA were called Zenergy, a dynamic fusion class that brings together the benefits of traditional yoga poses with powerful athletic movements, using creative sequencing. According to the company's former national director of group exercise, Zenergy was so well received by both instructors and club members that the company went ahead and created a second signature class called Zencore, which was a 30-minute version of Zenergy.

The response to these first two signature classes was so overwhelmingly enthusiastic that the company decided to evolve the signature class brand further, and by 2011 had formed a partnership with Aspen/Snowmass to develop a new signature class, Aspen Ascent. Aspen Ascent was designed to prepare members for skiing and boarding by providing a structured class to enhance cardiovascular capacity and concurrently improve balance, agility, and core strength. As part of the partnership that led to the creation of Aspen Ascent, Sports Club/LA members and instructors became eligible to receive discounts on lift tickets, ski school, and ski rentals at Aspen Snowmass. Even though the company had no clubs in the vicinity of Aspen, its members frequently travel to Aspen and Snowmass, and as a result, the classes offered the clubs an opportunity to separate themselves from the competition.

Reflections

The stories in this chapter bring to life many of the principles shared in earlier chapters in this book, especially those chapters on member retention, staging memorable experiences, and programming. Each of the clubs featured in this chapter took the initiative to create and execute strategies and actions that would distinguish it from the competition. In every instance, their strategies involved an unrelenting commitment to engaging members and providing unique experiences that could not be obtained at the competitors' clubs and gyms.

> Each of the clubs took the initiative to create and execute strategies and actions that would distinguish it from the competition.

39 Words of Wisdom From Boutique Fitness Studio Operators

Introduction

> Nothing speaks louder or resonates more profoundly than the words, actions, and results of entrepreneurs who have been successful in bringing their dream to life.

Nothing speaks louder or resonates more profoundly than the words, actions, and results of entrepreneurs who have been successful in bringing their dream to life. This chapter shares the stories of six fitness studio entrepreneurs, each of whom has created a uniquely differentiated, as well as highly successful, fitness studio. These stories were first published in a book entitled, *Studio Success*, written by this author, and published by the Association of Fitness Studios (AFS). Their stories speak volumes about the journey to success, as well as the many challenges that arise during that journey. Their stories are insightful, not to mention inspirational.

Each of our entrepreneurs has provided a highlight reel of their business. This highlight reel provides insights into their business concept, their revenue model, and their general approach to creating a loyal client base. In addition to sharing their story, each entrepreneur has generously provided personal insights into the lessons they've learned and the challenges they have faced with the intent that these insights will assist other studio operators in successfully pursuing and achieving their vision.

THE STORY TELLERS: STUDIO OPERATORS WHO HAVE BEEN SUCCESSFUL

EZIA Performance Labs

Web address: www.eziahp.com
Phone number :   760-845-1400
Owner: Isaiah Truyman
Years in business: 5
Size of studio: 6,000 square feet

Chapter Thirty-Nine
Words of Wisdom From Boutique Fitness Studio Operators

❏ Market Position

EZIA provides physical therapy and performance training to moms, weekend warriors, and professional athletes. We have something for every ability level (e.g., personnel training, sports performance, group exercise, yoga, Pilates).

❏ Business Model

EZIA was created in 2009 to help people achieve elite performance in all aspects of their life. Our portfolio includes EZIA Performance Labs, EZIA Mobile Network, and EZIA Enterprise Solutions. Although our foundation is built on athletic training for action sports such as rugby, golf, triathlon, and team sports, today our programs inspire and infect the champion in everyone. EZIA's team of experts includes performance coaches, physical therapists, nutritionists, and tech geeks. Together, we've created a family of services that personalizes the holistic approach we've used with Olympic-level athletes for any level of fitness

❏ Competitive Advantages

- We are better, and we can deliver on the promise of achieving health and wellness with pinpoint accuracy.
- We are faster, smaller, lighter, and more agile; we can respond to our customers and the market quickly.
- Our people are deeply passionate and go beyond the call in creating an exceptional experience and interaction for each client.
- Our facilities, training philosophy, community, and culture are all genuine and authentic; we are focused on delivering results for our customers. This is very real and creates exceptional engagement and retention numbers at our facilities. Our members get upset when we refer to them as customers; they prefer to be called "family members."

> Our members get upset when we refer to them as customers; they prefer to be called "family members."

❏ General Information on Pricing and Packaging

- We currently offer two memberships. The first is a personal training membership for $199 a month that includes two private training sessions a month, after which training can be purchased for $85 per session. The second is a small group training membership for $149 a month that provides access to all of our small group training sessions.
- We offer individual private training for $85 per session.
- We offer a variety of small group training classes as well as larger classes that encompass functional training, bike club, nutrition seminars, etc.

❏ The Initial Sources of Capital for the Business

- My partner and I each contributed $20,000 in personal equity to the business.
- We raised approximately $160,000 from friends and family.
- We raised another $240,000 from angel investors.
- We are now in the process of raising and additional $1.5 million with plans to raise $5 million in the next 18 to 24 months.

❑ The Three to Five Most Valuable Lessons You Have Learned in Your Business

- Start with the end in mind (planning is critical).
- Excellence in execution is 90 percent of the battle (always keep a focus on the basics).
- Launch one new revenue stream at a time; avoid introducing too many new things at once.
- Slow and steady wins the race.
- Your customer is your best friend.

❑ The Three to Five Most Effective Strategies for Marketing and Selling Your Brand

- The most effective method is referral from existing satisfied customers.
- The second most effective marketing approach has been good Internet marketing.
- The third most effective marketing strategy is grass roots guerilla marketing: stickers, postcards, door hangers, posters etc.

❑ The Three to Five Strategies That Have Proven Most Successful in Retaining Your Clients

- Hire and retain the best employees.
- Support your awesome employees with the best possible tools for their job (taking care of customers).
- Focus on seeing the experience of your business through the eyes of a customer.

❑ The Three to Five Most Important Lessons That Have Driven Your Profitability

- Maintain really good spreadsheets so you can "see" what the heck is going on; this may sound basic, but it is much harder and more time-consuming than it seems, especially for the small club operator.
- Be sure to have a working deal in place with someone who has skill in modeling businesses, or you will find yourself in the dark trying to put the pieces together after the fact.
- Don't waste money on pipe dream marketing.
- Paying more doesn't always get you more. Be sure you are incentivizing people to perform, not just paying them and hoping they are focused.

❑ When You First Started Your Business, What Were Your Three Greatest Challenges?

- The greatest challenge was and is trying to do all things at once, open new facility, get all financing, get staff, and get customers all at once.
- In the beginning, we really didn't have any infrastructure in place, so this meant two to three times as much work because we did everything manually until we learned to automate our systems.
- Never having enough money, or business. "Success is the art of engaging others in your vision."

❑ The Three to Five Greatest Challenges That You Face Day to Day

- Focusing on the basics, while also innovating for the future.
- Maintaining total customer satisfaction.
- Growing, growing, and the growing pains associated with it. Seems like every time we are finished with something, it's time to start updating it again.

❑ If You Were Starting Over Again, What Would Be the Three to Five Things You Wish That You Understood Better?

- The importance of raising more money than you think you will need.
- The importance of having an exit strategy as part of your business plan.
- The importance of having experienced mentors and advisors who you can call on for assistance. It is all about who you know!
- The importance of making sure you are having fun all the time; no one wants to work for a sourpuss.
- The importance of being an inspiring and contagious leader.

❑ Additional Insights

- It's a tough business, so be sure you really love what you do, and have a vision for the future. Then kick butt, and make it happen.

> **Make sure you are having fun all the time; no one wants to work for a sourpuss.**

Fitness Quest 10

Web address:	www.fitnessquest10.com
Phone number:	858-271-1171
Owner:	Todd Durkin
Years in business:	15
Size of studio:	8,000 square feet

❑ Market Position

Health and human performance studio built around programs that combine personal training, sports performance, Pilates, yoga, classes, teaching, and rehabilitation. Our studio's approach is built around a mind/body approach, with a blend of Western and Eastern philosophies, a place where clients can reach their health and fitness potential, but also be empowered to reach greatness in their life.

❑ Business Model

Fitness Quest 10 was launched in January 2000 as a one-man show. Today, FQ 10 is a team comprised of more than 35 trainers, coaches, therapists, and administrators, all uniquely educated and certified and all sharing one common goal: to motivate, educate, and empower people to transform their lives and reach their full potential. Our unique culture and our expert and passionate team is driven to transform lives by empowering people to reach their full potential.

We guarantee to make each client's life better!

❑ Competitive Advantages

- World-class facility that provides world-class service in a boutique style facility.
- Our Mission: "We guarantee to make your life better."
- Providing value to our clients each and every day.
- Our passion, energy, and positivity. I don't think it can be matched in the industry. I don't just say that. Our team is unique and we have a great melting pot of backgrounds, energies, and experiences. But our passion is truly evident.

❑ General Information on Pricing and Packaging

- We offer three membership options:
  ✓ An $89 membership that provides full access to facility
  ✓ A $135 membership that provides unlimited access to classes
  ✓ A $297 membership that provides unlimited access to all small and large group classes
- We offer individual personal training costs $60 to $75 per hour.
- We offer a variety of fee based small group and large group classes.
  ✓ Miss Fit Boot Camps: 12 sessions over four weeks for $250
  ✓ Large group training: Four sessions for $72; eight sessions for $130; unlimited sessions $150, and unlimited sessions with EFT for $135
  ✓ Small group training: Four sessions $148; eight sessions for $280; unlimited sessions for $360, and unlimited sessions with EFT for $297
  ✓ Youth Summer Camps: range from $85 to $275

❑ The Initial Sources of Capital for the Business

- Got a $5,000 loan from a family member, and the rest I took out on credit card loans.
- Additionally, I had negotiated three months free rent starting from the time I opened the business.
- Several of my payments (i.e., equipment) had three months deferred payment, so I didn't have to start making payments until three months after I received it.

❑ The Three to Five Most Valuable Lessons You Have Learned in Your Business

- Systems are critical for your success. Even if you are going to have one studio and it's only 1,500 square feet, it's imperative that you develop systems.
- The key to long-term success is selling your system, not selling yourself.
- Be slow to hire and quick to fire. Hiring plays a critical role in achieving success. Once you hire someone, you need to provide expectations, give ongoing feedback, and acknowledge and praise them when deserving.

- The best way to grow a business is by developing a fanatical culture filled with raving fans. And the way you do that is by focusing on extraordinary results, a phenomenal experience, and a culture that breeds family, fun, and positivity.
- Regardless of how big or successful you get, you must always know what's going on in your business.
- You need to know your vision and purpose in life. If your purpose is to create your own business, than you must find a way to get it done. Risk is an important element in anything worthwhile. At the same time, you do not need to be a brick-and-mortar business owner to create success either.
- How important it is to have mentors in your life. I have been extremely fortunate to have some great ones. From the time I opened my business, I have always surrounded myself with people smarter than me. From the Wayne Cottons of the world to the different mastermind groups I was associated with, to the teachers and professionals I learned from. Learning never stops. It sure helps when you have people that you can turn to that have "been there, done that."

❏ The Three to Five Most Effective Strategies for Marketing and Selling Your Brand

- Building customers for life and providing world-class service so they will bring friends and family, as well as provide testimonies.
- Donations and gifts to community (e.g., charities, schools, silent auctions).
- Connecting with local businesses and events.
- Implementing social media campaigns.
- Having feeder programs (e.g., Biggest Winner program, 10-Day Fit Camp, and Skinny Jeans).
- Word of mouth! This comes from great results.
- A great website. People use Google all the time to search out information, and it plays an important part in people getting eyeballs on your site. Your site is one of the most important touch points for your brand, and if it's great, people will immediately know if it fits them.

> Your website is one of the most important touch points for your brand, and if it's great, people will immediately know if it fits them.

❏ The Three to Five Strategies That Have Proven Most Successful in Retaining Your Clients

- Provide them great results; it matters.
- Give them what they want, and give them what they need.
- Giving world-class service, honoring our word (integrity), and exceeding customer expectations.
- Having a highly educated and motivated team that delivers world-class service.
- Retention rewards program.
- Providing continuing education for staff along with providing staff cutting edge tools and programs.
- As Ken Blanchard says, "Take care of your customers, take care of your team, and take care of you."

Know your numbers, but do not let the numbers run you or your business.

❏ The Three to Five Most Important Lessons That Have Driven Your Profitability

- Know your numbers, but do not let the numbers run you or your business.
- Have someone you trust helping you take care of the accounting and money.
- Having systems will help create time freedom and money freedom. Systems, systems, systems!
- It's not how much you bring in; it's how much you keep after your expenses.
- Every little thing counts!

❏ When You First Started Your Business, What Were Your Three Greatest Challenges?

- I had no money, no clients, and no business plan. That's not how you typically want to start a business. I had to find ways to get clients and get them quickly to create cash flow.
- I needed to create systems quickly because I had very little business experience before opening up my studio.
- Once I got busy in the first 6 to 12 months, everyone wanted me. I was so busy selling "me," I got so busy delivering training sessions that I couldn't grow the business. So I raised my rates, hired other people, and started selling my system.

❏ The Three to Five Greatest Challenges That You Face Day to Day

- Focus, focus, focus on the most important items that are going to move the needle for Fitness Quest 10 and Todd Durkin Enterprises. I have a ton of things going on. Identifying which are the most important and not getting distracted remain at the forefront.
- Leadership of my team. We have 38 teammates on board, and it's my job to continually "feed them" what they need: vision, expectations, feedback, motivation, culture. Yes, everyone is important in driving these aspects of the business. If the leader is not doing it, you can't expect anyone else to do it.
- Family time. It's easy for me to work 16 hours a day. I need to also prioritize time with my lovely wife Melanie and kids Luke (10), Brady (8), and McKenna (5). I realize that these treasures in my life also need my time, and I love spending time with them. Like anything, I need to prioritize it and put it in my schedule.

❏ If You Were Starting Over Again, What Would Be the Three to Five Things You Wish That You Understood Better?

- The importance of having a business plan. Had no clue how to do one and didn't take the time to do it.
- The importance of systems. I did not have one single system written down when I started.
- The importance of leadership. I always considered myself a leader but I didn't have the first clue in how to run a business. I was able to get by in the beginning with shear passion and energy. Now I mix that with a much more sophisticated approach to leadership

❏ Additional Insights

- Bigger isn't better.. Better is better!
- Be the best version of you.
- Planning and strategizing is critical. You must take the time to plan your work and work your plan. I spend a lot of time strategizing and then executing. But it starts with planning. I do my annual roadmap and strategic plan at the beginning of each year; I do a 90-day wonder at the start of every quarter; I do a goal-setting exercise called the "3 in 30" every 30 days. And every Sunday, I dial in the week with an in-depth plan of my week. All of these exercises overlap to make sure I'm executing on the right things.
- Mastermind groups and mentorships. Be part of mastermind groups and mentorships. They will accelerate your learning curve majorly. You can check out www.ToddDurkin.com for the ones that we offer.
- IMPACT. I live by this motto. It's the title of my first book, sIt stands for:

    I = Live INSPIRED
    M = MASTER your craft
    P = PLAY at world class
    A = ACTION
    C = CONDITION for greatness
    T = Be TENACIOUS!!!

The Exercise Coach

Web address: www.exercisecoach.com
Phone number 847-707-2281
Owner: Brian Cygan
Years in business: 17 with first studio opened in 2000
Size of studio: 1,300 to 1,900 square feet

❏ Market Position

At Exercise Coach, we have positioned ourselves to serve a sedentary population whose prior experiences with fitness have be unsatisfactory, whether it was due to not meeting a fitness goal, or the result of an intimidating and unpleasant workout experience. We are focused on providing an efficient and effective workout regime that produces results.

> Our focus is to serve people who are busy, sick of gyms, afraid of getting hurt, and who just plain hate exercise.

❏ Business Model

Our passion is to be the perfect fit for people for whom conventional fitness wisdom has failed. Our focus is to serve people who are busy, sick of gyms, afraid of getting hurt, and who just plain hate exercise. Guided by the science which proves "muscle quality matters more than movement quantity," we help our clients get the results that matter most to them with just two, 20-minute workouts per week. The Exercise Coach is now franchising and has 35 locations open or in development in six states with plans for at least 200 units nationwide.

❑ Competitive Advantages

- We aren't driven and guided by our own personal preferences as it relates to exercise and nutrition. We go where we believe ideal exercise and consumer challenges meet.
- We fully understand and empathize with the emotions of the sedentary and deconditioned market. We aren't interested in making people love exercise; we simply want to help them leverage it in the smartest way possible for their own benefit.
- Our programs and processes flow from this perspective and are ultra-safe, time-efficient, and startlingly effective. We help our clients get the results that matter most to them with just two, 20-minute workouts per week. Our proprietary fitness technology platform is unlike anything our clients have ever seen or felt. The unforgettable experience we deliver creates loyalty and buzz.

❑ General Information on Pricing and Packaging

- Personal training rates vary by market, ranging from $34 to $39 per session.
- Team training rates range from $22 to $29 per individual per session.
- We allow clients to purchase packages through EFT.

❑ The Initial Sources of Capital for the Business

- Personal capital of founder and also capital raised through individual private investors who were people that believed in my vision, passion, and plan (e.g., family and friends). They also had a personal interest in the services we would provide.

❑ The Three to Five Most Valuable Lessons You Have Learned in Your Business

- Business is leadership. True leadership is having personal drive along with the ability to influence others for their good, the good of the company, the good of customers, and the good of the community.
- Optimal business results occur where corporate passion and customer wants align.
- Your vision and values must be contagious. If they aren't, you need to rethink them.
- Businesses are revenue-generating vehicles. Some are better than others, but the person in the driver's seat still makes it or breaks it.

❑ The Three to Five Most Effective Strategies for Marketing and Selling Your Brand

- Be fully committed to well-defined target market.
- Design your marketing messages around those needs that your target market is acutely aware of.
- Craft a compelling story that your entire team can participate in and passionately communicate.

- Learn best practice advertising tactics from professionals with fitness marketing experience and seek out mentoring in these area
- Differentiate. Differentiate. Differentiate.

❏ The Three to Five Strategies That Have Proven Most Successful in Retaining Your Clients

- Get them the results that matter most to them.
- Cultivate a genuine relationship between clients and your whole team.
- Never take even your most loyal, long-term clients for granted.
- Be fully committed to positivity and being a source of energy for your clients every single session.
- Use a process-driven approach that makes your brand—not one individual—the object of your client's loyalty.

> Never take even your most loyal, long-term clients for granted.

❏ The Three to Five Most Important Lessons That Have Driven Your Profitability

- Create a career staffing model. Staff transitions cost time and money. Create a healthy family atmosphere for the team. Take an interest in their development and future.
- Never take advertising marketing holidays.
- Hire salaried full-time coaches versus paying per session rates.
- Understand your target demographics, and do what it takes to adequately research your service area before opening. Get help if you need it.
- Staff for the revenue you want, not for the clients you have.
- Optimize your economic variables. We have created a win-win-win. Our clients pay less, we collect more, and our coaches have career opportunities.

❏ When You First Started Your Business, What Were Your Three Greatest Challenges?

- It was a challenge not to have anyone to turn to from a best practice perspective.
- It was a challenge to not have standard procedures and systems in place and instead having to create our own.
- It was a challenge not to have any relevant HR experience or processes in place. This includes recruiting and hiring.

❏ The Three to Five Greatest Challenges That You Face Day to Day

- Wearing multiple hats and spending valuable time on administrative-type tasks.
- Keeping track of advertising deadlines and planning ahead to avoid last-minute scrambling.
- Putting in the time it takes to communicate effectively and fairly with the entire team.

❑ If You Were Starting Over Again, What Would Be the Three to Five Things You Wish That You Understood Better?

- The importance of hiring the right people.
- The keys to cultivating employee satisfaction and unshakable employee loyalty.
- The need for mentors and peer support.
- It would have been nice to go into a business knowing what to invest and exactly how to invest it.

Blockhead Fitness

Web address: www.blockheadfitness.com
Phone number: 312-217-3476
Owner: Sean Block
Years in business: 8
Size of studio: 3,000 square feet

❑ Market Position

Blockhead is a personal training and group training studio.

❑ Business Model

Blockhead Fitness goal is to provide a friendly clean environment where all age groups are welcome. The studio promotes a healthy lifestyle through convenience, qualified trainers, and most of all, getting oneself on the track to be healthier lifestyle through diet, exercise, and making workouts safe and fun.

❑ Competitive Advantage

> The advantage of owning a small business (studio) is being able to know your clientele on a personal level.

The advantage of owning a small business (studio) is being able to know your clientele on a personal level. We believe one of our greatest advantages is being able to offer free memberships to clients as long as they are using a trainer once a week.

❑ General Information on Pricing and Packaging

- Tier 1 Trainers
  - ✓ 6 private sessions: $480
  - ✓ 12 private sessions: $900
  - ✓ 12 tandem sessions: $1440
- Tier 2 Trainer
  - ✓ 12 private sessions: $1080
  - ✓ 12 tandem sessions: $1680
- Group Training
  - ✓ 12 sessions for a monthly rate of $180

- Krav Maga
  - ✓ 4 classes for a monthly rate of $80
- Boxing
  - ✓ 6 Sessions: $480
  - ✓ 12 Sessions: $900
- M.A.T.
  - ✓ 5 Sessions: $475

❑ The Initial Sources of Capital for the Business:

- I used my own money. Started small and kept overhead low.

❑ The Three to Five Most Valuable Lessons You Have Learned in Your Business

- Keep overhead low. Don't spend on things you absolutely don't need.
- Never negotiate on prices.
- Never hire anyone without doing a proper background check.
- Don't let just anyone come in because you need the extra money from trainers paying rent.
- Education, Education, Education.

❑ The Three to Five Most Effective Strategies for Marketing and Selling Your Brand

- I believe what makes our *studio success*ful is having educated trainers, a clean environment, and treating clients like they're at home. In return, our clients provide referrals.

❑ The Three to Five Strategies That Have Proven Most Successful in Retaining Your Clients

- Educated and friendly staff has kept clients coming back, many of them since we opened six years ago.

❑ The Three to Five Most Important Lessons That Have Driven Your Profitability

- This business is based on clients having disposable income.
- Knowledgeable staff, a great location, and good leadership are essential to generating a profit.
- Continually educate your staff as they are the engine that drives the business.

> **Knowledgeable staff, a great location, and good leadership are essential to generating a profit.**

❑ The Three to Five Greatest Challenges That You Face Day to Day

- Making sure all trainers arrive on time for their clients and show up.
- Making sure clients are connected with the trainer who is the best fit for them.
- Time management. Running a business and training clients 30 to 40 hours a week takes time management.
- Keeping the studio clean all the time.
- Not bringing personal life inside the workplace.

- ❏ If You Were Starting Over Again, What Would Be the Three to Five Things You Wish That You Understood Better?

  - How difficult it is to go from something you love doing (e.g., personal training) to managing people who don't share your vision or your passion.
  - If I had to do it all over again, I would have spent more time hiring the right person for the job; this would have saved me countless nights of sleep. There are a ton of bad trainers out there, trainers who think it's an easy gig and the money is great. For someone who hasn't gone to college yet can pick up a certification allowing them to earn $30 to $75 an hour, being a personal trainer is enticing. Unfortunately, they don't realize how difficult it is to generate a steady flow of clients.
  - Stand firm, and don't try to be your staff's best friend. Huge mistake I have made, and unfortunately, I probably will continue to do it.
  - Hire a manger.

- ❏ Additional Insights

  - Find out as much as you can about the trainers who you are considering hiring and/or retaining. There is not enough information in the marketplace about the credentials and work performance of trainers, especially in regards to trainers who are truly qualified to work with clients. Some of the trainers working in the market are horrible and give the industry a bad name. If I would have cared more about the backgrounds of trainers I hired, I could have weeded out half my anxiety attacks.

Reflections

As one studies the insights shared by the four highly successful entrepreneurs showcased in this chapter, it becomes evident that successfully opening and operating a boutique fitness facility takes passion, discipline, commitment, patience, and fortitude.

Appendices

A. Leading Health/Fitness Industry Associations and Organizations
B. Leading Health/Fitness Industry Trade Publications
C. Profiles of Leading Global Health/Fitness Facility Companies
D. Profiles of Leading U.S. Club and Boutique Fitness Facility Companies
E. Sample Marketing Materials From Leading Global Health/Fitness Operators
F. Profiles of Leading U.S. Health/Fitness Club Equipment Manufacturers
G. Sample Job Descriptions
H. Sample Structured Interview Questioning Format for a Fitness Director Applicant
I. Selected Operational Forms
J. Sample Design and Construction Checklist
K. Sample Member Satisfaction Survey
L. Sample Corporate Sales Checklist
M. Selected Risk Management Forms
N. Suggested References

Leading Health/Fitness Industry Associations and Organizations

American College of Sports Medicine 401 West Michigan Indianapolis, IN 46202 317-637-9200 www.acsm.org	Research, education, and certification for fitness professionals, physicians, and individuals in related sports medicine fields
American Council on Exercise 4851 Paramount Drive San Diego, CA 92123 800-825-3636 www.acefitness.org	Education and certification for fitness professionals
Aerobic and Fitness Association of America 15250 Ventura Blvd. Suite 200 Sherman Oaks, CA 91403 877-968-7263 www.afaa.com	Education and certification for fitness professionals
Association for Fitness Studios 300 North LaSalle Street, Suite 4925 Chicago, IL 60654 www.afsfitness.com	Association dedicated to serving the business needs of fitness studio owners and operators. AFS offers educational programs, networking opportunities, and other relevant resources to assist fitness studio operators achieve success.
Europe Active Rue Washington 40, B-1050 Bruxelles Belgium +32–(02) 649 90 44 www.ehfa.eu	Association involved in public policy, education, standard development, and public relations for the European club industry

IDEA Health and Fitness Association 10455 Pacific Center Court San Diego, CA 92121-4339 800-999-4332 www.ideafit.com	Education for fitness professionals
International Health, Racquet & Sportsclub Association Seaport Center, 70 Fargo Street Boston, MA 02210 800-228-4772 www.ihrsa.org	International trade association involved in providing public policy, education, industry benchmarking, and networking services for health/fitness, racquet, and sports clubs
International Spa Association 2365 Harrodsburg Road, Suite A325 Lexington, KY 40504 888-651-4772 www.experienceispa.com	Trade association for the spa industry; education for the spa industry
National Academy of Sports Medicine 123 Hodencamp Road, Suite 204 Thousand Oaks, CA 91360 800-460-6276 www.nasm.org	Education and certification for fitness professionals
National Strength and Conditioning Association 1885 Bob Johnson Drive Colorado Springs, CO 80906 800-815-6826 www.nsca-lift.org	Education and certification for fitness professionals
National Wellness Institute 1300 College Ct., P.O. Box 827 Stevens Point, WI 54481-0827 800-244-8922 www.nationalwellness.org	Association involved in delivering education, resources, and communication for professionals with an interest in wellness and health promotion

Leading Health/Fitness Industry Trade Publications

B

ACSM's Health and Fitness Journal Published by Lippincott Williams & Wilkins 16522 Hunters Green Parkway Hagerstown, MD 21740 800-638-3030	Publication for fitness professionals; can be obtained by non-ACSM members; published six times a year
ACE Certified News 4851 Paramount Drive San Diego, CA 92123 800-825-3636	Publication of ACE; published six times a year for certified members of ACE; covers a wide array of health and fitness-related topics
ACE Fitness Matters 4851 Paramount Drive San Diego, CA 92123 800-825-3636	Bimonthly publication of ACE that is geared to the consumer; provides information on health, wellness, and exercise
Aquatics International Hanley Woods LLC 6222 Wilshire Blvd Los Angeles, CA 90048-5100 888-269-8410	Monthly publication for aquatics professionals serving in all market segments
Athletic Business 4130 Lien Road Madison, WI 53704 800-869-6882	Monthly publication for athletic, fitness, and recreational professionals; focuses on issues concerning recreation centers, universities, military, and commercial health/fitness clubs
Club Business International Magazine of IHRSA Seaport Center, 70 Fargo Street Boston, MA 02210 800-228-4772	Monthly publication for members of IHRSA; focuses on the commercial club industry

Club Industry Penton Media 9800 Metcalf Avenue Overland Park, KS 66212 913-341-1300	Online publications serving various segments of the health/fitness and recreational industry, including commercial facilities, community centers, not-for-profits, and university-based facilities. Online publications include Club Industry Newsbeat (weekly) and Club Industry Trendbeat (monthly)
Club Insider News Box 681241 Marietta, GA 30068 770-850-8506	Monthly publication for anyone involved in the health/fitness club industry; offers inside news typically not provided by other publications; available in both hard copy and online
DaySpa Creative Age Communications 7628 Densmore Avenue Van Nuys, CA 91406 1-800-624-4196	Monthly publication that is dedicated to serving day-spa operators; features practical information about the spa industry
Exercise Standards and Malpractice Reporter PRC Publishing 3976 Fulton Drive, N.W. Canton, OH 44718 330-492-6063	Monthly publication targeted at professionals in the fitness industry; focuses on legal and risk management issues
IDEA Fitness Journal 10455 Pacific Center Court San Diego, CA 92121 800-999-IDEA	Monthly publication for personal trainers and group-exercise instructors
Health Club Management Published by Leisure Media Company, LTD Portmill House, Portmill Lane Hitchen Herts SGF 1DJ, England www.healthclubmanagement.co.uk	Monthly publication targeted at health/fitness professionals in all segments of the leisure and fitness industries. Targeted primarily at UK and European operators.
Pulse 2365 Harrodsburg Road, Suite A325 Lexington, KY 40504 888-651-4772	Monthly publication of ISPA targeted at professionals who own and operate spas
Recreation Management CAB Communications 50 North Brockway Street, Suite 4-11 Palatine, IL 60067 847-963-8740	Monthly publication targeted at recreation professionals
Strength and Conditioning Journal Professional Journal of NSCA 1885 Bob Johnson Drive Colorado Springs, CO 80906 800-815-6826	Bimonthly publication targeted at NSCA members

Profiles of Leading Global Health/Fitness Facility Companies

C

This section provides examples of some of the leading global players in the health/fitness industry.

❑ *24 Hour Fitness, San Ramon, California* (www.24hourfitness.com). 24 Hour Fitness was originally founded in 1983 in Northern California. It emerged as an industry leader in the 1990s after bringing on a private equity firm and purchasing Ray Wilson's Family Fitness Centers of California. Since the 1990s, it has been able to acquire regionally based club groups, as well as drive organic growth through a combination of debt and equity. In 2005, the company was sold to Forstmann Little, a New York–based private equity firm, for a reported $1.6 billion. In the summer of 2014, the company was sold by Forstmann Little to private equity investors (AEA Investors, Global Leisure Partners, and the Ontario Teacher's Pension Fund) for an estimated $1.9 billion. As of the 2014, the company operated over 413 clubs in the U.S. and overseas, serving approximately 3.8 million members. The company has several different types of club offerings, including active and express clubs (fitness-only clubs), sport clubs, super sport clubs, and ultra sport clubs (a level of club based on types of facilities and amenities offered). The company also offers a unique group of celebrity-branded clubs, such as Andre Agassi, Jackie Chan, Magic Johnson, and Derek Jeter. Depending on the type of club and market served, dues for an individual could range from under $30 a month to around $70 a month in its branded urban clubs. The company had estimated revenues of $1.4 billion in 2015, making it one of the five largest global companies when measured by revenues, along with LA Fitness International, Equinox, Lifetime Fitness, and Virgin Active.

❑ *Equinox Clubs, New York, New York* (www.equinox.com). Equinox is based in New York. As of December 2016, it operated over 90 Equinox branded clubs in several domestic and international markets, including New York, Chicago, Northern California, Southern California, Florida, Texas, London, and Toronto. Equinox clubs are premium gyms that serve an affluent, middle-aged, urban market. The Equinox brand slogan is: "It's not Fitness. It's Life." The brand is built on trendy modern facilities, innovative programs and services, and association with the "celebrity wannabes" in their respective communities. The typical facility ranges from 25,000 to 45,000 square feet, with a few approximating 100,000 square feet. Some facilities offer pools, and most have a spa. The clubs have between 4,000 and 6,000 memberships per club. Although pricing varies by market, in all instances, an individual membership costs in the range of $125 and $185, with additional fees for gaining full access to other Equinox clubs either in the region, nationally or internationally. Equinox is known for its innovative group-exercise and excellent personal-training services, with an estimated 15 percent to 20 percent of members enrolled in personal training. In 2014, Equinox purchased six Sports Club/LA clubs for approximately $110 million. Equinox leads the U.S. club industry with regard to leveraging technology. It also has one of the most dynamic websites in the industry. The company also owns and operates three other brands: Blink Clubs (budget clubs located in urban markets), Soul Cycle (group cycling studios), and Pure Yoga (mind and body studios). The company is estimated to have generated $1.07 billion in revenue in 2015.

- *Konami Sports, Tokyo, Japan* (www.konamisportsclub.jp). Konami Sports was founded in 1973. Originally, the clubs were operated under the People Company banner, but later, after being sold, were rebranded as Konami Sports. The company is public. As of 2014, the company operates 385 clubs in Japan, of which 196 are owned, 185 are managed, and four are franchised. In 2008, the company reported serving a membership base of nearly 980,000. In 2014, the company reported revenues of approximately $788 million, which when measured by revenues, places it among the top six globally.

- *LA Fitness International, U.S.* LA Fitness currently operates over 700 clubs throughout the U.S. The company, which was founded in the 1980s, really took off in the early part of the 21st century, when it acquired considerable private equity and debt financing. The company model was to build large, suburban multipurpose clubs that offered limited amenities and service at a very low price ($29 to $59 a month, depending on the regional market). While the company keeps its metrics private, it is estimated that their clubs serve over 3 million members and in 2015 generated just over $1.9 billion in revenue, making it the largest global fitness business by revenues. Some financial professionals have estimated LA Fitness's enterprise value at well over $3 billion. In late 2011, LA Fitness purchased 171 Bally Total Fitness clubs, and in 2012, 2013, and 2014 they purchased several regional U.S. club chains. As measured by the number of clubs that an organization has, as well as the revenues it generates, LA Fitness is the largest club company in the world.

- *Lifetime Fitness, Minneapolis, Minnesota* (www.lifetimefitness.com). Lifetime Fitness was founded in 1992 by Bahram Akradi. The company revolutionized the suburban club market by introducing the first family-oriented, high-volume sales club in the U.S. market. The company's typical clubs range in size from 110,000 square feet to as large as 140,000 square feet. The company was privately held until 2004, when it went public. The company's growth has primarily been through organic development, though since around 2010 it has made strategic acquisitions to grow its portfolio. As of 2016, the company owned and operated over 112 clubs throughout the U.S and Canada. The company has approximately 22,000 employees, who serve a membership base of over 800,000 members (approximately 8,000 to 10,000 members per club). In 2015, the company generated approximately $1.35 billion, making it the third largest club company by revenues. The company's reported EBITDA in 2013 was $345 million giving it a 28 percent EBITDA margin.

- *McFit, Germany.* McFit was founded in the 1990s. The company established the benchmark for budget clubs in Europe. The company model revolves around fitness-only clubs, offering 24-hour access, limited staffing (usually one staff person during staffed hours), no amenities (members actually pay for showers), lots of equipment, and self-directed exercise programming. One of its unique selling propositions is its technology platform, which may be among the best in the industry. As of 2016, McFit owned and operated over 240 clubs in Europe, the majority of which are located in Germany. As of 2016, McFit served 1.3 million members and in 2015 reported revenues of approximately 237 million Euro ($313 million U.S.). It also reports having an EBITDA margin in excess of 30 percent.

- *Virgin Active, United Kingdom* (www.virginactive.com). Virgin Active was founded in 1998, with the acquisition of the assets of the former Healthland chain of clubs in South Africa. Since its founding, the company has expanded into England, as well as into mainland Europe. In 2010, the company purchased Holmes Place, an operator of premium and luxury clubs in the U.K. and then in 2012 it purchased another prominent UK operator, Esporta. By 2016, the company owned and operated 270 clubs and had over 1.2 million members. The Virgin Active chain includes both Virgin Active and Virgin Active Classic clubs (premium and luxury). Virgin Active reported 2014 revenues of just over $1.05 billion U.S., making it only one of five health and fitness club companies to generate revenues equal to our exceeding $1 billion in 2013.

D Profiles of Leading U.S. Club and Boutique Fitness Facility Companies

This appendix provides an overview of several leading club and boutique fitness companies in the U.S.

- *Active Sports Clubs (formerly Club One), Sausalito, California* (www.activesportsclubs.com). Active Sports Clubs (formerly Club One) was founded in 2014. The company purchased the assets of Club One in 2014. As of 2014, it owns and manages 58 clubs (7 owned and 51 managed). In addition to operating commercial clubs in Northern California, it also manages community recreation centers and sports clubs for local municipalities and non-profit associations, as well as on-site corporate fitness centers for some of the nation's largest corporations. The company serves a member base of over 200,000. In 2015, the company generated approximately $45 million.

- *Anytime Fitness, Hastings, Minnesota* (www.anytimefitness.com). Anytime Fitness is a fitness franchise organization with over 2,400 fitness franchises around the world. The company's mission is to enrich lives through better health, convenience, community, and inspiration-driven franchise owners. As of 2016, the company had over 3,000 franchisees, serving approximately 1.8 million members around the globe. In 2015, the company reported total revenue from all franchisees in excess of $1.1 million.

- *Bay Club Company (formerly Western Athletic Clubs), Northern and Southern California* (www.bayclubs.com). The Bay Club Company was founded in 1977 by Jim Gerber, who ran the company until 2010, when it was sold to KSL. In 2014, KSL sold the company to York Capital and JMA Ventures. The company operates a total of 12 clubs, with a collective membership base of approximately 56,000. The company operates premium and luxury sport resorts that range in size from 40,000 square feet to over 100,000 square feet. Their clubs are multipurpose and offer fitness, aquatics, spa services, extensive youth programs, and tennis. The company reported 2015 revenues of just over $219 million.

- *Core Power Yoga* (www.corepoweryoga.com). Core Power Yoga opened its first studio in 2002 in Denver, Colorado. Since its inception, it has grown to over 100 studios in 13 states. The company employees over 1,800 instructors committed to delivering on the company's mission of sharing its passion for yoga and healthy living to inspire everyone to live their most extraordinary life. The company not only owns and operates studios, but it offers and extensive array of instructor development and training programs.

- *Crossfit, Washington, D.C.* (www.crossfit.com). Crossfit's mission is to fuel a revolution in fitness based on the pursuit of function, not form, on measurements of performance. The Crossfit community is comprised of over 12,000 affiliates worldwide who promote and teach the principles espoused by the parent organization. Crossfit is not a franchise, nor is a group of corporate-owned studios; instead, it is a loose grassroots association of affiliates who are committed to offering their communities the Crossfit approach to exercise.

- *DMB Sports Clubs (Village Health Clubs and Spas), Scottsdale, Arizona* (www.villageclubs.com). DMB is a chain of three clubs, based in Scottsdale, Arizona. Its clubs are high-end, sport resort-type clubs, serving an affluent family market. Its facilities are multipurpose clubs that range from 50,000 to over 100,000 square feet. Its brand is built on family offerings and a service level that have a resort-feel to them. Its clubs have between 2,000 and 4,000 memberships per club. Overall, the company has a membership base of 8,500. While pricing varies, individual dues at each of their respective clubs may range between $75 and $150 a month. The company reported 2015 revenues of just over $38 million. The company's clubs are known for their family programs and customer service.

- *Fitness Formula, Chicago, Illinois* (www.ffc.com). Fitness Formula owns and operates 15 clubs in the Chicago market that collectively have over 30,000 members. Its clubs are located primarily in an urban setting, although it does have suburban clubs. Fitness Formula facilities are premium clubs that serve an upper-middle class audience, composed of individuals and families. Its brand promise is to enrich people's lives and deliver results. Its clubs are primarily multipurpose and include gymnasiums and pools. Each facility ranges in size from 30,000 to 100,000 square feet. Its clubs offer group exercise, personal training, physical therapy services, spa services, and cafes. The company offers members for an additional incremental fee to have full privileges to all of the Fitness Formula clubs. Pricing ranges from $70 to just over $100 a month for an individual. Its clubs market in the local media. In 2015, the company reported generating revenues of nearly $50 million.

- *Leisure Sports, Pleasanton, California* (www.clubsports.com). Leisure Sports operates 10 (8 owned and 2 managed) high-end, multipurpose clubs in California, Oregon, and Nevada that collectively serve a membership base of slightly over 61,000. Leisure Sports focuses on the affluent (over $100,000 HH income) family market by offering a full-service, multipurpose facility. Its brand is distinguished by the connection of a high-end sports club with a high-end hotel, creating what the owners refer to as a sport resort. Its facilities range from 70,000 to over 100,000 square feet, with over 5,000 members on average per club. Monthly dues vary, but in most instances, individual dues will fall between $90 and $150 a month. Its focus is on service and programming. In 2015, the company reported revenue of just over $100 million.

- *Midtown Athletic Clubs (MAC), Chicago, Illinois* (www.midtownathleticclub.com). The MAC was originally founded in 1969 by Alan Schwartz and his father, when they opened the Mid Town Tennis Club in Chicago. The company changed its name to Midtown Athletic Clubs around 2012. The company currently operates 30 clubs (10 owned and 20 managed), in addition to a corporate-wellness entity that manages wellness and fitness centers for large corporations. The company's owned and managed clubs target an affluent upper-middle class demographic. The company is known for its outstanding tennis programs, high level of customer service, and commitment to employee education. The company reported 2013 revenues of approximately $87.6 million.

- *Pure Barre* (www.purebarre.com). Pure Barre is a franchise company that offers entrepreneurs the opportunity to own and operate a Pure Barre studio. As of 2016 there were over 300 independently owned Pure Barre studios throughout the U.S., each offering consumers a uniquely branded group exercise experience that offers a full-body workout using the ballet barre and other functional movements derived from Pilates.

- *Orange Theory, Boca Raton, Florida* (www.orangetheoryfitness.com). Orange Theory is a franchise of the Ultimate Fitness Group, LLC. The Orange Theory business model revolves around providing a scientifically designed high intensity interval (HIIT) program that is delivered in a 60-minute session. As of 2016, the company has opened over 500 studios in the U.S., making it the largest boutique fitness studio franchise in the U.S. In 2015, the company reported revenues in excess of $47 million.

- *Wisconsin Athletic Clubs (WAC), Milwaukee, Wisconsin* (www.thewac.com). WAC owns and operates seven clubs in the Milwaukee, Wisconsin market. WAC clubs serve primarily a family market, targeting a middle-class demographic. Its clubs vary in size, but most are under 40,000 square feet and offer either a fitness-only experience or, in the case of a few clubs, a multipurpose-club experience. Over the past several years, the company has partnered with the local hospitals in creating large complexes that include a medical component as well as the club. The company's first facility was a racquetball club that opened in the 1970s. The key mission of the company is to make a difference in people's lives. Its brand is based on accessibility in the local market, convenience, good facilities, a focus on service, and programming. Monthly dues for an individual are $55 to $75 a month.

The statistical and numerical data included in this section are based on information from the IHRSA 2016 Global Report as well as other publically available reports. The company overview was generated from observations made through first-hand knowledge of each company.

Sample Marketing Materials From Leading Global Health/Fitness Operators

E

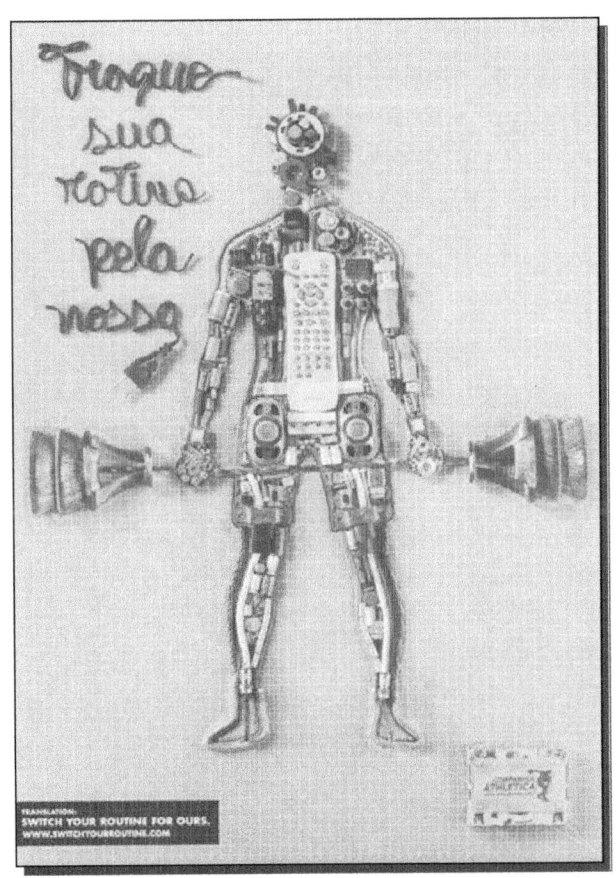

"Switch Your Routine" ad campaign, Companhia Athletica, Brazil

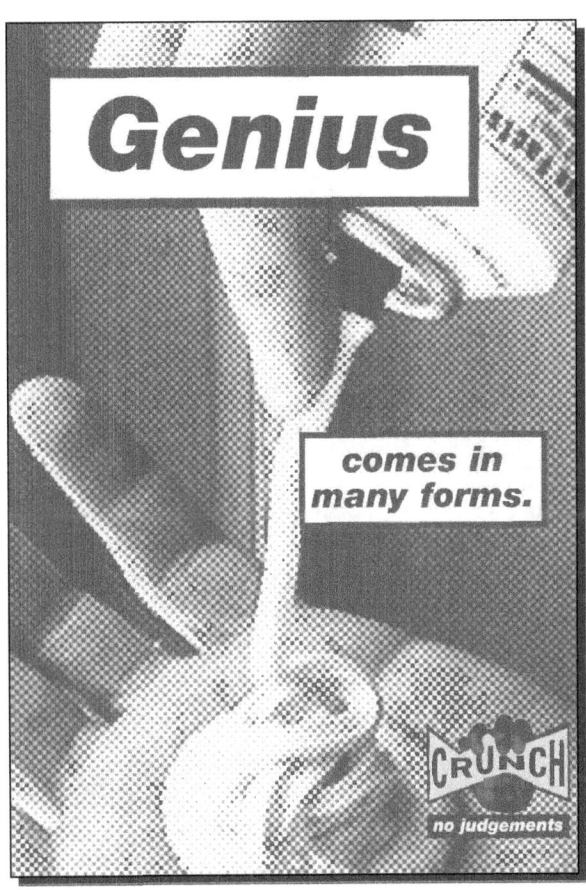

Direct mail piece, Crunch

Direct mail piece, Companhia Athletica, Brazil

"Fat Imprisonment" ad campaign, Companhia Athletica, Brazil

Smart phone application, Planet Fitness

Employees ad campaign, World Class, Russia

Member reward program, Club One

F Profiles of Leading U.S. Health/Fitness Club Equipment Manufacturers

This appendix provides an overview of several of the leading manufacturers of equipment for health/fitness club facilities in the world.

❑ *Cybex International, Medway, Massachusetts*

Cybex is a full-service equipment manufacturer that offers a complete array of cardiovascular and resistance training equipment. Cybex originated in the 1960s as the Cybex Ergometer Company and was later purchased by Lumex. Originally, Cybex manufactured medically based isokinetic equipment used in rehabilitative medicine. In 1983, Cybex purchased Eagle Resistance Equipment, a step that moved the company into a new manufacturing arena that focused on variable-resistance equipment and free-weight equipment. During its first several years of business, Eagle made significant inroads into the resistance-training equipment market that had been dominated at the time by Nautilus. Subsequently, during the early 1990s, Cybex became the biggest player in the resistance-training arena. Cybex also created a line of isokinetic cardiovascular equipment that was targeted specifically for the fitness/health club industry. At the time, the Cybex Upper-Body Ergometer was considered one of the best, if not the best, of its type in the industry. During the early 1990s, Cybex was known for its quality, service, and its isokinetic cardiovascular equipment. In 1997, Cybex merged with Trotter to form a new company, called Cybex International. In the process, the new company, Cybex International, inherited the treadmills and other cardiovascular equipment that Trotter had developed over the years. In the early part of the 21st century, the company released its most popular piece of equipment—a modified elliptical trainer, appropriately called the Arc Trainer. At the present time, Cybex sells over $120 million in equipment annually. Its line of equipment offerings includes variable-resistance equipment, free-weight benches, plate-loaded equipment, treadmills, bicycles, and the ARC Trainer. Much of Cybex's popularity in the club industry is a result of the variety of its equipment offerings (i.e., it can outfit an entire club), the quality of its resistance-equipment lines, and its ability to provide financing to clubs for the purchase of its equipment. Cybex was formerly a publically traded company. In 2016, the company was sold to Life Fitness for $195 million dollars.

❏ *Life Fitness, Franklin Park, Illinois*

Life Fitness was founded by Augie Neito, who built the company from the original Lifecycle company established by Ray Wilson, when he purchased the rights to market the original Lifecyle, which was invented in 1968 by Keene Dimmick. At the time, Lifecycle became the "band-aid" brand for the fitness industry when it was introduced in 1974. In the process, Life Fitness became the first manufacturer to establish a leadership position in the cardiovascular equipment arena. The Lifecycle later led to the development of the Lifestep and subsequently to a full line of cardiovascular equipment, including treadmills, recumbent bikes, and elliptical trainers. The cardiovascular equipment manufactured by Life Fitness was branded by its unique control panel and the special programming features on each machine, including hill and random programs. Life Fitness became and, to this day, remains the largest manufacturer of cardiovascular equipment in the industry. In the early 1990s, Life Fitness bought a resistance company, called High Tech, and created the Life Fitness strength line. In the later half of the 1990s, Life Fitness purchased Hammer Strength. The merger of the cardiovascular, variable resistance, and Hammer products created the largest equipment company in the industry. In 2015, Life Fitness acquired SciFit Systems, a manufacturer of fitness equipment. In 2016, Life Fitness purchased Cybex for a reported $195 million. As of year-end 2015, Life Fitness reported sales of approximately $770 million, making it the largest in the industry based on sales volume. Sales for 2016 are expected to exceed $800 million as a result of its 2016 purchase of Life Cybex. Life Fitness is known as a leader in several of its product categories. For example, the Hammer line is regarded as the gold standard in the plate-loaded category; its bikes are the top in their category, and its treadmills are among the top three in their category. Life Fitness's strength is based on its ability to completely outfit a club (e.g., treadmills, bikes, stair climbers, elliptical trainers, resistance machines, and free weights), the quality of its product from a technical and customer perspective, the innovative nature of its products, the respect that its team garners, and its marketing and sales.

❏ *Matrix Fitness, Cottage Grove, Wisconsin*

Matrix Fitness, a subsidiary of Johnson Health Tech, LTD, is a global leader in equipment manufacturing that introduced its first piece of fitness equipment in 1975. Matrix Fitness is the commercial fitness division of the company, having entered the commercial fitness industry in the early part of the 21st century. The company manufactures and sells a complete line of commercial fitness equipment including treadmills, elliptical trainers, stair climbers and a full line of strength equipment (selectorized resistance machines, free weight benches, and plate-loaded machines). The company's worldwide sales make it one of the three largest equipment companies in the health and fitness club industry.

❏ *Precor, Inc., Woodinville, Washington*

Initially, Precor started out by making cardiovascular equipment for the home market. At the time, it was among the leaders in home equipment, such as bikes and treadmills. Precor entered the commercial club market in the 1980s with its treadmills, bikes, and stair climbers. The Precor treadmill established a unique niche when it was introduced due to its ability to adjust to both positive and negative grades. Precor became an even bigger player in the market when it introduced the EFX Elliptical Trainer in 1995. In the process, the EFX became a landmark for the equipment industry that changed the club industry. By the late 1990s and early 21st century, Precor became one of the top three players in the cardiovascular arena, with the EFX and its treadmills. During this period, Precor also introduced its Stretch Trainer. Over the years, Precor has been renowned for its innovation in equipment design, its equipment esthetics, and its desire to introduce new concepts to the market. In 2004, Precor purchased Icarian, a leading manufacturer of variable-resistance equipment and free-weight benches. In turn, it established its own line of resistance equipment. Precor bought Cardio Theater in 2004, expanding its reach into the entertainment and technology sectors. Currently, Precor, which is owned by Amer Sports, a Finnish company that also owns brands, such as Atomic and Wilson, offers an extensive line of exercise equipment (e.g., treadmills, elliptical trainers, bikes, stair climbers, and resistance equipment). Not only can the company outfit an entire club, it also has the ability to offer cardio entertainment. It is among the four largest players in the industry, with approximately $200 million in annual sales. Precor's strength lies in its approach to innovation, its ability to offer a complete package, the aesthetics of its product offering, and its marketing and sales efforts.

❏ *Star Trac, Irvine, California*

In the early 1980s, Star Trac got its start as a company named Unisen. As Unisen, it produced the electronics for Life Fitness equipment during the early years of Life Fitness. Around 1990, Star Trac entered the market as Star Trac by Unisen, whereupon it positioned itself as a leading producer of commercial treadmills. Star Trac introduced one of the first commercial treadmills in the industry that was customer-friendly, technically sound, and reasonably affordable. Since its inception, Star Trac has subsequently expanded its line of commercial treadmills, as well as added other types of exercise equipment to its inventory, including stationary cycles, stair climbers, elliptical machines, and group-exercise bikes. Star Trac established itself as a leader in the area of cardiovascular equipment by offering quality equipment that had innovations that served the needs of the end-user. Star Trac's treadmills are the only ones with built-in fans, while its bikes and recumbent bikes are the only ones with an innovative design that includes fans and comfort seating. Star Trac obtained rights to the "Johnny G" line of group-exercise bikes in the early part of the 21st century. In 2005, Star Trac expanded its offerings into the cardio-entertainment arena, as well as the resistance-equipment segment of the market, with its purchase of Flex. The company took the Flex line and created its own line of resistance equipment. In 2010, Star Trac experienced some financial troubles and was sold to a new owner, who renamed the company—Star Trac Health and Fitness. The company continues to provide quality equipment to the global marketplace. Star Trac's strengths lie in its product innovation, its focus on producing user-friendly products, its level of customer service, and its positive relationships with its customer base.

❑ *Technogym USA, Seattle, Washington*

Technogym, an Italian-based firm, is the leading fitness equipment manufacturer in Europe and is second only to Life Fitness in total global sales, with reported sales of $582 million in 2015. Technogym released its first product, the isotonic line of resistance training equipment, in 1983, the year that the company was founded. Within five years of launching its isotonic line, the company introduced its first line of cardiovascular equipment. Shortly thereafter, Technogym became the leading manufacturer of exercise equipment in Europe.

Technogym burst on the U.S. scene in the early 1990s after establishing itself as the leading manufacturer of commercial cardiovascular and resistance equipment in the European market. Technogym set itself apart when it entered the domestic U.S. market on two fronts. First, it branded itself as the "wellness" company and provided educational support to the industry. Second, it introduced the technology platform that tied its equipment together through a "key" that contained all of a user's workout information. The "key," which continues to be a benchmark for Technogym, is still offered as an upgrade. Technogym also introduced the flare of contemporary European design to its resistance machines and free-weight benches. In the process, it changed the way that other manufacturers design their resistance-training equipment. Among the factors that Technogym has become a leader in the area of equipment innovation and technology are its built-in LED media systems and its cloud-based software platform for monitoring member activity. Technogym's various product offerings include treadmills, bikes, stair climbers, elliptical machines, variable resistance equipment, and free-weight equipment. Technogym's primary strengths lie in the technical quality of its equipment, its innovative design, its focus on wellness, and its ability to equip an entire club.

G Sample Job Descriptions

SAMPLE POSITION #1
Position Title: Child Center Attendant

Position Summary:
The child center attendant is responsible for supervising and caring for the children of members and guests who are left in the club's child center, as per the policies and rules of the club.

Essential Accountabilities and Functions:
- To greet each member, guest, and child who enters the center with a service attitude and ensure that they get to know that member and child by name
- To provide personal supervision of the child center area to help ensure the safety and enjoyment of the children in accordance with club policies and rules
- To facilitate educational and other types of activities for the children while they are in the child center

Specific Job Accountabilities:
- To greet each member, guest, and child by name when they enter and leave the children's center
- To make sure that each child under the club's supervision has been properly registered for the child center and that the parent and/or legal guardian has completed the required forms pertaining to the child being left under the club's supervision
- To monitor the activities of the children under the club's supervision and ensure that they are provided with the safest possible environment
- To provide an enriching and rewarding environment for the children while they are under the club's supervision
- To assist with the organization and preventative maintenance of the children's center
- To willingly step in and assist with responsibilities attendant to other services offered by the club, as may be required to help ensure that the club delivers upon its brand promise

Reporting Relationships:
- Reports to: Member services director
- Indirectly reports to: Operations manager

Work Experience:
- Minimum of six months experience working with or caring for children between the ages of six months and eight years of age preferred
- Prior experience in licensed day care a bonus

Continued

Education:
- High school education preferred, but not required
- Classes in early childhood development a plus

Certification/License:
- AED/CPR certification

Working Conditions/Environment:
- The job involves supervising young children within a club child center that is geared toward basic child supervision. The job involves registering children in the center, monitoring their activities while in the center, facilitating children's activities and games, reading to children, and cleaning the children's area, on occasion.

Specific Working Conditions:

Squatting:	Bending:	Kneeling:
Occasionally	Occasionally	Occasionally
Reaching:	Twisting:	Crawling:
Occasionally	Occasionally	Occasionally
Ladder climbing:	Stair climbing:	Other climbing:
NA	Rarely	NA
Walking on rough ground:	Exposure to temperature change:	Exposure to dust, fumes, and gas:
NA	Rarely	Rarely
Near moving machinery:	Working from heights:	Cleaning/scrubbing:
NA	NA	Occasionally
Dialing:	Collating:	Filing:
Rarely	Occasionally	Occasionally
Opening/closing:	Sorting:	Stamping:
Occasionally	Rarely	Rarely
Stapling:	Folding/unfolding:	Inserting/removing:
Rarely	Rarely	Rarely
Walk—hrs./day:	Walk—frequency:	
2–4 hours	Throughout shift	
Standing—hrs./day:	Standing—frequency:	
1–3 hours	Throughout shift	
Sit—hrs./day:	Sit—frequency:	
Less than an hour	Throughout shift	
Max. weight lifted occasionally:	State weight lifted if above 100 lbs.:	
25 pounds	NA	

Continued

Max. weight lifted frequently:	State weight lifted if above 100 lbs.:
15 pounds	NA
Max. weight carried occasionally:	State weight carried if above 100 lbs:
25 pounds	NA
Max. weight carried frequently:	State weight carried if above 100 lbs.:
15 pounds	NA
Max. weight pushed occasionally:	State weight pushed if above 100 lbs.:
50 pounds	NA
Max. weight pushed frequently:	State weight pushed if above 100 lbs.:
10 pounds	NA
Max. weight pulled occasionally:	State weight pulled if above 100 lbs.:
50 pounds	NA
Max. weight pulled frequently:	State weight pulled if above 100 lbs.:
10 pounds	NA

Employee signature: _____ Date: _____

Staff signature: _____ Date: _____

SAMPLE POSITION #2
Position Title: Fitness Director

Position Summary:
The fitness director is accountable for the club's fitness and group-exercise programs and in particular, for achieving the budgeted financial performance of the fitness department.

Essential Accountabilities and Functions:
- To oversee the development of the annual business plan and financial targets for the fitness department, along with monitoring actual financial performance of key revenue and expense areas to ensure achievement of the business plan and financial plan targets
- To be accountable for the recruitment, selection, and development of the club's fitness and group-exercise staff and to help ensure that the employees work as a team in achieving the department's and club's goals
- To be accountable for fostering a fitness environment that leads to member delight
- To make sure that every member who is on the fitness floor is served in a manner that helps ensure them of a memorable experience in the club
- To be accountable for the overall condition and cleanliness of the fitness and exercise equipment areas in the club

Specific Job Accountabilities:
- To develop the department's annual business plan and financial targets
- To manage the daily, weekly, and monthly revenue activities of the department in order to enable the club to achieve its fitness-revenue targets
- To oversee the financial activities of the department in a manner that will bring about achievement of the department's financial goals, including driving revenues and managing department expenses
- To oversee and monitor, on a daily, weekly, monthly, and YTD basis, new member screenings and orientations and to help direct members into activities that will engage them in a long-term fitness program
- To recruit, select, develop, educate, and lead the fitness and group-exercise team, including conducting regular meetings, providing continuing education activities, and performing semi-annual performance reviews on all direct reports
- To establish relationships with the members by engaging members with a service attitude while they are on the fitness floor
- To oversee the care of the fitness areas, including inspecting the equipment, making sure that the proper preventative maintenance for equipment is addressed, replacing and updating equipment as needed, and otherwise ensuring that the fitness area is clean, well-maintained, and safe for the members
- To oversee the day-to-day operations of the department, including completing all necessary administrative functions required by the club
- To serve as a role model for the fitness staff, including performing any necessary job responsibilities, as may be required to help ensure that the club delivers upon its brand promise

Reporting Relationships:
- Reports to: Club general manager
- Indirectly reports to: NA
- Directly supervises: Fitness instructors, personal trainers, and group-exercise staff
- Indirectly supervises: Housecleaning staff

Continued

Work Experience:
- A minimum of one year's experience in a supervisory role within the fitness industry
- A minimum of three years' experience as a personal trainer or fitness instructor

Education:
- College degree in exercise science, fitness, health, kinesiology, or recreation
- Graduate work in fitness or related field preferred

Certification/License:
- Certification as a personal trainer, fitness instructor, or conditioning specialist from a nationally recognized and third-party accredited certification organization (ACE, ACSM, NASM, NSCA)
- Secondary certification in fitness specialty area preferred, but not required
- AED/CPR certification

Working Conditions/Environment:
The club environment consists of a cardiovascular area, resistance training area, free-weight area, group-exercise studio, locker rooms, reception area, and office space. The fitness director will be involved in walking through the club on a regular basis, assisting members on the floor, leading personal training sessions with clients, teaching a group-exercise class, as needed, and, on occasion, performing activities that include lifting weights off the floor, picking up towels, and similar housekeeping-oriented tasks.

Specific Working Conditions:

Squatting:	Bending:	Kneeling:
Occasionally	Occasionally	Occasionally
Reaching:	Twisting:	Crawling:
Occasionally	Occasionally	NA
Ladder climbing:	Stair climbing:	Other climbing:
NA	Occasionally	NA
Walking on rough ground:	Exposure to temperature change:	Exposure to dust, fumes, and gas:
NA	Occasionally	Rarely
Near moving machinery:	Working from heights:	Cleaning/scrubbing:
NA	NA	Occasionally
Dialing:	Collating:	Filing:
Frequently	Occasionally	Occasionally
Opening/closing:	Sorting:	Stamping:
Occasionally	Occasionally	Occasionally
Stapling:	Folding/unfolding:	Inserting/removing:
Occasionally	Occasionally	Rarely
Walk—hrs./day:	Walk—frequency:	
3–4 hours	Throughout the day	

Continued

Drive—hrs./day:	Drive—frequency:
NA	NA
Sit—hrs./day:	Sit—frequency:
1–2 hours	Throughout the day
Max. weight lifted occasionally:	State weight lifted if above 100 lbs.:
100 pounds	NA
Max. weight lifted frequently:	State weight lifted if above 100 lbs.:
45 pounds	NA
Max. weight carried occasionally:	State weight carried if above 100 lbs.:
100 pounds	NA
Max. weight carried frequently:	State weight carried if above 100 lbs.:
45 pounds	NA
Max. weight pushed occasionally:	State weight pushed if above 100 lbs.:
100 pounds	NA
Max. weight pushed frequently:	State weight pushed if above 100 lbs.:
45 pounds	NA
Max. weight pulled occasionally:	State weight pulled if above 100 lbs.:
100 pounds	NA
Max. weight pulled frequently:	State weight pulled if above 100 lbs.:
45 pounds	NA

Employee signature: _____ Date: _____
Staff signature: _____ Date: _____

SAMPLE POSITION #3
Position Title: Group-Exercise Coordinator/Director

Position Summary:
The group-exercise coordinator is responsible for supervising the club's group-exercise program, including leading and instructing the various group-exercise classes offered to the members and guests of the club

Essential Accountabilities and Functions:
- To ensure that the club offers a dynamic, state-of-the-art group-exercise program that attracts high member participation
- To select, develop, and supervise the group exercise staff, with input from club management
- To ensure that classes are well received by the membership
- To greet each member and guest who enters the group-exercise studio with a positive attitude and ensure that they get to know that member by name
- To provide members with an entertaining, effective. and safe group-exercise experience whenever they participate in a class
- To provide support in properly maintaining the group-exercise studio

Specific Job Accountabilities:
- To oversee the development of the club's group-exercise program, including developing the class schedule and format, monitoring class attendance, and recommending programs that would enhance the overall experience of members in the group-exercise program
- To recruit, develop, and supervise the group-exercise staff, including overseeing all new instructor orientations, performing semi-annual performance assessments, and making sure that all classes have an instructor
- To greet each member and guest by name when they enter and leave the group-exercise classroom
- To come to the class at least 10 minutes in advance and to be prepared to provide an entertaining, effective, and safe group-exercise program for the participants
- To promote and sell the club's services to members and guests
- To assist in facilitating personal contact between members when they are in the classroom
- To assist with the organization and preventative maintenance of the group-exercise equipment and the classroom
- To willingly step in and assist with responsibilities attendant to other services offered by the club, as may be required to help ensure that the club delivers upon its brand promise

Reporting Relationships:
- Reports to: Fitness director
- Indirectly reports to: General manager

Work Experience:
- A minimum of three years' experience as a group-exercise instructor
- A minimum of one year's experience in developing or overseeing a group-exercise program
- Experience teaching, which should include classes similar to those to be instructed at the club

Education:
- A minimum of a high school education, with an undergraduate collegiate degree in fitness, kinesiology, or related field preferred
- Participate in at least one fitness continuing education program annually

Continued

Certification/License:
- Current certification as a group-exercise instructor by a third-party accredited certifying body in the group-exercise and fitness field (ACE, AFAA, etc.)
- If instructing classes in yoga, Pilates, Spinning, or related specialty class, either a nationally recognized certification in that specialty area or evidence of training in that specialty area
- AED/CPR certification

Working Conditions/Environment:
The job involves instructing group-exercise classes in an enclosed group-exercise studio with a cushioned wood floor. Class instruction involves a combination of low-impact and some high-impact movements, as well as movements involving lifting, stretching, and performing physical exercise.

Specific Working Conditions:

Squatting:	Bending:	Kneeling:
Occasionally	Occasionally	Occasionally
Reaching:	Twisting:	Crawling:
Occasionally	Occasionally	NA
Ladder climbing:	Stair climbing:	Other climbing:
NA	Occasionally	NA
Walking on rough ground:	Exposure to temperature change:	Exposure to dust, fumes, and gas:
NA	Rare	Rare
Near moving machinery:	Working from heights:	Cleaning/scrubbing:
NA	NA	Rare
Dialing:	Collating:	Filing:
Occasionally	Rarely	Rarely
Opening/closing:	Sorting:	Stamping:
Occasionally	Rarely	Rarely
Stapling:	Folding/unfolding:	Inserting/removing:
Rarely	Rarely	Rarely

Walk—hrs./day:	Walk—frequency:
1–2 hours	During class
Standing—hrs./day:	Standing—frequency:
1–3 hours	During class
Sit—hrs./day:	Sit—frequency:
Less than an hour	Either before or after teaching a class
Max. weight lifted occasionally:	State weight lifted if above 100 lbs.:
25 pounds	NA

Continued

Max. weight lifted fequently:	State weight lifted if above 100 lbs.:
10 pounds	NA
Max. weight carried occasionally:	State weight carried if above 100 lbs.:
25 pounds	NA
Max. weight carried frequently:	State weight carried if above 100 lbs.:
10 pounds	NA
Max. weight pushed occasionally:	State weight pushed if above 100 lbs.:
100 pounds	NA
Max. weight pushed frequently:	State weight pushed if above 100 lbs.:
10 pounds	NA
Max. weight pulled occasionally:	State weight pulled if above 100 lbs.:
100 pounds	NA
Max weight pulled frequently:	State weight pulled if above 100 lbs.:
10 pounds	NA

Employee signature: _____ Date: _____

Staff signature: _____ Date: _____

SAMPLE POSITION #4
Position Title: Personal Trainer

Position Summary:
The personal trainer is responsible for providing members of the club with a personalized fitness-lifestyle program, which includes an assessment of their fitness needs, as well as a prescription of an exercise and dietary plan that will assist the members in achieving their goals.

Essential Accountabilities and Functions:
- To greet each member and guest who enters the fitness floor with an engaging and enthusiastic attitude and ensure that they get to know that member by name
- To provide members with a personalized fitness program, including the development of the fitness program, instruction in the execution of the program, and, finally, support for the member to follow the program
- To achieve monthly personal training and related revenue program targets, as established by the club
- To provide support in properly maintaining and cleaning the fitness equipment and fitness floor
- To assist members, when sought out, in addition to those involved in personal training

Specific Job Accountabilities:
- To greet each member and guest by name when they are on the fitness floor, including establishing a relationship with each member greeted
- To conduct new member assessments and orientations
- To promote and sell the club's personal training and related fitness services to members and guests
- To provide personal training and any related personal instruction for members and guests
- To assist in facilitating personal contact between members when they are on the exercise floor
- To assist with the preventative maintenance and cleaning of the fitness equipment
- To assist with the cleaning and care of the fitness area
- To willingly step in and assist with responsibilities attendant to other services offered by the club, including teaching group-fitness classes, as may be required to help ensure that the club delivers upon its brand promise

Reporting Relationships:
- Reports to: Personal training director and/or fitness director
- Indirectly reports to: Fitness director

Work Experience:
- A minimum of one year's experience as a personal trainer and/or fitness instructor

Education:
- A minimum of a two-year degree, with an undergraduate degree in fitness, kinesiology, or related field highly preferred
- Participate in at least one fitness continuing education program annually

Certification/License:
- Current nationally accredited certification as a fitness instructor and/or personal trainer (ACE, ACSM, Cooper, NASM, and NSCA)
- Successful completion of the club's internal training within 90 days of employment

Continued

- Level 2 personal trainers must show evidence of having earned a second nationally accredited fitness certification
- AED/CPR certification

Working Conditions/Environment:

The job involves working in a fitness center that includes cardiovascular equipment, resistance machines, free weights, and other associated fitness training devices. The job often involves the lifting of weights, assisting members with lifting movements, and cleaning equipment. On occasion, personal trainers may be expected to lift and/or move objects that weigh between 45 pounds and 100 pounds.

Specific Working Conditions:

Squatting:	Bending:	Kneeling:
Occasionally	Occasionally	Occasionally
Reaching:	Twisting:	Crawling:
Frequently	Occasionally	NA
Ladder climbing:	Stair climbing:	Other climbing:
NA	Occasionally	NA
Walking on rough ground:	Exposure to temperature change:	Exposure to dust, fumes, and gas:
NA	Rarely	Rarely
Near moving machinery:	Working from heights:	Cleaning/scrubbing:
NA	NA	Occasionally
Dialing:	Collating:	Filing:
Frequently	Occasionally	Occasionally
Opening/closing:	Sorting:	Stamping:
Occasionally	Occasionally	Occasionally
Stapling:	Folding/unfolding:	Inserting/removing:
Rarely	Rarely	Occasionally

Walk—hrs./day:	Walk—frequency:
2–4 hours	Throughout the day
Standing—hrs./day:	Standing—frequency:
1–3 hours	Throughout the day
Sit—hrs./day:	Sit—frequency:
1 hour	Throughout the day
Max. weight lifted occasionally:	State weight lifted if above 100 lbs.:
100 pounds	NA
Max. weight lifted frequently:	State weight lifted if above 100 lbs.:
45 pounds	NA

Continued

Max. weight carried occasionally:	State weight carried if above 100 lbs.:
45 pounds	NA
Max. weight carried frequently:	State weight carried if above 100 lbs.:
25 pounds	NA
Max. weight pushed occasionally:	State weight pushed if above 100 lbs.:
100 pounds	NA
Max. weight pushed frequently:	State weight pushed if above 100 lbs.:
45 pounds	NA
Max. weight pulled occasionally:	State weight pulled if above 100 lbs.:
100 pounds	NA
Max. weight pulled frequently:	State weight pulled if above 100 lbs.:
45 pounds	NA

Employee signature: _____ Date: _____

Staff signature: _____ Date: _____

SAMPLE POSITION #5
Position Title: Spa Director

Position Summary:
The position of Spa Director is responsible for the overall marketing, sales, and financial success of the club's day spa.

Essential Accountabilities and Functions:
- To oversee all financial aspects of the day spas operations, including pricing, sales and accounting of all revenue and expenses
- To oversee the merchandising and marketing of the day spa to both club members and the public at large
- To select, hire, and educate the spa staff in a manner that reinforces the club's values and philosophies and helps ensure that the operation of the spa business is both profitable and exceeds the expectations of its clients

Specific Job Accountabilities:
- To select, hire, educate, and lead the spa department employee partners, which includes managing all aspects of the selection, hiring, and education process and providing the leadership for the team on a daily basis
- To conduct regular meetings and education sessions for the employee partners
- To develop the spa services menu, including the development of the specific services and the education of the employee partners in performing those services
- To oversee the financial success of the spa department by means of several steps, including the correct pricing of services; the monitoring and management of employee partner payroll and lesson payments; daily and period audits of sales; forecasting department performance on a specific period basis; and undertaking whatever other actions must occur for the department to meet its budget and forecast goals
- To handle the daily, weekly, and specific period payroll functions for the spa, including, but not limited to, collecting and auditing employee partner commission sheets, doing all payroll activities, managing payroll and commission expense to plan, etc.
- To oversee the marketing and merchandising of the spa to both club members and the public at large, including development of appropriate marketing brochures, media material, gift certificates, etc.
- To oversee the sales efforts of the spa in order to ensure that the spa meets its revenue and sales targets
- To assist in the delivery of spa services as required, including providing specific services, as qualified to do so by training (e.g., hairstyling, manicures, facials, etc.)
- To meet regularly with the fitness director and other department heads to make sure that complete cooperation exists between departments in the club and to ensure that regular communication occurs with other employee partners in the club regarding the spa's services and operation
- To assist with any required job activity of the spa, as may be needed, in order to help ensure that members and clients are always served in accordance with the club's overall service philosophy
- To conduct oneself at all times in a manner of professionalism that aligns with the values, philosophies, and standards of the club, including being in uniform and nametag

Reporting Relationships:
- Reports to: Fitness director/general manager
- Directly supervises: Massage therapists, estheticians, and spa support staff
- Indirectly supervises:

Continued

Work Experience:
- Minimum of one years' supervisory experience in the spa, massage, or cosmetology environment
- Minimum of three years' experience in the spa, massage, or cosmetology business

Education:
- Degree from accredited massage or cosmetology school
- College degree in related field preferred, but not required

Certification/License:
- Licensure as either massage therapist or esthetician
- AED/CPR certification

Working Conditions/Environment:
The spa director will spend the majority of the day working in the spa area, which includes treatment rooms, manicure area, pedicure area, and related retail area. On occasion, the job will involve working in an area that has wet surfaces and may expose the director to items that have been exposed to bodily fluids such as perspiration.

Specific Working Conditions:

Squatting:	Bending:	Kneeling:
Rarely	Occasionally	Rarely
Reaching:	Twisting:	Crawling:
Occasionally	Occasionally	NA
Ladder climbing:	Stair climbing:	Other climbing:
NA	Rarely	Rarely
Walking on rough ground:	Exposure to temperature change:	Exposure to dust, fumes, and gas:
NA	Rarely	NA
Near moving machinery:	Working from heights:	Cleaning/scrubbing:
NA	NA	Occasionally
Dialing:	Collating:	Filing:
Frequently	Occasionally	Occasionally
Opening/closing:	Sorting:	Stamping:
Occasionally	Occasionally	Rarely
Stapling:	Folding/unfolding:	Inserting/removing:
Rarely	Rarely	Rarely
Walk—hrs./day:	Walk—frequency:	
1–3 hours	Throughout the day	
Drive—hrs./day:	Drive—frequency:	
NA	NA	

Continued

Sit—hrs./day:	Sit—frequency:
4–6 hours	Throughout the day
Max. weight lifted occasionally:	State weight lifted if above 100 lbs.:
25 pounds	NA
Max. weight lifted frequently:	State weight lifted if above 100 lbs.:
1–2 pounds	NA
Max. weight carried occasionally:	State weight carried if above 100 lbs.:
25 pounds	NA
Max. weight carried frequently:	State weight carried if above 100 lbs.:
1 pound	NA
Max. weight pushed occasionally:	State weight pushed if above 100 lbs.:
25 pounds	NA
Max. weight pushed frequently:	State weight pushed if above 100 lbs.:
10 pounds	NA
Max. weight pulled occasionally:	State weight pulled if above 100 lbs.:
25 pounds	NA
Max. weight pulled frequently:	State weight pulled if above 100 lbs.:
10 pounds	NA

Employee signature: _____ Date: _____

Staff signature: _____ Date: _____

Sample Structured Interview Questioning Format for a Fitness Director Applicant

- ❏ General Fitness
  - Please indicate what steps you would normally take to ensure that prospective exercisers receive a safe and effective exercise program when they first decide to begin exercising.

Key elements of response:

_____ Have the individual complete a pre-activity screening, such as health history, Par Q, or similar tool.

_____ Have the individual obtain medical clearance, if that person is at high risk.

_____ Perform a fitness test to obtain baseline information on the physical abilities and fitness level of the individual.

_____ Complete an exercise prescription, and then lead the individual through the actual prescription.

_____ Follow-up with the individual on a regular basis to ensure that the person is correctly following the program, and make adjustments to the program, if needed.

  - A significant portion of the exercising and non-exercising population at this club is over the age of 50. What special precautions might you need to take when programming physical activity for a population of this age?

Key elements of response:

_____ Make sure that the individuals have received the appropriate screening, including medical clearance and screening, when indicated.

_____ Make sure that the staff is familiar with the special physical requirements of this population and provide the necessary training, if needed.

_____ Make sure that the activity programs for this age group are characterized by certain attributes, including the following: lower impact, include lower-intensity activity, are monitored by qualified staff, include all of the basic components of the fitness spectrum (flexibility, muscular fitness, cardiovascular fitness, and body composition), and are programmed to be conducted at a time that is convenient for the exercisers.

_____ Make allowances for more personal attention.

- Please describe the critical elements involved in developing an exercise program for a 45-year-old male who has been diagnosed as having type II diabetes. Assume that he has been cleared to exercise by his physician.

Key elements of response:

_____ Would make sure that he establishes a regular time to exercise each time he visits.

_____ Would make sure that he exercises at a lower-intensity level and for a longer duration, as opposed to at a high-intensity level and for a relatively shorter duration.

_____ Would make sure to monitor performance and check for signs of fatigue, dizziness, etc.

- According to the most recent literature, what are some key steps that can be undertaken to assist exercisers in their efforts to maintain their exercise program?

Key elements of response:

_____ Have each individual complete an interest questionnaire to obtain information about that person's goals, interests, support structure, etc.

_____ Establish realistic short-term and long-term goals (process and outcome) with the individual exerciser.

_____ Develop a behavioral contract that commits the exerciser, as well as the exercise leader, to certain process goals and actions; in addition, establish a self-monitoring or tracking program.

_____ Make the exercise program progressive by starting out easy and gradually increasing the demands (via intensity and duration) placed on systems of the exerciser's body.

_____ Establish a reward system to recognize achievement of process and reward goals.

- What are the top four or five current trends in the fitness/club industry, including group exercise?

Key elements of response:

_____ Group cycling

_____ Pilates

_____ Yoga and related activities

_____ Spa services, such as massage and related activities

_____ Personal training

_____ Sports-performance training

❏ Employee Relations

- You have just been hired as the fitness director. What steps would you take to ensure that the employees under your responsibility are aware of your expect ations and are prepared to perform as a team?

Key elements of response:

_____ Would arrange to have a meeting with the entire group to provide an overview of my expectations.

_____ Would meet one-on-one with each of the employees to get to know them and better understand their roles and individual needs.

_____ Would establish some basic ground rules for performance with the team.

_____ Would establish job descriptions and performance models for each employee.

_____ Would communicate with each employee on a regular basis through individual meetings, team meetings, etc.

- You have an employee who is responsible for the group-exercise program. Over the past month, you have noticed that the overall program is not being well-received by the members. In addition, you have had complaints from members and employees about the quality of the program and their feeling that the individual in charge is not concerned about it. What steps would you take to address the perceived problem?

Key elements of response:

_____ Would meet with the employee to gather information about the situation from that individual's perspective and share with that person some of the concerns brought up by the members and fellow employees.

_____ Would set up an action plan for performance, with some 30-, 60-, and 90-day goals. This plan would include expectations and actions that would be undertaken if those expectations were not met.

_____ Would provide additional coaching and training to address specific areas of need.

_____ Would meet with on a regular basis with that employee to review performance, counsel, redirect, and hold accountable.

_____ Would inform all others who have expressed concern about this situation that matters are being addressed and that the situation is being dealt with in a proactive manner.

- ❏ Financial Management

  - Please describe the primary streams of revenue and the largest expense areas for a fitness department in a typical health/fitness and sports club.

Key elements of response:

_____ The primary sources of revenue would be personal training and program fees.

_____ The largest expenses would be payroll, commissions, program supplies, etc.

  - Please describe the primary steps that you would take to prepare a budget for your department, including the difference between a zero-based budget and a trend-line budget.

Key elements of response:

_____ Would gather information on existing financial performance and usage patterns.

_____ Would identify opportunities for revenue growth and expense control, including targets for specific revenue and expense areas.

_____ Would create a preliminary budget, based on the historical information and projected targets.

_____ A zero-based budget is when you start from scratch and build budget on projected targets, while a trend-line budget is when you project budget targets off of prior historical trends.

  - The net financial performance of your department is 10 percent behind plan after the first six months of the year. Please briefly describe actions that you would take to get back on plan before the year was over.

Key elements of response:

_____ Would gather information on performance, and identify specific strengths and weaknesses.

_____ Would identify revenue opportunities, and set up action plans to achieve.

_____ Would identify expense-control opportunities, particularly in payroll, and then establish action plans for making the necessary changes.

_____ Would monitor the situation each week and make necessary adjustments.

❑ Member Relations

- Please describe, from your perspective, the key elements in creating great service and memorable experiences for members using the club.

Key elements of response:

_____ Make sure that all employees are trained in providing great service.

_____ Make sure that all members are greeted by name.

_____ Make sure that the club provides programs and services that interest the members and address their needs.

_____ Make sure that the club has enough equipment and that it is in good working condition.

_____ Make sure that the programs in which the members participate are monitored and that feedback from members concerning those programs is both elicited and considered.

_____ Listen to the members and try to meet or exceed their expressed expectations.

- A member comes to you complaining that another member is making excessive use of the equipment and not allowing other individuals to use the equipment when they are in the club. Furthermore, the member says the other member has exhibited rude behavior. The member believes that you should remove this other member from the exercise area. Please describe how you would address this member issue.

Key elements of response:

_____ Would listen to the member's concerns and make note of them.

_____ Would let the offended member know that I would address the concern provide a response as soon as feasibly possible.

_____ Would then meet with the other member and gather that person's perspective, without letting that individual know who had brought the issue to my attention.

_____ Would determine the appropriate course of action, and then meet with the offending member and inform that person of the action that I feel needs to be undertaken.

_____ Would meet with the offended member and let that individual know what action was taken.

❑ Marketing and Sales

- Please describe the strategies that you would use to increase personal-training participation and revenue.

Key elements of response:

_____ Would first gather information about current participation and why members either used or did not use personal training.

_____ Might employ a variety of tools to gather information, for example, focus groups, a survey, one-on-one discussion, etc.

_____ Would establish targeted quotas for the department and each of the trainers. Would also monitor these targets on a regular basis.

_____ Would package personal training to appeal to members, including having the right pricing.

_____ Would market, using specific strategies, such as pictures of the trainers with bios, a brochure on personal training, personal training bulletin board, etc.

_____ Would provide personal trainers with sales training.

- What do you consider to be the most critical elements of promoting fitness programs to members so that participation levels are maximized?

Key elements of response:

_____ Making sure to communicate to members in advance the programs that are available, using such tools as an annual program calendar or a monthly program calendar.

_____ Making sure that every employee is aware of the programs in the club and talks it up with the members (i.e., make each employee a salesperson).

_____ Getting members aligned with the programs and have them become spokespersons for the programs (committees, loyal member programs, etc.).

_____ Developing the appropriate mix of promotional materials, such as flyers, posters, statement stuffers, email, etc.

APPENDICES *Fitness Management*

Selected Operational Forms

SAMPLE OPERATIONAL FORM #1

[Club Name]
New Member Profile

The information provided on this profile will help us to get to know you better and create a foundation for personalizing your club experience.

Name: _____

Address: _____
_____

Email (optional): _____

Contact Phone #: _____

Please place a check mark by the appropriate response.

❑ Interests and Hobbies:

1. Which types of fitness activities/health promotion programs interest you?

   _____ Back fitness   _____ Group-exercise classes   _____ Health promotion programs
   _____ Martial arts   _____ Nutrition programs   _____ Personal training
   _____ Pilates   _____ Racquetball   _____ Spinning
   _____ Weight management   _____ Yoga

2. What kinds of services that the club might offer interest you?

   _____ Alternative health care   _____ Basketball leagues and events
   _____ Café   _____ Day spa services
   _____ Massage   _____ Nursery service
   _____ Racquet sport leagues and programs _____ Tennis leagues and programs
   _____ Youth programs and camps   _____ Other (_____)

Continued

3. What kinds of adventure and social activities if made available would interest you?

   _____ Golf outings   _____ Networking events   _____ Rock climbing

   _____ Scuba diving/snorkeling   _____ Skiing trips   _____ Sporting event outings

   _____ Whitewater rafting   _____ Social events (e.g., wine tasting, book club, etc.)

   _____ Other (_____)

4. What goal(s) would you like to achieve during your first 30 days, 90 days, and 360 days, as a result of your membership at the club?

   30-day goals:
   - _____
   - _____

   90-day goals:
   - _____
   - _____

   360-day goals:
   - _____
   - _____

5. Please describe your top three expectations that you have for your membership experience.
   - _____
   - _____
   - _____

❑ Membership Communication:

1. What are your preferences with regard to receiving prompt information and communication from the club (please check all responses that are appropriate)?

   ____ Cell phone. If checked, please provide number: _____

   ____ Email message. If checked, please provide email address: _____

   ____ Text message. If checked, please provide number: _____

   ____ Other. If checked, please provide information for reaching you:
   _____

2. Which social media outlet would you most likely use to obtain information about what is happening at the club?

   ____ Facebook page   __ Member blog

   ____ Website   __ Other

Continued

3. Are you likely to reference the club's website for information? ___ Yes ___ No
   If yes, can you describe the type of information you would like to be able to access through the website?

   _____

   _____

   _____

4. What services could the club offer through its website or intranet site that would make your membership experience more enjoyable and productive?

   ___ Ability to check account status   ___ Post class schedules

   ___ Schedule personal training appointments ___ Schedule spa appointments

   ___ Sign up for events   ___ Submit complaints and suggestions to management

❑ General Demographic Information:

1. Gender: _____ Male   _____ Female
2. Age segment: _____ Under 18   _____ 18 to 34
                        _____ 35 to 54   _____ 55+
3. Marital status: _____ Single   _____ Married
4. Number of children (if applicable): _____
5. Household income category (annual):

   ___ Under $50,000   ___ $50,000 to $74,999   ___ $75,000 to $99,999

   ___ $100,000 to $149,999   ___ $150,000 to $199,999   ___ Over $200,000

6. Highest level of education earned:

   ___ High school   ___ Undergraduate   ___ Graduate   ___ Postgraduate

Member signature: _____

Staff signature: _____

Date: _____

SAMPLE OPERATIONAL FORM #2

Purchase Order Request Form

Staff member completing purchase order request: _____

Day and date of request: _____

Time of request: _____

Signature of staff person making request: _____

❑ Supplier/Vendor Information:

> Name: _____
>
> Address: _____
> _____
>
> Contact person: _____
>
> Phone number: _____ Email: _____
>
> Federal Tax ID #: _____
>
> Have we purchased from this supplier in the past? _____ Yes _____ No
>
> Payment terms: _____

❑ Purchase Order Request Detail (Attach Any Applicable Forms From Supplier):

Item Being Requested	Amount of Item
1.	
2.	
3.	
4.	
5.	
Sub-total	
Freight	
Taxes	
Total amount of purchase order	

Continued

❑ Purchase Order Approval Information:

Person approving the purchase order: _____

Signature of person approving: _____

Date of approval: _____ Purchase order # assigned: _____

Date purchase order placed: _____

❑ Purchase Order and Invoice Verification:

Purchase order #: _____ Purchase order amount: _____

Invoice #: _____ Invoice order amount: _____

Variance between purchase order and invoice: _____

Explanation of variance: _____

_____

Person verifying purchase order to invoice: _____

Signature: _____ Date: _____

SAMPLE OPERATIONAL FORM #3

Weekly Report: Pool and Whirlpool

Date	Day	Time	Pool Chemistry	Whirlpool Chemistry
	Monday		pH level: Chlorine level: Alkalinity level: Temperature: Filter PSI:	pH level: Chlorine level: Alkalinity level: Temperature: Filter PSI:
	Tuesday		pH level: Chlorine level: Alkalinity level: Temperature: Filter PSI:	pH level: Chlorine level: Alkalinity level: Temperature: Filter PSI:
	Wednesday		pH level: Chlorine level: Alkalinity level: Temperature: Filter PSI:	pH level: Chlorine level: Alkalinity level: Temperature: Filter PSI:
	Thursday		pH level: Chlorine level: Alkalinity level: Temperature: Filter PSI:	pH level: Chlorine level: Alkalinity level: Temperature: Filter PSI:

Continued

APPENDICES *Fitness Management*

Date	Day	Time	Pool Chemistry	Whirlpool Chemistry
	Friday		pH level: Chlorine level: Alkalinity level: Temperature: Filter PSI:	pH level: Chlorine level: Alkalinity level: Temperature: Filter PSI:
	Saturday		pH level: Chlorine level: Alkalinity level: Temperature: Filter PSI:	pH level: Chlorine level: Alkalinity level: Temperature: Filter PSI:
	Sunday		pH level: Chlorine level: Alkalinity level: Temperature: Filter PSI:	pH level: Chlorine level: Alkalinity level: Temperature: Filter PSI:

J Sample Design and Construction Checklist

I. FACILITY DESIGN

____ Select an architect.

____ Complete agreement with architect (AIA Document B101™ Standard Form of Agreement Between Owner and Architect).

____ Have initial meeting with architect and share strategic conversation and marketing information. Complete architect program questionnaire.

____ Architect will do three phases of planning: schematic design, design development, and construction documents.

____ Team should meet with architect once during each of the phases. All plans should be reviewed and signed off on before the next phase begins. Last sign-off is at 90% construction documents.

____ Identify with architect the need for additional specialists such as landscape architect, civil engineer, acoustical engineer, etc. (Architect provides mechanical, electrical, plumbing, and structural engineers.)

____ Any changes in architect services are to be handled through AIA ASP form signed by architect and owner.

____ Architect will work with owner to identify contractors for bidding documents. Bidding should take about three weeks.

____ Architect and owner should interview each contractor before selecting the final contractor.

____ Contractor will be selected by owner and architect.

II. CONSTRUCTION

____ Once the contractor is selected, a pre-construction meeting is held to review and clarify plans, clarify contract terms and responsibilities, establish timelines, etc.

____ Sign legal agreement with contractor (AIA Document A101™ Standard Form of Agreement Between Owner and Contractor where the basis of payment is a Stipulated Sum).

____ Owner and architect should meet with contractor at least once a month. If club/owner has a construction manager, then the construction manager should meet with the contractor weekly. Meetings should focus on work progress, schedules, delays, inspections, change orders, etc.

____ Contractor will meet with subs on a weekly basis. Owner should get relevant notes and pictures from meetings.

____ All clarifications on construction documents are done between architect's construction administrator and contractor's construction manager. Often, contractor will issue a request for information (RFI) as part of the process.

____ Any change to project scope, whether a credit or cost, is handled through a change order. Only the architect requests a change order after talking with the owner and contractor. A change order, to be completed, must be approved by both architect and owner. Recommend keeping a change order log.

____ Contractor will submit monthly pay applications (in triplicate) using standard AIA form. To be paid, the pay application must be notarized, signed by contractor, and approved by architect.

____ Contractor will submit partial lien waivers starting with the second pay application. The liens must match up with previous pay application before current pay application is processed.

____ Each pay application will have retainage taken out, usually equal to 10% until 50% of the project is completed, after which retainage is reduced to 5%.

____ Final pay application will be for retainage and must be accompanied by final lien waivers.

____ Contractor must submit letter of substantial completion when the work is 95% to 98% completed and prior to punch list. All warranties are effective this date.

____ At completion of construction, a punch list is done with architect, owner, and contractor. The punch list should be done off the approved construction documents.

____ Contractor, as part of closing project, must conduct an HVAC balance report.

____ Prior to final contract payment, contractor must provide three sets of closing documents. These contain:
- As-built construction drawings
- All subcontractor warranties on work
- All equipment manuals
- All permits and certificates
- All final lien waivers
- Signed punch list and balance report

Sample Member Satisfaction Survey

Please tell us how the following areas of the club are meeting your needs and expectations.
Please rate only those areas that you have experienced personally, otherwise check the "no experience" box.

	Strongly Disagree	Disagree	Neutral	Agree	Strongly Agree	No Experience
Sports Desk						
Greeting is friendly, warm and sincere	1	2	3	4	5	○
Staff is well-trained	1	2	3	4	5	○
Information is readily available	1	2	3	4	5	○
Staff is able to problem solve effectively	1	2	3	4	5	○
Staff is service-oriented	1	2	3	4	5	○
Locker Rooms						
Locker room is kept clean, well-stocked and maintained	1	2	3	4	5	○
Steam room and sauna are kept clean and in working order	1	2	3	4	5	○
Spa is clean and well maintained	1	2	3	4	5	○
Showers are clean and well maintained	1	2	3	4	5	○
Staff is service-oriented	1	2	3	4	5	○
Café						
Quality of food meets expectations	1	2	3	4	5	○
Variety of food meets expectations	1	2	3	4	5	○
Café is kept clean and well maintained	1	2	3	4	5	○
Speed of service meets expectations	1	2	3	4	5	○
Value for your money meets expectations	1	2	3	4	5	○
Staff is service-oriented	1	2	3	4	5	○
Dining Room for Lunch						
Quality of food meets expectations	1	2	3	4	5	○
Variety of food meets expectations	1	2	3	4	5	○
Dining room is kept clean and well maintained	1	2	3	4	5	○
Speed of service meets expectations	1	2	3	4	5	○
Value for your money meets expectations	1	2	3	4	5	○
Staff is service-oriented	1	2	3	4	5	○
Club Activities and Programs						
Club sponsored events are valuable to me	1	2	3	4	5	○
I am satisfied with the parties offered	1	2	3	4	5	○
I am satisfied with the social/athletic outings offered	1	2	3	4	5	○
Programs are effectively promoted	1	2	3	4	5	○
I would like the club to offer more social events	1	2	3	4	5	○

	Strongly Disagree	Disagree	Neutral	Agree	Strongly Agree	No Experience
Business Office						
Staff is professional, knowledgeable and helpful	1	2	3	4	5	○
Staff is able to problem solve effectively	1	2	3	4	5	○
Staff is service-oriented	1	2	3	4	5	○
Tennis						
Tennis courts and surrounding areas are kept clean and well maintained	1	2	3	4	5	○
Pro staff is knowledgeable, enthusiastic and available	1	2	3	4	5	○
I would like the department to offer more social events	1	2	3	4	5	○
The department effectively promotes its programs	1	2	3	4	5	○
I am satisfied with the USTA league structure	1	2	3	4	5	○
I recommend the department to others	1	2	3	4	5	○
Aquatics						
Pool deck and surrounding area are kept clean and well maintained	1	2	3	4	5	○
Water quality in pool and spa meets expectations	1	2	3	4	5	○
I am satisfied with the adult aqua classes	1	2	3	4	5	○
I would like the department to offer more classes, clinics, programs	1	2	3	4	5	○
Staff is service-oriented	1	2	3	4	5	○
Spa						
Massage staff are professional, knowledgeable and helpful	1	2	3	4	5	○
Skin care staff are professional, knowledgeable and helpful	1	2	3	4	5	○
Value for your money meets expectations	1	2	3	4	5	○
Group Exercise Program						
Studios and equipment are kept clean and well maintained	1	2	3	4	5	○
I am satisfied with the variety of classes and programs offered	1	2	3	4	5	○
Staff is knowledgeable, enthusiastic and friendly	1	2	3	4	5	○
The department effectively promotes programs and communicates class changes	1	2	3	4	5	○
Fitness						
The fitness center and equipment are kept clean and well maintained	1	2	3	4	5	○
I am satisfied with the variety of equipment offered	1	2	3	4	5	○
Availability of fitness equipment meets expectations	1	2	3	4	5	○
Staff is knowledgeable, enthusiastic and friendly	1	2	3	4	5	○
Staff is service-oriented	1	2	3	4	5	○
Children's Center						
The center and equipment are kept clean and well maintained	1	2	3	4	5	○
Staff is knowledgeable, enthusiastic and friendly	1	2	3	4	5	○
The security/safety of the center meets expectations	1	2	3	4	5	○
I would like the department to offer more programs	1	2	3	4	5	○

APPENDICES — Fitness Management

	Strongly Disagree	Disagree	Neutral	Agree	Strongly Agree	No Experience
Squash						
The squash courts and surrounding area are kept clean and well maintained	1	2	3	4	5	○
Pro staff is knowledgeable, enthusiastic and available	1	2	3	4	5	○
I am satisfied with the variety of programs offered	1	2	3	4	5	○
The department effectively promotes its programs	1	2	3	4	5	○
I recommend the department to others	1	2	3	4	5	○
Pro Shop						
Staff is friendly, knowledgeable and enthusiastic	1	2	3	4	5	○
The Pro Shop carries merchandise that meets my needs	1	2	3	4	5	○
Staff is service-oriented	1	2	3	4	5	○
Gymnasium						
The gymnasium is kept clean and well maintained	1	2	3	4	5	○
I am satisfied with the variety of programs offered	1	2	3	4	5	○
Club Overall						
I am satisfied with the overall club appearance	1	2	3	4	5	○
The club is kept clean and well maintained	1	2	3	4	5	○
Repairs and maintenance are completed quickly and efficiently	1	2	3	4	5	○
Staff is knowledgeable, friendly and enthusiastic	1	2	3	4	5	○
Value for your money meets expectations	1	2	3	4	5	○
The club meets my needs and expectations	1	2	3	4	5	○
Staff is service-oriented	1	2	3	4	5	○

Please share with us your experience with other Club programs and services.

	Aware of		Have Tried		Will Try		Not Interested	
	Yes	No	Yes	No	Yes	No	Yes	No
Pilates								
Individual	○	○	○	○	○	○	○	○
Group Allegro	○	○	○	○	○	○	○	○
Group Mat	○	○	○	○	○	○	○	○
Personal Fitness Training								
Individual	○	○	○	○	○	○	○	○
Group	○	○	○	○	○	○	○	○
Bay Sport								
Physical Therapy	○	○	○	○	○	○	○	○
Executive Physical Exam	○	○	○	○	○	○	○	○
Cholesterol Screening	○	○	○	○	○	○	○	○
Complimentary Injury Check	○	○	○	○	○	○	○	○

	Aware of		Have Tried		Will Try		Not Interested	
	Yes	No	Yes	No	Yes	No	Yes	No
Adult Swim Classes								
Individual	○	○	○	○	○	○	○	○
Group	○	○	○	○	○	○	○	○
Nutrition Consultation w/Dietician	○	○	○	○	○	○	○	○
Yoga Classes	○	○	○	○	○	○	○	○
Gymnasium								
Basketball Leagues	○	○	○	○	○	○	○	○
Badminton Individual Lessons	○	○	○	○	○	○	○	○
Badminton Group Lessons	○	○	○	○	○	○	○	○
Social/Athletic								
Golf outings	○	○	○	○	○	○	○	○
Club seminars	○	○	○	○	○	○	○	○
Club parties	○	○	○	○	○	○	○	○
Electronic Funds Transfer	○	○	○	○	○	○	○	○

(Automatic payment from your checking account)

The following questions are for classification purposes only:

Gender: _____ Male _____ Female   Age: _____   Please indicate the year you joined DC: _____

How many visits to the Club do you make during a typical week? _____

What time of day do you most frequently utilize the Club? _____ before 9:00am _____ 9–12:00pm _____ 12:00–4:00pm
_____ 4:00–8:00pm _____ 8:00pm–close

What type of membership do you have? _____ Individual _____ Family _____ Racquet _____ Fitness

Please circle your two most preferred methods for the Club to communicate with you about programs and events.

Special Mailing	Statement Insert	Email	Sports Desk Bulletin
Club Bulletin Boards/Posters	Newsletter	DC Website	Activity Information Center

What one improvement would make visiting the Club a significantly better experience for you?
_____
_____

Please share any additional comments you may have.
_____
_____

Optional: We may wish to contact you about a comment or suggestion that you've made.

Name: _____   Member number: _____

Email address: _____

Thank you for your comments! Please return your completed survey by _____

Sample Corporate Sales Checklist

Step 1: Decide What It Is You Are Going to Sell

_____ Memberships

_____ Brown bags

_____ Seminars

_____ HRAs

_____ Testing

Step 2: Develop a Presentation Package That Can Be Used During Any Initial Contacts

_____ Industry data on savings achieved

_____ Pamphlet and/or sheet on services

_____ Club brochure

_____ Business cards

_____ Generic sales presentation

Step 3: Target Your Companies

_____ Companies already using the club or with member in the club

_____ Local chamber of commerce business listing

_____ Utilize specific criteria outlined in handbook and prioritize!

Step 4: Learn All You Can About the Companies

_____ Interviews with members

_____ Check with PR departments

_____ Library

_____ Chamber of commerce information

Step 5: Decide What It Is You Want to Accomplish With Your First Contact

_____ Make a sale

_____ Get an appointment to introduce your services

_____ Get them to visit the club

Step 6: Get the First Appointment

_____ Get current member to arrange appointment

_____ Write a short letter as outlined

_____ Include with your letter a nice reminder item (book, etc.)

_____ Mention you will follow up with a call; give day and time period (Tuesday through Thursday)

_____ Make the follow-up phone call

_____ Send a thank you after scheduling appointment

_____ Follow up regularly and include small gift

Step 7: The First Appointment—Make It Work for You

_____ Get them to the club if you can

_____ Bring a generic presentation package

_____ Make sure you bring your homework on the company

_____ Arrive early

_____ Bring a partner

_____ Keep presentation short and to the point

_____ Get a commitment for a next step

_____ Listen for needs

Step 8: Immediate Appreciation Is a Hallmark of Any Appointment

_____ Send a brief handwritten thank you upon returning to the club

_____ Express appreciation for their time and let them know when your proposal will arrive

Step 9: Get Your Proposal in the Person's Hands

_____ Customize your proposal and include the following:
- Executive summary
- Services/products you will provide
- Delivery system for services
- Timetable
- Benefits
- List of clients
- List of members who work for that company
- Fees and schedules

_____ Deliver your proposal in person; try to hand it to the person who makes the decision

_____ Send proposal only if delivering in person is impossible; your proposal must be accompanied by a cover that outlines your next step, including date(s) of follow-up

Step 10: Follow Up Your Proposal With a Call

_____ Allow two or three weeks before you call

_____ Find out their feelings toward the proposal

_____ Answer any questions

_____ Try to schedule an appointment

_____ Continue to follow up

Step 11: Take Your Proposal to an Agreement

_____ Make your next appointment effective by being prepared for further questions

_____ Realize that you may have to make additional presentations before signing

_____ Have an agreement prepared ahead of time in the event you have a chance to sign

_____ Realize it might take 6 to 12 months to finalize

Step 12: Service the Sale

_____ Deliver what you promise

_____ Provide regular feedback to the company

_____ Maintain contact with company representatives

_____ Perform evaluation of their services

M Selected Risk Management Forms

SAMPLE RISK MANAGEMENT FORM #1

Pre-Activity Screening Form

Name: _____   Member number: _____

Address: _____

Telephone (W): _____   Telephone (H): _____

Fax: _____   Email: _____

Gender: _____   Birthdate: _____

Regular physical activity is enjoyable, safe, and healthy for most people. However, some individuals may have health-related risks that might be aggravated by participation in a program of physical activity, and as a result, might require them to check with their physician prior to embarking on a program of physical activity. To help determine if a need exists for you to see your physician before beginning an exercise program, please answer the following questions carefully. All information will be kept in the strictest confidentiality.

PRE-ACTIVITY SCREENING QUESTIONS

Yes	No	
❏	❏	1. Has your physician ever told you that you have a heart condition?
❏	❏	2. Do you experience pain in your chest when you are physically active?
❏	❏	3. In the past month, have you experienced chest pain when not performing physical activity?
❏	❏	4. Do you lose balance because of dizziness or do you ever lose consciousness?
❏	❏	5. Do you have a bone or joint problem that could be aggravated by a change in your level of physical activity?
❏	❏	6. Is your physician currently prescribing medications for your blood pressure or heart condition?
❏	❏	7. Do you know of any other reason why you should not participate in a program of physical activity?

If you answered yes to any of these questions, it is recommended that you consult with your physician, by phone or in person, before having a fitness test or participating in physical activity program.

SAMPLE RISK MANAGEMENT FORM #2

Cardiovascular Health Pre-Activity Screening

For each of the following questions, please place a check by each item that has direct application to you.

_____ Age: Men $>$ 45   Women $>$ 55

_____ Family history: MI or sudden death before 55 years of age for father or other first-degree male relative or 65 years of age for mother or female first-degree relative.

_____ Cigarette smoker (current or have quit in the previous 6 months)

_____ Dyslipidemia: (one or more of the following):
- Blood cholesterol $>$ 200 mg/dl
- LDL cholesterol $>$ 130 mg/dl
- HDL $<$ 40 mg/dl
- LDL/HDL ratio $>$ 3 to 1
- Triglycerides $>$ 150

_____ Hypertension: Blood pressure – systolic $\geq$ 140 or diastolic $\geq$ 90 on blood pressure medication

_____ Impaired fasting glucose: Fasting glucose $\geq$ 100 mg/dl or presence of diabetes

_____ Sedentary lifestyle: Do not participate in at least 30 minutes of moderate physical activity at least 3x a week.

_____ Obesity: BMI $>$ 30, waist circumference $>$ 102 cm for men and $>$ 88 cm for women

Place a check by the appropriate category that applies to this individual.

_____ Low-Risk: Men $<$ 45 years of age and women $<$ 55 years of age who are asymptomatic and have no more than one risk factor, as indicated above.

_____ Moderate-Risk: Men $>$ 45 years of age and women $>$ 55 years of age or those who have two or more risk factors as indicated above.

_____ High-Risk: Individuals with one or more symptoms of cardiovascular disease or known cardiovascular, metabolic, or pulmonary disease.

Any individual classified as either moderate-risk or high-risk needs to receive a physician's clearance prior to participating in a program of structured physical activity.

** Physician's Note Required**   Date contacted: _____

SAMPLE RISK MANAGEMENT FORM #3

Physical Activity Readiness Questionnaire

I. General Information (Please check the appropriate box.)

Gender	❏ Male	❏ Female	
Age	❏ ≤45	❏ 45 to 55	❏ ≥55

II. Predisposing Coronary Risk Factors (Please check yes or no for each of the questions in this section.)

Yes No

1. Has your physician or other healthcare professional ever indicated that you have one of the following?
   ❏ ❏ a. High blood pressure (e.g., systolic equal to or over 140 and/or diastolic equal to or over 90)
   ❏ ❏ b. Elevated or abnormal blood lipids (e.g., cholesterol, triglycerides, LDL, HDL, etc.)
   ❏ ❏ c. Overweight (e.g., waist circumference over 40 inches for men and 35 inches for women)
   ❏ ❏ d. Elevated blood sugar (e.g., levels greater than 100 mg/dl)

❏ ❏ 2. Do you have a sedentary lifestyle (e.g., do not exercise at all or perform less than 150 minutes of moderate activity weekly)?

❏ ❏ 3. Do you smoke cigarettes or are you a former smoker who has quit in the last six months?

❏ ❏ 4. Do you have a family history of heart disease (e.g., father/first-degree male relative under age 55 or mother/first-degree female relative under age 65)?

_____ **Total number of Yes checks**
Note: If you are male and over the age of 45 or female and over the age of 55 and have checked at least one Yes in this section, it is recommended that you consult with your physician or healthcare professional before engaging in a program of regular physical activity.

III. Signs and Symptoms (Please check yes or no for each of the questions below.)

Yes No

❏ ❏ 1. Has your physician ever told you that you have a heart condition and that you should only do physical activity recommended by a physician?

❏ ❏ 2. Do you experience pain in your chest or radiating into your jaw, neck, or arms when you are physically active?

❏ ❏ 3. In the past three months, have you experienced chest pain at rest or when asleep?

❏ ❏ 4. Do you lose balance because of dizziness or do you ever lose consciousness?

❏ ❏ 5. Do you experience shortness of breath at rest or with mild exertion?

❏ ❏ 6. Is your physician currently prescribing medications for your blood pressure, blood lipids, or a heart condition?

❏ ❏ 7. Do you currently have or have you recently experienced swelling in the ankles or other extremities?

❏ ❏ 8. Do you experience pain or severe discomfort in your lower extremities when walking that subsides within one to two minutes after you stop?

❏ ❏ 9. Do you have diabetes?

❏ ❏ 10. Do you have asthma or another respiratory condition that causes difficulty with breathing?

❏ ❏ 11. Do you currently have or have you experienced within the past six months back pain/discomfort or other joint-related problems that prevented you from carrying out normal daily activities?

❏ ❏ 12. Are you pregnant?

_____ **Total number of Yes checks**
Note: If you answered yes to any of the questions in this section, *you will need to consult with your physician* prior to becoming physically active and/or before the club can prescribe an exercise program for you. The club does provide a form that your physician can complete and forward to us indicating how best to prepare your exercise program.

SAMPLE RISK MANAGEMENT FORM #4

Health History Inventory

Name: _____

Membership number: _____

Address: _____

_____

Telephone (W): _____ Telephone (H): _____

Fax : _____ Email: _____

Gender: _____ Birthdate: _____

Regular physical activity is enjoyable, healthy, and for most people, safe. However, some individuals may have health-related risks that might require them to check with their physician prior to starting an exercise program. To help determine if a need exists for you to see your physician before starting an exercise program, please read the following questions and answer carefully. All information will be kept in the strictest confidentiality.

I. PHYSICAL ACTIVITY SCREENING QUESTIONS

Yes   No
❏   ❏   1. Has your physician ever told you that you have a heart condition?
❏   ❏   2. Do you experience pain in your chest when you are physically active?
❏   ❏   3. In the past month, have you experienced chest pain when not performing physical activity?
❏   ❏   4. Do you lose balance because of dizziness or do you ever lose consciousness?
❏   ❏   5. Do you have a bone or joint problem that could be aggravated by a change in your level of physical activity?
❏   ❏   6. Is your physician currently prescribing medications for your blood pressure or heart condition?
❏   ❏   7. Do you know of any other reason why you should not participate in a program of physical activity?

If you answered yes to any of the aforementioned questions, it is recommended that you consult with your physician, by phone or in person, before having a fitness test or participating in a physical activity program.

Continued

II. GENERAL HEALTH HISTORY QUESTIONS. (PLEASE ANSWER YES OR NO TO EACH OF THE FOLLOWING QUESTIONS.)

Yes No

☐ ☐ 1. Have you ever experienced a stroke?

☐ ☐ 2. Do you have diabetes? If yes, are you currently taking any medications or receiving other treatment related to the diabetes? _____

☐ ☐ 3. Do you have asthma or another respiratory condition that causes difficulty with breathing? If yes, please describe. _____

☐ ☐ 4. Do you have any orthopedic conditions that would restrict you in performing physical activity? If yes, please describe. _____

☐ ☐ 5. Have you ever been told by a physician that you have one of the following? (check applicable boxes)
- ☐ High blood pressure
- ☐ Elevated blood lipids, including elevated cholesterol
- ☐ Cardiovascular disease
- ☐ Cancer
- ☐ Other health/medical condition (please describe): _____

☐ ☐ 6. Do you currently smoke or have you smoked in the past and stopped within the last six months?

☐ ☐ 7. Do you currently or have you experienced back pain or discomfort within the past six months that prevented you from carrying out normal daily activities? If so, describe. _____ _____

☐ ☐ 8. Are you currently taking any medications for a health or medical related condition? If yes, please indicate the medications you are taking. _____

☐ ☐ 9. Are you pregnant?

If you answered yes to any of the aforementioned questions, it is recommended that you consult with your physician, by phone or in person, before having a fitness test or participating in a prescribed physical activity program. In some instances, depending upon the answers you provide to the aforementioned questions, you may be required to obtain a physician's written clearance before an exercise program can be prescribed for you.

SAMPLE RISK MANAGEMENT FORM #5

[Club Name]

Waiver and Release (Adult)

The undersigned individual agrees to abide by the rules of the club, including the completion of a pre-activity screening questionnaire and/or health/medical information questionnaire prior to participation in any physical activities at the club. The undersigned individual agrees that all use of the club's facilities, programs, and services shall be undertaken at his/her sole risk and that the club shall not be liable for any injuries, accidents, or death occurring to said individual, arising either directly or indirectly out of participation in the club's facilities, programs, and services. The undersigned, for himself/herself and on behalf of his/her executors, administrators, heirs, and assigns, does hereby expressly release, discharge, waive, relinquish, and covenants not to sue club, its officers, and agents for all such claims, demands, injuries, damages, or causes of action, with respect to use of the club's facilities, programs, and services.

    The undersigned individual declares that they have completed the club's pre-activity screening questionnaire and/or health/medical information questionnaire and that they declare they are physically able to participate in physical activity. Furthermore, the individual declares that the club has advised them to obtain a physician's clearance in the event that their answers on either the pre-activity screening questionnaire and/or health/medical information questionnaire indicate that they should not participate in a program of physical activity without a physician's clearance, or if they are unsure of their physical health and maintain that he/she is physically capable of pursuing physical activity in the club without such steps being taken or has done so.

Individual's signature: _____

Date: _____

Staff witness signature: _____

SAMPLE RISK MANAGEMENT FORM #6

Physician's Statement and Clearance Form

Individual information requested for: _____
Physician's name: _____
Physician's address: _____
Physician's phone #: _____ Physician's e-mail: _____

1. ❑ I concur with my patient's participation, if he or she restricts activities to those that are moderate.

2. ❑ I do not concur with my patient's participation in this program.
   (If checked, the individual will not be accepted.)

Comments: _____
_____
_____
_____

3. ❑ Other: _____

Comments: _____
_____
_____
_____

Physician's signature: _____ Date signed: _____

Return form to: _____
_____
_____

© 2006, American Council on Exercise. Due to copyrights, you are not allowed to modify this form in any way. You are not allowed to sell this form.

Source: Tharrett, S.J. (2006). *The ACE Fitness and Business Forms Handbook.* Healthy Learning: Monterey, CA. Used with permission.

SAMPLE RISK MANAGEMENT FORM #7

[Club Name]

Authorization for Release of Protected Health Information

I, _____, hereby authorize _____ to release the following health information:

[   ]

and forward it to the following person/facility:

Name of person or facility: _____

Address (street, city, state, and zip code):

[   ]

Phone #: _____   Email: _____

This information is for the purpose of:

[   ]

This authorization is in effect until _____, when it expires.

I understand that by signing this authorization:

- I authorize the use or disclosure of my individually identifiable health information as described above for the purpose listed. I understand that authorization is voluntary.
- I understand the notice of privacy practices provides instructions should I choose to revoke my authorization.
- I understand that if the organization I have authorized to receive the information is not a health plan or healthcare provider, the released information may no longer be protected by federal privacy regulations.
- I understand that I have the right to receive a copy of this authorization.
- I understand that I am signing this authorization voluntarily and that treatment, payment, or eligibility for my benefits will not be affected if I do not sign this authorization.

Continued

I declare under penalty of perjury that the information on this form is true and correct.

Signature: _____ Date: _____

Identifying Information
_____ Copy of identification attached.
Type of identification: _____
(e.g. driver's license, birth certificate, passport, federal ID card, managed care card, etc.)
Number on identification: _____

If no identification is attached, your signature must be notarized.

Notarized by: _____

On: _____

Notary Public Number: _____

Notary must stamp in the space provided.

SAMPLE RISK MANAGEMENT FORM #8

Emergency Medical Authorization (Adult)

I hereby give consent, in the event I am incapacitated and unable to provide such consent and approval for a situation requiring medical attention and action for the administration of any treatment or care deemed necessary, and my designated representative, _____ cannot be reached in a reasonable period of time to extend such consent and approval on my behalf for attention and action for the administration of any treatment and/or care deemed necessary for the listed above by Dr. _____, or any of his/her associates, the preferred physician, or Dr. _____, or any of his/her associates, the preferred dentist, or in the event the appropriate preferred physician, dentist or other identified healthcare professional is not available, by another qualified physician, dentist or healthcare professional; and the transfer of myself to _____ hospital, the preferred hospital, or any hospital reasonably accessible.

This authorization does not cover non-emergency medical situations or non-emergency major surgery, unless the opinions of at least two other licensed physicians, dentists, or healthcare professionals concurring in the necessity of such emergency medical action are obtained prior to the performance of such emergency medical action/surgery and unless all reasonable attempts to obtain my approval, and in the event I am incapable of providing such approval, then efforts to contact my designated representative have been exhausted, defining such period for non-emergency medical action/surgery as 24 hours.

The following information is being released by me in the event that the physician, dentist, healthcare professional, or hospital is unable to access my medical history:

Allergies:

Medications:

Physical limitations/restrictions:

Other critical information (e.g. blood type, health conditions, etc.):

Insurance coverage:

Insurance provider		Policy number	

Continued

I, the undersigned, hereby agree appoint and constitute the club, and its duly authorized representative(s), namely _____, for the period of _____, 20____, through and including _____, 20____, and do hereby authorize them to obtain any x-ray examination, anesthesia, medical, or surgical diagnosis or treatment, and hospital care to be provided for me in the event I am unable to provide approval and my designated representative cannot be reached for approval in a reasonable period of time, under the general and special supervision, and on the advice of a licensed physician, dentist, or other qualified healthcare professional, acting under their supervision.

Signature: _____

Name (print): _____

Club representative (witness) signature: _____

Club representative name (print): _____

Date: _____   State of _____

                                                 Country of _____

SAMPLE RISK MANAGEMENT FORM #9

Emergency Medical Authorization (Minor)

I/we, the undersigned, am/are the parent(s)/legal guardian(s) of the minor(s) listed below:

_____   _____

_____   _____

I/we hereby give consent, in the event I/we can not be contacted within a reasonable period of time, for the administration of any treatment and/or care deemed necessary for the minor(s) listed above by Dr. _____, or any of his/her associates, the preferred physician, or Dr. _____, or any of his/her associates, the preferred dentist, or in the event the appropriate preferred physician, dentist, or other identified healthcare professional is not available, by another qualified physician, dentist, or healthcare professional; and the transfer of any of the above listed minor(s) to _____ hospital, the preferred hospital, or any hospital reasonably accessible.

This authorization does not cover non-emergency medical situations or non-emergency major surgery unless the opinions of at least two other licensed physicians, dentists, or healthcare professionals concurring in the necessity of such emergency medical action are obtained prior to the performance of such emergency medical action/surgery and unless all reasonable attempts to contact me/us have been exhausted, defining such period for non-emergency medical action/surgery as 24 hours.

The following information is being released by me/us on behalf of the minor(s) listed above in the event that the physician, dentist, healthcare professional, or hospital is unable to access the medical history of the above listed minor(s):

Allergies:

Medications:

Physical limitations/restrictions:

Other critical information (e.g. blood type, health conditions, etc.):

Insurance coverage:

Insurance provider		Policy number	

I/we, the undersigned parent(s)/legal guardian(s), hereby agree to appoint and constitute the club, and its duly authorized representative(s), namely _____, as temporary custodians of the minor(s) listed above for the period of _____, 20___, through and including _____, 20___, and do hereby authorize them to obtain any x-ray examination, anesthesia, medical or surgical diagnosis or treatment, and hospital care to be provided to my/our minor(s) in my/our absence, under the general and special supervision of, and on the advice of, a licensed physician, dentist, or other qualified healthcare professional acting under their supervision.

Parent/guardian signature: _____

Parent/guardian name (print): _____

Club representative (witness) signature: _____

Club representative name (print): _____

Date: _____   State of _____

Country of _____

SAMPLE RISK MANAGEMENT FORM #10

Incident Report Form for _____

Date and day of incident:		Time of incident:	

Location of incident:	

Information on Individual Experiencing the Incident:

Name:		H Phone #:	
Email:		W Phone #:	
Address			
Gender:	Age:	Member or Guest?	

Specific Information About the Incident

1. Describe how the incident occurred (details on what happened):
2. Describe the nature of the injury that occurred (what happened to the individual(s)):
3. Describe how the incident was discovered or observed:
4. Describe the resulting actions taken in response to the incident (actions by staff, witnesses, medical personnel, etc.):

Information About Witnesses

Names of witnesses:

Witness Statements

Witness: _____
Statement:

Witness: _____
Statement:

Witness: _____
Statement:

Staff Responder and Supervisor Information

First staff responder:	
Second staff responder:	
Supervisor on duty:	

First Responder Signature: _____

Supervisor on Duty Signature: _____

Member/Guest (person involved) Signature: _____

Date signed: _____

Please make copies and place in both the member's file and in the club's incident report log.

SAMPLE RISK MANAGEMENT FORM #11

[Club Name]
Incident Report Form

I. General Incident Information:

Month Day Year Time of Incident A.M. P.M.		Club Member: ____ Yes ____ No	Club Name: Club location:
Name of injured person:	First M.I. Last	Hospital/EMS or physician notified? ____ Yes ____ No Name of caller: _____ Time of initial call: _____ Time of any follow-up calls: 1. _____ 2. _____ 3. _____ Time of EMS arrival: _____	
Street Address:		Time of EMS departure: _____ Hospital taken to: _____ Name of EMS contact: _____	
State/City/Zip:			
Phone #'s:			
Email address:			

Continued

II. General Description of the Incident:

Description of Incident:
_____
_____
_____
_____

Bleeding-related injury? _____ Yes _____ No
Visible injury? _____ Yes _____ No
Not outwardly noticeable injury, but person expressed pain? _____ Yes _____ No
If an eye injury, was eyewear/protection being worn? _____ Yes _____ No

III. Incident Details, Including Club Response to the Incident:

Description of the injury/injuries:	Description of club response/first aid:

IV. Responder, Supervisor, and Witness Information:

First responder (name):

Responder's position/title:

CPR certified? _____ Yes _____ No   AED certified? _____ Yes _____ No

First aid certified? _____ Yes _____ No

Signature: _____

Continued

Manager on duty (name):	
Manager on duty position/title:	
CPR certified? _____ Yes _____ No AED certified? _____ Yes _____ No	
First aid certified? _____ Yes _____ No	
Signature: _____	

WITNESS (NAME): _____

Witness address: _____

Witness phone: (O) _____ (H) _____ (C) _____

Witness email: _____

Signature: _____

WITNESS (NAME): _____

Witness address: _____

Witness phone: (O) _____ (H) _____ (C) _____

Witness email: _____

Signature: _____

V. Details on Location of Incident:

1. Specific location: _____ fitness center   _____ studio   _____ gymnasium

   _____ pool   _____ tennis court   _____ locker rooms

   _____ spa   _____ lobby/circulation area

   _____ children's area   _____ steam/sauana/whirlpool (circle)

   _____ outside

Continued

2. Please describe the conditions of the environment during the time of the incident (e.g. was it a wet surface, was it extremely hot, etc.)

3. Other comments:

VI. Miscellaneous:

1. Did the police investigate? _____ Yes _____ No

If yes, please give name, rank, and contact information of the person on the lines below.

Name: _____ Rank: _____

Contact phone number: _____

2. Did another agency investigate (fire department, etc.)? _____ Yes _____ No

If yes, please give name, rank, and contact information for that individual on the lines below.

Name: _____ Rank: _____

Contact phone number: _____

3. Report submitted by: _____

Signature: _____

Date and time submitted: _____

Please make multiple copies, including one each for the person's file, the club's incident files, the insurer, and the individual involved in the incident.

N Suggested References

- *22 Immutable Laws of Branding: How to Build a Product or Service into a World Class Brand.* Al Reis and Laura Reis. Harper Collins. New York. 1998.
- *101 Strategies for Improving Member Retention in Health/Fitness Clubs.* Stephen Tharrett and Patricia Amend. Healthy Learning, Monterey, CA. 2012.
- *101 Programming Strategies for Engaging Members in Health/Fitness Clubs.* Stephen Tharrett and Teresa J. Thomason. Healthy Learning, Monterey, CA. 2012.
- *2002 Profiles of Success; IHRSA's Industry Data Survey of the Health and Fitness Club Industry.* Compiled by the International Health, Racquet & Sportsclub Association and Industry Insights, Inc. Boston, MA. 2002.
- *2003 IHRSA Global Report: State of the Health Club Industry.* Compiled by the International Health, Racquet & Sportsclub Association. Boston, MA. 2003.
- *2003 Profiles of Success; IHRSA's Industry Data Survey of the Health and Fitness Club Industry.* Compiled by the International Health, Racquet & Sportsclub Association and Industry Insights, Inc. Boston, MA. 2003.
- *2004 IHRSA Global Report: State of the Health Club Industry.* Compiled by the International Health, Racquet & Sportsclub Association. Boston, MA. 2004.
- *2004 Profiles of Success; IHRSA's Industry Data Survey of the Health and Fitness Club Industry.* Compiled by the International Health, Racquet & Sportsclub Association and Industry Insights, Inc. Boston, MA. 2004.
- *2005 Guidelines for Cardiopulmonary Resuscitation and Emergency Cardiovascular Care. International Consensus on Science Part III: Adult Basic Life Support.* Circulation 2005. American Heart Association in collaboration with International Liaison Committee on Resuscitation. Dallas, TX. 2005.
- *2005 IHRSA European Market Report: The Size and Scope of the Health Club Industry.* Compiled by the International Health, Racquet & Sportsclub Association. Boston, MA. 2005.
- *2005 IHRSA Global Report: State of the Health Club Industry.* Compiled by the International Health, Racquet & Sportsclub Association. Boston, MA. 2005.
- *2007 Profiles of Success; IHRSA's Industry Data Survey of the Health and Fitness Club Industry.* Compiled by the International Health, Racquet & Sportsclub Association and Industry Insights, Inc. Boston, MA. 2007.
- *2008 IHRSA Asia Pacific Market Report: The Size and Scope of the Health Club Industry.* Compiled by the International Health, Racquet & Sportsclub Association and Deloitte. Boston, MA. 2008.

- *2010 IHRSA European Market Report: The Size and Scope of the Health Club Industry.* Compiled by the International Health, Racquet & Sportsclub Association and Deloitte. Boston, MA. 2010.
- *The 2013 IHRSA Global Report: The State of the Health Club Industry.* Compiled by the International Health, Racquet & Sportsclub Association. Boston, MA. 2013.
- *2013 IHRSA Latin American Report.* Compiled by the International Health, Racquet and Sportsclub Association and Mercado Fitness, Boston, MA. 2012.
- *2013 Profiles of Success; IHRSA's Industry Data Survey of the Health and Fitness Club Industry.* Compiled by the International Health, Racquet & Sportsclub Association. Boston, MA. 2013.
- *2013 Sports, Fitness and Leisure Activities Topline Participation Report.* Compiled by the Sport and Fitness Industry Association and Sports Marketing Surveys, Silver Springs, MD. 2013.
- *2014 IHRSA Global Report: The State of the Health Club Industry.* Compiled by the International Health, Racquet & Sportsclub Association. Boston, MA. 2008.
- *2014 IHRSA Health Club Consumer Report.* Compiled by the International Health, Racquet and Sportsclub Association and ClubIntel, Boston, MA. 2014.
- *2015 AFS Benchmarking Study of Boutique Fitness Studios.* Compiled by the Association of Fitness Studios, Chicago, IL. 2015.
- *2015 IHRSA Health Club Consumer Report.* Compiled by the International Health, Racquet and Sportsclub Association and ClubIntel, Boston, MA. 2015.
- *2015 Profiles of Success; IHRSA's Industry Data Survey of the Health and Fitness Club Industry.* Complied by the International Health, Racquet and Sportsclub Association and Industry Insights, Inc. Boston, MA. 2015
- *2016 Fitness Studio Marketing Best Practices Research Report.* Compiled by the Association of Fitness Studios, Chicago, IL. 2016.
- *2016 Fitness Studio Operating and Financial Benchmarking Report.* Compiled by the Association of Fitness Studios, Chicago, IL. 2016.
- *2016 Global Fitness Industry Trend Report.* Compiled by ClubIntel, Dallas, TX. 2016.
- *2016 IHRSA Health Club Consumer Report.* Compiled by the International Health, Racquet and Sportsclub Association and ClubIntel, Boston, MA. 2016.
- *The ACE Fitness and Business Forms Handbook.* Stephen Tharrett. Healthy Learning. Monterey, CA. 2006.
- *ACSM's Health/Fitness Facility Standards and Guidelines. 4th Edition.* Steve Tharrett and James A. Peterson. Human Kinetics. Champaign, IL. 2012.
- *AED Position Paper. ClubCorp Internal Document.* Dallas, TX. 2002.
- *"Best of HBR on Leadership; It Is Hard Being Soft."* Harvard Business Review. Boston, MA. 2001.
- *Beyond the Universe.* Bill Pearl. Bill Pearl Enterprises, Inc. Agni Press. New York. 2003.
- *Building Membership Best Practices.* IHRSA Publication. Boston, MA. 2000.

- *ClubCorp Athletic Operations Manual.* ClubCorp Internal Document. Dallas, TX. 1998.
- *ClubCorp Standards of Operation for Athletics and Tennis.* ClubCorp Internal Document. Dallas, TX. 2003.
- *Discovering the Soul of Service.* Leonard Berry. The Free Press. New York. 1999.
- *Employee Compensation and Benefits Survey Results for the Commercial Health and Fitness Industry.* IHRSA and Industry Insights. Boston, MA. 2010.
- *Europe Active European Health and Fitness Market Report 2016.* Compiled by Deloitte and Europe Active. Europe Active, Brussels, Belgium. 2016.
- *The European Health and Fitness Market*, EHFA/Deloitte, December 2013.
- *The Experience Economy.* Joseph Pine, II, and James Gilmore. Harvard Business School Press. Boston, MA. 1999.
- *Fitness American Style: A Look at How and Why Americans Exercise.* Prepared for IHRSA by Roper Starch Worldwide. Boston, MA. 2001.
- *Health and Fitness Club Review.* Granville Baird Ltd. London, England. 2000.
- *The Health/Fitness Club Operator's Guide to Recruiting and Retaining Great Employees.* Stephen Tharrett. Healthy Learning, Monterey, CA. 2007.
- *IHRSA/ASD Health Club Trend Report (1987-2003).* American Sports Data, Inc. Hartsdale, NY. 2004.
- *IHRSA's Guide for Health Club Operators: How to Prevail in Competitive Markets.* John McCarthy. International Health, Racquet & Sportsclub Association. Boston, MA. 2006.
- *IHRSA's Guide to Lenders and Investors.* 2nd edition. IHRSA. Boston, MA. 2004.
- *IHRSA's One Million Strong: An In-Depth Study of Health Club Member Retention in North America.* Compiled by the International Health, Racquet & Sportsclub Association. Boston, MA. 2015
- *ISPA 2004 Consumer Trends Report.* Complied and prepared by the International Spa Association and the Hartman Group, Inc. Lexington, KY. 2004.
- *ISPA 2008 Global Consumer Study.* Commissioned by the International Spa Association, Lexington, Kentucky. Prepared by Research International. 2008.
- *ISPA 2010 U.S. Spa Industry Study.* Commissioned by the International Spa Association, Lexington, KY. Prepared by Price Waterhouse Cooper. 2010.
- *Karaoke Capitalism: Daring to Be Different in a Copycat World.* Jonas Ridderstrale and Kjell A. Nordstrom. Praeger Publishers. Westport, CT. 2005.
- *King of Clubs: Grow Rich in More Than Money.* Robert Dedman with Debbie Deloach. Taylor Publishing. Dallas, TX. 1999.
- *Leadership and the One-Minute Manager.* Ken Blanchard, Patricia Zigarmi, and Drea Zigarmi. William Morrow and Company, Inc. New York. 1985.
- *Legal Aspects of Preventative and Rehabilitative Exercise Programs.* 2nd Edition. Herbert and Herbert. Professional Reports Corporation. Canton, OH. 1989.
- *Legends of Fitness.* Stephen Tharrett, Frank O'Rourke, and James A. Peterson. Healthy Learning, Monterey, CA. 2011.
- *Marketing for Results: A Common Sense Approach for Health Clubs.* Brenda Abdilla. CBM Books. Fort Washington, PA. 1996.

- *Marketing Health and Fitness Services.* Richard Gerson. Human Kinetics. Champaign, IL. 1989.
- *Marketing Outreach Techniques for Clubs.* Management Vision, Inc. Internal Document. New York. 2002.
- *Muscletown USA.* John Fair. Pennsylvania State University Press. University Park, PA. 1999.
- *The One Minute Manager Builds High Performing Teams.* Ken Blanchard, Don Carew and Ernie Parisi-Carew. William Morrow and Company. New York. 1990.
- *Opening a Spa.* Melinda M. Minton. Minton Business Solutions. Fort Collins, CO. 2002.
- *Programming Best Practices.* ClubCorp Internal Document. Dallas, TX. 2003.
- *Raving Fans.* Ken Blanchard and Sheldon Bowles. William Morrow and Company, Inc. New York. 1993.
- *The Seven Habits of Highly Effective People.* Stephen Covey. Fireside Publishing. New York. 1989.
- *Spa Industry Survey.* Conducted and prepared by Price Waterhouse Coopers for the International Spa Association. Lexington, KY. 2002.
- *Sports and Fitness Programming Manual.* ClubCorp Internal Document. Dallas, TX. 1999.
- *Sports Club Bell Notes.* ClubCorp Internal Document. Dallas, TX. 2003.
- *Studio Success.* Stephen Tharrett. Association of Fitness Studios, Chicago, IL. 2014.
- *A Study of Consumer Attitudes Toward Physical Fitness and Health Clubs.* American Sports Data, Inc. Hartsdale, NY. 2002.
- *A Study of Former Health Club Members.* Conducted for IHRSA by American Sports Data, Inc. Hartsdale, NY. 1998.
- *Trends in Physical Fitness Behavior (1987–2002).* American Sports Data, Inc. Hartsdale, NY. 2003.
- *Uniform System of Accounts for the Health, Racquet & Sportsclub Industry.* Copyrighted by the Educational Institute of the American Hotel and Motel Association. Lansing, MI. 1998.
- *Why and Where People Exercise.* An IHRSA study conducted by American Sports Data, Inc. Hartsdale, NY. 1995.
- *Why People Join, Leave, and Stay with Health/Fitness Clubs: The Ultimate Handbook of Member Retention.* Stephen Tharrett and Paul Bedord, Ph.D. Healthy Learning, Monterey, CA. 2012.
- *Why People Quit.* An IHRSA Study conducted by American Sports Data, Inc. Hartsdale, NY. 1998.
- *Why People Stay: Health Club Member Retention Research and Best Practices.* IHRSA Publication. Boston, MA. 2000.
- *Winning the Retention Battle: Parts One through Four.* Conducted by the Fitness Industry Association and Leisure Industry Week with assistance from Gladstone MRM. London, England. 2001.

About the Author

Stephen J. Tharrett, MS, is currently the owner and president of Club Industry Consulting, a global consulting business established in 2006 and based in the U.S. Tharrett is also the co-founder of ClubIntel, a brand and member insights firm that is focused on providing the global club industry with insight, inspiration, and impact revolving around the emotional power of a brand and its ability to establish a powerful base of advocates and fans. From 2008 to 2010, Tharrett served as the chief executive officer for the Russian Fitness Group, a privately held health/fitness club company that was, at the time, the largest in Russia.

Prior to forming Club Industry Consulting in 2006, Tharrett had a 20-plus-year career with ClubCorp, a billion-dollar private club company based in Dallas, Texas, where he served in several roles, ranging from director of athletics to senior vice president for athletics, golf, and tennis, as well as serving on the company's leadership cabinet and business planning committee.

Tharrett is the author or co-author of nine other management textbooks: *The ACE Fitness and Business Forms Handbook; CSFA's Private Club Spa and Fitness Management Resource Manual; The Health/Fitness Club Operator's Guide to Recruiting and Retaining Great Employees; Legends of Fitness: The Forces, Influencers, and Innovations That Helped Shape the Fitness Industry; Studio Success: AFS' Authoritative Guide to Owning and Operating a Fitness Studio; The Ultimate Resource Manual for Implementing Health/Fitness Facility Standards and Guidelines; Why People Join, Leave, and Stay With Health/Fitness Clubs; 101 Programming Strategies for Engaging Members in Health/Fitness Clubs;* and *101 Strategies for Improving Member Retention in Health/Fitness Clubs.* Tharrett is also the co-editor of the second, third, and fourth editions of *ACSM's Health/Fitness Facility Standards and Guidelines.* He is a former president of IHRSA, having served as president of the international association from 1996 to 1997, and presently serves on the advisory boards for *Club Industry* magazine and the Association of Fitness Studios.